KING STEPHEN

Also in the Yale English Monarchs Series

*Available in the U.S. from University of California Press

KING STEPHEN

Edmund King

YALE UNIVERSITY PRESS
NEW HAVEN AND LONDON

For information about this and other Yale University Press publications, please contact:
U.S. Office: sales.press@yale.edu   www.yalebooks.com
Europe Office: sales @yaleup.co.uk   www.yaleup.co.uk

Set in Baskerville by IDSUK (DataConnection) Ltd
Printed in Great Britain by TJ International Ltd, Padstow, Cornwall

Library of Congress Cataloging-in-Publication Data

King, Edmund.
    King Stephen / Edmund King.
    p. cm.
    ISBN 978-0-300-11223-8 (cl : alk. paper)
    1. Stephen, King of England, 1097?–1154. 2. Great
Britain–History–Stephen, 1135–1154. 3. Great Britain–Kings
and rulers–Biography. I. Title.
    DA198.5.K54 2010
    942.02'4092—dc22
    [B]

                                                        2010017511

A catalogue record for this book is available from the British Library.
10 9 8 7 6 5 4 3 2 1

For Michael and Frances

CONTENTS

ILLUSTRATIONS

PLATES

MAPS

ACKNOWLEDGEMENTS

One of the monks of Peterborough, writing during the 1150s, noted that the English church and his own monastery had suffered much sorrow and tribulation during King Stephen's reign. But he would not go into too much detail, he said, "for many have written much thereon." Since I studied the monastery of Peterborough for my doctorate, it might have been thought incumbent on me to have followed his example. That I failed was due initially to the fact that the extensive writings on the reign, greatly extended since his day, provided admirable material for undergraduate teaching. I taught an advanced course on the reign at the University of Sheffield for the majority of the years between 1971–2 and (while in retirement) 2007–8. My first thanks are to those students who worked with me in these classes, helping me to structure the "nineteen long winters in which Christ and his saints were asleep". We have worked in a strong and happy department, in which medieval history has always been valued. The list which follows could easily be extended but in this connection I thank in particular: Clyde Binfield, Patrick Collinson, Sarah Foot, Mark Greengrass, Ian Kershaw, David Luscombe, R. I. (Bob) Moore, Daniel Power, and Martial Staub. The University has provided much practical support also, offering regular research leave, from 1977 onwards, and two periods of special leave. A semester of leave was funded by the Arts and Humanities Research Board.

It is a pleasure to turn now to thank other friends and colleagues who have offered material support to the present volume. The list is a long one and many of them in their turn "have written much thereon." I owe a particular debt to those who have read drafts of the book: Kathleen Thompson and Nicholas Vincent read it all, and Marjorie Chibnall read several chapters. Their close, at times critical but always supportive, reading has been invaluable. It is a pleasure but also humbling to note that Marjorie Chibnall has been assisting me in this way for nearly fifty years. Among those who have generously shared research findings and new texts with me I thank: David Crouch, Judith Green, Kimberly LoPrete, Daniel Power, Richard Sharpe, and Nicholas Vincent. The support of the following has been no less valuable: Emilie Amt, Marion Archibald, Julia Barrow, Janet Burton, Thomas N. Bisson, Martin Brett, Stephen Church, Charles Coulson, Paul Dalton, John Gillingham, Christopher Harper-Bill, Barbara Harvey, Sandy Heslop, Katherine Keats-Rohan, Nicholas Karn,

Brian Kemp, Paul Latimer, David Roffe, Matthew Strickland, Keith Stringer, Heather Tanner, Elisabeth Van Houts, Graeme White, and Kenji Yoshitake.

I can no longer thank but remember with affection: Robert Boucher, Ralph Davis, Kenneth Haley, C. Warren Hollister, Robin Jeffs, Tom Keefe, Edward Miller, Gareth Roberts, Eleanor Searle, and Simon Walker. Each of these offered me much appreciated support and encouragement.

The following libraries and institutions have generously supplied research materials (and facilitated the supply of illustrations): at Cambridge my own college, St John's (Mark Nicholls, Malcolm Underwood), King's College (Patricia McGuire, Tracy Wilkinson), The Fitzwilliam Museum (Martin Allen, Mark Blackburn), and the University Library; at Oxford, All Souls College (which elected me to a Visiting Fellowship in 1990), and The Bodleian Library; The British Library; The Dean and Chapter of Westminster (Richard Mortimer, Christine Reynolds); The National Museum Wales (Edward Besly, the late George Boon, Kay Kays); The Huntington Library, San Marino, U.S.A. (where I spent that first study leave, generously supported by a Fulbright Fellowship); and the Sheffield University Library. It has been invaluable to me to have the continued use of an office in retirement, for which further thanks are due to my colleagues in the department, and especially to James Pearson, who has guided me to the beginnings of a competence in computing.

This book is a biography of King Stephen not a "life and times." It was commissioned by Robert Baldock for the Yale English Monarchs series several years ago. I am grateful to him for his patient wait for it and for his positive welcome. Within the press Rachael Lonsdale and Tami Halliday have been ideal editors, taking immense care and providing just the right mix of tenacity and tact. I could not have been more fortunate in my publishers.

My family never quite lost confidence that the book would be finished. I am grateful to them for that and for so very much more. My thanks here go to my wife Jenny, to our children Michael and Frances, and to Tim, Freddie and Lily. They know how much I owe to them.

University of Sheffield
August 2010

ABBREVIATED REFERENCES

Aelred, *Genealogia*   Aelred of Rievaulx, *De genealogia regum Anglorum*, in *PL* 195, cols. 711–38

Aelred, *Relatio*   *Relatio venerabilis Aelredi, abbatis Rievallensis, de Standardo*, in *Chronicles*, iii

Amt, *Accession*   Emilie Amt, *The Accession of Henry II in England: Royal Government Restored 1149–1159* (Woodbridge, 1993)

Ann. Mon.   *Annales Monastici*, ed. H. R. Luard, 5 vols (RS, 1864–9)

ANS   *Anglo-Norman Studies*

ASC   *The Anglo-Saxon Chronicle*, ed. Dorothy Whitelock, rev. edn (London, 1965), cited by regnal year

Battle   *The Chronicle of Battle Abbey*, ed. Eleanor Searle (OMT, 1980)

Biddle, *Winchester*   *Winchester in the Early Middle Ages*, ed. Martin Biddle (Winchester Studies 1; Oxford, 1976)

BL   British Library

Book of Seals   *Sir Christopher Hatton's Book of Seals*, ed. Lewis C. Loyd and Doris Mary Stenton (Oxford, 1950)

Brooke, *London*   Christopher N. L. Brooke, *London 800–1216: The Shaping of a City* (London, 1975)

Camden   Camden Society: Royal Historical Society, London

Castellarium Anglicanum   David J. Cathcart King, *Castellarium Anglicanum: An Index and Bibliography of the Castles in England, Wales and the Islands*, 2 vols (Millwood, NY, 1983)

Charters of David I   *The Charters of King David I: The Written Acts of King David I King of Scots, 1124–53, and of his son Henry Earl of Northumberland, 1139–52*, ed. G. W. S. Barrow (Woodbridge, 1999)

Chester Charters   *The Charters of the Anglo-Norman Earls of Chester, c.1071–1237*, ed. Geoffrey Barraclough (Rec. Soc. of Lancashire and Cheshire 126, 1988)

Chibnall, *Matilda*   Marjorie Chibnall, *The Empress Matilda: Queen Consort, Queen Mother and Lady of the English* (Oxford, 1991)

Christina   *The Life of Christina of Markyate*, ed. C. H. Talbot (OMT, 2002)

Chronicles   *Chronicles of the Reigns of Stephen, Henry II and Richard I*, ed. R. Howlett, 4 vols (RS, 1884–9)

Chron. Ramsey   *Chronicon Abbatiae Rameseiensis*, ed. W. D. Macray (RS, 1886)

Councils and Synods   *Councils and Synods with Other Documents Relating to the English Church* 1, part 2: *1066–1204*, ed. D. Whitelock, M. Brett, and C. N. L. Brooke (Oxford, 1981)

CP   *The Complete Peerage of England, Scotland, Ireland, Great Britain and the United Kingdom*, by. G. E. C., rev. edn, 13 vols in 14 (London, 1910–59)

Crouch, *Beaumont Twins*   David Crouch, *The Beaumont Twins: The Roots and Branches of Power in the Twelfth Century* (Cambridge, 1986)

Crouch, *Stephen*	David Crouch, *The Reign of Stephen, 1135–1154* (London, 2000)
Dalton, *Yorkshire*	Paul Dalton, *Conquest, Anarchy and Lordship: Yorkshire, 1066–1154* (Cambridge, 1994)
Davis, *Stephen*	R. H. C. Davis, *King Stephen 1135–1154*, 3rd edn (London, 1990)
DB	*Domesday Book: A Complete Translation*, ed. Ann Williams and G. H. Martin (Harmondsworth, 2002)
Dialogus	*Dialogus de Scaccario*, ed. Charles Johnson (NMT, 1950)
Diceto	*Radulphi de Diceto Opera Historica*, ed. W. Stubbs, 2 vols (RS, 1876)
Eadmer	Eadmer, *Historia Novorum*, ed. Martin Rule (RS, 1884)
EEA	*English Episcopal Acta*, 34 vols (London, 1980–2009)
EHR	*English Historical Review*
EMC	Early Medieval Corpus of Coin Finds, 410–1180 <http://www.fitzmuseum.cam.ac.uk/dept/coins/emc>
English Lawsuits	*English Lawsuits from William I to Richard I*, ed. R. C. Van Caenegem, 2 vols (Selden Soc. 106–7, 1990–1)
EYC	*Early Yorkshire Charters*, 1–3, ed. W. Farrer (Edinburgh, 1914–16); 4–12, ed. C. T. Clay (Yorkshire Arch. Soc., 1935–65)
Eynsham	*Eynsham Cartulary*, ed. H. E. Salter, 2 vols (Oxford Hist. Soc. 49, 51; 1907–8)
Fasti	John le Neve, *Fasti Ecclesiae Anglicanae, 1066–1300*, ed. Diana E. Greenway et al., 10 vols (London, 1968–2005)
Galbert	Galbert of Bruges, *The Murder of Charles the Good, Count of Flanders*, ed. James Bruce Ross, rev. edn (New York, 1967)
GASA	*Gesta Abbatum Monasterii S. Albani*, ed. H. T. Riley, 3 vols (RS, 1867–9)
Gervase	Gervase of Canterbury, *Historical Works*, ed. W. Stubbs, 2 vols (RS 73, 1879–80)
GF Letters	*The Letters and Charters of Gilbert Foliot*, ed. A. Morey and C. N. L. Brooke (Cambridge, 1967)
GND	*The Gesta Normannorum Ducum of William of Jumièges, Orderic Vitalis and Robert of Torigni*, ed. Elisabeth M. C. Van Houts, 2 vols (OMT, 1992–5)
GS	*Gesta Stephani*, ed. K. R. Potter and R. H. C. Davis (OMT, 1976)
Haskins	Charles Homer Haskins, *Norman Institutions* (Cambridge, Mass., 1918)
Heads	*The Heads of Religious Houses: England and Wales* 1: *940–1216*, ed. David Knowles, C. N. L. Brooke, and Vera C. M. London, 2nd edn (Cambridge, 2001)
HH	Henry, Archdeacon of Huntingdon, *Historia Anglorum: The History of the English People*, ed. Diana Greenway (OMT, 1996)
Hollister, *Anglo-Norman World*	C. Warren Hollister, *Monarchy, Magnates and Institutions in the Anglo-Norman World* (London, 1986)
Holyrood	*A Scottish Chronicle known as the Chronicle of Holyrood*, ed. M. O. Anderson (Scottish Hist. Soc. 3:30; Edinburgh, 1938)
Howden	Roger of Howden, *Chronica Rogeri de Houedene*, ed. W. Stubbs, 4 vols (RS, 1868–71)
HR	*Bulletin of the Institute of Historical Research* (until 1986); *Historical Research* (from 1987)
HSJ	*Haskins Society Journal*
Hugh the Chanter	Hugh the Chanter, *The History of the Church of York 1066–1127*, ed. Charles Johnson, rev. M. Brett, C. N. L. Brooke, and M. Winterbottom (OMT, 1990)

JH   John of Hexham, Continuation of Simeon of Durham's *Historia regum*, in SD, *Opera*, ii

JL   Philip Jaffé, *Regesta pontificum Romanorum*, ed. S. Löwenfeld, F. Kaltenbrunner, and P. Ewald (Leipzig, 1885–8)

JS, *Entheticus*   John of Salisbury, *Entheticus Maior and Minor*, ed. J. Van Laarhoven, 3 vols (Leiden, 1987)

JS, *HP*   John of Salisbury, *Historia Pontificalis: Memoirs of the Papal Court*, ed. Marjorie Chibnall (NMT, 1956)

JS, *Letters*   *The Letters of John of Salisbury*, ed. W. J. Millor, H. E. Butler, and C. N. L. Brooke (OMT, 1955–79)

JS, *Policraticus*   *Johannis Saresbiensis Episcopi Carnotensis Policratici*, ed. C. C. J. Webb, 2 vols (Oxford, 1909); trans. John of Salisbury, *Policraticus*, ed. Cary J. Nederman (Cambridge, 1990)

JW   *The Chronicle of John of Worcester*, ed. R. R. Darlington and P. McGurk, vols 2–3 (OMT, 1995–8)

Kealey, *Roger*   E. J. Kealey, *Roger of Salisbury: Viceroy of England* (Berkeley, 1972)

King, *Anarchy*   Edmund King, ed., *The Anarchy of King Stephen's Reign* (Oxford, 1994)

King's Works   *The History of the King's Works* 1–2: *The Middle Ages*, ed. H. M. Colvin (London, 1963)

Law and Government   *Law and Government in Medieval England and Normandy: Essays in Honour of Sir James Holt*, ed. George Garnett and John Hudson (Cambridge, 1994)

Lewes   *The Chartulary of the Priory of St Pancras of Lewes*, ed. L. F. Saltzman, 2 vols (Sussex Rec. Soc. 38, 40; 1933–5)

Liber Eliensis   *Liber Eliensis*, ed. E. O. Blake (Camden 3:92, 1962)

LoPrete, *Adela*   Kimberley A. LoPrete, *Adela of Blois: Countess and Lord (c.1067–1137)* (Dublin, 2007)

Melrose   *The Chronicle of Melrose*, facsimile edn, ed. A. O. Anderson and M. O. Anderson (London, 1936)

Monasticon   W. Dugdale, *Monasticon Anglicanum*, ed. J. Caley, H. Ellis, and B. Bandinel, 8 vols (London, 1817–30)

MTB   *Materials for the History of Thomas Becket*, ed. James Craigie Robertson, 7 vols (RS, 1875–85)

Newburgh   William of Newburgh, *Historia rerum Anglicarum*, in *Chronicles*, i; trans. *The History of English Affairs*, ed. P. G. Walsh and M. J. Kennedy (Warminster, 1988)

NMT   Nelson Medieval Texts, London

North   J. J. North, *English Hammered Coinage* 1: *Early Anglo-Saxon to Henry III, c. 600–1272* (London, 1980)

OMT   Oxford Medieval Texts, Oxford

OV   Orderic Vitalis, *The Ecclesiastical History*, ed. Marjorie Chibnall, 6 vols (OMT, 1969–80)

OxDNB   *Oxford Dictionary of National Biography*, ed. H. C. G. Matthew and Brian Harrison (Oxford, 2004)

Peter the Venerable   *The Letters of Peter the Venerable*, ed. Giles Constable, 2 vols (Cambridge, Mass., 1967)

PL   *Patrilogia cursus completus, series Latina*, ed. J. P. Migne (Paris, 1841–64)

PR   *Pipe Roll*

PUE   *Papsturkunden in England*, ed. Walter Holtzmann, 3 vols (Berlin and Göttingen, 1930–52)

Reg. Ant.	*The Registrum Antiquissimum of the Cathedral Church of Lincoln*, ed. C. W. Foster and Kathleen Major, 10 vols (Lincoln Rec. Soc., 1931–73)
Regesta	*Regesta Regum Anglo-Normannorum*, ed. H. W. C. Davis, C. Johnson, H. A. Cronne, and R. H. C. Davis, 4 vols (Oxford, 1913–69)
RH	Richard of Hexham, *De gestis regis Stephani et de bello standardii*, in *Chronicles*, iii
RHF	*Recueil des historiens des Gaules et de la France*, ed. M. Bouquet et al., 24 vols in 25 (Paris, 1738–1904)
Romanesque	*English Romanesque Art 1066–1200*, ed. George Zarnecki, Janet Holt, and Tristram Holland (London, 1984)
Round, *Geoffrey*	J. H. Round, *Geoffrey de Mandeville* (London, 1892)
RS	Rolls Series, London
Saltman, *Theobald*	Avrom Saltman, *Theobald Archbishop of Canterbury* (London, 1956)
SD, *Libellus*	Simeon of Durham, *Libellus de Exordio atque Procursu istius hoc est Dunhelmensis Ecclesie*, ed. David Rollason (OMT, 2000)
SD, *Opera*	Simeon of Durham, *Historical Works*, ed. T. Arnold, 2 vols (RS, 1882–5)
Stenton, *First Century*	F. M. Stenton, *The First Century of English Feudalism 1066–1166*, 2nd edn (Oxford, 1961)
Strickland, *War*	Matthew Strickland, *War and Chivalry: The Conduct and Perception of War in England and Normandy, 1066–1217* (Cambridge, 1996)
Suger, *Louis VI*	Suger, *Vie de Louis VI le Gros*, ed. Henri Waquet (Paris, 1929)
TBGAS	*Transactions of the Bristol and Gloucestershire Archaeological Society*
Templars	*Records of the Templars in England in the Twelfth Century*, ed. Beatrice A. Lees (British Academy Records of Social and Economic History 11, 1935)
Torigni	Robert of Torigni, *The Chronicle of Robert of Torigni*, in *Chronicles*, iv
TRHS	*Transactions of the Royal Historical Society*
UGQ	*Ungedruckte Anglo-Normannische Geschichtsquellen*, ed. F. Liebermann (Strasbourg, 1879)
VCH	*Victoria History of the Counties of England*
Walden	*The Book of the Foundation of Walden Monastery*, ed. Diana Greenway and Leslie Watkiss (OMT, 1999)
Walter Daniel	Walter Daniel, *The Life of Ailred of Rievaulx*, ed. F. M. Powicke (NMT, 1950)
Waltham	*The Waltham Chronicle*, ed. Leslie Watkiss and Marjorie Chibnall (OMT, 1994)
WM, *GP*	William of Malmesbury, *Gesta Pontificum Anglorum: The History of the English Bishops*, ed. R. M. Thomson and M. Winterbottom, 2 vols (OMT, 2007)
WM, *GR*	William of Malmesbury, *Gesta Regum Anglorum: The History of the English Kings*, ed. R. A. B. Mynors, R. M. Thomson, and M. Winterbottom, 2 vols (OMT, 1998–9)
WM, *HN*	William of Malmesbury, *Historia Novella: The Contemporary History*, ed. Edmund King, trans. K. R. Potter (OMT, 1998)

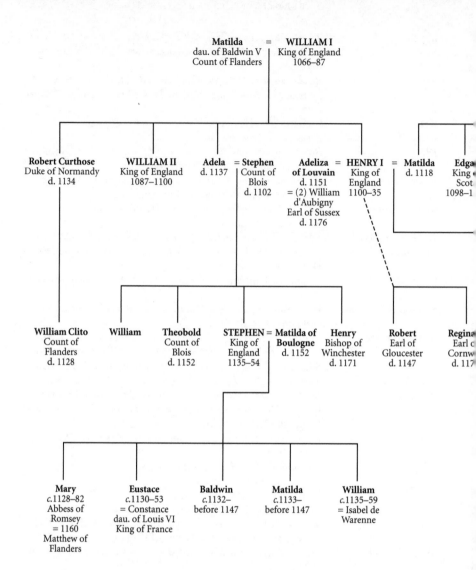

The Anglo-Norman Succession

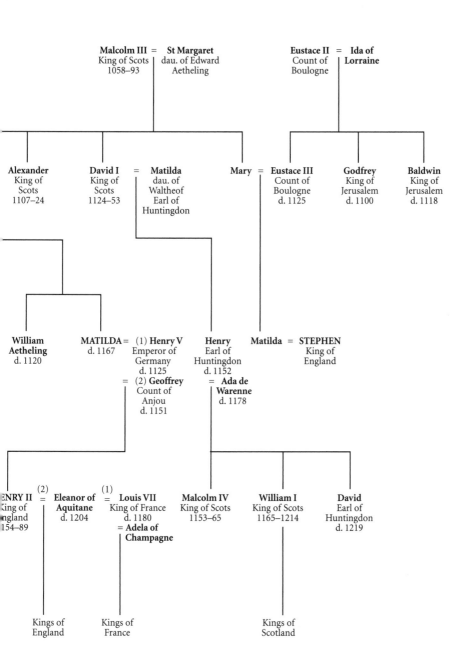

Malcolm III = **St Margaret**
King of Scots | dau. of Edward
1058–93 | Aetheling

Eustace II = **Ida of**
Count of | **Lorraine**
Boulogne

Alexander
King of
Scots
1107–24

David I
King of
Scots
1124–53

= **Matilda**
dau. of
Waltheof
Earl of
Huntingdon

Mary = **Eustace III**
Count of
Boulogne
d. 1125

Godfrey
King of
Jerusalem
d. 1100

Baldwin
King of
Jerusalem
d. 1118

William
Aetheling
d. 1120

MATILDA = (1) **Henry V**
d. 1167 | Emperor of
Germany
d. 1125
= (2) **Geoffrey**
Count of
Anjou
d. 1151

Henry
Earl of
Huntingdon
d. 1152
= **Ada de**
Warenne
d. 1178

Matilda = **STEPHEN**
King of
England

(2)
ENRY II = **Eleanor of**
King of | **Aquitane**
ngland | d. 1204
154–89

(1)
= **Louis VII**
King of France
d. 1180
= **Adela of**
Champagne

Malcolm IV
King of Scots
1153–65

William I
King of Scots
1165–1214

David
Earl of
Huntingdon
d. 1219

Kings of
England

Kings of
France

Kings of
Scotland

Chapter 1

FAMILY AND HONOUR

Stephen, count of Blois, married the daughter of William I, a woman of note, and had four sons by her. After he had died in the east, that remarkable mother wisely set aside her first-born because he was deficient in intelligence and seemed second-rate, and advanced her son, Theobald, who was her favourite, to the full inheritance. She entrusted Stephen, who was still a boy, to his uncle the king to be brought up and advanced, and she had the fourth son Henry tonsured at Cluny so that she would not seem to have begotten children merely for the world.[1]

When the young man's death became known, the face of things was wonderfully changed.[2]

Everyone knew the story of the battle of Hastings. It had given the English a new ruling house. That much was clear as the dust settled on the battlefield, after a long engagement, on 14 October 1066. It would give the English a new ruling class. That was less clear on the day but it followed inexorably. New Norman lords brought their relatives and their followers. Among them were two clerks, who would marry English women, and whose sons would become the greatest historians of their day. The first of these was Ordelerius of Orléans, one of the learned clerks of Roger of Montgommery, vicomte of the Hiémois and the first earl of Shrewsbury. His son was baptized at Atcham, on 16 February 1075, and given the name of the local priest, Orderic. The boy received his first education in Shrewsbury, but when he was aged just ten years he was sent to the monastery of St Evroul in Normandy.[3] In his last days, he still remembered being dragged from his family in tears, coming into Normandy "as an exile" and hearing "a language which I did not understand."[4] The other historian gives us less by way of biographical detail. This was William, a monk of Malmesbury Abbey in Wiltshire. He was certainly younger than Orderic, being born around 1090,[5] but their education was

---

[1] Newburgh, 31, ed. Walsh and Kennedy, 50–3.
[2] WM, *GR*, i. 762–3, writing of the death of William, son of Henry I, in the White Ship disaster, 1120.
[3] OV, i. 1–44; vi. 552–7.
[4] OV, vi. 554–5.
[5] On this date see WM, *HN*, xviii; Thomson, *William of Malmesbury*, 199–201.

similar. He was a bookish child, he says, "thanks to the encouragement of my parents and my own bent for study", and he credits his father's influence particularly; he was probably educated first at the local grammar school, and then sent to the monastery as a boy.[6] These two boys became learned men, immensely hard working, and conscious of the responsibilities of their craft. They lived through exciting times.

William of Malmesbury could write of "the fateful day" of the battle of Hastings, so he claimed, with a measure of detachment, "for the blood of both peoples flows in my veins."[7] Midway through his narrative of the battle, at half-time as it were, he stopped to consider what was at stake. He offered a verdict not on two armies but on two peoples. The English had inherited a rich tradition of sanctity. "Does not the whole island gleam with so many relics of its own natives, that you can scarcely pass through any town of note without hearing the name of some new saint?" But zeal for religion had cooled and the whole condition of the country had suffered with it. The aristocracy lived a life of debauchery: "drinking in company was a universal practice, and in this passion they made no distinction between night and day." The men of the day lived in small houses, little better than hovels, "unlike the French and the Normans, who in proud great buildings live a life of moderate expense." The Normans were in every way a contrast to the English. They were habituated to armed conflict: "the whole nation is familiar with war, and hardly knows how to live without fighting." The outcome of the battle was inevitable in William's view and its consequences beneficial. "The standard of religion, dead everywhere in England, has been raised by the arrival of the Normans; you may see everywhere churches in villages, and monasteries in towns and cities rising in a new style of architecture; and with new devotion our country flourishes."[8] Orderic's judgement was similar, though he knew the Normans from close at hand and continually stressed that their military qualities needed to be kept in check by strong rulers.[9] He saw his native land in 1066 as suffering from tyranny, since it was "deprived of lawful heirs"; "so she provided a mournful theme of ruin for the pen of true historians."[10]

A select few would learn of the story of the battle of Hastings through a visual record. At Canterbury, at some point in the reign of William the Conqueror, an embroidery was produced telling the story of the battle and the events that had led up to it.[11] Headlines in Latin helped the viewer to find the way, though they offered and still offer much scope for interpret-

---

[6] WM, *GR*, i. 150–1; Thomson, *William*, 2; Winterbottom, "The *Gesta regum* of William of Malmesbury."

[7] WM, *GR*, i. 424–5.

[8] WM, *GR*, i. 456–61.

[9] OV, iii. 98–9; iv. 82–3; v. 24–5; vi. 456–7; Chibnall, *World of Orderic*, 118–19.

[10] OV, ii. 190–1.

[11] Brooks and Walker, "The Authority and Interpretation of the Bayeux Tapestry."

ation. "Here Harold swore an oath to Duke William" – but what exactly did he swear?[12] "Here the king addressed his faithful men" – but what exactly did Edward the Confessor say as he lay on his deathbed?[13] The work was commissioned by Odo, bishop of Bayeux, the Conqueror's half-brother, and it was at Bayeux that it was preserved and is now on display. The Bayeux Tapestry is the only survivor of its type, but it cannot have been the only one made. According to Baudri de Bourgueil, abbot of Bourgueil in the Touraine and later bishop of Dol in Brittany, a similar embroidery was to be found on the walls of his patron, Adela, countess of Blois.[14] It was one of a number of similar hangings, for she also possessed scenes from the Bible – a salvation history – a history of Rome, and the siege of Troy. The history of the Conquest, as Baudri told it, followed closely the narrative found in the Bayeux Tapestry and was probably based upon it.[15] The abbot had never been admitted to the countess's private quarters and his description of them is entirely fictitious; nonetheless, it represents "what a contemporary courtier would expect to see in a noble household,"[16] and it is perfectly possible that Adela had commissioned a copy of the Bayeux Tapestry. For she was the daughter of the Conqueror and very conscious of the status this gave her. She was "Adela, countess of Blois and daughter of William, the glorious king of the English."[17]

Adela was named after her maternal grandmother, who was the daughter of Robert "the Pious," king of France (996–1031). This Adela was married to Baldwin V, count of Flanders; and their daughter, Matilda, was married to William, then duke of Normandy, around 1050. What were claimed to be their wedding dresses were displayed in Bayeux Cathedral.[18] William and Matilda had a large family, four sons and at least five daughters.[19] The sons were Robert, Richard, William, and Henry; the daughters were Adeliza, Matilda, Cecily, Constance, and

---

[12] "Vbi Harold sacramentum fecit Willelmo duci": *Bayeux Tapestry*, ed. Stenton, plate 29; ed. Wilson, plates 25–6 (breaking up this crucial scene).

[13] "Hic Eadwardus rex in lecto alloquitur fideles": *Bayeux Tapestry*, ed. Stenton, plate 33; ed. Wilson, plate 30.

[14] Baudri de Bourgueil, *Oeuvres poétiques*, 196–253; translated and discussed, Otter, "Baudri of Bourgueil, 'To Countess Adela.'"

[15] This is seen as certain by Brown and Herren, "The *Adelae Comitissae* and the Bayeux Tapestry."

[16] George Wingfield Digby, "Technique and Production," in *Bayeux Tapestry*, ed. Stenton, 47.

[17] *Documents historiques inédits*, 2/ii. 5: "Ego Adela comitissa Willelmi regis Anglorum et Matildis reginae filia"; cf. *Cart. Marmoutier pour le Dunois*, 69: "Ego Adela Blesensium comitissa et Willelmi gloriosi regis Anglorum filia"; and *Cart. Molesme*, ii. 25–6; "Adela comitissa, regis Anglorum filia."

[18] On the date of the marriage, see *Handbook of British Chronology*, 34; Bates, *William the Conqueror*, 34; *GND*, ii. 129 note 5. On the wedding dresses, Wingfield Digby, in *Bayeux Tapestry*, ed. Stenton, 45.

[19] Barlow, *William Rufus*, 441–5.

Adela.[20] The birth order of the daughters is uncertain but Adela was certainly the youngest of them. She was long thought to have been born around 1064,[21] well before the conquest of England, but Godfrey of Rheims states clearly that she was born only after her father had been crowned as king of England. This means that she was born early in 1067.[22] She was "born to the purple," as was her younger brother, Henry, in the following year.[23] Ivo, bishop of Chartres, in his first letter to her, stated that she had inherited royal blood from both lines.[24] It was what she wanted to hear.

Adela was married around the year 1083, when she was about sixteen years old. Her husband was Stephen-Henry, the eldest son and chief heir of Theobald III, count of Blois. It was an alliance between two of the greatest families in northern France, designed primarily to strengthen each of them against a third of those families, that of the counts of Anjou. The lands of the counts of Blois lay west, south, and east of Paris, the seat of the Capetian kings of France. It might have appeared that the marriage was also designed to counter their authority, and this is how the alliance of Henry I and his sister, Adela, would later appear to Suger, abbot of St Denis, in his *Life* of the French king, Louis VI.[25] When Theobald died in 1089, Stephen took the lion's share of the family lands, the historic centres at Blois, Châteaudun, and Chartres, together with lands in northern Berry, and Meaux and Provins. The eastern block of lands, the later county of Champagne, was divided, with Troyes (as the main centre), Epernay, Bar-sur-Aube, and Vitry, being granted successively to Stephen-Henry's half-brothers, Odo and then Hugh. Whilst a single title served as shorthand for the authority of each of the brothers, Blois for the one and Troyes for the other, these were federations of territories, which gave them lordship over and responsibility for scores of vassals. It was said of Count Stephen-Henry that "he controlled as many castles as the year has days." In making his dispositions in 1089, Count Theobald was able to take account of the qualities of his children. Stephen-Henry was the model of pacific lordship: "his generosity was unexcelled, his presence very pleasing, his performance in council sober, steady, and thoughtfully mature."[26] By 1089 Stephen-Henry and Adela already had two sons, and they must have hoped that they too would show signs of statesmanship.

---

[20] Robert, duke of Normandy (d. 1134); Richard; William (Rufus), king of England (d. 1100); Henry (I), king of England (d. 1135); Adeliza; Matilda; Cecily, abbess of Caen (d. 1127); Constance, countess of Brittany (d. 1090); Adela, countess of Blois (d. 1137).

[21] *Handbook of British Chronology*, 35.

[22] Boutemy, "Trois Oeuvres inédits," 340–4.

[23] Henry was born shortly after their mother's coronation at Whitsun, 1068: Hollister, *Henry I*, 30–1.

[24] Ivo of Chartres, e 5, *Correspondence* 1, ed. Leclercq, 14–17; LoPrete, *Adela*, 25–9.

[25] Suger, *Louis VI*, 142–9.

[26] Guibert of Nogent, *Dei Gesta per Francos*, 131–2; *The Deeds of God through the Franks*, trans. Levine, 54.

Adela and Stephen-Henry would go on to have at least six children, five boys and one girl; two other girls are mentioned who are probably the daughters of Stephen-Henry but not of Adela. Four of the five boys lived to adulthood and their birth order is not in doubt. The first-born was named William, the second Theobald, the third Stephen, and the fourth Henry.[27] There was another boy, Odo, who died young, but old enough to attest one of his mother's charters in 1101; he was either the third or the fourth son. The girl, Matilda, was married around 1115. It is likely that all of these children were born in a twelve-year period between 1085 and 1096, in the autumn of which year Stephen-Henry would depart on the First Crusade. A possible order is as follows: William, born *c.*1086; Theobald, born *c.*1088; Odo, born *c.*1090; Stephen, born *c.*1092; Matilda, born *c.*1094; Henry, born *c.*1096. They were a family, being described first as "the boys" and then as "the brothers," and contemporaries thought of them and wrote of them as a family unit.[28] No one was in any doubt as to the overarching influence of their mother on her children's development. Adela was independently wealthy, one of the great political hostesses of her day. She entertained kings and popes, bishops and abbots. They were impressed: "the most wise of women"; "a wise and spirited woman"; "a powerful woman with a reputation for her worldly influence"; "no more prudent, better constituted, or more virile woman had been seen in France for many an age."[29] She most certainly showed qualities of statesmanship. Circumstances would dictate that her influence over her children was particularly close.

Adela's husband would be one of the first crusaders. This also, like the battle of Hastings, was a story that everyone in the early twelfth century knew well by report and many had experienced at first hand. An Anglo-Norman magnate, Brian Fitz Count, would recall it when writing to one of Adela's sons early in the 1140s:

When Pope Urban came to Tours and held a council of the clergy, by God's command he spoke of the city of Jerusalem, saying that Christian pilgrims who went there in secret were being beaten, robbed, and killed. The pope promised that all who went to liberate it, wherever they came from, would be granted an indulgence and absolution from all their sins. Therefore, many powerful men arose and went on pilgrimage by the apostolic command, leaving their castles and cities,

---

[27] OV, iii. 116–17; vi. 42–5; *GND*, ii. 262–3. LoPrete, "Adela of Blois as Mother"; eadem, *Adela*, 549–53.

[28] They are "the boys" in their parents' charters and letters, e.g. *Cart. Notre-Dame de Paris*, ii. 264–5: "uxore mea filiisque meis unanimiter annuentibus"; they are "the brothers" in *GS*, 12–13; WM, *HN*, 52–3, 78–9.

[29] OV, v. 324–5: "mulier sagax et animosa"; Guibert of Nogent, *Dei Gesta per Francos*, 132: "sagacissima feminarum" (trans. Levine, 54); WM, *GR*, i. 504–5: "laudatae in seculo potentiae uirago"; Hugh the Chanter, 154–5: "nulla prudencior nec melius composita nec magis uirilis uirago ex multa retro etate in tota Gallia exstiterat."

their wives and children, and their great honours. Such were Count Stephen your father, Robert duke of Normandy, Raymond count of Toulouse, Bohemond, Robert count of Flanders, Eustace count of Boulogne, Duke Godfrey, and numerous of the richest and most important of the knights.[30]

The main ideas of the crusade, as they have been identified and discussed in great detail,[31] are found here in cameo. The pope "spoke of the city of Jerusalem": in order to liberate it an armed pilgrimage would be made, its members sustained by "an indulgence and absolution for all their sins." It was a common topos that they left behind all that they held most dear. According to William of Malmesbury, the Welshman left his hunting, the Danes their drink, the Scots their fleas, and the Scandinavians their raw fish.[32]

The northern French set out on crusade in the autumn of 1096. They met Pope Urban, who had preached the crusade, at Lucca in late October, and then travelled on to southern Italy. Advised that it was too late in the season to cross the Adriatic, both Stephen-Henry and Robert, duke of Normandy, sat out the winter at Brindisi, and would have had the chance to receive and send correspondence while there. They resumed their journey in April 1097 and reached Constantinople in the early summer. That their loved ones remained very much in their minds is nowhere more clearly shown than in a couple of letters which survive from the correspondence of the count of Blois.[33] "To Adela, his most sweet and most loved wife, and to his very dear children and all his vassals, noble and common, the grace and blessing of his whole greeting."[34] These are full, chatty letters, giving much detail of military affairs, but with homely touches too. His wife was not to worry about him. He had sailed on the Bosphorus, but, contrary to popular report, it was quite calm: "one need feel no more uncertainty upon it than on the Marne or the Seine." As to the climate, whatever the popular report of the scorching heat of Syria, this was false, "for winter among them is like our western winter."[35] Stephen reported, with some pride, that he had been warmly received by the emperor at Constantinople. The emperor had enquired about their family and had evidently been impressed by the number of their sons. "Verily, my darling, his Imperial Highness has very often urged, and urges, that we commend one of our sons to him; he promises, moreover, that he will accord him such great and such distinguished honor that he will not in the least envy

---

[30] King, "Brian Fitz Count," 89–90.

[31] The classic survey is Erdmann, *Origin of the Idea of Crusade*. See also, Riley-Smith, *First Crusade and the Idea of Crusading*; Blake, "Formation of the 'Crusade Idea'"; Cowdrey, "Urban II's Preaching of the First Crusade"; Robinson, "Gregory VII and the Soldiers of Christ."

[32] WM, *GR*, i. 606–7.

[33] Hagenmeyer, *Kreuzzugsbriefe*, 138–40, 149–52.

[34] Ibid., 138; trans. Krey, *The First Crusade: The Accounts of Eye-witnesses and Participants*, 100.

[35] Hagenmeyer, *Kreuzzugsbriefe*, 139, 150; trans. Krey, 107, 156.

our own standing."[36] In any other context this might have seemed patronizing, but Stephen was evidently stage-struck at the wealth and splendour of the imperial court. If a boy had been handed over, it might have been Stephen, the fourth son, but nothing came of the offer.

The second letter was sent from the crusader camp at Antioch. It is a dispatch from the front line, its tone darker than the earlier, its cheerfulness more forced. Stephen knew well enough that by the time his wife received the letter he might be dead. "Farewell, make excellent arrangements for your land, and treat your children and your vassals with honor, as befits you, for you will surely see me as soon as I can possibly come."[37] In fact she did see him, and quite soon, but therein lay a tale that was much repeated and gained much in the telling. Stephen had been elected leader of the crusading army, and when he abandoned the siege of Antioch, at a time when there was news of a strong force coming to relieve it, his companions felt bereft and betrayed, the more so when it was reported that he had advised the emperor that there was no point in his offering further support.[38] He "was an object of contempt to almost everyone, and was continually reproached because he had fled disgracefully from the siege of Antioch, deserting his glorious comrades who were sharing in the agonies of Christ."[39] Stephen would be told on his return that, whatever excuses he might offer, and he claimed that he had been ill, these were immaterial. He had not discharged his crusading vow, the definition of which had only become clear after he left, for in the event Antioch had been captured and the crusading army had gone on to capture Jerusalem. With his wife's very active encouragement,[40] Stephen returned and fell at Ramla on 19 May 1102. He had fulfilled his vow and made a good end: "the dishonourable act was rectified by martyrdom."[41] The stories were told and retold and among those close to Adela and her court a more sympathetic view would be taken of Stephen's actions at Antioch.[42] The count's reputation would not be a burden to his children. That was why he had returned to the Holy Land and almost courted death.

Adela will have learned that she was a widow by the end of the year 1102. She was then thirty-five years old. The instruction in her husband's earlier letter, that she should govern her lands well and take good care of

---

[36] Hagenmeyer, *Kreuzzugsbriefe*, 138; trans. Krey, 100.

[37] Hagenmeyer, *Kreuzzugsbriefe*, 152; trans. Krey, 157.

[38] *Gesta Francorum*, 63–4; Guibert of Nogent, *Dei Gesta per Francos*, 131–2, trans. Levine, 54; Albert of Aachen, *Historia Ierosolimitana*, 96–9, 266–9, 304–7.

[39] OV, v. 324–5: "turpiter aufugerit"; *Gesta Francorum*, 63–4: "turpiterque recessit"; Strickland, *War*, 122.

[40] OV, v. 268–9, 324–5.

[41] Guibert of Nogent, *Dei Gesta per Francos*, 228: "indecens factum martirii repensione correxit" (trans. Levine, 104); Albert of Aachen, *Historia Ierosolimitana*, 592–5, 644–5.

[42] LoPrete, "Adela of Blois (*ca.*1067–*ca.*1137)," App. 2, "Stephen of Blois in Twelfth-Century Crusading Narratives," 548–628; Brundage, "An Errant Crusader."

her sons, was hardly necessary. She had acted as almost an equal partner to her husband in his lifetime; she would control his lands as her sons grew to adulthood; and she remained a dominant figure long after they had reached it. It is a career that challenges many of the stereotypes of medieval lordship. High birth of itself does not explain her authority: her elder sisters are shadowy figures. Her birth gave her prestige but it was aptitude, her own character, that was the key. She was widowed when at the height of her powers and also at the height of her responsibilities. In 1102 her two surviving brothers, Robert, duke of Normandy, and Henry I, king of England, disputed control over the Anglo-Norman realm, and the time was approaching when her sons would need to be established in lordships of their own. Her overarching authority gave direction and allowed for flexibility. She was subtle and she was persuasive. In over twenty years, between her husband's second departure on crusade in the winter of 1098–9 and her retirement to the nunnery of Marcigny in the spring of 1120, she did not put a foot wrong.

In establishing the sons, flexibility was the key. The eldest son, William, would expect a substantial endowment. His first appearances suggest that he was starting to be groomed as lord of the western territories, as successor to his father, while it was intended that his younger brother, Theobald, would in due course succeed his uncle, Hugh, as count of Troyes.[43] We do no more than glimpse William and Theobald in these roles, however, and all is changed. William had been married to the heiress of Sully, and had appeared on public occasions as count,[44] but by 1107 Theobald had been knighted and was recognized as count of Blois, taking all of his father's territories.[45] Another brother, Odo, died around this time,[46] and it may have been around the same time that the youngest son, Henry, was sent as an oblate to the Cluniac house of La Charité-sur-Loire.[47] The disparagement of William was sufficiently remarkable to call for comment. According to William of Newburgh, the countess "wisely set aside her first-born because he was deficient in intelligence and seemed second-rate."[48] The chronicler wrote many years later, and many miles away in northern England, but there is no doubt at all that he reflected the language of the day, specifically the language of the Anglo-Norman court

---

[43] LoPrete, *Adela*, 122, 147–9.

[44] Ibid., 102–3, 143–50, 212–14. William had married Agnes, daughter of Giles de Sully, by November 1104: ibid., 468–9 (no. 49); OV, vi. 42–3.

[45] LoPrete, *Adela*, 152–3; Suger, *Louis VI*, 74–7.

[46] He is last mentioned in 1107: *Cart. Saint-Père de Chartres*, ii. 454–5 (date from LoPrete, *Adela*, 481, no. 69); his anniversary was kept on 25 December: *Un Manuscrit chartrain du XI siècle*, 149.

[47] Henry is found with his mother *c.*1104: *Cart. Saint-Père de Chartres*, ii. 411–12 ("annuentibus suis filiis G. et H."; date from LoPrete, *Adela*, 484, no. 74); and with his abbot in 1111: *Cart. La Charité-sur-Loire*, 119–24 ("presente domno Odone, priore de Charitate, cum monachis suis, Henrico filio comitis Stephani . . .").

[48] Newburgh, i. 31.

around the year 1106. In that year, Henry I's most influential adviser, Robert, count of Meulan, settled his estates on his twin sons and had his arrangements confirmed by the king. He sought to factor in two areas of uncertainty, the first that they should lose their territories, "on one side of the Channel or the other," the second that one of the sons would "not prove suitable for the governing of land."[49] At just this time also, Henry himself justified his capture of Normandy from his brother Robert, following the battle of Tinchebrai, in terms of Robert's patent unsuitability for office. He had "occupied his lands like a barren tree"; he was "a duke in name only, openly mocked by his own servants, incapable of avenging the insult implicit in their scorn."[50] It was good knockabout stuff, but the point that was being made was deadly serious. A man who could not manage his own household could not run a duchy. It cannot be coincidence that Adela, who is known to have been in close touch with Henry at this time, made a similar judgement of her own eldest son, William. The one story that we have of William, possibly not by coincidence, was of his violent conduct towards his bishop, Ivo of Chartres. This was in 1103.[51] William was still young and he might grow out of it, but why take the risk, when you had sons and to spare? Lordship was a professional business. The lands of the counts of Blois did not lie in frontier regions but in prosperous, well-established communities, which would become more prosperous from the profits of agriculture and trade. And their tenants, the local lords and castellans, had to be persuaded, not constrained.[52]

Adela's third surviving son, Stephen, observing these changes, which would determine the future course of the lives of his brothers, will not have felt that the future pattern of his own life had become any clearer. He was a part of the family team, but the position in which he would play was yet to be determined. In the interim he would obtain the training appropriate to a boy of high rank: formal instruction in Latin letters, from clerks trained in the schools;[53] instruction in horsemanship from male relatives or retainers; and much time would have been spent in listening to tales from the Bible and of the deeds of the heroes of antiquity and of the more recent past.[54] Stephen occurs alongside his

[49] *Regesta*, ii, no. 843, and text 319: "si . . . talis fuerit quod non sit idoneus ad terram regendam"; "si . . . non sit idoneus ad terram possidendam."

[50] OV, vi. 84–91; and the same ideas were rehearsed in front of Pope Calixtus II at Gisors in late 1119, ibid. vi. 284–9 ("non possidebant sed deuastabant").

[51] LoPrete, *Adela*, 216, 258–61, where it is suggested that William's mistake was to act against the interests of his mother.

[52] "It has been said of them that 'they knew how to appear at the head of their *fideles*, they did not care to administer their subjects; in short, they commanded but did not govern' ": Dunbabin, *France in the Making*, 195; citing Chédeville, *Chartres et ses campagnes*, 288.

[53] *Documents historiques inédits*, 2/ii. 5–7: "dono et illos septem hospites in Franca Villa quos prius habuit Willelmus Normannus magister filii mei"; this clause is not found in the version of the charter printed in *Cart. Conques*, 352–3.

[54] LoPrete, "Adela of Blois as Mother," 318–20.

brothers throughout the first decade of the twelfth century. There has to be an element of policy in this; the sons were on parade on a variety of "state" occasions; their involvement with grants was put on record in case their future responsibilities might change; they become used to the inter-related ceremonial of the liturgy and of land transfer. In the earliest of these records that survive their father was still alive. This is an agreement in favour of the chapter of the cathedral of Chartres, and it names four sons, William, Stephen, Odo, and Theobald.[55] The agreement may date from late 1099 and, if so, it is the first time that Stephen is mentioned by name. Another grant around the same time is witnessed by Stephen and William along with their parents.[56] Subsequent charters were issued in the name of Adela. In charters of 1102 for Bonneval there is a dynamic in the witness list: "Adela; William her son; Theobald; Stephen their brother."[57] A charter for Conques was issued around 1108 by Adela, "with count Theobald and with my other sons."[58] And very solemnly, in 1109–10, a further charter for Bonneval was issued at Chartres by Adela, "with the consent and at the wish of my sons Theobald, the count, and Stephen," and then confirmed by the French king at Etampes.[59] This is the last mention of Stephen in such a context, his interest noted but at the same time constrained by piety, protocol, and patrimony. There were other great occasions at Chartres which he might well have attended, including the marriage in spring 1106 between the great Bohemond I, prince of Antioch, a hero of the crusade, and Constance, daughter of Philip, king of France, whose first marriage to Hugh, count of Champagne, had been annulled. After, we may imagine, the bishop had preached suitably on the benefits and obligations of Christian love, the bridegroom mounted the pulpit and "related to the huge throng that had assembled all his deeds and adventures" on crusade. The event was long remembered.[60]

---

[55] *Cart. Notre-Dame de Chartres*, i. 104–8: grant by Stephen and Adela *cum filiis nostris*, who all signed ("+ Signum Guillelmi. + Signum Stephani. + Signum Odonis. + Signum Teobaldi"). On this document, see LoPrete, "Adela of Blois and Ivo of Chartres," 141–2; eadem, *Adela*, 451–2 (no. 20).

[56] *Cart. Notre-Dame de Paris*, ii. 265–6: "S. Stephani filii comitis. S. comitis Stephani. S. comitisse A. S. Willelmi filii comitis"; LoPrete, *Adela*, 457–8 (no. 28).

[57] *Cart. Molesme*, ii. 25–6: "Idem quoque donum Adela comitissa, regis Anglorum filia, et eius tres filii Guilelmus, Teotbaldus et Stephanus concesserunt ... S. Adela comitisse +. S. Guilelmi eius filii +. S. Teotbaldi +. S. Stephani eorum fratris"; LoPrete, *Adela*, 462–3 (nos. 38b, 39).

[58] *Cart. Conques*, 353–4: "Ego Adela Blesensis comitissa cum Teobaldo comite et aliis filiis meis."

[59] *Histoire de Bonneval*, 57–8: "concedentibus et volentibus filiis mei Theobaldo comite et Stephano"; LoPrete, *Adela*, 518–19 (no. 127); *Recueil des actes de Louis VI*, i, no. 46: "quam Adela nobilis comitissa, mater prefati comitis Theobaldi, approbantibus eodem comite et fratre suo Stephano, fecit monachis."

[60] OV, i. 26; iii. 182–3; vi. 70–1.

COUNT OF MORTAIN

Stephen in 1110 was around eighteen years old. The course of his adult life would start to be determined over the next few years, in the light of the interests of his family at this time. They were years of warfare between Henry I of England and the recently crowned king of France, Louis VI. Theobald of Blois took the part of Henry as that conflict developed and in the eyes of Abbot Suger of St Denis, the biographer of the French king, he was simply his uncle's pawn. Yet he fought for his own family's interest, to offer good lordship to vassals on the frontiers of his lands and in particular to check the ambition of Fulk V, the count of Anjou.[61] There were sieges and skirmishes in Brie, to the north-east of Paris, in the Chartrain and on the frontiers of Normandy. At the end of 1112, Henry re-took Alençon, having earlier imprisoned its lord, Robert of Bellême.[62] Stephen may have been with his uncle at this point, for it is known that he received the arms of knighthood from him, and it seems likely that this significant "rite of passage" occurred shortly after Henry crossed over to Normandy in August 1111. Stephen was certainly with Henry when the great lords of northern France, the kings of England and France, and the counts of Anjou and Blois-Chartres came to terms. At Candlemas, 2 February 1113, Henry I came to St Evroul, "accompanied with a great number of his magnates," and was admitted into the house's fraternity. "With him were his nephews Theobald and Stephen . . . and several other earls and magnates with their noble vassals."[63] At the end of that same month, Henry I met with the count of Anjou, near Alençon. There a peace was arranged, and it was agreed that the king's son, William Adelin, would be betrothed to the count's daughter, Matilda; at the same time Fulk himself swore fealty to Henry in respect of the border county of Maine. This put pressure on the French king, at whose request a meeting was arranged near Gisors, late in March 1113. As seen by Suger, "the king of England, the king of France, and count Theobald" were the three parties to it. Louis recognized Henry's overlordship not just of Maine but also of Bellême and of Brittany.[64] These lands would still need to be defended and in the key area of south-west Normandy in particular Henry would need strong support. The children of his sister, Adela, were to have a key part to play in the arrangements which he now made to secure this frontier. Matilda, her eldest daughter, was married to Richard, earl of Chester and vicomte of Avranches.[65] Stephen, her third son, was invested as count of Mortain. He had now acquired an established lordship of his own, with tenants,

---

[61] This is the case argued, with great learning and panache, in LoPrete, *Adela*, 304–40; cf. also eadem, "Anglo-Norman Card of Adela of Blois."

[62] Suger, *Louis VI*, 142–9; OV, vi. 176–9.

[63] OV, vi. 174–7.

[64] Suger, *Louis VI*, 170–3; OV, vi. 180–1; Hollister, *Henry I*, 229–33; LoPrete, *Adela*, 336–9.

[65] LoPrete, *Adela*, 339–40, 551.

castles, and a charismatic hermit. If this happened in 1113, he was around twenty-one years old.

Orderic is the only chronicler specifically to mention the grant to Stephen of the county of Mortain. He did so when he spoke of Stephen's mother, who had welcomed the pope at Chartres in 1103. Adela, he said, had "carefully brought up her young sons to defend the church."[66] He named William, Theobald, Stephen, and Henry. Stephen, the third son, "received the arms of knighthood from his uncle the king, and after William count of Mortain was captured at Tinchebrai, was given the county by the king." In this broad view, the grant of the county of Mortain was consequential on the battle of Tinchebrai, fought on 28 September 1106, in which Robert Curthose had been captured. It was not an immediate consequence, however. The king took his time, keeping his options open, and when he did grant this Norman frontier lordship to his nephew, he also granted him a significant estate in England. It is known that Stephen obtained the honour of Eye in Suffolk around the year 1113. The date comes from an interesting charter of Hervey, count of Léon in Brittany, in which he lists his predecessors as lords of Eye, saying that Stephen had succeeded Henry I, who had held the honour for seven years.[67] Stephen was also granted the lands which later would be referred to as the honour of Lancaster, for he occurs as lord of the honour in the Lindsey Survey, which has been closely dated to 1115–16.[68] These two honours, of Eye and of Lancaster, were reunited in common ownership, having previously been held by Roger the Poitevin under William Rufus.[69] All this suggests that Eye and Lancaster were granted to Stephen as a package; and it is tempting to suggest that this was part of a broader "package deal," as in some measure compensation for his not obtaining the English lands of the count of Mortain. In this analysis Eye and Lancaster should not be added, after Mortain, to a sequential list of Henry I's benefactions to Stephen, but be seen as part of a single grant: together they formed the new Anglo-Norman fee of the count of Mortain. There were advantages for both parties in the creation of this Anglo-Norman estate. For the king, it meant that Stephen had the same responsibilities as the men who now became his peers, a personal interest in "the union" of England and Normandy, which Henry had reforged with the capture of his brother in 1106. For the new count, it meant that he would have bases and revenues in the more prosperous parts of England, in particular in East Anglia, to support his holding of frontier terrritories both in Normandy (Mortain) and in England (Lancaster). Such arrangements were not made without discussion and negotiation and it would be surprising indeed if Adela herself was not involved in them.

[66] OV, vi. 42–5.

[67] *Eye Priory Cartulary*, ii. 24; cf. Lewis, "The King and Eye."

[68] *Lincolnshire Domesday*, 237–60; for the date see Foulds, "The Lindsey Survey."

[69] Lewis, "The King and Eye"; Chandler, "The Last of the Montgomerys"; Green, "Earl Ranulf II and Lancashire," 99.

It is not certain when Stephen first travelled to England. If he crossed to England with the royal court, as was quite likely for a young man still in need of introductions, then this would have been in July 1113 or July 1115. A late chronicle from Crowland Abbey in the English fenland states that he and Count Theobald, his brother, came there in 1114 to visit their former tutor, Geoffrey of Orléans, who was then abbot.[70] It may be that they did. Stephen was certainly at the court for one of the great state occasions of 1115, the Christmas court at St Albans, which saw the consecration of the new abbey church.[71] The king and queen were present, along with William, their son, then twelve years old. There were six earls: Robert, count of Meulan, Stephen himself (named second), Richard, earl of Chester (Stephen's brother-in-law), William of Warenne, Walter Giffard, earl of Buckingham, and David, son of the king of Scots (brother of the queen, who held the honour of Huntingdon). There were bishops, and royal officers, and barons, some of them with estates that marched with Stephen's own. One of them was Ranulf Meschin, vicomte of Bayeux.[72] Many of these were men of wide experience and long memories, which they may well have been prepared to share over supper.[73] At Salisbury, the following March, Henry had his magnates do homage to his son William as his heir, just as the Normans had done the previous year.[74] We may imagine the count of Mortain swearing this oath on one of these occasions. He and his peers will have sworn willingly enough. It was in everyone's interest that the succession should not be in doubt.

Stephen would be in Normandy for the next four years. These years have been seen as the crisis period of Henry I's reign, in which the English king would have the continuing support of Count Theobald and the new count of Mortain, as against the king of France and the count of Anjou, while he faced difficulties also, and most damagingly, with some of his own vassals. Henry had to offer his lordship in a highly competitive environment. Stephen in this period seems very much the agent of others, contin-

---

[70] *Rerum Anglicarum scriptorum veterum*, 121, in the context of Theobald and Stephen having been in England in 1114. There is no other evidence for this visit, but it is accepted as "plausible" in LoPrete, "Anglo-Norman Card of Adela of Blois," 587 and n. 70. On Geoffrey, see OV, ii. 346–51; *Heads*, 41–2, 246–7.

[71] HH, 460–1, 624–5; *ASC*, s.a. 1116. This was one of the great churches of the day: Fernie, *Architecture*, 111–15; it reused material from the Roman city of Verulamium: *GASA*, i. 52–4, 70–1. For those present, see *Regesta*, ii, no. 1102, the text of which is highly inflated but with a witness list which may be taken as genuine

[72] King, "Ranulf, Third Earl of Chester."

[73] Robert de Beaumont, earl of Leicester, had fought at the battle of Hastings: William of Poitiers, *Gesta Guillelmi*, 130–1, 178–9; OV, ii. 174–5. He had fought also at Tinchebrai, as had William de Warenne: OV, vi. 84–5. William had been an early suitor of Edith-Matilda, who was now queen of England: OV, iv. 272–3; *EYC*, 8: *Warenne*, 7–9. The bishop of Durham, Ranulf Flambard, could describe how he had escaped from the Tower of London, and exactly how he had been involved in the making of Domesday Book: OV, v. 312–13; iv. 170–3; Roffe, *Domesday: The Inquest and the Book*, 245–7.

[74] Eadmer, 237; *ASC*, s.a. 1115.

ually on the move, responding to crises as they occurred. This was the perspective of the French court.

> The king of England joined efforts with count Theobald and attacked the nearest border district of the king. The nearness of Normandy to the countryside of Chartres made them neighbours. They sent Stephen count of Mortain, nephew of one and brother of the other, at the head of a host to other districts, namely into Brie, for they were afraid that the king would suddenly seize that land in the absence of count Theobald.[75]

Orderic at St Evroul noted the brothers closer to home. The forfeited lands of Robert of Bellême, which would need to be defended, were granted by Henry I to Count Theobald, but then, by a family agreement and with Henry's consent, they were given to Stephen in exchange for "his claims on the ancestral inheritance in France."[76] And thus "young Stephen took possession of Sées and Alençon and Le Mêle-sur-Sarthe and Almenèches with La Roche-Mabile."[77] These, when added to Mortain itself, gave Stephen responsibility for some of the key fortresses on the southern frontier of Normandy. In the latter part of 1118 that frontier was fast slipping away and the English king suffered a series of reverses. In the second week of November he was at L'Aigle. Theobald was captured by the garrison there, but "the king and count Stephen came up with a force of knights, and by their chivalrous behaviour rescued the count from the enemy's hands."[78] Orderic tells the story from the point of view of Henry I, with some vividness, for these were struggles that came very close to his own monastery. Yet it would be wrong to see the count of Mortain henceforth solely as an agent of the king of England. He was seldom far apart from his elder brother, the count of Blois, and his brother was not yet married. In these circumstances, Stephen himself would have been seen as his brother's heir.

In the next year, 1119, Theobald would find himself once again in danger of his life and his brother, Stephen, would face the first test of his own mettle as a lord of men and as a military commander. Orderic set the scene in the following way:

> At that time the townsmen of Alençon rebelled against King Henry, and I will explain why they offended the king by such a crime. Stephen count of Mortain, who was their lord at the time, was a young man who neither loved the burgesses as he should have done nor showed them the respect that was their due. He was guided, like Rehoboam, by the

---

[75] Suger, *Louis VI*, 184–5; trans. Cusimano and Moorhead, 111.
[76] OV, vi. 196–7: "ipse uero eundem honorem permittente rege Stephano fratri suo pro portione paternae hereditatis quae in Gallia est donauit."
[77] Ibid.
[78] Ibid., 204–5.

fawning of sycophants, not the counsel of the elders, and formed the opinion that the townspeople were disloyal to him and to the king. Consequently he oppressed them with burdens and unaccustomed exactions, foolishly blind to the consequences that would follow. Finally he summoned them all and ordered them to give him their sons as hostages.[79]

The hostages, both male and female, were treated improperly, and the townsmen appealed for assistance to the count of Anjou: "Count Fulk readily agreed to this," came to Alençon, and laid siege to the castle. Henry brought up troops to relieve the siege, and his nephews, Stephen, count of Mortain, Theobald, count of Blois, "eager for glory and anxious to show their mettle," according to the Angevin *Gesta*, headed the advance guard.[80] They engaged the Angevins outside the town walls, and were defeated. Count Theobald was wounded by an arrow which struck him on the forehead and made him a grisly spectacle, with blood streaming over his face.[81] It was an image of defeat and the garrison was forced to surrender after just three days.[82]

  The battle of Alençon was a serious reverse for the king and his policy. Henry, and Stephen as his lieutenant, had lost Alençon and probably the other castles also. If Stephen is to be seen thereafter as compromised by what had happened at Alençon it will have been not by the military defeat but by his behaviour earlier. There is no reason to question the judgement of Orderic, that Stephen had been badly advised, and that his men had dishonoured those who had been held as hostages (the Angevin chronicle concurs).[83] He might have been tempted to observe that the townsmen's subsequent behaviour proved the taking of hostages to have been wise. He may not have known whom to ask for advice, for he had been lord of Alençon for just a few weeks and had no networks on which to draw. The history that he inherited he found was not that of his own family (as might be claimed for the county of Mortain) but that of the house of Montgommery-Bellême. It was still a potent force. Roger of Montgomery's brother, Arnulf, was closely associated with the court of the count of Anjou, and it was he who acted as the go-between in the townsmen's discussions with the count of Anjou.[84] Roger's son, and Arnulf's nephew, was William Talvas: he was count of Ponthieu (between Normandy and Boulogne) and had lands in northern Maine over which the English king

---

[79] OV, vi. 204–9.

[80] *Chroniques des comtes d'Anjou*, 156: "cupidi glorie et probitates suas voluntarii ostendere."

[81] Ibid., 158–9: "quidam jaceret in incerto sagittam, vulneraretque levi ictu in fronte consulem Theobaldum; sanguis autem defluebat super oculum nec videre poterat ex illa parte, sanguine oculum coperiente."

[82] Ibid., 160; Bradbury, "Battles in England and Normandy," 7–8.

[83] *Chroniques des comtes d'Anjou*, 155: "burgensium uxores et filias deshonestabant."

[84] OV, vi. 206–7; Thompson, "Arnoul de Montgommery."

had no control.[85] At the same time Reginald of Bailleul, a man with close
and long links with the family – for he had been the Domesday sheriff of
Shropshire – came to Falaise and renounced his fealty to the king. He and
others acted in this way, says Orderic, because it was being reported that
"almost all the Normans had deserted the king."[86] Henry had to negotiate.
"He sent envoys of peace to Fulk, count of Anjou." In May 1119 Henry's
son married Fulk's daughter, and in the following month, "the king, at the
count's request, received William Talvas . . . back into favour, and restored
to him all his father's lands in Normandy." Orderic makes no great claims
for these arrangements but he says that they offered "a much-needed
breathing space to the hostile peoples."[87]

    Stephen remained with the royal court. He is next noted in July 1119 at
Evreux, one of those "summoned by the king" to attack the garrison of
Amaury de Montfort, whose claims to the county Henry refused to
accept.[88] Thereafter, in what would be a significant twelve months diplomatically, he is nowhere mentioned, though members of his family were
much involved behind the scenes. He was not in the royal army in late
August at the battle of Brémule.[89] Though the forces involved were small,
and the battle lasted less than an hour, this was a decisive battle, for it
involved the leaders of both kingdoms.[90] The English king, Henry, lined
up against the French king, Louis. The son of the English king, William,
set himself against his rival for the succession, William Clito, son of
Robert of Normandy. The Anglo-Norman forces won the day. The
French king lost his standard, and his warhorse, and wandered from the
field dazed, being protected by a peasant who did not recognize him and
escorted him to safety. It is a nice story and it makes a point about
medieval kingship, that kings for the majority of their subjects were names
but not faces, effigies on coins but never seen in the flesh. Louis, once
behind his own lines, would regain his dignity but not the initiative. A few
weeks later the pope, Calixtus II, arrived in France and held a council at
Rheims.[91] He was concerned to make peace between the two kings but
found the parties intransigent. He was briefed initially by the French side,
and when he came to meet Henry at Gisors in November reproached him
for his treatment of his brother, "whom you have kept in fetters for many
years"; he should be released immediately and the duchy restored to him
and his son. The pope met an absolute rebuttal from Henry. As the scene
was realized by Orderic, here very much at the top of his game, Henry set
out in detail his title to rule the duchy. He had rescued Normandy from
the anarchy to which his brother had reduced it and given its inhabitants

---

[85] Thompson, "William Talvas," 172.
[86] Ibid., vi. 214–17.
[87] Ibid., 224–5.
[88] Ibid., 228–9.
[89] Ibid., 234–43.
[90] Hollister, *Henry I*, 263–5.
[91] SD, *Opera*, ii. 254–6.

peace and security; he had not "held his brother in fetters like a captured enemy" but had placed him "as a noble pilgrim, worn out with many hardships, in a royal castle"; he had made every effort to conciliate his nephew, William Clito, and would continue to do so; the duchy was his by right of battle as the just inheritance of his father.[92]

The remaining points of difference between the kings of England and France were resolved in the spring of 1120, and a key figure in the making of the peace was Adela, countess of Blois. She offered hospitality to the exiled Thurstan, archbishop of York, who had the trust of the French king; Thurstan mediated with Cuno, a member of the pope's entourage; Cuno mediated with the French king.[93] A peace was made and concluded in June 1120. The French king accepted the homage of William, the king's son, for the duchy of Normandy, and in so doing recognized him as Henry's heir. The peace has been described as "a dazzling diplomatic triumph for Henry I."[94] "At the king's command," the Norman nobles then did homage and swore allegiance to William.[95] His position as his father's heir could not have looked more secure. Adela of Blois, one of the instigators of the peace, chose this moment to retire from the world, taking up residence in the Cluniac nunnery of Marcigny.[96] Her public career was over but her interest in politics was not. She could receive regular messages and the occasional visit from her sons.[97]

All was set fair for Henry I in the summer of 1120. And yet on one winter night, that of 25 November 1120, many of his achievements were set to naught, and "the face of all things was wonderfully changed."[98] The court had set out to return to England, sailing from Barfleur, near Cherbourg. One of the last vessels to depart was the White Ship, only recently refitted, and carrying – it was estimated – around three hundred passengers and crew, along with some of the royal treasure. On a clear but moonless night the ship foundered on a rock close to the shore.[99] There were only a couple of survivors. It was the loss of a litany of young lives and expectations. There were three of the king's children: William, his son, recently married and recognized as his heir; Richard, his natural son, the new lord of Breteuil; Matilda, his natural daughter, countess of Perche. There was the king's niece, and Stephen's sister, Matilda, countess of Chester, along with her husband, Earl Richard, and his half-brother,

---

[92] OV, vi. 282–91; see also Eadmer, 258.

[93] Hugh the Chanter, 152–9. WM, *GR*, i. 758–9, also noted the importance of Adela and Theobald in the discussions.

[94] Hollister, *Henry I*, 274.

[95] SD, *Opera*, ii. 258: "Normanniae principes jubente rege filio suo Willelmo . . . hominium faciunt et fidelitatis securitatem sacramentis affirmant."

[96] Hugh the Chanter, 152–5; Wischermann, *Marcigny-sur-Loire*, 317–20.

[97] *Peter the Venerable*, i. 175–7; ii. 24, 136 (letter no. 15).

[98] WM, *GR*, i. 762–3: "iuuenculi ergo morte cognita res mirum in modum mutatae."

[99] On the loss of the White Ship, see OV, vi. 294–307; WM, *GR*, i. 758–63; JW, iii. 146–9; HH, 466–7; *ASC*, s.a. 1121. On the "ferry service" across the Channel, see Le Patourel, *Norman Empire*, 163–72; for the site of the disaster, ibid., 177–8.

Othuer, son of Hugh of Avranches, earl of Chester. Stephen lost not only a sister but many of his own friends and vassals. "The castellans of Mortain were particularly assiduous in the search for their kinsfolk, for almost all the barons and chief nobles of that county perished."[100] Stephen himself had initially planned to sail in the White Ship but had disembarked, "because there was too great a crowd of wild and headstrong young men on board."[101] Orderic a little later gives more detail and provides a slightly more pressing reason for Stephen to disembark. "As I have said, only the count because he was suffering from diarrhoea, and two knights, Robert of Saqueville and Walter, had left the vessel, and by God's will made the crossing safely in the king's ship."[102] There is a hunger for news after disasters of this kind and many such stories were in circulation.

One of the stories was that Thomas, the skipper of the sunken vessel, had died rather than survive to face the king's anger and consuming grief. The task of telling the king was swiftly delegated by the magnates to his nephew, Count Theobald, and even he balked at the task, arranging for a child to be brought before the king and innocently blurt out the news.[103] The king was desolate (see plate 1). The support of his close family was important to him and both Theobald and Stephen are found in his company in the following weeks. They may have been with him when he spent Christmas without state at his house at Brampton near Huntingdon.[104] They were certainly with him at councils held in January 1121. The king had been away from England for nearly five years and there was work to be done as well as condolences to be received. Stephen was one of those present at the Epiphany court, to which all the bishops of England had been summoned; he was the senior layman to witness the grant of the bishopric of Hereford to Richard, keeper of the king's seal,[105] and the grant of privileges to Shrewsbury Abbey.[106] Theobald was also at court.[107] The chief advice given by the bishops the king hardly needed and may already have acted upon. His wife, Matilda, "a truly incomp-

---

[100] OV, vi. 306–7.

[101] Ibid., 296–7.

[102] Ibid., 306–7.

[103] Ibid., 300–1; Hugh the Chanter, 164–5.

[104] HH, 466–7; ASC, s.a. 1121.

[105] Regesta, ii, no. 1243.

[106] Ibid., ii, no. 1245; printed Cart. Shrewsbury, i. 36–7 (no. 35), where it is argued that Epiphany 1121 and Whitsun 1121 are "equally possible" as dates. Twelve bishops are listed here, however, and there is no sign of the same number being present at the later council at Whitsun. Moreover, in Regesta, iii, no. 819, Stephen as king says that he was there when the grant was made. It is not made clear that what is printed ibid., is only the conclusion of a lengthy document, printed in full and discussed in Cart. Shrewsbury, i, pp. xiii–xvi, ii. 254–62. Once the witness list is accepted as genuine it must follow that it was the Jan. 1121 council of which it was intended as a record.

[107] Regesta, ii, no. 1244 (for Peterborough Abbey), possibly later in the month, since the charter is witnessed by Geoffrey, archbishop of Rouen, who is next recorded at the king's marriage.

arable woman," had died in the spring of 1118.[108] He needed to marry again and produce an heir who would have the same unquestioned legitimacy as William Adelin, so cruelly taken away when "both the love of his father and the hope of the people were confidently fixed on him." Adeliza, the daughter of Godfrey I, duke of Louvain, "a maiden of great beauty and modesty," was on her way.[109] She was met at Dover and escorted in state to Windsor. Adeliza and Henry were married on 29 January by the bishop of Winchester, and on the following day they were crowned by the archbishop of Canterbury. The king's nephews were there and alongside them, now given a more prominent role at court, was the king's eldest illegitimate son, Robert, who would shortly thereafter be granted the earldom of Gloucester. The exact precedence between Stephen, count of Mortain, and Robert, earl of Gloucester, cousins who were close in age and equal in rank, would exercise both clerks and courtiers over the coming years.

Thurstan of York returned just after the coronation of the young queen and was warmly received by the king. The dispute with Canterbury over the primacy, which had kept him from his see for six years,[110] had a political cost, for Norman lordship north of the Humber needed an archbishop of York to take an active role. Stephen, as the lord of Lancaster, would work closely with Thurstan. In the ensuing five years there are few direct references to Stephen, but what there is shows a pattern. It was at this time that he started to establish himself in his lordships.[111] It may be that some of his vassals from the county of Mortain who died in the White Ship disaster were on their way to take up lordships in England.[112] Simeon of Durham records that in the autumn and winter of 1122, Henry I went from York into Northumbria and then across the Pennines to Carlisle, whose fortifications he ordered to be strengthened, returning thence to York, where he conducted "important meetings of the citizens and men of the province."[113] There are indications, not without difficulties of interpretation, that Stephen was with the royal court for part of this time, and that he should be seen as one of the "lords of the province" noted by the Durham chronicler.[114] In the same period Archbishop Thurstan was

[108] Huneycutt, *Matilda of Scotland*, 145–6, citing *Liber Monasterii de Hyda*, 312–13.

[109] JW, iii. 148–9: "puellam uirginem decore modesti uultus decenter insignitam."

[110] Nicholl, *Thurstan*, 41–74.

[111] There are also notifications to him as the lord of Eye and as one of the leading magnates of Normandy: *Regesta*, ii, nos. 1337, 1356, 1406.

[112] OV, vi. 306–7; cf. the way the family and vassals of Ranulf Meschin were established in Cumbria a little earlier: Phythian-Adams, *Land of the Cumbrians*, 34–5. For the prosopography of the tenants of the county, Pouëssel, "Les Structures militaires du comté de Mortain."

[113] SD, *Opera*, ii. 267: "post graves civium et comprovincialium inplacitationes." OV, vi. 324–5, says that the king was at York on 6 Dec. 1122.

[114] He witnessed *Regesta*, ii, no. 1338, but this document is suspicious, for it is highly unlikely that John, bishop of Lisieux, another witness, was in York at this time; the witnesses are those addressed and those witnessing ibid., no. 1337, from which it may have been constructed. The latter document is given by Orderic and it is he who notes that Stephen, abbot of Chartres, was at York at this time: OV, vi. 324–5.

similarly engaged in establishing his authority in the north-west of his diocese; and the foundation of new religious houses was one of the means by which he did so. Stephen contributed to the endowment of what was to be an important Augustinian house at Nostell near Pontefract.[115] The king's confessor, Athelwold, would join the community shortly thereafter as its prior, and it may already have been envisaged at this point that he should become the first bishop of a new diocese at Carlisle.[116]

COUNT OF BOULOGNE

A man in this society would marry when his prospects could be measured and when a partner of appropriate rank became available. Stephen's bride was Matilda, the daughter and heiress of Eustace III, count of Boulogne. Matilda was a lady of high lineage, for her mother Mary was a daughter of the saintly Margaret, queen of Scots, whose grandfather had been Edmund Ironside, king of England. Any children born to Stephen and Matilda would carry the DNA of both the Anglo-Saxon and the Anglo-Norman kings. Matilda was also a niece of Henry I, for another of the daughters of Margaret of Scotland had been Matilda, his first queen. The marriage took place in 1125, the date known from an interesting charter which Count Eustace made in that year, in which he notes that he had given his inheritance to Stephen along with his daughter in marriage.[117] The union was seen as suiting Henry I's policy objectives, but the marriage itself was not in his gift. As William of Malmesbury put it, while the county of Mortain had been given to Stephen by the English king from his own possessions, the county of Boulogne was acquired through Henry's enterprise.[118] Henry had an interest, for the inheritance was not just the county of Boulogne but "the honour of Boulogne" in England. This was one of the great estates at the time when Domesday Book was made, valued at £770 a year in annual income. It was eleventh in rank at that date,[119] but the league tables tell only a part of the story, for the two largest estates had been dissolved by 1125 and – no less importantly – a high proportion of the Boulogne manors remained under the direct control of its estate officials.[120] The centre of the honour was in East Anglia and when supplemented by some of the estates of Eudo Dapifer and combined

[115] *Lancashire Pipe Rolls*, 301; Nicholl, *Thurstan*, 130–2; cf. Burton, *Monastic Order in Yorkshire*, 71–7. The grant was of a church dedicated to St Oswald, at Winwick in Makerfield (Lancs.).

[116] See the discussion in Nicholl, *Thurstan*, 134–5, 146–7; *EEA* 30: *Carlisle 1133–1292*, xxxv–xxxvi.

[117] *Recueil des chartes de Cluny*, v. 340–1: "laudante simulque confirmante Stephano comite Boloniensi, cui hereditatem meam cum Mathildi filia mea dedi."

[118] WM, *HN*, 98–9: "et pariter Bononiensem comitatum industrie adquisiuit; nam ante Moritoliensem in Normannia ex suo dederat." According to Robert of Torigni, Stephen "heres factus est," he was made the heir: *GND*, ii. 262–3.

[119] Hollister, *Anglo-Norman World*, 82 n. 2.

[120] There is a useful list of the estates in Tanner, "Eustace II," 280–5.

with the honour of Eye, it would make Stephen one of the dominant landowners in south-east England. Boulogne, and more particularly Wissant, were the chief continental ports on the short sea-crossing from France to England, one of the major thoroughfares in the commercial life of northern Europe (see plate 3).[121] The marriage brought Stephen to the centre of Anglo-Norman political life.

About the same time that Stephen was married a vacancy was created at the abbey of Glastonbury, through the promotion of its abbot Seffrid to the bishopric of Chichester. It was filled in 1126 by Henry, the younger brother of Theobald, count of Blois, and of Stephen, count of Mortain and Boulogne. Henry was a Cluniac monk. He had been professed at the mother-house, having spent his earliest years at La Charité-sur-Loire, where he can be glimpsed just the once as a monk in 1111. He was appointed to Glastonbury, so he himself said, "with God's approval and through the favour of Henry, king of the English."[122] It was a substantial favour. Glastonbury was the richest monastery in England. Its Domesday valuation of £828 was comparable to the £770 valuation of the honour of Boulogne.[123] This was princely preferment. The estate, however, was run down and not reaching its potential: "its buildings reminded him of peasants' huts; its monks were struggling to maintain the necessities of life: and it had been deprived of many of its possessions."[124] Henry set himself to recover lost estates, to reinforce the house's privileges, and to bring in professional managers; he would later write an account of his stewardship in his own hand. He saw at the same time the need to project the image of his own house abroad, to make it once again a place of renown. He invited William of Malmesbury to stay and research the house's history. William was impressed by the young abbot and remained closely attached to him.[125] As abbot of Glastonbury, Henry was not just a dominant figure in his local community; he was a lord of knights and a tenant-in-chief of the crown. He would be able to establish himself within the royal court and he kept in close touch with his family.[126]

[121] Grierson, "Relations between England and Flanders," 73–81. At Wissant, waiting for a fair wind to England, you might imagine at any one time, "more than a hundred abbots and monks, and a great multitude of military men and merchants": Hariulf, *Chronique de Saint-Riquier*, 241.

[122] "Scriptura Henrici abbatis," in *EEA*, 8: *Winchester 1070–1204*, 204–13, at 205: "annuente deo, favente Anglorum rege Henrici."

[123] Knowles, *Monastic Order*, 702–3.

[124] William of Malmesbury, *The Early History of Glastonbury*, 1.

[125] The preface to *De Antiquitate*, ibid., 40–3, conveys very skilfully that Henry had put many people's backs up when he first arrived; the conclusion, ibid., 165–7, provides a more conventional eulogy.

[126] He is found in Normandy with the king in 1128–9, obtaining privileges for his own monastery and for his mother's house at Marcigny: *Regesta*, ii, nos. 1590, 1599a. He was in the company of his brother, Count Theobald of Blois, and of Andrew of Baudemont. He is recorded in the company of his other brother, Count Stephen, at Bermondsey Priory, which he may have used as his London club until he had a property of his own: Oxford, Bodleian Library, Dodsworth MS 78, fo. 25v.

Stephen and his wife can be seen in the records of their own lordship. Over twenty of the count's own charters survive and an equal number of documents issued by him are referred to but no longer survive. Each of these provides a snapshot, more or less sharp, with more or less detail, depending on when they were taken and the circumstances in which they were preserved. Of the charters which are lost, but of which there remains a basic record, a substantial number come from the county of Mortain.[127] They relate in particular to two religious foundations. The first of these was the ancient collegiate church in Mortain itself.[128] The second was the new monastery at Savigny, founded on the southern boundary of the count's territory. We get from these charters a picture of an early twelfth-century lordship, accustomed to its routines, able to function whether the count was present or not.[129] The count's officials controlled the market at Mortain, and 15 shillings a year from its tolls were given for the lighting of two altars in the church. The count supported the gifts of his men, some made within the confines of Mortain,[130] others in the full gaze of the ducal court at Rouen.[131] The count had a small army of officials: a steward, bailiffs in the main centres of the estate, foresters and justices. There were clergy also, a dean and a sacristan, the master of the school, and a small cadre of clerks, some of whom can be named, for it was they who drafted the count's charters. Whenever the canons of Mortain were with the count – so they were careful to keep on record – if he was residing at Mortain, they would receive the same provisions as his domestic chaplains and eat with them at his table. His was a privileged, cosmopolitan world and for a few heady days they could be a part of it.

[127] There are numerous references to lost *acta* of Stephen as count of Mortain in later confirmations: of Henry II in 1156–8, in *Recueil des actes de Henri II*, i. 184–8; of the bishop of Avranches in 1179, in Hill, "The Counts of Mortain and Savigny," 249–51 (Savigny); *vidimus* of Philip VI of France in 1333, in Boussard, "Le Comté de Mortain," 253–79 (the canons of Mortain); Van Moolenbroek, *Vital l'Ermite*, 138 and n. 118 (the nuns of Mortain).

[128] Boussard, "Le Comté de Mortain," 253–79.

[129] Power, *Norman Frontier*, 58–61: "the local aristocracy maintained local order in this corner of Normandy."

[130] The relevant documents here are: (i) Bibliothèque nationale, MS lat. 5441, ii. 416 (transcript kindly supplied by Daniel Power); printed *Gallia Christiana*, xi. 478–9: "acta sunt hec apud Moret' in aula comitis anno incarnati uerbi M°c°xxx°viiii°"; (ii) Desroches, *Mont-Saint-Michel*, i. 229: *actum* dated 1128, in which Ranulf Avenel headed a list "de baronibus comitis." The charter cited by Desroches, in *Annales du pays d'Avranches*, 133, dated 1121 "in curia comitis de Moretonio coram Guillelmo Avenel tunc temporis senescallo eiusdem comitis et clericis et militibus multis," has been shown by Power, *Norman Frontier*, 52 n. 158, to date from 1191.

[131] Stephen's own charters issued at Rouen are: (i) Evreux, AD Eure H. 10 (transcript kindly supplied by Daniel Power); calendared *Regesta*, ii, no. 1547: "apud Rothomagum facta fuit hec concessio in presentia domini et auunculi mei Henrici regis Anglorum" (Bec Abbey); (ii) BL, Cotton MS Cleopatra C. vii, fo. 76v; printed Round, "Bernard, the King's Scribe," 424–5 (Bernard the scribe). Royal charters referring to his earlier confirmations are: *Regesta*, ii, nos. 1544 (Aunay Abbey), 1546 (Furness Abbey), 1588 (Virey Abbey), 1973 (Savigny Abbey).

"The venerable Vitalis," a former canon of Mortain and a former chaplain of Robert, count of Mortain (the half-brother of William the Conqueror), renounced this world but never quite escaped from it. He settled in the forested area south of Mortain, at Savigny, and there he attracted followers by the simplicity of his life and the power of his preaching. A key stage in what would be the foundation of a new order is marked by Henry I's confirmation to "Vitalis the hermit" of the grant of the site of the monastery by Ralph of Fougères. This was a substantial diploma, bearing the *signa* of many of the great and the good, which is seemingly precisely dated to 2 March 1112.[132] Henry in making the grant was asserting his authority on the frontiers of his lordship and his appointment, in the following year, of Stephen as count of Mortain was part of the same process. Stephen would become a key supporter of Savigny; indeed in the record the careers of the charismatic hermit and the pious count seem intertwined. Stephen and his tenants are found time and again in the abbey cartulary, said the abbé Desroches, with the abbey cartulary in front of him as he wrote – an exercise that cannot be repeated, for the cartulary was destroyed by Allied bombing of the town of St Lô in 1944.[133] They would protect the monastery, and, after the death of Vitalis in 1119, they – and the other lords of western Normandy – would offer land for new foundations. In all, at least forty-seven Savignac houses were founded. One of these was at Virey, west of St Hilaire-du-Harcouët, where a fine privilege sets out in an exemplary way what such a foundation involved.[134] Three brothers, Ralph, William, and Roger de Virey, made a series of grants to the church of Savigny, most substantially their rights over a long list of local churches, which included the tithes owing to them, with other grants including 20 shillings of rent in England, "of the fee of the count of Mortain." They did this, they said, "with the agreement and consent of their lords, namely Stephen, count of Mortain, and Henry of Fougères, who wish each of them to share in these benefits along with their ancestors and their wives." The grant was made specifically so that, at Virey, "by the ordering and under the command of the monastery of Savigny, under a prior or under an abbot (if that prove possible), and by the grace of God, the monastic life shall be followed." Another charter for a new monastery, at Furness in Lancaster, was of similar date and contains many of the same formulas, just as a charity might now suggest a standard form of words for use in a bequest.

The abbey of Furness was Stephen's own foundation. According to the house's foundation history, the first monks set out immediately after the consecration of the abbey church at Savigny on 1 June 1124 and arrived in their new home early in July.[135] It will have helped smooth their path that

---

[132] *Regesta*, ii, no. 1015; Haskins, 311; Green, *Henry I*, 124–5.

[133] Desroches, *Annales du pays d'Avranches*, 108, 130.

[134] *Monuments historiques*, no. 409.

[135] *Monasticon*, v. 246–7 (giving the date of foundation as 7 July 1127); *Coucher Book of Furness*, i. 21. SD, *Opera*, ii. 267, places the original foundation in 1123.

their leader was an English-speaker.[136] The site chosen for them was at Tulketh near Preston, on the banks of the Ribble. Three years after that, finding the site inconvenient, the monks moved even further north, to Furness. Such moves were not unusual, as new communities sought to bed down, and this community will have needed little encouragement, for what they were now offered was on a quite different scale from what they had previously enjoyed. At Furness they were given not a township but a whole province, the count's demesne lands there, his forests and his hunting rights, extending in the north to Ulverston and to the south to his fisheries at Lancaster. There was much for the early monks to do but the economic potential of this grant was huge and Furness would become one of the richest monasteries in northern England.[137] It may be significant that the more generous grant of land came only after Stephen's marriage, for this left Lancaster more peripheral to his concerns. The charter of foundation of Furness, which survives in a fine seventeenth-century facsimile, is dated to the last months of 1127 (see plate 2).[138] The offering was made for the salvation of the souls of himself and his wife, of his lord and uncle, Henry, king of the English and duke of the Normans, and of all the faithful, living and dead. At this point there was no mention of any children.

While in his *acta* as count of Mortain and as lord of Lancaster Stephen may appear a distant figure, as count of Boulogne he seems personally more engaged. He had joined an established family business. He is mentioned invariably in the company of his wife and it seems clear that – to use a modern analogy – she was the full-time managing director while he was the part-time chairman. Colchester, the site of one of the earliest and the finest of post-Conquest castles, served as the administrative centre of the honour of Boulogne in England. It had been held as a discrete estate, "the lands of count Eustace," in the early years of Henry I's reign, and additional lands had been acquired after the death of Eudo Dapifer in 1120.[139] This history was in the minds of Stephen and Matilda when they confirmed to St John's Abbey, Colchester, "whatever they held under Eudo Dapifer, whatever they held under count Eustace, of the fee which now is in our power"; they made the grant for the salvation and well-being of themselves and their children; and they remembered in their prayers Count Eustace and Countess Mary and other of their ancestors.[140] They confirmed Countess Mary's deathbed bequest of the manor of

---

[136] This was Ewan, "a monk of Savigny, who had been born at Avranches of English parents": Poulle, "Savigny and England," 163; *Heads*, 133–4.

[137] There is a fine treatment of the abbey's history by F. M. Powicke in *VCH Lancashire*, ii. 114–30.

[138] *Book of Seals*, no. 423: SIGILLUM STEPHANI COMITIS BOLONII ET MORITONII.

[139] Round, "The Counts of Boulogne as English Lords"; King, "Stephen of Blois," 280–3.

[140] *Cart. Colchester*, i. 48–9.

Kingweston in Somerset to Bermondsey Priory, where she was buried.[141] They similarly confirmed to the monks of Christ Church, Canterbury, freedom from customs duty at the port of Wissant, which Count Eustace had granted them. The fact that this was a confirmation was shown clearly by the way that the clerk copied from the earlier charter the provision that the grant would be valid, "whether there was peace or discord between the king of the English and the count of that land."[142] The reservation seems hardly necessary by the late 1120s but the monks had long memories.

The count and the countess were at Canterbury in person: they placed their sealed charter on the high altar of the abbey church, and it remains in the chapter archives to this day. The seal, although damaged, is the only original of Stephen's seal which survives. The archbishop of Canterbury, presiding over this ceremony, was William of Corbeil. They knew him well, since before his appointment to Canterbury he had been prior of the Augustinian house of St Osyth's, Chich, in Essex, one of whose chief benefactors was Baldwin d'Austry, the constable of the honour of Boulogne.[143] They wrote to the archbishop and the bishop of Ely, "their most dear fathers and brothers," notifying them that they had transferred all secular rights, what they termed the "earthly honour," of the church of Gamlingay in Cambridgeshire to the Augustinian canons of Colchester. They did so, they said, "for the remission of our sins and those of our ancestors and for the safe preservation of our son, Eustace, and our other offspring and for our temporal well-being."[144] This is the first mention of their eldest son, Eustace, who must have been born before August 1131, when their good friend Hervey, the bishop of Ely, died. The heads of local religious houses were frequent guests at their table, following traditions of hospitality set on both sides of their family. This may help explain their strictures on hereditary benefices, which are unusual for lay people at so early a date.[145] The same point can be made when Stephen and Matilda were in the county of Boulogne. They are found holding court in the small town of Desvres in the Boulonnais, presiding over a recognition of the personal freedom of tenants of Longvilliers, where a new Savignac

[141] BL, Harley MS 4757, fos. 8v–9r. The manor was held by Countess Ida of Boulogne in 1086, when it was worth £6: *DB*, 248b–249a.

[142] Canterbury Cathedral Library MS Cartae Antiquae F129: "donatio autem ista rata semper erit. siue pax sit siue discordia inter regem Anglorum et comitem ipsius terre." The same phrase is found in Count Eustace's grant, ibid., F130. Heather Tanner kindly informed me of this grant by Stephen and Matilda, in advance of its listing in her *Boulogne and Politics*, 322.

[143] Stephen and Matilda confirmed his grant: *EYC* 8: *Warenne*, 49. St Osyth's is eight miles from Colchester, on the Colne estuary. The story of its foundation is well told in Bethell, "Richard of Belmeis and the Foundation of St Osyth's." On the archbishop see, Barlow, "William de Corbeil."

[144] Oxford, Merton College Muniments, no. 5525, i–ii.

[145] As Christopher Harper-Bill has kindly pointed out to me.

abbey was under construction.[146] They made grants also to the monks of St Wulmer, Samer, which survive in copies that are much improved but which have a sound, and local, set of witnesses, including Osto of Boulogne, who has been identified as an early master of the Templars in England.[147] The Boulogne estate had capable and long-serving managers. The steward, Heinfrid, had previously served as steward of Count Eustace, and joined the larger team under Stephen and Matilda after 1125.

"Stephen was the greatest of English territorial magnates and needed an administrative organisation hardly less elaborate than that of the king himself."[148] Sir Frank Stenton was here commenting on just a small archive of Stephen's charters, relating to East Anglia and most specifically to the Cluniac priory of Eye in Suffolk, but his point is only strengthened by an examination of the continental honours from which Stephen derived his titles. Stephen was perforce much reliant on his household officers, men who provided the interface with the many local communities in which he exercised his lordship. The charters show their professionalism and the flexibility with which they operated. To Stephen, his deputy (*vicecomes*) in Mortain, he writes from a distance but reaches from the parchment to grab him, as it were, by the collar: "you, Stephen, I firmly order you that you should not force them [the nuns of Mortain] to answer on any matter, other than by my authority and in my presence."[149] He could send firm instructions also to men of higher rank than that, such as Geoffrey Blund, the sheriff of Suffolk, who was one of those instructed to return a church to the monks of Eye.[150] He writes in a different register, but still gives an instruction, to his friend the local bishop too.[151] If the local officials did not act on his orders, then their supervisor would do so.[152] This is not just an estate administration as elaborate as the king's but one closely in touch with that administration and borrowing many of its

---

[146] Haigneré, "Chartes de l'ancien Boulonnais," 413–14; printed from abbey cartulary AD Pas-de-Calais H 2 Mi 5, fo. 114v (manuscript reference kindly supplied by Heather Tanner); Auvry, *Savigny*, ii. 247–8.

[147] Haigneré, "Chartes de l'abbaye de Samer," 117–23. These are charters of Stephen as count dated "1141" and "1145." These dates will have been supplied later, to fit them into a sequence of dated charters, at a time when the dates of Stephen's kingship were long forgotten. For the identification of Osto see, Green, "Financing Stephen's War," 105.

[148] Stenton, *First Century*, 68.

[149] Paris, Archives Nationales JJ48, fo. 59v (no. 103), from an inspeximus by Philip IV at Mortain, April 1310 (a copy of which was supplied by Nicholas Vincent); printed Haskins, 127 note 17. On the situation of the house, see Desroches, *Mont-Saint-Michel*, 257–8.

[150] BL, Add. MS 8177, 134a–b; Stenton, *First Century*, 266, and *Eye Priory Cartulary*, i. 30–1.

[151] Oxford, Merton College Muniments, no. 5525, i–ii.

[152] His justice at Coutances would hear any further complaint about William de Vernon and his foresters and agents, if the monks of Bec were not allowed to take timber for building and fuel: Caen, AD Calvados, MS J non coté: Cartulaire de St-Etienne, Caen, fo. 23r ("si supra idem aliquid feceritis quod eis noceat, precipio quod iusticia mea de Constanc' rectum faciat"). The cartulary is Stein, *Cartulaires français*, no. 712. I owe my knowledge of the manuscript and a photocopy of the relevant folio to the continued kindness of Nicholas Vincent.

formulas and its procedures. The monks of the tiny priory of Bromholm, no less than the monks of the great abbeys of Normandy, would enjoy the count's firm peace throughout his lands.[153] The prior and the monks of Eye in Suffolk were to enjoy their possessions, "as they best and most honourably held in the time of Robert Malet, and on the day on which I received the lands of Robert Malet from the king, and on the day on which I most recently crossed the Channel"; and they should only answer to the count in person. There may have been a case for the monks to answer – it was, after all, against the count's local officials that the monks had complained – but they were promised a personal hearing when the count was next in England, and in the meantime they were not to be disseised of their property.[154] It is only a short step from this writ, which has every appearance of authenticity, to the writ of *novel disseisin*, one of the possessory assizes introduced by the English royal court half a century later. This would similarly use the phrase, though specifically as a limitation of time, about the king's "last crossing the sea."[155] It hardly seems anachronistic to speak of the emergence of best practice.

Best practice is certainly to be seen in the workings of the exchequer. This provided settled routines for the management of the estates and the prerogatives of the English monarchy, which were able to draw upon a continuing financial record. The pipe roll of 1129–30 survives as a record of good housekeeping on the national scale.[156] The routine entries on this roll are those which show sums allowed to the sheriffs of the various counties in respect of Danegeld, the national land tax. Stephen was the dominant lay landholder in Suffolk, had a significant presence in the adjacent counties of Essex and Norfolk, as in Lincolnshire, and lands in twenty different counties in all. He also had urban property in London, Southwark, Winchester, Bedford, and Colchester.[157] The count of Mortain, Stephen's invariable title in this record, could expect to be exempted from Danegeld, but still it had to be properly accounted for and in some counties his officers seem to have been slow in filing their returns.[158] The London account is a social history in microcosm, with staple foodstuffs and exotic goods being bought for the king's table and sent to him at Woodstock.[159] The sheriff of London paid the officials of the count of Mortain £12 12s 6d in cash, whilst the cost of fine cloth from London drapers, supplied to the count, was charged to the king's account.[160]

---

[153] BL, Harley MS 2110, fo. 67v; printed, *Monasticon*, v. 63: "volo et precipio ut firmam pacem meam habeant per totam terram meam."

[154] BL, Add. MS 8177, fo. 134b; Stenton, *First Century*, 265–6, and *Eye Priory Cartulary*, i. 31 (no. 21).

[155] *Glanvill*, bk. xiii, cap. 33, ed. Hall, 167–8.

[156] *PR 31 Henry I*; Green, "Praeclarum et magnificum antiquitatis monumentum."

[157] There is a useful table in Davis, *Stephen*, 8.

[158] King, "Stephen of Blois," 285.

[159] *PR 31 Henry I*, 143–52

[160] Ibid., 143.

Traders from Provins, one of the fairs of Champagne, described as "the merchants of count Theobald," had their tolls remitted.[161] There are other marks of royal favour to Stephen and his estate officials, such as the fine of 15 marks owed by Roger Gulafre for a breach of the peace being pardoned "for the love of the count of Mortain."[162] There are a number of entries also, perhaps the most interesting of all in this account, in which the count's tenants ask for the king's support. Fulcher of Playford, one of the barons of the honour of Eye, offers 10 marks, "to have justice in England in the court of the count of Mortain."[163] Robert Gresley offers 20 marks, "that the king assist him in a certain lawsuit against the count of Mortain," along with a further 60 marks for the subsequent agreement (*convencio*).[164] And, "between the Ribble and the Mersey," Lesing and his brother, Edward de Cordiner, Ailsi son of Ulf, Roger of Ranchil, Osbert son of Edmund and Uctred his brother, all described as "men of the count of Mortain," each offered significant sums – 30 or 40 marks – "for concord between them and the count."[165] It is easy to offer a bland translation of these entries, more difficult to guess at the circumstances that lie behind them. Undoubtedly, however, they reflect the harsher side of the count's lordship; for the most part the activities of his officials and of his court were not subject to external review.

THE SUCCESSION

The generous grants made both to Stephen and to his younger brother, Henry, giving each of them significant prestige and landed wealth within the Anglo-Norman realm, came at a time when the succession to it had become a key policy issue for Henry I. He lacked an heir. In 1126 he had been married to Adeliza of Louvain for more than five years and no child had been born to them. William Clito, the son of Robert of Normandy, had always been a reproach to Henry and was now a direct rival. Many in the Anglo-Norman realm viewed William as Henry's legitimate successor. It was a prospect that Henry would resist at all costs, and his other nephews, Stephen especially, were agents of his policy. If Stephen is to be viewed as a player in the family team, now – so it must have appeared – he had been set to mark William Clito. It is not necessary to see Stephen, in default of William Clito, as Henry's chosen successor. Henry in promoting

---

[161] Ibid., 144. Note also a pardon granted at the instance of Andrew de Baudemont, ibid., 147. Andrew was the steward of Theobald of Blois: Bur, *Champagne*, 431–2.

[162] *PR 31 Henry I*, 97. Roger Gulafre was the steward of the honour of Eye: *Eye Priory Cartulary*, i. 58–9.

[163] *PR 31 Henry I*, 99. Fulcher of Playford had recently succeeded his brother in his fee and it is possible that the justice he sought related to his inheritance: *Eye Priory Cartulary*, i. 30 (no. 19), 246–7 (nos. 346–7); ii. 75–6

[164] *PR 31 Henry I*, 114. Robert Gresley had lands in Nettleton (Yarborough wapentake) and Calcote in Legsby (Wraggoe wapentake), in both of which places the count of Mortain had lands also: Lindsey Survey, 11/16, 22; 16/5, 8, in *Lincolnshire Domesday*, 237–60.

[165] *PR 31 Henry I*, 33.

Stephen was making a rather different point. Orderic Vitalis reported at length on an episode which preceded the Anglo-French peace of 1120, when the English king met the pope at Chaumont. Henry declined the pope's request that he release his brother, Robert of Normandy, from captivity but he was anxious to stress that he would do what was proper for Robert's son. What was proper for a man of this high rank was control over three English counties and a place within Henry's court.[166] It was an offer that William Clito, the eldest son of the Conqueror's eldest son, proudly declined. It cannot be an accident that, over a period of time, just such substance and rank would be given to Stephen. It was what was appropriate. It was appropriate also that Stephen's younger brother, Henry, once he had proved himself as abbot of Glastonbury, should be promoted to a bishopric.[167] Henry was nominated as bishop of Winchester following the death of William Giffard in 1129.[168] While he should, strictly, have resigned Glastonbury on his appointment, no pressure was put on him to do so, and the combined resources of the richest monastery in the country and what was close to being the richest diocese made him unquestionably the wealthiest man in the country after the king.[169] The king, as he grew older, felt most comfortable with his close family. It helped that the nephews themselves were very confident and assured as courtiers; they were charming and could hold their own in any company.

The king's chosen successor was not one of his nephews but his daughter, Matilda. Matilda had been married in 1114 to the German emperor, Henry V.[170] It was a wonderful match and a heavy tax was laid

---

[166] OV, vi. 288–9: "Tres etiam comitatus in Anglia optuli ut illis principaretur et inter aulicos oratores educatus lucenter experiretur."

[167] The suggestion has been made that Henry was prior of Montacute in Somerset for a few years before he was appointed abbot of Glastonbury. This is unlikely. Contemporaries were quite clear as to Henry's c.v. He had been a Cluniac monk from his boyhood; as a young man he was appointed abbot of Glastonbury; and then he was made bishop of Winchester: SD, *Opera*, ii. 283; OV, vi. 42–5; *GND*, ii. 262–3; Newburgh, i. 31–2. The statement that he was prior of Montacute is found in a note from Faversham Abbey printed in *Red Book of the Exchequer*, ii. 752. It was viewed sceptically in *Heads*, 121, but more benignly in the additional text, 269. The discussion there centres on the Montacute annals. These are found in BL Cotton MS Tib. A x, fos. 145–76, where, it is stated, "fos. 163v–164 show an interest in Henry compatible with his having been prior of Montacute – the part of the MS which might have related to his priorate is too much burnt to be legible." The manuscript, however, can be read sufficiently to establish that the only references to Henry are to his appointment as bishop of Winchester in 1129, in succession to William Giffard, and to his death in 1171. The annals record the death of Prior Arnold on 5 Nov. 1139 but no successor. This was the year in which Henry of Winchester became papal legate and the most likely explanation of the Faversham entry is that at this point he took the estates of Montacute in hand.

[168] JW, iii. 188–9; *ASC*, s.a. 1129; *Ann. Mon.*, i. 12 (Margam), ii. 49 (Winchester), 221 (Waverley), iii. 434 (Bermondsey); *UGQ*, 79 (St Augustine's, Canterbury).

[169] Knowles, *Monastic Order*, 702–3; Hollister, *Anglo-Norman World*, 82 n. 2; Howell, *Regalian Right*, 34–5. Vincent, *Peter des Roches*, 55, describes the see of Winchester as "one of the greatest prizes to which any churchman could aspire."

[170] On Matilda as empress see Chibnall, *Matilda*, 18–44.

on England to pay for it. Matilda, however, was widowed on 23 May 1125, and within a year of this Henry had determined that she would be his heir. He "sent men of distinction and called his daughter home";[171] she was with the royal court when it crossed from Normandy to England in September 1126.[172] There was a lot to be done if the king's plans were to be realized. They had to be sold, as best they could be, to the wider political community. The royal court was summoned to Windsor for the Christmas feast of 1126 and after the celebrations the court moved the short distance to London. There, on 1 January 1127, oaths were sworn in support of the empress.[173] We have some idea of the proceedings. Roger, bishop of Salisbury, acted as the master of ceremonies. He called the great magnates up one by one. A form of words was probably read out, to which each of the magnates assented briefly, rather as a bridegroom might answer "I do" to a priest's reading of his marriage vows. It would be interesting to know the exact form of words, but there is more commentary than exact reporting in the many records of the proceedings which survive. John of Salisbury, though writing at some distance in time, may come closest to an answer. He stated that Stephen, like the other magnates, "had sworn fealty to the empress Matilda, Henry's daughter, and had undertaken to help her secure all England and Normandy against all men after her father's death."[174] This is quite close to the earlier of the two versions given by John of Worcester, who was writing close to the event: "they swore fealty and an oath to the king's daughter that they would defend the kingdom of England to her against all others."[175]

Whatever the exact form of words, Stephen, count of Mortain, was one of the magnates who assented to them. The 1st of January 1127 is a fixed date in his biography, though it became so only after Henry died. William of Malmesbury sought to fix the date by attaching a story to it. "There was a noteworthy contest, it is said, between Robert and Stephen, who as rivals in distinction strove with each other for the honour of swearing first, the one claiming the prerogative of a son, the other the rank of a nephew."[176] John of Worcester later heard a rather different version of the same story:

The regulator of the proceedings spoke to Robert, earl of Gloucester, who was sitting to the left of the king, saying, "Get up, get up, and swear

[171] WM, *HN*, 4–5.

[172] SD, *Opera*, ii. 281; *ASC*, s.a. 1126; HH, 476–7.

[173] JW, iii. 164–7; SD, *Opera*, ii. 281; Hugh the Chanter, 218–19; *ASC*, s.a. 1127 (mentioning Windsor only).

[174] JS, *HP*, 82–3: "Iurauerat enim Matildi imperatrici . . . fidelitatem et quod post decessum patris illam in adoptione et conseruatione Anglie et Normannie contra omnes homines adiuuaret."

[175] JW, iii. 166–7: "fide et sacramento spoponderunt filie regis se totum regnum Anglorum illi contra omnes defensuros."

[176] WM, *HN*, 8–9: "notabile fuit ut fertur certamen" (AB); "notabile ut dicitur fuit certamen" (Ce).

the oath as the king wants!" Robert replied, "No, rather Stephen, count of Boulogne, was born before me and should do this first, he who is sitting to the right of the king." This was done.[177]

The story of the two men sitting on their hands, and needing to be cajoled into taking part, rings true, and it draws attention to two related points, first the king's will as the key determinant in what happened,[178] second the lack of enthusiasm among some of those whom the king constrained. Each of these chroniclers was writing early in the civil war which followed Henry's death and they reflect the circumstances of that war.[179] Their readers wanted information on exactly what was said and done at the council. If there is a basis of fact in these stories it may have to be read between the lines. It may be that what was reported as a dispute over precedence shows a reluctance of the great magnates, not just Robert of Gloucester and Stephen of Mortain, to have any part at all in these proceedings. They will have heard of, and some of them may have taken part in, similar events in the past,[180] but there was no precedent for what was done here, with the right to succeed the king being passed to the king's daughter. The ceremony would have raised more questions than it answered. On what terms would the empress succeed? Did the king have any plans for her marriage? Even if so, was she capable of having children of her own (for she had had none so far)? If she were to marry, what would be the status of her husband? And of any children they might have? The oaths were conditional in any event, in that the king might still have an heir by Queen Adeliza. The queen was present at these proceedings, which were predicated on her infertility (quite wrongly, as it would turn out); she was treated with proper respect and had her income increased.[181]

Whatever the form of words, the message to the outside world was clear enough. Henry would do anything to resist the claims of William Clito, his nephew, to succeed him as king. The response of the French king was immediate. He "addressed the nobles of the realm at his Christmas court and asked them urgently to give sympathy and help to William the Norman." The most practical help was given by the king himself. He gave William Clito "in marriage the sister of his own queen"; "moreover he gave him Pontoise and Chaumont and Mantes and all the Vexin."

---

[177] JW, iii. 178–81.

[178] *ad iussum regis* (JW, iii. 166–7; later toned down, *ad uelle regis*, iii. 176–7); he caused archbishops [etc.] to swear (*ASC*, s.a. 1127); *jubente illo* (SD, *Opera*, ii. 281); *fecit episcopos* [etc.] *hoc pacto promittere* (*GND*, ii. 240–1). Stephen's party would claim that the oath had been extorted by force: JS, *HP*, 83–4.

[179] The passages just cited, from William of Malmesbury and John of Worcester, were written in the early 1140s: WM, *HN*, xxxii–xxxiii; JW, iii, p. xxxii.

[180] Most recently, the oaths sworn to William Ætheling in 1115 (in Normandy) and 1116 (in England): *ASC*, s.a. 1115; Eadmer, 238; Green, *Henry I*, 134–6.

[181] SD, *Opera*, ii. 281–2; WM, *HN*, 6–7; *VCH Shropshire*, iii. 10–11.

"This was done in January," and so was clearly a direct response to reports of events in England.[182] The French diplomatic service may already have had intelligence of the next move by the English king. This was the marriage of the empress to Geoffrey, the son of the count of Anjou. After negotiations, in which Robert of Gloucester and Brian Fitz Count were involved, the couple were betrothed in the cathedral church of Rouen in May 1127.[183] In the meantime there was another death and another opportunity, possibly a decisive one, for the French king to advance the career of William Clito.

On Wednesday, 2 March 1127, Charles, count of Flanders, was assassinated. This was a most shocking crime, for he was killed as he knelt at prayer, "in order to hear the early mass in the church of St Donatian" at Bruges; "following his pious custom he was giving out alms to the poor," and he had just recited the Lord's Prayer when he was struck down by Borsiard and his accomplices, members of the Erembald clan. The news travelled fast. It reached England early on the Friday and Laon later in the same day. "We learned this," says Galbert of Bruges, "through our students who at that time were studying at Laon, as we also learned it from our merchants who were busy carrying on their business on that very day in London."[184] The French king was the overlord of Flanders and the count had died without heirs. He claimed the right to oversee the election of the new count. This took place at Arras, where he heard the various claimants, took counsel from the barons of Flanders and the representatives of the cities, and secured the election of William Clito. The king and "the new count" then moved via Lille and Ghent to Bruges. The count granted privileges to the cities, including a confirmation of the rights of their sworn associations, the communes, and homage was sworn to him in impressive public ceremonies.[185] No one was in any doubt as to the wider political significance of this election. It was a direct challenge to the English king, Henry I, who responded in kind, using "all his strength and cunning to try to diminish the count's power."

In the dispute that followed the election of William Clito as count of Flanders, which was in large measure fostered by the English king, Stephen – not for the first time – would act as Henry's chief lieutenant. Henry "sent his nephew Stephen of Blois, count of Boulogne and Mortain, who with other of his party influenced the opinion of many of the great men by many gifts and even greater promises."[186] Stephen was well placed for such work and he had a proper interest in it, for he himself was one of the barons of Flanders. He formed an alliance

[182] OV, vi. 368–71; Chibnall, *Matilda*, 54–6.
[183] HH, 476–7; WM, *HN*, 8–9; *ASC*, s.a. 1127; Chibnall, *Matilda*, 55–6.
[184] Galbert, caps. 12, 15.
[185] Ibid., caps. 47, 52–6.
[186] Walter of Thérouanne, cap. 45.

with the duke of Louvain,[187] the count of Hainault,[188] Thomas de
Coucy,[189] and William of Ypres.[190] "All these men and their allies worked
against the [French] king's wishes and dispositions, and impeded the
progress of the new count in every way that they could."[191] All those
named here may have received money-fiefs from the English king.[192] In
addition to this, the economic interests of the townsmen of Flanders were
gravely affected by the hostilities between their count, William Clito, and
the king of England and count of Boulogne. The "new count" promised
the burgesses of St Omer that, were he to make peace with the king of
England, by the terms of that agreement he would ensure that they were
granted freedom from tolls and taxes throughout the kingdom of England.
Similarly, if he should make peace with Stephen, count of Boulogne, he
would ensure that they were free from tolls "at Wissant and throughout his
land."[193] It is clear that he offered the same terms to the burgesses of the
other cities of Flanders.[194]

Stephen came to terms with William Clito later in the year. Orderic
describes the peace being made:

> In August [William Clito] led an army against Stephen count of
> Boulogne, and in an attempt to force him into subjection began to lay
> waste his lands relentlessly with fire and sword. But in time, trustworthy
> negotiators were sent out and the two men joined hands because they
> were kinsmen, and laid down their arms after agreeing on a three-year
> truce.[195]

By this time Henry I's original coalition had fallen apart. Galbert records
William of Ypres being captured by "our count" William Clito on

---

[187] Godfrey, duke of Lower Lorraine (1106–40), father of Adeliza, who married Henry
I in 1121.

[188] Baldwin IV, of Mons, count of Hainault (1120–71), "the boy from Mons": Galbert of
Bruges, caps. 67, 96.

[189] Also known as Thomas de Marle or Thomas de La Fère, count of Amiens (1118–30),
homo perditissimus (Suger, *Louis VI*, 30–1): Duchesne, *Histoire généalogique*, 197–205, preuves
325–36.

[190] Also known as William of Loo (illeg. son of Philip of Loo, the second son of Count
Robert the Frisian), "the false count of Ypres" (Galbert, cap. 67), "the bastard" (Suger, *Louis
VI*, 248–51), a neighbour of Stephen as count of Boulogne and closely associated with his
cause as king of England.

[191] Walter of Thérouanne, cap. 45.

[192] Baldwin of Mons certainly received a fee of 100 marks from Henry I: Gilbert of
Mons, 63; for comment Lyon, *From Fief to Indenture*, 34–7. William of Ypres had "five
hundred pounds of English money," either directly from Henry or purloined from the
treasure of Count Charles (Galbert, cap. 49), and a force of 300 knights (ibid.; Suger, *Louis
VI*, 248–9).

[193] *Actes des comtes de Flandre 1071–1128*, no. 127, caps. 7, 16.

[194] Galbert mentions a grant to Bruges, what he calls a "little charter of agreement,"
cap. 55.

[195] OV, vi. 370–3.

26 April, while about the same time Baldwin of Mons had withdrawn from his attack on Oudenaarde.[196] But other claimants to the county remained, Henry's pockets remained deep, and William Clito could not establish his authority. For all this we would appear to have his own words:

> Behold my my powerful and inveterate enemy, namely the king of the English, who has long grieved at my success. Now he has brought together innumerable knights and vast amounts of money; and out of pure spite he labours to take away from you and from ourselves a section of the most faithful and powerful men of your realm, confident in the number of his men and still more in the quantity of his cash. In this way he has been able to subvert the hearts of the Flemings with gifts, so that not only do they not hold firm, but in fear they have come to resist me.[197]

Galbert provides chapter and verse for these complaints.[198]

If 1127 had been a year of mixed fortunes for Henry I, 1128 would be a good one. On 10 June he knighted his future son-in-law, Geoffrey of Anjou, and a week later he was present at the marriage of Geoffrey to Matilda, the empress.[199] Almost immediately thereafter, Geoffrey became count of Anjou when his father left for the Holy Land. Some claimed that the empress had married below her station, but then it was hardly possible not to disparage an empress, and supporters of the marriage would argue that Geoffrey was "a young man of very high birth and remarkable strength."[200] In the month after the empress's marriage, William Clito died. Flanders had descended into civil war, with Thierry of Alsace having been elected as count by the men of Ypres and Bruges. Late in July, William Clito died at the siege of Aalst, at a time when he seemed to be gaining the upper hand against the rival count. "In his short life this most noble of youths gained eternal fame."[201] His death, however, resolved the civil war; Henry had, fortuitously, seen his objectives realized; and Louis, who had failed in his more recent interventions in the duchy, was happy to back off. Both kings recognized Thierry as count of Flanders. Orderic concluded his treatment of events in Flanders in 1127–8 by saying that "King Henry exercised his royal authority to bring under [Thierry's] control Stephen, count of Boulogne, and the other Normans who had lands in Flanders."[202] This may mean no more than that the king, having

---

[196] Galbert, caps. 79–80.

[197] *RHF*, xv. 341, letter addressed to the king of France.

[198] Galbert, caps. 96–101.

[199] John of Marmoutier, "Historia Gaufredi ducis," 177–80.

[200] WM, *HN*, 8–11; *GND*, i, lxxxvii–lxxxviii; ii. 242–5.

[201] HH, 482–3.

[202] OV, vi. 378–9: "Rex Henricus ei *subiugauit* regali justicia." I translate *subiugauit* here as referring to *control* rather than *rule*, as better expressing the authority of the counts of Flanders at this date.

mustered these men against William Clito, now gave Thierry of Alsace assurances of their loyalty.[203] The king of England and the count of Boulogne were now at peace with the count of Flanders, and normal trade resumed.[204]

Stephen's most significant involvement in Henry I's diplomacy, up to this stage in his career, had been at times when the king of France was most actively promoting the claims of William Clito as the English king's successor. It may, then, be no coincidence that a period of apparent disengagement from the royal court followed William Clito's death. This may have lasted for more than four years. William of Malmesbury selected just three events as worthy of notice during this time. The first was the papal schism of 1130. "On the death of pope Honorius in that year the church at Rome was agitated by a great dispute about the papal election."[205] One group of cardinals elected Gregory as Innocent II, the other Peter Pierleoni as Anacletus II. The party of Anacletus gave him control of Rome, but Innocent gained the support first of the king of France, then of the German emperor, and then of Henry I of England. Henry accepted Innocent at Chartres in January 1131 and then received him at Rouen the following May, when he "honoured him with gifts."[206] Henry then returned to England and

---

[203] It has been suggested that it did mean more than this. "Henry had made Stephen do homage to Count Thierry": Le Patourel, *Norman Empire*, 99–100. It is just possible that Stephen did homage but it is highly unlikely. Marjorie Chibnall's note on this passage referred to the earlier treaties between the king of England and the count of Flanders, concluded in 1101 and 1110; and it is these that provide the best indication of the relationship of the count of Flanders and the count of Boulogne at this date. It can only be seen as highly conditional. In the 1101 treaty, the count of Flanders undertook that his troops coming to England would not be impeded by "his men, in particular the count of Boulogne", and this is one of a number of such exceptions. *Diplomatic Documents* I, no. 1; Ganshof, "Le premier traité Anglo-Flamand," 257: "Ces clauses relèvent combien le comté de Bouulogne s'était en fait détaché de la Flandre à la fin du XIe siècle." The count of Flanders could not speak for the count of Boulogne. In the 1110 treaty, the count of Boulogne was nominated as an arbitrator, but only if he was in good standing with the king of England. *Diplomatic Documents* I, no. 2. He might not be. It was his choice. Count Eustace III would thereafter remain in good standing with both the king of England and the count of Flanders, at times attending their courts. At the court of the count of Flanders he would be given a place of honour and referred to as "my faithful man", but still he was one of "my barons": *Actes des comtes de Flandre 1071–1128*, nos. 62, 86, 90, 95, 108, 118–19. This was how the world was ordered: "Barones vero, iuxta generalem consuetudinem in curia regum Francorum comitumque Flandrensium ab antiquo tempore constitutam, adiudicaverunt": ibid., 214 (no. 95). The implications of this ordering would not change while Matilda of Boulogne had control of the county. Thierry might wish to return to the matter when she died.

[204] One of the copies of the chirograph issued by William Clito for St Omer was used as a draft for Thierry of Alsace's charter, and the clauses which restricted trade are crossed out: Giry, *Saint-Omer*, 371–8.

[205] WM, *HN*, 12–13.

[206] Ibid., 18–19, and references there cited. There is an extensive literature on the papal schism of 1130, summarized in *Councils and Synods*, 754–7 (no. 135), and surveyed in Robinson, *Papacy*, 69–78.

in early September 1131 he convened a major council at Northampton. At this, the empress "received an oath of fealty from those who had not given one before and a renewal of the oath from those who had."[207] William of Malmesbury gives this information without context, which is unlike him, the reason being that to explain the context would be to lay bare a severe check to the king's diplomacy. Matilda was living apart from her husband, Geoffrey, count of Anjou, in part at least because the business arrangements – and marriage at this level was a very serious business – were not satisfactory to the count. The king and his council resolved to send her back, presumably with a better offer.[208] At just this time of particular uncertainty as to the English succession, William of Malmesbury, as his third selection, noted the coronation first of Philip, and then, "when this son was killed not long afterwards through falling from his horse," that of Louis, the sons of the French king, Louis VI.[209] The establishment of the heir, and his coronation during his father's lifetime, was the custom in France. The chronicler contrasted the situation in France and in England for very good reason. The English succession was far from secure. Why otherwise the repeated insistence that oaths be sworn in the empress's support?[210]

Stephen was not at the Northampton council meeting in September 1131; if he had been, this fact would have been recalled later.[211] He was at the Christmas court of 1132, at Windsor, which a charter for the Cistercian monastery of Rievaulx in Yorkshire shows to have been well attended. The archbishop of Canterbury, William of Corbeil, was present along with diocesan bishops from England, Wales, and Normandy. There were five earls, Robert, earl of Gloucester, William earl Warenne, Stephen, count of Mortain, Ranulf, earl of Chester, and Robert, earl of Leicester. The barons were mostly members of the royal household: Miles of Gloucester, Humphrey de Bohun, Robert de Courcy, Eustace Fitz John, Payn Fitz John, William Maltravers, Geoffrey Fitz Pain, Jordan Painel, and

---

[207] WM, *HN*, 18–21.

[208] HH, 486–9; Chibnall, *Matilda*, 57–60.

[209] WM, *HN*, 20–1. The two coronations were in fact separated by more than two years. Philip was crowned on 14 Apr. 1129 and died on 13 Oct. 1131; Louis (VII) was crowned on 25 Oct. 1131: *Recueil des actes de Louis VI*, iii. 215–16; OV. vi. 390–1 (1129), 446–7 (1131).

[210] Only two oaths are certain, however, those of Jan. 1127 and Sept. 1131. Ralph of Diceto would later mention an oath s.a. 1133, and Roger of Howden one s.a. 1134: Diceto, i. 246–7; Howden, i. 187. In each case, a later chronicler, wanting to record the oaths, has inserted them in what seemed to be an appropriate point in his text: see further, WM, *HN*, xcvii–xcviii; Chibnall, *Matilda*, 61. Those accustomed to using the "cut and paste" facility on their word processor will readily see how such confusion could occur.

[211] There is a positive "control" here in the very full list, of 47 names, witnessing *Regesta*, ii, no. 1715, granting the abbey of Malmesbury to Roger, bishop of Salisbury, and so subjecting the monks to what William of Malmesbury would describe as a form of slavery: WM, *HN*, xxvii–xxix, 70–1. Note also *Regesta*, ii, nos. 1713 (for the abbey of Cluny), 1736 (for the archbishop of Canterbury).

Aubrey de Vere. In 1133 Stephen is noted first at Westminster,[212] then at Winchester in the spring,[213] and finally at Woodstock outside Oxford in the early summer, a period marked by a "whirlwind of appointments, benefactions, and confirmations."[214] One of these was the appointment of Nigel, one of the nephews of Roger of Salisbury, and previously treasurer, as bishop of Ely. He was being set up to succeed his uncle as the king's chief administrative officer and he would need to be continually at court.[215] No less frequently at court was Henry, bishop of Winchester. He would find it necessary to purchase an estate in Southwark to provide himself with a base in the capital. London prices were a bit steep, he was at pains to explain, but he needed his own place, since he was often at court on royal business.[216] The brothers were often found together. Money talked. Henry issued a significant privilege in favour of the Londoners, the first substantial grant to them, allowing them their own officers but stopping short of granting a commune of the kind that the counts of Flanders had recently offered to their chief cities. The grant was made before the king left, once again, for the duchy of Normandy.[217]

Henry crossed to Normandy, for what would prove to be the last time, on 2 August 1133.[218] This event almost demanded a suitable portent, and it was not difficult to find one, for there was a full eclipse of the sun on that day, the best recorded eclipse of the middle ages.[219] It is not known whether Stephen accompanied the king. The empress had had her first child at Le Mans in March 1133, and he was christened Henry. A second child, Geoffrey, was born at Rouen at Whitsun 1134, after a difficult childbirth in which the mother nearly died. Henry of Huntingdon described the king at this point as rejoicing in his grandchildren.[220] This might seem a sentimental comment from a chronicler who was a married man himself. It may, however, represent the accurate reporting of remarks made to him by his bishop, Alexander of Lincoln, for he had crossed the Channel and was with the king in late summer 1134, first at Verneuil, where he was on campaign, and then at Rouen.[221] Here the king heard a case between the bishop of

---

[212] *Regesta*, ii, nos. 1761, 1795 (for St Bartholomew's, Smithfield). The texts are much improved, but the dating clauses reflect the style of *scriptor* xiii and the witness lists may be accepted as genuine.

[213] *Regesta*, ii, no. 1830 (diocese of Evreux).

[214] *Regesta*, ii, no. 1757 (Reading Abbey); Hollister, *Anglo-Norman World*, 206.

[215] *Liber Eliensis*, 283–5.

[216] *EEA* 8: *Winchester 1070–1204*, no. 24: "altiori precio comparaui"; Carlin, "Winchester House, Southwark." The remains of the palace may be seen by those walking along the South Bank, between the London Dungeon and Southwark Cathedral.

[217] *Regesta*, ii, no. 1645. Both the date of this charter and its authenticity are debated. I follow Hollister, "London's First Charter of Liberties."

[218] JW, iii. 208–11; WM, *HN*, 22–3 and n. 64.

[219] Newton, *Rotation of the Earth*, 99, 160–3.

[220] HH, 488–9.

[221] HH, 490–1; OV, vi. 438–9; *Regesta*, ii, no. 1895.

Lincoln and the abbot of Peterborough. The abbot admitted the rights which the bishop claimed in the parish church at Peterborough; he agreed, when they were back in England, to attend the bishop's court.[222] The full text of the agreement is given in the king's charter, and there are several others like it, all drafted by the same scribe.[223] At Falaise, another high-status clergyman appeared, in search of lodgings. Henry had given Abbot Anselm of Bury a plot of land to serve as lodgings, which lay next door to that of another of his officers, Geoffrey Fitz Pain. "In my presence and with my agreement," the king said, "he has given this to Rainer his chamberlain," who was the abbot's Norman agent.[224] Another chamberlain, William of Houghton, gave a manor to Ramsey Abbey, retaining it for his lifetime only. He promised, when he got home, to surrender his title by placing the relevant charters on the high altar of the abbey church. All this happened *coram me*, in the king's presence.[225] In all these transactions, carefully worked out and carefully recorded, there are no elements of high policy; instead the king was providing good lordship for "his men," in the specific sense of those who held their lands directly of him. When Abbot Anselm returned home to Bury St Edmunds, he would make provision for mass to be said every day in his abbey church, "for the most glorious Henry, king of the English, for as long as he shall live, for his safety and the prosperity of his empire." He did this, he said, "for the friendship and the familiarity that there has always been between us."[226]

Abbot Anselm had good grounds for concern. The relaxed lordship of 1134 had given way to a tense anxiety by the spring of 1135. There had been a rupture between the king on the one hand and his daughter and son-in-law on the other. Matilda and Geoffrey were calling into question the old king's policy. The story could not be kept from the press, but the press, particularly in England, were highly reticent in what they reported. William of Malmesbury, who could be a masterly political commentator, took refuge in a short phrase, saying that the king in his last days was "somewhat angry" with Geoffrey, since he showed him no respect.[227] Henry of Huntingdon referrred to "a number of issues" and blamed the empress, not her husband, for the dispute.[228] Orderic Vitalis, close to the theatre of war, provides more information. He says that Geoffrey had "demanded castles in Normandy, asserting that the king had covenanted with him to hand them over when he married his daughter." He says that some of "the Norman magnates" favoured "the Angevins" and mentions

[222] *Reg. Ant.* 1, 35–6 (no. 52), and plate V (= *Regesta*, ii, no. 1911).

[223] This is *scriptor* xiii: Bishop, *Scriptores Regis*, plates v, xvii(a); *Regesta*, iii, pp. xiii–xiv.

[224] *Feudal Documents*, ed. Douglas, 79–80 (no. 56 = *Regesta*, ii, no. 1913)

[225] *Cart. Ramsey*, i. 250 (= *Regesta*, ii, no. 1915).

[226] *Feudal Documents*, ed. Douglas, 112–13 (no. 112): "pro eodem glorioso rege Anglorum quamdiu uixerit pro salute sua ac prosperitate imperii sui"; "pro maxima amicicia ac familiaritate que semper erat inter nos."

[227] WM, *HN*, 24–5: "marito eius subiratus."

[228] HH, 490–1: "discordiis uariis que oriebantur pluribus causis."

William Talvas and Roger of Tosny as falling under suspicion. By the autumn of 1135 William Talvas had defected and the king is described at this time as "prowling around" the area of Sées, taking Alençon in hand and strengthening the fortifications of Argentan.[229] It was an area that Stephen, count of Mortain, knew well and he may have been with the king at this time.[230] He was certainly with him earlier in the year, when Henry confirmed the provisions of the Truce of God for the duchy of Normandy. This has been described as "the only surviving monument" of Henry's Norman legislation.[231] This document was issued, "in the presence of the bishops . . . and of all my barons who undersign, by common counsel and agreement."[232] The phrase provides a counterpoint to the clear evidence of divided counsels later in the year.

What was the real story that lay behind the anger and the harsh words, which would die by the end of the year, when the king's own voice was silenced? The closest to an explanation is provided only much later by Robert of Torigni, abbot of Mont St Michel. He mentions Henry's refusal to hand over the fortifications of William Talvas. He then goes on:

> There was another and more significant cause of dispute between them. The king had refused to do fealty to his daughter and her husband when they required it, for all the fortresses of Normandy and England; and this they did on behalf of their sons, who were King Henry's lawful heirs.[233]

There is some hindsight in this passage but its central thrust must accurately reflect the politics of the autumn of 1135. The dispute between the king and Matilda and Geoffrey was intimately linked to the succession. They asked for the castles, whether of the dowry or of all Normandy,[234] as security, to ensure that the king's wishes as to the succession would be carried out. Without them – this has to be the view being taken – they would struggle to succeed. Did they ask for more? Did Geoffrey and Matilda focus on the claims of their sons and specifically that of Henry, the elder, at the cost of their own expectations? It may be so but it is likely that what Robert of Torigni, writing in the early 1150s, represented as an agreed view was in the early 1130s just one view among many: a contribution to a discussion, had any such discussion been allowed. It seems to have been the view of the empress's brother, Robert

---

[229] OV, vi. 444–7; Chibnall, *Matilda*, 60–2.

[230] *Regesta*, ii, nos. 1934, 1941.

[231] Haskins, 120–1.

[232] *Regesta*, ii, no. 1908 (calendared); full text in *Coutumiers de Normandie*, 1/i. 65–8, and largely reproduced in *Regesta*, iii, no. 608. On the background, see Boüard, "La Trève de Dieu en Normandie."

[233] Torigni, 128.

[234] OV, vi. 444–5 (Normandy); Torigni, 128 (dowry).

of Gloucester, who remained loyally at the king's side;[235] it may also have
been the view of her uncle, David, king of Scots.[236] Whatever the requests
that were made the old king categorically refused them. He had designated
his daughter as his successor; he had required his magnates to fall into line;
and that would be his last word on the subject.

[235] *GS*, 12−15: "dicens aequius esse filio sororis sue, cui iustius competebat."

[236] RH, 145, referring to Geoffrey of Anjou's marriage to the empress, "cuius filio Anglia
ac Normannia iurata fuit."

Chapter 2

THE ACCESSION

Stephen, count of Boulogne, having been chosen by the nobles of the kingdom, with the sanction of the clergy and people, was crowned king in London on Christmas Day by William, archbishop of Canterbury. The beginning and course of his reign was overwhelmed by so many and such violent commotions, that how to describe them, or how they may be concluded, no one yet knows.[1]

You are known to be descended, in almost a direct line, from that king's lineage.[2]

Everyone knew the story of what had happened on the death of William the Conqueror.[3] The greatest king in western Christendom, he had been left on his deathbed naked and neglected, bereft of basic decency. The great men immediately looked to their own interests. They mounted horse and rode away to their own castles. The king's own servants stripped his corpse, stole his possessions, and then abandoned him. It was one of the local knights, Herluin,[4] a man not bound to him by service, who arranged for the king to be laid out, and his body taken for burial in the church of St Etienne at Caen. This was the king's intended resting place, in a monastery of his own foundation, one of the finest buildings of its day. But as the funeral service progressed fate had more tricks in store. A local man – Ascelin Fitz Arthur – stood up and claimed that the king's burial place was on his land; and compensation was paid to him on the spot. And when finally the king's body was placed in the tomb, the space proved too small, so that when he was doubled up to fit in it, his intestines burst, and the finest incense could do little to mask the stench of decay. There was a moral tale here, and certainly it had lost nothing in the telling. Earthly honour meant nothing. The earls and the counts whose closeness to the king defined their roles, the officers of the household, the domestic servants – all had abandoned their duty. Orderic, who told the tale, would have expected his lay readers to pick all these images up. And he

---

[1] RH, 144–5.
[2] Letter of Pope Innocent II, confirming Stephen's election, RH, 148.
[3] It is found in Orderic who is followed in some particulars by Wace: OV, iv, xxi–xxii, 100–9; Wace, *History of the Norman People*, ed. Burgess, 195–6. There are some echoes also in WM, *GR*, 512–13.
[4] OV, iv. 104–5: "quidam pagensis eques."

would have expected even the novices at his monastery to recognize some echoes from the scriptures, for example the knight Herluin filling the role of Joseph of Arimathea who had taken charge of Christ's body after the crucifixion. But if it has been emboidered a little, the essence of the story is clearly accurate: the king was abandoned; money was paid for his burial place; and those who went to the funeral would never forget the smell.

So when the Conqueror's youngest son lay on his deathbed all were concerned that there be no repetition of these sordid scenes. "The news of his illness quickly brought the magnates together."[5] The following earls are mentioned as having been at the king's deathbed: Robert of Gloucester, William of Warenne, Rotrou of Mortagne, Waleran of Meulan, and Robert of Leicester, "as well as other magnates and officers and noble castellans."[6] The archbishop of Rouen was sent for and he would later describe to the pope, Innocent II, a model Christian death. Henry renounced his sins and on each of three successive days he was absolved and took communion; he made arrangements for restitution to his creditors; and finally at his own request received the sacrament of Extreme Unction.[7] The king died on the night of 1 December 1135.[8] The following day his body was taken the short distance to Rouen, with a very large escort,[9] and with "the nobles acting as bearers in turn." He had left instructions that he be buried at Reading, and since no date of burial could be fixed and the journey was a long one, privately within the episcopal enclosure at Rouen necessary precautions were taken.[10] The king's body was reduced to little more than a skeleton, with his brain, entrails and eyes being removed and buried at the convent at Rouen.[11] It was then taken to rest for a time in Caen, among the tombs of his ancestors, awaiting a fair wind and the royal command.[12]

[5] WM, *HN*, 24–5.

[6] OV, vi. 448–9.

[7] WM, *HN*, 24–5. The messenger carrying this letter to the pope very likely went via Cluny, for shortly thereafter the abbot wrote to Adela of Blois, notifying her of her brother's death in similar terms: *Peter the Venerable*, i. 22; ii. 103–5 (letter no. 15); trans. Davis, *Stephen*, 12–13. The emphasis on repeated access to the sacraments is interesting. It may be that the king was not just absolved and took communion but was also anointed on each day. The repetition of anointing was a custom particularly associated with Cluny, which some commentators found otiose: *Catholic Encyclopedia*, s.v. Extreme Unction: Repetition.

[8] WM, *HN*, 22–5; HH, 490–1 (he had eaten a dish of lampreys, "of which he was very fond, though they always made him ill"), 702–3; OV, vi. 448–9. The fact that Henry died during the night explains the references in several authorities to his having died on 2 Dec., because they "started the day at sunset": *Peter the Venerable*, ii. 104–5.

[9] Orderic gives the impossibly large figure of "twenty thousand men": OV. vi. 448–51.

[10] WM, *HN*, 26–7: "in a corner of the cathedral"; OV vi. 450–1: "in the archbishop's chamber."

[11] Notre-Dame-du-Pré, in the suburbs of Rouen, a dependent priory of the abbey of Bec, patronized by Henry I, and the home of the empress in her retirement: Chibnall, "The Empress and Bec-Hellouin," 37–9.

[12] HH, 702–3; OV, vi. 450–1; WM, *HN*, 26–7.

The nobles may have done the decent thing in conducting the king's body to Rouen but at this point their involvement ceased. Their interest was in the succession and they knew that, in spite of all the old king's efforts, the succession was not agreed. The successful candidate was Stephen, and before looking at why the choice of his peers fell on him, it will be useful to work out a chronology and establish the main stages in his route to power. Stephen was "in his county of Boulogne" when he learned of the king's death, and he crossed immediately to England. Henry had died during the night of Sunday, 1 December. A messenger setting out at first light on Monday and riding post-haste would have made short work of the hundred-mile journey from Lyons-la-Forêt to Boulogne. We may imagine him arriving on Wednesday comfortably before nightfall, bringing news that came as no surprise. Stephen will have made what again was a familar crossing, from Wissant to Dover, no later than Thursday, 5 December. There was a need for speed, and all the chroniclers emphasize this,[13] but once in England he will have wanted to appear as the rightful king claiming his own and not as a postulant, so an excess of speed might have been counter-productive. He will have made for London with all deliberate speed. A late but a local source says that he applied at the main royal castles en route, at Dover and at Canterbury, but was turned away.[14] So he may have done, but he did not need to wait long for an answer, for he will have had his own routine for getting to London, and a choice of comfortable beds in his own houses. He could have got to his own base in the capital, in Southwark south of the Thames, as early as Sunday, 8 December, less than a week after Henry I had died.

There then followed what in organizational terms was the key week in Stephen's rise to power. This was the second week of December. The detail comes from a pro-Stephen source, the *Gesta Stephani*, whose author may have been based in London.[15] It states that in both the capital cities of the kingdom, first at London and then at Winchester, Stephen was recognized as the rightful king. Indeed, it is suggested that he was received as such in each place. At his arrival, in London, "the citizens were filled with excitement and came out to meet him with acclamation."[16] And when he came to Winchester, "the chief among the citizens came out to meet him, and after a brief discussion they gave him an honourable escort into the city."[17] This is the language of the royal *adventus*, the formal cere-monies – adapted from those of ancient Rome – in which a ruler was received. At such a time the city became the new Jerusalem. "City, be

---

[13] HH, 700–1: "sine mora"; WM, *HN*, 26–7: "maturauit aduentum"; OV, vi. 454–5: "protinus transfretauit"; Torigni, 127: "transfretauit citissime"; *GND*, ii. 274–5: "ueliciter transfretans."

[14] Gervase, i. 94.

[15] King, "*Gesta Stephani*."

[16] *GS*, 6–7: "cum læto strepitu obuiam ei occurrit."

[17] *GS*, 8–9: "[Bishop Henry] cum dignioribus Wintonie ciuibus obuius ei aduenit . . . in ciuitatem secundam duntaxat regni sedem honorifice induxit."

happy, Heavem, rejoice! / Rejoice, [London] at the King's Advent. / The king of Peace arrives at your gate / To bring for ever blissful joy."[18] The Christian prototype of such an entry is Christ's entry into Jerusalem on Palm Sunday. The Church will have held back from the full ceremonial, granted that Stephen came as a postulant; nonetheless it seems clear that both in London and in Winchester he was given a royal reception.

London was the great prize. With a population of at least 25,000 it was one of the largest cities of northern Europe, "abounding in the wealth of its citizens, and crammed with the wares of merchants from every land."[19]

> Amid all the noble cities of the world, the city of London, throne of the English kingdom, is one that has spread its fame far and wide, its wealth and merchandise to great distances, raised its head on high. It is blessed by a wholesome climate, blessed too in Christ's religion, in the strength of its fortifications, in the nature of its site, the repute of its citizens, the honour of its matrons; happy in its sports, prolific in noble men.

This is William Fitz Stephen, writing in the early 1170s, describing the environment in which Thomas Becket, recently canonized, had been raised. He went on to note that two miles to the west of the city the royal palace of Westminster rose by the water's edge, "a building of the greatest splendour with outworks and bastions."[20] Adjacent to the palace was the abbey of Westminster, the expected coronation site of the English kings. The physical and intellectual topography shaped the welcome that Stephen received.[21] The Londoners claimed rights of election: "it was their own right and particular privilege," they claimed, "that if their king died from any cause, a successor should immediately be appointed by their own choice." There was an urgent need for an election, and Stephen was the man on the spot: "all regarded him as suited to the position on account both of his high birth and of his good character."[22] And so they agreed to receive him as king. There was a *pactum*, an agreement, made between them. The citizens agreed to support him, while he promised – a necessary part of any coronation promise – to pacify the kingdom in the common interest. To make these arrangements involved a great deal of consultation and communal discussion. There was much talk at the time of a commune, a sworn association of the citizens recognized as a corporation by the public authority. Stephen knew the issues better than most, for in 1127 William Clito had recognized the communes of the major

---

[18] Kantorowicz, "King's Advent," 41, where the text cited is from Metz.

[19] WM, *GP*, i. 222–3; Keene, "London to 1300," 196.

[20] *MTB*, iii. 2; trans. in Brooke, *London*, 113, 115.

[21] Most fully described in *GS*, 4–7, 12–13; and see also the discussion in McKisack, "London and the Succession," 78–9.

[22] *GS*, 6–7.

Flemish towns, including Bruges and St Omer.[23] The Londoners undoubtedly aspired to the same rights, and might have hoped that in accepting his election Stephen was accepting their claims. But it is most unlikely that Stephen made a formal grant of a commune.[24] This would have been unwise. The real electors, largely unseen in London but never out of mind, were the great magnates of the Anglo-Norman world. They were very distrustful of communes, which they saw as threats to their own lordship. For Stephen to grant a commune to the Londoners would have sent quite the wrong signals to these men, at a time when he needed their support.

At London Stephen had been carried along by the tide of the citizens' hopes and aspirations. It would be a similar story at Winchester. Stephen would not have rushed from London, which provided a good base for communications, but by the middle of the week – perhaps on Wednesday, 11 or Thursday, 12 December – he will have been en route for Winchester, which he could have reached with just one overnight stop. His business there was no less important than in London. Winchester had been the capital of Wessex. It was still recognizably the administrative centre of the kingdom, though it faced increasing competition from London. It was there that Domesday Book, the "Book of Winchester," was kept. Winchester represented the historic memory of the English kingship. It was there also that the exchequer was accustomed to meet, when twice a year the sheriffs were required to render account of every penny they had received as agents of the crown, an experience that few of them enjoyed. Here difficult matters were decided and precedent became custom: here was developed "the science of the exchequer," what a London taxi driver would now call "the knowledge." Here was the main royal treasury.[25] When the treasury chamberlain, the man with the keys, William de Pont-de-l'Arche, surrendered the royal treasure to Stephen, he was recognizing Stephen's claim and giving him the resources to pursue it. Behind him we need to see the *éminence grise* of the English administration, Roger, bishop of Salisbury. Roger was the administration. The exchequer was his power base. He promised continuity; and the promise of continuity was all that he required of Stephen. He and his circle would claim that he had been the key figure in Stephen's rise to power. Henry of Huntingdon, an archdeacon of his nephew Alexander of Lincoln, said that he had brought

---

[23] The "little charter of agreement" for Bruges is referred to in Galbert, cap. 55. The charter for St Omer issued by William Clito in 1127 is in *Actes des comtes de Flandre, 1071–1128*, no. 127; that of Thierry of Flanders in 1128 in *De Oorkonden der Graven van Vlaanderen, 2/i*, no. 2: "I order that the commune that they have sworn will endure and I will allow no one to dissolve it."

[24] As was suggested by Davis, *Stephen*, 54, and in his edition of *GS*, 6–7. McKisack, "London and the Succession," 79, refers rather to the "new communal aspirations of the Londoners," which puts the matter very well.

[25] Biddle, *Winchester*, 291, 304–5; Hollister, "Origins of the English Treasury"; *Dialogus*, 50.

Stephen the crown and strong material support.[26] Well might he say this. That the power of the crown had to be securely founded on worldly wealth was a part of this family's world-view.[27]

It was not, however, Roger of Salisbury, whom most people mentioned first when they came to discuss how Stephen had come to power. They highlighted rather the part played by Stephen's brother, Henry, bishop of Winchester. Henry was described as the man "on whom his enterprise entirely depended," without whose support "all his efforts would have been in vain."[28] Henry was able to orchestrate the support of the Church. He managed to make a virtue of what the Londoners and the civil servants (whom we have examined) and the lay magnates (who remain to be discussed) might have regarded as necessity. He did so by presenting his brother as a man sympathetic to current ideas of church reform. On Sunday, 15 December or in the days that followed Henry worked on an agreed text that promised to put an end to disputes between church and state. Stephen promised "canonical" election, which meant that the body of clergy who served as "electors" to a bishopric or an abbacy should be allowed to select a candidate free of any secular interference. He renounced "simony," which meant that no trace of money would enter into his dealings with the Church. He granted churches their possessions and churchmen free disposition of their – often very considerable – moveable wealth. He granted bishops control over the – sometimes unchaste – bodies of their clergy and jurisdiction over them. Henry had been a Cluniac monk, and this document can be seen as a "master-stroke of Cluniac policy,"[29] but he was now also a bishop, and it was the episcopal order that would be the main beneficiary of this programme. The chairman of the episcopal bench, and the pope's legate within England, the archbishop of Canterbury, whose role it was to crown a new king, agreed to do so on these terms.[30]

Seen from the perspective of England, Stephen's accession has all the appearance of a coup, of which his brother Henry served as the mastermind. The *Gesta Stephani* may be thought to hint at this when it speaks of "those who before his accession had bound themselves in friendship to him or his brothers,"[31] but this may be only to say that the new king had a wide affinity, which was undoubtedly the case. In December 1135, however, the brothers were not of one mind. While in England the main electors turned to

---

[26] HH, 700–1: "diadema ei et uires auxilii sui contribuit." So also at Ely, where Roger's other nephew was bishop, *Liber Eliensis*, 285: "ad cuius nutum pendebat totum regni negotium."

[27] *Dialogus*, 1: "hec subueniunt"; Hudson, "Richard FitzNigel and the Dialogue of the Exchequer."

[28] *GS*, 8–9; WM, *HN*, 28–9. *GND*, ii. 274–5, also mentions Henry of Winchester's support.

[29] Davis, *Stephen*, 18.

[30] WM, *HN*, 28–9: "The terms of that oath were afterwards put in writing"; cf. HH, 704–5, which says that Stephen repeated these promises on the day of his coronation.

[31] *GS*, 8–9.

Stephen, with his brother's prompting and the support of the chief administrators, in Normandy they turned to Theobald. After Henry died the Norman magnates seem to have been largely observers, meeting in small groups, unsure of the future and agreed only that that future was not Angevin. Orderic says that the Normans meeting at Le Neubourg wished to prefer Theobald but then a messenger appeared, sent by Stephen to inform them that he was the choice of the English: not that he was yet king but that they wished to make him so.[32] Robert of Torigni gives Theobald's movements. He came first to Rouen, the capital of Normandy, and then to Lisieux, where he arrived on Saturday, 21 December. But then on the following day, while he and Robert of Gloucester were talking, a messenger appeared saying that Stephen was by now king.[33] It was the very day of the coronation. The sudden appearance of this messenger provides the final clues as to the chronology. He will have come from London and crossed from Dover, or perhaps more likely Winchester, and crossed from Portsmouth. In either event, he would have made first for Rouen, his mission to broadcast the word of what had been agreed. He cannot have set off later than Wednesday, the 18th. By then the die was cast, the date of the coronation fixed. We may date the agreement with the Church, which determined that date of the coronation, with some confidence to Sunday, 15 December,[34] or at most a day or two thereafter.

The coronation took place on Sunday, 22 December 1135, at Westminster Abbey (see plate 5).[35] All the emphasis was on continuity and it seems likely that the rite used for the coronation of Henry I was used here also.[36] It was a religious ceremony which gave the king power, a sacramental authority that would sustain him against all challenge for the rest of his life. It started with the king prostrating himself before the high altar, just as did a candidate for ordination to the priesthood. He then read out a series of promises, as kings had done before him, that he would keep the peace, that he would protect his people from arbitrary behaviour, that he would maintain the just laws of his predecessors. The reference to his predecessors was far from routine and the chancery clerks set out to reinforce it. He would maintain "the liberties and good laws of King Henry." There followed the ritual of election, those present in the church standing for the whole community in accepting Stephen as their king. No more was this routine. Stephen was the choice of clergy and people alike: their voices echoed through the church

---

[32] OV, vi. 454–5: "regem preficere uellent."

[33] Torigni, 128–9: "iam esse regem."

[34] It is interesting that this is the date that Orderic gives for the coronation: OV, vi. 454–5.

[35] This is the date given in WM, *HN*, 28–9; JW, iii. 214–15; *Melrose*, s.a. 1135; *Battle*, 140–1; Annals of St Augustine's, Canterbury, *UGQ*, 79. It is to be preferred to Christmas Day, 25 Dec., as given in RH, 144, and *ASC*, s.a. 1135.

[36] The main studies are: Richardson, "The Coronation in Medieval England"; Nelson, "The Rites of the Conqueror"; Brückmann, "The *Ordines* of the Third Recension of the Coronation Order"; Garnett, "The Third Recension of the English Coronation *Ordo*"; and there is a fine realization of the ceremonial in Green, *Henry I*, 44–5.

and were taken up by the Londoners outside. He would not forget them and would not allow others to forget. Immediately after the election the king was anointed and symbols of royal power, of the resources which would allow him to perform his role, were placed in his hands. He was then crowned by the archbishop of Canterbury, William of Corbeil. Other symbols were handed to him as he was enthroned, and these together made up the tableau which was then circulated, on the king's seal and more selectively on the king's coins. A solemn High Mass followed and the kiss of peace was exchanged between old friends.

After the coronation there was much to do. There was the need to publicize what had been done and to secure the new king's position against challenge. That challenge might come on the frontiers of his power – and those in the minster may already have known of more than one such challenge – or it might strike direct at the king's title to rule. It would be wise to give priority to the latter and this is what seems to have been done. The first document to be issued by Stephen's chancery was a short charter addressed, in customary fashion, "to all his men both French and English." He granted "to all his barons and men of England" all the liberties and good laws that King Henry "my uncle" had granted them along with "the laws of Edward the Confessor." All those addressed and their heirs would be protected by the new king and his heirs in their position.[37] It was a simple statement of continuity, which took care to allude to the new king's blood link to his predecessor. Only one copy of this charter survives but it would have been distributed widely and certainly sent to each shire court to be read at its next monthly meeting. Those hearing it might have been reassured but they still have wanted to know more. They will have wanted to know the story of how Stephen had come to power. His spin doctors were happy to oblige.

Again there is only the one text. It is embedded in one of the charter narratives of the great monasteries, written at Ely in the heart of the fenland. It returns us to the deathbed of Henry I:

> While King Henry sickened unto death, a great number of powerful and noble men gathered about him, sorrowfully contemplating the last hours of their lord, and increasingly concerned about what dispositions he would make about himself and the kingdom. To them at the last he indicated what ought to happen. "To you," he said, "great and wise men, I give as king the worthy knight Stephen, my count, my most dear kinsman, a virtuous nobleman, yet firm in his faith in the Lord, for you to receive from me by right of inheritance, and you are all to be witnesses of this." Immediately thereafter the king breathed his last. The count took up this commission, and having gathered a large body of knights, he hastened to England and came before the Londoners. Since he was a renowned count and valiant knight, of

[37] *Regesta*, iii, no. 270.

proven integrity and greatly loved, and was descended from the stock of
kings, and with the great men and the citizens won over by rewards and
promises and the clergy fearing great disorder should he be turned
away, he was received by the English as king of England. It greatly
aided him in achieving this outcome that, just as the king his uncle had
ordered, Hugh Bigod swore on the holy gospels before the clergy and
people that he had been present at the king's deathbed, and had heard
him conceding the kingdom to Stephen his nephew, and had been sent
by him to witness to this within England.[38]

Just where this text came from it is hard to determine. It may just be the
Ely tradition. But it seems too sharp to be based on oral memory, and if it
is based on a written text that text has all the hallmarks of an official
newsletter. The local bishop was one of the nephews of Roger of
Salisbury. This is the official history. Just how much credence was given to
the claim that the king had changed his mind was another matter. It had
become a part of the case for Stephen's acceptance by the time his kingship came under challenge, and so he was forced to defend it. But that it
played a key role in his coming to power in December 1135 is unlikely.
Henry's plans for the succession had been dead in the water long before
the king himself died. Those among the clergy who wished to accept
Stephen need do no more than recall the dominating personality of their
deceased ruler. The king had required the oath to be sworn. From there it
was but a short step to claiming that the oath had been extracted by force.
And, as anyone who had done even a freshman course in canon law knew
very well, it was no perjury to break a forced oath.[39]
  Although the monks of Ely kept the text of the newsletter safe, they
were not its intended audience. The positive case for Stephen was made
succinctly and it was designed to appeal to the concepts of honour which
governed the lives of the lay aristocracy. It was they who needed to be won
over. Other general promises may have been made to them. In the version
of Stephen's coronation promises that was disseminated in the spring of
1136 the lay estate learned of particular concessions of some value to
them.[40] The new king said that he would keep in his hands the areas
placed under forest law by William I and William II, but – he said – those
that King Henry had added he would restore "to the churches and the
kingdom." As the story of the king's promise spread this precise distinction tended to be lost sight of. Henry of Huntingdon said that the king had
broken his coronation promise by holding forest pleas.[41] The importance
of the forest in English politics in the twelfth and thirteenth centuries is

[38] *Liber Eliensis*, 285.
[39] *GS*, 12–13: "constat omne iusiurandum a quolibet cum uiolentia extortum ipsam peri-
urii efficaciam penitus amisisse."
[40] *Regesta*, iii, no. 271.
[41] HH, 708–9.

difficult to overstate.[42] Almost every county of England was affected, and
in each county almost every local landowner and religious house. And the
forest was a royal prerogative: there were no constraints of custom on
what kings could do there. As Richard Fitz Nigel – the son of Nigel,
bishop of Ely – put it: "What is done in accordance with forest law is not
called 'just' without qualification, but 'just, according to forest law.' "[43]
Any promise of relaxation was welcome in this area, as also in the local
administration of justice. The king promised that he would root out "all
exactions and injustices and miskennings maliciously introduced by
sheriffs and others." He would observe and he would require his own
agents to observe "good laws and established and just customs with regard
to *murdrum* and pleas and other legal cases." Stephen and his vassals had
suffered their share of the arbitrary behaviour of royal agents in the past.
He knew how his new subjects felt. He promised them a lighter touch. As
word got about, these general promises were generously interpreted. It
was even claimed that the king had promised to remit Danegeld.[44]

The promises made to the Church had one particular audience in
mind. That was the papacy. One of the first tasks of the team that
Stephen gathered about him in the days after his coronation was to draft
a letter to the pope, Innocent II.[45] What was said in it can be reconstructed
from the circumstances in which it was sent and from the contents of the
letter which the pope sent in reply.[46] The pope referred to the firm peace
that Henry I had kept and how it had been destroyed after his death. On
the initiative of the clergy, with the unanimous assent of the magnates and
the people, Stephen had been elected as king and consecrated by the
bishops. He had heard great things of Stephen, had been told of the
promises he had made on the day of his coronation, and knew that he was
close kin to the previous king.[47] He knew all this, the pope said, from letters
he had received from the bishops of the English province, "as also from
those lovers of the holy Roman church, the glorious king of the Franks
and that illustrious man, count Theobald," and also from the personal
testimony of men of substance. It is likely that the royal delegation to the
pope, who was in Pisa not in Rome, went via Paris and Chartres, and
obtained the letters here referred to as part of the dossier in Stephen's

---

[42] A useful monograph is Young, *Royal Forests.*

[43] *Dialogus*, 60.

[44] HH, 704–5; JW, iii. 202–3. Generosity in individual cases and chancery style may
have contributed to this impression. There are specific exemptions from Danegeld in charters for the monasteries of Fountains, Rievaulx, and Warden, drafted by *scriptor* xiii: *Regesta*,
iii, nos. 335, 716, 919.

[45] On the politics of the royal court, *Christina*, 160–1.

[46] RH, 147–8; JL, no. 7804. This is an important text, for it is the closest we get to what
was said at the time. R. L. Poole was prepared to accept the document as based on "good
information," though critical of it on diplomatic grounds: John of Salisbury, *Iohannis
Saresberiensis Historiae Pontificalis*, ed. Poole, 107–8.

[47] RH, 148: "de prefati regis prosapia prope positu gradu originem traxisse dinosceris";
GS, 6–7: he was seen as "idoneus tam generis dignitate quam animi probitate."

support. There is no mention in the pope's letter of the previous king's plans for the succession, and no mention anywhere of the empress taking her case for the succession to Rome. The pope's endorsement was strong and he would not waver in his support for Stephen.[48] All this diplomatic discussion and the need to travel in the depths of winter will have prevented any speed records being broken,[49] and it was in all probability after Easter before the pope's letter of endorsement was received in England. In the three months the royal embassy was on the road the new king had gone a long way towards securing his authority in England.

The first public function of Stephen as king was to attend the burial of his predecessor at Reading Abbey. The king and his barons went out to meet the body and he himself served as one of the pall-bearers, "for the love of his uncle."[50] The funeral took place on Monday, 5 January 1136, five weeks after Henry had died.[51] The place was that determined by the old king, but the timing suited the new king well. Reading was an old monastic site, refounded by Henry, and by him given the resources to put it in the front rank. These allowed the rapid completion of the monastic buildings: all but the monastery church had been completed within five years. Surviving sculptures reveal craftsmanship of the very highest quality.[52] It had the beginnings of what would become one of the finest relic collections in England, its showpiece the hand of St James, which the empress Matilda had brought back from Germany and given to the monastery.[53] Although the monastery had been founded little more than ten years before it had developed a high reputation for the purity of its monastic life and for its hospitality. Visitors were impressed.[54] Reading served as a showpiece for the monastic order in England. The king's obsequies were celebrated with all due solemnity: masses were said, various precious offerings made, alms handed out to crowds of the poor, Henry's body was exposed on a hearse, and "placed with great honour in a tomb" before the high altar of the abbey church.[55] On the first anniversary of his

---

[48] The reasons for the pope's support are well discussed in Holdsworth, "The Church," in King, *Anarchy*, 209–10.

[49] The journey from England to Rome could take up to seven weeks: Poole, *Studies in Chronology and History*, 263–4.

[50] JW, iii. 214–15.

[51] The date was established by Brian Kemp: *Reading Abbey Cartularies*, i. 14 n. 1.

[52] *Romanesque*, 167–71 (no. 127a–o).

[53] It would not be on show for much longer, for Henry of Winchester removed it, presumably claiming it as part of Henry I's regalia, and it was only restored at the end of the reign: Kemp, "The Miracles of the Hand of St James," 1–4; Leyser, "Frederick Barbarossa, Henry II and the Hand of St James."

[54] WM, *GR*, i. 746–7: "a model of inexhaustible and delightful hospitality"; WM, *GP*, i. 304–5.

[55] JW, iii. 214–17. Simon, bishop of Worcester, was closely attached to Queen Adeliza, first as her chancellor and then as her confessor: ibid., iii. 156–9. "He was pious, upright, pleasant, and generous": Barlow, *English Church 1066–1154*, 86.

death his widow gave Aston (Herts.) to the abbey and later she and her second husband would give money for lights to burn in front of the tomb of her dear lord.[56]

Gathered around him at Reading, in these hospitable surroundings, Stephen had a very strong nucleus of support, including officers of the royal household.[57] There were three royal stewards: William Martel, who had witnessed the coronation charter; Hugh Bigod, who had testified to the king's change of mind (it was his household office that gave credence to the story, whether it was true or not); and Robert Fitz Richard, a member of the family of Clare, lord of Little Dunmow in Essex and of Baynard's Castle in London.[58] There was the royal constable, Robert de Vere, who had served in this office since c.1127, and had acquired by marriage the barony of Haughley. Haughley like Clare was in Suffolk, a county in which Stephen as lord of Eye was the dominant landowner. There was the chamberlain of the exchequer, William de Pont-de-l'Arche, an important member of the treasury team, while the new treasurer was Adelelm, another member of the clan of Roger of Salisbury.[59] There was at least one senior clerk, Roger of Fécamp, a man with wide experience of the Norman administration under Henry I, whose body he may have accompanied to Reading. (Robert de Vere certainly had.) There was a second royal constable, Miles of Gloucester. His father and grandfather before him had been sheriffs of Gloucester, and had control of the royal castle. Gloucester was a centre with strong royal associations, the third of the centres – along with Westminster and Winchester – where the Anglo-Norman kings were accustomed to wear their crowns.[60] Stephen treated Miles with great generosity and it is the charters which record the grants made to him that allow us to reconstruct Stephen's early court. At Reading also was Payn Fitz John, an important servant of the late king, especially associated with the west country, a man whose experience went back twenty years; and possibly accompanying Payn there was Ingelram de Say, lord of Clun in Shropshire.[61] From the north midlands there was Robert de Ferrers, lord of Tutbury in Staffordshire, with whom the king had kinship ties.[62] Some of these men would shortly die, to the satisfaction of later moralists, who wished to see the seeds of decay present from the

---

[56] The first anniversary charter is particularly interesting, for she prays also for "our lord Stephen by the grace of God king of the English": *Reading Cart.* i, no. 370; cf. also ibid. nos. 371, 459, 535.

[57] A short account on the main departments of the royal household at the beginning of Stephen's reign is found in the "Constitutio Domus Regis," *Dialogus*, 128–35.

[58] Ward, "The Clare Family," 272–3. Other members of the house of Clare closely associated with Stephen were Walter Fitz Richard and Baldwin Fitz Gilbert, lord of Bourne in Lincolnshire: ibid., 273–4.

[59] *Fasti* 3: *Lincoln*, 8–9.

[60] Biddle, "Seasonal Festivals and Residence."

[61] As suggested by Round, *Geoffrey*, 11–13.

[62] Jones, "Charters of Robert II de Ferrers," 8–9.

beginning of the reign.[63] But the clear image from these early days is of the ready take-up of the apparatus of government.

It was part of the case for Stephen that considerable disorder had followed Henry I's death. At Reading intelligence would already have been at hand to prove that this was no figure of speech. At Hexham, the prior of the Augustinian canons, Richard, noted the incursion of David, king of Scots.[64] David had brought a large army and taken five strategic castles: Carlisle, Newcastle upon Tyne, Wark, Alnwick, and Norham. He had done so "around Christmas time," which shows that the stimulus to this incursion, whatever its stated agenda, was Henry's death, not Stephen's coronation. At St Evroul, close to the southern frontier of Normandy, Orderic noted the events that followed Henry I's death. "In the first week of December Geoffrey of Anjou, on learning of King Henry's death, immediately sent his wife Matilda into Normandy." As was to happen in northern England, a number of strategic castles were taken. These included Argentan, Exmes, and Domfront, whose custodian received the empress as his "true lady"; also the episcopal city of Sées and other adjacent castles.[65] The empress's title was mentioned also by the king of Scots. "He took security and hostages from the great men and the nobility of the region that they maintain their faith to the empress his niece."[66] In these two risings, uncoordinated but linked in their refence to the empress's claims, there was a challenge not just to the integrity of the Anglo-Norman realm but also to Stephen's title to rule over it.

Stephen responded quickly, as he was in every respect well equipped to do. He had long experience leading troops over long distances. He knew the Great North Road well, for it was the road to Lancaster as well as to York. He was able to bring to York and then on to Durham the largest army that had been seen there in living memory,[67] in which mercenary troops, paid for from the treasury, played a prominent role. He arrived at Durham on 5 February, the day after Ash Wednesday. The size of his army made a statement but every other consideration urged caution: the Scots were not likely to offer battle, the baronage of the area had mixed allegiances, and the two rulers were kinsmen. Men of the day were very used to making agreements, about marriage and property rights: agreement was always preferable to litigation. With men of high status there was a ritual involved: the terms of a settlement were agreed between their men, and only when they had agreed to agree would they meet in person. In the case of the agreement between the English and Scottish kings in 1136, it

---

[63] HH, 700–1, noted that William of Corbeil, who had consecrated Stephen, died within the year. GS, 24–5, noted the deaths, "in a pitiful way without profit from repentance," of Payn Fitz John (in 1137) and Miles of Gloucester (in 1143).

[64] RH, 144–6.

[65] OV, vi. 454–5: "naturalem dominam."

[66] RH, 145. Other chroniclers also mention the oath: Barrow, "The Scots and the North of England," 244 n. 62.

[67] HH, 706–7.

was stated that there had been prior discussions and that one of the matters discussed, the claim of Henry of Scots to hold the earldom of Northumberland, had not been included in the final communiqué.[68] A compromise agreed would be structured in terms of matching concessions, each party giving ground in turn to allow a settlement. This is just what is found here. The agreement was verbal. The terms negotiated would be read out, and each party would swear to accept them, in the presence of witnesses: at this point "the peace was made."[69]

The text in Richard of Hexham is sufficiently close to events and sufficiently precise to preserve the clear structure of an agreement of this kind.[70] The first concession was made by the king of Scots. "Henry the son of king David of Scots did homage to King Stephen at York." You did homage for something, in return for a grant of land or other rights. What Henry did homage for represents the matching concession of the king of England; and it was a handsome one. "The king gave him his father's earldom of Huntingdon, and Carlisle, and Doncaster." The homage was probably for Huntingdon and for Doncaster. In return for this the Scottish king released four of the five towns that he had taken, including Newcastle, where he had probably been based while the discussions were taking place. Carlisle was the prize, its possession valuable in itself and a vindication of the Scottish version of the history of Cumbria. Carlisle was "given" to the Scottish king, not his son, after he had given security in the form of hostages and after the men of both sides had undertaken to hold their principals to the terms of the agreement. This too was standard form. The grant of Carlisle was a major concession by the king. The most careful observer of the day, however, William of Malmesbury, a man moreover sympathetic to the empress's cause, said simply that Stephen in this "peace or pretended peace" had "got what he wanted."[71] If we use this clue to look at the Treaty of Durham, as it has come to be called, what Stephen wanted could only be the homage of the son of the king of Scots. David had justified his attack in terms of the oaths that had been sworn to the empress. In this treaty he dealt with Stephen as king of England, and his son and heir became the man of the king of England.[72] In every way that men of the time would have recognized, both David and Henry of Scots had accepted the legitimacy of Stephen's title.

It is a confident king who is found first at Durham and then at York, the great metropolis of northern England. The charters that were issued in his name at this time, several of which survive as originals, were carefully

[68] RH, 146.

[69] On *conventiones* during this period, see Chibnall, "Anglo-French Relations"; Crouch, "A Norman *convencio*"; King, "Dispute Settlement."

[70] RH, 146.

[71] WM, *HN*, 30–1.

[72] Henry of Huntingdon, whose diocesan bishop had been involved in the deliberations, laid stress on this point: "filius autem regis Dauid, Henricus, homo regis Stephani effectus est" (HH, 706–7).

drafted to give this impression.[73] There were charters for the York archdiocese itself, and for its minster churches at Beverley and at Ripon; for the Cistercian monasteries of Fountains and Rievaulx; for Whitby Abbey on the coast of North Yorkshire; for the cathedral at Durham; and for Tynemouth Priory in Northumberland. This might seem to represent a narrow clerical constituency, but it was not. In the confirmation for Fountains he confirmed the gifts not just of Archbishop Thurstan but of Eustace Fitz John, a northern magnate and the brother of Payn Fitz John; he remitted all earthly service (here including Danegeld) due to himself or the archbishop of York or Eustace or to his or their successors.[74] The same goes for Walter Espec, who had been with Stephen the last time a king of England held court at York, in 1122. Stephen now confirmed his foundation charter for Rievaulx and his more recent foundation of Warden Abbey in Bedfordshire.[75] The same goes for William de Percy at Whitby. The great men brought their affinities: one of the grants to Whitby was made by a Percy tenant before Stephen in person,[76] while Walter Espec, it was claimed, was surrounded "by all his relatives and heirs then living."[77] Stephen, the lord of Lancaster, was an integral member of the northern community. As in every way full members of that community there were some powerful saints, Wilfred at Ripon, Hilda at Whitby, John at Beverley, and Cuthbert at Durham: "I do not wish," the king said, "that St Cuthbert should lose anything of his right."[78] He expected that the northern saints would be there when he had need of them, and so it would prove.

There are a number of firsts in the charters which Stephen issued at this time. There is the first mention of the new royal chancellor Roger le Poer, who, as William of Malmesbury diplomatically put it, was "a nephew or perhaps even a closer relation" of Roger, bishop of Salisbury.[79] The job of the chancellor was to act as keeper of the royal seal, and of this group of charters issued at York two survive as originals and are sealed. The York seals are now little more than fragments but one of the Durham seals has an almost perfect copy of the king's new seal.[80] It was double sided. It showed the king on the one side enthroned in majesty, wearing a crown, holding in his right hand a sword and in his left hand an orb surmounted by a cross on which a dove perches a little uncertainly. These are the

---

[73] *Regesta*, iii, nos. 99, 255–7, 335, 373a, 716, 717, 906–7, 942, 975, 979, 990. In these charters Stephen underlines his kinship to the earlier Norman kings; he prays for their souls and the safety of his kingdom; he emphasizes that he has made his grants "by royal authority and by the power that has been bestowed on me by God."

[74] *Regesta*, iii, no. 335; Dalton, "Eustace Fitz John."

[75] *Regesta*, iii, nos. 716, 919.

[76] Ibid., no. 942: "quam Alanus Busel eis concessit coram me."

[77] Ibid., no. 919: "et aliis omnibus nepotibus et heredibus Walteri tunc viventibus."

[78] Ibid., no. 257: "nolo quod Sanctus Cudbertus quicquam perdat de jure suo."

[79] WM, *HN*, 48–9: "id est filius," "i.e. son," was added by one early reader.

[80] Greenwell and Hunter Blair, "Durham Seals, Part VI," 120–1 (no. 3019) (= *Regesta*, iii, nos. 255–6): I have largely reproduced the elegant brief descriptions given here.

symbols of his kingship, with which he had been invested at his coronation. This (the "majesty") side of the seal bore the legend: STEPHANUS DEI GRATIA REX ANGLORUM.[81] On the other side he appears as a mounted warrior, kitted out for battle. He has a mail hauberk and a hood, a pointed helmet with two ribands streaming behind. In his right hand he brandishes a sword, while, resting on his left shoulder, he has a kite-shaped shield with a projecting spike. The horse seems to pace the ground. The team is ready for action. The legend on this (the "equestrian") side was: STEPHANUS DEI GRATIA DUX NORMANNORUM.[82] These are the classic images of the equestrian order. They had been used by Stephen on his own seal as count of Mortain and Boulogne, and as constructed here on his seal as king would influence the seals made by Stephen's own earls.[83] The message of these early months was continuity and Stephen's first seal was modelled closely on the seals of Henry I (see plate 4).[84]

At York Stephen held court. Alongside Thurstan in his cathedral city are found his suffragan, Athelwold, bishop of Carlisle, previously prior of Nostell, and the two bishops of eastern England, Alexander of Lincoln and Nigel of Ely (the two nephews of Roger of Salisbury); also two of the bishops of Normandy, Audouin of Evreux (Thurstan's brother), and John of Sées. The Norman bishops may have come more as refugees than as courtiers, but still they came. They will have told him, if he did not know already, what had happened on the southern frontier of Normandy after Henry's death. Among the laymen present were Robert de Vere, William Martel, Hugh Bigod, Robert Fitz Richard de Clare, Robert d'Oilly, William Mauduit, and Robert Avenel. If we are searching for the intermediaries in the treaty with the Scots we may look at the names in that group. The bishop of Ely was certainly at Durham and involved in the discussions.[85] It was at York in a ceremonial setting, in a city "still showing Roman elegance," that Henry of Scots performed homage to Stephen as he had promised to do.[86]

The king, accompanied by Henry of Scots, then came south to hold his Easter court at Westminster.[87] Easter Day was 22 March, the earliest day possible under the Gregorian calendar. "During the Easter festival in London he held his court, which was more splendid for its throng and size, for gold, silver, jewels, robes, and every kind of sumptuousness, than any that had ever been held in England."[88] Stephen was here taking

---

[81] "Stephen by the grace of God king of the English."

[82] "Stephen by the grace of God duke of the Normans."

[83] Heslop, "Seals," 303 (no. 331): "Here the equestrian image, which had evolved slowly up to this point, finds its first classic statement on the royal seal." He notes that the image was copied by the Clare earls of Hertford and Pembroke, citing Hunter Blair, "Armorials in English Seals," plate IIg; note also the second seal of Waleran of Meulan: plate 17.

[84] Birch, "The Great Seals of King Stephen," 4; Heslop, "Seals," no. 331.

[85] *Regesta*, iii, no. 832 (for Spalding Priory).

[86] WM, *GP*, i. 324–5; RH, 146.

[87] HH, 706–7; RH, 146, 148; *GS*, 24–9.

[88] HH, 706–7.

up the tradition of holding major courts, at which the king wore his crown, at Christmas, at Easter, and at Whitsun, the great feasts of the Christian year. He had been crowned just before Christmas, with only a few magnates present,[89] and this court had not really come to life until the funeral of Henry I at Reading. He had now established himself.

> Now that the feast day was imminent, and delighted at his great triumph, he decided to hold court immediately, wearing the royal crown upon his head, and summoned the kings and dukes subject to him to the same ceremony, to mark it solemnly and to establish lasting peace among his nobles.

This extract is from another contemporary writer, Geoffrey of Monmouth, and the king referred to is Arthur.[90] It is a court of the kind that Geoffrey's earliest listeners would have recognized, a court of the kind that King Stephen held at Easter 1136.[91] It had as its centrepiece the crown-wearing. The king robed and was escorted into church, with the two archbishops, those of Canterbury and York, leading him by the hand, one on either side. The queen was escorted into church in a separate procession, "wearing her own regalia." Stephen's queen had not previously been crowned and so the Easter 1136 ceremony involved a coronation and not just a crown-wearing.[92] The ceremonial verses in praise of the king, the *laudes regiae*, would have been sung. "The king and queen then removed their crowns and put on lighter robes." They then feasted; according to Geoffrey of Monmouth they did so in their separate quarters, "for the Britons used to observe the old Trojan custom, that men and women should celebrate feast days separately." This may not have happened in 1136, but we can be sure that "all were seated according to their rank."[93] We can be sure also that the feast attracted its own elaborate ceremonial, the steward at the head of the noblemen bearing in the principal dishes, followed by the menial servants, all filling their allotted roles. The meal served formally in this way was a standard image of medieval lordship. Everyone would have been familiar with it.

[89] WM, *HN*, 28–9: "paucissimis optimatibus"; *Liber Eliensis*, 285, says that Henry, son of the king of Scots, was the only man of comital rank present (confusing the Christmas court of 1135 with the Easter court of 1136, which Henry did attend).

[90] This extract, and the remaining quotations in this paragraph, are from Geoffrey of Monmouth, *History of the Kings of Britain*, 208–15. Henry of Huntingdon read this work at Bec early in 1139: HH, clxviii, 582–3.

[91] Tatlock, *Legendary History*, 272–3: "If a historian wishes accurate depiction of a twelfth-century crown-wearing and all its festivities, it is doubtful if he can find it anywhere so vivid as here in the *Historia*."

[92] Gervase, i. 96.

[93] John of Hexham reported that at the Easter 1136 court Stephen placed Henry, son of the king of Scots, in the place of honour, which angered the archbishop of Canterbury and a number of the nobles, including Ranulf of Chester, and led to them withdrawing from court: JH, 287.

That those of highest rank should receive an individual summons to such gatherings was clearly established by this date and was particularly significant in the circumstances of 1136.[94] Care was taken to preserve a full and ordered record of those present. This Easter court saw the most complete gathering of the higher clergy of the Anglo-Norman *regnum* that had ever been held. They were headed by the three archbishops: of Canterbury, York, and Rouen. All the English bishops were present, save for two, those of Chester and of Exeter. The senior of the Welsh bishops, Bernard of St Davids, was there, while of the Norman bishops, in addition to those of Sées and Evreux, who had been with him at York, Coutances and Avranches were also at the Easter court.[95] Two English sees were vacant, those of Bath and of London, and steps were taken to fill them. An attempt to translate the abbot of Bury St Edmunds to the see of London ran into difficulty.[96] The appointment of Robert of Lewes to the see of Bath, by contrast, was presented as a very model of an appointment following the new concordat with the Church, which the royal court ratified. A charter of Stephen records what happened.[97] Every word was chosen with care. "Know that I give and concede to Robert bishop of Bath the bishopric of Bath with its lands and its men, its demesne lands and its knights' fees, and all other things pertaining to the bishopric." He did this, he went on to say, after a canonical election had been held and after full consultation. The bishop was granted all the rights which his predecessors had enjoyed under the king's predecessors. The document concluded: "All this was done, at Westminster during the celebration of a general council and in the solemnity of the Easter festival, with all my faithful men listed below hearing and approving." The language used makes it clear that Stephen saw this as, and the clergy accepted that it was, a royal appointment. But before the king granted the territorial possessions of the see and took the homage of the elect for them, there had been a canonical election, just as the king had promised there would be. We may suspect there was only one candidate, for Robert of Lewes was closely associated with Henry of Winchester,[98] but still the formalities had been gone through.

---

[94] WM, *GR*, i. 508–9: "omnes . . . magnates regium edictum accersiebat" (writing of William the Conqueror); *GF Letters*, 63, ll. 87–8 (no. 26): "eorum namque qui statuto consilio propriis, ut dicitur, consueuerant appellari nominibus" (of Christmas 1126); RH, 148: "episcopos et proceres sui regni regali edicto in unum convenire præcepit" (of Easter 1136); *GS*, 24–5: "edicto per Angliam promulgato, summos ecclesiarum ductores cum primis populi ad concilium Londonias consciuit" (of Easter 1136); ibid., 14–15 (of summonses to Robert of Gloucester); and the comments of Maddicott, " 'An Infinite Multitude of Nobles,' " 23 and n. 33.

[95] Of the Norman bishops only those of Lisieux and Bayeux were not at the Easter court. John of Lisieux was the head of the Norman administration; Richard of Bayeux was the illegitimate son of Robert, earl of Gloucester: Haskins, 99; OV, vi. 428–9, 442–3.

[96] Diceto, i. 248–52.

[97] *Regesta*, iii, no. 46.

[98] *Fasti* 7: *Bath and Wells*, 2; JW, iii. 212–13: "sic enim disposuit Wintoniensis episcopus Heinricus."

The higher clergy were a small and close-knit group. Several owed their promotion to powerful connections, but still they were a meritocracy. They sang from the same hymn-sheet. (When they did not – as later in the time of Thomas Becket – they would find themselves in some difficulty.) With the laymen it was another matter. The king had to deal with them individually: it was a part of etiquette that he did so, and in the circumstances of Stephen's accession it was political necessity also. At the head of this group were the earls: they were a distinct social order; some were close kin, all had a close relationship to the king – that was a part of the job description. There were five earls in this court, and each name resonated to a degree. First was "Henry, the son of the king of Scots," an English earl with regard to the honour of Huntingdon, given precedence here because of his royal birth.[99] Alongside him was Ranulf, earl of Chester.[100] He reputedly resented the precedence that Henry was given but the real point of difference lay in their competing claims to Carlisle,[101] for his father had been the first northern governor of this city and his name was on the land.[102] Next came William, Earl Warenne. An old man, he had been an earl and frequently in arms for nearly fifty years. He had commanded divisions at the battles of Tinchebrai (1106) and Brémule (1119); he had been one of the earls at Henry I's deathbed; and on the king's death he had been placed in charge of the defence of Rouen and upper Normandy.[103] Also at Henry's deathbed had been Waleran, count of Meulan, along with his twin brother Robert, earl of Leicester. They too had taken a major role in the defence of Normandy since that time, and while Waleran had now crossed – briefly – to England Robert had remained in the duchy, following a pattern that would recur. According to a Norman chronicler, Stephen at this Easter court arranged the betrothal of one of his daughters to Waleran, an obvious sign of royal favour to him, though his intended bride was still an infant. Roger, earl of Warwick, another member of the Beaumont clan, was the son-in-law of William of Warenne.[104]

There yet remained more than thirty names, part of the common counsel of the land, and testifying to the new king's support.[105] Listed first

[99] Keith Stringer, "Henry, Earl of Northumberland'; on the Huntingdon honour, see Stringer, *Earl David of Huntingdon*, 106–10; for his *acta*, *Charters of David I*.

[100] Dalton, "*In neutro latere*"; *The Earldom of Chester and its Charters*; for his *acta*, *Chester Charters*.

[101] On the tension at the Easter court, see RH, 146, and JH, 287 (adding the name of Ranulf of Chester). Ranulf's ambition to regain Carlisle provides one of the storylines in John of Hexham's chronicle.

[102] King, "Ranulf of Chester"; for "the boundary of Ranulf Meschin," *Charters of David I*, 61–2 (no. 16).

[103] OV, vi. 448–51; *EYC* 8: *Warenne*, 7–9.

[104] OV, vi. 456–9; Crouch, *Beaumont Twins*, 29–31; Crouch, "Roger, Second Earl of Warwick."

[105] They are taken from *Regesta*, iii, nos. 46 (for Robert, bishop of Bath: March 1136), 271 (the "coronation charter": April 1136), 944 (for Winchester Cathedral: March 1136). The names are tabulated in Round, *Geoffrey*, 262–6.

were the noble officers of the household: the constables Robert de Vere, Miles of Gloucester, Robert d'Oilly, and Brian Fitz Count; the stewards William Martel, Hugh Bigod, Humphrey de Bohun, Simon de Beauchamp, Robert Malet, and Robert Fitz Richard de Clare; the butlers William d'Aubigny and Eudo Martel; the chamberlains: Aubrey de Vere and William de Pont-de-l'Arche. Then there are the barons Robert de Ferrers, William Peverel of Nottingham, Simon of Senlis, Geoffrey de Mandeville, William d'Aubigny Brito, Payn Fitz John, Hamo de St Clair, Ilbert de Lacy, Geoffrey Talbot, Walter Espec, Roger of Valognes, Henry de Port, Walter Fitz Richard de Clare, Walter de Gant, Walter de Bolebec, Walchelin Maminot, William de Percy. A number of these men came from the west country and the north of England: if at court for the first time, they will have "done homage and sworn fealty as was the custom."[106] We may imagine them being called out one by one, just as Roger of Salisbury had called out those swearing fealty to the empress on 1 January 1127. The witness lists that are being drawn on here are unusually explicit in indicating the rank of individuals and the offices which they held, a further indication of the formality of this Easter court.

There is no royal charter datable from this court for the great majority of the individuals whose homage the king received. It cannot have been expected or required. The coronation oath – perhaps repeated as a part of the ceremonial – said enough on the subject. Charters would record agreements that were to some degree exceptional. We know of the terms in which the king had, in the very first days of the reign, dealt with Miles of Gloucester.[107] These relate to Miles's specific concerns but are also valuable as indicative of baronial ambition more generally. The gist of the matter is contained in the shorter of the two charters:

Know that I return and concede to Miles of Gloucester and his heirs after him, in fee and inheritance, all the honour of his father and the custody of the towers and the castle of Gloucester, to hold in the same manner as he rendered [service] for them in the time of King Henry, as his patrimony. Also the whole of his honour of Brecon, and all his offices and all his lands, as he best and most honourably held them on the day on which King Henry was alive and dead.

The charter concludes by saying that this was an agreement (*convencio*) that the two men had made.[108] The other charter sets out the terms of the agreement more fully. "You are to know that I as lord and as king have made

---

[106] This is Henry of Winchester in his *libellus* speaking of Robert Fitz Walter, "after my brother Stephen succeeded to the kingdom": *English Lawsuits*, i. 246. There is a similar form of words in *GS*, 12–13: "they devoted themselves wholly to his service by a voluntary oath, after paying homage"; and later very briefly in Diceto, i. 248: "fidelitates exigit."

[107] On Miles, see Walker, "Miles of Gloucester"; the relevant charters are *Regesta*, iii, nos. 386–8, issued at Reading around the time of Henry I's burial.

[108] *Regesta*, iii, no. 387.

this agreement with him as my baron and justiciar that for so long as I live I will not implead him concerning any tenancy which he held on the day on which King Henry was alive and dead, nor [will I implead] his heir." This charter for "offices" reads "sheriffdoms and other things."[109] These when taken together are sweeping grants. They represent an agreement, the result of discussions, and for this reason even though the drafting is that of a royal clerk the thought patterns are those of the greater aristocracy. Miles had two main bases, at Gloucester and at Brecon. At Gloucester his power was greatly increased by the fact that he held additionally the two royal offices, that of sheriff and that of castellan. It is the grant of the royal offices, in inheritance, intended to descend to his successors for all time, that is remarkable here. The whole tendency of this society was for offices to become fees, as Marc Bloch long ago pointed out.[110] It was a tendency that Henry I had set himself resolutely against. In so doing he cut against the grain of baronial thinking. Miles of Gloucester had put it succinctly. Both the lands and the offices were his patrimony, part of the complex of rights and duties – which went under the other shorthand phrase, his "honour" – which it was his bounden duty to defend. It was an exceptional grant of Stephen, in circumstances that related in general to his control of the west country and the Welsh March, and specifically to one individual. This was Robert of Gloucester.

Robert of Gloucester did not attend the Easter court.[111] His problems of allegiance are highlighted by William of Malmesbury in the *Historia Novella*.[112] Robert – it is here suggested – was worried about the oath he had sworn to his half-sister but found himself now presented with a *fait accompli*. Stephen had control of the resources of the Anglo-Norman *regnum*; he was an extremely popular figure; and by now almost all the great men had come over to him. This was indeed the case and finally, after having being summoned to court many times, Robert did appear. According to the *Gesta Stephani*: "He was received with favour and distinction and obtained all he demanded in accordance with his wish, on paying homage to the king."[113] The *Historia Novella*, paving the way for Robert's later renunciation of his fealty, puts the matter rather differently. "He did homage to the king conditionally, that is to say, for as long as the king maintained his rank unimpaired and kept the agreement, since having long observed the king's disposition he foresaw that he would be likely to break his word."[114] The *Gesta Stephani* and the *Historia Novella* are here offering two different interpretations of a single event, for it is not in doubt

[109] *Regesta*, iii, no. 386.
[110] Bloch, *Feudal Society*, 190–210.
[111] On Robert, see Crouch, "Robert of Gloucester and the Daughter of Zelophehad"; idem, "Robert, First Earl of Gloucester"; and, for his *acta*, *Earldom of Gloucester Charters*.
[112] WM, *HN*, 30–3.
[113] *GS*, 12–15.
[114] WM, *HN*, 32–3: "quamdiu ille dignitatem suam integre custodiret et sibi pacta seruaret."

that Robert of Gloucester did pay homage to Stephen. That the king promised to "maintain his rank unimpaired" is not in doubt either, for Stephen was constituting a court and was highly conscious of rank. In Normandy in the following year the king "addressed the earl jovially and emphasised his rank."[115] But Robert wanted more than this: he wanted influence, such as he had enjoyed in his father's day. The medieval equivalent of the smoke-filled committee room, the close identification with decision-making in a royal court that lay at the centre of the political life of the Anglo-Norman world, this was Robert's natural habitat. That was what Robert meant by "keeping his rank unimpaired," while for Stephen it was a simple matter of precedence. In explaining the rupture that followed, there is no need to charge either man with a breach of faith; they simply interpreted what was said – which was what was agreed – differently. Even had Robert accepted Stephen more readily – as he was apparently prepared to accept Stephen's brother, Theobald – his days of dominance at court were over. Robert was never able to come to terms with his loss, but his struggle to do so was to be an important feature of the politics of the next decade.

Robert of Gloucester appeared at court at some time in April 1136, when he is found at Oxford. This suggests that he paid homage either at Oxford or when he joined the court as it travelled through the Thames valley. If we look for such an intermediate stop the obvious one is Wallingford, where the borough and castle were under the control of his close associate Brian Fitz Count. Somewhere along this route also there was received, brought back by the royal agents from Pisa, the pope's confirmation of Stephen's election. This was what Stephen's advisers had been waiting for, with a measure of confidence, and what they read allowed them now to notify the whole political community that Stephen was their lawful king. The draft was ready. "I Stephen by the grace of God and with the assent of the clergy and the people having been elected as king of the English, and consecrated by William archbishop of Canterbury and legate of the holy Roman church, and thereafter having been confirmed by Innocent pontiff of the holy Roman see," was the opening of the initial statement. The key words here were *elected, consecrated*, and *confirmed*. The king was emphasizing that he had been elected in the proper way, by clergy and people. He had been consecrated by the proper person, the archbishop of Canterbury, who was the pope's representative in England, and – he might have added – in the proper place, at Westminster. He had been confirmed, the case for his election having been heard and accepted, by the papal court, the supreme court of Western Christendom. The main body of the text then recorded the promises he had made, which involved all of his subjects in some way. He concluded by reserving the rights of the crown. "All this I concede and confirm saving my rightful royal dignity." This is "the 'Oxford' charter of liberties for the

---

[115] WM, *HN*, 38–9: "coram pulchre iocundeque comitem illum appellans."

Church" but is is no less a "coronation charter" than that which had been issued four months earlier. Three originals of this charter survive, along with a number of copies, both in charter collections and in chronicles.[116] It was widely disseminated.

This charter, which emphasized Stephen's legitimacy and started to define his rule, came from a court in session, the king and magnates "in common council." The meetings of the court were governed by strict rules. Magnates were expected to come in response to the royal summons, and to leave only when they had permission to do so. When the court became the camp and was put on a war footing, the need for discipline was reinforced. If a magnate wished to cross the Channel, then – if he was in any way unsure of his standing – it would be prudent to obtain a formal permission to do so; while the royal court as it was about to transfer as a body had a special status. If this claim to control and this formality seem surprising, it should be remembered that there were a limited number of natural ports in England, as in Normandy, and there were royal agents in each of them. It was not a figure of speech when Robert of Gloucester claimed that he needed to give undertakings as to his loyalty before being allowed to cross to England.[117] If you were an official emissary from another court, such as a papal legate, you might be asked to wait or you might be refused entry. These were "ancient customs," established rights, of the English crown and Stephen would be particularly tenacious of them.[118] It is therefore quite possible that, as Round suggested,[119] the Easter court was prorogued, remaining formally constituted as it travelled along the Thames valley to Oxford, and that those attesting the Oxford charter were physically present there. There are enough variations between the London and the Oxford witness lists to give credence to this. Robert of Gloucester, Brian Fitz Count, and Robert d'Oilly (the royal castellan at Oxford) are new names. The archbishop of York, Henry of Scots, and some of the northern magnates, who had been with the court from York, had gone home. Oxford was not on their way, but for the magnates of the west country and the Marches it was, and they are here, along with the officers of the royal household. At Oxford, the court was dissolved; but not everyone had permission to leave. Robert of Gloucester had taken his time in arriving and it would be some time before he was allowed to leave. He is found with the king at the royal lodges of

[116] *Regesta*, iii, no. 271. Originals survive from the archives of the cathedrals of Exeter, Hereford, and Salisbury, and copies in the collections of the two archdioceses, Canterbury and York. These are "no doubt specimens of similar charters preserved in at least all cathedral churches, and, it may be assumed, deposited there on behalf of the counties": Poole, "The Publication of Great Charters by the English Kings," 311. There is a full text in Richard of Hexham and an all but full text in William of Malmesbury: RH, 148–50; WM, *HN*, 34–7 and n. 94.

[117] WM, *HN*, 32–3.

[118] See further below, Chapter 10.

[119] Round, *Geoffrey*, 22.

Hurstbourne in Hampshire,[120] Gillingham in Dorset,[121] and at the siege of Exeter.[122]

A lot of rumours were flying around in the spring of 1136. "At Rogationtide [26 April] it was rumoured that the king was dead." This news led Hugh Bigod, who had been with the court until recently, to occupy Norwich castle. It is possible, though not likely, that the king went to Norwich to require its surrender from him.[123] "After Pentecost [10 May] King Stephen made ready his fleet for crossing to Normandy, and as he was waiting near the port for a favourable wind a messenger arrived, who informed him of the death of Roger, bishop of Salisbury." The king may have made such plans but he did not cross and the bishop was perfectly well.[124] Messengers also came from the city of Exeter, asking for the king's help against Baldwin de Redvers, "a man of eminent rank and birth," who was acting in a novel and arbitrary way: he was claiming lordship over the city and the surrounding countryside, and he had occupied and was provisioning the royal castle. These reports were accurate and the king most certainly did act upon them. He "was enraged at the rash presumption of Baldwin, especially because it was clearer than daylight that his rebellion against him was unjust, since the king had a reasonable claim to the castle at Exeter, which had always been a royal possession." He sent an advance party of 200 cavalry and followed it in short order,

[120] *Regesta*, iii, no. 340, for the abbey of St Peter, Ghent, was issued at *Huche Lesbiam*. The editors suggest this might stand for Hittisleigh in Devon but Hurstbourne in Hampshire is the more likely identification, for two reasons: (i) Hittisleigh is a minor village west of Exeter while Hurstbourne is a royal lodge (*King's Works*, ii. 963); (ii) Nigel, bishop of Ely, who attests this charter, may then have gone on to Salisbury, but he was not with the royal court thereafter.

[121] *Regesta*, iii, no. 818 (for Shaftesbury Abbey). Other charters issued here are ibid., nos. 434 (for Launceston Priory), 800 (for Buckfastleigh Abbey), and 953 (for Winchester Cathedral). The presence of religious from houses in Devon and Cornwall suggests that the tenants-in-chief of those counties had been summoned to Gillingham. The "housekeeper" had a penny a day and was earning his keep: *King's Works*, ii. 944–6.

[122] *Regesta*, iii, nos. 337 (for Furness Abbey), 952 (for Winchester Cathedral). Other charters issued here are ibid., nos. 572 (for the burgesses of Lympstone and Kenton), 592 (for Montacute Priory).

[123] The authority for this episode is Henry of Huntingdon. He says that Hugh Bigod entered the castle of Norwich and was reported to have said that he would not surrender it unless the king came in person, and then only reluctantly. HH, 706–7: "Hugo Bigod in castellum Norewic subintrauit, nec reddere uoluit, nisi ipsi regi aduenienti, ualde tamen inuitus." Those who followed Henry took this as a firm statement that the king had indeed gone to Norwich: Torigni, 129: "reddidit regi"; *Ann. Mon.*, i. 45 (Tewkesbury: "[exercitum movit] postea ad Norwiche, et redditum est ei castellum"); ii. 225 (Waverley: "rex illuc ivit, et redditum est ei castellum, et ad Pentecosten moratus est in provincia illa"). Against adding this to Stephen's itinerary: (i) it is not corroborated elsewhere; (ii) there is no cluster of charters issued in favour of the religious houses of the region such as mark the king's travels elsewhere in 1136. All the indications are that the king did not go to East Anglia until the winter of 1136–7.

[124] OV, vi. 462–3. A version of the same rumour must have reached northern England, for Richard of Hexham states that Stephen crossed to Normandy in Aug. 1136: RH, 150.

being received by the citizens with proper ceremonial and escorted within the walls.[125]

Everyone knew something at least of the city of Exeter. It was "a large city with very ancient walls built by the Roman emperors, the fourth place, so it is said, in England."[126] It was "a vigorous centre for every sort of trade."[127] It was a provincial capital and the seat of a diocese. Some might have known that it had a history of rebellion. It had opposed William the Conqueror early in 1068, surrendering only after an eighteen-day siege, though by now the challenge was remembered as amounting to very much at all. William of Malmesbury preserved little more than the story that part of the castle wall had collapsed of its own accord, while a member of the garrison appeared on another part of the wall, "bared his bottom and made the enclosure resound with an enormous fart, to show his contempt for the Normans."[128] Baldwin de Redvers in 1136 represented more of a threat. The possessor of three distinct honours, of Plympton in Devon, Christchurch in Hampshire, and the Isle of Wight, all granted by Henry I, he was the greatest landowner in the south-west and, now that Robert of Gloucester was on board (and indeed outside), he was the greatest magnate who had been summoned to court and had refused to attend.[129] What lay behind his dispute with the king, which can certainly be called a rebellion from the point at which his garrison refused to surrender the castle when the king arrived, was not – we can be reasonably confident – Stephen's refusal to confirm Baldwin in "his lands."[130] Rather it was his refusal to grant him office, certainly the castellanship of Exeter castle – for it was as castellan that he claimed rights over the citizens and the surrounding countryside – and possibly also control of the sheriffdom of Devon. Baldwin may have been aware of the hereditary grant of these two offices to Miles of Gloucester and have hoped for similar treatment; but in this county the case was very different. The office of sheriff of Devon was held by, and a better hereditary claim lay with, Richard Fitz Baldwin. He was the son of Baldwin de Meules, lord of Okehampton, sheriff of Devon and castellan of Exeter.[131] He was, moreover, a member of the house of Clare. The king was closely identified with this family; he would not wish to condone the unauthorized seizure of a royal castle; and as count of Mortain he had a residual interest in some of Baldwin de Redvers's estates, which had previously formed part of the Mortain fee.[132]

[125] *GS*, 30–3.
[126] *GS*, 32–3.
[127] WM, *GP*, 314–15.
[128] WM, *GR*, i. 462–3 (giving a more fastidious translation).
[129] On Baldwin, see Bearman, "Baldwin de Redvers."
[130] As is argued in Davis, *Stephen*, 22.
[131] On the families involved see here, Green, "The Empress's Party in South-West England," 157–8.
[132] *Charters of the Redvers Family*, 24–5.

The siege of Exeter was the main news item of the summer of 1136.[133] It was a long siege, lasting nearly three months, and enormously expensive, costing the king in all £10,000. It left its mark on the landscape, for the earthworks of Stephen's siege castle can still be seen.[134] Our main authority was very interested in the technicalities of siege warfare.[135] The king

> vigorously and energetically pressed on with the siege of the garrison; sometimes he joined battle with them by means of armed men crawling up the rampart; sometimes, by the aid of countless slingers, who had been hired from a distant region, he assailed them with an unendurable hail of stones; at other times he summoned those who have skill in mining underground and ordered them to search into the bowels of the earth with a view to demolishing the wall; frequently too he devised engines of different sorts, some rising high in the air, others low on the ground, the former to spy out what was going on in the castle, the latter to shake or undermine the wall.[136]

The castle was a strong one; it was well provisioned; and it was only as the wells ran dry that surrender was forced on it. As the water ran out, wine had to be used as a substitute, for cooking and for firefighting among other things. As the position of the garrison grew parlous, and it became clear that they would have to surrender, divisions appeared in the royal camp as to the terms that should be offered. Several reasons have been suggested for these divisions. It is suggested, more than once, that some were "serving in the king's army with treacherous designs," while others "were bitterly grieved for their relations who were shut up within." All approached the king together, there was lively discussion, and "suddenly they changed him to another man." This despite the efforts of his brother, Henry of Winchester, to stiffen his resolve, saying that the garrison would very soon be forced to surrender on any terms they could get. He was not the only cleric who felt this way. According to Henry of Huntingdon, the king "took the very worst advice, and did not execute punishment on those who had betrayed him"; had he done so, there would have been fewer castles held against him.[137] All the garrison were released on honourable terms, and there were no reprisals. One reason argued for leniency was that the defenders had no ties of lordship to the king, but the royal standard was

---

[133] *GS*, 30–47, is the main source for the following paragraph; the siege is noted also in RH, 146–7, JW, 218–19, *ASC*, s.a. 1135, HH, 708–9 (thence Torigni, 129, *Ann. Mon.* i. 45 (Tewkesbury), ii. 225 (Waverley), Newburgh, i. 33).

[134] This is now known as Danes Castle, Exeter, recently excavated and incorporated in the Exeter Heritage Trail: *Medieval Archaeology*, 38 (1994), 203–4; <http://www.exeter.gov.uk/timetrail/06_norman/defence.asp>.

[135] This was one reason why Barlow thought that the author of the *Gesta Stephani* was unlikely to be the bishop of Bath: *English Church 1066–1154*, 21 and n. 83.

[136] *GS*, 34–5.

[137] HH, 708–9. JW iii. 218–19, makes no comment but records that terms of surrender were agreed and Baldwin and his family disinherited.

raised in clear sight of them, and that could have been reason enough for severity. Those defending Baldwin's honorial castle, at Plympton, were also allowed to leave without penalty. Baldwin "at length left England as an exile and went to the count of Anjou." While Stephen pursued Baldwin, Henry of Winchester was left in charge of the south-west. He saw the local leadership of the crown as culpable in Baldwin's revolt and both the bishop of Exeter and the sheriff of Devon were eased into early retirement.[138]

John of Worcester also noted the king's leniency and he had another problem area in mind. "When all should be at peace through fear of the king, who should be as a roaring lion, there is in many places, particularly in Wales, depopulation and devastation."[139] The native historians of Wales took as a key event in the Welsh uprising against the Norman settlers the ambush and killing, near Abergavenny, of Richard Fitz Gilbert de Clare, by Morgan ab Owain, a "descendant of the royal line that had once ruled in Glamorgan."[140] In response, Stephen sent two trouble-shooters, Richard's younger brother Baldwin and Robert Fitz Harold of Ewyas. Baldwin stopped at Brecon, and "gave himself over entirely to gluttony and sloth."[141] Robert was rather more successful and was able to secure the castle of Carmarthen. Worse was to follow. Widespread warfare broke out in the Marches, and the "watershed" of this war, according to David Crouch,[142] was a pitched battle near Cardigan in October 1136, in which the leaders of the Anglo-Flemish force escaped with their lives but the majority of their followers were slain. It was only after this that the heavyweight marcher lords appeared on the scene. Miles of Gloucester was able to relieve Cardigan, but Carmarthen was taken, and it was possibly in this campaign that Payn Fitz John was slain.[143] Robert of Gloucester, a living link with the previous king and the authority which he had exercised, was detained at Stephen's court through the summer, a diminished figure, deliberately kept away from the sources of his power.[144] There was a powerful force behind this Welsh resurgence, which crucially would not be dissipated by dynastic disunity: in Deheubarth, the sons of Gruffudd ap Rhys "forged an unusual unity of purpose in their anxiety to

[138] William Warelwast, the *bishop* of Exeter, after a distinguished career as a diplomat and churchman, was now elderly and blind, and he would retire to Plympton Priory, where he died on 26 Sept. 1137. It is said that in his last days he resigned his ring and staff into the hands of Henry of Winchester: Plympton Annals, *UGQ*, 27. William Warelwast's death was notified to Baldwin de Redvers in Angers and prayers were said for him there: "Chronicon Sancti Sergii Andegavensis," s.a. 1138. The *sheriff*, Richard Fitz Baldwin, "chose this very moment to disengage himself altogether from worldly cares" and he was buried on 25 June 1137: Finberg, "Uffculme," 214 and n. 2; Oliver, *Monasticon Exoniensis*, 342.

[139] JW, 216–17.

[140] Crouch, "The March and the Welsh Kings," 258.

[141] GS, 20–1.

[142] Crouch, "The March and the Welsh Kings," 269.

[143] JW, iii. 228–9; GS, 24–5; Crouch, "The March and the Welsh Kings," 272; Mason, "Pain Fitz John."

[144] Crouch, "Robert of Gloucester and the Daughter of Zelophehad," 229–30.

recover their inheritance."[145] The news of events in Wales in the summer and autumn would have arrived at the royal court piecemeal; it may have taken some time for a pattern to emerge; and by then it was too late. It is easy to explain Stephen's choice of priorities. But he had promised the protection of tenancies to the marcher lords as to all others, and was not able to deliver. When a systematic challenge to his authority did appear it would be amongst the marcher lords, but that time was not yet.

Stephen's itinerary in the winter of 1135–6 had seen him rushing across the Channel to secure the crown and then immediately thereafter hastening up the Old North Road to treat with the Scots. In the summer he personally conducted a long siege outside Exeter. This represented a long period "on the road" and at other times of the year he sought to settle and to establish his routines. His brother, Henry of Winchester, and Roger of Salisbury remained close to him. It may have been as early as Whitsun that he issued at Winchester a fine diploma in favour of the monks of Cluny, granting to them the manor of Letcombe Regis in Berkshire in place of the pension of 100 marks a year granted to them by "King Henry of venerable memory, my uncle and ancestor, for the soul of his father, my grandfather."[146] This was a diploma in solemn form, bearing an impressive set of subscriptions, crosses made by the hands of Stephen, his queen, and his son Eustace (possibly his earliest attestation), and attested also by Henry of Winchester, his nephew Henry de Sully, Roger of Salisbury, his nephews Alexander of Lincoln and Nigel of Ely, two earls, Alan of Richmond and Roger of Warwick, Aubrey de Vere, Robert de Vere, William Peverel, and Ilbert de Lacy. Perhaps on the same occasion, allowing copies to be sent to Burgundy by the same messenger, there was issued the king's protection of the abbey of Marcigny, "where my mother is a nun"; its demesne lands in England were to be treated as those of the king himself.[147] His family never seem far from his thoughts. At London he made a grant to the almonry of Westminster Abbey. "I do this," he said, "for the good of my soul, for the safe-keeping of my wife and children, for the repose of the soul of my dear father, for the welfare of my mother, and for the soul of my uncle King Henry."[148] The king was confident in the power of prayer.

It was in the south-east of England, in and around London, where many of his family lands lay, that Stephen was most secure and could feel most relaxed. This was his base throughout the winter of 1136–7. His presence could start to be spoken of as routine. Thus the preamble to the

---

[145] Davies, *Wales 1063–1415*, 45–51, at 50–1; Crouch, "The March and the Welsh Kings," 255–74.

[146] *Regesta*, iii, no. 204: "rex Henricus avunculus meus et antecessor meus pro anima patris sui, avi mei, . . . dedit." The monks used the money to tend their vines: Duby, "Le Budget de l'abbaye de Cluny," 75.

[147] *Regesta*, iii, no. 576.

[148] *Regesta*, iii, no. 936: "hoc concessi pro anima mea et pro salute uxoris mee et filiorum meorum et pro requie et redemptione dilecti patris mei et incolumitate matris mee et pro anima avunculi mei regis Henrici."

narrative of a court case affecting the priory of Holy Trinity, London and its claim that the castellan of the Tower of London, Hasculf de Tany, had encroached on land that was rightfully theirs. The prior sought out the king, "on one occasion when he was at Westminster."[149] When he was ushered into the king's presence he found there: Queen Matilda, Algar, bishop of Coutances, Roger, "the then chancellor," Arnulf, archdeacon of Sées, William Martel the steward, Robert de Courcy, Aubrey de Vere, Geoffrey de Mandeville, Hugh Bigod, Adam de Beanay, as well as "Andrew Buccuinte and many other burgesses of London."[150] It is an impressive court for what seems to be a routine meeting. The castellan was asked what right he had to the land and replied simply: "I hold it." The king then viva voce required Andrew Buccuinte, who was the justiciar of London, to have an enquiry made into the site of the land in dispute. As a result of this the priory recovered possession. At some later time the hereditary claim of Geoffrey de Mandeville, one of those present here, to the castellanship of the Tower was recognized by the king.[151]

The king spent some time outside the capital in these winter months. There is no reason to doubt Henry of Huntingdon's statement that he hunted from the royal lodge at Brampton near Huntingdon,[152] and he may have held a court at Bury St Edmunds, a substantial town that had grown around one of the great monasteries of England.[153] There was also the opportunity to reside on family manors and some important business was transacted during these visits. At Witham in Essex, one of the estate centres of the queen's honour of Boulogne, he had three bishops in his entourage. Henry of Winchester, Bernard of St Davids, and Robert of Bath. Messengers were sent from there to Normandy, confirming to Hugh, archbishop of Rouen, and all the bishops of Normandy, all their "episcopal and synodal rights," and specifically fines due from breaches of the Truce of God, in just the same terms as King Henry his uncle had granted them.[154] At the centre of one of his honours, at Eye in Suffolk, "by the counsel of his barons," he granted to the priory of Eye all the rights and privileges they had enjoyed first under Robert Malet and then "in my day." The "barons" named are: Nigel, bishop of Ely, Roger the chancellor, Henry de Sully, Waleran, count of Meulan, Robert Fitz

---

[149] *Regesta*, iii, no. 506: "quadam vice cum esset rex Westmonasterii."

[150] *Regesta*, iii, no. 506; *English Lawsuits*, i. 244–5; Round, *Commune of London*, 97–102.

[151] Hollister, "The Misfortunes of the Mandevilles," 126.

[152] HH, 708–9. Henry is almost certainly mistaken in saying that Stephen spent Christmas 1136 at Dunstable, for this is where he spent Christmas 1137.

[153] *Regesta*, iii, nos. 287 (for Eye Priory), 756, 767 (for Bury St Edmunds Abbey: a grant of the king's revenues in the manor of Beccles, Suff., made for the soul of King Henry his uncle).

[154] *Regesta*, iii, no. 609, dated by the editors 1136–9, but the grant would not have been necessary once these privileges had been confirmed within the duchy, at Evreux, in 1137: ibid., no. 608. The date must be late 1136, for Henry of Winchester crossed to Normandy in Advent and spent the winter there: OV, vi. 478–9. This was a significant privilege and it may be that Henry of Winchester delivered it to Hugh of Rouen in person.

Richard, William Martel, Adam de Beaunay, John the Marshal, Hubert de Muntchesney, John Fitz Robert the sheriff, Geoffrey son of Walter, William son of Roger, Hervey de Glanville, Richard of Alençon, and Roger Hose. This is a substantial court and it must have met some time in the early weeks of 1137.[155] We may think that we see here Stephen able for the first time to relax just a little, visit his comital lands, and call to mind "the day on which I came to the crown of England."[156]

NORMANDY

In March 1137 Stephen crossed to Normandy.[157] "The wretched people," says Orderic, "after suffering a whole year of oppression and neglect, were overjoyed at the news of his coming."[158] The king had a large following.[159] He needed to show himself and demonstrate his authority; he needed to come to terms with his neighbours; and he needed if possible to meet the Angevin military threat. He crossed from Portsmouth to La Hogue, the medieval equivalent of the Portsmouth–Cherbourg ferry, the most westerly of several well-established Channel crossings. This allowed him to progress slowly through western and central Normandy, through the towns that stood at the head of main rivers, to the capital at Rouen. The towns on his route included Caen, the burial place of the Conqueror, and Bayeux, where the tapestry commissioned by the Conqueror's half-brother Odo may have been on view. These two towns, and the claims to the memories of Norman authority that their fine buildings evoked, were centres of the power of Robert of Gloucester. The bishop of Bayeux was an illegitimate son of his. But Robert of Gloucester was not in the king's

[155] *Regesta*, iii, no. 288, where the editors give a date a year later, after the king's return from Normandy. The charter is dated to 1137, in the king's second year, and whatever conventions are followed for the calendar year the king's second regnal year was 22 Dec. 1136–21 Dec. 1137. The editors discount the earlier date on the assumption that Waleran of Meulan "was in Normandy during the winter 1136–7" but this charter and ibid., no. 827 (which has been misdated for the same reason) demonstrate that he was not. Robert Fitz Richard was dead by 1138.

[156] Ibid.: "die qua ad regni coronam perveni."

[157] Orderic says that the crossing was in the third week of March (presumably the week beginning Sunday, 14 Mar.): OV, vi. 480–1; cf. JW, iii. 228–9 ("in March"); HH, 708–9 ("in Lent"); WM, *HN*, 36–7 ("at the beginning of Lent").

[158] OV, vi. 480–1.

[159] Ibid.: "cum magno comitatu." Some of those in his entourage just before he crossed the Channel are given as witnesses to a charter he issued for the abbey of St Denys, Southampton, at Portsmouth *in transitu meo*: *Regesta*, iii, no. 827. These are: Roger, bishop of Salisbury; Alexander, bishop of Lincoln; Bernard, bishop of St Davids; Roger the chancellor; Waleran, count of Meulan; Roger of Fécamp; William d'Aubigny *pincerna*; William Martel; Robert Fitz Richard; Robert d'Oilli; Aubrey de Vere; William de Pont de l'Arche; Robert de Courcy; Ingelram de Say; Martin Fitz Atso; Warin of Hampton. The editors date this charter to *c*.28 November 1137, on the king's return, again on the assumption that Waleran of Meulan had not returned to England. The phrase *in transitu* was invariably used for when the king was about to cross the Channel; the presence of Roger of Salisbury, who will not have crossed, further supports the date of March 1137, as given by Haskins, 124–5 and n. 5.

entourage at this point. According to William of Malmesbury, the earl had waited behind in England to sort out various business, before making the crossing to Normandy, "actually on Easter Day itself."[160] Easter Day fell on 11 April, about three weeks after the main court had crossed. The image of the great man, hearing an early mass and then scurrying across the Channel, missing out on all ceremonial and festivity, is at first sight a little incongruous. But in fact it was completely in character. Robert missed the ceremonial of Stephen's Easter court of 1137 in Normandy, as he had done the Easter court of 1136 in England, arriving in each case just a few days late, in time for his apologies to be accepted but not believed.

We are not told to which centre in Normandy the Easter court was summoned, but Stephen would have been concerned to follow precedent and normal expectations, and all such considerations would have directed his path to Rouen. Rouen was the undoubted capital of the province of Normandy. It was the seat of the archbishop, Hugh, previously prior of the Cluniac house at Lewes in Sussex, who had no rival as head of his province and would remain a loyal supporter of Stephen in his early years.[161] It was an important port, at the head of the Seine, one of the great rivers of northern Europe, at a time when trade was booming. Just one charter survives, for one of the minor guilds, to give quite inadequate testimony to the bustle of the city, but it is likely that Stephen granted more substantial privileges.[162] It had an important Jewish community.[163] The citizens needed the protection of a strong ruler, and the same considerations that had led the Londoners to support Stephen should have secured similar support for him from the men of Rouen. Almost a half of the small number of charters that Stephen issued in Normandy in 1137 were issued at Rouen, and while it is likely to have been his base in the autumn before his return to England, some at least of them should be associated with this initial

---

[160] WM, *HN*, 36–9. I would not doubt this clear statement, on the basis of Robert of Gloucester's attestation of two of Stephen's charters which are dated "anno incarnationis dominice mcxxx sexto, regni mei vero secundo": *Regesta*, iii, nos. 69, 594. As had happened a year before (ibid., no. 818), and as would happen again a year later (ibid., no. 132), *scriptor* xiii is responsible for dates which though reliable as to regnal years give calendar years that conflict with other evidence. It is interesting to note that in the two original charters which survive from this sample these idiosyncratic dates are written over an erasure, altering the years which the other chancery scribes and later historians would view as correct: ibid., nos. 69 (Bishop, *Scriptores Regis*, 21 n. 6 and plate XX), 132 (*Regesta*, iv, plate XI).

[161] Spear, *Norman Cathedrals*, 198–9; WM, *HN*, 48–9: "maximus regis propugnator."

[162] *Regesta*, iii, no. 727, for the cordwainers guild. The one surviving charter for the citizens of Rouen issued in Stephen's time is that granted by Henry, duke of Normandy, c.1150: *Regesta*, iii, no. 729. This refers back to a charter of his father, Geoffrey of Anjou, issued soon after he became duke in 1144. There are hints that a charter of Stephen or Henry I lay further back. In particular, the grants of privileges in London make more sense if made by a ruler who claimed authority there.

[163] Golb, *Jews in Medieval Normandy*, 147, suggests that there would have been no fewer than 2,000 Jews in Rouen at this time.

visit.[164] While at Rouen, Stephen was joined by his brothers, Theobald, count of Blois, and Henry, bishop of Winchester. We know of this from their attestation of a grant to the Angevin house of Fontevraud, confirming that made by King Henry, "my lord and uncle and predecessor," a document pervaded by a sense of family: "I grant this for the remission of my sins and those of my wife, my children and my brothers."[165] Also present in Normandy for a time was Andrew de Baudemont, who had been Count Theobald's steward and was now, at the end of his days, a monk of the Cistercian abbey of Ourscamp, near Noyon, where his son Waleran was the abbot. Their business was to facilitate the transfer of the Norman monastery of Mortemer to the Cistercian order. The king readily agreed to this request when it was put to him by Andrew, for he was a very good friend "and had been his close associate before he entered religion"; and the archbishop of Rouen confirmed this in the king's presence. The king made generous grants in support of the house, "and the queen then promised to build a church in that place, which she went some way to completing."[166] A narrative of this kind helps to animate the dry lists of names and places found in the charters. The brothers were coming together in their common interest. They had just lost their mother, Adela of Blois, who had died at Marcigny on 8 March 1137.[167] She was the last survivor of the children of William the Conqueror.

Amongst the early diplomatic business of Stephen's visit to Normandy, and intended as a prelude to military endeavour, were the agreements he made with Theobald, count of Blois, and with the king of France. Each had written to the pope a year earlier in Stephen's support.[168] Nothing had happened in the interval to change their minds but Stephen's presence in Normandy allowed each to draw on promises that will already have been made. The agreement with Theobald, according to Robert of Torigni, was made at Evreux. It involved the payment of a money-fief of 2,000 marks a year, and it was necessary to restore wounded pride, "since count Theobald was indignant that Stephen, who was the younger, had received the crown which – he said – was rightfully his."[169] The story of the tension between the

---

[164] This was clearly the view of the editors of the *Regesta*, in their itinerary, but was not spelt out by Davis in his book. There should be added to the materials for this visit an agreement between the canons of St Evroul and the monks of Notre-Dame de Mortain, made in the presence of King Stephen, Hugh, archbishop of Rouen, "and very many counts and magnates": Power, *Norman Frontier*, 59 and n. 203; Haskins, 126 n. 9.

[165] *Regesta*, iii, no. 327: "pro remissione peccatorum meorum et uxoris et filiorum et fratrum meorum"; for prayers for his brothers see also ibid., nos. 281, 594, 598. Note also the reference to Count Theobald's involvement in the issue of ibid., no. 749, for the canons of Ste Barbe-en-Auge: "precibus venerabilis viri Hugonis Rothomagensis archiepiscopi et Teobaldi comitis Blesensis dilectissime fratris mei."

[166] The charter here is *Regesta*, iii, no. 598. The context is provided by "Le Récit de la fondation de Mortemer," ed. Bouvet, 154–5.

[167] LoPrete, *Adela*, 526–8.

[168] RH, 147–8.

[169] Torigni, 132.

two brothers was certainly current in Normandy at the time, for Orderic also speaks of it, saying that Theobald was disgruntled at having the crown snatched from his grasp in December 1135.[170] The balance of power and of wealth and of prestige between the brothers had changed rapidly in recent months. There was necessarily a process of adjustment. The same thing can be seen in Henry of Winchester's ambition to succeed to the see of Canterbury, vacant since the death of William of Corbeil on 21 November 1136.[171] The chroniclers showed the instincts of good journalists and made the tensions into headline news. The historian can take the advantage of a longer view, and perhaps detect sibling rivalry within a very tightly knit family. To the king of France they put up a united front. "In May King Stephen had a meeting with King Louis, received the duchy of Normandy from him as his right, and made a pact of friendship with him, as his predecessor had done."[172] As a part of the ceremonial of this pact Eustace, Stephen's son, a boy perhaps seven years old, did homage for Normandy.[173] This eased the tensions between two powerful monarchies that until quite recently had been at war. There will have been little tension in this particular meeting. Louis VI would be dead before the summer's end, and in the south of France his son, Louis, accompanied by Count Theobald, went to meet his bride. We know her as Eleanor of Aquitaine. For contemporaries with a sense of history and no knowledge of what would come later, this was a diplomatic triumph for the French crown, for not since the days of Charlemagne had their influence extended so far south.[174]

In the spring and early summer of 1137 Stephen's court was being placed on a war footing. The challenge came from the Angevins. "Geoffrey of Anjou invaded Normandy with four hundred knights and caused widespread damage, acting as his wife's stipendiary commander."[175] Orderic while critical of Stephen is completely loyal to him, and the empress's claim to the succession is seen merely as a pretext for her husband to engage in plunder. The Angevins brought a much bigger army than they had in the previous year and it caused considerable damage.[176] Various religious houses had to pay the count of Anjou to spare their outlying properties, for the duke of Normandy could not protect them.[177] Initially Stephen stayed in and around Rouen, and sent his Flemish troops under William of Ypres to engage with the Angevins. Both sides were to be disappointed of their wider ambitions. Geoffrey wanted to strike north through the centre of the

---

[170] OV, vi. 454–5: "indignatus quod regnum non habuerit."
[171] *Fasti* 2: *Monastic Cathedrals*, 4 (William's death); OV, vi. 478–9 (Henry's ambition).
[172] OV, vi. 482–3: "fœdus amicitiae sicut antecessor eius tenuerat pepigit."
[173] HH, 708–9: "homo regis Francorum effectus est de Normannia"; Torigni, 132: "fecit ei hominium de Normannia"; for important discussion of this homage and the issues involved, see Gillingham, "Doing Homage to the King of France," 65–7.
[174] WM, *HN*, 20–1; OV, vi. 490–1.
[175] OV, vi. 482–3: "stipendiarius coniugi suæ factus."
[176] Torigni, 132.
[177] OV, vi. 482–3, noting payments made by the monks of Dives and Fécamp.

duchy and take Caen, hoping that Robert of Gloucester would give him support. The castle garrison at Caen, however, was loyal to the king, and the rumours of Robert of Gloucester's defection proved premature. William of Ypres was also disappointed, for without Norman support his troops were no match for the Angevins, and this was not forthcoming. And so William, "turning his back on his faithless allies, joined the king across the Seine." Stephen, meanwhile, had had some success. He gained the support of Rabel de Tancarville, the chamberlain of Normandy, after he had at first refused to come to court or to surrender his castles.[178] As Lillebonne – the chief of these – was at the mouth of the Seine, downstream from Rouen, this was a confrontation from which Stephen could hardly back off. His success further south, at the episcopal city of Evreux, was more significant. "He won to his side Rotrou, count of Mortagne, and Richer of L'Aigle his nephew by giving them everything that they in their greed eagerly demanded."[179] The Perche was a small county on the south-central frontier of Normandy, whose independence was carefully cultivated by its counts during the twelfth century. In the context of summer 1137, with the south-east frontier of Normandy so permeable, some concession to the counts of the Perche might well be counted an investment.[180]

Thereafter Stephen's army, and with it his ambitions, fell apart. The trouble may have started, according to one later witness, with the most commonplace aggravation in any army, a quarrel between two individuals after the taverns closed, which turned to violence and then escalated. "There was great discord in the army at Livarot on account of a barrel of wine, which one of the Flemings had taken from a knight of Hugh of Gournay. [This led to] a major quarrel between the Normans and the Flemings."[181] Orderic also states that there was a serious quarrel, "and men on both sides were violently slain."[182] Shakespeare in *Henry V* would dramatize similar tensions, and made their resolution by the king himself, prowling in the camp, a demonstration of his leadership. Not so any of the several writers here. It was not just the troops but the generals who were divided amongst themselves. The witness to this is William of Malmesbury, with his keen interest in what we now call "high politics," and his particular focus on Robert of Gloucester. According to William, there was an attempt to ambush Earl Robert, which was instigated by William of Ypres, and which the earl avoided because he had been forewarned: "for some days he kept away from the court, to which he was frequently invited."[183] It needed the mediation of the archbishop of Rouen to bring the two men together;

---

[178] OV, vi. 484–5; Torigni, 132.
[179] OV, vi. 484–5.
[180] On the context, see the excellent discussion in Thompson, *The County of the Perche*, 78–81.
[181] Torigni, 132.
[182] OV, vi. 484–5.
[183] WM, *HN*, 38–9.

there was a further ceremony to demonstrate their unity; but again few were convinced that it was any more than a charade. The result of all this, going back to Orderic to provide the narrative drive, was that "the whole army was in a ferment and most of the leaders went off without taking leave of the king, each one followed by his own troops of dependants. When the king saw his army melting away without a battle he was furious and went in hot pursuit of the deserters as far as Pont Audemer."[184] Those whom Orderic mentions as hot-headed youths with whom the king reasoned but whom he could not mollify were William de Warenne – the heir to one of the great Anglo-Norman estates, to which he would succeed in the following year – and Hugh de Gournay. These divisions within his army forced the king to come to terms with the Angevins, which he did in late June. Messengers were again at work, riding between the two parties. Stephen agreed to pay the Angevins 2,000 marks a year for the duration of the truce, and was able to pay the first year's subsidy in ready cash. Concerning how long the truce was to last, the sources differ, Orderic saying two years and Robert of Torigni three. Their uncertainty was quite understandable, for in fact it would last less than a year.[185]

We have a close if possibly not an exact date for this truce, for it ran until the nearest feast day, which was that of St John the Baptist, on 24 June.[186] And Orderic says that peace returned in July.[187] We know also that Stephen returned to England in early December. As to what he did during the intervening five months there is little precise information. In itself this is not surprising, for Christmas to Whit Sunday – which fell on 30 May in 1137 – contained the main feasts and fixed reference points in the political calendar. Moreover, this would long be remembered as a parching hot summer which saw a severe drought.[188] The king might wish to sit in the shade, confident that the routines of the harvest, of getting and spending, and of tax collection in England and Normandy, proceded as they had done in the previous reign. Soon after his accession, he had granted the nuns of Fontevraud 100 marks of annual revenue from the farms of the capital cities of London and Winchester, 60 from London and 40 from Winchester: "and of that 100 marks they are to have half at Easter and the other half at Michaelmas."[189] He now gave the hospital at Chartres 10 *livres* from the revenues of Rouen, to be paid promptly each year, "at Michaelmas when my farms and monies are collected."[190] The monks of Bec were to be free of all customs dues at Wissant and the other Channel ports of the county of Boulogne, "for in this regard they have charters of

---

[184] OV, vi. 484–7.
[185] On the truce see, OV, vi. 486–7; Torigni, 132–3. RH, 151, also has two years.
[186] Torigni, 132–3.
[187] OV, vi. 486–7.
[188] Suger, *Louis VI*, 282–3; OV, vi. 480–1; Torigni, p. 133; *Recueil d'annales Angevines*, 9; *Chronicon Turonense*, s.a. 1137 in *RHF*, xii. 47; *Chronique de Saint-Pierre-le-Vif de Sens*, 198–9, and the pseudo-Godel (ibid., xlv n. 1), in *RHF*, xiii. 675.
[189] *Regesta*, iii, no. 327.
[190] Ibid., no. 69. The *livre* of Rouen was worth a half that of the pound sterling.

count Eustace and myself."[191] The bishop of Evreux would split with the
king the profits of the annual fair at Evreux, while from day to day boats
plied their trade on the Seine and the bishop took a tithe of the port of
Vernon.[192] The king, surrounded by his family,[193] could pray for the safety
and well-being of his kingdom of England and duchy of Normandy.[194]

FIRST IMPRESSIONS

As the king came to the end of his second year of rule, his contemporaries
had seen him confront many challenges to the safety and well-being of the
Anglo-Norman *regnum*. They had started to draw up a balance sheet. This
was their contribution to the political process. Of the king's temperament,
they had perhaps learned little that they did not expect. As a courtier,
before he became king, he had thrived on his networks and was an
immensely popular figure.[195] As king he would look for consensus. The
author of the *Gesta Stephani* stopped to reflect in 1136 that "the king
preferred to settle all things in the love of peace and concord rather than
encourage the schism of discord in any way"; then, when the king was
seen at first hand in Normandy in 1137, Orderic said the same, that
Stephen "judged it prudent to make small concessions to preserve what
mattered than to grasp at everything and deservedly forfeit the support of
friends."[196] We can be confident that these were early judgements.

The most high profile of the peace settlements that he made were with
the kings of Scotland and France. The grant of Carlisle, as a part of the
peace with the Scots, which reduced its recently appointed bishop to the
status of a refugee and left the interest of Ranulf of Chester in the city
unacknowledged, was far from being a "small concession." Nonetheless,
William of Malmesbury, who has claims to be the sharpest political
commentator of the day, and who was not seeking to pay Stephen any
compliments, said in a matter-of-fact way about the peace with the Scots
that Stephen "had got what he wanted."[197] What he wanted here, and for
which he was prepared to pay a price, was the recognition of his kingship

---

[191] *Regesta*, iii, no. 73: "quia garantizo quod habent de hac quietatione cartam comitis
Eustachii et meam" (probably a reference to a lost charter of Stephen as count of
Boulogne).

[192] Ibid., no. 281. The king and the bishop would split the profits of the fair of
Nonancourt: ibid., no. 282.

[193] The queen is found at Rouen, Lyons-la-Forêt, and Evreux: ibid., nos. 327, 598, 843
(her own charter granting Cressing in Essex to the Templars); "Récit de la fondation de
Mortemer," 155. Eustace will have been with her much of the time but his presence is
noted only in ibid., no. 327, and when he did homage to the king of France.

[194] Ibid., no. 594: "pro statu et incolumitate regni et ducatus mei"; ibid., no. 598: "pro
. . . incolumitate regni mei Anglie et ducatus Normannie."

[195] WM, *HN*, 32–3: "amorem tantum demeritus quantum uix mente aliquis concipere
queat"; *GS*, 4–5: "diues et humilis, munificus et affabilis"; *Liber Eliensis*, 285: "quia famosus
et comes largus et probus et multum dilectus"; RH, 145.

[196] *GS*, 36–7; OV, vi. 484–5.

[197] WM, *HN*, 30–1.

by the king of Scots and the homage of that king's son and heir in respect of the lands which he held – most notably the honour of Huntingdon – in England. In dealing with Stephen's visit to Normandy in 1137, William says nothing of his agreement with the king of France. Yet he had been at his most magisterial when writing of the agreement that Henry I had made with the French king in 1120, before the loss of the White Ship. This he saw as the work of a true statesman, the culmination of diplomacy which had involved – among others – Theobald, count of Blois, and his mother Adela.[198] It had ended four years of conflict between the two rulers. Without any conflict at all, again with the mediation of Count Theobald, and intially perhaps of Adela, Stephen had made an agreement on the same terms with the king of France, and Eustace had done homage for Normandy. This involved an acknowlegement of Stephen's legitimacy as king of England and of Eustace's rights as the heir to Normandy.[199] The pope had accepted him also. Stephen could claim international recognition.

Contemporaries were in no doubt that Stephen was able to cut this figure on the international stage because of the wealth he had inherited from his predecessor. "The coins, which were of the highest quality, were reckoned to amount to nearly a hundred thousand pounds."[200] Possibly included in this estimate, but more likely in addition to it, was the Norman treasure, estimated at 60,000 pounds, delivered to Robert of Gloucester as his father's executor.[201] There were jewels, piled up in precious vessels, "jacinths, sapphires, rubies, emeralds, and topazes," some of which Stephen would give to his brother Theobald and which eventually came to Abbot Suger of St Denis.[202] There were other "vessels of gold and silver," the inherited wealth of earlier kings, and ingots of silver ready for use.[203] A coin hoard discovered in 2002 in northern France gives some specificity to broad statements of this kind. It was found at Pimprez, near Compiègne, a manor of the Templars, and was deposited around the year 1140. The hoard contained 374 pennies of Henry I, 72 of Stephen, as well as coins from the mints of Metz, Liège, Maastricht, Trier, and Zürich. It also contained twelve silver ingots, or silver "cakes," which were evidently traded at monetary value and could be divided into halves and quarters as required; these amounted to a little over half of the bullion value of the hoard.[204] All this would suggest that we should at least double the figures

[198] WM, *GR*, i. 758–9: "ordinabat haec et effitiebat prudentissimi patris prudentia."
[199] Gillingham, "Doing Homage to the King of France," 67.
[200] WM, *HN*, 30–1.
[201] OV, vi. 448–9.
[202] They flooded the market and the abbot bought them at cut price: Suger, "De Administratione," in *Oeuvres* 1, ed. Gasparri, 128–31.
[203] WM, *HN*, 30–3; HH, 10–11. The most profitable business of the Jews in England at this time may have been in plate: Stacey, "Jewish Lending," 83–5.
[204] See the catalogue of the sale by Spink London on 6 and 7 Oct. 2004: *The Coinex Sale: The Pimprez Hoard and Other Important Properties* (catalogue no. 170), 74 and nos. 387–492, 832–64.

of the chroniclers to get any idea of the wealth on which Stephen could draw. He could for the first time in his life think in terms of five figures. But it would not last and when the money was spent there was little to show for it. This too is what we are told. "He squandered his money like a fool," was the verdict of a monk of Peterborough,[205] while William of Malmesbury commented that Stephen "always managed to settle business with more loss to himself than to his opponents."[206] William had close contacts with those who would shortly declare their opposition to the king.

Stephen was an accomplished courtier. He knew how to behave. When he became king, he placed great emphasis on court ceremonial, and his Easter court of 1136 was the most splendid in living memory.[207] There is an emphasis in documents surviving from this time on the "common counsel" of his barons. This is how kings were expected to take decisions. Yet we do not travel far from Westminster before we hear of divided counsels, a theme that would become almost routine during the reign; we only pick up the language of common counsel again late in 1153, and then very much as a commentary on the intervening period. At Exeter in 1136 there had been a plethora of opinions, some urging exemplary treatment of the defeated garrison, others opposing this, and there was talk of treachery. It was reported that he had been "changed into another man."[208] So also in Normandy in the summer of 1137. We are told of the Normans and the Flemings, under different leadership, pulling in different directions. Robert of Gloucester appeared as a semi-detached member of the court,[209] and in justification for his detachment claimed there was a conspiracy against him. The archbishop of Rouen was forced to mediate. This episode was symptomatic of wider divisions. When the king stood ready to attack the Angevins many of the magnates simply took off without leave. All observers were shocked.[210] The king was angry.[211] He was angry because he placed great emphasis on court ceremonial and etiquette. And yet when he caught up with Henry de Gournay and the other "young men" he spoke calmly to them. It was a family characteristic, for William of Malmesbury would say of Stephen's brother Henry that whatever the provocation he would never show anger.[212] The king kept smiling.[213] The style was the man.

The very first generalization that contemporaries made of Stephen's coming to power was that the great churchmen had supported his

[205] *ASC*, s.a. 1137.

[206] WM, *HN*, 40–1.

[207] HH, 706–7.

[208] *GS*, 42–3: "in alterum eum hominem repente mutauerunt."

[209] WM, *HN*, 38–9: "curia quo sepe inuitabatur aliquantis diebus abstinuit."

[210] OV, vi. 484–5: "gravissima seditio"; Torigni, 132: "magna dissensio"; *Chroniques des comtes d'Anjou*, 225: "contentio gravis." This determined the outcome: "qua seditione confusus rex expeditionem solvit" (ibid., 225).

[211] OV, vi. 486–7: "nimis iratus est."

[212] WM, *HN*, 110–11.

[213] *GS*, 38–9: "leni animo quod acciderat ferens"; *HN*, 38–9: "serenitate uultus."

candidacy. Henry of Winchester could be seen as "the man on whom his enterprise entirely depended."[214] Roger of Salisbury had "brought the royal crown to Stephen as well as the strength of his support."[215] In return, Stephen had made many promises. Some of them were marketable. Henry of Winchester gained privileges as abbot of Glastonbury, with the restoration of the manor of Uffculme, and as bishop of Winchester, with the restoration of the manors of East Meon and Wargrave, along with the extension of "his fair" at Winchester and exemption from toll for "his burgesses" of Taunton.[216] Roger of Salisbury, now at the height of his pomp, could seemingly get anything that he asked for.[217] What he asked of Stephen was the borough of Malmesbury, "with all its hundreds and its lands and its customs."[218] He would make this a second centre of his diocese and build a castle there.[219] The bishop of Norwich, with Robert of Gloucester watching, was given broad privileges in which economic rights figured prominently. He gained the prolongation of his fair at Norwich, "with all customs that pertain to the right of fairs," along with new fairs at the thriving port of King's Lynn and the market town of Hoxne.[220] A charter for Eye Priory – to move from the bishop of Norwich to a monastery in his diocese – shows a little more clearly what those rights were held to comprise; here, "during the time of the fair no one shall have authority save the monks and their men." The monks also had rights to tithes of the port of Dunwich. Stephen was happy to spell them out: "their tithe in Dunwich will increase each year in pennies and in herrings and in all other things in proportion to the increase in my own resources in that place."[221] You could not say fairer than that. The wealth of the country was growing and the churchmen sought to corner and channel this growth, bringing trade within the remit of their fairs, and attaching to those fairs comprehensive privileges. An indication of how comprehensive these "customs" could be is found at Winchester, whose fair was extended for six further days, making fourteen days in all, by this latest privilege of Stephen for his brother.[222] For the whole of the period thus extended, the bishop enjoyed the rights of the crown throughout the city.[223] Later, to symbolize the transfer of power, the official measures were solemnly taken

---

[214] GS, 8–9; cf. WM, HN, 28–9.

[215] HH, 700–1.

[216] Regesta, iii, nos. 341, 947–8, 952–3.

[217] William of Malmesbury reported the king as saying that the bishop would grow tired of asking before he grew tired of giving: WM, HN, 68–9.

[218] Regesta, iii, no. 784.

[219] WM, HN, xxvii–xxviii.

[220] Regesta, iii, no. 616: "cum omnibus consuetudinibus que ad jus feriarum pertinent et hoc per totam leucam circa Norwicum."

[221] Regesta, iii, no. 288. There is nothing in the small print to say that the value of herrings could go down as well as up.

[222] Regesta, iii, no. 952.

[223] Biddle, Winchester, 286–8.

up St Giles Hill, where the fair was held.[224] Such theatre was in every way characteristic of Henry of Blois.

These grants of economic privilege were generous but they were for the king to give. More difficult issues were raised by the grants of land that he made to churchmen at this time, most notably again to his brother. These involved estates that had fallen into the hands of laymen prior to the death of William the Conqueror. The king in his coronation charter had reserved such cases to himself, saying that he would either restore the property or at very least investigate the claim. Under this provision the monastery of Glastonbury reclaimed the manor of Uffculme (Devon), "which of old was of the right of the church but which King William my grandfather took from it."[225] Henry had been waiting his moment, as he explained in his first-person narrative explaining how he had restored his church's rights.[226] Robert of Bampton had rebelled and this rebellion had allowed Henry to reclaim the church, which was restored to him by the royal court. Henry is here being somewhat economical with the truth. The manor may subsequently have been granted to Glastonbury by the royal court but initially it had been taken from the lay tenant, a man of baronial rank, without any form of process. Robert of Bampton had sworn homage at the Easter court. Those who sought documentary evidence of what the homage had been sworn for could obtain a writ from chancery that spelt out for the individual the implications of the king's coronation oath. He should hold peaceably what he had held, either from the king or from others, on the day that Henry was alive and dead. The king would permit no legal challenge to land so held.[227] Robert of Bampton had held Uffculme on 1 December 1135. His ancestor had held in the time of Domesday Book.[228] Yet this counted for nothing against the acquisitiveness of Henry of Winchester. Robert refused to surrender the manor and this refusal was reported as rebellion.[229] He cuts a sorry figure in the pages of the *Gesta Stephani*, "a winebibber and a gourmand, and in peacetime devoted only to gluttony and drunkenness."[230] But he had a case, and that case had not been heard. As Finberg commented, there was not even "a pretence of equity when churchmen were encouraged to reclaim their property while the layman with perhaps as good a case might seek redress in vain. So one-sided a concession was bound to provoke resentment and may have added fuel to the anti-clerical spirit that blazed up

---

[224] Keene, *Winchester Survey*, ii. 1115.

[225] *Regesta*, iii, no. 341: "tanquam ea que de antiquo jure ipsius erant ecclesie et que predictus avus meus Willelmus ab eadem abstraxit ecclesia."

[226] *English Lawsuits*, i. 246 (no. 292); Stacy, "Henry of Blois and the Lordship of Glastonbury," 14–17.

[227] *Regesta*, iii, no. 39, for Eustace de Barrington, may be taken as exemplary of such charters: "et super hoc non ponatur in placito."

[228] *DB*, 317a, when the manor was worth £18; for the houses in Exeter ibid., 318b.

[229] In HH, 706–9, he is a traitor without a past, "Robertus quidam proditor."

[230] *GS*, 28–9.

during the civil war."[231] The resentment helped lead to the siege at Exeter, where Robert of Bampton held property.

The privileges that the clergy obtained in the early months of Stephen's reign are a part of the political history of the period as well as of its economic history. So also with the restitution of property that the churchmen had lost. Henry of Winchester's claims in respect of Uffculme must have seemed very reasonable when presented first to the royal and then to the papal court,[232] but what his success in fact proved was that a powerful churchman could be allowed to short-circuit due process of law. The king was the loser from such charity. Individual cases such as this were widely reported and commented upon. This is how political attitudes are formed. The power of the clergy over their neighbourhoods as the civil war came to them can be contrasted with the attempts of the laity to compete on equal terms. When William of Malmesbury stated, wanting to provide a generalization as he started a new chapter, that some powerful men were vexed at the bishops because of their wealth and the size of their castles,[233] this is not a statement that needs to be glossed. He meant just what he said.

---

[231] Finberg, "Uffculme," 218. This study is required reading for the politics of 1136.
[232] *Regesta*, iii, no. 341; *Great Chartulary of Glastonbury*, i. 125–6
[233] WM, *HN*, 44–7.

Chapter 3

MIXED FORTUNES

These two years [1136 and 1137] were very prosperous for King Stephen; but in the third year [1138], about which I am going to speak, he had mixed fortunes and things were beginning to fall apart.[1]

The start of the year was distinctly low-key. At Christmas 1137, the second anniversary of his coronation, the king of England was at Dunstable, "a township in Bedfordshire."[2] It was a town that Henry I had developed, and when he founded an Augustinian priory there he reserved "the houses in the town and the garden where I am accustomed to stay."[3] Stephen had come to stay because he was en route north, to face a renewed challenge from the Scots. He had stopped because the garrison of Bedford castle had refused to surrender to him when instructed to do so. The king besieged the castle on Christmas Eve, and throughout the Christmas festival, in atrocious weather. "Many considered this displeasing to God, since he was treating the most solemn of festivals as of little or no importance."[4] It can hardly have been a great occasion,[5] for most of the magnates were absent, the county community was divided, and it was mainly the officers of the household who accompanied the king.[6] At the same time the French king, Louis VII, wore his crown at Bourges, "attended by nobles and middling men from all over France and Aquitaine and other regions round about."[7] Louis had married Eleanor of Aquitaine earlier in the year at Bordeaux and a series of crown-wearings witnessed the extension of his authority.[8] The contrast between the Christmas festivities at the two courts could not have been more marked.

[1] HH, 710–11.
[2] JW, iii. 234–5: "uillam quandam in Bedefordensi prouincia sitam."
[3] *King's Works*, ii. 924–5. Henry had spent Christmas here in 1122 and again in 1131: HH, 468–9, 488–9.
[4] HH, 710–11. On the weather OV, vi. 510–11: "hibernis ingruentibus pluuiis."
[5] As claimed by *GS*, 46–7: "curia splendide et solemniter . . . celebrata."
[6] The main evidence is a charter which Stephen issued for Henry, bishop of Winchester, "at Goldington during the siege of Bedford": *Regesta*, iii, no. 342. It is witnessed by Robert, bishop of Bath (who has a charter issued for himself at the same place, ibid., iii, no. 47), Robert de Neufbourg (steward of Normandy), Aubrey de Vere (chamberlain), Robert de Vere (constable), and John the Marshal.
[7] OV, vi. 508–9. Louis had succeeded his father, Louis VI, the previous summer, immediately after his marriage to Eleanor of Aquitaine: Suger, *Louis VI*, 278–87; OV, vi. 490–1.
[8] Martindale, "Eleanor of Aquitaine."

The year which followed would indeed be a year of mixed fortunes for the king of England. At Bedford he succeeded in making a drama out of what should have been at best a minor managerial crisis. At some point in 1137, Simon de Beauchamp, one of the royal stewards and the castellan of Bedford castle, died. It was decided that Simon's daughter should be married to Hugh *pauper*, the younger brother of Waleran, count of Meulan, and Robert, earl of Leicester. The intention was that Hugh be given not just the Beauchamp lands but the – comparatively limited – royal resources in the county and perhaps along with these the title of earl. Other members of the Beauchamp family felt themselves disparaged by these arrangements, notably Miles and Payn, who were the sons of Simon's brother, Robert de Beauchamp. When Miles de Beauchamp, who had control of the castle, was required to surrender it to Hugh *pauper*, he refused, claiming that it was "the hereditary possession of himself and his family,"[9] while at the same time protesting his loyalty to the king. The stand-off was resolved only when Henry, bishop of Winchester, arrived and – probably after the king had left – settled the issues in dispute. The castle had to be surrendered – there was no doubt as to the king's entitlement to it – but the garrison's profession of good faith was accepted and they left on honourable terms.[10] It had clearly been the intention of the family that Miles de Beauchamp should be Simon's heir rather than his daughter; and he was the man in possession when the king arrived. This may well have been conceded by the bishop. Certainly the estates continued under the control first of Miles and then of his brother Payn.[11] Hugh *pauper* never did become earl of Bedford.[12]

The siege of Bedford was not seen by most commentators as a major event.[13] They had their eyes fixed on the king, then moving north "with a strong force to Northumbria."[14] Stephen arrived in the region around the Feast of the Purification, 2 February 1138.[15] It was just two years after he had last travelled the same, familiar roads and had made peace with the Scots at Durham. That peace had been broken within the year, and with Stephen being in Normandy for most of 1137, it was left to Archbishop Thurstan, meeting with the king of Scots at Roxburgh, to renew the truce until Stephen returned.[16] When Stephen arrived back in England, in December 1137, he refused outright the main demand of the Scots, that Henry, the son of the king of Scots, be granted the earldom of

---

[9] *GS*, 48–9: "ex paterno iure sibi et suis debita."

[10] OV, vi. 510–11.

[11] Stenton, *First Century*, 237–8; Faulkner, "Beauchamp Family."

[12] On Hugh *pauper*: *GS*, 50–1, 116–17; White, "King Stephen's Earldoms," 77–82; King, "Waleran of Meulan," 177–8.

[13] It is noted in passing in JW, iii. 234–7; HH, 710–11. Missing text in *GS*, at 47–8, means that the episode is not put in context.

[14] JW, iii. 236–7.

[15] RH, 150–5, is the main source for this paragraph.

[16] JH, 288.

Northumberland. In January 1138 the Scots invaded the territory to which they laid claim. The king of Scots was at Corbridge on the Tyne when the king of England approached with an impressive force, "a great multitude of earls and barons and a powerful army of knights and footsoldiers." David retreated before him and Stephen followed. It was reported that David of Scots had hatched a plot to attract Stephen into Roxburgh and catch him and his forces unprepared. Stephen, however, bypassed the town, and "harried and burned a great part of the land of the king of Scotland." He then returned to southern England. It was not just that it was the beginning of Lent, when Christian kings did not fight, and that his supply lines were in any event extended, but also – and this is what had given credence to the story of the Roxburgh ambush – that the loyalty of some of his men was suspect. The man of whom there was the gravest suspicion was Eustace Fitz John, the lord of Malton in the Vale of York; he was required to remain in the king's court and to surrender Bamburgh, a castle important both strategically and symbolically, because of its association with Northumbrian separatism.[17]

The royal court spent Easter 1138 at Northampton. Archbishop Thurstan was there, along with "bishops, abbots, earls, barons, and many nobles of England."[18] There was routine business done at this court,[19] but the main task for the king and his counsellors was to review such intelligence as they had of the objectives of their opponents and to work out a strategy to counter them. Should he go back to Normandy? It can hardly have been an option, so soon after he had left, but the truce with the Angevins had been violated and Waleran of Meulan and William of Ypres were sent across the Channel to "bring relief to the sorely vexed province."[20] Should he go back north once again? This must have been a serious option, for it was clear that hostilities would continue. Thurstan, archbishop of York, had come south for a purpose, however, and he would be sent back, and would be furnished with a substantial contingent of household troops, to counter the Scottish threat.[21] That threat was being

[17] Eustace complained that he was detained in the king's court, which was against custom: Aelred, *Relatio*, 191 ("ab eo in curia contra morem patrium captus"); *Aelred of Rievaulx: The Historical Works*, trans. Freeland, ed. Dutton, 259–60.

[18] JW, iii. 240–1. Charters which might be associated with this court are *Regesta*, iii, nos. 466, 623, 671, 885–6, and 963, in favour of Lincoln Cathedral, Nostell Priory, Ramsey and Thorney abbeys, and Worcester Cathedral, including as witnesses and beneficiaries Alexander, bishop of Lincoln, Simon, bishop of Worcester, Athelwold, bishop of Carlisle, Nigel, bishop of Ely, Adam de Beaunay, Aubrey de Vere, Hugh Bigod, John the Marshal, and Robert Fitz Walter de Chesney. Henry, bishop of Winchester, and Roger, bishop of Salisbury, may also have been present: JW, iii. 230–1.

[19] There were elections to the bishopric of Exeter (Robert Warelwast, nephew of the previous bishop), and the abbeys of Winchcombe (Robert, a Cluniac and possibly a relative of the king) and St Mary's, York (Savaric): *EEA* 11: *Exeter 1046–1184*, xxxiv–xxxvii; *Heads*, 79, 84.

[20] OV, vi. 514–15.

[21] RH, 161.

reported in the most lurid detail. "The king of Scots, under cover of piety, on account of the oath he had sworn to the empress's daughter, commanded his men in barbarous deeds – they ripped open pregnant women and tore out the unborn foetuses; they tossed children on the points of their lances; they dismembered priests on their altars."[22] The *Life* of St Godric of Finchale recorded that the tribesmen of David's army had broken into the hermit's small oratory, torn down its furnishings and trampled on the sacred Host.[23] These atrocities provided the main news story of the early summer,[24] both in Normandy and in England, and the shrewder commentators could see that events on both sides of the Channel were linked. Orderic Vitalis described David of Scots as aiding "the pernicious disturbers of the realm in support of the Angevins."[25] The empress herself was the main loser from this association. The royal court might well have hoped that the northern English and the Normans would make common cause against her and her allies.

The main threat lay in the third frontier region of the Anglo-Norman realm, the Marches of Wales. In the southern Marches, Henry I had relied principally on two men, Miles of Gloucester and Payn Fitz John, who would later be described as his "privy counsellors"; they were seen as the dominant – and domineeering – figures "from the river Severn to the Sea, all along the border between England and Wales."[26] It was clearly Stephen's intention that they should continue in this role and he had made it a priority to secure their support. Payn Fitz John had died, however, killed by the Welsh as he pursued a raiding party, on 10 July 1137,[27] while the king was in Normandy. This left a power vacuum, particularly in Herefordshire and Shropshire, the two counties which Payn controlled, at a time when there were additional suspicions about the loyalty of several of the marcher lords. The king needed to show his face. And so from Northampton he set out for Gloucester. He was received there with the full honours due to a king, the citizens coming out to meet him and escorting him into the city. He came first to the church, giving his royal ring as an offering, which his chaplains later redeemed, and then Miles of Gloucester "led him with honour to the royal palace." The following day the citizens swore fealty to him, and later in the week, on Ascension Day, the king and his followers "gladly assisted at processions and masses" for the solemn feast.[28] The king was in his element here – he was "delighted" at his reception, according to our eyewitness account – but he was never able to relax for long.

---

[22] HH, 710–11.

[23] Reginald of Durham, *Vita S. Godrici*, 114–16.

[24] *Scottish Annals*, 179–82, translates relevant passages from the Durham chroniclers, Aelred of Rievaulx, Henry of Huntington, and John of Worcester.

[25] OV, vi. 518–19.

[26] Gerald of Wales, *Opera*, vi. 34: "secretarii et praecipui consiliarii"; *GS*, 24–5.

[27] JW, iii. 228–9.

[28] Ibid. 240–3. For the context here, see Hare, "Gloucester as a Royal Ceremonial Centre," 56–8.

It was while the king was at Gloucester that "he learned that Hereford castle was being fortified against him," so he took a large army there and pitched camp.[29] There was both a local and a broader national dimension to this episode. The local arose from the death of Payn Fitz John. Payn left no son and it was agreed between the two families that his elder daughter, Sibyl, should be married to Roger, the son and heir of Miles of Gloucester. This agreement – set out in considerable detail – Stephen had recently confirmed.[30] Among the estates that Roger and Sibyl would thus acquire was the barony of Weobley in Herefordshire. This, however, would have been the second time in succession that the barony had descended in the female line, and there were other relatives who nursed claims to it, which the shire community of Hereford supported, and which the current political uncertainty allowed them to pursue. The chief among them was Gilbert de Lacy, who held the Norman lands of the family. Associated with him was his cousin, Geoffrey Talbot.[31] It seems to have been Geoffrey Talbot who held Hereford against the king. A siege was started and, while it was going on and within sight of the castle walls, in the cathedral church of the diocese Stephen celebrated the Whit feast and wore his crown.[32] This can hardly have seemed auspicious, but if there was a wider rebellion planned at this time, the king's presence gave the more senior figures pause. Brian Fitz Count, an important marcher lord who was also lord of Wallingford, was among those at court.[33] Stephen stuck with the siege of Hereford, and after two or three weeks the garrison "made terms and surrendered" to the king. As had happened at Exeter in 1136, and more recently at Bedford, the garrison was allowed to leave unharmed.[34]

"The king lingered for a while at Hereford and then left with his army," making for London.[35] It was either while he was at Hereford or on his way to the capital that a small delegation arrived at the court, announced that they came from Robert, earl of Gloucester, and asked for an audience with the king. What they had to say will have come as no surprise. The earl was defying the king, that is to say he was renouncing the homage and the fealty that he had sworn to him in the spring of 1136.[36] He did so, the

[29] JW, iii. 242–3.

[30] *Regesta*, iii, no. 312; iv, plate xxi.

[31] Coplestone-Crow, "Payn FitzJohn and Ludlow Castle"; Wightman, *Lacy Family*, 167–94; Crouch, *Stephen*, 79 and n. 21.

[32] JW, iii. 242–3.

[33] *Regesta*, iii, nos. 383, 385, the former addressed by the king to "his justices and all his sheriffs and reeves and *ministri* throughout England and Wales."

[34] "Since King Stephen was, no rather is, a pious and peaceable man, he did not injure anyone but allowed his enemies to depart freely": JW, iii. 242–3.

[35] Ibid. 244–5, 248–9; *GS*, 56–7.

[36] The main authority for this paragraph is WM, *HN*, 40–3. William of Malmesbury here states that the messengers set out from Normandy "immediately after Whitsun" (28 May). Robert of Gloucester had by this time already come to terms with Geoffrey of Anjou, according to Robert of Torigni, but John of Worcester and Orderic Vitalis confirm that his defection only became public knowledge in June: Torigni, 136; JW, iii. 248–9; OV, vi. 514–17.

messengers were instructed to say, because the king had unlawfully claimed the throne, having previously sworn the oath to the empress in the most public of ceremonies. The earl's homage to the king was to be taken as null and void, for the king had broken all the promises he had made to the earl. The earl had done this after taking advice from his counsellors, and after consulting his confessors, for in all matters of oaths it was the clergy who claimed jurisdiction. No less an authority than the pope had insisted that the oath to the empress be kept.[37] The emissaries will have been asked to withdraw while the king conferred with his counsellors and then, after the mimimum interval necessary for decency, they were given a message to take to Earl Robert in reply: the oath sworn to the empress was invalid, for it had been forced from the magnates; and in any event it had been conditional, and the king had changed his mind. These arguments that the earl now adduced had been heard after Henry had died, and rejected by the clergy and the pope himself, all of this before Earl Robert had come to court and paid homage to Stephen. The king had treated the earl well, had given every recognition of his high rank, and had never refused him justice. The earl should be left in no doubt of the severe consequences of his actions, for himself and for his family. The king's counsellors were advising his total disinheritance, and unless the earl immediately reconsidered his position, the king would have no choice but to accept their advice. He should come to court and the case he made would be properly heard, but in the meantime and as security all his castles should be surrendered to the king.

While the king continued back to London, the messengers of the earl of Gloucester were allowed to travel to "his headquarters" at Bristol. Bristol was one of the great towns of England. It had "a harbour able to receive ships coming from Ireland, Norway and other lands overseas,"[38] reportedly with anchorage for a thousand ships. On the land side, it had "a castle rising on a vast mound, strengthened by walls and battlements, towers and divers engines."[39] Here in the castle were the earl's private apartments, the knights and foot soldiers of his garrison and the officials who ran his English estates. The messengers brought instructions, which perhaps had been anticipated, that the castle should be provisioned, that "they should accept as allies all who came in to them," and should go on the offensive against the king and his party. Amongst those welcomed was Geoffrey Talbot, who had been driven from the castles first of Hereford and then of Weobley. Earl Robert's offensive when it came was directed at the city of Bath. A Roman city, famous for its restorative waters, it had for

---

[37] WM, *HN*, 42–3. William of Malmesbury says that he will insert a text of the papal letter later on in his own text, but he does not do so. David Crouch suggests that "there may have been a general papal injunction to the English magnates (Robert included) secured by Henry I to back up the oath they had sworn": "Robert of Gloucester and the Daughter of Zelophehad," 242 n. 8.

[38] WM, *GP*, i. 446–7.

[39] *GS*, 56–7.

the past half-century been the seat of a bishopric.[40] It will have seemed a soft target and the intention of Earl Robert's supporters was evidently to capture the castle in the city, strengthen its defences, and use it as an outpost to control access to Bristol via the Avon Valley.

The attack on Bath in 1138, which in the end proved inconsequential, was the first engagement in what must now be described as a civil war.[41] The chief protagonists were on the one hand Geoffrey Talbot and his cousin Gilbert de Lacy, and on the other the bishop of Bath, only recently appointed to the episcopal bench and now in the front line.[42] Geoffrey and Gilbert went out from Bristol with a small force to reconnoitre outside the Bath city walls. "They made their way round the city slowly and cautiously, so they thought, when behold the bishop of Bath's knights, who had caught sight of them, suddenly appeared." Gilbert escaped but Geoffrey was captured and brought into Bath under armed guard. "The Bristol garrison was much angered by this and advanced threateningly to Bath." They asked to parley with the bishop, on neutral ground between the two cities, and sent him a safe conduct. This they immediately broke. They took the bishop into custody, insulted him, "and threatened him and his followers with hanging if their companion at arms, Geoffrey, were not freed as soon as possible." The bishop, terrified, gave orders for Geoffrey's release. "When the king heard of this, he raged against the bishop as an accomplice of his enemies. He would probably have taken away his pastoral staff if he had yielded more to resentment than to his love of peace." The king took a few weeks to raise an army and he then came to Bristol by way of Bath. As he approached Bath, the bishop came out to meet him as courtesy required, and there was an awkward conversation before his explanations were accepted; "having at length appeased him and restored their accustomed friendship he brought him into Bath." Robert of Lewes would not be the last bishop whose loyalty to the king would be called into question.

The chroniclers now describe a general conflagration and what followed was of necessity less a military campaign than a firefighting exercise. Bristol was a particularly difficult town to take by siege. The king's forces could "waste and burn the lands and the townships in the area belonging to the earl of Gloucester."[43] This was classic military tactics, intended to demoralize the garrison and deprive it of supplies. But Bristol could be supplied by water, both from the south-west peninsula and from South Wales. Elaborate schemes were dreamt up to block the mouth of the River Avon, but none were found practicable, and in the event the king "tired of the siege and turned to besiege the earl's other castles." These were easier

[40] WM, GP, i. 304–9; GS, 58–9.

[41] This paragraph is based on the accounts in GS, 58–65, and JW, iii. 248–9.

[42] R. H. C. Davis, drawing on the account of this episode, saw Robert, bishop of Bath, as the author of the Gesta Stephani: GS, xxxvii–xxxviii. An outline of the case against this identification will be found in King, "Gesta Stephani."

[43] JW, iii. 250–1.

targets, though each needed some time and effort. Castle Cary and Harptree in Somerset were taken, Castle Cary by an agreement, and Harptree after its garrison had been surprised in open country.[44] The earl of Gloucester had other castles in the south-east of England that were more exposed. The most significant of them was Dover, held by Walchelin Maminot. Here, by contrast to Bristol, the king's forces did have command of the sea. They were led by the queen, who showed none of her husband's indecisiveness. She "besieged Dover with a large force on the land side, and sent word to her friends and kinsmen and dependants in Boulogne to blockade the foe by sea."[45] They came very readily, and in considerable numbers. Faced with this determination, and in fear for their lives, the garrison surrendered.

They did so because they had heard what had happened to the garrison of Shrewsbury some time before.[46] Shrewsbury was one of the three marcher earldoms that the Conqueror had established in the face of the three Welsh princedoms. After the fall of the house of Montgommery-Bellême, it had come after its disgrace in the early years of Henry I's reign to a member of a family on the Norman–Breton border, Alan, son of Flaad, and from him to his son, William Fitz Alan. William "had married a niece of Robert earl of Gloucester and inclined to his party."[47] Fresh from success in taking Dudley from Ralph Paynel, the king brought "a big force" by water to besiege Shrewsbury. "William learnt in advance of the king's coming, and secretly escaped with his wife, children, and some others, leaving in his castle men who had sworn to be loyal to him and never to surrender it."[48] The chief of these was Arnulf de Hesdin, William's uncle, and "a bold and headstrong" knight. There was clearly nothing chivalric in the language that he used in rejecting the king's order to surrender the castle and his offer of terms.[49] After a short siege, and amid scenes of some confusion, the castle was taken. The motte was filled in, a siege engine was prepared, fires were started around the walls, and the main gate was stormed. "The king, because many unruly men regarded his gentleness with contempt and many great lords scorned to come to his court when summoned, commanded in his anger that Arnulf and about ninety-three of the men who had defied him should be hanged on gibbets or be put to death in some other fashion without delay."[50] The majority of those who suffered this penalty were the common foot soldiers,

---

[44] *GS*, 66–9, has the most detail; also JW iii. 250–1, and, for Castle Cary, HH, 712–13. The Ce text of WM, *HN*, 72–3, notes that the king had captured Harptree "from some of the earl's knights before he came to England."

[45] OV, vi. 520–1.

[46] HH, 712–13.

[47] OV, vi. 520–1.

[48] JW, iii. 250–1.

[49] OV, vi. 522–3, says this ("superbe respuit, insuper et iniuriosa regi uerba iaculari presumpsit"), and the sequel establishes as much.

[50] Ibid. 520–1.

but "five men of rank were killed."[51] It was to other men of rank that this statement of intent was addressed. It was a straightforward one. The king's opponents should consider their position, and mind their language.

No one disputed that however many were slain at Shrewsbury the king was within his rights, for whatever their allegiance, they were defying the king in person, and insulting language to him was in itself treasonable.[52] The king's followers were delighted at the news of his severity at Shrewsbury and it had the desired effect. It certainly encouraged the surrender of the Dover garrison,[53] and it may have discouraged some whose loyalty was wavering, such as Brian Fitz Count, from declaring their hand. The king had strong support at Shrewsbury, including that of the bishops of Hereford, Chester, and Worcester, Robert, earl of Leicester, Simon of Senlis, earl of Northampton, Robert de Ferrers, Miles of Gloucester, William d'Aubigny *pincerna*, Hugh de Gournay, and Philip de Belmeis.[54] He offered special prayers at this time, "for the soul of King Henry, his uncle and lord, for his own safety and that of his wife and his brothers and his sons, and for the integrity and well-being of his kingdom."[55] The threat to that integrity offered by Robert of Gloucester had for the moment been contained. The main threat would now come from Scotland and the king and his followers waited anxiously for news from the north.

THE BATTLE OF THE STANDARD

Soon after Easter 1138 the Scots made renewed incursions into northern England.[56] They ravaged the coastal areas of Northumbria as far south as Durham. There were then rumours that a large army had been mustered in southern England, and so they retreated to the banks of the Tweed. Soon afterwards, a separate war-band was detached under the leadership of William Fitz Duncan, who was King David's nephew. This did great damage in Cumbria and the Craven district of Yorkshire. It seems to have

[51] JW iii. 250–1; those hanged included Arnulf himself, according to OV, vi. 522–3, and perhaps others of the embassy at which the king had taken such offence; HH, 712–13.

[52] Hollister, "Royal Acts of Mutilation."

[53] GS, 68–9. The king should have showed such severity earlier, was the view of HH, 708–9.

[54] *Regesta*, iii, no. 132, in favour of Buildwas Abbey, given "apud Salopesbiriam in obsidione"; Cox, "Charters for Wenlock Priory," 56–8, given at Bridgnorth "in reditu obsidionis Salop." The charter for Wenlock, not known to the authors of the *Regesta*, confirms the authenticity of the Buildwas charter, which they had questioned. Both charters give the date as "1139, in my third year," where the regnal year is correct but the calendar year is wrong: see the discussion earlier, p. 71 n. 160.

[55] Cox, "Charters for Wenlock Priory," 56: "et specialiter regis Henrici domini et avunculi mei et pro salute mea et uxoris et fratrum et filiorum et pro statu et incolumitate regni mei."

[56] On these campaigns see RH, 155–9; JH, 291–2.

travelled via Carlisle, moving down the west coast and attacking the possessions of "the fine monastery at Furness." The Scots will have been well aware that this was Stephen's own foundation, a symbol of his lordship in a region which he no longer controlled.[57] On 10 June 1138, at Clitheroe in the Ribble valley, William's forces defeated a band of Norman knights; "they carried off great spoil and a large number of captives."[58] It is known that the following day, the king of Scots himself was besieging Norham, for he issued letters of protection to a number of northern monasteries. The monks of Tynemouth Priory were to enjoy his peace. "And anyone who declines to keep this peace, as I have conceded and confirmed it, shall be completely cast off from myself, and Henry my son, and all within our household and network of friendship."[59] This phrasing suggests the influence and may indicate the presence of Aelred, monk and later abbot of Rievaulx, one of the counsellors of David of Scots and later the author of a treatise on friendship.[60] It is even possible that Aelred helped negotiate the surrender of Norham shortly thereafter.[61]

The castles of Wark and Norham, in the valley of the Tweed, had been among the castles captured by David after the death of Henry I and then restored to Stephen by the Treaty of Durham early in 1136. They came under renewed pressure in 1138. The garrison at Wark had attacked the supply train of the Scottish army as it travelled south, gaining valuable supplies, and it was able to withstand the first retaliatory attack. The garrison at Norham was less resolute, and it surrendered to David's army a little later in June, which to some seemed shameful since "as yet the wall was in good condition, the tower very strong and their provisions abundant." These were the men of the bishop of Durham, Geoffrey Rufus. It was intimated to him that he could secure the return of the castle and be given full restitution for all of his losses if he would only abandon his allegiance to Stephen and swear fealty to the king of Scots. The bishop refused. While he remained loyal, suspicions about the loyalty of Eustace Fitz John, which had caused him to be relieved of the custody of Bamburgh, proved justified. As the Scottish army once again headed south, Eustace accompanied it, surrendering his own castle at Alnwick,

---

[57] RH, 156.The monks of its daughter-house at Calder were forced to migrate and would finally settle at Byland: *Foundation History of Byland and Jervaulx*, 1–2.

[58] JH, 291. Clitheroe was the *caput* of a group of Lacy estates: Dalton, *Yorkshire*, 189.

[59] *Charters of David I*, no. 66: "Et quicunque hanc pacem tenere noluerit sicut ego concedo confirmari de me et Henrico filio meo et nostra familiaritate et nostra amicicia sit omnino alienatus." Richard of Hexham says that the monks paid 27 marks for this privilege; he notes that his own house had charters from both David and Henry, couched in similar terms, but these do not survive: RH, 153–4.

[60] *De Spirituali Amicitia*, written 1158 x 1163: Walter Daniel, xcii.

[61] In mid-Nov. 1138, William, abbot of Rievaulx, negotiated the surrender of of Wark on behalf of Walter Espec, and Powicke suggested that Aelred was with his abbot at this time: RH, 171–2; Walter Daniel, xlvi, xc.

helping to attack Bamburgh, and promising the surrender of his castle at Malton in the Vale of York. And now, it was reported, these different warrior bands had joined together as a single force, 26,000 strong, and proposed to attack not just Yorkshire "but also the greater part of England."[62] To those living in the north, the stories of atrocities grew stronger with every passing week, and the places mentioned as under threat came ever closer to home.

In this situation Thurstan summoned the leading northern barons to a meeting at York to decide on strategy.[63] There would be an impressive roll call when they convened: William of Aumale, Walter de Gant, Robert de Bruce and his son Adam, Walter Espec, Ilbert de Lacy, Roger de Mowbray, William de Percy, Richard de Courcy, William Fossard, Robert de Stuteville, "and many other powerful and sagacious men."[64] They were joined by a contingent from the royal household, under Bernard de Balliol, and troops from the north midlands, the militias of Nottinghamshire under William Peverel and of Derbyshire under Robert de Ferrers.[65] The archbishop assured them and their followers that they would be fighting for king and country, in what could be represented as a holy war. The muster was carefully choreographed to convey this impression. The local militias marched under the banners of their local saints. They would intercept the Scots just south of the Tees, the point at which a raid became an invasion, at Cowton Moor near Northallerton. There they raised their standard. It was in the form of a ship's prow, and on it were hung a silver pyx containing the Host, and the banners of St Peter the Apostle (the patron of the York diocese), St John of Beverley, and St Wilfred of Ripon.[66]

[62] RH, 159.

[63] JH, 292; RH, 159–60; JW, iii. 252–3; Aelred, *Relatio*, 181–2, states that he called out the shire levies; HH, 712–13. The relevant section of the *Gesta Stephani* has been lost. William of Malmesbury ignores.

[64] RH, 159–60, has the fullest list of names. Aelred, *Relatio*, 182, mentions also Adam, the son of Robert de Bruce; HH, 718–19, says that a brother of Ilbert de Lacy was the only man of equestrian rank who was killed in the subsequent battle.

[65] RH, 162. William Peverel (who is also named as one of the protagonists in HH, 718–19) and Robert de Ferrers are here distinguished from the great men of "the province." Nottinghamshire was in the diocese of York, and it was closely linked with Derbyshire, which was in the diocese of Coventry. There is the problem that Robert de Ferrers is recorded also at the siege of Shrewsbury, and thereafter at Bridgnorth, and according to Orderic the siege was raised "in the same week" as the battle of the Standard: OV, vi. 522–3. It is possible that the same man was in both places, as Nicholl, *Thurstan*, 225, and Crouch, *Stephen*, 80. It may be noted, however, that Robert de Ferrers died in 1139, and was succeeded by his son, another Robert de Ferrers: RH, 178; Jones, "Charters of Robert II de Ferrers." It may be that both men were active in Aug. 1138, the father accompanied by knights of the honour with the king, his old associate, at Shrewsbury, and the son with levies from Derbyshire at the Standard.

[66] RH, 162–3; Aelred, *Relatio*, 181, refers to "the royal ensign that is commonly called the Standard."

The battle was fought on 22 August 1138. It lasted no more than three hours.[67] In this respect it was typical of most medieval battles. The Scots, according to Aelred of Rievaulx, formed up in three groups. In the front line were the Galwegians, who insisted on leading the charge; behind them Henry of Scots "and the knights and archers with him formed a second line with great shrewdness, and the men of Cumbria and Teviotdale joined them"; in the next line were miscellaneous forces, including the men of Lothian, while King David "retained the Scots and the men of Moray in his own line and assigned some of the English and French knights as his bodyguard." The Scots had the advantage of numbers, but they had far fewer cavalry and, compared with the English, were poorly organized and poorly equipped. The royal forces had their best knights in the front rank, along with archers and lancers. The archers did great damage. "You might see a Galwegian stuck all around by arrows like the spines of a hedgehog, but shaking his sword nonetheless, now rushing forward to slaughter the enemy as if in a blind madness, now beating the empty air with futile blows."[68] It is a vivid image of Scottish impotence. "The whole Norman and English host stood its ground unmoved, in one dense formation round the standard." Several of the generals on the Scottish side were killed early on, some by their own men. Henry of Scots, "longing for glory and honour," led a cavalry charge but was quickly driven back.[69] There was no overall co-ordination, and once the first attack was repulsed, panic spread through the ranks, and both the king of Scots and his son Henry, casting aside their baggage and the emblems of their rank, fled the field.[70] "The king's son came on foot with one knight only to Carlisle, while his father escaped with difficulty through woods and passes to Roxburgh."[71] It was reported that at least 10,000 of the Scots were slain, either on the battlefield or during the retreat, while on the English side the losses were minimal.[72]

The battle had become a rout. Yet its outcome, after lengthy negotiations, was a settlement more favourable to the Scots than the one they had achieved in 1136. Why was this? If it is accepted that politics is the art of the possible, then it is necessary to ask why the position of the English king was so constrained. The reason is that those making the peace had their own agendas. Those most closely involved were the northern barons. It was they who had fought the battle and they who would make the peace. Without an agreement they would remain vulnerable. Even after the defeat in North Yorkshire, the Scots had been able to enter Northumbria, place the castle of Wark under siege, and harry as far as the Tyne.[73] Many

---

[67] There are descriptions of the battle in RH, 163–5; HH, 712–19; Aelred, *Relatio*, 181–99; and there is valuable discussion in Strickland, "Securing the North."

[68] Aelred, *Relatio*, 189–91, 196.

[69] HH, 716–19; Aelred, *Relatio*, 196.

[70] RH, 164; Aelred, *Relatio*, 197–8.

[71] JW, iii. 254–5.

[72] RH, 164; JW, iii, 254–5; HH, 718–19.

[73] RH, 165–6; JW, iii, 256–7.

of the northern barons had close ties to the Scottish royal court. Aelred of Rievaulx would dramatize these in his own account of the battle of the Standard, having Robert de Bruce prior to it going as an emissary to the king of Scots, urging him not to attack. He did not wish to see an old comrade and close friend place himself in danger, "after the childhood games in which we trained together, after the practice of arms in which we always joined in many dangers, after the splendid banquets that the kingdom provided us both, after the pleasure which the hunting of birds and beasts brought us both."[74] In so far as it was a matter for them, so the northern barons intimated to David of Scots, they had no objection to one of his main demands, that Henry his son should become earl of Northumberland.[75] Their offer remained on the table. There was scope for diplomacy here and by chance a senior diplomat, whose authority both kings could accept, was on hand.

This was Alberic, cardinal bishop of Ostia, an eminent Cluniac, one of a cadre of such who formed the international peacekeepers of their day. He had come to announce the end of the papal schism, following the death of the antipope Anacletus II in January 1138, which had allowed Innocent II to return to Rome. Alberic had arrived earlier in the summer and, once his credentials had been accepted, he travelled northwards through England. He arrived at Carlisle on 26 September, accompanied by Robert, bishop of Hereford, and Athelwold, bishop of Carlisle, who was seeking to be restored to his see. There he spent three days in discussion with the Scottish king. The unity of Western Christendom was at the top of the legate's agenda, and any impediment to that unity he would wish to remove. The dispute between the two kings was a major impediment. Once David had accepted Pope Innocent, and had agreed to protect non-combatants, he could shine forth as a model Christian king, and the legate could encourage an accommodation with him. A truce was made and Alberic returned to southern England.[76]

THE CHRISTMAS COURT 1138

In the months December 1138 and January 1139, first at London and then in and around Oxford, the royal court was called in session, its most

[74] Aelred, *Relatio*, 192–5, in *Historical Work* trans. Freeland, 261–5. The king rejected his appeal and so Robert withdrew his homage.

[75] RH, 162: "quem postulaverat comitatum Northumbriae Henrico filio suo se impetraturos a rege Angliae firmissime promiserunt."

[76] On Alberic's legation the main authority is Richard of Hexham, who met him and was impressed by him; he is followed by John of Hexham, and John of Worcester is also well informed: RH, 167–77; JH, 297–9; JW, iii. 236–7, 244–5, 260–3. The council of Westminster in Dec. 1138, over which the legate presided, is widely noted: *Councils and Synods*, 768–79 (no. 139). Other evidence of Alberic's activity is found in *Eynsham*, i. 66; *GASA*, i. 114–15; *EEA* 14: *Coventry and Lichfield 1072–1159*, 89–93; *Letters of Osbert of Clare*, 80–3; *Customary of Bury St Edmunds*, 117 (showing him at Bury on 19 Nov.); *Battle*, 140–1; *Memorials of Fountains*, i. 70–2; Diceto, i. 250–1.

important meeting since the Easter court of 1136. It was preceded by a church council and over these two months the business of church and state can be seen to be intertwined.[77] The churchmen initially met apart, under the chairmanship of the papal legate, Alberic of Ostia. His letter to the prior and the monks of Canterbury gives an outline of the agenda:

> We wish to inform you that we have summoned by papal authority the bishops, abbots and all the other religious persons of this kingdom to a council which we have arranged to be held in London at Westminster on 11 December. There, God willing, we shall consecrate the bishop-elect of Exeter and discuss the appointment to Canterbury and other ecclesiastical and papal matters, with divine assistance.

The legate also outlined the procedure to be followed in the matter which particularly concerned them, the election of a new archbishop of Canterbury. The monks were to make his instructions public on 27 November; they were then, after a suitable fast and alms-giving, to proceed to an election. But that was not seen as determinative in itself. They should send a delegation with the authority to speak to the wishes of and to commit the whole community. The legate suggested that they come two or three days early and said that he would be grateful for a quiet word. The actual decision would be made at the council. A great army of churchmen came to it, several of them via Reading, where they had joined the monks of that house in commemorating the third anniversary of the death of Henry I. All stayed in their own houses or took lodgings in and around the city. Many of the great magnates, though summoned to the Christmas court a fortnight later, will have come early to share vicariously in the deliberations. And at a discreet distance ambitious men awaited the call to high office.[78]

The majority of the time in the council was taken up with the "other matters" to which Alberic referred in his letter. A variety of items of church discipline were discussed and provisions made under sixteen headings (for which the technical term was "canons"): these became canon law, the law of the Church. For the most part the canons followed well-established lines, repeating those of the last important councils, held at Westminster in 1125 and 1127. Some followed the established agendas of the reform movement. No one should receive a church or any ecclesiastical benefice from a layman. Specifically, such benefices should not pass

---

[77] *Councils and Synods*, 768–79 (no. 139). This prints Alberic's letter of summons, from Gervase, i. 106, which is found also in translation in Saltman, *Theobald*, 9–10.

[78] Theobald, abbot of Bec, was over in England on a business trip: Saltman, *Theobald*, 6; Walter, the brother of Richard de Lucy, was staying with one of his relations, the abbot of St Albans: *Battle*, 140–3; Arnulf, the archdeacon of Sées and later bishop of Lisieux, is shown to be present by *Regesta*, iii, no. 667.

from father to son by right of inheritance. As to those in holy orders who were married or living with mistresses – the council accepted a distinction in their secular status but as clergy their fate was the same – they were to lose their benefices. Those who refused to pay their tithes, the single tax that did most to support the mission of the Western Church, were to be excommunicated. At a number of points in the council, however, legislation can be seen developing in response to secular change. Excommunication would also be the fate of nuns "who wear furs of vair, gris, sable, marten, ermine or beaver, put on gold rings, or braid or make up their hair."[79] It was to fall also on those who killed, imprisoned, or assaulted anyone in holy orders of any degree, though they could by canon law only be excommunicated after they had received three summons to make satisfaction. This provision was timely and it would make a lot of work, and create a lot of correspondence, for the local bishops in the months ahead. Another provision would later be seen as aimed as much against the bishops as against the clergy whom they disciplined. No one in holy orders should bear arms or engage in warfare. "No one that warreth for God entangleth himself."[80] It was a text for the times.

The main news item from this council was the name of the new archbishop of Canterbury. It was well known that Henry of Winchester wanted the job. Orderic picked up the story straight away after William of Corbeil died in November 1136; he reported that Henry was elected as archbishop at that time. There had been no election, but in the winter of 1136–7 Henry placed himself conveniently in France in case of any summons to Rome,[81] and at least twice during the vacancy he sent emissaries who came back with minor privileges:[82] they will have sought a private audience with the pope to ascertain his views on the primacy, and they may well have offered cash to help with his expenses. Henry did not get the job, which went instead to Theobald, abbot of Bec. The election, so the story was later told, was carefully orchestrated. Henry was sent by the legate to ordain Richard de Belmeis to the diaconate in St Paul's Cathedral; while he was out of the way and in total ignorance of what was proposed, Theobald was elected; and when word was brought to Henry during the ordination he abandoned the ceremony in disgust.[83] This

[79] A passage discussed as important early evidence for the fur trade in Brooke, *London*, 258–61.

[80] 2 Tim. 2:4.

[81] OV, vi. 478–9.

[82] A papal confirmation of the restoration of two manors to Winchester (see *Regesta*, iii, nos. 947–9) was given at Viterbo on 8 Apr. 1137, and a privilege relating to the College of the Holy Cross, Winchester, was given at the Lateran on 10 Mar. 1138: *PUE*, 2/ii, no. 16; iii, no. 31. Similar in form to the first grant, and of like date, was the restoration of the manor of Uffculme to Glastonbury (see *Regesta*, iii, no. 341): *Great Chartulary of Glastonbury*, i. 125–6.

[83] Diceto, i. 252 (and in facsimile in Brooke, *London*, plate 51); Gervase, i. 109.

makes a nice story and later historians have been happy to accept it;[84] but it does not ring true. Henry was not a man to betray anger in this way;[85] he was not a man from whom secrets could be kept; and by Christmas Eve, when the election took place, Theobald's name was probably not a secret at all. The clue to what was going on may be provided by the further statement of Ralph de Diceto, that the election was announced by Alexander, bishop of Lincoln. Henry of Winchester was the sub-dean of the province. It was his job – in the absence of the dean – to preside over the election and to announce its result. He would do this twenty years and more later, after Theobald died, when Thomas Becket was elected.[86] Such conspiracy as there was in 1138 was just as likely intended not to humiliate him but to save his face: he was allowed to claim a prior engagement. Theobald can hardly have been a surprising choice. His previous office as abbot of Bec gave him major standing in the Anglo-Norman world. He had been abbot for just two years, but prior for ten years before that, under an abbot who suffered from ill health.[87] Even in those two years, he admitted forty-seven monks as novices, to what was widely viewed as a model monastic establishment.[88] Those recognized as the two great archbishops of Canterbury of the post-Conquest period, Lanfranc and Anselm, had been his predecessors, and the latter was viewed as a saint. Theobald was a man of evident capacity even if he had none of the charisma of Henry of Blois. In any bench of bishops one charismatic is enough.

A number of other clerical appointments were made at the Christmas court. It was accepted that the king himself would have the last word. Alberic had spelt this out to the monks of Canterbury though they knew it well enough. They needed to come up with a name "whose appointment the authority of canon law cannot resist, to which the bishops of the province ought similarly to assent, and to which the king could not – indeed should not – properly refuse his assent." The canon law had developed a set of procedures that allowed lay involvement in church appointments to continue while seeking to set some limits on it. So the canons said that you should not receive a church from a layman. But a monk at Battle, with no element of censure, explains why Walter de Lucy was appointed: "he had attracted the royal attention and the favour of the magnates

---

[84] "The move must have been prepared in advance by the pope, the legate, the king, and some of the bishops, but had been carefully concealed from Henry": Barlow, *English Church 1066–1154*, 93–4. "[Henry] obviously thought that the whole business was a dirty trick, and that the person responsible was Stephen": Davis, *Stephen*, 27.

[85] "He could not be induced by any severity of language to betray anger" was the verdict of William of Malmesbury, who knew him well: WM, *HN*, 110–11.

[86] Diceto, i. 306–7; Barlow, *Thomas Becket*, 70–1; *Councils and Synods*, 843–5 (no. 156). The dean of the province was the bishop of London, but both in Dec. 1138 and in late May 1162 the see of London was vacant.

[87] Saltman, *Theobald*, 3–7.

[88] WM, *GP*, i. 238–9: "famosum gimnasium."

through the assiduity of his brother," Richard de Lucy.[89] And the monks at Gloucester were similarly open about how Gilbert Foliot, a monk of Cluny, was appointed abbot of Gloucester a few weeks later: "hearing of this man's eminence and probity, Stephen, at the request of his constable Miles, had given him the abbacy of Gloucester at London."[90] The reason for the request was that Gilbert was a kinsman of Miles of Gloucester.[91] Canon law said there should be no family influence on appointments. Yet Stephen's illegitimate son Gervase, who had perhaps been nominated earlier, was now consecrated as abbot of Westminster by the papal legate (see plate 21).[92] He would be safe for just so long as his father lived, though it was wise of him to take an early opportunity to go to Rome to resolve any queries his appointment might be thought to have raised. This reshuffle in the clerical boardroom was made possible by some clerics being stood down. The abbots of Battle, Crowland, and Shrewsbury were deposed, for misdemeanours unstated,[93] and it seems to have been at this council that the appointment of Anselm, abbot of Bury, to the diocese of London was overruled.[94] Canon law allowed for all of this. It was sufficiently flexible to adjust to the realities of power.

The clergy took a close interest in clerical promotions but there was much other business to consider at this Christmas court. While the council was in session there were several long discussions about the peace terms which Alberic had worked out with the northern magnates but which the king needed to confirm. These involved many courtiers, but Stephen's queen, Matilda, was seen as being particularly influential. Some of the southern barons were opposed to any peace settlement, and the king himself was initially reluctant, so the legate used the queen as an intermediary and they finally got their way. "Her glowing woman's breast, refusing to admit defeat, ceased not from prompting him, night and day, in every way she could, until she bent the royal mind to her wish. For she greatly loved her uncle, David king of Scotland, and Henry, his son and her cousin; and so she endeavoured the more to make peace between them

[89] *Battle*, 142–3.

[90] JW, iii. 262–5.

[91] Morey and Brooke, *Gilbert Foliot and his Letters*, 35–7.

[92] JW, iii. 262–3; *Heads*, 77. His mother, Dametta, was installed in the abbey manor of Chelsea: Harvey, "Abbot Gervase de Blois," 131. The name *Damet* is "found as a baptismal name in the Low Countries and in Saxony": Clark, *Selected Writings*, 274 and n. 79. His abbacy is fully discussed in Mason, *Westminster Abbey*, 37–51.

[93] JW, iii. 262–3: "infamati degradantur." *Shrewsbury* had been held against Stephen earlier in the year, and unparliamentary language had been used by the emissaries, of whom the abbot may have been one: OV, vi. 520–3. The abbot of *Crowland* was the brother of Cospatric, earl of Dunbar, who may have been "the leader of the men of Lothian" who died at the battle of the Standard: OV, ii. 350–1; HH, 716–17; "fenland annals" in *Chronicon Angliae Petriburgense*, 90; while RH, 175–6, also notes the deposition. As to the abbot of *Battle*, the house's chronicle states that he had fallen victim to factions at court and that he resigned: *Battle*, 140–1.

[94] Diceto, i. 249–50; Nicholl, *Thurstan*, 232–3; Brooke, *London*, 356–7.

and her husband, the king of England."[95] This passage could be read in purely conventional terms. Peace-making after all was generally acknowledged to fall within a woman's proper role, but the queen's active involvement is not in doubt, and the ties of kin here referred to are part of the network of family ties and friendship that we have seen the king of Scots himself playing upon. At least one further emissary from the pope had arrived in December, announcing a universal council of the Western Church to be held at Rome the following Easter. Notice that the empress wished to challenge Stephen's title at the papal court may have been served at the same time. There needed to be discussions as to who should be sent to Rome and what instructions they should be given, and this represented further business for the king and the great men.[96] The papal emissary will have brought fresh instructions for the legate. It may have been at this time that a way was found to compensate Henry of Winchester for his not being translated to Canterbury. Certainly within days of Alberic's return to Rome, Innocent II wrote privately to Henry offering him the very considerable prize of the standing papal legation in England, the appointment to be activated as soon as there was need.[97] It is more than likely that this deal was made, or at least that the possibility was floated, at the Christmas court when the appointment to Canterbury was confirmed.

Early in the New Year, the legate and the bishops then left London and headed for Canterbury, where Theobald was consecrated and enthroned on 8 January 1139.[98] They must, however, have left on the understanding that they would immediately retrace their steps and rejoin the royal court at Oxford. On 18 January, "there came together the king and his wife Queen Matilda, and not a few earls and barons and prelates," for the consecration of the new church of Godstow Abbey.[99] Godstow lay just outside the north walls of the town of Oxford. There, at the end of Henry I's reign, a local man, John of St John, had given land to a community of nuns under Edith. The abbess was a lady of some standing, according to the tradition of her own house "born of the worthiest blood of this realm," and she was good at getting things done: "she has built the church of this place by her own expense and labour and by collecting alms from the faithful."[100] Even with such advantages, however, nunneries usually had to make do on small endowments, and it may have been largely by

[95] RH, 176; trans. *Scottish Annals*, 213.

[96] *Christina*, 162–5.

[97] Richard of Hexham says that Alberic and his delegation left England shortly after 13 Jan. 1139 while William of Malmesbury gives 1 Mar. as the date of grant of the legation: RH, 176–7; WM, *HN*, 50–1.

[98] Gervase, i. 109.

[99] *EEA* 1: *Lincoln 1067–1185*, 20 (no. 33): "conuenerunt predictus rex et uxor eius Matildis regina, comites et barones necnon et pontifices."

[100] For the nuns' own history, see *English Register of Godstow*; for the bishop's charter see the following note; and for an excellent modern commentary see Elkins, *Holy Women*, 62–5.

chance that at the time of the dedication of the abbey church the royal court was in session and determined to make a show. Quite how good a show can be seen from charters of the king and of the local bishop.[101] Not only does the bishop's charter give the donors' names but it specifies their gifts, graded according to their status and indicating the type of wealth they thought it appropriate to transfer. The king stood at the head of the list, giving 100 shillings "from his own demesne lands," followed by the queen, who gave 10 marks' worth of land, and then Eustace their son who gave 100 shillings "in cash until such time as he should have land of his own." The higher clergy then made their contributions: Archbishop Theobald gave 100 shillings; Alexander of Lincoln also gave 100 shillings, "from the tolls of Banbury";[102] the bishop of Exeter gave 40 shillings from two churches;[103] the king's son Gervase, abbot of Westminster, gave 60 shillings, as did the abbot of Abingdon. The two local laymen, John of St John and Robert d'Oilly, and the citizens of Oxford, confirmed the gift of the monastery site and local resources to support it, and a long list of local men added their gifts. The one earl noted as making a gift was Robert, earl of Leicester, who together with his wife, the countess Amice, gave 60 shillings. Otherwise the largest lay gift was that of Miles, the constable of Gloucester, who gave 20 shillings. All these gifts the legate blessed, the king fortified with royal power, and Theobald and the whole bench of bishops confirmed. One point that will not have escaped the crowds present on another of the ceremonial occasions that the king so enjoyed was the wealth of the higher clergy. The new archbishop and the local bishop matched the gifts of the king and his son shilling for shilling, whilst what most of the layman could give was small change.

The events of these winter days of 1138–9 are lit up by a range of sources that are almost unique in their domestic detail. They show the life of the court with men of influence, both clergy and laymen, fixing things and discussing policy.[104] At the centre of the court is the royal family. The king appears at his most presidential. The queen was highly active, with her own agenda and the resources to back it up. Their son Eustace, perhaps eight years old, makes one of his earliest recorded appearances. It would have been possible to compare his features with those of

[101] *EEA* I, 20–2 (no. 33); *Regesta*, iii, no. 366.

[102] *EEA* I, 23–4 (no. 35), is a later confirmation of this gift.

[103] *EEA* II: *Exeter 1046–1184*, 37–8 (no. 38), which has the king as its first witness.

[104] Royal charters accepted as indicating the composition of the court at this time are *Regesta*, iii, nos. 366–7 (Godstow Abbey), 390 (Miles of Gloucester), 473 (Lincoln Cathedral), 638 (St Frideswide's, Oxford), and 667 (Ramsey Abbey). These suggest the presence of the papal legate, the archbishop of Canterbury, the bishops of Lincoln, Ely, Exeter, Salisbury, Bath, Worcester, and Coutances; the earls of Leicester, Warwick, Northampton, and York; William Martel, Aubrey de Vere, William d'Aubigny *pincerna*, William Mauduit, Ingelram de Say, and Henry de Tracy. Ibid., nos. 850–1, may show the royal court, with the bishops absent, at Reading for the third anniversary of the burial of Henry I on 5 Jan. 1139; in which case, the names of William of Ypres and Richard de Lucy, until recently in Normandy, may be added to the list.

Stephen's illegitimate son, Gervase, now provided to the great abbey of Westminster with papal support. Another cohesive body is the bench of bishops. Alberic's letter summoning the council had drawn attention to their role as the leading figures in the council. And Alexander of Lincoln's first-hand account of events at Godstow seems anxious to stress the collegiality of the bench of bishops under the leadership of the new archbishop.[105] Neither the cohesion of the king's own family nor this collegiality was seriously compromised by the attitudes of the one man common both to that family and to the episcopal bench: Henry, bishop of Winchester. His disappointment at the election to Canterbury would soon be placed to one side. To most of those looking back on 1138 it must have appeared that the king had had a pretty good year.

THE LATERAN COUNCIL

In late January and February 1139 the king was almost certainly in London, for it was there that he gave the abbacy of Gloucester to Gilbert Foliot. A number of the senior clergy set off for the Lateran Council. It had been agreed that "since it seemed dangerous that in times when war was imminent all the prelates of England should leave the country and make the difficult crossing of the Alps, certain ones, and they the more prudent, were chosen to undertake an embassy for themselves and the rest."[106] The new archbishop, Theobald, headed the list, and at Rome he received the pallium which was the distinguishing mark of an archbishop.[107] With him went Simon, bishop of Worcester, Roger, bishop of Chester, John, bishop of Rochester, Robert, the newly consecrated bishop of Exeter, and four abbots.[108] There were at least two archdeacons, Henry of Huntingdon, the historian,[109] and Arnulf of Sées,[110] along with representatives from other dioceses and religious houses.[111] Theobald

[105] *EEA* 1, 21: "hec Teobaldus archiepiscopus totusque noster episcoporum conuentus episcopali auctoritate confirmauerunt."

[106] *Christina*, 162–3.

[107] Diceto, i. 252.

[108] RH, 176–7. JW, iii. 264–5, confirms the names of the bishops, with the exception of Rochester (who might have been viewed as a suffragan of Canterbury), and names Reginald of Evesham (who is probably his source) as one of the abbots. Another was Richard, first abbot of Fountains, who accompanied the legate and died in Rome on 30 April 1139: *Memorials of Fountains*, i. 70–2, 130. Geoffrey, abbot of St Albans, was originally nominated but was excused: *Christina*, 162–7.

[109] HH, liv–lv.

[110] JS, *HP*, 83.

[111] Aside from those known to have attended, charters were issued at the council in favour of the bishops of Lincoln, Salisbury, and Ely, and the abbots of St Augustine's, Canterbury, Ramsey, and Westminster: W. Holtzmann, note in *Reg. Ant.* 1, 293. The emissary from Ely was the monk Alexander, "a most religious man and fluent in Latin, French, and English," along with other dignified and learned figures: *Liber Eliensis*, 315–16. William Thorne, *Chronicle of Saint Augustine's Canterbury*, 69–70, does not suggest that his abbot attended the council.

certainly and probably all of the English contingent travelled via his monastery at Bec. There his brethren could congratulate him on his new dignity and he could arrange for the election of his successor.[112] There Henry of Huntingdon met up with Robert of Torigni, the historian of the community, and was shown a first edition of a recently published work on the history of Britain. This was Geoffrey of Monmouth's *History of the Kings of Britain*. He was staggered by what he read there.[113]

The Second Lateran Council met in Rome in the first half of April 1139.[114] It was "a triumphant celebration of the end of a schism."[115] It was a victory for one man above all: the pope, Innocent II. His opening address to the council fathers owed little to any notions of collegiality:

> You recognise that Rome is the head of the world and that the high honour of an ecclesiastical office is received by the permission of the Roman pontiff, as it were by feudal law and custom: without his permission it is unlawful to hold office. You also know that it belongs to him to pacify those who are in contention and to arrange and order according to his wisdom whatever is in confusion.[116]

It was in this atmosphere and in this context that the empress Matilda's challenge to the legitimacy of Stephen's kingship was heard. There are two authorities for this, a letter of Gilbert Foliot written in 1143–4, and a vignette from John of Salisbury's *Memoirs of the Papal Court*, written perhaps twenty years later.[117] Both these eyewitnesses say that the case on each side was argued very forcefully, in front of a wide audience.[118] The case for the empress was made by Ulger, the bishop of Angers. He seems to have been a holy man, "a lily among thorns,"[119] but he had none of the qualities of an advocate and at the papal court he was out of his depth. He was quite taken aback both by the force of the case made against him and by some of the arguments used. The case for the empress, which he made dutifully enough,[120] turned on two main arguments, her hereditary right and the oath that had been sworn to her. On the other side, those trained in the fine distinctions of the schools immediately got to work. The primary argument was the hereditary right. If that fell, then the oath sworn in terms of that

---

[112] Torigni, 135; Saltman, *Theobald*, 13–15.

[113] HH, liv–lv, 558–9: "stupens inueni"; *GND*, i, lxxvii–lxxix; Tatlock, *Legendary History*, 433–4.

[114] Foreville, *Latran*, 73–95, 180–94; *Councils and Synods*, 779–81 (no. 140).

[115] Robinson, *Papacy*, 138.

[116] *Chron. Morigny (1095–1152)*, 70–2; in French translation in full in Foreville, *Latran*, 180–2; these opening remarks quoted from Robinson, *Papacy*, 138.

[117] *GF Letters*, 60–6 (no. 26); JS, *HP*, 83–5.

[118] *GF Letters*, 65: "in medium deducta est et aliquamdiu uentilata."

[119] *Actus Pontificum Cenomannis*, 430: "qui tunc temporis sapientia, moribus, sanctitate, quasi lilium inter spinas . . . prevalet"; JS, *HP*, 84.

[120] *GF Letters*, 65: "diligenti percurrisset oratione."

right would have to be invalidated. And so it should be, so those arguing for the king claimed. Henry in marrying had deviated from the true path and since his marriage had not been legitimate those born to it could claim no hereditary right. The word went unsaid, but the meaning could not be more clear: the empress was a bastard. These arguments clearly shocked the empress's counsel; he started to bluster, and the hearing broke up in disarray. The case against the empress went unanswered on the day.[121]

The bishop of Angers may not have known the story on which the allegation of illegitimacy was based, though it was well enough known in northern Europe.[122] The empress's mother was Matilda of Scotland. A pious lady, she was one of the large family produced by Malcolm II, king of Scots, and a notably pious lady – indeed, it would turn out, a saint – Margaret of Scotland. Matilda had been educated in England by the nuns of Wilton, alongside her sister, Mary, the future mother of Stephen's queen. The earliest witness, Eadmer, monk of Canterbury, starts his version of the story at this point: "many believed that she had been dedicated by her parents to God's service, as she had been seen walking abroad wearing the veil like the nuns with whom she was living."[123] One of those who believed this was Anselm, the archbishop of Canterbury, who in 1094 heard that Matilda had left the cloister and was living shamelessly in secular garb, and expressed his concern.[124] And so when in 1100 Matilda was selected as Henry's future bride, her eligibility to marry was a matter for debate. That debate was held in a church council, from which Anselm scrupulously absented himself. Matilda appeared in person and argued her own case with some spirit. She claimed that she had only been veiled, "to preserve me from the lust of the Normans, which was rampant and at that time ready to assault any woman's honour." The future queen's protestations that she had never been committed to the religious life were accepted and the council ruled in her and the king's favour.[125] Anselm did then celebrate the marriage and crown the queen in a most solemn ceremony. Moreover, the empress's supporters could reasonably claim, as they started to collect themselves, the sanctity of the late archbishop gave further proof – if any were needed – that he could never have been involved in any actions contrary to the canon law.

---

[121] Ibid.: "hoc in communi audientia multorum vociferatione declamatum est et nichil omnino ab altera parte responsum." On the other hand, John of Salisbury says that the case was answered: *HP*, 84–5. Poole was sceptical of Gibert Foliot's clear statement, but Chibnall accepted it and was followed by Brooke: *Johannes Saresberiensis Historiae Pontificalis*, ed. Poole, 111–12; JS, *HP*, xliii n. 1; Morey and Brooke, *Gilbert Foliot and his Letters*, 119–20.

[122] Eadmer, 121–6; OV, iv. 272–5; WM, *GR*, i. 754–7; Herman of Tournai, 31–3; Walter Map, *De Nugis Curialium*, 474–5. The stories are forensically examined in Sharpe, "King Harold's Daughter," 14–19.

[123] Eadmer, 121, trans. Bosanquet, 127.

[124] *Letters of Saint Anselm of Canterbury*, ii. 91–2 (no. 177), describing Matilda as "a fallen daughter" (*filia perdita*). When she became queen the letter was suppressed.

[125] Eadmer, 121–6, at 122, trans. Bosanquet, 127.

Even had Bishop Ulger been better informed, and had he been more nimble in debate, he was fighting a losing battle. While the reports of the discussions at the council might make it appear that the case for the empress was being heard for the first time, in fact it was not. Stephen reportedly had three advocates. They were Roger de Clinton, bishop of Coventry in England, Arnulf, archdeacon of Sées in Normandy, and Lupellus, a clerk of the former archbishop of Canterbury, William of Corbeil.[126] Why were these men chosen? Most probably because they had been members of the original delegation from the royal court that had announced Stephen's election at the papal court in late February and early March 1136.[127] The case they made had been accepted and the pope had confirmed the election. A further question would then present itself. What was the exact status of the proceedings at the time of the council in 1139? The most likely answer is that what the pope and cardinals viewed themselves as doing was hearing an appeal against the original decision. If this line of reasoning is accepted then the result of the appeal must have been a foregone conclusion, for there was no new information on which to reverse it. As the outcome became clear, the bishop of Angers reportedly lost his temper, saying to Arnulf of Sées, "I would marvel at the shamelessness of your lies were it not that your whole race is garrulous and deserves to be held up as an example of sinful life and skill and effrontery in lying. In these arts you are conspicuous among the Normans." A good story perhaps, but it shows the weakness of the empress's case. She was claiming the lordship of England and Normandy but she had only a marginal interest in this territory and her counsel had none at all. Confronted by conflicting testimony, with counsel engaged in personal abuse, the pope reacted in the way that both parties must have expected. He declined to hear further argument, and "accepted king Stephen's gifts and in friendly letters confirmed his occupation of the kingdom of England and the duchy of Normandy."[128] The losing party claimed bribery but in truth it had lost the argument.

The empress had lost on more than one level. The pope's decision in Stephen's favour should not be seen as the more attractive of two unattractive options, since a decision for the empress would have made civil war quite certain. Innocent will have viewed the matter much more positively. Alberic of Ostia's legation had served as a model of what he wished to achieve. The king of Scots had been at the same time rescued from schism and reconciled with the king of England. The legate, though initially greeted with scepticism, had won golden opinions from all with

[126] He had also been a clerk of Archbishop Ralph (d. 1122): *EEA* 28: *Canterbury 1070–1136*, xlvii and n. 70, nos. 36, 80, 81,

[127] Roger of Coventry was a conspicuous absentee from the Easter court of 1136: *Regesta*, iii, no. 271; *EEA* 14: *Coventry and Lichfield 1072–1159*, xl. On discussions at the royal court on the composition of the delegations, *Christina*, 160–1 (1136), 162–5 (1139).

[128] JS, *HP*, 83–5.

whom he came in contact.[129] All this reflected well on the pope. And while much business crowded in on the council, at its core lay the progress of reform. Stephen's identification with reform was a highly positive feature of his kingship. A strong contingent had come to the council from the English Church. Some had sent their apologies by envoys who might be furnished with charters for papal confirmation. On several occasions in issuing these privileges the papal chancery had broken from its routine formulas to stress the concessions that Stephen had made to the Church. Here is one such, in a document issued for Alexander, bishop of Lincoln, on 28 April 1139:

> Moreoever we validate with our own authority the liberty granted to the church by that illustrious man Stephen, king of the English. Amongst its provisions we are led to make special mention here of the following: that after your death and that of your successors, while the episcopal see shall be vacant, no one should presume to usurp the goods of the bishopric or those of the church, but rather those belonging to the church and their possessions shall remain in the free custody and power of the clergy, with everything being preserved for the use of future bishops and for the good of this church.[130]

The council had decreed that kings should do justice in consultation with the bishops.[131] England could be represented as a model of good practice in this regard also. When the pope wrote after the council to the king and his brother, the papal legate, on a variety of matters,[132] he will have been in no doubt that he had made the right decision.

THE ARREST OF THE BISHOPS

As one set of royal agents travelled to Rome to attend the Lateran Council another embassy made its way north to work on the fine print of a new treaty with the Scots. When the terms were settled, a meeting was convened at Durham on 9 April 1139 to ratify the agreement. The English delegation was headed by the queen, who was accompanied by "many earls and barons of southern England." The Scots were led by Henry, the king's son, who was the main beneficiary of the terms agreed. He was granted the earldom of Northumberland and, although an attempt was

---

[129] RH, 167: he was wise, learned, and eloquent, and – not least – he knew how to behave; for a less colloquial translation see Robinson, *Papacy*, 161.

[130] *Reg. Ant.* 1, 190–3 (no. 249). There are further references to "the illustrious king" in bulls issued at the same time for Nigel of Ely and Roger of Salisbury: *Liber Eliensis*, 302–5; *PUE*, 2, no. 19.

[131] Foreville, *Latran*, 192.

[132] Letters to the king and to the legate survive in *Liber Eliensis*, 316–17. The "friendly letters" sent concerning the succession, according to John of Salisbury, have not survived: JS, *HP*, 85.

made to exclude its chief town, Newcastle, from the grant, he soon gained control over it. It was agreed further that those of the northern barons who wished could then do homage to Henry, saving their fealty to the king of England, "and this many of them did." Eustace Fitz John was one of those who took advantage of this provision. The Scots for their part offered little more than promises. The king, and his son, and all their subjects, "were to continue at peace with and most loyal to king Stephen of England in all things." But they were required to offer hostages that they would keep to their word, and sons of several of the earls were surrendered. As had happened with the earlier Treaty of Durham, and as was clearly part of the terms agreed on each occasion, Henry of Scots – with the hostages – then came south to join the court of the English king. He will have come the more readily because he had a high-status bride waiting for him in the person of Ada de Warenne, "whom he loved dearly."[133]

Henry of Scots met up with Stephen at Nottingham and it may have been here that the royal court celebrated Easter. A week later, on 30 April, the court moved on to Worcester. The king could enjoy the ceremonial. He was received "by the clergy and people of the surrounding area in a festive procession." He came to the cathedral church, laid his ring on the altar as an offering and a mark of respect; this was returned to him the following day. "The king wondered at the humility and devotion of the monks," and the monk John took care to put his brethren's piety on the record.[134] The king was well attended.[135] He had with him Roger, bishop of Salisbury, and Robert, bishop of Bath, as well as the local bishop, Simon of Worcester. He had five earls, including Henry of Scots, the newly made earl of Northumberland, Simon of Senlis, earl of Northampton, Robert of Leicester, Roger of Warwick, and Waleran, count of Meulan. The king made Waleran additionally earl of Worcester around this time, offering him the crown's resources within the shire in return for his military support.[136] Miles of Gloucester was at court also and it may have been at his instance that Stephen with parts of his army then moved to attack the castle at Ludlow, up country from Worcester, "which was held against him," possibly by Gilbert de Lacy.[137] Siege castles were set up and the king withdrew, intending to travel to London, but he was kept back by difficulties in the army. It seems that some kind of tournament was arranged, in the course of which Henry of Scots "was pulled off his horse by an iron hook" and had

[133] The main source for this paragraph is RH, 177–8, trans. *Scottish Annals*, 214–15; also JH, 299–300; *Melrose*, s.a. 1139; OV, vi. 522–5.

[134] JW, iii. 266–7.

[135] Taking as evidence for this court the witness list to *Regesta*, iii, no. 964, a diploma for Worcester Cathedral, whose authenticity is questioned by the editors of that volume but defended in *Cart. Worcester*, xxii, lxvii–lxix (with facsimile); RH, 178.

[136] King, "Waleran of Meulan," 168.

[137] JW, iii. 266–7, with Gilbert de Lacy suggested as the custodian in Coplestone-Crow, "Payn Fitz John and Ludlow Castle," 180 and n. 95.

to be rescued by the king.[138] It was an incident typical of the brash behaviour of the troops at this time, "relentless in their cursed fighting, and driven by their boastful strength."[139] The diversions nearly made the king late for a meeting of the court that had been convened at Oxford on the feast day of the Nativity of St John the Baptist, 24 June 1139.

"There an extraordinarily scandalous and quite unprecedented affair took place."[140] This affair has become known as "the arrest of the bishops," the bishops being Roger, bishop of Salisbury, and his two nephews, Alexander, bishop of Lincoln, and Nigel, bishop of Ely. All had been active in Stephen's administration in the first three years of the reign, and there is no reason to doubt their continuing interest as the royal court travelled away in the spring of 1139, first to the east and then the west midlands. The story was later told that they left for the Oxford court with some foreboding, Roger of Salisbury setting off from Malmesbury having confided to the monks that he felt he would be less use at court than a colt in battle.[141] It seems an odd image for a man who had lived and breathed the life of the court for forty years. It signalled that he felt the court was now a hostile environment. It will be necessary to explain why, but first it may be useful to set out in outline what happened. There is no shortage of witnesses, for this was a sensational story, involving – as do all the best stories in any age – a struggle for power at the very heart of the establishment, high drama, low farce, and even a modicum of sex.[142]

Oxford was a major town, but unlike London-Westminster, Winchester, or even Gloucester, it had only recently become a regular meeting point for the royal court. When we are told that trouble flared up there over claims to lodgings this is in every way credible. The brawl involved the men of the bishop of Salisbury and Earl Alan of Richmond.[143] The bishop of Salisbury had some bases in the town but he may have come with a larger contingent than usual and so have needed additional accommodation; Earl Alan and his men may have been in this town for the first time and unsure of their bearings.[144] Particularly after a good lunch. "The contest was carried on first

---

[138] HH, 718–19. The story as it was reported is put in context by the fuller information from the local chronicler, JW, iii. 266–7. This makes it likely that any threat to Henry of Scots came not from the Ludlow garrison but from other members of the royal army, which included the men of his rival, Simon of Senlis. In what may be another version of the same story, it was reported that Ranulf of Chester had tried to entrap Henry on his return to Scotland: JH, s.a. 1140, 306.

[139] JW, iii. 266–7.

[140] HH, 718–19.

[141] WM, *HN*, 46–7. The Gloucester chronicle has the story also: JW, iii. 246–7.

[142] The fullest account of "the arrest of the bishops" is in Kealey, *Roger*, 173–89.

[143] WM, *HN*, 46–7. Other sources say that the dispute was between the king's men and the bishop's men: Gloucester chronicle, in JW, iii. 246–7; *GS*, 76–7.

[144] Alan III, a count of Brittany and earl of Richmond, succeeded his father, Stephen, in 1135–6, but did not attest the "Oxford" charter of liberties: *EYC* 4: *Richmond* 1, 87–9; *Regesta*, iii, no. 271.

with abusive language, then with swords. Alan's followers were put to flight and his nephew almost killed."[145] The brawl had taken place in a court that should have been protected by the king's peace. Still, it chiefly involved men at arms and it might have been resolved by military discipline. It was not. The last time a brawl at court had captured the headlines, in Normandy in the summer of 1137, it had done so because it was seen as symptomatic of divisions between the great men. So here. The bishops were required to surrender their castles in satisfaction for their men's behaviour. This was a massive indemnity for a comparatively minor offence. It called in question their loyalty. The bishops protested that loyalty and offered to give an alternative satisfaction, possibly to pay a monetary penalty. This was refused. Roger of Salisbury, Alexander of Lincoln, and Roger the chancellor were placed under arrest.[146] Nigel of Ely, the third of the bishops, was lodged outside the city. This allowed him the time to make his escape but rather than retreat to the fenland he made for Devizes in Wiltshire, one of the castles of Roger of Salisbury, who lived there in domestic comfort.[147] It was a futile and counter-productive gesture, and in short order all the bishops' castles were surrendered.[148] The bishops were then released, but Roger of Salisbury was a broken man and both Nigel of Ely and Alexander of Lincoln had the threat of deposition hanging over them.[149]

What was the meaning of all this? Those closest to these events when they came to put them in context did so in the same way.[150] Everyone was on tenterhooks. "Reports were being spread in England that Earl Robert might arrive from Normandy at any moment with his sister." The uncertainty in the political situation meant that individuals were looking to their own, garrisoning their castles, and strengthening them in readiness for any siege. It was not just laymen who were behaving in this way but several of the higher clergy. Indeed if you viewed the world from the perspective of Winchester, as the monk who kept the annals of that house necessarily did, then the clergy loomed large. This is his entry for 1138:

> In this year Bishop Henry built in Winchester a town-house which was rather a palace, with a strong tower; also the castles of Merdon, and Farnham, and Waltham, and Downton, and Taunton. Roger, bishop of Salisbury, fortified the castles of Salisbury, Sherborne, Devizes, and

---

[145] WM, *HN*, 46–7. JH, 301, states that the nephew died.

[146] JW, iii. 246–7, 266–7; OV, vi. 532–3; *GS*, 76–9; WM, *HN*, 68–9; *Christina*, 166–7.

[147] Roger kept large quantities of cash at Devizes: HH, 720–1. And he also kept his mistress, Matilda of Ramsbury, the "wife of whom no one spoke," in Sir Richard Southern's nice phrase: OV, vi. 532–3; Southern, *Medieval Humanism*, 231. Such understandings with the press seldom last for long.

[148] *GS*, 78–9; OV, vi. 532–3; Gloucester chronicle, in JW, iii. 246–7.

[149] HH, 722–3: "tam merore quam senio confectus" (of Roger); OV, vi. 534–5: "Eliensis publicus hostis totius patriae factus est" (of Nigel); *Regesta*, iii, no. 493: "vel si evenerit quod Alexander episcopus mecum pacem fecerit, vel alius episcopus Lincolnie substitutus fuerit" (of Alexander).

[150] WM, *HN*, 44–7; *GS*, 72–7, with some introductory matter missing; OV, vi. 530–5.

Malmesbury; the earl of Gloucester those of Gloucester, Bath, Bristol, Dorchester, Exeter, Wimborne, Corfe, and Wareham; Brian [Fitz Count], Wallingford and Oxford; Bishop Alexander, Lincoln; John the Marshal, Marlborough and Ludgershall; Geoffrey de Mandeville, the Tower of London and Rochester. There was no man of any standing or substance in England who did not either build or strengthen a fortification in England.[151]

Not every one of these entries is exact, but that is not the point.[152] Wherever you looked there were castles being fortified or newly erected. And a number of the bishops were taking a prominent role.

Roger of Salisbury had quite a small diocese but it contained no less than four major fortifications.[153] On his own demesne manors he had made new castles at Devizes and at Sherborne. He had encircled a wide area, and had made ranges of buildings surmounted by great towers. Devizes is now totally gone but the visitor to what is now an English Heritage site at Sherborne can at least pace out the circle and see substantial remnants of one of those great towers.[154] Roger had also built fortifications in his cathedral city of Salisbury (Old Sarum) and Malmesbury, "in the churchyard itself, hardly a stone's throw from the abbey."[155] Alexander "the magnificent" of Lincoln had the largest diocese in the country, extending over eight counties, and he had a network of private residences about a day's journey apart. His main castle was at Newark on the Trent, which he had made his second capital, spotting its economic potential and contributing to its rise as one of the chief towns of the midlands. No diocese in England has kept its archives better, or been better served by historians, so it is quite certain that the inception of Alexander's great project at Newark dates from the early 1130s, i.e. from the later years of Henry I and not from Stephen's reign.[156] His archdeacon, Henry of Huntingdon, mentioned another castle of his at Sleaford, and he was engaged in building a new palace at Lincoln.[157] All these castles were

---

[151] *Ann. Mon.*, ii. 51.

[152] It was Miles of Gloucester who held Gloucester: WM, *HN*, 62–3; William of Ypres held Rochester: JW, iii. 302–3; Robert d'Oilli held Oxford: *GS*, 116–17; and at this date royal garrisons controlled Bath and Exeter: *GS*, 44–5, 64–5, 70–1.

[153] On Roger's castles, see Kealey, *Roger*, 86–91; Stalley, "A Twelfth-Century Patron of Architecture."

[154] *Devizes* was the finest castle in Europe, according to Henry of Huntingdon: HH, 720–1 ("non erat aliud splendidius intra fines Europe"); cf. *GS*, 78–9 ("mirando artificio sed et munimine inexpugnabili firmatum"); *VCH Wiltshire*, x. 237–8; *Castellarium Anglicanum*, ii. 498. At *Sherborne*, "the dominating tower keep was 70ft high, and may date from around 1130," Kealey, *Roger*, 87–8; for the plan see the English Heritage guide; *Castellarium Anglicanum*, i. 128.

[155] WM, *HN*, 44–5. On *Old Sarum*, which had a quadrangle similar to that at Sherborne, *VCH Wiltshire*, vi. 53–7; *King's Works*, ii. 824–6; *Castellarium Anglicanum*, ii. 500. On *Malmesbury*, *VCH Wiltshire*, iii. 216; *Castellarium Anglicanum*, ii. 502.

[156] *Regesta*, ii, nos. 1660–1, 1770, 1772–3, 1791; Braun, "Notes on Newark Castle"; *Castellarium Anglicanum*, ii. 380.

[157] HH, 720–1; also in the Ce text of WM, *HN*, 48–9; *Castellarium Anglicanum*, i. 262; *Regesta*, iii, no. 463.

state of the art, as much palaces as castles or private dwellings: a single word could not cover their range. Indeed they could deceive the eye. The quality of the masonry was so fine that they seemed to be built of a single block of stone.[158]

In the wrong hands, these castles could do great damage to the king's cause. The question was asked whether the three bishops, so closely associated with the king until this time, could still be trusted. If there was doubt about even one of them questions would be raised against the others, for their association was so close that if one faltered the cry would immediately go up that this was a conspiracy.[159] The bishops could protest their loyalty, but all their protestations could be countered. They could say their castles were built for display, as ornaments to their dioceses, and so in a sense to the greater glory of God, but that was not how anyone else saw it. How did this conspicuous consumption fit with the Christian message? They could say they would fight resolutely for the king in any emergency, but was it their job to fight and should not that task be left to the professionals? And how secure was their title? Certainly the castle at Salisbury should be seen as royal,[160] and the king would be quite entitled and following precedent in his treatment of laymen if he were to claim it back. In Normandy at any rate it was accepted that the king could put a royal garrison in any castle, not reducing the title of its owner but accepting that all fortifications were in some sense public dwellings. So at least in any time of military emergency.[161] The very garrisoning and provisioning of the castles showed the country being put – not by any central authority but by a great number of private decisions – on a war footing.

The bishop of Salisbury and his nephews had great power, great wealth, but few friends. "Some powerful laymen, vexed that they would be surpassed by clerks in the amassing of wealth and the size of their castles, nourished within their hearts an unseen grudge of envy."[162] They had acquired this wealth in the royal service, and it could be claimed that some of it was the king's.[163] It appeared that they stood above the law, gaining property at the expense of both laymen and clergy, as has been seen.[164] They had been generously treated at the beginning of the reign, "the king repeating to his friends from time to time: 'By the birth of God! I would

[158] This was William of Malmesbury's comment on his fortifications at Old Sarum and at Malmesbury: WM, *GR*, i. 738–9

[159] Roger of Salisbury deplored Nigel of Ely's defence of Devizes for this reason: OV, vi. 532–3.

[160] WM, *HN*, 44–5: "quod cum regii iuris proprium esset"; the respective rights of the king and the bishop in the borough and castle of Salisbury are discussed in *VCH Wiltshire*, vi. 51–3.

[161] On the "rendability" of castles, see Haskins, 277–84; Yver, "Les Châteaux forts en Normandie," 60–3, 80–1, 94–5; Coulson, *Castles in Medieval Society*, 163–73.

[162] WM, *HN*, 44–7, slipping in a quotation from Ovid. *GS*, 72–5, also speaks of the envy of the king's councillors at the bishops' wealth and ostentation.

[163] WM, *HN*, 56–7.

[164] Note the comments at the end of Chapter 2.

give him half of England if he asked for it, until his time shall pass: he will grow tired of asking before I do of giving.' "[165] William of Malmesbury here dramatizes what everyone knew, that the power base of the bishops came from their close identification with the king. If they could be prised away from him, then that power base would collapse like a stack of cards. This is what happened at Oxford. It seems to have been planned. As to the identity of the "powerful laymen," the chief responsibility was attributed to "the two brothers," the count of Meulan and the earl of Leicester, along with "Alan of Dinan and a number of others."[166] The king against his better judgement had been persuaded that the bishops needed to be called to account. "The king, though easily swayed owing to his excessive favour towards them, pretended for some time not to listen to their smooth words, softening the bitterness of his delay either through regard for religion where bishops were concerned or, as I think more probable, because he disliked exposing himself to censure."[167] The bishops had been manhandled at the very least; their loyalty had been questioned; they had been deprived of their property without trial; and the arrests had taken place at court.

Henry of Winchester, the newly appointed papal legate, decided to make an issue of the arrests. There is no sign that he had been at Oxford in late June, and he needed a little time to come to terms with the implications of the arrests and possibly to take soundings, but finally he convened a council to meet in Winchester – his own cathedral city – on 29 August 1139.[168] It was a church council, and practically all the bishops came, headed by Archbishop Theobald, though some apologized, Thurstan of York on the grounds of ill health, whilst "others made the war their excuse."[169] If recent precedent was followed then the bishops would have come with some of their archdeacons and the more important of the abbots would also have been summoned. One of those present was William of Malmesbury, perhaps representing his monastery, which was then vacant, or perhaps the subject of a special invitation from the legate, a man with a high regard both for his own reputation and for William's historical skills.[170] It was a church council, but its chief purpose was to call the king to account. So whilst the king and his councillors were not formally members of this council they were resident in the city at the same time and delegations went to and fro. This "inter-communing" would become routine as the two systems of law, the canon law of the Church and the common law of England, drifted apart.

[165] WM, *HN*, 68–9.
[166] OV, vi. 530–3. *GS*, 72–7, refers to "the crafty count of Meulan and some others." On the Beaumont dominance of court at this time, see Crouch, *Beaumont Twins*, 43–5.
[167] WM, *HN*, 46–7. *GS*, 74–5, also says that the king prevaricated.
[168] *Councils and Synods*, 788–92 (no. 142). The main authority is WM, *HN*, 50–9; noted also in HH, 722–3; *Christina*, 166–7; JH, 301.
[169] WM, *HN*, 50–1.
[170] WM, *HN*, xxiii–xxiv.

The legate started with a long speech in Latin complaining on procedural grounds about every aspect of the treatment of the bishops. "It was a lamentable crime, he said, that the king had been so led astray by those who instigated him to this as to order hands to be laid on his men, especially when they were bishops, in the peace of his court." Not only this but then, "under pretence of the bishops' being at fault, churches were being robbed of their property." If the bishops had committed any offence, they should be tried by their peers, and any property taken away should be restored until such time as the trial was held.[171] The legate made a powerful case but there were good lawyers on the other side and they could answer in terms of case law. The arrest at court was a problem. It was a particular problem for Stephen for he was an experienced courtier and he made much of the routines of the court. This was why it was necessary to say that the peace had been breached initially by the men of the bishop and not by the king or his agents. Who could be sure? As to immunity for the clergy, in these circumstances it simply did not apply. Remember the trial of Odo of Bayeux in 1082:

> Once when William [the Conqueror] was complaining to [Archbishop] Lanfranc of his brother's treachery, the archbishop's reply was: "Arrest him and lock him up." "What," said the king, "lock up a clergyman?" The archbishop laughed . . . "No," he retorted, "you will not be arresting the bishop of Bayeux, you will be taking into custody the earl of Kent."[172]

When William of St Calais, bishop of Durham, was tried in 1088, Lanfranc cited the trial of Odo as a precedent: "We do not judge you because of your bishopric but because of your fief; and in this way we have judged the bishop of Bayeux concerning his fief before the father of the present king; and the king did not call 'bishop' in that suit but 'brother' and 'earl.' "[173] In the case of Roger of Salisbury in 1139 it was argued that he was a royal officer, and that any cash and valuables confiscated were the property of the crown, acquired by him in his official capacity. The bishop, said those arguing on the king's side, had readily accepted this. The chief of them was Aubrey de Vere, an experienced lawyer: he "spoke with restraint and without abusive language, though some of the earls, standing by his side, often interrupted his speech by hurling insults at the bishop."[174]

---

[171] WM, *HN*, 50–3.

[172] WM, *GR*, i. 544–5. The split personality of Odo of Bayeux is clearly apparent on his seal, which shows him in his vestments on one side and as a mounted warrior on the other: *Book of Seals*, no. 431, plate facing 304.

[173] *English Lawsuits*, i. 90–106, at 99 (no. 134); discussion in Barlow, *English Church 1066–1154*, 281–7; Cowdrey, *Lanfranc*, 219–24.

[174] WM, *HN*, 54–7.

In this instance it was the castles that were the key. Henry of Winchester was trying to make it appear that a castle was just another piece of church property. He had his own interest in doing so, as those listening to him will not fail to have remarked, though it would have been politic to do so privately. But were not the castles a special case? It was all very well going on at length about canon law, but what was its attitude to the bishops as holders of castles? The king's party produced as their star witness one of the outstanding churchmen of the age. This was the primate of Normandy, Hugh of Rouen.[175] On the subject of the bishops and their precious castles he produced the medieval equivalent of catch-22. They should have their castles, he said, if they could prove by canon law that they were entitled to hold castles, but this was a position that canon law did not support. And:

> Even granted that it is right for them to have the castles, yet certainly, as it is a time of uncertainty, all the chief men, in accordance with the custom of other peoples, ought to hand over the keys of their fortifications to the disposal of the king, whose duty it is to fight for the peace of all. So the bishops' whole case will fall to the ground. For either it is unjust, according to canon law, for them to have castles, or, if this is permitted by the king as an act of grace, they ought to yield to the emergencies of the times by delivering up the keys.[176]

The king and his own canon lawyers were confident enough in their own case to say that if any judgment were given against them by the legate and the English bishops then the king himself would appeal to Rome. He had, after all, not lost a case there yet. For a time it did look likely that some censure would be imposed and that it would be suspended while the king appealed over the head of the legate directly to the pope. And here was another catch-22, for the clergy were warned that if they went to Rome without the king's permission they would find it difficult to return. This was one of the historic rights of the crown which the king had specifically reserved when he made his famous agreement with the Church at the very beginning of the reign. He was very tenacious of these rights.

The bishops had no choice but to back off. William of Malmesbury saw the legate and the archbishop as making their appeal in the following terms. "They fell as suppliants at the king's feet in his room, and begged him to take pity on the Church, pity on his soul and reputation, and not suffer a divorce to be made between the monarchy and the clergy."[177] This was the real risk, that the tight alliance between "church" and "state" that had brought Stephen to power would now be weakened. As the council

[175] Luscombe, "Hugh (d. 1164)," *OxDNB*; Waldman, "Hugh of Amiens," 147; Spear, *Norman Cathedrals*, 198–9.

[176] WM, *HN*, 58–9.

[177] Ibid.: "inter regnum et sacerdotium."

broke up, however, the king's party would have seen this as a threat that could be contained. The press releases were entirely favourable to their case: "it was decided that all towns, castles and fortified places throughout England where secular business was conducted should submit to the jurisdiction of the king and his barons."[178] The castles had royal garrisons placed in them, men who became particular targets of the clergy's ire.[179] In just a few days king and barons would be able to claim the ultimate justification for what had been termed their precipitate action. They had acted just in time. Hard on their heels, as they rode back to their homes, came the news that the empress, accompanied by Robert of Gloucester, had landed on the south coast.

[178] JW, iii. 266–9; cf. *GS*, 80–1: "it was stringently enacted that any receptacles of war and disturbance in the hands of any of the bishops should be handed over to the king as his own property."

[179] They were "laymen and moreover men of little religion," according to Henry of Winchester: WM, *HN*, 50–1. *Sherborne* was under the control of William Martel, who had "mightily exasperated the legate by seizing and stealing much of his property": WM, *HN*, 96–7; *GS*, 148–9. *Malmesbury* may have been entrusted first to John the Marshal, "that scion of hell and root of all evil"; thereafter it was captured by Robert Fitz Hubert, who was driven out, and a royal garrison was restored: JW, iii. 284–7; *GS*, 168–9; WM, *HN*, 62–3. *Salisbury* may have come first to William of Salisbury, who did much damage to the church, died, and left his parents to foot the bill: *GS*, 148–9; *VCH Wiltshire*, vi. 53–4. *Devizes* was initially garrisoned for the king; then disputed between Robert Fitz Hubert and Robert of Gloucester; and then came briefly to Hervey Brito: JW, iii. 286–9; *GS*, 104–9; WM, *HN*, 74–7. *Newark* was surrendered "into the custody of strangers," who can be identified as a garrison of Robert of Leicester, who was excommunicated by the bishop and censured by the pope: HH, 720–1; *Reg. Ant.* 1, 239–41 (no. 283). *Sleaford* may have been under the control of Alan of Richmond, "a man of the greatest cruelty and craft": *GS*, 102–3; WM, *HN*, 54–5 and n. 130.

Chapter 4

WAR AND PEACE

And thus it came to pass in England, what we see the Lord saying in the Gospels: "A kingdom divided against itself cannot stand."[1]

The king, it was reported, was often quick to say of his opponents: "When they have chosen me king, why do they abandon me? By the birth of God, I will never be called a king without a throne!"[2]

The empress Matilda, accompanied by her brother Robert, earl of Gloucester, landed at Arundel in Sussex on 30 September 1139.[3] She would later speak of how she had come to England, "after the death of my father,"[4] as though she had waited just a matter of days before she crossed the Channel. In fact it had been nearly four years. In the meantime Stephen had been crowned, and recently her appeal to the papacy had been diplomatically but nonetheless firmly rejected. She was forced to take direct action, hoping to establish a base in England and to fight Stephen from there. In failing to take Bristol castle after Robert of Gloucester had renounced his allegiance, the king had opened this opportunity for her. It was still an enterprise that was fraught with danger. She was expected. The king had given "orders to keep a careful watch, night and day, on all the approaches to the harbours."[5] The coast of Dorset, specifically the port of Wareham, which was under the control of Robert of Gloucester, would later provide safe access to the west country for those who had crossed over from Normandy. But Baldwin de Redvers had used this route when he had returned to England a few weeks earlier. Wareham most certainly was being watched and the king with his army was in the vicinity. Southampton and Portsmouth, the main ports on the Solent, were out of the question. The empress and Robert of Gloucester chose to land further

---

[1] *Liber Eliensis*, 320: "Constat tunc de Anglia verissime completum fuisse quod Dominum in evangelia legimus dixisse: 'Omne regum in se ipsum divisum desolabitur.' " So also, "Vita Roberti de Betune," in *Anglia Sacra*, ii. 313; Newburgh, i. 39.

[2] WM, *HN*, 38–41.

[3] Ibid., 60–1. Those writing closest to the event support this date, Orderic saying that it took place "in autumn," Henry of Huntingdon that it was immediately after the Winchester council, and John of Worcester that it was "in the month of October": OV, vi. 534–5; HH, 722–3; JW, iii. 268–9.

[4] *Regesta*, iii, no. 391: "quando in Angliam veni post mortem Regis Henrici patris mei."

[5] *GS*, 84–5.

east, at Arundel in West Sussex. It may be that this was the only port open to her.[6] The king was "much displeased" at the news of her arrival and he vented his anger particularly on "those responsible for watching and guarding the ports."[7]

Arundel was a part of the dower lands and the normal residence of Adeliza of Louvain, the widow of Henry I. She was an active manager of the estates that Henry had given her.[8] While devoted to the memory of her late husband, she had not so far seen this as incompatible with loyalty to the new king. She was to marry again, to William d'Aubigny *pincerna*, and have children with him, but whether she was married when the empress landed is unclear. It does not appear that the empress was expected and the castle had not been fortified. It could hardly provide a permanent base for her and her supporters; they would need to move on, if they could. Robert of Gloucester moved on straight away. He had come with only a small contingent of troops,[9] and as soon as he had news of the king's approach, he abandoned his sister and made for Bristol, using minor roads to try to escape detection. Before he had gone far, he was intercepted by an important figure, someone who knew the minor roads of Hampshire like the back of his hand. This was no less than the local bishop and papal legate, Henry of Winchester. What occurred between them nobody knew, or at least nobody was saying, but when they parted Robert continued on his way to Bristol and Henry rejoined his brother at Arundel. The author of the *Gesta Stephani*, firmly taking the royal line, says that Henry, "at length met the earl – so it was rumoured – and after a compact of peace and friendship had been firmly ratified between them let him go unharmed." He still found the bishop's behaviour difficult to understand: "to any man of any sense it must be doubtful, or rather quite incredible, that a brother should greet the invader of his brother's kingdom with a kiss."[10] Henry's behaviour makes most sense here, and it also helps to make sense of the year which follows, if he is seen as preoccupied with the need to make peace. This represented a political judgement on his part, that the claims the empress was making, wherever she

[6] Thus Torigni, 137.

[7] JW, iii. 268–9.

[8] It is a particular feature of the documents issued by her chancery that, in her grants to religious houses, she underlines her title, that Henry had held these lands in demesne, and had given them to her: *Reading Abbey Cartularies*, i. 404–5 (no. 535): "cum omnibus liberalibus consuetudinibus cum quibus dominus meus nobilissimus rex Henricus ea in dominio tenuit et mihi dedit"; ibid., i. 301–2 (no. 370): "ut regine et sponse sua"; *Cart. Afflighem*, 104–6 (no. 67).

[9] William of Malmesbury, who had close contacts with the quartermasters in Robert of Gloucester's camp, says that he had brought 140 knights and that he set off for Bristol with no more than a dozen of them: WM, *HN*, 60–1. Torigni, 137, says that he took ten knights and ten archers.

[10] *GS*, 88–9.

was based, would not go away. He would have seen it as a moral imperative too. It was his responsibility.

At Arundel, once Henry of Winchester had returned there, the discussions did not last long. The alternatives were a siege or some kind of
compromise agreement. It will not be surprising to find – by now – that it
was the language of love that was used and not that of conflict. Adeliza
seems to have had no stomach for a fight. "The ex-queen was awed by the
king's majesty, and was afraid that she might lose what rank she had in
England, and solemnly swore that no enemy of the king had come to
England through her doing, but that, saving her dignity, she had provided
hospitality to those in authority who were known to her."[11] Nor did several
of those advising the king wish to fight. Henry of Winchester reportedly
urged that the empress be let go. However inappropriate it seems now, and
seemed at the time to those outside court circles, they played the game
according to the rules. "An agreement was made and a truce accepted
under sanction of an oath."[12] Under the terms of that agreement the
empress left the castle at Arundel, unharmed, and was given an escort
appropriate to her rank on her journey on to Bristol. The escorts were
Henry, bishop of Winchester, and Waleran, count of Meulan. It is unnecessary to see the first of these as the empress's nominee and the second as
the king's.[13] The route crossed the bishop's diocese. When it left it, about
halfway, Robert of Gloucester – under a safe conduct that was equally a
part of the agreement – met up with his sister, Waleran of Meulan turned
back, and legate and earl escorted her to Bristol. Robert of Gloucester let
it be known that he had not abandoned his sister at Arundel. Rather, he
claimed, Adeliza "with a woman's fickleness" had abandoned the faith
that she had sworn.[14] Stephen then stayed at Arundel, with an entourage
which included the bishops of Winchester and Chichester, Waleran, count
of Meulan, Ranulf, earl of Chester, Earl Gilbert, Robert de Ferrers,
earl of Nottingham, William of Ypres, William Martel, Robert de Vere,
William d'Aubigny *pincerna*, and Eudo Martel.[15] It may have been only at

---

[11] JW iii. 268–9: "iureiurando iurat neminem inimicorum suorum per se Angliam
petisse, sed, salua dignitate sua, uiris auctoritatis utpote sibi quondam familiaribus hospi-
tium annuisse."

[12] *GS*, 88–9.

[13] Davis, *Stephen*, 38 n. 7a; *GS*, 88–9 n. 1.

[14] WM, *HN*, 60–3.

[15] Stephen issued only the one charter at Arundel, and the seal used and the witnesses
suggest that it was on this occasion: *Regesta*, iii, no. 679, iv, plate x. Davis and Cronne, ibid.,
iv, plates i–ii, viewed the seal as a forgery based on Stephen's first seal, but it has been established that the seal was genuine and should be seen as Stephen's second seal: *Cart. Worcester*,
lxvii–lxviii; Heslop, "Seals," 303 (no. 332). Granted this, it would seem logical to see this as
the seal of Stephen's second chancellor, Philip of Harcourt, who succeeded Roger le Poer
(who was arrested in June 1139: WM, *HN*, 48–9), and served until he was nominated as
bishop of Salisbury in Mar. 1140, when he was succeeded in his turn by Robert de Gant:
Regesta, iii, p. x; *Fasti* 4: *Salisbury*, 2.

this point that it was arranged that William d'Aubigny should be married to Adeliza of Louvain.[16]

If there was any element of strategic thinking in letting the empress travel to Bristol, if there was any sense that the threat could be contained more easily thereby, then it was misplaced. Her arrival was followed by several major defections. Some of these individuals may have been, or at least claimed themselves to have been, sleeping partners in the enterprise, awaiting the opportunity to declare their support. Others may have joined her less willingly. The result was the same. The empress and her party gained a power base in the west country which Stephen and his party were not strong enough to attack head on. Rather their ambition had to be to stop the rot, to set up some kind of quarantine zone. Here the castles gained by the crown consequent on the arrest of the bishops proved invaluable. This might have been the intention behind their seizure.

The key defection to the empress was that of Miles of Gloucester. It was important in terms of his personality and energy, and because of the resources that he controlled. It was also important symbolically, for this was a major defection: he was someone whom Stephen had worked hard to win over, had rewarded well, and who had become closely identified with his kingship. The change of allegiance caused complications for him and had to be carefully prepared. There was his relationship to Robert of Gloucester, which was a little too close for comfort, for while Robert claimed that Gloucester "was the chief place of his earldom,"[17] it was in fact the power base of Miles; and when the Gloucester monk writes of Robert as "earl of Bristol" rather than as "earl of Gloucester," as he is inclined to do,[18] we can be confident that he is following local usage. An accommodation was worked out before the empress landed. Elias Giffard, on behalf of Miles, and Humphrey Fitz Odo, on behalf of the empress, acted as intermediaries. It was agreed that Miles's existing offices, notably his sheriffdom and castellanship, would be protected, along with his lands. In addition he was to be given "the castle of St Briavels and the whole Forest of Dean," with all the royal demesne lands between the Severn and the Wye, including Rodley, Awre, and Dymock, and additionally the royal

---

[16] Torigni, 137, says that William d'Aubigny was married to the queen at this point and that it was he who had invited the empress to come to England. His statement has been generally accepted but there are good grounds to question it. (i) The more strictly contemporary chronicles do not mention William d'Aubigny, only the queen: WM, *HN*, 60–1; JW, iii. 268–9 (*GS*, 86–91, and HH, 722–3, do not name names). (ii) William's involvement would have raised suspicions as to his loyalty, but there is no indication of this; rather his stock was on the rise. These points were noted by Wertheimer, "Adeliza of Louvain," 112–13. (iii) *Regesta*, iii, no. 679, as is argued in the previous note, is unusually specific as to politics and to place. It does not name William as an earl, and *Waltham*, 78–9, states that he was not an earl at the time of his marriage (see further Round, *Geoffrey*, 324). An alternative view would see the couple as married late in 1139. On them see further Thompson, "Queen Adeliza and the Lotharingian Connection."

[17] WM, *HN*, 62–3: "eadem ciuitas caput est sui comitatus."

[18] JW, iii. 252–3, 298–9, 300–1.

manor of Cheltenham. All this was the subject of a formal agreement, made at Domfront before Elias Giffard and Humphrey Fitz Odo, secured by the empress and the count of Anjou, with the earl of Gloucester acting as a pledge that they would perform their undertakings. The *conventio* was very likely made in the summer of 1139. It was activated when the empress landed in the autumn. She now speaks viva voce:

> I wish you to know that when I came to England after the death of king Henry my father, Miles of Gloucester just as soon as he could came to me at Bristol and received me as lady and as she who was acknowledged to be the rightful heir of the kingdom of England; and he brought me with him to Gloucester and there he did me liege homage against all men.[19]

In return for this homage Miles was granted the Forest of Dean with its castle and the other lands from the royal demesne that had been promised to him.[20] The empress was not always so accommodating. At Bristol, she "received homage from all sides and dispensed the laws of the English kingdom as she pleased." At Gloucester, "tortures worthy of Decius and Nero, and deaths of various kinds were imposed on those unwilling to submit to her, and firm in their allegiance to the king."[21] The empress's personality, rather than just her theoretical claim, was now a factor in English politics.

The other major defection to the empress's cause was that of Brian Fitz Count, the lord of Wallingford.[22] The *Gesta Stephani* mentions him even before Miles of Gloucester, and says that he was "delighted" to hear that the empress had arrived. Brian showed a devotion to the empress's cause that shines through to the present day. It had been he and Robert of Gloucester who had escorted her to Le Mans in 1127 for her betrothal to Geoffrey of Anjou.[23] He had had little choice but to throw in his lot with

---

[19] *Regesta*, iii, no. 391.

[20] It had been known that the empress had granted to Miles of Gloucester St Briavels castle and the Forest of Dean, in 1139; and that Henry II in 1155 had granted Miles's son, Roger, then earl of Hereford, various royal demesne manors in Gloucestershire: *Regesta*, iii, no. 391; *Rotuli Chartarum*, 53; Walker, "Honours of the Earls of Hereford," 180–2. The discovery by Nicholas Vincent of a much fuller text of the empress's charter for Miles of Gloucester, in BL, Sloane MS 1301, fo. 422r–v, supplies the missing link. And a good deal more. It proves that the defection of Miles of Gloucester was carefully negotiated in advance of the empress's landing; it gives the names of those "who carried messages between us"; it makes it likely that other key defections were similarly negotiated; and, if taken at face value, it suggests that even in 1139 these key supporters were asking that the empress's husband, Geoffrey, count of Anjou, associated himself with her promises. I am most grateful to Nicholas Vincent for sending me a text of this charter and discussing it with me.

[21] Gloucester chronicle, in JW, iii. 270–3.

[22] *GS*, 90–3; JW, iii. 272–3; WM, *HN*, 60–1; Torigni, 137; JH, 302.

[23] WM, *HN*, 10–11.

Stephen in 1136. And as Stephen in his early years came to make Oxford almost his second capital, so the royal court moved of necessity back and forth from London up the Thames valley, where Wallingford was a key centre. When he declared for the empress immediately on her landing he was offering himself as a target. Stephen moved immediately to Wallingford and placed the castle under siege.

> He came to Wallingford with an innumerable host, and was minded to shut them in persistently with a ring of besiegers that could not be broken, when he was deterred by better advice from his barons and gave up his intention for the time being. For they said (what was the truth) that the castle was most securely fortified with impregnable walls, that supplies had been put into it in very great abundance, . . . that the garrison consisted of a very strong force of invincible warriors, and that he could not linger there any longer without the greatest injury to himself and his men.[24]

The positive threat seems overstated but a long siege was required and it was taking the king away from the main theatre of war. So he set up two siege-castles and moved westwards to attack Trowbridge the *caput* of Humphrey de Bohun. At very much the same time, for the same chronicle injects some pace into the story here, Miles of Gloucester, "a man of the greatest spirit and active and very ready for mighty enterprises, arrived at Wallingford by night with a superb force of soldiers, and by a bold and vigorous attack at length compelled the surrender of the troops that the king had left there."[25] The *Gesta Stephani* is at times a difficult source to use. The author paints in big, bold colours. He sometimes seems to say less in a long paragraph than William of Malmesbury conveys in a single phrase. But sometimes, as here, he has the heart of the matter. Miles of Gloucester was "active." He was a dynamic force.

As a centre for activity Gloucester was well placed. It stood in the midst of the Vale of Gloucester, a land which "bears crops in abundance and is fertile in fruit," its wines almost as sweet tasting as those of France.[26] It could exercise its historic role as a centre of communications and control. Depending on which side you supported, the communications were not always peaceful, the control often far from beneficent. There was nothing of the pastoral in the language used by the king's supporters: Gloucester was "the source of all evil";[27] it had become "a shit-house."[28] John of Worcester describes graphically the impact of the empress's arrival at Gloucester on his own monastery and on the town. "There were frequent reports that Worcester would soon be devastated by its enemies, despoiled

---

[24] *GS*, 90–3.
[25] *GS*, 92–3.
[26] WM, *GP*, i. 444–5.
[27] JW, iii. 274–5, translating "e uagina malitie."
[28] *GS*, 100–1: the king's enemies "quasi in sentinam conuenerant."

of its goods, and consumed by fire." The townsmen sought refuge within the monastic precinct.

> Then could be seen all the goods of the citizens carried into the cathedral. Oh what miseries were beheld! Lo, the house of God into which offerings should be brought, and where the sacrifice of praise should have been offered, and the most solemn vows made, seems now but a furniture warehouse. Behold the principal monastic house of the diocese has become a hostel and a debating chamber for the citizens. There is scarcely any room left for the servants of God in an inn so filled to abundance with chests and sacks.[29]

The attack that they had long feared came on 7 November, "the first day of winter."[30] For all the talk of the army's strength this was a raiding party, designed to intimidate, to gather booty, to show the citizens they could hope for no protection from the king. Where the protection came from, belatedly, was from Waleran of Meulan, who had recently been granted the earldom of Worcester. He "grieved when he saw the firing of the city, and felt as if the damage had been done to himself." The king appeared only a few days later, and when he saw what had happened he too "was much grieved."[31]

Sympathy was not much help. No more was it for the royal garrison at Hereford. "The city of Hereford was gained without difficulty: a few knights, resolutely shutting themselves up in the castle, were besieged from outside. The king approached on the chance of being able to devise some help for them in their difficulties, but was disappointed of his wish, and departed ignominiously."[32] He came as far as Leominster or Little Hereford, 12 miles from Hereford. "There, taking counsel, some of the inhabitants swore allegiance to the king, while others refused, saying to the king: 'The king may, if he wishes, trust in the truth of our words, if not in our oath.' " A truce was made between them, and the king went back to Worcester. There also he had to listen to some home truths. The newly elected bishop of Bangor, Maurice, arrived and the king confirmed his appointment. Initially, however, Maurice refused to perform homage to the king, and it took some persuasion by the bishops of Hereford and Chichester before he did so.[33] When townsmen and bishops prevaricate in this way the outlook for royal authority can only appear precarious in the extreme. This after all was the coalition that had brought Stephen to power. He should have been able to bank on their support. It is not difficult, however, to see what justification townsmen on the Welsh

---

[29] JW, iii. 272–3.
[30] This is the date given by Bede: *Oxford Companion to the Year*, 545–6.
[31] JW, iii. 274–7.
[32] WM, *HN*, 64–5.
[33] JW, iii. 278–9; *Fasti* 9: *Welsh Cathedrals*, 2.

Marches and a recently consecrated Welsh bishop could have provided for their insubordination. The king had broken his part of the compact. He had offered to them, as to all, his firm peace and protection.[34] He had not delivered.

ROGER OF SALISBURY AND ROBERT FITZ HUBERT

In the last days of the year 1139 Roger of Salisbury lay close to death. With his chaplains around him, he considered his past life, and as Christians should he vowed to make a good end. He knew, for he was an experienced confessor as well as a magnate of enormous power, that before he came to the final judgement seat he should make restitution to those whom he had wronged. He thought it best, for the habits of a lifetime died hard, to send precise written instruments to all those clerical corporations whom he discovered to be on his conscience. These were documents that it was well worth keeping.[35] The canons of St Frideswide's, Oxford, received charters restoring "whatever I have taken from them unjustly" and making other gifts: these included mead-owland, a mill, rights over three churches, and – perhaps most significant in monetary terms – control over their fair in Oxford and rights in the suburbs while the fair was being held.[36] Oxford was not in his diocese but still he wrote of this house in the most proprietary terms. In a short charter he returned to the abbey of Cirencester all the churches in which he had a life interest. We know from other sources that it was a long list, of churches previously in the hands of Regenbald the priest, names redolent of the history of England: Frome in Somerset, Avebury in Wiltshire, and Shrivenham, Cookham, and Bray, all in Berkshire. The vicar of Bray, as of the other churches, would be allowed only a life tenancy, and it would revert thereafter to the canons.[37] To the chapter of his own diocese, "in my free power" and struggling just a little with the language of collegiality, he returned all the prebends which he had in his hands. He specified the prebend of Cannings, the manor in which the castle of Devizes was situated, and the church of Lavington, which he had only recently received from the king.[38] Anything he wanted he could obtain, had been the assessment of William of Malmesbury, and he was none too scrupulous about the methods that he used.[39] In the last and most revealing of this series of charters he seems to confess as much:

---

[34] See, e.g., *Regesta*, iii, nos. 395–8, in favour of St Guthlac's Priory, Hereford. In no. 397 Roger of Salisbury is acting in a viceregal capacity. Not any more. Miles of Gloucester would ensure that the alms were paid. Not any more.

[35] Kealey, *Roger*, nos. 26–31, 262–9, gives texts; listed also in *EEA* 18: *Salisbury 1078–1217*, nos. 7, 9–11, 17, 21.

[36] Kealey, *Roger*, nos. 29 ("quicquid eisdem iniuste abstuleram"), 30–1.

[37] Ibid., no. 27, with detail in the royal confirmation, *Regesta*, iii, no. 189.

[38] Kealey, *Roger*, no. 26: "in libera potestate mea."

[39] WM, *HN*, 66–7.

Roger, bishop of Salisbury, to all the faithful men of Holy Church greeting. You should know that through ambition and secular power I have unjustly and without judgement deprived the monks of the diocese of Worcester of their church of Wolverhampton which Bishop Sampson gave them following the gift of King Henry. Moreover, I recognise that because of this great sin and on account of my misdeeds, the hand of the Lord has touched me and rightly afflicted me. Therefore, fleeing to the mercy of Mary, the most pious mother of God, I ask pardon for my great crime and I beg the brothers of Worcester out of respect for the divine mercy to forgive this injury which I have done against them and to pardon me in the presence of God at whose tribunal I now stand.[40]

This letter carried a general address but most of this group of charters were addressed first to Henry of Winchester, the papal legate, and to Theobald, archbishop of Canterbury. It is almost a last-gasp defiance, carefully drafted, asserting that these were matters for the Church.

This was not the view of the king and the barons, and when they had news of Roger's death, which occurred on 11 December, they hastened to Salisbury.[41] Here Stephen "celebrated Christmas and wore his crown as was the royal custom,"[42] and here he asserted the full range of his regalian rights. He had promised that during such a vacancy the resources of the bishopric should not be confiscated by the crown but given into the hands of "clerks and pious men" of the Church. Stephen on his arrival was surrounded by such, but he drove a hard bargain with them. The bargaining chips were in plain view for, piled up on the high altar of the cathedral, there was an enormous treasure.[43] It was intended, so the canons protested, as the building fund for the new cathedral church. Its only protection was a shared piety, and – in the last resort – fear of the wrath of the saints whose relics lay in the church. One of the miracles of St Edmund at Bury was to freeze in their tracks robbers who entered the church overnight. They were caught the next morning and promptly hanged. Their fate might be represented as a graphic symbol of the power of a government whose standards had been set by Roger himself.[44] Stephen's officers gathered up the treasure without the slightest qualms. This was money, they said, that Roger had gained as a royal agent. He had

[40] Kealey, *Roger*, no. 28, trans. 203, and for discussion of its authenticity *EEA* 18, no. 21.
[41] WM, *HN*, 64–5, for the date; JW, iii. 278–9, says that the court had previously been at Oxford. Roger's death is also noted in HH, 722–3; *GS*, 96–9; OV, vi. 533–4; JH, 302; Tewkesbury Annals, *Ann. Mon.*, i. 46 (which say that he died in prison); Winchester Annals, ibid., ii. 52.
[42] JW, iii. 278–9: "Dominicam Natiuitatem celebraturus et pro more regio coronam dignitatis portaturus."
[43] WM, *HN*, 68–9; *GS*, 96–7: "infinitam nummorum quantitatem," estimated by the Gloucester chronicler at 40,000 marks (JW, iii. 258–9), along with silver and gold plate.
[44] New York, Pierpont Morgan Library, M 736, made *c.*1130: *Romanesque*, 95 (no. 20).

admitted as much, they went on, and had surrendered it to the king. The canons, faced with this pressure, with the arguments of the council at Winchester now introduced into their cloister, made the best deal that they could. They got a royal confirmation of their possessions, including the restorations made by Roger, on which the ink was hardly yet dry.[45] It was cast as a royal benefaction, given "in charity and with good-will," but the price of this confirmation alone was £2,000. The nearest the canons got to an apology was the acknowledgement that the king was overriding his earlier promises, because of the necessity of the times. "If peace should return," he would make restitution.[46] In this almost casual phrase there was a big admission. The country was at war.

The royal court went next to Reading, for the anniversary of the burial of Henry I.[47] The monks were always hospitable, and after the major disjuncture of the death of Roger of Salisbury the reporting of this continuity could only be seen as advantageous to the regime. There may have been an additional reason for this visit, for it is about this time that the regular series of grants made by Queen Adeliza in memory of her late husband starts to make mention of lights burning at Henry I's tomb.[48] It could be that the fine effigy of the king, which Richard II would later insist be kept in better repair,[49] was now on view for the first time. And at the same time also Adeliza wrote to her dear friend Alexander of Lincoln telling him of how she had divided the manor of Stanton Harcourt, giving shares not just to Reading Abbey but to the Templars, to her cousin Milicent, the wife of Robert Marmion, and to William of Harfleur.[50] This division will have made administration difficult for the monks, but when they were tempted to farm out their rights they received a peremptory writ from the queen forbidding them from doing so.[51] It transpired that this was another church over which Roger of Salisbury had laid his hand. Among the business done while the royal court was at Reading was the appointment of new abbots for Malmesbury and Abbotsbury.[52] The

---

[45] *Regesta*, iii, nos. 787–8, two important charters, both of which survive as originals (ibid., iv, plates xlviii–xlix): the latter is the more detailed, but there is no reason to suspect it as a "forgery" (as do the editors) for it closely follows Roger of Salisbury's own grant, whose authenticity is supported by the other documents he issued shortly before his death. Amongst the grants was a rare exemption from Danegeld. The two charters for Salisbury are clearly of a pattern with ibid., iii, no. 189, for Cirencester, also confirming a deathbed request of Bishop Roger.

[46] JW, iii. 278–9: "si pacem optinuerit."

[47] Ibid. iii. 278–81.

[48] *Reading Abbey Cartularies*, i. 404–5 (no. 535): "ad continua luminaria ante . . . corpus domini mei nobilissimi regis Henrici"; confirmed by her husband, William d'Aubigny, as earl of Lincoln, ibid. i. 302–3 (no. 371).

[49] Ibid. i. 107–8 (no. 116).

[50] Ibid. i. 405–6 (no. 536).

[51] Ibid. i. 407 (no. 558), printing BL Add. Ch. 19574, which has a fine impression of Queen Adeliza's seal.

[52] WM, *HN*, 70–1; JW, iii. 278–81; *GS*, 98–9.

building of a castle had been but the most visible aspect of the way Roger had squeezed all life out of the monastery of Malmesbury, removing its abbot and reducing an independent house to the status of a cathedral priory. The house's librarian, William, had watched all this with despair and ultimately with resignation. He recorded the restoration of the abbacy in almost triumphalist terms. The new abbot, he said, had removed the house from slavery.[53]

Soon after the death of Roger of Salisbury, his nephew Nigel, bishop of Ely, was driven from his see and disgraced. Henry of Huntingdon, a close neighbour of Bishop Nigel, said simply that the king's hatred of Roger was now transferred to his kin.[54] This, though undoubtedly true, was only a part of the story. It must not be forgotten, for no one at the time had forgotten, how Nigel had behaved at the time of "the arrest of the bishops" the preceding summer. He had turned tail, had taken over Devizes, and his behaviour must have given credence to claims that "the bishops" were disloyal. When Stephen and his forces approached the Isle of Ely in January 1140 Nigel would inevitably behave in exactly the same way and inevitably the same conclusion was drawn by those on the king's side. And so they said: that he was anxious to avenge the wrongs the king had done to his uncle, "and also help King Henry's children, as far as he could, to obtain the kingdom more quickly";[55] that he had hired knights and had molested his neighbours, in themselves routine enough claims; that he had fortified a castle at Ely, and a further one at Aldreth on the approach to the Isle, and formed a confederation with the local men to defend these castles and the whole area against the king.[56] This information comes from the monks of Ely themselves, anxious to stress that the bishop's actions were none of their doing. The author of the *Gesta Stephani* gives a vivid picture of how the king's army slowly and patiently, aided by those who had local knowledge of the causeways, made its way into the fens, took the castle of Aldreth and seized all the resources of the diocese. They found "booty of great value and treasures in extraordinary quantity." The bishop was driven out, escaping by night with just three companions, and making his way to Gloucester.[57] The royalists claimed a great victory but it was nothing of the kind.[58]

Nigel would be back. He was too sharp and inventive not to be. But he would never enjoy under Stephen the role for which he had been trained. He was the obvious successor to his uncle; he wanted nothing more than to be an insider, presiding over the exchequer board, just as his uncle

---

[53] WM, *HN*, xxvi–xxviii, 70–1; WM, *GR*, i. 4–5; Farmer, "William of Malmesbury's Commentary on Lamentations."

[54] HH, 722–5.

[55] *GS*, 98–9.

[56] *Liber Eliensis*, 314–15, trans. Fairweather, 388–90.

[57] *GS*, 98–101; *Liber Eliensis*, 314–15; JW, iii. 280–1; HH, 722–5.

[58] *GS*, 100–1: "mire et gloriose de aduersariis uictoria"; JW, iii. 280–1: "uane glorie."

had done; his behaviour was that of a man who sees his destiny snatched from him.[59] He had served as treasurer; he had brought the best practice of the exchequer into his diocese, making a careful survey immediately on his appointment;[60] he was establishing himself as a central figure in Stephen's administration.[61] Now for a decade and more the disciplines of the exchequer would be absent. There were even rumours that the coinage was being deliberately devalued, on the orders of the king himself, since his treasure was now exhausted.[62] And to complete the disjuncture of the dead of winter 1139–40 there came news – long expected – of the death of Archbishop Thurstan of York. He was a bishop like no other.[63] Thurstan and the baronage of Yorkshire had been partners in a common enterprise, their security in this world and their salvation in the next, and to all aspects of his role he had shown a complete commitment. He took the cowl at Pontefract, the one Cluniac house in his diocese, on 25 January 1140, and almost a fortnight later, on 6 February, he died.[64] The partnership was dissolved. "After his death, forthwith sprang up the insolence and roving licence of unrestrained disputes, shameless contempt of the clergy, irreverence of the laity towards ecclesiastical laws and persons; the unity of the kingdom was destroyed, because each man's will was his law."[65]

The lordship exercised in England, both by those who could claim they were engaged in campaigning and those who were not, now starts to be described in the sources in the most lurid of terms. The tyranny of those engaged in castle warfare, the sufferings of the poor, and the violence

[59] JW, iii. 280–1, comments that with the death of Roger of Salisbury, "it was as though he had lost his right hand."

[60] Hollister, *Anglo-Norman World*, 218–19; *English Lawsuits*, i, no. 287, 241–2.

[61] This is the clear evidence of the charters, which show him in attendance on the king at the time of his coronation, in 1136/early 1137 at Durham, York, Westminster, Oxford, Woodstock, Hurstbourne (Hants.), Eye, Bury St Edmunds, and Fareham, as then remaining in England and acting for the king while he was in Normandy, less frequently while the king was in the north and the west country in 1138, but thereafter at Westminster, London, and Oxford (both early in 1139 and at the time of "the arrest"), and acting and being addressed in an "executive" capacity: *Regesta*, iii, nos. 46, 99, 119, 121, 204, 271, 278, 284, 287–8, 340, 389, 468, 616, 638, 667, 671, 673, 717, 819, 832, 842, 878–81, 891, 936, 944–5, 949, 975–7, 989–90. And it makes sense. It does not make sense, in my view, to see the bishop as the prime mover in a plot "to kill all the Normans on a fixed day and hand over the government of the kingdom to the Scots," word of which reached Orderic Vitalis in Normandy and of which there is a full and circumstantial account in *Liber Eliensis*: for the sources OV, vi. 494–5; *Liber Eliensis*, 286–7, 294–9; Diceto, i. 253. The monks, who were no friends to the bishop, said this happened while he was away, on the king's business: *Liber Eliensis*, 294, "causis regni urgentibus, que episcopum assidue inquietum reddebant, diu extra monasterium morari inpellebant." Orderic, though sympathetic to the king in the matter of "the arrest of the bishops," says that Nigel put the rising down: OV, vi. 494–5, 530–5. The evaluation in Kealey, *Roger*, 167–8, is very fair.

[62] WM, *HN*, 74–5.

[63] In the judgement of John of Hexham: JH, 302–5 ("rarus in his diebus").

[64] JH, 305; JW, iii. 280–3, has 21 Jan. and 5 Feb.

[65] JH, 305, and for comment, Dalton, *Yorkshire*, 151–2.

offered to them and to the clerical order, feature in all the accounts. The description in the *Anglo-Saxon Chronicle* is much the best known of these. "Every powerful man built himself a castle, and these they held against [the king], and they filled the country full of castles. They oppressed the wretched people of the country severely with castle-building. When the castles were built, they filled them with devils and wicked men."[66] Now this passage, at least as it has come down to us, was written in the 1150s, after the civil war had concluded. William of Malmesbury, however, was writing much closer to the event, and he says much the same thing:

> That whole year [1140] was troubled by the brutalities of war. There were many castles all over England, each defending its own district or, to be more truthful, plundering it. The knights from the castles carried off both herds and flocks, sparing neither churches nor graveyards. After plundering the dwellings of the wretched countrymen to their very foundations, they bound the owners and imprisoned them, and did not let them go until they had spent for their ransom all they possessed, or could in any way obtain. Many breathed forth their dear lives during the very tortures by which they were being forced to ransom themselves, lamenting their sufferings to God, which was all they could do.[67]

This is a characteristic passage of William's, even down to the throwaway remark at the end. All were seen as implicated in this local tyranny. The worst offenders, however, and those for whom the worst opprobrium of contemporary writers was reserved, were the mercenary troops who now flocked to England from abroad. William had one particular mercenary in mind, a man exemplary for his cruelty and lack of faith. He had seen him in action.[68]

The mercenary was Robert Fitz Hubert. He was a Fleming, of good family, and reportedly a relation of William of Ypres.[69] If so, it is likely that he first came to England in William's entourage. Increasingly, however, and this was seen as typical of the breed, he fought for himself. He first, on 7 October 1139, attacked the castle at Malmesbury.[70] This was one of the castles of Roger of Salisbury and after his arrest a royal garrison had been installed there. Robert appeared and gained possession of the castle by "a cunning ploy." The royal garrison fled for sanctuary to the monastery. The king then appeared in person and laid the castle under siege. This placed Robert in some difficulty. The castle, though secure, was not designed for a long siege. He had no lord to whom he could appeal for help. It was his relation William of Ypres who acted as a go-between, securing him his liberty in return for the surrender of the castle. A royal garrison was then

[66] *ASC*, s.a. 1137.
[67] WM, *HN*, 70–3.
[68] WM, *HN*, 76–7: "hisce auribus audiui . . . audiui inquam eum respondisse."
[69] JW, iii. 286–7.
[70] WM, *HN*, 62–3, part of the Ce text.

placed in the castle once again, with the proviso that when peace returned it would be destoyed.[71] It was a small episode, but at Malmesbury the story would grow in the telling. How in one monastery eighty monks had perished inside their church: this perhaps to be explained by Robert's wish to smoke out the royal garrison. And much more. Some at first hand. "He used to smear prisoners with honey, and expose them naked in the open air in the full blaze of the sun, stirring up flies and similar insects to sting them."[72] He would come to a suitably sticky end.

There is now a break in the career of Robert Fitz Hubert until Passiontide, 26 March 1140, when – again by a cunning plot – he took the castle of Devizes.[73] Devizes was another of the castles of Roger of Salisbury and a much more formidable proposition. It also, after the bishop's fall, had been placed under the control of a royal garrison. These troops were surprised by Robert Fitz Hubert and his men, and once they gained the inner courtyard the design of the castle dictated that the defenders could only take refuge in one of the towers, which they were forced to surrender after just a few days. Devizes was a great prize and its new commander quickly discovered that he had powerful friends. He was first approached, with offers of assistance, by troops of Robert of Gloucester under the command of one of his sons, but they were treated with disdain and driven off. Robert Fitz Hubert seems then to have sought help from – or perhaps he was sought out by – John Fitz Gilbert the Marshal, the castellan of Marlborough. John was most likely at this time viewed as an Angevin supporter, though not an active one. Just how he captured Robert Fitz Hubert is not certain; possibly by giving him a safe conduct to Marlborough, then closing the gates behind him and putting him "in a narrow dungeon to suffer hunger and tortures."[74] The earl of Gloucester again became involved and made an agreement with the marshal, promising him a cash sum of 500 marks and appropriate hostages in return for the opportunity to persuade Robert Fitz Hubert to surrender the castle. These efforts failed.

It is a complex story and our three good authorities each have their own version of it.[75] On its outcome, however, all are agreed. Robert was produced in front of the castle walls and when the garrison refused to surrender he was hanged like a common thief and his body left swinging in the wind. "Those who brought about his death must be given the praise they deserve," said William of Malmesbury, "for ridding the country of such a plague and so justly punishing an enemy in their midst." Just what

---

[71] On these events see, *GS*, 92–5; JW, iii. 284–7; WM, *HN*, 62–3.

[72] WM, *HN*, 76–7.

[73] WM, *HN*, 74–5, gives the date. JW, iii. 286–7, says that the taking of Devizes followed "non multo post" events in Malmesbury, but *GS*, 94–105, has a good interval between the two events, in which *inter alia* Roger of Salisbury died and the king attacked the Isle of Ely. Robert Fitz Hubert had in the meantime been with Robert of Gloucester.

[74] *GS*, 106–7.

[75] WM, *HN*, 74–7; JW, iii. 284–91; *GS*, 104–9.

was his offence? His father in his own country may have been a man of standing but he himself was not a gentleman. He was "a man of great cruelty and unequalled in wickedness and crime."[76] He fought for himself; he could not claim in mitigation of his behaviour that he had acted in the support of a lord. More than this – and perhaps this was his real offence – he started to develop ideas above his station.

> Such was the cunning intention of this turncoat, not to keep the earl's side, nor to proclaim himself a supporter of the king, but to bring into the castle a large body of his own people and either to ensnare by craft or seize by force all the surrounding country.[77]

The chroniclers exaggerate Robert's ambition.[78] He wanted to establish his own lordship. He might have hoped for something from the king, but in the poorer and perhaps more puritanical court of the empress he stood little chance of promotion. He had his own code of values and he died – so at least his enemies would have us believe – because he had a sworn agreement with his own followers that under no circumstances would they surrender the castle. On Robert's death, however, they too turned out to have their price, for "on receiving very large sums of money from the king" they surrendered to him. The royal agent was Hervey Brito, "a man of distinction and soldierly qualities and the king's son-in-law."[79] Hervey, the vicomte of Léon in Brittany, was generously treated by Stephen at this time; with his marriage, it is presumed to one of Stephen's illegitimate children, there came the grant of the honour of Eye, and with the castellanship of Devizes there came for a time the earldom of Wiltshire.[80] There seemed to be new earls everywhere.

THE EARLDOMS

Stephen was seen as increasingly profligate in the granting of land and of office. "There were many, impelled to wrong-doing by high birth or lofty spirit, or rather the recklessness of youth, who did not hesitate to ask the king for estates or castles or in fact anything that had once taken their fancy." One aspect of this general profligacy was the granting of earldoms: "he established many as earls who had not been earls before, with endowments of landed estates and revenues that had belonged directly to the king."[81] This was William of Malmesbury, writing of 1138 but in a

---

[76] *GS*, 92–3.

[77] *GS*, 106–7.

[78] WM, *HN*, 76–7, says that holding Devizes would allow him to control the whole territory (*totam regionem*) from Winchester to London.

[79] *GS*, 108–9.

[80] The main references may be taken from WM, *HN*, 54–5 and n. 129; for charters attested by Hervey as earl, *Regesta*, iii, nos. 16, 477.

[81] WM, *HN*, 40–1.

chapter that extended up to the end of 1140. In this period the number of earldoms perhaps doubled. It is difficult to be precise, not least because the same Latin word *comes* applied both to earls within England, who normally but not invariably took their title from a county, and to counts within northern France, who normally took their title from their place of lordship. They ranked equally. Thus Ranulf, earl of Chester, "the city of the legions," ranked alongside William, Earl Warenne, who took his name from a hamlet in Normandy;[82] whilst of the Beaumont twins, Waleran was count of Meulan on the Seine within the French Vexin and Robert was earl of Leicester in the English midlands. Their father, Robert de Beaumont, made earl of Leicester, and Robert, the king's son, made earl of Gloucester, served successively as Henry I's chief counsellors and were the only new earls he created in a reign of thirty-five years. In 1138–40, by contrast, Stephen advanced seven men to this rank and granted comital rights to perhaps seven others.[83] The new creations were all within England. It is clearly no coincidence that these grants by Stephen were made in the years when his authority first came under threat and as the circumstances and the attitudes of civil war took root in people's minds. But there is no agreement as to how the grants are best explained.

The main discussion has been about what rights were given by the grants of earldoms.[84] In the view of Sir Frank Stenton, "by the beginning of Stephen's reign an earldom gave to its holder little more than a title and the precedence which it implied."[85] That in itself was no small thing. Individuals might date their charters by comital years, just as kings did by regnal years;[86] their seals would reflect the dignity;[87] and they would take

---

[82] WM, *GP*, i. 466–7; *EYC* 8: *Warenne*, 1.

[83] Davis, *Stephen*, 125–41: (new creations) nos. 8 (Northampton: Simon of Senlis), 11 (Nottingham: Robert de Ferrers), 12 (Pembroke: Gilbert Fitz Gilbert de Clare), 13 (Hertford: Gilbert Fitz Richard de Clare), 16 (Lincoln: William d'Aubigny), 19 (Essex: Geoffrey de Mandeville), 25 (Norfolk: Hugh Bigod); (existing *comites*) nos. 10 (York: William of Aumale), 14 (Worcester: Waleran of Meulan), 15 (Northumberland: Henry of Scots), 17 (Cambridge: William de Roumare), 20 (Cornwall: Alan of Brittany), 21 (Wiltshire: Hervey Brito), 22 (Hereford: Robert of Leicester).

[84] On Stephen's earldoms the main stages in the argument are represented by: Round, *Geoffrey*, 267–77; Stenton, *First Century*, 227–34; Davis, *Stephen*, 125–41; and, with full bibliography, White, *Restoration and Reform*, 57–67.

[85] Stenton, *First Century*, 233.

[86] Miles of Gloucester in 1141, "apud Bristodium positus iamque consulatus honorem adeptus": *Monasticon*, vi. 137; William de Roumare on 31 January 1142, "septimo anno Stephani regis et tercio consulatus mei": *EYC* 10: *Trussebut*, 114–15 (no. 66); Alan of Brittany in 1140, where Sir Charles Clay suggested a reading such as "*anno primo* conquisitionis mee": *EYC* 4: *Richmond* 1, 15–16 (no. 12); and Henry, earl of Northumberland, in 1141, refers to "ea die qua comitatus de Norhimberland mihi datus fuit": *Charters of David I*, 103 (no. 103).

[87] Seal of Waleran of Meulan, as below. Henry, son of the king of Scots, had a seal made to reflect his new title as earl of Northumberland. SIGILLVM HENRICI COMITIS NORHVMBERLANDIE FILII REGIS SCOCIE: *Charters of David I*, 31.

pleasure in the promotion of members of their family.[88] Yet when in 1140 Geoffrey de Mandeville was made earl of Essex, it was stated that he was to hold in the same way "as other earls of my land best and most freely and most honourably hold the counties of which they are earls, with all the dignities and liberties and customs which other of my earls most honourably and most freely hold."[89] He was commenting on a period in which he had observed, just as William of Malmesbury had observed, that many of his peers had been granted not just a title but some of the rights of the crown in their counties. There was money in this. And, according to Ralph Davis, there was policy also, that of moving the balance of authority away from the sheriffs and towards the earls, whom he saw as "an essential necessary part of government in a kingdom divided by war."[90] In an extreme version of this case, asserted rather than argued, it was claimed that Roger's fall, and the devolution of authority from the centre to the localities, was a part of the programme of Stephen's government, agreed with the great magnates at the beginning of the reign and just awaiting a convenient opportunity for its realization.[91]

The origins of the definition of the earl come from the war-band, the *comitatus*; the earls are the king's companions-in-arms. In times of peace they would act as royal emissaries. In time of civil disturbance, they would accompany the king and give him counsel. In time of war, they would fight. Administrative trainees later in the century would be told, succinctly, that new earls were created "in consideration of their services or of their sterling character."[92] Some of Stephen's grants were explicitly related to military service. William, already count of Aumale, and Robert de Ferrers were made earls following the battle of the Standard.[93] Other grants were made to the king's close companions. William d'Aubigny *pincera*, who had additional seniority as the husband of a queen, and Simon of Senlis certainly fell into this category. There were grants of earldoms, largely off the radar of the chronicles, to Gilbert Fitz Gilbert de Clare and Gilbert Fitz Richard de Clare, members of a family closely associated with the king. The grants were made over a short period of time, and that time was the beginning of the civil war in England. Several of the grants, particularly those of comital rights, are quite specific as to time and place and they can be used to show

---

[88] Waleran of Meulan, in *Eynsham*, i. 53 (no, 34): "soror mea comitissa de Penbroch per litteras suas requisiuit me."

[89] *Regesta*, iii, no. 273: "sicut alii comites mei de terra mea melius vel liberius vel honorificentius tenent comitatus suos unde comites sunt cum omnibus dignitatibus et libertatibus et consuetudinibus cum quibus alii comites mei prefati dignius vel liberius tenent."

[90] *Regesta*, iii, p. xxvi.

[91] Warren, *Governance*, 92–5; for a case-study arguing against this approach see Dalton, "William Earl of York."

[92] *Dialogus*, 65: "regum munificentia obsequii prestiti uel eximie probitatis intuitu comites sibi creat."

[93] JH, 295: "Rex eciam Angliae laetatus super his successibus suis Willelmum de Albamarla comitem in Eboraci sciria fecit et Rodbertum de Ferers comitem in Derbiscira."

how the political situation was viewed by the king and his companions at that time and place. The grants of earldoms are considered here as a part of the dynamic of Stephen's court. They may have been the actions of a weak and increasingly desperate man. But there was an element of strategy to them. It was a strategy for survival, for securing the loyalty of individuals and for strengthening key areas to contain the Angevin advance.

One of the first of those granted an English county by Stephen, and one of those most full of his new dignity, was – like William of Aumale – already a count. This was Waleran of Meulan, who was granted the earldom of Worcester. In charters and in most chronicles he continues to appear as count of Meulan, but John of Worcester notes his activity as the local earl, and most graphically the earl changed his seal. In place of a seal with the legend SIGILLUM GUALERANNI COMITIS MELLENTI there was now a double-sided seal bearing both this legend and on the counter-seal the legend SIGILLUM GUALERANNI COMITIS WIGORNIE (see plate 17). The second seal was in all likelihood made in the summer of 1139. This is a likely time also for the grant of the earldom.[94] To use the categories of the 1990s, Waleran was to be a "working peer" not a figurehead in his capacity as earl of Worcester. And in the circumstances of the 1140s he would need and he expected to be given the resources to support the dignity and his exercise of his rights. These were royal rights. He was most emphatic about this, as the charters which he issued as earl make clear. In one of these he conceded to Worcester Priory exemption from forest pleas in the manor of Tibberton and then continued: "I concede and I pardon to the prior and the monks the king's geld which I am entitled to and all customs and services and forest rights which were once the king's and are now mine in that township."[95] He needed to spell them out because in the 1140s he had to exercise his rights at second hand. It means his voice comes across very strongly. It is not lacking in confidence.

Robert, earl of Leicester, Waleran's twin brother, was a more cautious character. A little later than his brother became earl of Worcester he was invited to take similar responsibility for the county and the city of Hereford, which the king had lost soon after the empress landed.[96] The invitation can be tied to a place and time with some confidence for the charter recording it survives.[97] The place is Newtown, eight miles from Hereford, on the road from Worcester. The time, almost certainly, is during Lent 1140, when the royal court was recorded at this place. The royal forces must have come across country from Ely, and Newtown may have been the point at which they thought better of a direct attack on Hereford and turned back to Worcester. From there Waleran of Meulan,

---

[94] King, "Waleran of Meulan," 165–81, with the two seals reproduced as plates 3 and 4.
[95] Davis, "Some Documents of the Anarchy," 168–71: "que prius regis erant et postea mea"; *Eynsham*, i. 52–3 (no. 33): "que mei iuris est donatione regis Stephani."
[96] WM, *HN*, 64–5: "ciuitas Hereford sine difficultate recepta."
[97] *Regesta*, iii, no. 437; facsimile iv, plate xxv.

described simply as "the earl," sought to avenge the ignominies inflicted on "his citizens." On a raid south he attacked the two most impressive buildings associated with Robert of Gloucester's lordship, his "magnificent house" a mile distant from Gloucester and the town of Tewkesbury. Though he spared the monastery he caused much damage and when he returned to Worcester he told all who would listen "that he had hardly ever caused such a conflagration either in England or in Normandy."[98] The king had powerful support on this campaign, for the Newton charter for Robert of Leicester was attested by five further earls: his brother Waleran of Meulan; William, Earl Warenne; William (d'Aubigny *pincerna*), earl of Lincoln; William, count of Aumale and earl of York and Earl Simon, along with other magnates. The charter itself is carefully drafted.

> Know that I return and concede to Robert earl of Leicester and his heirs the borough of Hereford and the castle and the whole county of Herefordshire excepting the land of the bishopric and the land of the abbot of Reading and of the other churches and abbeys who hold of me in chief, and except the fee of Hugh of Mortimer, and the fee of Osbert son of Hugh, and the fee of William de Briouze, and the fee of Gotso de Dinan once that of Hugh de Lacy.[99]

The word "return" looks a little odd here, but it is later explained by the statement that the earl and his heirs should hold "as William Fitz Osbern once best and most freely held." William, "the bravest of the Normans, renowned for his generosity, ready wit, and outstanding integrity," had been the first earl of Hereford, given regal power in the southern March.[100] The earl had a form of hereditary claim through his wife.[101] The meaning of the grant is that Robert was allowed, if he could, to take over all royal rights in the county.[102] The exceptions to his control were those of the greater tenants-in-chief, the chief suitors of the county court (someone on the campaign trail must have had a list of these), who would have seen themselves disparaged if forced into subjection to the earl.[103] The grant was

---

[98] JW, iii. 282–5.

[99] *Regesta*, iii, no. 437.

[100] The eulogy is from Orderic Vitalis, recording William's death at the battle of Cassel in Feb. 1071: OV, ii. 280–5; on William also, Wightman, "The Palatinate Earldom of William Fitz Osbern."

[101] The claim "added a touch of legitimacy to the proceedings": Crouch, *Beaumont Twins*, 48–9, 87.

[102] This follows the argument of Paul Latimer that what was granted here, and in similar cases, was not an earldom but the *comitatus*, the royal rights in the county: Latimer, "Grants of 'Totus Comitatus'."

[103] This is the explanation of the reservation of named individuals, which is always found in grants of this kind, not that Robert of Leicester "was instructed to take over the land of the king's enemies, the few tenants-in-chief who were still loyal to Stephen being named," as in *Regesta*, iv, plate xxv. The same consideration underlay the terms agreed when the *comitatus* of Northumberland was granted to Henry, son of the king of Scots, in 1139: RH, 178.

similar to that made to Waleran of Meulan in the previous year, and it offered the potential for development in a similar way, but the territory was more distant and more hostile. There is no evidence of Robert's subsequently campaigning in Herefordshire and no evidence of his control of royal resources there.

There was campaigning in these months in the south-west of England. It may have involved the king, "taking every opportunity to defend his own,"[104] but his personal involvement can only have been brief. Robert of Gloucester and his supporters had significant power bases in the four south-western counties: Cornwall, Devon, Somerset, and Dorset.[105] Until now, Stephen's one reaction had been to campaign in north Somerset around Dunster, which was held by William de Mohun, but he had not managed to take the castle from him.[106] When Baldwin de Redvers had returned to England in the autumn of 1139, shortly before Robert of Gloucester and the empress, he had landed on the coast of Dorset. Stephen had attempted to invest him there but had no success, and so moved to Arundel, cursing those whose duty it was to watch the seaports.[107] Baldwin was able to establish effective control of his Dorset lands, centred on his *caput* at Carisbrooke,[108] though perhaps not immediately of the provincial capital at Exeter, where his earlier ambition had led to his exile. In Devon Stephen had a resolute supporter in Henry de Tracy, one of his own men, who was based at Barnstaple.[109] Cornwall, however, now came under the control of another of the illegitimate children of Henry I. This was Reginald of Dunstanville. As the story was told, William Fitz Richard, "who had control of the county of Cornwall under the king, treacherously broke the faith he had promised on oath to the king and admitting Reginald, a son of King Henry, into a castle that had always been in the king's power and jurisdiction and marrying his daughter to him, he thus delivered to him the whole county of Cornwall."[110] William of Malmesbury also saw this episode as one of the significant events of the early months of 1140 but he has a rather different take on it. He says that Robert, earl of Gloucester, "in view of the great difficulties of the time," made his brother Reginald earl of Cornwall.[111] The phrase indicates that it was not the place of an earl, however high his birth, to make another earl, but necessity made its own rules.

[104] WM, *HN*, 74–5.
[105] Green, "The Empress's Party in South-West England," 147–64.
[106] WM, *HN*, 64–5; *GS*, 80–3.
[107] *GS*, 84–5; JW, iii. 268–9.
[108] *Charters of the Redvers Family*, 7, 64–7 (no. 15).
[109] *GS*, 82–5. Henry de Tracy, "a man of war and well tried in all martial exercises," was a Mortain tenant in Normandy, and was granted by the king additionally the confiscated baronies of Castle Cary and Great Torrington: *GS*, 210–11; Loyd, *Origins*, 104–6; Vincent, "The Murderers of Thomas Becket," 239–41.
[110] *GS*, 100–3 (translating *comitatus* as "county" and not as "earldom").
[111] WM, *HN*, 72–5.

The attempt to regain control of Cornwall followed the template that was becoming established. The king asked one of his loyal supporters to shore up his power in a region that he seemed set to lose. This was Alan, earl of Richmond. Alan was called many things by the chroniclers of the day but none of them suggest that diplomacy was his strong point, and it may be significant that for a time at least when he was in Cornwall he was accompanied by a "minder" in the shape of Richard de Lucy. This is known from a charter that Alan issued, as earl of the county, in favour of the priory of St Michael's Mount.[112] Just as Robert of Leicester had referred his claims in Herefordshire back to the time of William Fitz Osbern so Alan of Richmond referred his back to his uncle Brian, a much more shadowy figure but "of whose inheritance I possess the land of Cornwall."[113] In encouraging such "hereditary" claims in particular cases of difficulty, the king was raising expectations universally, for the news of the grants travelled without the small print. Still, for a few weeks at least, Alan could reside at Bodmin and monks and chaplains could pray not just for his own ancestors but for "the stability of his lord king Stephen and his sons and his wife."[114] Others took their own view of the stability of the king's control of the south-west in this year. When Ralf the butler of Robert, earl of Leicester, founded Alcester Abbey in Warwickshire in 1140, he prayed for a very wide range of donors, including Stephen and his queen, but he granted the new foundation a substantial estate in Dorset, leaving the monks to defend property which he might otherwise have lost.[115]

The king, who had been in and around Worcester during February, then returned to Oxford. A court must have been summoned, for the archbishop of Canterbury here consecrated two bishops of Welsh sees, Maurice of Bangor and Uhtred of Llandaff, and obtained professions of obedience from them.[116] He would not let the civil war compromise the integrity of his province. It may have been on this visit by the king that a recognition was made by the burgesses of Oxford, "in my presence and in the presence of my earls and barons," concerning the rents held in the town by St Frideswide's Priory.[117] The court is then recorded in Winchester and in London, though the order of the meetings and the dates cannot be fixed with any certainty.

---

[112] *EYC* 4: *Richmond* 1, 15–16 (no. 12), 90.

[113] Ibid., 15: "de cuius hereditate terram Cornubie possideo."

[114] Ibid.: "pro stabilitate domini mei regis Stephani et filiorum et uxoris sue."

[115] *Monasticon*, v. 174, dated 1140, a very fine charter but its authenticity is questioned by Styles, "Early History of Alcester Abbey," printing a slimmer version of the foundation charter, 22–3; cf. Holdsworth, "The Church," in King, *Anarchy*, 224; Crouch, *Beaumont Twins*, 142–3, suggesting that Ralph retired into the monastery that he had founded.

[116] JW, iii. 284–5; *Canterbury Professions*, nos. 82 (Llandaff), 83 (Bangor, dated 3 Dec. 1140). The bishop of Llandaff "was married and his daughter subsequently married one of the more prominent Welsh chieftains": Saltman, *Theobald*, 93.

[117] *Regesta*, iii, no. 640: "burgenses mei de Oxeneford recognoverunt coram me et coram comitibus et baronibus meis per sacramentum suum"; the same phrase is used ibid., iii, no. 639. Other charters which might have been issued at this time are ibid., iii, nos. 264, 452–3.

Around the time of one of his visits to Winchester in 1140 the king stopped at Waverley Abbey. This was the first Cistercian monastery in England, founded in 1128 by a colony of monks from L'Aumône, north of Blois, and there was already an impressive church and set of claustral buildings on this site.[118] Stephen confirmed all the grants already made or to be made by the faithful to this house, doing so, he said, at the urgent request of his brother, "the father and the founder both of his diocese and of this church."[119] The queen was present, and their son Eustace, who is pointedly referred to as the king's heir. This was an exercise in family solidarity in a year in which Henry of Winchester, as papal legate, would have an influential role.

On Whit Sunday, 26 May 1140, the king was at the Tower of London. This is the one secure date in his busy itinerary during this year. We may envisage him hearing mass in the fine chapel in the Tower. Even in this confined space there was room for him to be seated in proper dignity. But, we are told, there was only one bishop present; the others either could not be bothered to attend or they were afraid to do so.[120] Alexander of Lincoln may have been afraid: for a time at least, after "the arrest of the bishops," he had been deprived of the temporalities of his see,[121] and Stephen no longer featured in his prayers.[122] Henry of Winchester, the king's "most dear brother,"[123] may not have attended this court but he kept in close touch. He had succeeded Roger of Salisbury as dean of the collegiate church of St Martin-le-Grand in London, whose endowments supported the clerks of the royal chancery. The succession to the bishopric of Salisbury had provoked controversy. At least one meeting of the royal court, in March or April, had discussed the issue.[124] Henry de Sully, who had been waiting in the queue for preferment for some time, was supported by his uncle the legate but not by his other uncle, the king, who "for various reasons" accepted the nomination of the magnates that Philip of Harcourt, recently appointed as royal chancellor, should succeed. Philip may even have been consecrated but the legate vetoed his

---

[118] Halsey, "Architecture of the Cistercians in England," 70–1; Knowles, *Monastic Order*, 246–9.

[119] *Regesta*, iii, no. 921: "quod quidem feci prece et requisitione prefati fratris mei, patris et fundatoris et episcopi sui et ecclesie prefate."

[120] WM, *HN*, 76–7.

[121] *Regesta*, iii, no. 493: "habebo episcopatum Lincolnie in manu mea" (*scriptor* xx, telling it like it was).

[122] *EEA* i: *Lincoln 1087–1185*, 24–5 (no. 37): "pro consolatione et provectu nostre matris ecclesie et pro nobismet ipsis et amicis nostris et pro anima regis Henrici et avunculi mei Rogeri qui fuit episcopus Saresb' et pro animabus patris et matris mee et amicorum meorum defunctorum." Similar phrases ibid., 30 (no. 47).

[123] *Regesta*, iii, no. 790, one of the charters issued at Salisbury around Christmas 1139 is addressed by the king "dilecto fratri suo."

[124] The authorities here are: OV, vi. 536–7, which records the dispute but does not give a date or a place; JW, iii. 284–5, says that the king granted the see to Philip at Winchester, "consilio baronum suorum"; Waverley Annals, in *Ann. Mon.*, ii. 228, state that these events took place at a council in London in mid-Lent (17 Mar. 1140).

appointment, as he had done in the case of John of Malmesbury earlier in the year.[125]

After Whitsun the king set out for East Anglia. By tradition it was in June that the last regular meeting of the royal court was held before the summer break. That meeting in 1139 had been held at Oxford, and it had seen high drama; the meeting in 1140 was at Norwich, "a town remarkable for its trade and large population,"[126] and no excitement was looked for. The court was well attended.[127] Whilst there had been no bishop at the Tower at Whitsun, here at Norwich there was not just the local bishop, Everard, but Alexander of Lincoln, perhaps at court for the first time since his arrest, and also Athelwold of Carlisle, who had yet to find a secure role under the lordship of the king of Scots. There were four earls: Alan of Richmond, who cannot have stayed long in Cornwall; William of Warenne; Simon of Senlis and William d'Aubigny. These earls were there because it suited them. All save Simon of Senlis had significant estates in Norfolk.[128] William d'Aubigny could inspect the building works at his castles at Rising, close to the port of King's Lynn (see plate 14), and at Buckenham in the south of the county; William of Warenne could admire the no less extensive building works at his estate centre at Acre; and, on the other side of the Wash, Alan of Richmond had a secure income from the rapidly expanding port of Boston.[129] If these men were secure in their lordship of the region so also was the king. His queen, Matilda, retained in her own hand the lordship of the honour of Boulogne, the dominant estate in Essex, and as lord of Eye he had a significant and strategic lordship in East Anglia. No region was more rich at this time and in no region was the king more generous. "The king gave" is a phrase that we meet time and time again.[130] The king gave the second town of Essex, Maldon, with its burgesses, to his brother, Theobald of Blois.[131] The king

---

[125] WM, *HN*, xxx–xxxi.

[126] WM, *GP*, i. 151.

[127] Stephen's movements at this time are far from well recorded. The relevant folios from the *Gesta Stephani* have been lost; John of Worcester's chronicle stops at just the same point, and the Gloucester continuation takes its eye off the king; William of Malmesbury and Henry of Huntingdon focus on the horrors of the civil war. *Regesta*, iii, no. 399 (St Benet's, Holme), is taken as evidence for those at court.

[128] I am particularly indebted here to Latimer, "The Earls in Henry II's Reign," which made a special study of the earldoms in East Anglia.

[129] Liddiard, "Castle Rising, Norfolk"; Kenyon, *Medieval Fortifications*, 49–51; Hill, *Medieval Lincoln*, 314–20.

[130] Outside East Anglia, the king gave Bloxham (Oxon.), with its two hundreds and its forest rights, to Waleran of Meulan: (*Eynsham*, i. 52–3: "*rex* Stephanus *daret* michi Blocchesham"), and Weekley (Northants.) to Ralph, count of Vermandois (Northamptonshire Record Office, Montagu of Boughton, Box 7, no. 3/1: "michi *rex* Stephanus *dedit*"; reference from Nicholas Vincent).

[131] Mandate of Henry of Winchester, *EEA* 8: *Winchester 1070–1204*, 47 (no. 68): "die qua *dedit rex* comiti Theobaldo terram de Meldona"; and Stephen's own charter, *Regesta*, iii, no. 543: "die qua *dedi* manerium illud comiti Theobaldo."

gave the honour of Eye, at first to William of Ypres and then to Hervey count of Léon, who became his son-in-law.[132] The king gave Thetford, the second town of Norfolk, to William of Warenne.[133] The one man seemingly excluded from this circle of giving was Hugh Bigod. At one stage in this expedition his garrison was evicted from the castle of Bungay;[134] but the king was generous, and always ready to compromise, and a little later in the summer he may have granted Hugh the earldom of Norfolk.[135] At the same time he gave the earldom of Essex to another great lord of the region, Geoffrey de Mandeville, "a man who had always been loyal to him" and on whom he was increasingly reliant following the exile of Nigel of Ely. In Norwich, surrounded by his magnates, in a castle that has been described as being for its day "architecturally the most ambitious secular building in western Europe," the king could hope for his prayers to be answered: "for the remission of his sins, for his well-being and that of Eustace his son, for the stability of his kingdom, and for peace."[136]

ATTEMPTS AT PEACE-MAKING

It was a little while after Whitsun, and so must have been around midsummer 1140, that Henry of Winchester, as legate, arranged for a colloquium to be held near Bath "between the empress and the king, on the chance that peace might be restored by the inspiration of God."[137] As was normal in such situations, the protagonists would only meet face to face once the terms for any settlement had been agreed. The initial meeting was between a delegation from each side. The empress's side was headed by Robert, earl of Gloucester, accompanied by "the rest of her advisers," that phrase just possibly suggesting that those who came with the earl were neither numerous nor of high rank. On the king's side were Henry, the papal legate, Archbishop Theobald, and Stephen's queen,

---

[132] *Cal. Charter R.*, v. 366–7, a charter of "Herveius comes de Leonia et dominus honoris Eye" addressed "excellentissimo regi Anglorum Stephano karissimo domino suo"; discussion in Lewis, "The King and Eye"; *Eye Priory Cartulary*, ii. 16–17, 23–6.

[133] In *EYC* 8, 93–4 (no. 45), William of Warenne grants to Thetford Priory churches and tithes and all his rights in Thetford, "sicut uncquam *rex* Stephanus melius et liberius tenuit et michi *dedit.*"

[134] Waverley Annals, in *Ann. Mon.*, ii. 228: "ivit rex cum exercitu suo super Hugonem Bigod in Sudfolc et cepit castellum de Buneie"; for comment, Crouch, *Stephen*, 118–20.

[135] *Ann. Mon.*, ii. 228: "item in Augusto perrexit super eum et concordati sunt sed non diu duravit." Hugh is recorded as earl (*consul*) five months later: HH, 728–9, 736–7. Opinion is divided as to who granted Hugh Bigod his earldom. Round, *Geoffrey*, 50, n. 1, and Wareham, "The Bigod Family," 234, argued for the king, but Davis, *Stephen*, 138–9, and Crouch, *Stephen*, 119 n. 41, argued for the empress.

[136] Heslop, *Norwich Castle Keep*, 66; *Regesta*, iii, no. 399: "pro . . . remissione peccatorum meorum et incolumitate mea et Eustachii filii mei et pro stabilitate regni mei et pacis."

[137] WM, *HN*, 76–9, is the only source for the peace discussions of 1140. The Gloucester chronicler notes that Robert of Gloucester moved his forces to Bath before 15 Aug. 1140, and there was skirmishing thereafter between his forces and the king's: JW, iii. 290–1.

Matilda. The discussions proved fruitless and the two sides parted with mutual recrimination. It was only in September, after an interval that would have allowed the legate to have reported to the pope if he wished and receive instructions in reply, that the legate made another effort. He went on a diplomatic mission to France, where he had "long and anxious discussions on peace in England" with, amongst others, the French king, Louis VII, Count Theobald of Blois, "and many churchmen." While the earlier discussions had largely, so far as can be seen, involved talks about talks, Henry returned to England with a precise set of peace proposals.[138] To these proposals, the empress and Earl Robert "agreed at once," while on the other side the king at first havered and then finally rendered the whole deal null and void. If William of Malmesbury knew some at least of the detail – and with his close links both to Robert of Gloucester and to Henry of Winchester he was uniquely placed to know – he is not saying. If we want to know what was on the table, we have just the clues he offers as to the attitude of the parties, and rather more detail of later peace discussions. Later of course things had moved on. So there can be no certainty here.

Whilst there can be no certainty it is still worth considering the possibilities. We may start with the most precise information that William of Malmesbury gives us, the fact that Henry had discussions with his – and Stephen's – elder brother, Theobald of Blois, and with the French king. This was not the first time that Henry of Winchester had referred to this coalition of advisers. He had done so in the previous year, at the council which he had summoned following the "arrest of the bishops," seeking to add further weight to his own opinion. William of Malmesbury heard him address Stephen directly:

> Let him therefore tell his brother that, if he thought fit to acquiesce calmly in his advice, he would by God's will give him advice to which neither the church of Rome, nor the court of the king of France, not even Theobald, the brother of both of them, certainly a wise and religious man, could reasonably object, but which they ought to accept with favour.[139]

In the context of a council of the English Church these references seem almost incongruous, but for Henry they were completely in character. He was a cosmopolitan figure. He kept up a wide correspondence. And as legate, he saw it as his duty to consult widely. It was natural that he should consult Theobald. Some had seen them as a team in December 1135: "the wisdom of the brothers" would bring to perfection whatever was lacking in the king.[140] Theobald's *sapientia* was certainly needed now, with his

[138] WM, *HN*, 78–9: "salubria patriae *mandata* referens."
[139] WM, *HN*, 52–3.
[140] *GS*, 12–13.

brother's title and territory – in which he had his own interest – under threat. The links with the French king were more recent, for Louis VII had succeeded his father on 1 August 1137. He also now had a family relationship with Stephen and his brother, for in February 1140 Louis's sister, Constance, had been betrothed to Stephen's son, Eustace.[141] The union was described as following "the counsel of the barons" of both kingdoms. Henry of Winchester's reference to his links with the French court in September 1139 may indicate that the marriage was already under discussion then. Nor is it to be doubted that amongst the "many ecclesiastics" consulted both in 1139 and in 1140 was the chief counsellor of the French king, Abbot Suger of St Denis, who could claim to have been involved in diplomacy with Henry I for twenty years and more.[142] At the betrothal the queen was present with a proper magnate escort, though the king remained in England: this was the time when he was campaigning in the fens. It was widely reported in England that it was the cash taken from the altar of Salisbury cathedral that had been used to "purchase" the bride.[143]

What then of the terms which Henry of Winchester brought back from these discussions? It can be taken as axiomatic that there was no question in the autumn of 1140 of reversing the decision of December 1135, of Stephen abdicating and of either the empress Matilda ruling in her own right or a regency council acting on behalf of her eldest son, Henry. This did not reflect the balance of power between the two sides. And it was not how people thought. It would not just have been unacceptable to the king and his immediate family, who had been closely involved in the peace discussions; it would have caused problems for the whole political community. The pope had only recently rejected Matilda's claims, simply cutting short the arguments made on her behalf. The higher clergy had crowned the king and sworn fealty to him. The lay magnates had almost to a man done homage to him. William of Malmesbury represents Stephen as saying: "When they have chosen me king why do they abandon me? By the birth of God, I will never be called a king without a throne."[144] The use of direct speech is unusual in the text. If William had not heard the king speaking, as he had Henry of Winchester, still he felt he had good warrant for these words. They also seem every way in character.

[141] JW, iii. 284–5.

[142] Others may be looked for in the record of the reconciliation of Louis VII with his former chancellor, Algrin of Etampes. As well as Suger, this involved the mediation of Bernard, abbot of Clairvaux, Hugh, bishop of Auxerre, Imar, abbot of Montierneuf (later cardinal legate in England), Hugh of Crécy, prior of Cluny, Odo, sub-prior of St Martin-des-Champs, and "other religious men." Also involved, indicating the continuing interest of Theobald, count of Blois, was his steward, Andrew of Baudemont. *RHF*, xvi. 6–7; Luchaire, *Louis VII*, 120–1 (no. 67); *Peter the Venerable*, ii. 309 n. 28; Grant, *Suger*, 86, 148.

[143] HH, 720–1: "accipiensque thesauros episcopi *comparauit* inde Constantiam sororem Lodouici regis Francorum ad opus Eustachii filii sui"; followed by, but with independent commentary, Newburgh, i. 44; cf. OV, vi. 514–15 and n. 6.

[144] WM, *HN*, 38–41.

There is a note of desperation here, and a note of defiance. And in any discussion of peace, they show us the king's bottom line. Stephen never would be a king without a throne. But it would become a desperately close run thing.

Equally it must have been axiomatic that if there was to be agreement between the two parties then Stephen would have to concede, in his turn, that it was not just his sons who had an interest in the succession but the sons of the empress also. There were at least five, and possibly six, boys who had to be considered. The king's eldest son was Eustace, now betrothed, and aged perhaps ten or eleven. The second son was William, aged about six.[145] A third son, Baldwin, may already have died.[146] If Stephen may have had three sons living in the autumn of 1140, the empress most certainly did, and their birth dates are known. Henry at this time was aged seven, Geoffrey was six, and William was four. The key to any agreement would be the provision that was made for the eldest son of the king (Eustace) and the eldest son of the empress (Henry). The younger sons, and in particular the second sons, could not have been ignored, however. Not only were they their brothers' next heirs but they were seen as having some claim on the family lands. The discussions in 1140 concerned the future of these young boys. It is possible to get an idea of what might have been argued on their behalf at this date by looking ahead to what would be arranged in 1153. The settlement then involved the transfer of the English crown at a specific but uncertain date *in the future*, i.e. upon Stephen's death, while taking steps *immediately* to effect a territorial settlement which would underpin that transfer.[147]

In 1140 there were several possibilities as to how an agreement might have been framed along these lines, both concerning the rights to be transferred and the timing of the transfer. Might the 1140 draft settlement have been quite close in its terms to what would be agreed in 1153, with the rights in the crown that Henry I had enjoyed going to his grandson, Henry, with Eustace taking over his father's *comitatus*? It is possible, and indeed I have argued for it before,[148] but I am not sure now that it survives close analysis. Consider the likely reaction to this proposal of the two parties. Would this have taken their interests into account? The empress', certainly. There is no difficulty in envisaging her agreeing "at once," but in the circumstances of 1140 was this her "bottom line"? Would the king not have rejected it outright, rather than havering as we are told he did? The legate

---

[145] *EYC* 8: *Warenne*, 14–15.

[146] He was buried at Holy Trinity Priory, Aldgate. *Regesta*, iii, nos. 511–12: "pro requie animarum scilicet Baldwini filii mei et Matildis filii mee qui in eadem ecclesia sepulti requiescunt." Baldwin was buried to the north of the high altar: *Cart. Aldgate*, 232. *Regesta*, iii index, following *Handbook of British Chronology*, says that he was dead by 1137.

[147] *Regesta*, iii, no. 272.

[148] WM, *HN*, lx–lxi.

had brought back a package of proposals from France. What of the "French" imput, in particular that of the king of France himself? Such an arrangement, with Eustace's expectations being reduced to those of "a mere count,"[149] would have involved the disparagement of his sister, Constance, within a few months of her betrothal. Not only that, but a potential union of Anjou and Normandy and England, under one house if not under one individual, involved the strengthening of the Anglo-Norman *regnum*. Might the suggestion rather have been that it be divided? If there was any consistency in the policy of the French crown, such as Suger claimed, then this certainly would have been its objective.

If England and Normandy were to be once more under different lordship, then further questions come crowding in. Who was to get what? And when were they to get it? Would Eustace get Normandy (now) and Henry get England (when Stephen died)? Or would Henry get Normandy (now) and Eustace succeed his father as king of England? A division which – at a time to be determined – would have given Normandy to Henry and England to Eustace looks the more logical. Stephen had not made much of Normandy, whilst in England the empress was hemmed in in the west country and there was no sign of her making a breakthrough. The immediate transfer of Normandy to Eustace and the ultimate succession of Henry to England looks in the long term to give too little to Stephen but in the short term it would have produced peace. It is interesting to note that the *Anglo-Saxon Chronicle* under the correct year 1140 notes the marriage of Eustace and Constance, and says that by it the king's son "hoped to obtain all Normandy."[150] The year seems correct almost by accident, for all the entries for what have earlier been described as the "nineteen long winters" were written – at least in their present form – after the reign had come to an end. Granted this, in a passage written in the early 1150s, it is at first sight tempting to relate the observation to Eustace's hopes to recover Normandy after it had been lost in the mid-1140s. Still, there is sometimes sense in treating even the most disjointed of sources as meaning in a particular instance exactly what it says. What it says is that the marriage was seen as entailing Eustace's succession to Normandy.[151]

Each of these possibilities is difficult to envisage but perhaps more so now than it would have been at the time. It is difficult now to unthink "the Angevin Empire," though Holt's phrase about a set of territories that had been "cobbled together" through "an unholy combination of princely greed and genealogical accident" may resonate.[152] But in 1140 the division

---

[149] It was felt that there was a case that needed to be answered in the empress's marriage to the count of Anjou: see *GND*, i, lxxxviii; ii. 242–5; WM, *HN*, 8–11; Chibnall, *Matilda*, 55.

[150] *ASC*, s.a. 1140.

[151] Gervase of Canterbury, i. 112, s.a. 1140, largely following John of Worcester, here adds: "then [following the betrothal] Eustace received (*suscepit*) the duchy of Normandy and did homage for it to the king of France."

[152] Holt, *End of the Anglo-Norman Realm*, 19–20.

of England and Normandy can hardly have been unthinkable. The union had been the creation of the Conqueror but on his deathbed it had been dissolved, and when William Rufus died in the New Forest the division was maintained, at least for a time. Indeed, from 1087 "until the death of Robert Curthose in 1134, a defender of Robert's legitimacy might have argued that the two offices of king and duke were in different hands."[153] It is not surprising that there were "long and anxious discussions."[154] It might have been envisaged that there would be several dynasties that over a period of time would become distinct.

1. Henry, "the son of the empress, the daughter of King Henry," to be the future king of England, after King Stephen's death.
2. Eustace, the son of King Stephen, the grandson and the nephew of successive counts of Blois-Chartres, to be duke of Normandy when he came of age.
3. Geoffrey, the younger son of Geoffrey, count of Anjou, to be count of Anjou after his father's death.
4. William, the younger son of King Stephen, to succeed to "the lands of count Eustace," the honour of Boulogne, on his mother's death.

Such division would certainly have been thinkable, for each of the boys, if necessarily after circumstances had changed, would claim or enjoy the territories specified.[155] It would have been radical, but those formulating the proposals – Henry of Winchester and the other senior Cluniacs; Bernard of Clairvaux; Suger of St Denis and the other advisers of Louis VII of France – did not lack ambition. They were statesmen: widely experienced; highly confident; extremely articulate. They might have hoped that the boys were still young enough to be instructed in their expectations.

The proposals came to nothing and Henry of Winchester withdrew to watch upon events.[156] This is hardly surprising. Discussions should have taken place at court but the royal court had atrophied. According to

---

[153] Chibnall, *World of Orderic*, 189.

[154] WM, *HN*, 78–9.

[155] (i) Robert of Gloucester had argued in Dec. 1135 that Henry should be king of England; he brought him to Bristol in 1142 as "the lawful heir"; and Henry's claim was accepted in the autumn of 1153: *GS*, 12–15; WM, *HN*, 126–7; *Regesta*, iii, no. 272. (ii) When Henry became duke of Normandy in 1150, he was opposed by Louis VII "in the name of Eustace" and Eustace crossed to Normandy to challenge Henry: *GS*, 226–9 ("rege Franciae *sub nominee Eustachii* ducem impugnante, sed et ipso Eustachio pro seipso contra aemulum suum uiriliter et inuicte decertante"), 230–1; Torigni, 161. (iii) When Henry became count of Anjou in 1151, he was opposed by Geoffrey, who claimed that his father had willed that he should inherit Anjou if Henry were to inherit Normandy and England: Torigni, 165; Newburgh, i. 112–14; and interesting discussion in Hollister and Keefe, "The Making of the Angevin Empire," 264–6. (iv) William did become count of Boulogne, though only after the death of Eustace in Aug. 1153, and held the county until his own death in Oct. 1159: *EYC* 8: *Warenne*, 14–18.

[156] WM, *HN*, 78–9.

Henry of Huntingdon, it ceased to be important to state for the record where the king was at Christmas or at Easter, for "the ceremonies of the court and the custom of royal crown-wearings, handed down from the ancient line, had completely died out."[157] This weakened not just the king but the whole political community. This is because, as Geoffrey Koziol has argued, the court ceremonies and crown-wearings "are fundamentally misconstrued as rites of royalty. They are more accurately described as dramas for the political community as a whole, which tested its cohesiveness and measured the standing of its members."[158] Seen from this perspective, the focus for an agreement was simply lacking in the last weeks of 1140. In the short term, it is clear that both parties felt they had more to gain by fighting than by compromise. At the very beginning of the following year, the best hopes of one of the parties, and the worst fears of the other, would be realized.

[157] HH, 724–5
[158] Koziol, *Begging Pardon and Favor*, 306; cf. idem., "The Problem of Sacrality," 140–1.

Chapter 5

1141

So all this year, whose tragedies I have briefly related, was ill-omened and almost mortal to England, which, after thinking that it might now in some sort draw a breath of freedom, fell back again into misery, and thus, unless God's mercy sends a remedy soon, it will long remain.[1]

Of all the great cities of England, in the seventy-five years since the Norman Conquest, Lincoln had perhaps seen the most change. It was the largest city in eastern England, and in recognition of this the diocesan centre was moved there from Dorchester on the Thames, soon after the Conquest.[2] The length of the move is one indication of the scale of the diocese: it was 115 miles from Dorchester to Lincoln, while from one end of the diocese to the other was 160 miles. In the north of the city of Lincoln there was an area of high-status housing, in marked contrast to the narrow streets around the wharves on the River Whitham. This northern part of the city would become the administrative enclave, known as the Bail. Here the first bishop of Lincoln, Remigius, built a new cathedral with a west front modelled closely on that of St Stephen's, Caen. Here was the other power base in the city, the castle, where the sheriff had his offices and the records of government were kept. When Roger of Salisbury fostered the appointment of his nephew Alexander as the third bishop of Lincoln in 1123 he could reflect with some satisfaction that this diocese was "as rich perhaps as any that England holds."[3] Roger was in a position to know, for he presided over the exchequer, and of all the sheriffs who appeared before him it was the sheriff of Lincoln who was charged with the highest of the county farms.[4] Alexander of Lincoln, like the rest of his clan, was a vigorous economic manager. Newark on the Trent had

---

[1] WM, *HN*, 110–11.

[2] On the city and the diocese, see Hill, *Medieval Lincoln*; Owen, *Church and Society in Medieval Lincolnshire*; *EEA* 1. On the move of the diocese from Dorchester to Lincoln see WM, *GP*, i. 472–5.

[3] WM, *HN*, 66–7. The bishop's lands are shown as worth *c.* £600 in 1086 in Corbett, "Normandy and the Norman Conquest of England," 511. If the tenanted lands are included, however, the figure comes out at *c.* £765: *DB*, 396a–b (Bucks.), 425b–426b (Oxon.), 522a–b (Cambs.), 552a–553a (Hunts.), 565a–b (Beds.), 595b (Northants.), 629b–630b (Leics.), 763b–764a (Notts.), 897b–900a (Lincs.).

[4] £755 in 1129–30, and by late 1150s over £1,100; the next largest figure in 1129–30 was for the combined counties of Dorset and Wiltshire: Amt, *Accession*, 198–204.

become a new town under his stewardship.[5] Lincoln also had its link via the Fossdyke with the Trent at Torksey.[6] Its road communications, though travellers would hardly recognize this today, were also important, for it lay on one of the main routes from London to York, travellers going north from Lincoln and crossing the Humber by ferry.

Lincoln then was a city of great wealth and some strategic importance. If we ask why a decisive battle was fought at this place, at this time, we do not lack for witnesses. This is how Orderic introduced the protagonists:

> Ranulf earl of Chester and William de Roumare, his half-brother, rebelled against King Stephen and, by a trick, captured the castle which he held at Lincoln for the protection of the city. They cunningly found a time when the household troops of the garrison were widely dispersed, and then sent their wives ahead to the castle under the pretext of a friendly visit. While the two countesses were passing the time there, laughing and talking with the wife of the knight who should have been defending the castle, the earl of Chester arrived, unarmed and without his cloak, as though to escort his wife home, and three knights followed him without arousing any suspicion. Once inside the castle they suddenly snatched crowbars and weapons which lay to hand and violently expelled the king's guards. Then William burst in with a force of armed knights, according to a pre-arranged plan, and in this way the two brothers took control of the castle and the whole city.[7]

Orderic was writing just a few months after the battle and yet already the events that he describes had started to be transformed into legend. He speaks of the seizure of the castle but some of those closer to home knew that the matter was more complicated. The two brothers had rights within the castle and the city, some of which they had inherited, some of which the king had given them only recently. William of Malmesbury, introducing his description of the same events, says that Stephen "had gone away from Lincolnshire peacefully before Christmas [1140], when he had added to the honours of the earl of Chester and his brother."[8] The king's grants to the two men provided a context to the battle. Their interest in Lincolnshire was through their mother, "the countess Lucy." Lucy was possibly the daughter of Turold, sheriff of Lincolnshire in the 1070s. She had become "the countess" when her third husband, Ranulf le Meschin, had become earl of Chester after the loss of his cousin in the White Ship in 1120.[9] William de Roumare was Lucy's son by her second

[5] King, "Economic Development," 11.
[6] Hill, *Medieval Lincoln*, 307–9. Henry I had the Fossdyke recut in 1121: SD, *Opera*, ii. 260.
[7] OV, vi. 538–9.
[8] WM, *HN*, 80–1: "honoribus auxerat"; cf. OV, vi. 540–1: "magnos honores et dignitates auxerat."
[9] Brownbill, "The Countess Lucy."

husband, Roger Fitz Gerold. The two brothers had substantial estates in Lincolnshire.[10] A charter of Stephen in favour of William de Roumare, earl of Lincoln, has every appearance of taking us back to 1140, when "honours" were conferred. It granted him the royal manor of Kirton-in-Lindsey, a major centre with jurisdiction over twenty-six settlements, and valued even in 1086 at £80.[11] "Besides this I grant him his castle of Gainsborough and his bridge over the Trent, free and unmolested, to hold with all the free customs with which any earl in England best and most freely holds his castles." The witnesses are quite compatible with a meeting of the the royal court in the latter months of 1140.[12] It is likely that the earldom of Lincoln had been granted to him at the same time.[13]

It is the terms on which the castle of Lincoln was held which are the key to the controversy that blew up so suddenly during the Christmas feast of 1140–1. It is clear that Stephen had recently granted the constableship of the castle to Ranulf of Chester. A later charter of Stephen sought to reinstate Ranulf in the position he had enjoyed before the battle of Lincoln.[14] When (and if) he could do so: "then there shall remain to the king the tower and the city of Lincoln, and to the said earl there shall remain the tower which his mother had fortified along with the office of constable of the castle of Lincoln and of Lincolnshire by hereditary right." As the charter here states and as can still be seen, there were, unusually, two keeps or towers within the castle enclosure, and one of them in 1140 and long thereafter was known as Lucy's Tower. Put a little over-simply, Lincoln had a castle that was at the same time both royal and

---

[10] An impression may be gained from the map in Cronne, *Stephen*, 137, and there is full discussion in Dalton, "Ranulf of Chester and Lincolnshire."

[11] DB, 887.

[12] *Regesta*, iii, no. 494. The editors suggest dates of 1139–40 or 1146 and prefer 1146. The latter date rips the document right out of context. In favour of late 1140. (i) The place is right: The charter was issued at Stamford, and WM, *HN*, 80–1, states that the king had left "Lindocolina prouintia." *Regesta*, iii, no. 835, probably dates from the same occasion. (ii) The chancery style is right, with its reference to the earl's privileges being equivalent to those of his peers: cf. *Regesta*, iii, no. 273, of like date, for Geoffrey de Mandeville. (iii) The witnesses are right: Ranulf, earl of Chester; Gilbert, earl of Pembroke; Gilbert, earl of Hertford; Earl Simon; Roger, earl of Warwick; Earl Robert de Ferrers; William Martel; Baldwin Fitz Gilbert; William Fitz Gilbert; Richard de Canville; Richard Fitz Urse; Eustace Fitz John; Ralph de la Hay; Hugh Wake; William de Coleville. There is no evidence that Stephen could command a court of this size at any time in 1146.

[13] OV vi. 540–1 refers to "dignitates" as well as "honores." Clear evidence for the date of the grant of this dignity is provided by a charter of William de Roumare for Warter Priory, *EYC* 10: *Trussebut*, 114–16 (no. 66): in it he refers to the seventh year of Stephen's rule as the third year "consulatus mei," and separately to "anno uero quo effectus sum comes Lincolnie." Stephen's fourth regnal year was 22 Dec. 1139–21 Dec. 1140.

[14] *Regesta*, iii, no. 178. It is a calendared copy of an agreement made between the king and the earl and it does not include witnesses. Here the editors' arguments for a date of 1146 rather than 1140 are well made. It is likely, however, that this text represents the updating of a charter issued by Stephen at Stamford in 1140, the original of which has not survived.

seigneurial. To add to the complication, the bishop – only very recently restored to the king's favour – had reputedly turned his own cathedral church "into a castle."[15] While this may often be a loose phrase, in this case archaeology and architectural history support it.[16] The bishop was also building a new palace to the south and east of the cathedral, having obtained permission to demolish part of the walls of the upper city to make room for it.[17] In this crowded building site, with so many centres of power so close together and so loosely differentiated, it did not take much to provoke a confrontation. What seems to have inaugurated it was a complaint from the citizens of Lincoln, in this case in league with the bishop, that the brothers were inflicting unaccustomed burdens on them.[18] Whether or not the complaint was fair, it supports the view that the brothers were acting in some official capacity. The king, who had granted the offices, the constableship to Ranulf and the earldom to William, now had second thoughts. He asked for the castle back and it was perhaps in response to this that rather than surrendering Lucy's Tower Ranulf expelled the garrison of the royal tower.[19] The king marched fast up Ermine Street and at some point within the the twelve days of Christmas he arrived in the city unannounced.[20]

Ranulf of Chester managed to effect his escape from the castle and retreated to Chester. He sent messengers to Robert of Gloucester, his father-in-law, in the west country.[21] He promised in return for help to accept the empress and swear fealty to her. Not all in the empress's camp were convinced by his protestations, for – and this would be a cross that he would continue to have to bear – he was not trusted, having for some time appeared neutral in his loyalty.[22] It suited Robert of Gloucester, however, to respond to this appeal. Peace discussions had just failed. The accession of Ranulf of Chester offered important new territory and resources to the empress's party, particularly if his position in Lincolnshire could be defended. So Robert of Gloucester, along with Miles of Gloucester, "and all who had armed themselves against the king," set out, though they travelled along minor roads and their intended destination was not at first

---

[15] WM, *HN*, 82–3: "aecclesiam . . . incastellauerat."

[16] Gem, "Lincoln Minster"; Williams and Vince, "The Early Norman Castle at Lincoln and the West Tower of Lincoln Cathedral."

[17] *Regesta*, iii, no. 463.

[18] *GS*, 110–11: "ciuibus et affinibus dira iniungeret."

[19] The two best-informed authorities support this interpretation. *Liber Eliensis*, 320–1: "rex cum castellum Lincollie repeteret a comite Ranulfo Cestrie, quod ad custodiendum ei tradiderat, et ipse non solum illi reddere negavit, sed . . . agmine bellum parabatur inferre"; while JH, 306, states that he took possession of all the fortifications of Lincoln: "omnes munitiones Lincolniae occupauit sibi."

[20] Within the festival: WM, *HN*, 82–3; arrives unexpectedly: *GS*, 110–11; quickly and unexpectedly: JH, 307.

[21] WM, *HN*, 82–3; *mandatis* also in *GS*, 110–11; similarly OV vi. 540–1; only JH, 307, has him seeking out Robert directly.

[22] WM, *HN*, 82–3: "quia in neutro latere fidus uideretur esse."

revealed to the majority of the army. At some point, possibly at Castle Donington in Leicestershire, they met up with Ranulf of Chester.[23] From there the most obvious route would have taken them across the Trent at Newark – Robert of Leicester's castle garrison would have had neither the numbers nor any incentive to try to stop them – and thence along the Fosse Way to Lincoln. The twin towers of the castle and, more prominent still, the cathedral with its fortified west front, would be the first glimpses they gained as they approached the city from the south-west. There is no mention of the bridge over the Whitham either before or after their arrival, so it may have been destroyed to delay their passage. If so, the tactic was not successful, for a fording place was found a little to the west.

While it might help the drama to see this army fighting its way across and immediately engaging the king's forces, it seems that the confrontation was more deliberate than this, and that it was not until the day after their arrival at the earliest that the battle was fought. It is certain that it took place on an important feast day, that of the Purification of Our Lady, on 2 February 1141. The king's defeat on this day almost demanded a suitable portent, and it was found in the liturgy. The king had attended mass in the cathedral church, celebrated by the bishop, Alexander, whom a few months earlier he had threatened to depose.[24] This was the Feast of Candlemas, in which candles were blessed, carried in procession, and held up alight by the congregation for large parts of the service. It was widely reported that the king's candle had cracked and gone out and had to be relit.[25] The king would have heard more than once during the service the words of Simeon as he cradled the infant Christ in his arms. "Now Lord let thy servant depart in peace, according to thy word." As Stephen emerged from the cathedral porch and looked across to the castle, he could have reflected that his own days might be numbered and his end very far from peaceful.

By this date both sides – those envisaged at prayer within the cathedral, and those outside the city walls – had significant forces at their disposal. Those "who had armed themselves against the king" included the "big three," Robert of Gloucester, seen as the leader, Miles of Gloucester, and Brian Fitz Count, along with "the disinherited," chief among them Baldwin de Redvers, and Ranulf of Chester along with his brother William de Roumare. Ranulf had brought with him "a dreadful and unendurable band of Welshmen," but this degrades them, for they were led by three kings, Madog ap Maredudd of Powys, Cadwaladr ap Gryffyd ap Cynan, and Morgan ab Owain of Glamorgan, and their trained troops may have had a decisive impact on the battle.[26] The king's support had built up over

---

[23] *GS*, 110–11; WM, *HN*, 82–5.

[24] HH, 732–3; *Regesta*, iii, no. 493.

[25] The same story with only minor variants is in *GS*, 110–13; HH, 732–3; OV vi. 544–5.

[26] *GS*, 110–11 (for the degradation); *Liber Eliensis*, 320–1; OV, vi. 542–3 (for the names); discussed by Crouch, "The March and the Welsh Kings," in King, *Anarchy*, 277–8.

the previous few days. A charter which he issued in favour of Bordesley Abbey, a foundation of Waleran of Meulan, earl of Worcester, has the following lay witnesses: William of Ypres, Hugh Bigod, Baldwin Fitz Gilbert, Ingelram de Say, Richard de Courcy and Richard Fitz Urse.[27] These men had been with him from the time of his arrival, and by the time of the battle several other earls and quite a few of the northern baronage had joined them. Along with them was the archbishop-elect of York, William the treasurer, who was given the temporalities of the see by the king, and might have kept them had the outcome of the day been different.[28] There were reportedly divided counsels. Some advised the king to wait for reinforcements. But it seems clear that he already had a substantial army, fully the equal in numbers of that opposing him: had there been an obvious imbalance, battle would never have been offered. Still, the decision to fight was the king's own. He had backed away before and was a man conscious of his reputation. He could hope to enjoy a moral advantage, for it was treasonable to confront an anointed king in the field.

Henry, archdeacon of Huntingdon, was here on home territory and before his account of the battle he gave speeches to the leaders of both sides.[29] This is a rhetorical device but still it gives a view of the issues involved and the reputation of some prominent individuals. The king himself was softly spoken and so his address to his troops had to be delegated to Baldwin Fitz Gilbert. The royal troops, so they were assured, had right on their side, they were "the faithful against the faithless, those who remain true against those who are false." Nor if they considered the leadership qualities of the opposing generals did they have anything to fear. Robert of Gloucester was a blackguard, "with the mouth of a lion and the heart of a rabbit," while Ranulf of Chester was a loose cannon, "impetuous in battle, careless of danger, with designs beyond his powers, passionate in his pursuit of the impossible," and the Welshmen whom he led were poorly armed and had no discipline. On their own side, by contrast, were many earls and barons born and bred to feats of arms. The day would assuredly be theirs.

The speeches given to the opposing army, however, painted these same earls in a much less favourable light, as men possessing their full share of the weaknesses reported of some of the aristocracy in any age. So at least Robert of Gloucester, who named six earls, with not a good word to say of any of them. Alan of Brittany was simply detestable, unrivalled in his cruelty. Waleran of Meulan was more devious, "the last to muster, the first to decamp, slow to attack, quick to retreat," a twelfth-century precursor of W. S. Gilbert's Duke of Plaza-Toro. Then there was Earl Hugh Bigod, the arch-perjurer, for not only had he broken his oath to the empress but he had affirmed "that King Henry had granted the

[27] *Regesta*, iii, no. 114.
[28] JH, 307, giving the date as Jan. 1141.
[29] The quotations in this paragraph are from HH, 726–37.

kingdom to Stephen and set aside his daughter." The count of Aumale was a bounder and a cad: "because of his intolerable filthiness his wife left him and became a fugitive," only to fall on the rebound into the hands of a man even worse, a notorious adulterer and hopelessly addicted to the bottle. Neither the man nor the unfortunate lady are named, but by elimination this would seem to refer to William de Warenne, earl of Surrey. The last of the six earls was William of Ypres, a bête noire of the empress's supporters, for they knew of his importance to Stephen's cause. These men were all perjurers, as were the lesser men who supported them. Robert of Gloucester was fighting – the case is rehearsed yet again – against a king who had cruelly usurped the realm, "contrary to the oaths which he swore to my sister." The king could certainly not claim any moral superiority.

The royal forces offered battle. The exact place cannot be identified, but it must have been an open space, perhaps to the north or (more probably) the west of the city, seen as suitable for feats of arms.[30] They started "with that prelude to the battle that is called jousting, for in this [the royal forces] were accomplished."[31] It is possible that they expected the empress's forces to withdraw at this point;[32] battle had not been joined and so no honour had been lost; but if so they were disappointed. Again it is Henry of Huntingdon who is the best informed and he manages to give some structure to the battle. The empress's supporters formed up in strict classical formation in three squadrons. At the centre there were "the disinherited," among them Baldwin de Redvers, though no leader is named for this group. On the one flank there was Ranulf of Chester with his Welsh auxiliaries outflanking his own troops, while on the other there was Robert of Gloucester, *dux magnus*. The royal forces were disposed rather differently. The king placed himself at the back of the field, and fought on foot, surrounded by his household troops, also on foot – their horses were led away – for their greater security. In front was his cavalry: not his own troops but those brought by his earls, but these "false and factious earls" had brought limited forces with them. The mercenaries were under the command of William of Ypres, accompanied by at least one of the

---

[30] For discussion see Beeler, *Warfare in England*, 112–19; Hill, *Medieval Lincoln*, 178–9. There was a "battle-place" to the west of the castle, thought in the late thirteenth century to have been the scene of trial by battle but perhaps reflecting a tradition of this earlier engagement: ibid., 179, 359. It is "Battle Piece" in Marrat's map of 1817 and the key there identifies "entrenchments by King Stephen": Mills and Wheeler, *Historic Town Plans of Lincoln*, 26–9. This is not the only reference to the king having left his mark on the topography of Lincoln. A local man, over a century after the battle, would identify his tenement as having a boundary against the king's ditch, through which Stephen would habitually go on his way to the castle of Lincoln "during the last war": *Reg. Ant.* 9, 244–6: "ubi idem rex intrare et exire solebat versus castellum Lincolnie tempore veteris guerre."

[31] WM, *HN*, 84–5.

[32] This is the suggestion of Strickland, "Against the Lord's Anointed," 66.

northern earls, and these would face Ranulf of Chester and the Welsh.[33] The initial cavalry charges seem to have been decisive. "The disinherited" attacked those who had it all, the royal earls, and the king's forces were routed, their leaders fleeing the field. The troops under William of Ypres initially had greater success, forcing the Welsh auxiliaries into retreat, but they in turn were routed when Ranulf of Chester turned on them. William of Ypres then retreated, for by now the result was not in doubt: "as he was a great expert in warfare, he saw the impossibility of assisting the king and reserved his aid for better times."[34] With the result clear and given the high status of many who remained in the field, the second stage of the battle was less bloody and more deliberate, being devoted to the taking of prisoners. The king himself was the chief prize and was reported to have surrendered only after the most heroic struggle. He had been given a double-headed axe, a true Viking weapon, by one of the citizens of Lincoln, and with this he laid about him to good effect, killing several men. He had secured a reputation for bravery, but had lost the battle. Finally, late in the day,[35] he was surrounded and overpowered, his captor, William de Cahagnes, crying out in the melee: "Come here everyone, come here. I've got the king!"[36] So he had. Stephen would not surrender to a simple country knight but was brought before Robert of Gloucester and surrendered to him.[37]

In the aftermath of the battle no attempt was made to prevent the common soldiery from looting the city of Lincoln and slaying any of the citizens who had stayed to defend their property.[38] The majority fled in panic and they were no more fortunate, for many of them died when overloaded boats overturned and their occupants were drowned. In total, "according to some estimates about five hundred of the chief citizens perished."[39] The victorious warriors claimed to have right on their side, referring particularly to the "right of storm" which governed the treatment of towns taken after a defence.[40] It was stretching it more than a little to apply it in this instance and the main reason for the looting was simple greed. Still, William of Malmesbury comments, neither victors nor vanquished had any sympathy

[33] There are slightly different versions of the opposing forces in OV, vi. 542–3, HH, 736–7, and JH, 307–8. Henry of Huntingdon has the count of Aumale alongside William of Ypres; Orderic pits mercenary against mercenary, with Alan of Brittany and the Bretons alongside William of Ypres and the Flemings, and he names the two Welsh princes who accompanied Ranulf of Chester; John of Hexham supports the more local witness, saying that Alan of Brittany never took the field.

[34] So at least HH, 736–7; OV, vi. 542–3, says that William's troops were "the first to turn in flight, thereby encouraging the enemy and leaving their allies in a state bordering on panic."

[35] *Liber Eliensis*, 321, says that the battle lasted "pene tota die."

[36] HH, 738–9.

[37] OV vi. 544–5; this was the king's suggestion, JH, 308; the earl was much moved, *Liber Eliensis*, 321.

[38] For the sack see WM, *HN*, 86–7; HH, 738–9; OV vi. 544–7; *GS*, 112–13.

[39] OV, vi. 546–7.

[40] HH, 738–9: "lege hostili"; cf. Strickland, *War*, 222–4, on the "right of storm."

for the citizens, "since it was they who by their instigation had given rise to this calamity."[41] This is a chilling phrase and somewhat surprising at first sight coming from a cleric, one who might have been expected to sympathize with the sufferings of the poor. It gives an early indication of what would prove an important subtext in his treatment of towns and townsmen. Whilst he gave them their proper dignity as "citizens," in the circles for whom he wrote they were taken down a peg and became simply "burgesses."[42] The party of the empress was showing itself to be anti-mercantile, opposed to any manifestation of municipal liberty. Their feelings are quite understandable but for a party with pretensions to government they were ill advised. In any subsequent dealings they had with the major cities this reputation would come before them.

Along with the king on 2 February 1141 there were captured "a few barons of notable loyalty and courage."[43] They were more fortunate than the citizens of Lincoln. The northern chronicler, John of Hexham, gives quite a long list: Bernard de Balliol, Roger de Mowbray, Richard de Courcy, William Fossard, William Peverel, William Clerfeith (though he later escaped), and Gilbert de Gant.[44] Baldwin de Clare, Richard Fitz Urse, Ingelram de Say, and Ilbert de Lacy were also mentioned in dispatches.[45] It would appear that while the earls had turned tail many of the baronage had stood firm. The northern barons seem to have been particularly resolute. The presence and the tenacity of these men are explained in large part by the way that their interests were threatened by the brothers Ranulf, earl of Chester, and William de Roumare, the new earl of Lincoln. The Humber estuary was a thoroughfare not a boundary, and all but a few of the major tenants in Yorkshire had significant holdings in Lincolnshire also.[46] Roger de Mowbray was the main landholder in Gainsborough, where William de Roumare "had built his castle" and had its tenure confirmed to him by the king; Gilbert de Gant held lands at Folkingham and at Barton-upon-Humber, and his uncle Robert was the king's chancellor.[47] Royal favour to the brothers late in 1140, taken along with the recognition that the north midlands was now the frontier between the two parties, had destabilized the region. None of the men taken captive was detained for very long. The empress would now pursue her claim to be the rightful ruler of the kingdom. It was not in her interest to weaken the defence of its northern borders, as would assuredly have happened had all these men remained in captivity. And she had the main prize.

---

[41] WM, *HN*, 86–7.

[42] Ibid., *HN*, lxxxiv–lxxxv.

[43] Ibid., *HN*, 84–7. In the Ce version of the text the few (*pauci*) barons became many (*plures*). William's audience did not wish to have their bravery disparaged through having the enemy forces depleted.

[44] JH, 307–8.

[45] OV, vi. 524–5; HH, 736–9.

[46] Clay, "Lincolnshire and Yorkshire Connections."

[47] *DB*, 920, 923, 953; Dalton, "Ranulf of Chester and Lincolnshire," 118–19, 121–3.

The king was brought in captivity, accompanying the core elements of the army that had defeated him, to the west country. Robert of Gloucester took personal responsibility for his safety.[48] They came first to the royal city of Gloucester, arriving on 9 February, a week after the battle.[49] There the king was "presented" to the empress.[50] If they did converse, that conversation can only have been on familiar lines. The king was kept at Gloucester for a short time but then moved to Bristol. That castle was quite used to receiving high-status guests. It was there that Robert, duke of Normandy, had been kept during the last phase of his long captivity, from 1126 to 1134, when he died. Robert had been moved there "on the advice of [the empress] and that of David king of Scots, her uncle."[51] So also in the case of Stephen. Bristol was the more secure base, which Stephen himself had not been able to take earlier, and it was a seigneurial castle not a royal one. The king was kept there "at first in a manner that was honourable, except that he was not allowed to leave his quarters," but then, because he overstepped the boundaries appointed for him, "he was kept in chains."[52] There was every reason to believe that he would die in captivity, just as Robert, duke of Normandy, had done. Even so, he remained the king of England, a necessary point of reference in all political discussion.

News of the king's capture will have reached the empress two or three days before he appeared before her. She, so it appeared to a close observer, "was ecstatic at this turn of events."[53] This can be believed. From another of her charters we can capture something of her feelings at first hand. "I now have King Stephen in my custody at Bristol," she said later in the summer, "he who by the grace of God and with the aid of Robert earl of Gloucester my brother, and the aid of the same Miles [of Gloucester] and other of my barons was captured in battle at Lincoln on the feast of the Purification of Our Lady."[54] The king's capture was totally unexpected. But in this there lay a problem. No plans had been made for this eventuality. How now should she proceed? How both in practical and in theoretical terms should she seek to realize the claim that she should be ruler of England, as her father had intended? The practicalities were perhaps easier to manage. Stephen's own route to power had taken him via the two

---

[48] He would not let the king out of his sight, *Liber Eliensis*, 321; he was concerned that the king be properly treated, WM, *HN*, 86–7.

[49] JW, iii. 292–3.

[50] WM, *HN*, 86–7; on the treatment of prisoners see Strickland, *War*, 196–203.

[51] *ASC*, s.a. 1126.

[52] WM, *HN*, 86–7. Other sources refer simply to his imprisonment: *GS*, 114–15; HH, 738–9; OV, vi. 550–1; JH, 308; the Gloucester chronicle, in JW, iii. 292–3.

[53] JW iii. 292–3: "ob istiusmodi euentum uehementer exhilarata," written by a monk of Gloucester clearly on the basis of a first-hand report from his abbot, Gilbert Foliot.

[54] *Regesta*, iii, no. 393: "tunc habebam in captione mea apud Bristoll regem Stephanum qui, dei misericordia et auxilio Roberti comitis Glocestrie fratris mei, et auxilio ipsius Milonis et aliorum baronum meorum captus fuit in bello apud Lincoln die Purificationis Sanctae Mariae."

capital cities of Winchester and London to coronation at Westminster. She herself would follow the same route and perhaps as she went along the theoretical aspects of her governance could be worked out.

"She was advised to win the support of Henry, bishop of Winchester, the king's brother."[55] It was good advice. Henry was the papal legate. In this vacuum of authority he had a better claim than anyone to lead. He was moreover never a man to shirk responsibility and never a man readily to abandon a course of action once he had set himself to it.[56] The empress could now be persuaded that these were virtues. And so she sent messengers on ahead and set out. In these early days after Stephen's capture, time was of the essence. She left Gloucester on 17 February and had amongst her entourage Bernard, bishop of St Davids, Nigel, bishop of Ely, and Gilbert Foliot, abbot of Gloucester, a man who would become one of the main apologists for her authority. Still in high spirits she came to Cirencester, a Roman town with an important monastery, and this became the first main staging-post on her road to power.[57] The direct route would then have taken her via Marlborough and Ludgershall, which we know to have been safe houses. At some point she will have received a response to the letters she had sent to Henry of Winchester. Her negotiations with him were concluded ten days later, in an open space on the approaches to Winchester, on 2 March, the third Sunday of Lent.[58] The following day the bishop escorted her into Winchester:

The bishops of almost all England, many nobles, the chief magnates, innumerable knights, different abbots with their monks, from the same city monks from two houses, nuns from a third house, chanting in procession hymns and thanksgivings, and the clergy of the city with the citizens and crowds of people, all came to meet her with great state and pomp. Then the most famous city of Winchester was handed over to her, and the crown of the English kingdom was given to her rule. The legate cursed all who cursed her, blessed those who blessed her, excommunicated those who were against her, and absolved those who submitted to her.[59]

Henry of Winchester and Bernard of St Davids escorted the empress into the cathedral, one on either side.[60] It was a church built on an imperial scale, its nave 81 metres (266 feet) in length, seemingly designed for

[55] GS, 118–19. The Gloucester chronicler also notes that she took advice: JW, iii. 292–3.
[56] WM, HN, 108–9 ("qui quod semel proposuisset non ineffectum relinquere uellet"), 110–11 ("semel incepti, ut prius dixi, sui non segnis executor").
[57] JW iii. 292–5.
[58] WM, HN, 88–9; Regesta, iii, no. 343, but reading "dominica tercia quadragesime" for either intrantis or incarnacionis, which are the alternative readings of the Glastonbury cartularies.
[59] JW, iii. 294–5.
[60] WM, HN, 88–9.

processions of just this kind;[61] and the empress was clearly impressed. The
bishop took advantage of the occasion to obtain assurances in respect of
his monastery at Glastonbury, which had evidently been much on his
mind in the preceding months.[62] A charter she issued for him protected
the seisin of him and his men from the day on which "he came to me and
spoke with me at Wherwell, that being the day before the Monday on
which the said prelate and the citizens of Winchester received me
honourably in the church and the city of Winchester."[63] It was an important step forward and she was now surrounded with many of the trappings
of regality. The bishop had given her "the king's castle and the royal
crown, which she had always most eagerly desired, and the treasure the
king had left there, though there was not much of it."[64]

It was not just in respect of ready cash that the empress's resources were
limited. Her entourage was more impressive than it had been but it was still
not a national force. There was certainly a good turnout of bishops. Henry
of Winchester and Bernard of St Davids had formed the escort party; the
bishops of Ely and Lincoln, the nephews of Roger of Salisbury, and those
of Bath, Hereford, and Chichester were also present. The core of her lay
support was provided by Robert of Gloucester, Brian Fitz Count, and Miles
of Gloucester. They "and a number of others" had made the agreement
with Henry of Winchester, and the others mentioned in Henry's charter
from the empress were Reginald, earl of Cornwall, Humphrey de Bohun,
Ralph Lovel, Elias Giffard, and Robert Musard. This hardly represented,
however, "the chief magnates" and "many nobles." The empress had asked
that she be received immediately by both church and state. What she had
here was an agreement with the Church. And just as W. S. Gilbert's Lord
Chancellor had no doubt that he in his own person embodied the law, so
Henry of Winchester, as papal legate, was quite sure that he embodied the
Church. "The empress swore and gave assurance to the bishop that all
important business in England, especially gifts of bishoprics and abbacies,
should be subject to his control, if he and Holy Church received her as lady,
and he kept his faith to her unbroken."[65]

The deal was then that the legate would deliver the Church. His
personal undertaking to her was a first step in this. An immediate problem
appeared in that the archbishop of Canterbury kept himself at arm's
length from these proceedings, which he clearly felt to be precipitate.
Theobald came first not to Winchester but to Wilton. There he said that
he was not yet ready to swear fealty to the empress, since he thought it

---

[61] Fernie, *Architecture*, 32–3, 117–21, 304–7; Biddle, *Winchester*, 310–11: "no other church
in England or Normandy even approached this scale until the second half of the twelfth
century."

[62] Stacy, "Henry of Blois and the Lordship of Glastonbury."

[63] *Regesta*, iii, no. 343. There was a community of Benedictine nuns at Wherwell, who
would have cause to regret that the civil war had now come to their cloister.

[64] *GS*, 118–19.

[65] WM, *HN*, 88–9; *Regesta*, iii, no. 343.

"unbefitting his reputation and position to transfer his allegiance without consulting the king." Following this meeting the archbishop, together with many of the bishops and some of the laity, went to Bristol to speak with the king. There Stephen released them from their personal oaths to him "because of the necessity of the times."[66] All this made for delay, and Easter was approaching. The empress's party had been depleted by these discussions with the king, others had gone back to their homes, and she herself spent Easter at Oxford.[67] After Easter steps would be taken to consolidate her authority.

On the Sunday after Easter, Low Sunday, the clergy of England gathered at Winchester for a further council.[68] Coming hard on the rituals of Holy Week and Easter, and then allowing the clergy up to a week for travel, this was a traditional time for their gatherings (as it remains today). There were some absentees, who had sent letters of apology, but still it was an impressive gathering, which gained added solemnity from the importance of the business under discussion. This was nothing less than the succession to the realm of England. On the first day of the council proper, Monday, 7 April 1141, the legate called for a series of private meetings of each of the main estates among the clergy. First he talked with the bishops, then the abbots, then the archdeacons. The bishops were the most influential figures but the others were far more than a supporting cast. The senior of the abbots no less than the bishops were tenants-in-chief of the crown; they were dominant figures in their local communities, and several were significant in national and international politics. The abbot of St Albans, Geoffrey de Gorron, a former schoolteacher, the confidant and patron of the anchorite Christina of Markyate, and well known at the royal and papal courts, may be taken as representative of this group.[69] As to the archdeacons, their local power was no less entrenched, and there were several "notable men" amongst them, including Henry, archdeacon of Huntingdon, classmate of one of Henry I's sons and the best-selling historian of his day, and Walter, archdeacon of Oxford, "a man learned in rhetoric and with a liking for the history of foreign lands."[70] Each of

[66] WM, *HN*, 88–91; JW, iii. 294–5.

[67] So at least WM, *HN*, 90–1. The Gloucester chronicler, however, says Wilton, JW, iii. 294–5.

[68] *Councils and Synods*, 788–92 (no. 142). The council was not widely reported but William of Malmesbury, who was an eyewitness, provides a full account and there is a mention also in the Plympton annals: WM, *HN*, 90–7 (from which the quotations that follow); *UGQ*, 28.

[69] *GASA*, i. 72–106; *Christina*, 134–71; *Regesta*, ii, nos. 1426, 1715, 1740; *Regesta*, iii, nos. 819, 928; *Councils and Synods*, 770–1, 812–13; *ASC*, s.a. 1125.

[70] On the archdeacons as a group, see Brett, *English Church under Henry I*, 199–211; *Twelfth-Century Archidiaconal Acta*, ed. Kemp. On Henry of Huntingdon, see HH, xxiii–lvii, 594–5. On Walter of Oxford, Crick, "Oxford, Walter of"; described as one of the "notable men" in the Oxford of his day in Southern, "From Schools to University," 8; for his talents, Geoffrey of Monmouth, prologue, in *History of the Kings of Britain*, ed. Reeve and Wright, 4–5: "uir in oratoria arte atque in exoticis hystoriis eruditus"; and see also, *Regesta*, ii, no. 1000; *Regesta*, iii, no. 189; *EEA* i: *Lincoln 1067–1185*, nos. 33–4.

these groups could supply a different perspective from their own communities. They found themselves, it was reported on the following day, to be of one mind. They would now set aside the election of Stephen and appoint the empress in his stead. This amounted to a complete volte-face, for the clergy as for the political community at large. It is the duty of any politician in such a situation to ignore this fact, however generally it is recognized, and to show how an inherent consistency underlay the adaptation to changing political circumstances. Henry of Winchester was more than equal to the task.

The consistency came from accepting that Henry I had indeed confirmed, following an oath sworn by all the bishops and barons, that the kingdom of England and the duchy of Normandy should go to his daughter should he not leave a male heir. When the king died, however, he was in Normandy and so also was his daughter the empress, and she "made delays in coming to England." It was because of the danger of delay, said the legate, "that provision was made for the peace of the county and my brother allowed to reign." Stephen had taken up the kingship but his governance had been found wanting. His agreement with the Church and his coronation oath had alike been broken: "no judgement was enforced on transgressors, and peace was at once brought entirely to an end." The arrest of the bishops was symptomatic of the king's mercenary attitude to the Church and of his failure to follow good advice, such of course as had been offered him by these same churchmen at the earlier council of Winchester. Stephen's inconsequence up to this point served only to highlight the shining success of Henry I's rule. The more this was emphasized the more difficult it became to ignore the old king's views on the succession. The empress should be accepted because she was a chip off the old block. This in his peroration was how the legate summarized the case for her:

> Since God has executed his judgement on my brother in allowing him to fall into the power of the strong without my knowledge, so that the kingdom may not totter without a ruler, I have invited you all to meet here in virtue of my position as legate. The case was discussed in secret yesterday before the chief part of the clergy of England, whose special prerogative it is to choose and consecrate a prince. Therefore first, as is fitting, calling God to our aid, we choose as lady of England and Normandy the daughter of a king who was a peacemaker, a glorious king, a wealthy king, without peer in our time, and we promise her faith and support.[71]

The title the empress gained here was *domina Anglorum*, "lady of the English." This title she would now start to use in her charters, which

---

[71] WM, *HN*, 92–3.

suggests that this council was seen as giving her a new dignity that carried with it a new authority.[72]

When the legate had finished speaking there was polite applause from some and a studied silence from others. The clergy had exercised their claims to elect a new ruler. They had vindicated the empress's title to rule but there was much more to do before she could enjoy power. In particular, she needed the support of the Londoners, who also nurtured claims to elect. The legate invited them down to Winchester. He sent them a safe conduct, which they will not have needed but which indicates that the country remained divided and that they were viewed still as supporters of the king. Their security had always lain in their solidarity. Their language was full of this and particularly of their coming as representatives of the London commune. "They had been sent by what they call the commune of London, and brought not contentiousness but a request that their lord the king should be released from captivity."[73] The same request for the king's release was made by one of the queen's clerks. He politely handed a letter from the queen to her brother-in-law the legate. Henry, who had rejected the Londoners' demands at some length, repeating what he had said the day before, now launched into a further rebuttal. "While he was whittering on," says William of Malmesbury a little unkindly, the clerk read out the queen's letter anyway. It asked in emotional terms that the king should be released and restored to the throne. As to the Londoners, they said that they would report back the decision of the council to their colleagues, "and give it all the support they could." In the language of diplomacy this meant "forget it." The council was quickly wound up and the king's supporters excommunicated. The most prominent among them was the royal steward, William Martel, a particular bête noire of the legate.[74]

The council met in the second week of April. Everything might have been expected to urge the empress, once she had news of this formal approval, to move on to London. It was only in mid-June, however, fully two months later, that she arrived in the city. Why the delay? In part this must have been caution, a desire to be sure of support, a hope that her entourage would swell in numbers as word of the Church's approval spread. She needed to establish a court, to establish some routines, including a network of communication. If she could not immediately do that from London, then she needed another base. Oxford supplied the need. From there a first summons came for her supporters to meet up at

---

[72] Chibnall, "Charters of the Empress Matilda."

[73] WM, *HN*, 94–5: "missos se a communione *quam uocant* Lundoniarum." The legate was most reluctant to give any recognition to the London commune. He got around the problem diplomatically by saying that he had invited them not as representatives of the commune but because individually they were "quasi magnates," great men in their own right. See my discussion, ibid., pp. lviii–lix.

[74] WM, *HN*, 96–7 and n. 226.

Reading Abbey. This was for the Rogation Days, 6–8 May 1141.[75] They
were there to honour her father's memory, now inextricably bound up
with her own title. The empress prayed at her father's tomb, and her
prayers were not just for his soul, but for herself and "for the well-being of
Geoffrey count of Anjou, and the lord Henry my son and my other sons,
and the safety of the whole kingdom."[76] Among those who joined the
empress at Reading was William Mauduit, whom she described as "my
constable" and who paid her a relief of 100 marks.[77] Such a payment was
fully in accordance with a return to the customs of her father's day.

This thought was clearly not lost on the men of London. A delegation
came out to meet the empress at the abbey of St Albans in early to mid-
June, and "there they had lengthy discussions about the surrender of the
city."[78] As a result of these she did then come to London and "was
received with a magnificent procession at Westminster." There in the royal
palace she stayed for some days "deciding how to set the affairs of the
kingdom in order." There was London business to attend to. She filled the
vacancy in the bishopric of London, which had lasted for seven years, by
appointing Robert de Sigillo, who had served as chief clerk in her father's
chancery.[79] His experience might prove useful to her. She could also call
on the London die-cutters to produce coins in her name and those at court
with her obtained dies for their own moneyers.[80] She made a lengthy
agreement with Geoffrey de Mandeville, the custodian of the Tower of
London, confirming the king's grant to him of the earldom of Essex and
granting him extensive privileges.[81] The record of this agreement provides
evidence for her court, which she kept in permanent session.[82] Amongst
the earls, occurring for the first time and perhaps given these titles while
in London, were Baldwin de Redvers, earl of Devon, and William de

---

[75] JW, iii. 294–5.

[76] *Regesta*, iii, no. 699 (for Reading Abbey): "pro incolumitate Gaufridi Andegauorum
comitis, et domini Henrici filii mei et aliorum filiorum meorum, et pro statu totius regni."
The editors describe the charter as "unconvincing in every way," but these sentiments seem
right for this place at this time.

[77] *Regesta*, iii, no. 581, earlier printed and discussed by Davis, "Some Documents of the
Anarchy," 182–5.

[78] JW, iii. 294–5. *Regesta*, iii, no. 497, may be dated to this occasion. It is witnessed by
Henry, bishop of Winchester, Nigel, bishop of Ely, Robert, bishop of Hereford, Miles of
Gloucester, and Brian Fitz Count. Note also at the same time and place, ibid., no. 392, in
the hand of *scriptor* xiv, who has close associations with Miles of Gloucester.

[79] JW, iii. 296–7; *Dialogus*, 129. The delay in making an appointment was the result of
infighting in the chapter: Brooke, *London*, 356–7. It was also in the interest of Henry of
Winchester, who was administering the diocese during the vacancy: *EEA* 15: *London
1076–1187*, liv and no. 41.

[80] On the PERERIC coins see Blackburn, "Coinage and Currency," in King, *Anarchy*,
173–5. The mints were Bristol, Canterbury, Ipswich, Lincoln, London, Stamford, and
Winchester. *Regesta*, iii, no. 316, is a charter issued by the empress at Westminster for
William Fitz Otto, the official in charge of the die-cutters.

[81] *Regesta*, iii, no. 274.

[82] *GS*, 120–1.

Mohun, earl of Dorset. The record has also been used as evidence that the empress had by now taken the title of queen, but she never did so.[83] The position was not vacant.

The most urgent issue before the lady of the English and her followers was what was to be done with the king of England. Not just Stephen's family but others of his supporters, "the chief men and the highest nobles of England," took a close interest in his treatment. This after all would provide a model for their own. They asked for his release. "They promised to persuade him to give up the crown, and thereafter live devoted to God alone as a monk or pilgrim."[84] The empress flatly refused all such offers. The queen and the king's supporters cannot have been surprised by this. What concerned them far more was what should be done with what one source calls the *consulatus* of Stephen, the estate which he had held as count of Boulogne and Mortain, the power base that had helped him secure the crown.[85] The papal legate, though he had accepted Matilda as *domina Anglorum,* was the chief of those who argued that Eustace, as Stephen's son and heir, should – now that his father was in captivity and as it were dead to the world – be seen as inheriting these honours.[86] If, as is at least possible, some such arrangement had formed a part of the peace proposals that Henry as legate had put forward in the previous year, then he could claim to have been consistent and he might have hoped for some accommodation at this point. But this also was flatly refused.

The empress's refusal is understandable. The risks would have seemed too great. The memory of William Clito, whom many had seen as the legitimate heir after the wreck of the White Ship, might have been warning enough. And yet her refusal came at a heavy price. "She flatly refused, and – it was said – she had offered these lands to others."[87] If

[83] *Regesta,* iii, no. 274. The original charter, BL, Cotton Charter xvi. 27 (*Regesta,* iv, plate xiv), was severely damaged in the Cottonian Library fire in 1731 and the seal was lost. Richard Fitz George (d. 1635) sketched the seal and transcribed the legend as follows: MATILDIS IMPERATRIX ROM. ET REGINA ANGLIAE ("Matilda empress of the Romans and queen of England"): BL, Harley MS 5019, fo. 75r. Had the transcription been accurate it would have suggested that the empress had taken the title of queen, but when the sketch and the empress's known seal are compared it is clear that it is not and that she did not (see plate 10). St George has misread the correct legend: MATHILDIS DEI GRATIA ROMANORUM REGINA ("Matilda by the grace of God queen of the Romans"). The evidence here is magisterially treated in Chibnall, *Matilda,* 102–4; and for further examples of seal legends being "imaginatively reconstructed" (ibid., 104), see King, "Waleran of Meulan," 171–6.

[84] JW, iii. 296–7.

[85] The three main authorities all refer to this point, though in slightly different terms. The Gloucester chronicler, in JW iii. 296–7, refers to Henry of Winchester asking "ut consulatus qui fuerat sui fratris nepoti sue daretur"; GS, 122–3, to the queen's demanding "ex paterno tantum testimento hereditando," i.e. to the county of Boulogne only; but William of Malmesbury, in *HN,* 98–101, feels it important to set the matter out fully, and here refers to "hos comitatus," i.e. both Mortain and Boulogne.

[86] WM, *HN,* 98–101, and comment 98 n. 232.

[87] WM, *HN,* 100–1, and the matter is naturally put much more categorically in GS, 120–1: "quicquid rex decreto regali permissum statuerat ore imperioso destituere."

Stephen's heirs were to be disinherited, and the networks that had supported him were to unravel, what of all the others who in the past months had bound themselves to his service? They could only fear a similar fate. They would have seen then, and we must see now, that the treatment of Eustace was the key to any more general negotiated settlement. It was a situation that called for statesmanship and a readiness to forgive past injuries. Yet the running was being made by a woman who showed none of those qualities. When the Londoners said they lacked the resources to assist her and asked for time to pay an aid:

> She with a grim look, her forehead wrinkled into a frown, every trace of a woman's gentleness removed from her face, blazed into unbearable fury, saying that many times the people of London had made very large contributions to the king, that they had lavished their wealth on strengthening him and weakening her, that they had previously conspired with her enemies for her hurt, and therefore it was not just to spare them in any respect or to make the smallest reduction in the money demanded.[88]

She treated her closest advisers, who by now included David, king of Scots,[89] in just the same way, sending them away "with contumely, rebuffing them by an arrogant answer and refusing to hearken to their words; for by this time she no longer relied on their advice, as she should have, and had promised them, but arranged everything as she herself thought fit and according to her own arbitrary will."[90] The empress is clearly being typecast here. These extracts are from a source favourable to the king and hostile to the empress. It is tempting to suggest that what is being said should be discounted for this reason. This would be unwise. Other witnesses, undoubtedly close to the empress and sympathetic to her cause if not to the strategy that she pursued, say just the same thing.[91]

London, it soon appeared, was too hot for the empress to handle. No protestation of loyalty, however effusive, no processional welcome, however grand, could conceal a simple lack of trust. Compounding this was the external pressure that could be put on the Londoners by the queen and her supporters. The queen was shrewd and single-minded in her husband's cause. She mustered a large army on the south bank of the Thames, directly opposite the city, and started to plunder the surrounding countryside. "The people of London were then in grievous trouble."[92] They had accepted the empress but because of their past identification with

---

[88] *GS*, 122–3.

[89] *GS*, 120–1; SD, *Libellus*, 312–13; JH, 309. He issued a charter in favour of Westminster Abbey "at London in June": *Charters of David I*, no. 105

[90] *GS*, 120–1.

[91] JW, iii. 296–7: "she did not listen to good advice but harshly rejected their petition"; JH, 309: "in regem quoque Stephanum *truculenta* se acturam professa est"; WM, *HN*, 96–7, more obliquely.

[92] *GS*, 122–3.

Stephen's cause she saw them as her enemies. She had accepted as castellan of London Geoffrey de Mandeville, earl of Essex, and had made substantial grants to him, including the Tower and the other major fortification at the west of the city.[93] With Geoffrey too the Londoners were at daggers drawn.[94] Now the queen threatened to devastate their suburban properties and reduce them to "a habitation for the hedgehog,"[95] a nice image from the scriptures though more colloquial language was probably in use in the London taverns. It seems likely that some form of crown-wearing ceremony was intended at Westminster,[96] but on 24 June,[97] before it could take place, the empress was driven out. The Londoners rang the many bells of the city churches, unbarred the gates of the city, and set off down what is now the Strand, "like thronging swarms from beehives."[98] The palace and the abbey of Westminster, were – it must be remembered – outside the city walls. This distance allowed the empress the opportunity to escape. There seems to have been no chance for her to regroup her forces and fight back, for her followers were widely dispersed, some within the city and some outside. They all made off in haste. The story was told, and quickly went the rounds, that the empress had been surprised while eating a well-cooked feast.[99] She was forced to flee ignominiously,[100] so suddenly that the food was still lukewarm when the London mob broke in and ransacked her quarters. Once again she travelled up the Thames valley via Brian Fitz Count's stronghold at Wallingford to Oxford.[101] Her reputation went before her. The empress of the Romans, the daughter of the mighty Henry, the lady of the English, was now reduced to the ranks of the ladies who lunched.

The empress stayed in Oxford for a few days, then went on to Gloucester to consult with Miles of Gloucester,[102] before returning with

[93] *Regesta*, iii, no. 274.

[94] They were his mortal enemies, according to the empress, and, immediately after she had been driven out of London, the Londoners surrendered the city to the queen and set about besieging the Tower: *Regesta*, iii, no. 274 ("inimici eius sunt mortales"); SD, *Libellus*, 312–13; Brett, "Annals of Bermondsey, Southwark and Merton," 300.

[95] *GS*, 122–3, quoting Isa. 14 : 23.

[96] *GS*, 124–5, speaks with some relish of the discomfiture of those, "qui *ad dominam inthronizandam* pompose Londonias et arroganter conuenerant."

[97] The date is given in the London annals: Brett, "Annals of Bermondsey, Southwark and Merton," 300. It is also found in SD, *Libellus*, 286–7.

[98] *GS*, 124–5. The townsmen may have gained cover from the midsummer revels; for the later connection between popular rising and church festivals, see Walker, *Political Culture*, 166 and n. 68.

[99] *GS*, 124–5. It was a feast day after all.

[100] JW iii. 296–7: "ignominiosam cum suis arripuit fugam"; *GS*, 124–5: "impraemeditata fugae"; confirmed not contradicted by William of Malmesbury's tongue-in-cheek comment that she and her followers left calmly and "with a kind of military discipline": WM, *HN*, 98–9.

[101] *GS*, 124–7; JW, iii. 298–9.

[102] JW, iii. 298–9. It was probably at this point that she confirmed her earlier grants to Miles of Gloucester: BL, Sloane MS 1301, fo. 422r–v, a fuller version of *Regesta*, iii, no. 391.

him to Oxford, where on 25 July she granted him the earldom of Hereford.[103] The events at Oxford in July appear in the chronicles as an interlude between the dramas that had been acted out at London and would be again at Winchester, but this was a key period in strategic terms, one of anxious calculation and hard bargaining. The evidence for this is the charters.[104] The two most detailed are those which the empress issued in favour of Geoffrey de Mandeville and of his brother-in-law, Aubrey de Vere.[105] What is distinctive about these two charters is not just their detail but the fact that they are acknowledged to be composite documents, comprising not just a grant (*donatio*) but also an agreement (*convencio*). The empress took the hand of Earl Geoffrey and swore to accept the terms of each of the grants. She also, great lady though she was, was required to offer him security:

> I have made this agreement with the said earl Geoffrey, so far as I am able, that my lord the count of Anjou will offer security with his own hand to hold to this, and Henry my son likewise. And that the king of France will be a hostage if I am able to arrange this, while if I am not I will ensure that the said king gives his hand to hold to this.

A major part of the agreement is the lists that are given of those who would serve as hostages. All of them were to be hostages *per fidem*, as presumably the king of France was intended to be: such men would give their word, would offer their hand, but not surrender their persons or members of their families. A first group, of ten individuals, is stated to be both hostages and witnesses. These were Robert, earl of Gloucester; Miles earl, of Hereford; Brian Fitz Count; Robert Fitz Roy; Robert de Courcy the steward; John Fitz Gilbert; Miles de Beauchamp; Ralph Paynel; Robert d'Oilli the constable, and Robert Fitz Hildebrand. They were among the empress's leading lay supporters. It can be said of them that they were present, that they were apprised of the agreement, at least in general terms, and were prepared to stand security for it. Then came men "who should be hostages." These seem to divide further, first a group of members of her household, then several substantial figures, five of whom

---

[103] JW, iii. 298–9: "to bind him the more closely to her service and as an outstanding reward for it"; *Regesta*, iii, no. 393.

[104] They are discussed more fully in King, "A Week in Politics."

[105] *Regesta*, iii, nos. 275 (Geoffrey), 634 (Aubrey). The dating of these charters to July 1141 was first proposed by R. H. C. Davis in 1964, and defended by him in 1988 in reply to J. O. Prestwich, who wished to restore Round's earlier dating of them to the early months of 1142: Round, *Geoffrey*, 163; Davis, "Geoffrey de Mandeville Reconsidered"; J. O. Prestwich, "The Treason of Geoffrey de Mandeville," *EHR* 103 (1988), 283–312, and R. H. C. Davis, ibid., 313–17, and with a further exchange of views, ibid., 960–8; Davis, *Stephen*, 157–60. In support of Davis's date, see Chibnall, *Matilda*, 105–12; eadem, "Charters of the Empress Matilda," 281–3; King, "A Week in Politics," 65–8.

were of comital rank.[106] Their standing is evidently different from that of the first named. If they were present at Oxford – and granted the overlap with the names of those found with her at Westminster some at least may have been – they were not parties to the agreement. They were, however, men on whose support she could rely.

The empress could rely on those she named as hostages because they had come to her and had accepted her lordship. Others had not. Geoffrey de Mandeville and Aubrey de Vere were offered additional hostages, "other of my barons whom he [Geoffrey] may wish to have and whom I [the empress] am able to have."[107] The charters at Oxford recognize that there were limits to her authority. Some of what she granted she did not control. Aubrey de Vere would receive Colchester castle, the administrative centre of the queen's honour of Boulogne, "as soon as I am able to get hold of it"; Geoffrey de Mandeville would get (Bishop's) Stortford castle only if the bishop of London, who was present at Oxford, was able to agree.[108] Some of what she was able to give she might need to give back. The charter for William de Beauchamp, which granted him the sheriffdom of Worcester, had to take account of the fact that Waleran of Meulan, the earl of the county, might transfer his allegiance to her.[109] Individuals needed to come to her in order to make terms, and they would be granted title from the day on which they did so: "the day on which he became my man"; "the day on which they adhered to the service of my lord the count of Anjou and myself."[110] In all these calculations of the transfer of title, it must be noted, the deliberations of the council of Winchester, the empress's election as lady of the English, in April 1141, find no place. What had happened there was simply permissive: it had allowed individuals to offer support, had made honest men of them, had given them an answer to any charge of bad faith. The council had given the empress *authority* but not *power*. At Oxford – and it must have been a bitter pill to swallow – she acknowledges as much. Aubrey de Vere received a long list of grants, including an earldom, many of them qualified in some way.[111] When the empress gained real power, real authority, then she would do more.[112]

---

[106] The five earls were Reginald of Cornwall, Baldwin de Redvers, Gilbert of Pembroke, Hugh Bigod, and Aubrey de Vere.

[107] *Regesta*, iii, no. 275, for Geoffrey de Mandeville: "alii barones mei quos habere voluerit et ego habere potero"; the same phrase ibid., no. 634, for Aubrey de Vere.

[108] Ibid.: "turrim et castellum de Colecestria sine placito finaliter et sine escampa quam citius deliberare potero"; ibid., no. 275: "si potero perquirere erga episcopum Lundoniae et erga ecclesiam sancti Pauli castellum de Storteford per escambium ad gratum suum, do et concede illud ei et haeredibus suis."

[109] Ibid., no. 68; "semper ipse Willelmus de me in capite teneat nisi ipse bona voluntate et gratuita concessione de predicto comite tenere voluerit."

[110] Ibid., nos. 274 ("sicut tenuerunt die qua ipse homo meus effectus est"), 275 ("usque ad diem qua servitio domini mei comitis Andegavie ac meo adhesit").

[111] Ibid., no. 634. Even the grant of the earldom was vague, for Aubrey's choice of county was Cambridgeshire, but it was not known whether the king of Scots claimed it. He did, and so Aubrey became earl of Oxford, one of four counties on an alternative shortlist.

[112] Ibid.: "infra annum quo potestativa fuero regnum Anglie."

These charters give a sharp insight into the politics of the summer of 1141.[113] The empress is speaking but she is having to negotiate with the barons, and you can hear their voices no less clearly than hers. Some of them at least still expected a negotiated settlement, and this expectation influenced what they asked for. In the first of the empress's charters for Geoffrey de Mandeville, issued at Westminster before she was driven out of London, she granted him additional lands to the value of £100 a year. The greater part of this comprised the royal borough of Maldon in Essex, which Stephen had given to his brother Theobald, count of Blois, possibly in lieu of the pension granted him in 1137.[114] It was only natural that this should now be considered confiscate, and yet, the empress's charter goes on, "if I shall give back to count Theobald all the land which he held in England, then I will give earl Geoffrey an exchange of land . . . before he shall be disseised of the aforesaid lands."[115] Theobald was seen as having a claim to this land, by the king's grant, which would have to be taken account of in any settlement. This at least was the view of Geoffrey de Mandeville. He himself had earlier charters issued by the king and queen, and they were produced to the empress as containing valid title.[116] It is for this reason that in both her charters for Geoffrey the empress gives Stephen his title as king.[117] She had also to accept that she was constrained in granting out the estates of her opponents. To William de Beauchamp she says, "Also I give and concede to him the lands and inheritances of his close relatives who have been against me in my war and are not able to come to terms with me, unless another of his closer relatives shall have served me in that war."[118] Built into the agreement is his expectation of what is proper in determining the descent of land. There would be no free-for-all. It was claimed against the empress that:

> by reckless innovations she lessened or took away the possessions and lands of some men, held by grant of the king, while the fees and honours of the very few who still adhered to the king she confiscated altogether and granted to others; she arbitrarily annulled any grant

[113] The points in this paragraph are argued more fully in King, "A Week in Politics."

[114] *Regesta*, iii, no. 543; *EEA* 8: *Winchester 1070–1204*, nos. 68–9; on the pension, Torigni, 132.

[115] *Regesta*, iii, no. 274: "tali tenore quod si reddidero comiti Theobaldi totam terram quam tenebat in Anglia, dabo Galfrido comite Essexe escambium suum ad valentiam . . . antequam de praedictis terris dissaisiatur."

[116] Ibid., no. 275: "illas c libratas terrae de terris eschaetis quas idem rex et regina ei dederunt . . . sicut habet inde cartas eorum."

[117] Ibid., no. 274: "ipse et homines sui sint quieti de omnibus debitis quae debuerunt regi Henrico aut regi Stephano"; Ibid., no. 275: "illas cc libratas terrae quas rex Stephanus et Matildis regina ei dederunt, sicut habet inde cartas illorum." Prestwich, "The Treason of Geoffrey de Mandeville," 293: "from Geoffrey's point of view Stephen and his wife were still the king and queen whose charters he held."

[118] *Regesta*, iii, no. 68: "item dedi ei et concessi terras et hereditates suorum proximorum parentum qui contra me fuerint in werra mea et mecum finem facere non poterunt, nisi de sua parentela propinquiore michi in ipsa werra servierit."

fixed by the king's royal decree; she hastily snatched away and conferred on her own followers anything that he had given in unshakeable perpetuity to churches or to his companions in arms.[119]

In practice, as her own charters show, she could not do so.

The empress was losing the argument and losing territory at one and the same time. There is no doubt whom she felt was chiefly responsible for briefing against her. This was Henry of Winchester, the papal legate. She had been well advised to seek his support, immediately after the battle of Lincoln, "because he was reckoned to surpass all the great men of England in judgement and wisdom and to be their superior in virtue and wealth";[120] and she now determined not to lose that support without a fight. She went from Oxford to Winchester. It was a move that took her leading men completely by surprise. Robert of Gloucester knew nothing of it, while Henry of Winchester himself was "astonished" when she arrived.[121] She took up residence in the castle, in the south-west of the city, adjacent to the city gate used by travellers from the west.[122] Only then did she summon the bishop. He sent word that he would be along shortly, but immediately fled from the city. The story quickly spread that as the empress rode in through one gate he was escaping through another.[123] For anyone familiar with the topography of the city of Winchester the story will have made perfect sense. The main road ran through the city from west to east. The bishop's palace at Wolvesey was adjacent to the east gate (see plate 8). The nearest of his castles was at Merdon but it is most likely that on this occasion he made for Farnham. There he was secure from attack and there he could be in easy touch with those on whose support he could most rely. With the Londoners first of all. They had driven the empress out and had much to fear from her. They had admitted Stephen's queen to the city in the empress's stead.[124] The queen's other main base at this time was at Guildford. There Henry of Winchester had a "family conference" with the queen and now accepted the case that she had been urging for weeks.[125] The legate's breach with the empress was seen to be complete.

Henry of Winchester now watched as his episcopal city became a battleground. The initial focus of the fighting was the royal palace.[126] The site was important for several reasons. It was important strategically, being

[119] *GS*, 120–1.

[120] *GS*, 118–19.

[121] JW, iii. 298–9: "cuius inopinatum aduentum . . . miratus." Robert of Gloucester had earlier come to Winchester to try to make peace with the bishop: WM, *HN*, 100–1.

[122] *GS*, 118–19; JW, iii. 298–9; WM, *HN*, 100–1.

[123] *GS*, 126–7; JW, iii. 298–9.

[124] *GS*, 126–7; SD, *Libellus*, 312–13.

[125] WM, *HN*, 100–1.

[126] Ibid., *HN*, 102–3, refers to the "bishop's tower," and *GS*, 126–7, 130–1, to "the bishop's castle." These references are to a fortification at the royal palace: Biddle, *Winchester*, 297–8, 325–6.

at the centre of the city, and also controlling any access from the castle to the enclave in the south and east which included the cathedral church and the bishop's palace. It was important historically: it was the original, and continued to be the chief, centre of royal authority in the city. Here was a copy of the *Anglo-Saxon Chronicle*, chained and on permanent duty as testimony to the traditions of English kingship. Here was the royal writing office, with the monks of the cathedral priory standing ready with ink and parchment whenever there was need. Here the exchequer met for the first time around 1110, and the sheriffs were accustomed to come twice a year to render account. Here was the original treasury, which moved to the castle at some point, but which may still have been in the palace in 1141, though its reserves of cash were much depleted. Here, when the signs of civil war were first apparent, the bishop had built a fortified keep. The empress, as lady of the English, had clear title to control the royal palace, but the bishop defended it resolutely. He would fight fire with fire and the results for the city are described in cataclysmic terms:

> He decided to set fire to Winchester and raze it to the ground. . . . On 2 August, he set fire to the city and reduced to ashes the convent of the nuns with its buildings, more than forty churches together with the largest and best part of the city, and finally the monastery of monks devoted to the service of God and St Grimbald with its buildings. In the church of St Grimbald there was a large and holy cross, which long ago had been made on King Canute's orders, and beautifully enriched by him with gold and silver, gems, and precious stones. Marvellous to tell, the cross, as the fire drew near, and almost as though it was aware of the approaching danger, began to sweat and blacken before the eyes of the brethren present, and to convey the blackness of the incendiaries. Then just as it caught fire, three dreadful claps of thunder sounded as though from heaven.[127]

Inevitably there is some exaggeration here. Hyde Abbey was outside the city walls, moved there early in the reign of Henry I, and fire can hardly have spread as far.[128] But the monks had suffered greatly at the hands of the bishop and they ensured wide publicity for the complaints they made

---

[127] JW, iii. 298–301. The "convent of nuns" was St Mary's Abbey, or Nunnaminster: Biddle, *Winchester*, 321–3; Foot, *Female Religious Communities in England*, 243–52. The "church of St Grimbald" was Hyde Abbey: Biddle, *Winchester*, 313–21; *Liber Vitae of Hyde Abbey*, 16–48. The burning of the two houses is noted also in WM, *HN*, 102–5; *GS*, 130–1. "Over forty" represents a good estimate of the total number of parish churches within the city walls at this date: Biddle, *Winchester*, 329–35. The celebrated cross of Canute is shown in the frontispiece to the *Liber Vitae*, 35–7 and plate V. The cross was later, so it was claimed, stripped of its gold and silver "by the legate" and the proceeds used to pay the wages of the soldiers who had committed this atrocity: WM, *HN*, 104–5.

[128] It may have been the result of skirmishing between the opposing forces: Biddle, *Winchester*, 318–19.

against him.[129] Their great crucifix had been destroyed and even before the fire took hold it had wept at the suffering it perceived.

The suffering lasted for seven weeks. This was "the siege of Winchester" but over that time the nature of the siege changed. What had started as a siege by the empress's forces of the royal palace, which was being defended by the bishop's men, turned into a siege by the king's supporters of the royal castle, which was being defended by the empress and her forces. The armies grew in size and each side was later concerned to emphasize the strength of the opposition it had faced. The empress had come to Winchester "with as large a force as she could" muster, and this contained the core of her support. King David of Scots was there. So was Robert of Gloucester, seemingly quite secure in his own house in the centre of the city.[130] Among the other earls, according to the *Gesta Stephani*, were Baldwin, earl of Exeter; Roger, earl of Warwick; William, earl of Dorset and Reginald, earl of Cornwall. Among the barons, "who were in no way inferior to the earls in loyalty and worth, valour and distinction," were Brian Fitz Count, John Fitz Gilbert the Marshal, Robert d'Oilli, and William Fitz Alan.[131] This is the longest list of the empress's supporters at the siege. It was a time of confusion, when there was no certainty as to who was on which side. Particular uncertainty surrounds two magnates whom the empress had striven hard to bring over to her side. Ranulf, earl of Chester, "came late and was of little help,"[132] more watching on events than contributing resources. It was said that he had approached the queen but that the royal supporters distrusted him and he was turned away.[133] The position of Geoffrey de Mandeville is also unsure, though the "second edition" of the *Historia Novella* has him fighting alongside the Londoners on the side of the queen.[134] As to the queen's more certain support, "almost all the earls of England came, for they were young and frivolous, men who preferred the *chevauchée* to the pursuit of peace."[135] This also may be exaggerated, for only Simon of Senlis, earl of Northampton, Gilbert de Clare, earl of Hertford, William d'Aubigny, earl of Arundel, and William, Earl Warenne, are named.[136] There was a strong

[129] Just as Roger of Salisbury had done at Malmesbury, so Henry of Winchester had done at Hyde, suspending the abbacy and keeping the revenues of the house in his own hand: *Monasticon*, ii. 435–7; Biddle, *Winchester*, 319–20.

[130] WM, *HN*, 104–5 and n. 250; Keene, *Winchester Survey*, ii, no. 234.

[131] *GS*, 128–9: "uiribus mire et copiose undecumque secum conductis"; cf. WM, *HN*, 102–3: "pauci uero cum imperatrice uenerant."

[132] WM, *HN*, 102–3.

[133] JH, 310.

[134] WM, *HN*, 102–3 and n. 243.

[135] WM, *HN*, 100–3.

[136] Writing of events somewhat earlier, OV vi. 546–7, names Waleran of Meulan, William of Warenne, and Simon of Senlis as the core of the queen's support, and these are termed "the faithful three" by Round, *Geoffrey*, 145. Simon of Senlis and William of Warenne are mentioned by JW iii. 300–3, while Earl Gilbert captured William of Salisbury in the retreat, WM, *HN*, 116–17. *Liber Eliensis*, 322–3, gives William of Warenne, William, earl of Arundel, Geoffrey de Mandeville, and Earl Gilbert, "and other powerful helpers," as those who secured the king's release.

professional element in the royal army, with mercenary troops fighting under William of Ypres, and a force of a thousand men from the London militia.[137]

It was a professional campaign that royal forces conducted to drive the empress and her supporters out of Winchester. It was designed to cut off the supply route from the west to the royal castle. In order to protect this route the nunnery at Wherwell, where negotiations had been held prior to the empress's original reception at Winchester, now became the key to her survival. The empress sent out a party of troops to garrison the nunnery, "so that the king's forces might be more easily held in check and supplies brought into the city in more adequate quantities."[138] The nuns were driven from the abbey church, for their natural place of refuge in time of war was at the same time the most defensible part of their convent when the empress's troops (under John the Marshal) came under attack in their turn.[139] The cutting of the main supply line to the city from the west offered the possibility that the king's forces would be able to encircle the city, barricade the empress within the castle and prevent her escape. The city was lost to her. If she was to get away safely then there was no time to lose.

On the morning of 14 September the gates of the city were opened and the empress and her party broke out. Those named as being with her are the king of Scots, Robert of Gloucester, Miles of Gloucester, Reginald of Cornwall, and Brian Fitz Count. They "were in close column, all retreating as one body." The empress was placed towards the head of the column if not in the vanguard, with the escort of Reginald, earl of Cornwall; she needed protection from an attack from the flank, in case troops were sent across from Wherwell to intercept her. But the main threat could be expected to come from pursuit from the city, and so the rearguard would be the key to the empress's safety. So at least it turned out. For more than eight miles there was a running skirmish until the rearguard of the army came to cross the ford at Stockbridge. There it either found the long causeway barred against it and was forced to fight or it stopped voluntarily to confront its pursuers and give the empress more time to escape.[140] Robert of Gloucester and his bodyguard were captured by the Earl Warenne and a party of Flemings. All the others got away as best they could. The king of Scotland escaped only – so it was said – by bribing his captors. This was the third occasion on which he had been driven from

[137] WM, *HN*, 104–5; JH, 310; *GS*, 128–31; SD, *Libellus*, 312–13.
[138] *GS*, 130–3.
[139] On the fighting at Wherwell, both during the siege and the retreat, see, WM, *HN*, 104–5; JW, iii. 302–3; *GS*, 130–3; *History of William Marshal*, i. 12–15.
[140] The scene is well set, from local knowledge, in Hill, "The Battle of Stockbridge, 1141." The main sources, listed in order of writing, are, JW iii. 300–3; *GS*, 130–5; JH, 310–11; *History of William Marshal*, i. 12–15.

England with dishonour and it would be the last.[141] Even more ignominiously, some of the great barons "cast away all emblems of their knighthood and going on foot, in sorry plight, gave false names and denied that they were fugitives."[142] Miles of Gloucester may have been intended here, for he returned home "exhausted, tired, and half-naked."[143] John the Marshal lost an eye in the defence of Wherwell and was left for dead.[144] If the empress's best generals were shell-shocked, so too was the empress herself. She rode first to Ludgershall castle, arriving there "terrified and troubled" and being forced to move on "for fear of the bishop." After a night's disturbed sleep she was placed astride a horse and "riding like a man" – which offered both better speed and a measure of disguise – she came to Devizes, but lacking any intelligence as to what had happened behind her did not feel secure even there. And so she was placed on a litter "like a corpse" and in this sorry state she also came to Gloucester.[145]

The empress had retained her freedom but at a heavy cost. Any pretence at strategy had disappeared along the Stockbridge road. Her prestige had suffered a crippling blow. Her forces had been scattered.[146] Several of her prominent supporters had been captured. Among them was Robert of Gloucester. After his capture he had been presented to the queen, just as Stephen had earlier been presented to the empress, and then in the custody of William of Ypres taken to Rochester castle in Kent.[147] Negotiations were now put in hand for his release in exchange for the king. This might at first glance seem surprising. As Robert himself is reported to have said, "a king and an earl were not equal in rank,"[148] so a simple exchange would favour the king's party. Not only that, the release of the king inevitably would involve the restoration of his kingship, whereas the release of the earl was that of just one supporter of the empress's cause, a cause that was in retreat. The empress's panic, her fear of isolation, helps explain her readiness to compromise. When she got to Gloucester, in the last week of September, she witnessed a charter of Miles of Gloucester for

---

[141] The statement that he was captured for a third time, *GS*, 134–5, should be read in conjunction with ibid., 128–9, which says that he had already been twice "chased in shameful flight from England," rather than meaning that he was captured and ransomed three times in the rout: cf. Chibnall, *Matilda*, 114; Davis, *Stephen*, 60; Hill, "Battle of Stockbridge," 176; Strickland, *War*, 196. JH, 311, states that one of the king's godsons, David Olifard, protected him from the pursuers; the Olifards were tenants of the honour of Huntingdon and of Peterborough Abbey: Barrow, *Anglo-Norman Era*, 18, 45 and n. 69; *Henry of Pytchley's Book of Fees*, 54, 97–8.

[142] *GS*, 134–5.

[143] JW, iii. 302–3.

[144] So at least the *History of William Marshal*, i. 14–15.

[145] JW, iii. 300–3; the story of her riding "like a man" is also preserved in the *History of William Marshal*, i. 12–13; WM, *HN*, 105–7, notes her reaching Devizes "in the greatest haste"; so also *GS*, 134–5.

[146] SD, *Libellus*, 312–13: "ceteri quique huc illucque disperguntur."

[147] JW, iii. 303–4; WM, *HN*, 106–7, 114–17.

[148] WM, *HN*, 116–17.

the monks of Llanthony Secunda.[149] Robert of Gloucester was there alongside her, but in spirit only. Brian Fitz Count was there. Aside from Robert Fitz Martin the other witnesses are men of local rank. It is a small escort, not the nucleus of a fighting force. It is quite understandable that they feared that if they did not come to an agreement, and secure Robert of Gloucester's release, then they would be picked off one by one.[150] These were pragmatic arguments but no less important was Robert's prestige. In the retreat from Winchester he had taken the most dangerous commission and had shown great calmness under enemy fire. His spell of imprisonment helped his reputation grow apace. He still believed in the empress's cause. The empress's party had to get Robert of Gloucester out of prison because they could not face the future without him.

The negotiations were complex and at times quite heated.[151] It was accepted in these circumstances that the spouse spoke for her man. The queen had long been the focus of the king's party and was widely credited with securing her husband's release,[152] and now the countess of Gloucester rather than the empress negotiated the terms of her husband's release. The intermediaries in the negotiations themselves were "the earls and those who were also properly invoved in work of this kind," a phrase that would include the household officers of any high-status captive. They also involved Theobald of Canterbury and Henry of Winchester, "the archbishop and the legate," who now appear in the pages of William of Malmesbury as a double act.[153] The senior clergy had claimed the right to reverse the succession, in April 1141, when they nominated the empress as lady of the English. What had happened since had left the country still divided and their own reputations severely damaged. They were desperate to use the exchange of prisoners as the occasion to make peace. "It was finally agreed on both sides that the king should be restored to the royal dignity, and that the earl should be raised to the government of England under the king, that both should be just rulers and restorers of peace just as they had been instigators and authors of dissension and upheaval."[154] They got as far as agreeing the heads of a possible agreement, but no further than that. Robert of Gloucester declined to accept any such terms. He was not, he said, a free agent; it would not be right for him to abandon his sister and so (again) set aside the oath he had sworn to her.[155] The peace negotiations collapsed.

There would be an exchange of prisoners but even this was not a simple matter when it involved men of such high rank. Who was to be exchanged and what conditions, if any, would be attached to their release? Robert of

[149] "Charters of the Earldom of Hereford," 13–14 (no. 3).
[150] WM, *HN*, 118–19.
[151] For the heat, *HN*, 116–17; *GS*, 136–7.
[152] *Liber Eliensis*, 322.
[153] WM, *HN*, 116–21.
[154] JW, iii. 304–5. WM, *HN*, 116–17, confirms that such an offer was made.
[155] WM, *HN*, 116–19.

Gloucester asked for a general release of prisoners taken along with him, but at first this was refused.[156] The king's party asked that all territory taken by the empress and her party after the battle of Lincoln should be restored to him. There was method in this. The acceptance of the point would allow them to argue – what they in any case believed – that everything done by the empress or on her behalf was illegitimate. Thus Stephen when dealing with Geoffrey de Mandeville shortly after his release started by restoring to him all the tenancies he had possessed "on the day that I was held up at Lincoln and captured."[157] These requests were refused by those who spoke for the empress. There would be no general release of prisoners and no restoration of territory. Rather the two men "should be released on the same terms, no other condition being involved except each should guard his own region to the best of his ability, as before." This left the mechanics of the release to be determined. It was insisted that the king be released first and a complex provision of hostages was put in place to secure the release of the earl, "the archbishop and the legate" providing written sureties and offering their own persons as additional hostages that the king's party would keep its side of the bargain. They would not be required. On 1 November, All Saints' Day, the king was released from his imprisonment at Bristol castle, "leaving his queen and son with two men of high rank, there to serve as security for the earl's release." Robert of Gloucester had a little while before been brought from Rochester to Winchester. When the king reached Winchester, Robert was released, "leaving his son William there in the same manner until the queen's release." Robert then returned to his castle at Bristol; the queen and Eustace were released and returned to Winchester; and on their arrival Robert of Gloucester's son was allowed to go free.[158]

Stephen after his release returned to London, where he was given a rapturous reception.[159] The city with its adjacent palace at Westminster would thereafter provide his main base. There immediate steps were taken to restore his authority. A legatine council was summoned to meet at Westminster on 7 December 1141, in order to reverse the decisions made at the council at Winchester the previous April. It would prove an awkward meeting. The king himself appeared and complained that he had been captured and almost killed by his own men, even though he "had never refused them justice." The legate brazened it out, claiming – quite unconvincingly – that the decision of the earlier council had been reached under duress, because the empress and her men "had surrounded Winchester with noise of arms." He now addressed the delegates, "in the

---

[156] WM, *HN*, 116–21; the demand for ransoms is placed in context in Strickland, *War*, 191.

[157] *Regesta*, iii, no. 276: "die qua impeditus fui apud Lincolniam et captus."

[158] WM, *HN*, 106–9, 118–21.

[159] *GS*, 136–7: "when the king was restored a superb and magnificent procession of barons went out to meet him and accompanied him as an escort"; HH, 740–1: "the king . . . was received by the English nobility with great rejoicing."

name of God and the pope, and bade them aid zealously to the utmost of their power a king anointed with the goodwill of the people and the approval of the Apostolic See." He was heard out in virtual silence by the clergy and was roundly abused by an envoy of the empress, who charged him with double-dealing.[160] It was alleged that he had encouraged the empress even before the tumultuous events of the past year, and he had certainly during the year insistently enjoined the lay baronage to support her. "You yourself, a prelate of Holy Church," said one of them, Brian Fitz Count, "have ordered me to adhere to the daughter of king Henry your uncle, and to help her to acquire that which is hers by right but has been taken from her by force."[161] Henry and Theobald, witheringly described in the same letter as the "so-called archbishop of Canterbury," were henceforth held in contempt by the empress's supporters.

The council at Westminster was a shabby episode at the close of what had been a sordid year. It was not just that many prominent individuals had had their reputations diminished. It had been a year that had brought the whole political process into disrepute. If this seems a little too modern a phrase still it can be defended here, for it translates what the political commentators of the day wished to say. Orderic wrote with Stephen still in captivity, "languishing wretchedly in a dungeon," and Louis of France off on campaign: "I see the princes of this world overwhelmed by misfortunes and disastrous setbacks."[162] William of Malmesbury ended a chapter here and his life too was nearly at an end. "This year, whose tragedies I have briefly related, was ill-omened and almost mortal to England, which, after thinking it might now in some sort draw a breath of freedom, fell back again into misery."[163] The author of the *Gesta Stephani* had more cause to take pleasure in the king's release but still bemoaned the terms of the exchange of prisoners, which meant they would "return to the earlier position of the civil war: these indeed were harsh and ill-judged terms and bound to do harm to the entire country."[164] Herman of Tournai wrote that England had sunk "from earlier wealth into great poverty because of the devastation and expense of persistent dissension."[165] The monk of Gloucester, cut off in mid-sentence, is still conclusive enough: "for a whole year all over the kingdom and country, the poor were pillaged, men were slaughtered, and churches cruelly violated."[166]

---

[160] WM, *HN*, 108–11.

[161] Davis, "Henry of Blois and Brian Fitz Count"; and for translation and fuller commentary, King, "Brian Fitz Count."

[162] OV, vi. 550–1.

[163] WM, *HN*, 110–11.

[164] GS, 136–7.

[165] Herman of Tournai, 34.

[166] JW, iii. 304–5.

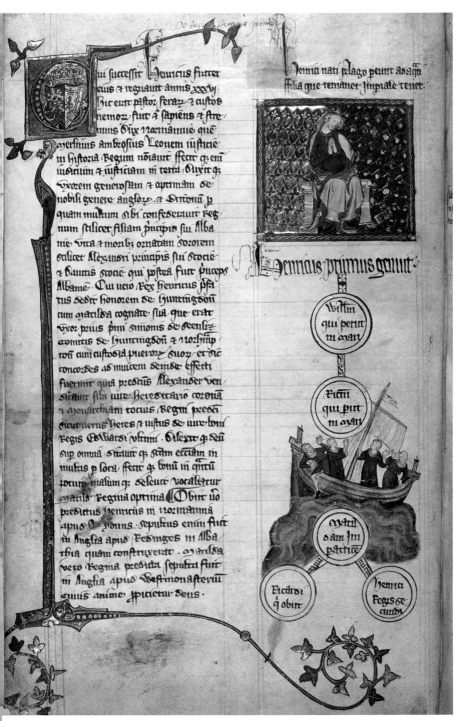

Henry I grieves at the sinking of the White Ship. Illustration to show the line of succession to Henry I, from a group of legal texts mȳe *c.*1320 for the corporation of the city of London. The line continues through the empress Matilda to Henry II.

2 The seal of Stephen before he became king, giving his title as "count of Boulogne and of Mortain." A facsimile from *Sir Christopher Hatton's Book of Seals*, mŸe 1640–1. It shows the seal as affixed to the foundation charter of Furness Abbey, which is dated to 1127. The seal is distinctive in that the rider carries a lance with pennon, rather than the more usual sword, and he carries his shield away from his body.

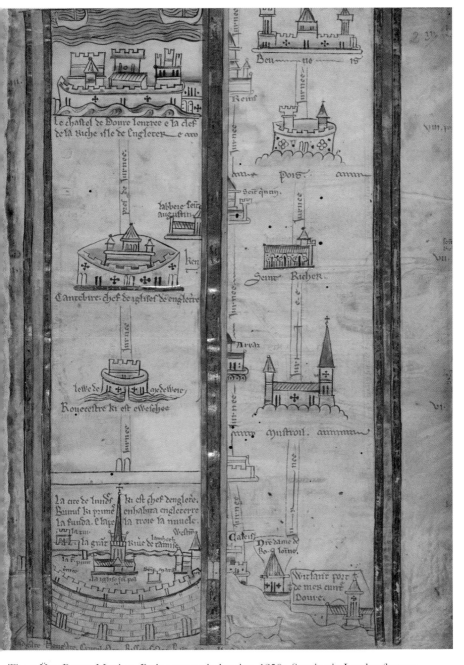

The roŸ to Rome. Matthew Paris autograph drawing, 1250s. Starting in London (bottom
left), the roŸ goes first to Rochester and Canterbury, thence to Dover, described as "the entry
and key to the rich island of England"; then across the channel, with its two boats, to (bottom
right) a choice of channel ports, Calais, Boulogne, or Wissant, and thence through the county of
Boulogne into France. Each day's journey is marked out, as are the main buildings of interest to
the discerning traveller.

4 First seal of King Stephen. (top) Obverse, seated in majesty. The king is seated on a throne, wearing a crown surmounted with three fleur-de-lys; he carries a sword in his right hand and in his left hand an orb surmounted by a cross on which a dove perches. He wears a tight-fitting tunic with belt, above it a mantle with an embroidered border, fastened on the right shoulder. (above) Reverse, equestrian. The king wears a mail hauberk and hood, a pointed helmet with two ribands flying behind. He carries in his right hand a deeply-grooved sword and on his left arm he holds in front of his body a convex pear-shaped shield.

The coronation of Stephen. Illustration from Matthew Paris, *Flores Historiarum*. The text which follows notes that Stephen was crowned by William of Corbeil, archbishop of Canterbury. The other bishop shown may be Henry of Winchester, the king's brother.

The judgement of Solomon capital, *c*.1120, from Westminster Abbey. The king at his coronation promised to rule with justice and equity. This vivid exemplar would have been visible to those walking in the abbey cloister on the day that Stephen was crowned.

7 Henry of Blois enamel plaques. Made by a Mosan goldsmith in England, during Stephen's reign, for Henry, bishop of Winchester (identified as HENRICUS EPISCOPUS in the lower plaque). The upper plaque shows two censing angels emerging from the clouds of Heaven. The Latin inscription asks that Henry be allowed entry to Heaven, "but not just yet, lest England suffer for it, since on him it depends for peace or war, agitation or rest." The lower plaque shows Henry, tonsured and with a fine beard, clutching his crozier, presenting an altarpiece or reliquary. The inscription draws attention to his fame, his character, his learning and his eloquence. In every way typical of Henry, these pieces show his connoisseurship, his piety, and above all his supreme confidence.

8 Wolvesey Palace, Winchester. A reconstruction of the building as it was when Henry of Winchester died here in August 1171. Henry was a great builder, and in the south-east corner of the walled Roman city he built "a palatial house with a strong tower." He added a new hall to the existing buildings, enclosing them to make a courtyard, making the complex defensible by the time of the siege of Winchester in 1141. Shortly after this, Henry demolished the royal palace and used the materials for further additions to his own palace.

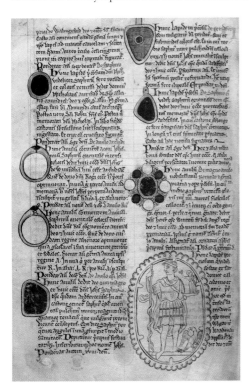

9 Jewellery at St Albans Abbey, illustrated and described by Matthew Paris, 1250s. The grandest of the rings is the pontifical ring (centre) given by Henry of Winchester. It is inscribed with his name on the hoop. The ring had an oval central sapphire in a gold setting, surrounded by four pearls and four garnets.

10 The seal of the empress Matilda. This fine seal (top) was made for Matilda whilst she was German empress. It shows her seated, crowned, holding a sceptre in her right hand. The legend, translated, reads: "Matilda by the grace of God queen of the Romans". The empress continued to make use of this seal after she came to England, even after she was given a further title "lady of the English" in April 1141. It has been suggested that she had a further seal made after this date, and that she took the title "queen of the English." This is based on the transcription of the legend (above) made by Richard St George in the early seventeenth century. The two legends are set out below (correspondence between them in bold):

(A) + MATHILDIS DEI GRATIA ROMANORUM REGINA

(B) **MATHILDIS** IMPE**RAT**RIX **ROM**' ET **REGINA** ANGLIAE

It seems clear that St George, faced possibly with a damaged seal, has misread the legend. He had no clue from the text of the document, for the empress uses the title "Mathildis regis Henrici filia" ("Matilda the daughter of King Henry").

11 Oxford Castle, St George's Tower. Engraving by A. W. N. Pugin. One of the earliest stone towers in England, built soon after the conquest. It was from here that the empress escaped in December 1142 and crossed the frozen river.

12 Coin of the empress Matilda. One of a number of coins issued in the name of the empress and struck at Cardiff, found in the Coed-y-Wenallt hoard in 1980. (left) Obverse. This regal image may be compared with that of the king (plate 13a-b). The legend reads: MA . IM . HE . The MA here clearly stands for MATHILDIS and the IM for IMPERATRIX. The extension of HE is more problematic. It may stand for HERES, in which case the legend would read "Matilda the Empress Heir (to England)". To most of her supporters, however, it was her son, Henry, who was the true heir. (right) Reverse. + IOLI: DE: BRIT: C(AIE)R. This gives the name of the moneyer, Joli de Breteuil, and the place of issue, Cardiff.

a

b

c

d

e

f

13 Miscellany of coins. It was the judgement of William of Newburgh that during Stephen's reign, "every magnate minted his own coins," and like a king, laid down the law for his subjects. A selection of these "magnate" coins are shown here, alongside the "official" issue of Stephen struck in the mid 1140s. (a-b) Stephen type 2; (c) William of Aumale, earl of York; (d) Patrick, earl of Salisbury; (e) Henry of Scots, earl of Northumberland; (f) Two Figure type: The second figure in this coin, struck in York, is uncertain – possibly it shows Stephen and his queen, Matilda, but more likely the two figures are Stephen and his son, Eustace.

14 Castle Rising, Norfolk. Mid-twelfth century. One of the residences of William d'Aubigny pincerna, earl of Sussex. The path leads to a ceremonial stairway, taking the visitor to the main living quarters on the first floor – the hall and great chamber of the lord, the chapel, and domestic offices. The keep is 50 feet high.

15 Castle Hedingham, Essex. Interior of the great hall, c.1140, built of stone from Barnack, Northamptonshire. The main residence of Aubrey de Vere, earl of Oxford. Stephen's queen, Matilda, died here in May 1152. What now survives of the great keeps of twelfth-century castles is usually stronger on defence than on domestic detail, but something of the feel of life in a magnate household can still be gained here.

16 The Lewis Chessmen. Found in the early nineteenth century on the Isle of Lewis, Outer Hebrides, Scotland. The pieces consist of finely carved walrus ivory and whales' teeth, showing seated kings and queens, mitred bishops, mounted knights, standing warders and pawns shaped as obelisks. These are amongst the most approachable images of mid-twelfth-century society, and as arranged here by the British Museum, with a bishop seemingly instructing a king and queen, they serve as a tableau of Stephen's reign.

17 Second seal of Waleran of Meulan, 1139–40. Affixed to a grant made in the mid-1140s to the abbey of St Victor, Paris. When he was appointed earl of Worcester by Stephen in 1139, Waleran commissioned a new seal to reflect his new dignity. The sword side (left) may be compared with Stephen's first seal (plate 4), with lappets hanging from the back of the helmet. The banner side (right) is comparable to that on Stephen's third seal, made in 1140. A checky device on the banner, shield, surcoat and saddle-cloth draws attention to the fact that Waleran claimed descent – through his mother – from Charlemagne.

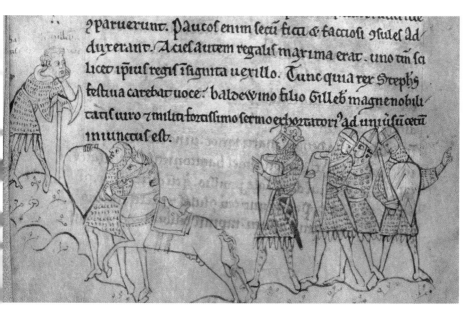

18 Battle of Lincoln, 1141. Baldwin Fitz Gilbert addresses the troops. Illustration *c*.1200 from a copy of the *Historia Anglorum* of Henry of Huntingdon. The sketch was prompted by an anecdote from the chronicle: the royal troops before the battle were exhorted to valour by Baldwin Fitz Gilbert (left), the king (centre) having delegated the task because he had a weak voice. The horse listens intently but the men seem distracted.

19 Lincoln Cathedral. Frieze on west front, 1140s, showing Noah's ark/Noah and his family leaving the ark/God's covenant with Noah. Another passage in Henry of Huntingdon's chronicle refers to Bishop Alexander restoring his cathedral "with such delicate craftsmanship that it seemed more beautiful than when it was newly built." He might have been thinking of this frieze, which shows the influence of the abbey of St Denis, rebuilt by Abbot Suger shortly before.

M). Di gra Regina Angl. Epo Lond. 7 Toti Clero. 7 Omib⁹ fidelib⁹ Sce Ecclie sal'
Sciatis me tradidisse hospitale meu iuxta Turri lud eccessu dni mei Regis Seph:
Ecclie Sce Trinitatis Lond. 7 priori. 7 Canoneis ibide do servientib⁹ in custodia
pperuam. 7 Volo ut illd ponant ubi oportum⁹ eis uisum fuerit. Concessi ⁊
ad ipsum hospitale manutenendu molendinu iuxta Turrim lond. 7 Totam
terram ad ipsum molendinu ptinentem. Et pdicta Ecclia Sce Trinitat tenebit
in ipso hospitali in pperuu. xiij. paupes p salute anime dni meu Reg Steph.
7 mee. necnon 7 p salute filior nror Eustach. 7 Willi. 7 Omiu nror. Con
cessi ⁊ eide hospitali in custodia pdicte Ecclie Sce Trinitatis xx. Lib. singtis
annis de reddiru de Edredeshytha in pperuam Elemosina. dno meo Rege
Steph id ipsu annuente. T. henr de Essexe Constab regi Ric de Chamuitt.
Warner de Lisor. A. Cancell. Thoma Capell. Ric de montedenro. Aps
haingeham.

20 Charter of Queen Matilda. Facsimile from *Sir Christopher Hatton's Book of Seals*. The queen grant
"her hospital next to the Tower of London" to the canons of Holy Trinity, Aldgate. Issued at
Castle Hedingham (plate 15). The seal shows the queen standing crowned in a mantle and gown, a
fleur-de-lys sceptre in her right hand and a falcon perched on her left hand.

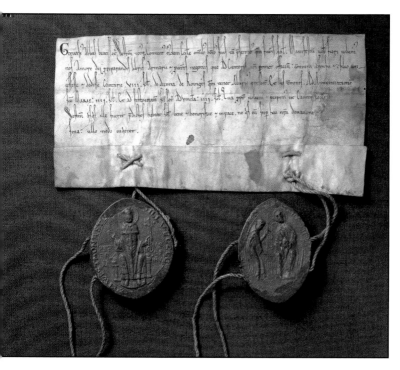

21 Seal of Gervase, abbot of Westminster, son of Stephen. Affixed to a charter in favour of the preceptor of the monastery granting his department 8 shillings a year for the repair of books. The seal (right) shows the abbot, holding his crozier, in front of the Virgin and Child. The legend reads SIGILLUM GERVASII ABBATIS SANCTI PETRI MONASTERII. Gervase was later criticised for granting out lands without the consent of his community but this transaction was for their benefit and it bears the seal of the convent also (left).

22 Seal of Mary, prioress of Higham, daughter of Stephen. This fine seal shows Mary standing, veiled, wearing a long close-fitting dress with long sleeves and supporting on her left forearm a closed book. The legend on the seal emphasises her rank as the king's daughter – SIGILLUM MARIE FILIE STEPHANI REGIS ANGLIE (The seal of Mary, daughter of Stephen king of England).

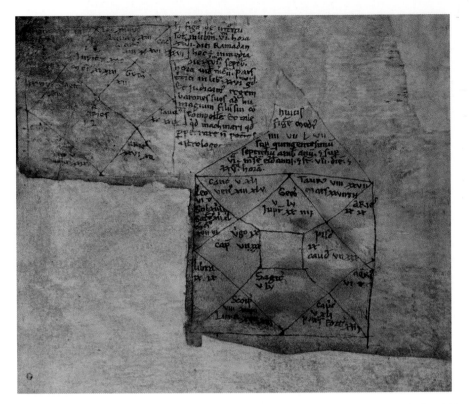

23 Two horoscopes for the king's party. Made *c.*1151. In the first of them (top, centre), dated 16 September 1151, it is stated that the king would shortly "compel his barons to perform homage to his son (Eustace)," but that he would not do so without consulting an astrologer.

24 Coins of the two contestants. (left) King Stephen type 7. It was a part of the peace process, agreed late in 1153, that a new coinage be issued for the whole of England. It would only be superseded in 1158, four years after the accession of Henry II. (right) Henry's succession is previewed in this unique coin, struck in the west country, which gives him the title REX FUTURUS, the future king. The two die-cutters make Stephen seem resigned to his fate while Henry looks supremely confident.

Chapter 6

PROVINCIAL GOVERNMENT

This lordship of his the earl very greatly adorned by restoring peace and quietness everywhere, except that in building his castles he exacted forced labour from all and, whenever he had to fight the enemy, appropriated everyone's help either by sending knights or by paying money. And there was indeed in those regions a shadow of peace but not yet peace complete, since nothing more grievously vexed the people of the country than working not for themselves but for others, and by their efforts adding to the resources for discord and warfare.[1]

With the king of England in captivity it was difficult to tell the time. 1141 was the sixth year of Stephen's kingship. The writers who structured their work in terms of the regnal year continued to do so,[2] even though the king himself was in captivity for nearly nine months of the year. It was his captivity that was the main news event of the year. When Simon Tuschet gave land to the new Gilbertine house at Haverholme he dated his grant to "the year in which a battle was fought between king Stephen and earl Ranulf of Chester, while the venerable bishop Alexander held rule over the diocese of Lincoln."[3] Many miles from Lincoln, near Châteaudun in the centre of the county of Chartres, Ursion of Fréteval gave to the monks of Tiron whatever they had of his fee, "in past days up to the year in which Stephen, king of the English, was captured in battle."[4] When Stephen was released this event in its turn became a point of reference. Robert, son of Gosbert, granted a small property, with full ceremonial, to the dean and chapter of St Paul's, giving the date as 1 November 1141, "that is, upon the release of King Stephen from the captivity of Robert the son of King

---

[1] *GS*, 150–1, writing of Robert, earl of Gloucester (translation modified).
[2] HH, 724–5: "sexto anno"; Torigni, 139: "Romanorum Conradus 4; Francorum Ludovicus 4; Anglorum Stephanus 6." On "dating documents" see Clanchy, *From Memory to Written Record*, 299–304.
[3] "Haverholme Priory Charters," ed. Foster, 37–8: "in anno quo commissum est prelium inter regem Stephanum et comitem Cestrie Ranulphum venerabili Alexandro episcopo monarchiam sedis Lincolnie tenente"; noted Stenton, *First Century*, 243.
[4] *Cart. Tiron*, ii. 35–7 (no. 267): "a retroactis diebus usque ad annum illum quo in bello captus est Stephanus rex Anglorum."

Henry."[5] And many miles from London, near Pontorson on the western frontier of Normandy, Gerduin of Aucey gave the tithes of one of his estates to the monks of Mont St Michel, dating the transaction to "the year in which Stephen king of the English was released from captivity."[6] Even after his release, the king himself could not avoid all reference to his imprisonment. He referred to the battle of Lincoln as "the day on which I was held up at Lincoln and captured."[7] That disastrous day needed to be specified because it was the limitation of secure title. And it lived long in the memory of his opponents. On a fine spring day in 1142, David, king of Scots, and his son Henry, and Richard, abbot of Melrose, walked the bounds of an estate on the south bank of the River Tweed, "on the Friday after Ascension Day in the second year of the captivity of Stephen, king of the English."[8] To the king of Scots 1142 was not Stephen's seventh year but the second year of his captivity.

It was important to alter this perception. It was important to re-establish the monarchy. The route to this was ceremonial. The king would be re-crowned and with the utmost solemnity, "because of the dishonour of his earlier captivity and because of the hopes inspired by his return." The ceremony took place at Canterbury on Christmas Day, 1141.[9] The choice of venue was not obvious, for it was at Westminster that Stephen had been crowned, as had his three predecessors. But the men of Kent had been the king's most loyal supporters in his captivity and, perhaps no less significantly, the anointing of the king was one job that the papal legate could not take from the archbishop of Canterbury. Theobald performed the ceremony himself, in his cathedral church. He made a point of holding up the proceedings, once all were assembled, while he himself robed, putting on the pallium which he had brought back from Rome, the sign of his authority as archbishop. He sat the king on his own chair, the queen facing him on the other side of the choir. There had been no time for a rehearsal. This, at least, seems to be the explanation of the story which became attached to the re-coronation, long after the event, as stories do.

---

[5] *HMC Ninth Report*, A i, 62: "super altare Sancti Pauli in die Omnium Sanctorum . . . anno mcxli, id est in exitu regis Stephani de captione Roberti filii regis Henrici." Round, *Geoffrey*, 136, saw this deed as showing the Londoners' pleasure at the king's release. This may have been so but the phrase says no more than that this was the very day of the king's release: "ea enim die rex eluctatus captionem."

[6] *Cart. Mont-Saint-Michel*, 162–3 (no. 87): "anno quo Stephanus rex Anglorum exiuit de captione."

[7] *Regesta*, iii, no. 276, granting to Geoffrey de Mandeville, earl of Essex, "omnia tenementa sua que tenuit de quocunque illa tenuerit die qua impeditus fui apud Lincolniam et captus."

[8] *Charters of David I*, nos. 120–1: "die veneris crastino Ascensionis domini anno scilicet secundo quo Stephanus rex Anglie captus est" (29 May 1142). These charters cannot have been drawn up before 1143 and it is possible that this "second year" was seen as being 1143, in which case the date would have been 14 May 1143 and the air perhaps a little more bracing.

[9] For the date, Gervase, i. 123; for the further details of the service, ibid., i. 526–7.

"There was a spot of bother between the monks and the clerks while each of them chanted *Christus Vincit.*"[10] The monks were the monks of Christ Church, Canterbury, the resident choir. The clerks were the clerks of the chapel royal, the visiting soloists. The *Laudes Regiae* were one of the high spots of the service. The *ordo* said simply that this was music for three voices.[11] Fine. The monks of Canterbury, like all monks, could sing antiphonally – i.e. the two sides of the choir singing verses alternately – with their eyes shut. They seem to have done so on this occasion and very loudly, quite drowning out the voices of their visitors.[12] The archbishop was horrified, for the ceremony was intended to stress his own dignity no less than the king's, and he excommunicated the offenders. The king spoke up for them. It had been a lovely service.

So indeed it had.[13] It had started in the king's private chamber. There, on a fine cloth, the tangible symbols of monarchy had been laid out. There were special sandals, stole bracelets, ceremonial swords, gilded spurs, the rod, the sceptre, and the royal crown itself. The king was solemnly invested with each of these, which will have taken some time, for each came accompanied with a special prayer and there was a longer discourse when this part of the ceremony had been completed. Then they processed into the church. Four barons bore lighted candles before the king. Four other barons bore a canopy above the king's head. "Three of the most noble earls of England bore three swords with gilded scabbards." Prayers were said over the king and queen as they knelt before the high altar; they were escorted to their seats; the archbishop robed and the mass commenced. Still the service remained focused on the king himself: there was a special collect in his honour; his escort formed up again for an offertory procession; and the *Laudes Regiae* were sung, not without incident, as has been seen. "After the mass the king took communion." At the end of this long service, the archbishop escorted him to the royal palace, clothed in lighter but still splendid garments. "Then the king put on a lighter crown and sat down to supper with the bishops and magnates of the land."

---

[10] Ibid., i. 527: "Facta est autem altercatio inter monachos et clericos dum utrique 'Christus Vincit' cantarent."

[11] Ibid., i. 526: "Deinde 'Christus Vincit' a tribus personis."

[12] This was not, of course, quite how the monks told it; they said, "clerici festinabant importune" – it was not their turn.

[13] The detail here comes from the description of the re-coronation of Richard I at Winchester on 17 Apr. 1194 given in Gervase, i. 524–7. He explains first that people had forgotten how to perform a coronation in these circumstances – "quia modus coronationis huiusmodi a multis retroactis diebus a memoria hominum sublatus est" – and so they looked to Canterbury, which was able to provide guidance, since Stephen and his queen had been crowned there. That guidance seems to have come in the form of an order of service. This is given in two chunks, the opening of each prayer or psalm serving as a short-hand for the texts to be used. All this relates to Richard's coronation – "haec fuit forma coronationis regis Ricardi" – but it followed what had been done for Stephen – "rex autem Stephanus . . . *sic* coronatus est."

The guest list for this occasion can be reconstructed with a fair degree of confidence. This is because a charter was issued at this time in favour of Geoffrey de Mandeville, consolidating the territorial gains that he had made in the previous year.[14] Those listed as witnesses were first the queen, then Henry, bishop of Winchester. The papal legate was the only bishop named. There were eight earls: William, Earl Warenne; Gilbert, earl of Pembroke; Gilbert, earl of Hertford; William, count of Aumale; Earl Simon; William d'Aubigny, earl of Sussex; Earl Alan, and Earl Robert de Ferrers. And there were eight barons, starting with the son of a count, William of Ypres, and then in order William Martel, Baldwin Fitz Gilbert de Clare, Robert de Vere, Faramus of Boulogne, Richard de Lucy, Turgis of Avranches, and Adam de Beaunay. The number of those listed here corresponds quite closely, the number of barons exactly, with those who had specified roles in the procession. There can be no certainty as to who exactly did what but the hereditary positions in the royal household were greatly valued by the magnates. Many years later, according to a story of Walter Map, William d'Aubigny strode into Henry II's lodgings in Paris, where he was dining with the king of France, and grasped the wine jug from the menial who waited at table. William was the royal butler: this was his job. "And from that great court he brought away the reputation of courtesy and not of presumption."[15] We may take it that William had served in the same capacity at Stephen's "Restoration Court" in 1141–2.[16] They put on a good show but this would be the last time for a decade and more that so many earls would come together in one place.

Stephen and his queen probably remained in or around London in the early weeks of 1142. The only reference to this time comes from William of Malmesbury, who says that both sides "behaved with calm restraint from Christmas to Lent, seeking rather to keep their own than assail what belonged to others."[17] The king's side could take some encouragement from rumours that began to circulate that the empress had suffered a nervous breakdown: "she had been greatly shaken by the rout of Winchester and worn out almost to the point of utter collapse."[18] These rumours, which would have been readily believed, they will have been happy to pass on, with suitable embellishment. They will have taken comfort also from the news that the north and east midlands, the scene of the battle of Lincoln, was territory that the king could still count as "his own" for the most part. A significant loss late in 1140 had been Nottingham, "a most noble city, famous for the size of its population and its wealth of all kinds."[19] It was taken by

[14] *Regesta*, iii, no. 276.

[15] Walter Map, *De Nugis Curialium*, 492–5.

[16] So called by Round, *Geoffrey*, 158.

[17] WM, *HN*, 122–3.

[18] *GS*, 138–9: "fuerat enim ex Wentoniense dispersione quassa nimis et usque ad defectum pene defatigata."

[19] JW, iii. 292–3: "urbs nobilissima . . . populosa multitudine et opulentia rerum omnium referta."

Robert of Gloucester, at the instigation of Ralph Paynel, and William Paynel was placed in charge of the garrison.[20] This was a castle popularly spoken of as being nearly impregnable.[21] Yet it seems to have been returned to the king with surprising ease. "Behold! In the darkness of the night, by the contrivance of two youths who had charge of the mills, the soldiers of William Peverel scaled the rock on which the citadel was built, obtained possession of the town, and expelled from Nottingham all who were in favour of the empress."[22] This is perhaps an extreme example of what would become a pattern over the next few years, with what seem to be major fortresses captured by just a few determined men. There were not the resources in men or money and perhaps there was no longer the will to keep so many castles in a defensible state.

The securing of Nottingham, the point at which northern and southern England might be held to divide, will have facilitated Stephen's first recorded action in 1142, which was to travel north to York. This he did probably in late March or early April.[23] Stephen had gone north immediately after his first coronation, in the early weeks of 1136. The reason for that expedition was clear, because of the challenge offered by David, king of Scots. Whatever brought him north in 1142 was less pressing. William of Malmesbury professed himself to have no idea what the king was up to.[24] John of Hexham said that while in the north he stopped a tournament arranged between the two earls in the region, William of Aumale, earl of York, and Alan, earl of Richmond.[25] He structured his story of the events of the early 1140s, with very little sense of chronology, in terms of the ambition of these two earls and that of Ranulf, earl of Chester, and the other great men. The tournament, whether real or not, provided an excellent image of the fragmented state of northern politics. Stephen will have hoped to provide a single focus and to have attracted support. There are no signs that he was successful. It did not help that church politics were if anything more messy than secular, in a region where the senior churchmen, particularly the archbishop of York, had been a rallying force. "After [Thurstan's] death . . . the unity of the kingdom was destroyed, because each man's will was his law."[26] Whatever was intended

---

[20] JW, iii. 290–1; JH, 308–9 (placing this after the battle of Lincoln). The two men named are Ralph Paynel of Dudley and William Paynel, possibly Ralph's brother: *EYC* 6: *Paynel*, 5–6, 48, 50–1.

[21] Newburgh, i. 89–90: "que natura loci inexpugnabilis videbatur."

[22] JH, 312.

[23] There can be no doubt that this visit took place. The king was seen as going north, arriving at York, and being taken ill at Northampton on his return. The times offered by the two sources are, however, contradictory. John of Hexham says that Stephen came to York after Easter ("post Pascha": ibid., 312); William of Malmesbury that the king was taken ill at Northampton just before Easter ("in ipsis pene Paschalibus feriis": WM, *HN*, 122–3).

[24] WM, *HN*, 122–3.

[25] JH, 312: "militares nundinas."

[26] JH, 305, cited in this context in Dalton, *Yorkshire*, 152.

as the broader strategy, whatever military objectives the king had for the summer of 1142, these had to be abandoned because he fell ill. We are not told the cause but it was a serious illness, so serious – now it was the turn of the empress's party to talk up the severity of the complaint – "that in almost the whole of England he was reported as being dead."[27] He was ill for several weeks, from before Easter until after Whitsun.[28] "Then the vigour of health gradually came back and put him on his feet again."[29] While the king was convalescent the queen and her son Eustace crossed the Channel in the company of William of Ypres, Richard de Lucy, and others of her household. She had her own lordship to reassert, after the instability of the previous year, and Eustace could be introduced to lands which it was hoped he would one day inherit.[30]

In the meanwhile, the empress and her advisers had been busy. Early in Lent a "secret conference" had been convened at Devizes, to discuss "how her cause was to be best maintained." The deliberations were not reported but at the end there was a bland press release, stating that "all her adherents approved sending for the count of Anjou, it being his duty to maintain the inheritance of his wife and sons in England."[31] Experienced political observers would have observed that these sentiments were very far from bland. They represented a comment on the past as well as a plan for the future. In terms of the definition of the empress's cause this marks a shift in thinking already observable – on the most likely dating of the relevant charters – in the summer of 1141. Geoffrey de Mandeville had asked that the empress's menfolk should play a more prominent role. And so she had promised that both the count of Anjou and Henry her son should swear to hold to the agreement. Exactly the same clause had appeared in the parallel grant of lands and an earldom to Aubrey de Vere.[32] That these were not just empty phrases but that active steps were taken to secure the involvement of Count Geoffrey and of Henry is shown by a charter issued by Henry confirming his mother's grants to Aubrey de Vere. As it is his earliest surviving charter it is a document of considerable interest, not least in the protocol which gives his own title. He is "Henry the son of the daughter of King Henry, the rightful heir of England and Normandy."[33] As such, "just as my lady that is to say my mother the

---

[27] WM, *HN*, 122–3: "grauis incommodum morbi apud Northamtonam detinuit, adeo ut in tota propemodum Anglia sicut mortuus conclamaretur"; cf. JH, 312: "praeventus vero infirmitate."

[28] Easter, as noted, was 19 Apr., and Whit Sunday was 7 June, in 1142. A precept to the queen ordered the canons of Arrouaise to be given seisin of the tithe of Marck, as he had given it to them "in infirmitate mea apud Norhantoniam": *Regesta*, iii, no. 25.

[29] WM, *HN*, 122–3: "Tunc enim sensim refusus salutis uigor eum in pedes erexit."

[30] *Regesta*, iii, nos. 25–6 (Arrouaise), 194–6 (Clairmarais).

[31] WM, *HN*, 122–3: "coniugis et filiorum hereditatem in Anglia iure defensitare deberet."

[32] *Regesta*, iii, nos. 275 (for Geoffrey de Mandeville), 634 (for Aubrey de Vere).

[33] Ibid., no. 635: "Henricus filius filie regis Henrici rectus heres Anglie et Normannie."

empress restored and conceded so I also restore and concede to Earl Aubrey" all the lands and tenements of his father, Aubrey de Vere. He gave these undertakings, "with my own hand in the hand of Hugh of Ing just as my mother the empress swore in the hand of earl Geoffrey." Neither Earl Geoffrey nor Earl Aubrey had gone in person to the court of the count of Anjou, but Hugh of Ing was one of Geoffrey de Mandeville's most prominent vassals and there can be no doubt that a similar charter was issued for Geoffrey.[34] This was impressive talk for a boy of nine but it was what people wanted to hear.

It was the count of Anjou, however, that "all the empress's supporters" in the spring of 1142 most wanted to see. If not much had changed in England in the past twelve months a lot had happened in Normandy. Those supporters will have factored these changes into their analysis of the political situation and we must do the same. The battle of Lincoln had given Geoffrey of Anjou the opportunity to realize his ambitions. Orderic here started a new chapter.[35] "When Geoffrey count of Anjou heard that his wife had won the day he came at once into Normandy, sent out envoys to the magnates and commanded them as of right to hand over their castles to him and keep the peace." The magnates, perhaps in response to this, perhaps as their own reaction to the crisis, "met at Mortagne and debated together about the state of the country." In what reads as in some ways a rerun of what had happened in December 1135, the Normans spurned the advances of Geoffrey of Anjou. "Archbishop Hugh and the Normans approached count Theobald and offered him the kingdom of England and duchy of Normandy." But circumstances had changed and Theobald saw no prospect of defending Normandy. He tried to make conditions for the release of his rights, asking for the restoration of Tours and the Touraine and the release of his brother and the restoration of the honour he had held in the time of Henry I. Theobald had no bargaining power and he made these requests purely for the record. His reluctance to act removed any faint prospect of a unified resistance to the Angevins. It was every man for himself.

There followed the takeover of Normandy by Geoffrey, count of Anjou. This was not an event but a process, one which stretched over three years. Normandy was lost to Stephen not in battle but as a series of Norman lords and Norman garrisons followed the example of the garrisons of the frontier castles of Verneuil and Nonancourt. They "gave thought to the fact that many who had resisted the Angevins had now given way to them" and then followed suit, recognizing "the lordship of count Geoffrey and

---

[34] It is interesting to note that Warin Fitz Gerald, who would later serve as Henry's chamberlain, was another prominent vassal of Geoffrey de Mandeville, acting as witness to several of his charters (Vincent, "Warin and Henry Fitz Gerald, the King's Chamberlains," 235 and n. 4), and tempting to suggest that he was a member of the same delegation.

[35] OV vi. 546–9, from which the quotations in this paragraph are taken.

Matilda."[36] The first of the great lords to come to terms with Geoffrey was Robert, earl of Leicester. He did not immediately transfer his allegiance, rather he "obtained a truce with the Angevins for himself and his brother Waleran until the latter should return from England."[37] That truce governed Waleran's behaviour in England also. The twin brothers here confronted the situation envisaged by their father in 1106: "if they should lose their inheritance on one side of the Channel or the other then as brothers together they should together share what remained."[38] They would now co-operate to keep their losses to a minimum. The bishop of Lisieux, the most experienced of the Norman clergy, came at the same time to the same conclusion as the shrewdest of the Norman barons. He "took the advice of his friends and made peace with the count in the last week of Lent." By the end of the year the Angevins "had established their authority everywhere up to the Seine," that is to say they had been accepted by the chief lords of central Normandy.[39] They had made important gains but they still had much to do.

This was the situation when the emissaries from the empress's court arrived in Normandy during the spring of 1142, saying – probably not for the first time – that Geoffrey of Anjou was required urgently in England if "the cause of his wife and his sons" was to advance. Courteous exchanges followed but the bottom line was that Geoffrey would not leave Normandy with the capture of the duchy incomplete: "he pleaded his own difficulties in objection, and they were many, one being that he was kept from coming to England because a number of castles were in revolt against him in Normandy." Geoffrey wanted help from England. Many of the empress's followers were happy to oblige: "they turned to entreat the earl [of Gloucester] to accept this task for the sake of the inheritance of his sister and his nephews." It gave them the opportunity to gain some prestige by joining a successful campaign. But Robert himself was most reluctant to go: "it would be dangerous for his sister, whom others could hardly protect when he was away, men who had practically abandoned her when he himself was captured, men without confidence in their own cause." Robert would only go if those urging him on, those on his own side, gave him hostages, "to be taken to Normandy with him and to serve as sureties both to the count of Anjou and the empress."[40] The taking of hostages, "namely the sons of the earls and magnates of England who

[36] OV vi. 548–51: "dominatum Iosfredi consulis et Mathildis susceperunt."

[37] Ibid. 548–9. Torigni, 142, says that it was Waleran – whom he describes as the greatest of the Norman magnates in terms of his revenues, his fortifications, and the size of his affinity – who made the agreement with Geoffrey and surrendered to him the castle of Montfort.

[38] *Regesta*, ii, no. 843, with full text 319: "si contigerit quod perderent hereditatem ex hac parte maris uel ultra tunc concedo et precipio ut sint fratres communes communiter participantes de residuo."

[39] OV vi. 550–1.

[40] WM, *HN*, 124–7, is the source for this paragraph up to this point.

favoured the empress," was also reported in Normandy.[41] The name of one of these sons is known. This was Mathiel, the son – but not the heir – of Miles of Gloucester, earl of Hereford.

It is known because the giving of the hostage was built into a much broader agreement between Robert of Gloucester and Miles of Gloucester, and that agreement survives. It is one of a series of agreements, chiefly but not exclusively concerning the English midlands, which helped keep the peace during the 1140s. They show the thought processes of members of the higher aristocracy in a way not mediated by the clergy who wrote the chronicles. As this is the earliest such agreement of which a written record survives, and as it has a precise political context, it repays close attention.[42] "All are to know," it starts off, "that this is a treaty of love between Robert earl of Gloucester and Miles earl of Hereford."[43] What follows makes clear that in truth little love was lost between the two men:

Robert earl of Gloucester assures Miles earl of Hereford in faith and on oath that he will guard him to the extent of his power without guile, in his life and members and landed honour, and that he will aid him to maintain his castles and his rights and his inheritance and his tenements and his acquisitions, those which he now has, and maintain his customs and rights and liberties in wood and plain and rivers. That part of his inheritance which he has not got he will help him to acquire. If anyone should wish to do ill to the earl of Hereford or in any way diminish his rights, and the earl shall wish to make war on him, then Robert earl of Gloucester shall hold to him and aid him in faith and to the best of his ability, without guile. Robert earl of Gloucester shall not make peace or truces with those who do ill to the earl of Hereford, without the free consent and guarantee of the earl of Hereford. And especially in the war which there now is between the empress and King Stephen he shall hold with the earl of Hereford and they shall work as one;[44] similarly with all other wars.

These assurances from the earl of Gloucester were backed up by the countess, the earl's wife, and by the major tenants of the earl. The latter undertook to withdraw their services if the agreement was breached, and both the countess and the honorial barons undertook "to make a legal record of the agreement if there was need." This seems an odd phrase, for here was the agreement in writing, almost certainly in duplicate, with the

[41] Torigni, 143, sees the hostages as being offered to Geoffrey of Anjou in return for his preparing to cross for England. As he declined to do so, it seems likely that the hostages remained in the custody of Robert of Gloucester.

[42] *Earldom of Gloucester Charters*, no. 95, from the facsimile in *Book of Seals*, no. 212, 151–3 and plate IV.

[43] Ibid.: "Noscant omnes hanc esse confederationem amoris inter Robertum comitem Gloecestrie et Milonem comitem Herefordie."

[44] Ibid.: "et nominatim de hac guerra que modo est inter imperatricem et regem Stephanum se cum comite Herefordie tenebit et ad unum opus erit."

seal of the one earl attached to the copy to be kept by the other. But what gave force to it were the verbal undertakings, when the two parties came together (*convenerunt* hence *conventio*); the text was simply an aide-memoire. A shorter set of undertakings were given by the earl of Hereford, for his good faith was embodied in the surrender of one of his sons.[45] And – so at least it was envisaged – not just for a single campaign but "until the war between the empress and King Stephen and Henry the son of the empress is over."[46] Henry, it will be noted, now comes into the discussions: the war "which there now is" concerned the empress and the king, but the war as it would develop concerned the king and the empress's son. "When the war is over and Robert earl of Gloucester and Miles earl of Hereford shall have their lands and their rights again, Robert earl of Gloucester shall give Miles earl of Hereford his son back again. Then the trustworthy men of both earls shall consider and take hostages and securities so that the love between these earls shall be maintained for ever."

The war was very far from over in the summer of 1142. Robert of Gloucester, with these hostages and "a force of knights ready for action," made his way via safe houses to Wareham in Dorset. Thence he sailed to Caen. Once there, "he summoned the count of Anjou" by messengers. The count came readily enough but he repeated his insistence that he could only consider coming to England if he was first given help to tighten his grip on Normandy. The request was expected. The forces from England joined with those under the command of the count of Anjou and together they captured "ten castles in Normandy."[47] In what seems almost like an extract from a letter home, later incorporated into the text of the *Historia Novella*, these ten castles are named: Tinchebrai, St Hilaire-du-Harcouët, Briquessart, Aunay, Bastebourg, Trévières, Vire, Plessis-Grimoult, Villers, and Mortain.[48] The last of these names makes clear the military objective of this particular campaign. It was to take Mortain, and the other fortifications of that county,[49] for this was the oldest of Stephen's titles and the bastion of his personal lordship within Normandy. Once this had been done, there was limited resistance to Count Geoffrey's takeover of the remainder of western Normandy.[50] The centres of the two counties, and the seats of their bishops,

---

[45] Ibid. The agreement allowed the earl to place another of his sons as hostage in the place of Mathiel if he so chose, provided that the replacement was healthy.

[46] Ibid.: "donec guerra inter imperatricem et regem Stephanum et Henricum filium imperatricis finiatur."

[47] On these events see WM, *HN*, 124–7.

[48] The **Ce** text of WM, *HN* gives the names of the castles as follows: Tenerchebrai, Seithilaret, Brichesart, Alnai, Bastonborg, Triueres, Castel de Vira, Plaiseiz, Vilers, Moretoin. These seem to be vernacular forms of the names.

[49] Torigni, 143: "maiori exercitu congregato pergens ad Moritolium, redditum est ei, et Tenechebrai, Cerences, Tiliolum, scilicet quatuor castella propria comitis Moritoliensis"; *Recueil d'annales Angevines*, 10; John of Marmoutier, "Historia Gaufredi ducis," 226–7.

[50] John of Marmoutier, 226–31, has a very full account of the remainder of the campaign, and there is useful discussion in Norgate, *England under the Angevin Kings*, i. 338–41; Haskins, 128–9.

were at Avranches and Coutances. At Avranches the count was met outside
the walls by the bishop and the citizens and escorted first to the cathedral and
then to the ducal apartments, where the castellans of the region came and
swore fealty to him. A similar story was told at Coutances, though the bishop
was absent and the garrison of his castle at St Lô on the River Vire put up a
brief resistance. The barons of the region also swore fealty, with the single
and significant exception of the garrison of Cherbourg, which was under the
command of the brothers Ralph and Richard de la Hay. Cherbourg was a
fortress and at first it was defended resolutely, but when Ralph was captured
by the count of Anjou and Richard, it was reported, was taken by pirates
while on his way to seek help from the king in England, the garrison lost
heart, negotiated terms of surrender, and in their turn accepted the count's
lordship. This has taken us to the depths of winter, 1142–3.[51]

By this time the earl of Gloucester had returned to England. The count
of Anjou had not returned with him, to the distress of the empress's
supporters, who felt that – in more than one sense – they had been taken
for a ride. So indeed they had, but no firm promises had been made to
them. The count, however, "as a great favour, allowed the boy's uncle to
take to England his eldest son by the empress, so that on seeing him the
nobles might be inspired to fight for the cause of the lawful heir."[52] This
was late in 1142, in late October or early November.[53] Henry, "the lawful
heir" and increasingly the focus of the hopes of his side, was still a few
months short of his tenth birthday. He was sent to Bristol. There, "in that
castle," he was brought up alongside Roger, another of the sons of Robert
of Gloucester – who would become bishop of Worcester – and "instructed
in the first elements of learning and good behaviour."[54] His tutor was a
graduate or *magister*, Master Matthew.[55] Henry would later claim to have
a special affection for the canons of St Augustine's Abbey, Bristol, who had
helped and protected him from his earliest years.[56] He gained a first-hand
knowledge of places and personalities within the kingdom he hoped one
day to rule, but his presence did not have the impact on the civil war that
his supporters had hoped for. He probably stayed little more than a year.

---

[51] John of Marmoutier, 230: "hiemi imminente cedendum arbitratur"; Torigni, 145,
places the surrender of Cherbourg s.a. 1143.

[52] WM, *HN*, 126–7. Torigni, 143, suggests that Henry had been in Robert of
Gloucester's household from the beginning of the Mortain campaign. The Annals of
Saint-Aubin, s.a. 1142, *Recueil d'annales Angevines*, 10, also note Henry's visit to England.

[53] Poole, "Henry Plantagenet's Early Visits to England," 448–9.

[54] *MTB*, iii. 104–5; for the context see Cheney, *Roger, Bishop of Worcester*, 48, and WM,
HN, xcii–xciii.

[55] *Regesta*, iii, nos. 329, 331, 666, 776. Matthew was later the chancellor of Henry's wife,
Eleanor of Aquitaine, and he may earlier have been the tutor of Henry's aunts: Vincent,
"Charters of Eleanor of Aquitaine," 35–6; Van Houts, "Les Femmes dans le royaume
Plantagenêt," 104.

[56] *Regesta*, iii, nos. 126, 996: "in initio iuventutis mee." On the history of the house see
Cart. St Augustine's Abbey, Bristol, xiv–xxii.

The year that Henry Fitz Empress was in England had seen his cause if anything set back. Robert of Gloucester had returned to England in late 1142 because reports were coming to him which confirmed his worst fears,[57] that in his absence the king's forces would make some headway against the empress's followers and "even attack her own person." The empress was based in Oxford. This was an important town in strategic terms and in the course of becoming a provincial capital. A few miles upstream lay the hunting lodge at Woodstock, "the favourite seat of [Henry I's] retirement and privacy," a place "made for the habitation of man and beasts," with a private zoo which included lions, leopards, lynx, camels, and a porcupine sent to him by William of Montpellier, "a kind of hedgehog covered with bristling spines."[58] The tenure of Oxford by the empress preserved this link with her father's day and offered some protection to Brian Fitz Count a few miles downstream at Wallingford. The empress can hardly, however, as her enemies claimed, have "felt excessive confidence in herself and her men because the castle and all the country round about were brought under her authority."[59] She was in fact highly exposed, at the furthest point east that her forces could hope to defend, and Stephen set about driving her out. He was able to disrupt her communications, taking Wareham in Dorset, from where Robert of Gloucester and his expeditionary force had sailed, and also Cirencester in Gloucestershire, on the road that led from Oxford through the upper Thames valley and then to Gloucester. These were important centres but also soft targets. Wareham had been left almost deserted, though Robert of Gloucester's retainers would later seek to deny this,[60] while at Cirencester "the garrison had stolen away." There were not the troops to defend these castles. Similarly with two castles close to Oxford itself, at Bampton and at Radcot, the latter the scene of a later skirmish in Richard II's reign: the first "was taken by storm, the other surrendered at discretion."[61]

Oxford was another matter. The author of the *Gesta Stephani* liked to provide a thumbnail sketch of each major settlement and he writes in what would now be thought of as estate agent's prose. "Oxford is a city very securely protected, inaccessible because of the very deep water that washes it all round, most carefully encircled by the palisade of an outwork on one side, and on another finely and very strongly fortified by an impregnable castle and tower of great height."[62] Its strength would now be tested. The king "appeared suddenly on the other side of the river," below the ford

[57] WM, *HN*, 126–9.

[58] *GS*, 138–9; HH, 470–1; WM, *GR*, i. 740–1, ii. 372–3; *King's Works*, ii. 1009–17

[59] *GS*, 140–1.

[60] WM, *HN*, 126–7, says that the king's men found the castle undefended ("uacuum propugnatoribus offendens"); in the Ce text this has been altered to say that it was not well fortified ("non bene munitum"). On the concern of this later recension to show the military followers of Robert of Gloucester in a good light see, ibid., lxxxiii–lxxxiv.

[61] *GS*, 140–1.

[62] Ibid.

suitable for ox-carts that had given the city its name. The empress's troops sent to defend the ford were driven back. Theirs was not an easy position to defend, for there was no single crossing of the river but several crossings of separate streams, the road running on a long causeway.[63] The king and his troops, "swimming rather than wading," so the story was told, crossed the river, entered within the town walls and intimidated the citizens. They commenced a siege of the castle that would last for three months, from the end of September to shortly before Christmas.[64] Its objective was the capture of the empress herself and it was pursued resolutely. No one was left in any doubt that Stephen intended to see this siege through. This know-ledge brought Robert of Gloucester, with – as has been seen – his nephew Henry, hotfoot back to England. He was able to recapture Wareham and establish secure control of the passage to the harbour there.[65] He then ordered the empress's forces to meet at Cirencester, prepared to march from there to relieve the siege.[66] Perhaps these extra men would have made a difference, perhaps this was no more than bluster, a side to Robert that his enemies picked on and that William of Malmesbury cannot quite conceal. We cannot know, for while he was there news came that the empress had managed to escape.

This was to be the last occasion on which the empress made headlines, the last and the most remarkable of her great escapes.

I have never read of another woman so luckily rescued from so many mortal foes and from the threat of dangers so great: the truth being that she went from the castle of Arundel uninjured through the midst of her enemies; she escaped unscathed from the midst of the Londoners when they were assailing her, and her only, in mighty wrath; then stole away alone, in wondrous fashion, from the rout of Winchester, when almost all her men were cut off; and then, when she left besieged Oxford, she came away safe and sound.[67]

The empress's escape from Oxford was seen as a miracle, and the story gained much circumstantial detail as it was told, in the midst of which one can glimpse a simple and secular explanation of what occurred. The

[63] For the geography see Salter, *Medieval Oxford*; Davis, "The Ford, the River and the City"; *Oxford before the University*, ed. Dodd.

[64] A precise date is given for the beginning of the siege, "three days before Michaelmas," i.e. 26 Sept. 1142: WM, *HN*, 126–7. It started "shortly after Michaelmas" and ended "shortly before Christmas": HH, 742–3. *GS*, 142–3, gives the length as three months without any fixed points.

[65] WM, *HN*, 128–31; also *GS*, 144–5. The royal garrison surrendered by agreement, having been allowed time to seek support: on the protocol here see Strickland, *War*, 208–12, discussing this episode. Gervase of Canterbury says that the siege of Wareham lasted three weeks and that the royal garrison was under the command of Herbert de Lucy: Gervase, i. 124.

[66] WM, *HN*, 130–1, giving the date as after the beginning of Advent, the first Sunday of which fell on 29 Nov.

[67] *GS*, 144–5.

questions came crowding in, one after another, and the chroniclers answered as best they could. How did she get out? The author of the *Anglo-Saxon Chronicle* says that "she was let down at night from the tower with ropes," but he was recalling the manner of St Paul's escape from his enemies at Damascus.[68] William of Malmesbury says, "as a matter of fact," that she sneaked out by a side door, with just four companions.[69] Why were they not stopped? There were "many watchers in the silence of the night"; but in fact the watch had been wound down and those that remained had grown careless, giving the empress her opportunity.[70] How did they get across the river? The empress "crossed dry-footed, without wetting her clothes at all, the very waters that had risen above the heads of the king and his men when they were going over to storm the town"; but this sounds more like the Israelites crossing the Red Sea than the traversing of an established thoroughfare.[71] The river may indeed have been frozen: "all the ground was white with an extremely heavy fall of snow and there was a very thick crust of ice on the water."[72] These wintry conditions offered further opportunity for the story to be embroidered. Here is Henry of Huntingdon getting in on the act. The empress, he said, was dressed for the conditions, for she "fled across the frozen Thames wrapped in white garments, which reflected and resembled the snow, deceiving the eyes of the besiegers."[73] It is only a short step from Henry of Huntingdon to the summary of the reign offered by Sellar and Yeatman. "After this Stephen and Matilda (or Maud) spent the reign escaping from each other over the snow in night-gowns while 'God and his Angels slept.' "[74]

The escape had evidently been carefully planned. In the cover of the night the empress with her companions made their way on foot to Abingdon, where they picked up horses and rode the further short distance to Wallingford.[75] The empress was then seen as being in safe hands, for Brian Fitz Count's devotion to her cause was well attested.[76] It would be acknowledged by the empress herself: grants were made to Reading Abbey, later in the reign, for his "loyalty and loyal service," and

---

[68] *ASC*, s.a. 1140; for the scriptural parallel, Acts 9 : 24–5, 2 Cor. 11 : 32–3; for the tower, plate 11.

[69] WM, *HN*, 132–3: "illud satis constat." *GS*, 142–3, speaks of her being accompanied by three sound chaps: "tribus prudentis ingenii se comitantibus militibus"; the number has grown to five in Gervase, i. 124.

[70] *GS*, 142–3; WM, *HN*, 132–3.

[71] *GS*, 142–3, for the empress; Exod. 14 : 15–31, for the Israelites.

[72] *GS*, 142–3.

[73] HH, 742–3; the same story picked up in JH, 317, where this appears as the final entry s.a. 1144; also in Gervase, i. 124: "ob frustrandos vigilum oculos nitidissimis lintheis simul omnes cooperti."

[74] Sellar and Yeatman, *1066 and All That*, 28: "Lax State of Affairs."

[75] WM, *HN*, 132–3. The work ends at this point. This is the only source to mention Abingdon, but *GS*, 142–5, says that "about six miles" were covered on foot, and Gervase, i. 125, says "no more than five miles."

[76] *GS*, 134–5.

her son Henry associated himself with these sentiments.[77] It would have been a false loyalty, however, to encourage the empress to stay long at Wallingford. This would have risked a further siege, with the possibility of her capture remaining a fear of her supporters and a constraint on their own actions. She moved very soon to Devizes, and some time in 1143, perhaps immediately on her arrival, she is found there together with Robert, earl of Gloucester, Miles, earl of Hereford, Brian Fitz Count, and Humphrey de Bohun. She addressed her men, both French and English, throughout the whole of England. She took under her special protection the nuns of Godstow Abbey, a house of the foundation of her father, Henry I, and herself. Specific grants that King Stephen had earlier given were now confirmed by her, "as they held them whilst I was besieged at Oxford."[78] This grant to a religious house in Oxfordshire, so soon after the siege, and referring back to the siege, is extremely interesting. We do not know the names of the men (or women) who bore this privilege back to Oxford, but we may suspect that they knew better than anyone just how the empress had managed her miraculous escape.

Stephen's own movements following the successful conclusion of the siege of Oxford are not easy to establish. It is known that he was at the legatine council held in London in mid-Lent 1143.[79] It is likely also that he spent some time at Oxford early in 1143, to mark his success in taking the city and to establish his position there.[80] This is probably the occasion when the monks of Abingdon obtained a confirmation of the early grant of the hundred of Hormer, after the relevant charter of Edward the Confessor was read out before the barons, and charters of confirmation of William the Conqueror and Henry I were tabled.[81] The barons named are Geoffrey de Mandeville, earl of Essex, Robert de Vere, William of Ypres, Richard de Lucy, Walter of Buckland, Adam de Beaunay, Mainfenin Brito, and Hugh

---

[77] *Regesta*, iii, no. 703 (with facs., ibid., iv, plate xlvi), a charter of the empress granted, "pro amore et legali servicio Briencii filii comitis quod mihi fecit"; ibid., no. 704, a charter of Henry Fitz Empress granted, "pro amore et legali servicio Briencii filii comitis quod domine Mathilde matri mee imperatrici et mihi fecit." Also calendared, with discussion, in *Reading Abbey Cartularies*, ii, nos. 667–8.

[78] *Regesta*, iii, no. 370: "sicut eam habuerunt quando apud Oxinfordiam obsessa fui." A similar phrase may lie behind a reference, in a document of 1175 x 1179, to a transaction made "before the empress was besieged by King Stephen at Oxford, which was about forty years ago": *Reg. Ant.* 9, 256 n. 6.

[79] HH, 742–3: "rex Stephanus interfuit concilio Lundonie in media Quadragesime." This council is discussed further at the beginning of Chapter 7.

[80] Dating to the early weeks of 1143 two charters, *Regesta*, iii, nos. 4 (for Abingdon), 858 (for the Templars). These two documents were earlier associated by Lees, in an excellent discussion of Stephen's itinerary after the battle of Lincoln, but placed at Oxford during the siege: *Templars*, xlv–xlvi.

[81] *Regesta*, iii, no. 4. Other charters for the house may have been issued on the same occasion, e.g. *Regesta*, iii, no. 7; in ibid., no. 10, however, the reference to "die qua primum coronatus fui" and to the king's doing justice not within the city (as ibid., no. 3) but when he was next in the neighbourhood, might suggest a date of 1142.

of Bolebeck.[82] The monks will have offered ready money for this confirmation, the more readily perhaps to rebut any suggestion that the empress had escaped through their town with their connivance. And it will have been received very readily, for in the early months after his release the king was short of funds. This on his own admission. It was at Oxford, perhaps at this time, that he granted to the monks of St Augustine's, Canterbury, a mill near the East Bridge of Canterbury, "in restitution for a loan of 100 marks which I took from that church in my urgent business."[83] The phrase used here – *in necessitate mea* – is a routine one in conveyancing, used to indicate borrowing by peasant and magnate alike, but it is rare indeed for a king to use it of himself. It states that the original transaction had been made "in the presence of my barons, namely William of Ypres, earl Gilbert, Ralph de la Hay, and many others." Around this time also, the queen mortgaged 10 marks' worth of land at Gamlingay in Cambridgeshire, to the London financier Gervase of Cornhill, "until I have repaid the debt which I owe him."[84] It never was repaid.

In the early part of the summer the pace picks up a little. The king was active in the south of England, in Wiltshire and Dorset, and also in northern Lincolnshire. These were the frontiers of his effective authority. It is likely that the visit to Lincolnshire came first. It can be dated from a charter that the king issued in favour of the abbey of Peterborough, confirming land clearances within the royal forest of Rockingham, "up until the day when I came to Peterborough on my return from Lincolnshire where I had once again fortified my castle of Caistor in Lindsey, namely on 7 June."[85] To fix this event in broader historic time the charter was dated to "the year of the incarnation 1143, from the Passion of St Oswald 501 years, and the eighth year of my reign." This visit of the king was remembered at Peterborough as the third occasion on which the monastery's most potent relic, the arm of St Oswald, had been displayed. "He gave it his ring" – this was following his normal practice, which required it to be bought back, but the king had no ready cash and so – "out of love for the church he remitted 40 marks of monies that were owing to him." The ritual involved the washing of the saint's arm, "and by the virtue of the water from the washing of his arm, many sick men were made whole, many were released from demons, and numb and palsied limbs were cured."[86] The

---

[82] These are the witnesses to the Abingdon charter; that for the Templars has Geoffrey de Mandeville, Robert de Vere, and Turgis of Avranches.

[83] *Regesta*, iii, no. 163: "in restauratione vadimonii centum marcarum quod ego pro necessitate mea ab eadem ecclesia cepi." The house chronicle associated this transaction with the king's financial difficulties after the battle of Lincoln: William Thorne, *Chronicle of Saint Augustine's Canterbury*, 81.

[84] *Regesta*, iii, no. 243; the witnesses were Earl Simon of Senlis, Richard of Boulogne, Simon de Gerardmoulin, and Warner de Lusors. On Gervase of Cornhill, see Round, *Geoffrey*, 304–12.

[85] *Regesta*, iii, no. 655.

[86] Hugh Candidus, 106; trans., 57–8.

charter lists those who witnessed the grant and this ceremonial. There were two bishops, Alexander of Lincoln and Athelwold of Carlisle, both of whom would attend the legatine council later in the year,[87] Daniel, abbot of St Benet's, Holme (near Norwich); then a group of barons headed by William Martel, the royal steward, Turgis of Avranches, a royal constable, Fulk d'Oilli, and William d'Aubigny Brito.

The king had viewed the refortification of Caistor as a significant occasion. He would have seen it as in some way reasserting his control over Lindsey, which had been compromised by the grants he had made to William de Roumare and his half-brother, Ranulf of Chester, and by his defeat at the battle of Lincoln. Stephen had with him at Caistor three earls, Gilbert de Clare, earl of Hertford, Geoffrey de Mandeville, earl of Essex, and Simon of Senlis, earl of Northampton, along with the officers of his household. Also present were the royal chancellor, Robert de Gant, and his nephew Gilbert de Gant.[88] Gilbert was a local castellan, and it may have been at this time that he built a castle at Barton overlooking the Humber estuary.[89] Around this time also he was married to a niece of Ranulf of Chester, and seen from the perspective of a northern chronicler this showed the earl of Chester extending his lordship in Yorkshire and Lincolnshire;[90] but it is possible to view this from another angle, for she was the sister of Earl Gilbert de Clare, who was accompanying the king at this time. The king's patronage of the Gant family was clearly intended to strengthen his affinity in competition with that of the sons of the Countess Lucy, and in this he had at least a measure of success. Ranulf of Chester's knights still controlled the castle of Lincoln but the king could hope to isolate them and, as if to make the point, the royal entourage on the way south from Caistor to Peterborough stopped at one of the Chester manors to the east of the city.[91] William de Roumare seems to have gone his own way. Around this time he went on pilgrimage to Compostela and thereafter, within Lincolnshire at least, he appears solely as a generous benefactor to religious houses.[92] One of them was at Revesby, close to his honorial centre of Bolingbroke, which was a daughter-house of Rievaulx and provided Aelred with his first command. Aelred's biographer, Walter

---

[87] *Councils and Synods*, 808.

[88] *Regesta*, iii, no. 861.

[89] BL, Cotton MS Vesp. E. xx, fo. 64r: "apud Bartona quando firmavit castellum in eadem villa."

[90] JH, 308; Dalton, "Ranulf of Chester and Lincolnshire," 121–6.

[91] *Regesta*, iii, no. 855, "apud Niwebelam," identified as Newball in Stainton by Langworth; for the Chester holding here see *Lincolnshire Domesday*, 255 (Lindsey Survey, 16/1). The royal charter confirmed a grant by Turgis of Avranches *regis constabularius* of "totum uastum de x libratis terre quas rex Stephanus mihi dedit in manerio de Hensintone" (Hensington in Woodstock, Oxon): *Templars*, 188.

[92] *Charters of the Earls of Chester*, 82–4 (no. 70); Dalton, "Roumare, William de, First Earl of Lincoln."

Daniel, saw the house's rapid rise in prosperity as due not just to Aelred's leadership qualities but to the confusion caused by civil war.[93]

By the end of June 1143 the king was in Wiltshire, evidently seeking to take the fight to his opponents.[94] With his brother the bishop of Winchester supplying troops to assist him, he came to Wilton, "thinking that the nunnery would be a suitable defensive base against incursions from the men of Salisbury, who were fighting strongly against the king's party in support of the empress." The intention must have been to move on to the attack and recapture Salisbury,[95] and thereafter perhaps even attack the empress in her stronghold at Devizes. The earl of Gloucester moved rapidly to meet the threat, "and on 1 July he arrived suddenly from the west and set fire to the city." What happened next depends on which authority is followed. The *Gesta Stephani* presents the outline of a set-piece battle, with the king, as at Lincoln, advancing outside the city to meet the threat, and the earl arranging his forces in three squadrons. Gervase of Canterbury has the king quartered within the nunnery itself, quite unprepared for an attack, and immediately fleeing the scene. That the king and the bishop did flee ignominiously is agreed.[96] They left their men to bear the brunt of the fighting; there were some casualties; and several of the commanders were captured. Again, as at Lincoln, there was considerable looting in the town, the king lost much of the machinery of war and some treasure,[97] and the goods of the townsmen were plundered, even those that had been placed for safekeeping within the nunnery itself. Among the prisoners taken during the battle and then brought to Bristol was the royal steward, William Martel.[98] He was ransomed for 300 marks and only with the additional stipulation that he surrender the castle of Sherborne.[99] "The king's party were utterly

---

[93] Walter Daniel, 27–32. The foundation charter of Revesby, which William of Roumare addressed to the king, is printed in *Facsimiles of Charters from Northamptonshire Collections*, 1–7 (with the facsimile as frontispiece).

[94] Henry of Huntingdon places these events in 1142, but this is clearly an error, as the evidence of the *Historia Novella* shows Robert of Gloucester to have sailed for Normandy in late June 1142, and William of Malmesbury would not have ignored an engagement which showed the earl in so positive a light: HH, 740–1; cf. WM, *HN*, 124–5, and the comments of Round, *Geoffrey*, 407. The other sources have 1143. *Gesta Stephani* says shortly after the empress's escape from Oxford, the Waverley Annals have "in the summer," and Gervase of Canterbury has the precise date of 1 July: *GS*, 144–9; *Ann. Mon.*, ii. 229; Gervase, i. 125–6. While Gervase is a late source he is evidently well informed on this engagement and his date can be accepted.

[95] The town was under the control of William of Salisbury: *CP*, xi. 375, citing *GS*, 148–9; also *Regesta*, iii, no. 791.

[96] *GS*, 148–9, says that "rex . . . ignominiose diffugerat"; Gervase, i. 126, says "fugam arriperet inhonestam."

[97] Gervase, i. 126, speaks of "uasis aureis et argenteis ceterisque rebus suis post terga relictis"; *GS*, 148–9, says that the earl of Gloucester arrived at Bristol "cum multis exeniis."

[98] Gervase, i. 126, describes him as "quidam prepotens et regem amicus"; *GS*, 146–7, calls him "uir illustris fide quoque et amicitia potissimum regi connexus."

[99] Gervase, *GS*, and HH all mention the surrender of Sherborne; only Gervase mentions the ransom.

dejected." Quite understandably. This was not a major engagement.[100] It is an overstatement to call Sherborne "the master-key to the whole kingdom," as it may have appeared from London.[101] Nonetheless the empress's main bases in the west country will for a time have seemed utterly secure. Her supporters could travel unchallenged to the coast, and then to Normandy, where the conquest of the duchy had become inevitable. Might the Angevins then move on to the attack and invade England? The atmosphere in the autumn of 1143 seems very similar to that in the autumn of 1139. In 1143 as in 1139 it was marked by a loss of nerve at the centre of the royal court and by a sudden arrest.

The meeting of the court was at St Albans. The time was "after Michaelmas," 29 September.[102] The man arrested was Geoffrey de Mandeville. Just as the bishops in 1139 had been required to surrender their castles, whose strategic importance subsequent events had demonstrated, so Geoffrey was forced to hand over his castles, most notably the Tower of London, but also Pleshey and Walden, as the price of his release. In the year between his arrest and his death he was a relentless and ruthless opponent of the king. The worse he behaved – and even the historian of the monastery of his own foundation admits that he and his men behaved very badly – the more the case against him seemed to be proved. But what exactly was the case? Why was the earl arrested? These were the first questions that would be asked. The historian who could not answer them, whether in the mid-twelfth or in the early years of the twenty-first century, was not up to his or her job.

William of Newburgh was never a man to shirk the challenge. He had the text of Henry of Huntingdon in front of him when he was writing, but this on its own did not provide an adequate motive for the arrest. This he supplied in the form of a story that the king was looking for revenge, because of the indignity suffered at the hands of Geoffrey by Constance of France, who had been betrothed to the king's son and heir Eustace in 1140. The time is presumably the summer of 1141.

Constance was in London with the queen, her mother-in-law, who it so happened wanted to take her somewhere else. Geoffrey, however, who had command of the Tower at the time, refused to allow this, seizing Constance from the queen, who did her best to resist. He detained Constance and let the humiliated queen go. Later Geoffrey reluctantly returned his notable prize when it was demanded of him by the king, her father-in-law, who concealed his righteous anger for the time being.[103]

---

[100] Round, *Geoffrey*, 146, 460, called this "the affair of Wilton" not "the battle of Wilton" and while later historians have not followed him there is something to be said for his reticence.

[101] *GS*, 148–9: "latissime prouincie indeptus fuit principatum."

[102] The date is found in Brett, "Annals of Bermondsey, Southwark and Merton," 300.

[103] Newburgh, i. 44–5.

This is a story that had become attached to the arrest. William of Newburgh had good links with the Augustinian priory of Holy Trinity, London, and he may have the story from a London source.[104] But a good story is what it is and it would be wrong to take it as an explanation. What else was charged against Geoffrey?

The author of the *Gesta Stephani*, who makes the best case that he can, says that "in the extent of his wealth and the splendour of his position Geoffrey surpassed all the chief men of the kingdom." He was less a baron than a viceroy: "everywhere in the kingdom he took the king's place and in all transactions was listened to more eagerly than the king and received more obedience when he gave orders."[105] The position he had gained from the crown is set out very fully in the charter issued for him at the Christmas court of 1141.[106] He had been given in inheritance the shrievalties of London and Middlesex, Essex, and Hertfordshire, along with the justiciarships of these three shires, and the custody of the Tower of London. The import of this was that "he had monopolized every link between London, and the counties near her, and the crown."[107] He was certainly very conscious of his dignity as an earl. A charter that he issued in favour of the see of London has the address: "Geoffrey by the grace of God earl of Essex and justiciar of London to Robert by the same grace bishop of London and to the archdeacon and to all his barons and men, and to his tenants and friends of London and Essex, both clerks and laymen, greeting."[108] The earl, like the bishop, enjoyed his power by the grace of God. Yet Geoffrey remained an assiduous royal agent. He was regularly at court in 1142 and 1143, just as he was at the time of his arrest.[109] It was he and "his sidekick, earl Gilbert," who early in 1142 "was despatched by King Stephen to Ely with a troop of soldiers" to expel the supporters of Bishop Nigel; they routed the soldiers and rounded up the knights, delivering them to Ely in humiliation, their legs tied under their horses.[110] He received orders to protect the monks of Colchester and on another occasion was asked to ensure that no excrement was thrown on to the streets of London.[111] His own orders as a royal official show an exact concern for

[104] Gransden, *Historical Writing in England, c.550–c.1307*, 267.

[105] *GS*, 160–1.

[106] *Regesta*, iii, no. 276.

[107] Brooke, *London*, 191.

[108] Kempe, *St. Martin-le-Grand*, 58–9 (trans.), 182–3 (text); also (corrected and abbreviated) in Round, *Commune of London*, 118. The document, as Nicholas Vincent has pointed out to me, ignores protocol by not giving the name of the bishop first. An earlier charter of Geoffrey's, more correctly addressed, is printed by Round, ibid., 119: "Domino ac patri Roberto Dei gratia Londoniensi episcopi . . . Gaufredus comes de Essexa salutem."

[109] *Regesta*, iii, nos. 4 (Oxford), 406 (Ipswich), 855 (Lincolnshire), 858 (Oxford), 861 (Caistor in Lindsey).

[110] *Liber Eliensis*, 319: "associante ei comiti Gileberto"; for comment, Miller, *Ely*, 171–2. The event clearly lived long in the memory but its exact date is uncertain.

[111] *Regesta*, iii, nos. 210, 533.

legal process.[112] He had at least a working relationship with his clerical equivalent as justiciar, William de Belmeis, the archdeacon of London.[113] The worst charge that can be proved against him, on the basis of the London charters at least, is that he encroached on lands of Holy Trinity Priory to plant a vineyard in the suburb of East Smithfield.[114]

If the appropriation of the royal prerogatives is not a charge that can be sustained, what of "the common report" that "he had determined to bestow the kingdom on the countess of Anjou"? It is likely that this charge was the crux of the matter and it is one that is very difficult to test. It was made to the king "in private conference," by those bound to him in personal friendship. While the *Gesta Stephani* makes this arrest a mirror image of that in 1139, with angry exchanges in a public forum and the king intervening to keep the peace,[115] this seems less likely than what we are told in the Walden chronicle, that the court had been disbanded and that Geoffrey was taken to one side when he was about to leave. In this account also, it was a small clique that caused his downfall. Geoffrey, it says, "supported the king's side for some time in most loyal service against his rival, but in the end, being maligned by some of the leading men of the kingdom, who were motivated by envy, he was falsely charged before the king, in secret, with being disloyal to the king and a traitor to his country."[116] He was then brought to London and detained until such time as his men could surrender to royal custodians the Tower of London, the *caput* of his honour at Pleshey, and the castle of his new power base at Walden. The Tower was thereafter in the custody of Richard de Lucy, who would inherit much of the authority that Geoffrey had enjoyed; Turgis of Avranches is found at Walden; the custodian of Pleshey is not known. Sources from St Albans preserve the names of William de Warenne, William of Ypres, William Martel, and (most especially) William d'Aubigny, earl of Arundel,[117] as those with the king at this time.[118] If this

---

[112] *English Lawsuits*, i. 260, no. 309, in favour of the canons of St Martin-le-Grand, ordering restitution of "their whole grain harvest of Good Easter" and an enquiry regarding their title to five acres of land.

[113] The archdeacon is an addressee and he and his brother Walter witnessed Geoffrey's charter for St Martin-le-Grand: Kempe, *St. Martin-le-Grand*, 182–3; he also witnessed the foundation charter of Walden Abbey: *Walden*, 171; *Fasti* 1: *St Paul's, London*, 9.

[114] *Regesta*, iii, no. 507.

[115] *GS*, 160–3.

[116] *Walden*, 14–15.

[117] One of the knightly families holding of St Albans preserved the legend that one of its members had unhorsed the earl of Arundel in defence of the sanctuary of the monastery: Matthew Paris, *Historia Minor*, i. 270–1; Round, *Geoffrey*, 204–5. *Waltham*, 76–81, speaks of disputes between the earl of Arundel and Geoffrey de Mandeville, "two of the leading barons of the land," and gives Geoffrey much the better press.

[118] Abbot Geoffrey of St Albans (d. 1146) was said *in necessitate* to have melted down the precious metal in an altarpiece and given it to the four men named, in response to threats that otherwise they would burn the town: *GASA*, i. 94. Round commented that "there is no episode to which it can be so fitly assigned as this of 1143": *Geoffrey*, 206 n. 3.

identification is correct, then William Martel had been released quite promptly after his capture at Wilton. These were all men "bound to the king in personal friendship" and several of them can be shown to have profited by Geoffrey de Mandeville's fall.

There had been arrests at court before but no layman had previously had his position destroyed in quite the way that Geoffrey de Mandeville was through the penalties inflicted on him by the king and his inner courtiers in the autumn of 1143. He lost his lordship and his power base. It is not surprising that he is thereafter found rather outside his earlier area of operations and in active revolt against the king.

> This high-minded man, having been tricked, as has already been said, by the underhand treachery of men who wished him ill, immediately enticed to join him, by gifts and promises, a considerable number of battle-hardened knights; he added archers, and hastened to gather together from wherever he could other retainers of the same kind notorious for their crimes. Whereupon, like a strong, unbridled horse ready to maim with teeth and hooves any who stood in its way, he first assailed manors, villages, and other things belonging to the king's estates, set them on fire, and then he lavishly distributed amongst his fellow-knights the not inconsiderable plunder stolen during his pillaging.[119]

The author's perspective here is very clear. Geoffrey and his supporters were in the wrong. But what exactly did they do? And how did their actions impact on the king's behaviour and on the position of the crown? These questions can be answered in part from accounts written at Ely and at Ramsey, the two monastic communities most involved in the revolt. These sources are vivid in their detail, if rather less strong on the wider picture. One instance of this is that they each reveal the attempted deposition of their religious superiors, the bishop of Ely and the abbot of Ramsey. It is hardly conceivable that these events were not connected in some way with alleged conspiracy in favour of the empress and with Geoffrey de Mandeville's revolt but that connection is not made in the sources and the chronology is very difficult to establish. Before introducing these matters it will be useful to look at the geography.

This was a fenland revolt. Geoffrey came first to the capital of the fens: "he took and pillaged the town of Cambridge, which was subject to the king, breaking into it when the inhabitants were off their guard." The doors of the churches were battered down and their plate and the treasure that the townsmen had stored in them were plundered.[120] He and his men next, it would appear, came to Ely and found this area already unstable because of the actions of the bishop. "The king's men were united in plotting against

---

[119] *Walden*, 14–15; there is a similar passage, more coloured but no more specific, in *GS*, 164–5.
[120] *GS*, 164–5.

the holy place of Ely."[121] Geoffrey now made common cause with the knights of the bishopric, men whom earlier he had humiliated. He besieged Aldreth, "the small castle at the entry to the island,"[122] and Ely itself and obtained possession of both fortifications. Centred there, like a spider in its web, he was able to move quickly from side to side. He moved via the network of waterways. It was by water that he came, perhaps at the beginning of November, to the abbey of Ramsey. His reputation preceded him: not his later reputation as an unprincipled and predatory feudatory, but his past history as a royal official. The monks thought he had come to restore their abbot, who had recently been deposed. They were wrong. Geoffrey immediately "occupied the monastery, drove out the monks, stole with sacrilegious hands the church's treasure and plate, made the monastic precinct into a stable, and gave the adjacent townships to his retainers as stipends."[123] To the west, close to the North Road, he then built a castle at Wood Walton and entrusted this to his eldest and illegitimate son, Ernulf, while to the east he built a castle at Benwick to control the river crossing.[124] With these arrangements in place, he and his men "were able to retreat unmolested to Fordham," to the east of Ely, which controlled communications between the fenland and East Anglia. When King Stephen was put in the picture, "he was beside himself with anger and reckoned it was all due to the machinations of bishop Nigel."[125] The king built a series of castles ringing the fenland, among them one at Burwell, in order to contain the threat.[126]

It is not surprising that the king saw the hand of the bishop of Ely behind the fenland revolt. Nigel had garrisoned Devizes against the king for a few dramatic days in the autumn of 1139; he had fled to the empress and been constant in his attendance on her in 1141; he had been received back in the fold in 1142 but his military following had been humiliated. Here if anywhere in 1143 there was a marked man. Any proceedings against him, however, would have to follow the letter of the canon law. So they would do. At one of the church councils of 1143, either in mid-Lent or in the autumn, the bishop faced grave charges.[127] It was said that he had incited rebellion in the kingdom and that the goods of his church had been given to his

---

[121] *Liber Eliensis*, 328.

[122] *GS*, 100–1: "castellulum quod erat in introitu insule."

[123] *Chron. Ramsey*, 329. A grant to the abbey of Thorney was dated to "proxima die veneris ante Pentecosten in ipsomet anno postquam comes Gaufridus ceperat abbatem et ecclesiam de Rameseye" (12 May 1144): Cambridge UL, Add. MS 3020, fo. 206r.

[124] Ibid., 332; *Liber Eliensis*, 328: "in transitu aquarum." On Wood Walton see Brown and Taylor, "Cambridgeshire Earthwork Surveys 3," 62–4.

[125] *Liber Eliensis*, 328: "rex Stephanus in iram graviter accensus omnia hec reputavit ab episcopo Nigello machinari."

[126] Lethbridge, "Excavations at Burwell Castle, Cambridgeshire," 121–33. "Giant's Hill" in Rampton shows many of the same features and dates from the same time: Brown and Taylor, "Cambridgeshire Earthwork Surveys 2," 97–9.

[127] *Liber Eliensis*, 324–6. On the councils see *Councils and Synods*, 794–810 (nos. 144–5), and on Nigel of Ely's movements see in particular the fine discussion ibid., 805–7; also *Liber Eliensis*, 433–6.

knightly followers. Those bringing the charge were Jocelin, the prior of Eye, one of the centres of Stephen's own lordship in Suffolk, and a much more substantial figure, Master Robert of Cricklade, prior of St Frideswide's, Oxford. It is possible that the bishop was suspended in mid-Lent. We cannot be sure. Nigel is certainly the conspicuous absentee at the meeting of the bishops at Winchester in late September.[128] According to the monks of Ely, his reaction to the charges against him was to seek a conference with the empress at Devizes. This did not turn out well. The king's men were on the lookout for him, came on him by chance at Wareham, and without compunction they stole his horses and his baggage, most notably all the goods of his chapel. He lost albs, copes, and chasubles, some of them decorated in gold, silver cruets and chalices, a gospel-book decorated with gold and encrusted with relics.[129] The bishop escaped, came back to Ely, told the story of his losses to a saddened and sceptical community, and thereafter set out for Rome. He cannot have left England before December 1143, for he took with him a letter from Gilbert Foliot, abbot of Gloucester, to the new pope, Celestine II.[130] It did not mention the war.

The abbot of Ramsey was also on the road to Rome at very much the same time and for very much the same reasons.[131] The context here has to be surmised but certainly the king was actively involved. At some point late in 1143 Stephen came to Stamford and there he was met by Walter, the abbot of Ramsey, who "resigned his pastoral staff into the royal hand." The person appointed in his place was Daniel, a monk of the house, a capable man who had guided the king through the fens earlier and was expected to do so again but – according to all the monastic writers – was a disgrace to his profession.[132] The king then brought the new abbot to Ramsey and intruded him in his new office, "which it was not proper for a king to do."[133] Abbot Daniel had only been in office for eighteen days when Geoffrey and his men sailed in silently from the east, whereupon, as has been seen, the abbot and the community were driven out. Both the old and the new abbot then took their cases to Rome.[134] Abbot Walter it was, after the necessary interval of three

---

[128] *Councils and Synods*, 804–10 (no. 145).

[129] *Liber Eliensis*, 324–5. These valuable goods had not been taken by the bishop at random. They would allow him to celebrate mass in any season and in style.

[130] *GF Letters*, no. 23: "pro domno et amico nostro Nigello Heliensi episcopo serenitate uestre supplicamus."

[131] The evidence here is a Ramsey Abbey memorandum, National Archives, E. 164/28, fos. 158r–160r, under the far from neutral heading "persecutio domini Galteri abbatis," printed in *Chron. Ramsey*, 325–36. There is an excellent discussion of this text in Paxton, "Charter and Chronicle in Twelfth-Century England," 144–55.

[132] *GS*, 100–1; *Walden*, 16–17: "quodam falsi nominis ac tonsure monacho."

[133] As the story was told, the election of Daniel could not have been more improper. He had only achieved office through simony and then he had been intruded by the king: *Chron. Ramsey*, 328–9.

[134] Walter took a small and select *familia* with him on his journey to Rome, his principal advisers being William, prior of St Ives, and two *magistri*, Michael of Burwell and Richard of Elton: ibid., 329.

months, who returned triumphant, a decision that made the king extremely unhappy.[135] It is only this aside, late in the day, that makes the royal involvement a major factor in the case. Up until that time the king was seen as taking sides in an internal dispute in the monastery, one that turned on effective stewardship of the resources of the community. This cannot be the whole story. Abbots were leaders of local communities. If their loyalty was suspect they could be and were removed without compunction, and some irregularity could always be alleged against those who lived by the Rule.

The fenland revolt, which so unsettled the region's monastic houses, came to an end in the late summer of 1144, with the death of Geoffrey de Mandeville. He had been besieging the royal garrison in the castle of Burwell and, so the story was told, he had taken off his head protection because it was a hot day. Thus exposed, he suffered a direct hit in the head, and although he made light of the injury he died a few days later at Mildenhall in Suffolk. He died excommunicate and it was the settled teaching of the Church, reinforced by the legatine council of 1143, presided over by Henry of Winchester, that excommunicates could not be buried in consecrated ground. His body was claimed by the Templars, taken to London, and then, according to different versions of the story, either cast into a ditch outside the churchyard or hung from a tree within the churchyard.[136] Either way it was an ignominious end for a very capable businessman who had given generously to charity.[137] We get a very clear picture of him, negotiating access to his market at Walden, carefully listing the nineteen churches he had given to the abbey he had founded there, and in due time making no less careful restitution to the canons of St Martin-le-Grand and the chapter of St Paul's, all of which might have been cited in mitigation had his end been less dramatic.[138] If we look for a political context for Geoffrey's fall we must go back to his arrest the previous autumn. That arrest seemed almost a rerun of the arrest of Roger of Salisbury in 1139, and the background to that was a divided court and the fear of invasion. It may be that a further invasion was expected in 1143, when the empress's husband would come to England in her support, as her followers had long desired.

There was no doubt in the autumn of 1143 that Stephen had lost Normandy. Geoffrey of Anjou now controlled "all of Normandy on the near side of the Seine,"[139] and some with lordships in upper Normandy had

---

[135] "rege super hoc multum murmurante," ibid., 330.

[136] HH, 744–5; Gervase, i. 128–9; *Waltham*, 78–81; *Chron. Ramsey*, 331–2; *Walden*, 16–19 and n. 31–4. Round's treatment of the earl's last days, in *Geoffrey*, 201–26, is a *tour de force*.

[137] HH, 742: "magne in mundanis diligentie"; *GS*, 160–1: "uir sicut prudentis animi ingenio spectabilis"; *Waltham*, 78–9: "rei sue familiaris prouidus dispensator."

[138] *Regesta*, iii, no. 274; *Walden*, 169–72; Kempe, *St. Martin-le-Grand*, 58–9 (trans.), 182–3 (text); Round, *Commune of London*, 118–19.

[139] A charter of Geoffrey of Anjou, dated 1143, "anno quo . . . partem Normannie que est citra Sequanam adquisivimus": Juenin, *Nouvelle Histoire de Tournus*, preuves, 156–7; similar phraseology, possibly from another charter of like date, is found in the Annals of St Aubin, s.a. 1143, *Recueil d'annales Angevines*, 10.

also come to terms with him.[140] In mid-January 1144 Geoffrey and his forces crossed the Seine at Vernon and a few days later he was received by the citizens of Rouen, the capital city of the duchy, with all the ceremonial due to its ruler.[141] The castle was garrisoned by troops under the lordship of William, Earl Warenne; they were besieged by among others the forces of Waleran of Meulan, who had fought alongside William de Warenne just three years earlier at the battle of Lincoln, "and by other of the Norman lords who had come to terms with the count." The castle of Rouen was strongly built and bravely defended and it was three months before the garrison surrendered, when their provisions were exhausted. It was at this point, according to Robert of Torigni, that Geoffrey, count of Anjou, now became additionally duke of Normandy. He notes that while the siege of the castle was proceeding Geoffrey had been joined by the count of Flanders, who had brought up 1,400 knights, by the king of France, who had also brought a contingent, and by Rotrou, count of the Perche, who died shortly after the siege was concluded.[142] The chronicler carefully says nothing about the exact title by which Geoffrey now held the duchy. One thing that is certain, however, is that he did not wish to be seen as holding by right of conquest. Rather the stress will have been on the hereditary rights of his wife and his son and on approval by the various estates in Normandy that approximated to a formal election.

A series of agreements, which involved a good deal of patient diplomacy, lay behind the smooth takeover of power. Geoffrey had worked with the grain of local custom and had shown himself ready to compromise and accept advice. He had come to terms with many of the magnates and had conceded territory in return for support.[143] He had negotiated an agreement with the citizens of Rouen.[144] He had also come to terms with the Norman Church, not without initial difficulty, for he had refused to accept the election of Arnulf, archdeacon of Sées, as bishop of Lisieux in succession to his uncle

---

[140] Walter Giffard and the men of the *pays de Caux*: Torigni, 145.

[141] Torigni, 147: "receptus est a civibus Rothomagi sollenniter," on 20 Jan.; *Annales de Jumièges*, 62–5: "Rothomagum cepit, consensu ciuium"; Annals of Rouen, s.a. 1144, *RHF*, xii. 785: "in ecclesia S. Marie Rotomagi honorifice susceptus est," giving the date as 19 Jan. The citizens of Rouen, Henry Fitz Empress would later confirm, had enjoyed certain of their privileges, "ab illo die quo cives Rothomagi homines ducis Galfridi patris mei effecti sunt": *Regesta*, iii, no. 729.

[142] Torigni, 147–8; "reddiderunt se et turrem, videlicet Gaufrido antea Andegavensi comiti, jam exinde Normannorum duci"; with the same phrase in the Annals of Mont-Saint-Michel, in *Robert de Torigni*, ed. Delisle, ii. 234; Annals of Rouen, *RHF*, xii. 785; Thompson, *The Country of the Perche*, 84.

[143] Cherbourg was surrendered after mediation between Geoffrey's own men ("comitis collaterales") and those who spoke for the garrison: John of Marmoutier, 230; Torigni, 148: "et ceteri principes Normannie qui iam cum duce concordati erant."

[144] The evidence here is Duke Henry's lengthy grant to the citizens of Rouen in 1150–1, which confirms an earlier grant of his father: *Regesta*, iii, no. 729 ("Omnes autem predictas concessiones affiduciavit G. dux Normannorum pater meus se tenere."); Haskins, 134.

John, who had died in May 1141.[145] The clergy called out the heavy artillery, with letters from Bernard of Clairvaux and Peter the Venerable attacking Geoffrey as "a tyrant" and as "an enemy of the church."[146] The quarrel had been defused by late 1143,[147] though it would not be the last of its kind.[148] Geoffrey had negotiated with Louis VII of France, first that he would not oppose the conquest of the duchy and then to have his assumption of power legitimized.[149] The details of the negotiations were kept confidential but it seems likely that Geoffrey held the duchy by grant of the French king and that in return for this grant he surrendered Gisors and the other castles of the Norman Vexin.[150] The capture of one of these, Lyons-la-Forêt, where Henry I had died, saw the end of the year's campaigning and the coalition forces went home. It was represented on the French side that it was Louis VII who had captured Normandy and then transferred the duchy to Henry Fitz Empress in return for liege homage.[151] This statement is so condensed as to be misleading and it is far from certain that Henry did homage for Normandy. It might have suited the French crown to reserve its position as to what should happen when Geoffrey of Anjou died.

The winter of 1143–4 was the ninth of the nineteen long winters when, according to the *Anglo-Saxon Chronicle*, "Christ and his saints were asleep." For Stephen it was the very worst of times. With the death of Pope Innocent II in September 1143 he had lost an ally who had never wavered in his support. Innocent's death meant that Stephen's brother, Henry of Winchester, lost the papal legation and with it a good deal of his political influence. Henry went to Rome to seek the renewal of the legation, but this was more in hope than expectation, for the new pope, Celestine II, was known to be a supporter of the empress, and Archbishop Theobald shadowed his every move.[152] Stephen had very little money. The one engagement that he had fought recently had seen his defeat and with it he had lost something of his reputation for bravery. And now he had suffered what

[145] OV, vi. 550–1; Torigni, 142.

[146] *Letters of St Bernard*, 332–3 (no. 252); *Peter the Venerable*, i. 261–2 (no. 101).

[147] On 18 Sept. 1143 Arnulf witnessed a charter of the count of Ponthieu, "regente in Galiis rege Ludovico, principante in Normannia duce Gaufrido": *Letters of Arnulf of Lisieux*, xix–xx, 209; *Recueil des actes des comtes de Ponthieu*, 44–7.

[148] A bitter and bloody contest followed the death of Arnulf's uncle, John, bishop of Sées, in 1144: Spear, *Norman Cathedrals*, 273–4; *Letters of Arnulf of Lisieux*, xxxiii–xxxiv.

[149] Newburgh, i. 39: "cum rege quippe Francorum, qui regi Stephano foederatus videbatur, prudenter colluserat, ne quid ab eo impedimenti pateretur quominus prosperaretur in iis quae intendebat."

[150] Robert of Torigni acknowledged the presence of the French king in 1144 but gave him no special status, but then in 1152 he says that Geoffrey had granted the Norman Vexin to the French king *ad tempus* in return for his support: Torigni, 148, 169. A charter of the French king shows him in control of Gasny on the Epte, "by grant of the count of Anjou," by 1147: Power, *Norman Frontier*, 392 and n. 23; and for discussion see also Chibnall, "Normandy," in King, *Anarchy*, 110 and n. 91.

[151] "Histoire du roi Louis VII," in *Vie de Louis le Gros*, ed. Molinier, 161–2.

[152] JS, *HP*, 85–6; HH, 742–5; Saltman, *Theobald*, 19–20; William Thorne, *Chronicle*, 77.

from his point of view was clearly "the loss of Normandy," that loss ratified by the French king, "to whom he had seemed to be allied." The loss of territory was serious but what was potentially fatal to his kingship was the manner in which it had been achieved. In the pages of Orderic, writing of 1141, it was "the Angevins" who were fighting both in England and in Normandy; they appear as an invading force.[153] By the time Geoffrey became duke of Normandy in 1144 that perception had changed. Geoffrey had changed it and his son Henry had watched him at work. Stephen had been given a second chance in 1141, very much against the odds, in part because his opponent had failed to build a consensus. Lessons had been learned. Geoffrey of Anjou, in taking over Normandy with the support of the Church, the magnates, and the mercantile community, provided a model of how the takeover of England might be achieved. The consensus that Geoffrey had secured meant that Stephen had no realistic hope of recapturing Normandy and those who supported him in England would have to adjust to this fact. Henceforth it would be the lordship of Geoffrey and his son Henry that allowed the Normans to tell the time.[154]

[153] OV, vi. 546–9: (Henry of Winchester) "ad Andegauos se protinus conuertit"; (Robert of Leicester) "pacem cum Andegauensibus procurauit"; "guerram Andegauorum."

[154] The archbishop of Rouen would date his charters by the regnal years of Geoffrey from 1144: Haskins, 129–30.

Chapter 7

A VARIETY OF COIN

Numerous castles had been raised in each region through the eager action of factions, and in England there were in a sense as many kings, or rather tyrants, as there were lords of castles. Each minted his own coinage, and each like a king had the power to lay down the law for his subjects.[1]

Stephen his nephew, a mild and humble man, reigned as king after Henry, and young men flooded the land, evil men and sinners, who troubled the land.[2]

Henry of Winchester, the papal legate, was never at a loss for words and in any situation he had a relevant text from the scriptures ready to hand. He would remind himself, when victorious in a lawsuit, that he should offer his adversary some compensation, since "a bruised reed should not be broken."[3] He expected constancy in those who had taken religious vows: they should not "take their hands from the plough" of divine service.[4] As political events changed in the country which his brother ruled, he encouraged his contemporaries to move on and not dwell on the past. "Remember the wife of Lot, who on turning back was turned into a pillar of salt." This had been his advice to Brian Fitz Count, in the autumn of 1142, and doubtless to others of the empress's supporters also.[5] "You are always looking back, but you take little notice of the offence which you see there, even though it may soon mean your downfall." The offence was a serious one in the bishop's eyes, for it affected in equal measure both his own pocket and his view of proper order. "I sent you letters only recently to ask you to provide a firm peace to all those coming to my fair, and your letters to me did not deny this; but in the meanwhile my goods have been taken by your men." These were goods bound for the fair at Winchester. It was one of the great fairs of medieval England and a major source of revenue for the bishop, who had viceregal powers in his cathedral city while the fair was being held.[6]

---

[1] Newburgh, i. 70.
[2] Hugh Candidus, 104–5: "et immerserunt super terram iuvenes, viri iniqui et peccatores," 57.
[3] *English Lawsuits*, i. 221 (no. 257). The text is from Isaiah 42 : 3.
[4] *Book of St Gilbert*, 146–7. The text is from Luke 9: 62.
[5] King, "Brian Fitz Count," 89–91. The texts are from Genesis 19: 26; Luke 17: 31–2.
[6] Biddle, *Winchester*, 286–8; Keene, *Winchester Survey*, ii. 1091–123.

Brian Fitz Count did not deny the charge but rather pleaded necessity. His own position in the world had been all but destroyed:

> King Henry gave me land. But it has been taken away from me and my men because I am doing what you ordered me to do. As a result, I am in extreme straits and am not harvesting one acre of corn from the land which he gave me. It is not surprising that I take from others to sustain my life and the lives of my men, and in order to do what you commanded of me. Nor have I taken anything from anyone who has left my own possessions alone. You should know that neither I nor my men are doing this for money or fief or land, either promised or given, but because of your command and the lawfulness of myself and my men.[7]

Here, honed in correspondence and heightened in adversity, is the reference to the reign of Henry I as the measure of prosperity, of good order, and of legitimacy. In these terms the empress had been accepted by Henry and the other higher clergy a little over a year before.[8] Brian wrote in the same terms, perhaps a little under a year later, to Gilbert Foliot, abbot of Gloucester, and found a more sympathetic audience. He spoke of the good and golden days of Henry I, now turned to base metal. He must have given a fuller biography, for the abbot in reply said that Henry "brought you up from boyhood, educated you, knighted you, enriched you."[9] Brian Fitz Count was not the only one of the empress's supporters looking back nostalgically to the time of Henry I. The same ideas can be seen in charters issued by Baldwin de Redvers, earl of Devon. In the privilege he gave to Christchurch, Twynham, Baldwin refers his own title back to the time when "King Henry most fully and most freely granted the whole fee to my father, Richard de Redvers, to hold by hereditary right,"[10] while he gave land to St James's Priory, Exeter, "for the soul of the most noble King Henry, who gave land to my father."[11] For these men the link to Henry I was integral to their sense of identity.

Brian Fitz Count and Baldwin de Redvers had served in the household of Henry I; they were his *familiares*, a part of his extended family. They were not his blood relatives. Henry of Winchester was. He was the old king's nephew. Brian lost no opportunity to remind him of this fact. Not

---

[7] King, "Brian Fitz Count," 90.

[8] WM, *HN*, 92–3.

[9] *GF Letters*, no. 26, at 61: "Non est tibi elapsum a memoria quod te promovit a puero, quod iuvenem educavit, et donatum militie cingulo, donibus et honoribus ampliavit."

[10] *Charters of the Redvers Family*, no. 15, dated 1139–41: "sicut rex Henricus patri meo Ricardo de Redveriis plenius et liberius habere concessit, quando ei primum hereditario iure habendum totum contulit feudum."

[11] Ibid., no. 25, dated 1143–4: "pro anima . . . nobilissimi Henrici regis qui terram patri meo dedit"; and the same phrase is found in no. 27, of 1146, for St Martin-des-Champs, Paris.

only was the bishop forgetting his uncle's benefactions to him, he was forgetting the instructions he and the higher clergy had given in the aftermath of the battle of Lincoln. "You yourself who are a prelate of Holy Church have ordered me to adhere to the daughter of King Henry your uncle, and to help her to acquire that which is hers by right but which has been taken from her by force." The bishop was now going back on his word, while at the same time lecturing Brian and his companions on concepts of good faith. William of Malmesbury spoke of the legate in late 1141 "trying to diminish by his great eloquence his unpopularity for what he had done."[12] It was characteristic understatement. What Brian Fitz Count shows in this letter is simple contempt. The bishop has forfeited the privileges of his order. Brian invites him to step outside.

> All faithful men of Holy Church should therefore know that I, Brian Fitz Count, whom good King Henry brought up and to whom he gave arms and an honour, am ready to prove what I assert in this letter against Henry, nephew of King Henry, bishop of Winchester and legate of the Apostolic See, either by combat or by judicial process, though a clerk or a layman.[13]

The challenge was simply an insult. Henry of Winchester could cope with that. What might have given him pause, however, was the reproach that preceded it. "I am sorry for the poor and their plight, when the church provides scarcely any refuge for them, for they will die if peace be longer delayed." It was not just the empress's supporters who felt that the higher clergy, headed by Theobald "the so-called archbishop of Canterbury" (as Brian Fitz Count calls him dismissively), were failing in their duty. The author of the *Gesta Stephani* excoriated the bishops for their moral cowardice and noted that some of them even "rode on horseback with the haughtiest destroyers of the country and took their share of the spoils." The bishop of Winchester was at the head of his list.[14]

Henry of Winchester was fully alive to the challenge. In a world dominated by private agreements and by self-help, in which their own moral authority was called in question, he and his episcopal colleagues sought to impose such order as they could. They met in council at London in mid-March 1143. The king himself took part in their deliberations. The meeting was necessary, according to the archdeacon of Huntingdon, "because of the clergy's urgent needs: for plunderers were paying no respect either to clerks or to God's church, and clerks were being taken captive and ransomed just like laymen."[15] The legislation produced at this

[12] WM, *HN* 108–9.
[13] King, "Brian Fitz Count," 91.
[14] *GS*, 154–7.
[15] HH, 742–3.

council survives.[16] The preamble states that "following in the footsteps of the Fathers we seek to provide new remedies for new diseases"; that is, it was necessary to react to the circumstances of a civil war. It was first necessary to protect the persons of the clergy themselves. Anyone who laid hands on them was to be excommunicated, and unless he was at death's door he could only be absolved by the pope himself. There was to be no escape from the sanctions applied to such men. No cleric might act for them or serve in their household. Mass was not to be said, nor bells be rung, "in town or in castle or in the countryside," in their presence. If priests persisted in doing so then they were to be degraded and would lose their benefices. The most public sanction for an excommunicate would come on his death. They were not to be given burial, and this applied not just to burial in consecrated ground: they were not to be buried at all. Those excommunicates who had been buried on church land were to be dug up no later than the following Christmas. Nor were these empty threats, as the fate of Geoffrey de Mandeville – which we have anticipated – was to show. Roger of Wendover, working on earlier chronicles and putting his own gloss on them, said at this point that the council intended that those working the ploughs in the fields should enjoy the same peace as if they were in a cemetery.[17] It seems a slightly odd phrase, but the image is that of consecrated ground as a protected space; he saw the clergy as seeking to extend that protection into the countryside. In certain respects some of the other provisions of the council did endeavour to do this. It prohibited "all exactions and unaccustomed works on castles." It refused to allow any priest or deacon to collect revenue or act as reeve for the laity. The Latin words used here were *exactor* and *prepositus*. An *exactor* was someone who almost by definition was taking some levy that was unauthorized and unaccustomed and so – by definition – improper. To list such in the same breath as a reeve is extremely suggestive of clerical attitudes. The very exercise of lay lordship, over the clergy, over their men and their possessions, was coming into question. In their deliberations the clergy hold up a mirror to what was happening in the English countryside.

REGIONAL LORDSHIP

It was at Peterborough on the edge of the fenland that one of the monks wrote what has become the classic description of the disorders of the reign of Stephen.

When the traitors understood that he was a mild man, and gentle and good, and did not exact the full penalties of the law, they perpetrated every

---

[16] *Councils and Synods*, 800–4 (no. 144).
[17] Roger of Wendover, *Chronica*, ii. 232.

enormity. They had done him homage and sworn oaths, but they kept no pledge; all of them were perjured and their pledges nullified, for every powerful man built his castles and held them against him and they filled the county full of castles. They oppressed the wretched people of the country severely with castle-building. When the castles were built, they filled them with devils and wicked men. . . . I have neither the ability nor the power to tell of all the horrors nor all the torments they inflicted upon wretched people in this country; and that lasted the nineteen years while Stephen was king, and it was always going from bad to worse. They levied taxes on the villages every so often and called it "protection-money."[18]

The word that has been translated as "protection-money" is *tenserie*. It appears as a rash at very much the same time as the castles, and it has been suggested that it refers to rights claimed by lords over the local peasantry for building and repairing their castles, or alternatively that it was an extension of the rights of lay advocates over local religious houses.[19]

Nigel of Ely, anxious to provide a national context for his local difficulties, told the pope about *tenserie*. It served as a shorthand for the arbitrary actions of the lay power, and the pope in return condemned that power. He wrote to Archbishop Theobald and all the bishops of England, on 24 May 1144.[20] Nigel's lands and possessions had been taken away, particularly when he had been expelled from his diocese. Some, in the name of *tenserie*, had despoiled his townships and his men, and oppressed them with unjust works and exactions. It mattered not that they claimed that such sacrilege took place with the express or tacit commission of the king or magnates. Might was not right. It was important to obey God rather than man. An identical letter, also preserved in the Ely archive, was sent to Archbishop Hugh and the bishops of Normandy.[21] Why it was sent and indeed whether or not it was actually delivered is very far from clear. Some of those complained of may have had Norman lands. But it is at least as likely that the message here was to be read between the lines and was directed at the archbishop himself: "See what a fine mess you've got us into." The bishop of Ely could trace all his troubles back to "the arrest of the bishops" in the summer of 1139. Hugh of Rouen had supplied his moral authority and suitable texts in support of the king. This was Nigel of Ely's reply. And in the west country, Gilbert Foliot is found complaining of two particular lords, who were once again taking *tenserie*. They were doing so, moreover, *imperiosa voce*, "with an imperious voice."[22] This could almost be read as "with the voice of the empress." Gilbert expected the reader or listener to admire the conceit.

---

[18] *ASC*, s.a. 1137.
[19] Strickland, *War*, 84–6; King, "Anarchy of King Stephen's reign," 135–7; Round, *Geoffrey*, 414–16; Bisson, "The Lure of Stephen's England."
[20] *Liber Eliensis*, 326–7.
[21] Ibid., 329–30.
[22] *GF Letters*, no. 27.

"They called 'it protection-money'." The author of the *Anglo-Saxon Chronicle* was a monk writing at Peterborough. *They* in his experience are likely to be men found closer to home, who spoke with the king's voice. Men such as Simon of Senlis, earl of Northampton, who sucked into his *tenseria* a cluster of the knightly tenants of Peterborough Abbey.[23] Simon issued a charter for Thorney, another of the fenland monasteries, in respect of their market at Yaxley, which they hoped against hope might rival the fair which the monks of Ramsey held at St Ives.

> Know that I give in perpetuity the market of Yaxley, held on the Monday, as also the wharf there, to the abbot of Thorney and the brethren there serving God, for my salvation and that of my ancestors. And I wish and I firmly command that all who come to this market whether by water or by land shall have my peace. This as the charter of king Stephen ordered. It is my wish also that the lands of the aforesaid monks should be quit of *tenserie* and all works.

A second charter, issued to a clerical audience and stressing that he had been admitted to the fraternity of the house, omitted the offending word and was in other ways more mollifying, but still it was the earl's peace that backed up the protection offered to the monks.[24] There is a similar pair of earlier charters, granting the same protection and many of the same rights, though lacking the word *tenserie*, from Henry, son of the king of Scots, issued in the period when he was earl of Huntingdon.[25] The monks of Thorney filed them together, and when in the thirteenth century they compiled their great "Red Book," while other magnate charters of the time were placed as appropriate in the county sections, these were placed amongst the royal charters. In doing so the compiler showed admirable historical sense.

The monk of Peterborough might also have been thinking of William, Earl Warenne. During the winter of 1146–7 the earl granted to the monks of Castle Acre, men who lived in the shadow of the imposing castle that he had built in west Norfolk, a confirmation of any acquisitions which they might make, "from my fee of whatever tenancy within my *tenseria*, whether by way of gift or purchase."[26] Baldwin de Redvers, earl of Devon,

---

[23] Hugh Candidus, 128: (abbot William) "pro confirmacione uero nouem militum quos comes Simon tenuerat centum marcas dedit regi."

[24] His two charters are found in the Red Book of Thorney, Cambridge UL, Add. MS 3020–1, fos. 21r–v. The charter of Stephen referred to is *Regesta*, iii, no. 884. In another charter, Earl Simon confirmed to "his monks" of St Andrew's Priory, Northampton, the grant of the manor of Sywell made by William of Avranches in 1147, "liberam et quietam de tenseriis et omnibus serviciis atque consuetudinibus mihi et heredibus meis pertinentibus": BL, Cotton MS Vesp. E. xvii, fos. 199v–200r.

[25] *Charters of David I*, nos. 63–4.

[26] BL, Harley MS 2110, fo. 4r: "omnibus que habent perquisita de meo feudo de cuiuscunque feudo sint infra meam tenseriam, siue de donis siue de emptionibus."

gave "his burgesses" of Christchurch in Dorset an exemption from customary payments "throughout all my land and *tenseria.*"[27] He saw his control as extending to knightly tenants as well as to the peasantry, for he responded to complaints by the bishop of Salisbury by relinquishing his claim to four churches in Devon and to the services of certain knights, who were described as living "beneath" and under the control of his castle of Crewkerne in Somerset.[28] The great magnates were relaxed in their exercise of authority, confident that their commands would be obeyed. The charters of William de Warenne are particularly instructive in this regard. The infirmarer of Lewes Priory was allowed to take fish for the benefit of the sick brethren of the house, under the supervision of one of the earl's officials. The earl's rents could safely be piled up on the altar of West Ardsley church, and left there until the claims of the canons of Nostell were satisfied. The canons of Thetford were to have a fair of two days, protected by the earl's peace. The formulas used are those of royal charters. The earl's markets and fairs were protected by the standard £10 penalty; the earl's agent, in one case his brother, would act if his instructions were disobeyed; his grant could not be challenged in any court. The very intimation of the earl's displeasure might be sanction enough. The earl could write in these terms "to his sheriff and all future sheriffs of Wakefield (in Yorkshire)," "to his barons of Norfolk," "to his minsters and burgesses of Thetford," and to his barons and ministers of the rape of Lewes (Sussex).[29]

The magnates of the empress's party were no less aggressive and no less assured. They lost an important general with the death of Miles of Gloucester, earl of Hereford, while out hunting on Christmas Eve, 1143. He was embroiled in controversy with his local bishop at the time, for he "needed a great deal of money for the hire of knights he had assembled against the king" and so "compelled the churches he had brought under the yoke of his lordship to pay unprecedented levies"; but he had the strong support of the local heads of house, including Gilbert Foliot, and he escaped what would be the fate of Geoffrey de Mandeville, receiving an honourable burial at Llanthony Priory.[30] He was succeeded by his son,

---

[27] *Charters of the Redvers Family*, no. 31: "per totam terram meam et tenseriam."

[28] Ibid., nos. 29–30.

[29] *EYC* 8: *Warenne*, nos. 31 (alms), 38 (fish), 43, 45 (fair); BL, Harley MS 2110, fo. 4r: "si ullus eius iniuriam faciat Rainaldus frater meus faciat ipsis in iusticia"; *Monasticon*, vi. 730: "prohibeo ne iidem canonici ulli homini aut femine inde respondeant uel in placitum intrent."

[30] JH, 315; *GS*, 148–9, 158–61. The bishop used all his weapons, imposing an interdict on the earl and his kinsmen, "and the whole city of Hereford," having "the doors of the church blocked by thorn-bushes and the crosses thrown down": *GF Letters*, no. 22; "Anglo-Norman Chronicle of Wigmore," 425. The earl was "brought back to the church," after payments by his guarantors: *GS*, 160–1; *GF Letters*, no. 22. He did not die excommunicate, as is stated in Walker, "Miles of Gloucester," 77.

Roger, "a young man distinguished by exceptional prowess,"[31] but he would not enjoy his father's influence. The dominant figure in the west country was now more than ever Robert of Gloucester, along with his sons:

> Without any resistance from anyone they put almost half of England, from sea to sea, under their own laws and ordinances. This lordship of his the earl very greatly adorned by restoring peace and quietness everywhere, except that in building his castles he exacted forced labour from all and, whenever he had to fight the enemy, he demanded everyone's help either by sending knights or paying money. And there was indeed in those regions a shadow of peace but not yet peace complete, for nothing more vexed the people of the country than working not for themselves but for others, and thus by their own efforts adding to the resources for discord and warfare.[32]

This, though sketched by one of the king's supporters, is quite a balanced portrait. In some ways Robert was behaving like many of his peers. In exacting forced labour on his castles he joined a long list. This was typical of the exactions about which the churchmen complained. But there was more. Robert of Gloucester had in effect set himself up as king of the west country. He provided peace, and peace was integral to the job description of any ruler. But he had redirected to himself rights that more properly belonged to the crown. And both he and his son after him issued coins in their own names.

In the 1140s the crown all but lost control over the English coinage.[33] That control, as it had been exercised hitherto, was formidable. Coins were minted locally, in a wide variety of towns, but the dies from which the coins were struck were issued centrally. Each issue of coin had some distinguishing features, from which numismatists can identify a type. Payments to the king, at the exchequer, were accepted only in coins of the current issue; this brought in most coins of the old issue, and all foreign coins, for re-minting. All coins were silver pennies, 92.5 per cent fine, with a weight of around 1.39 grammes. These coins, though small in size, are very precise historical documents. They bear on one side (known technically as the obverse) the king's head and his name. Stephen's first type shows the king with crown and diadem, holding a sceptre in his right hand. These were the symbols of kingship, as shown on the royal seal but stripped down to essentials, and this was the image of kingship which circulated most widely in medieval times. On the other side (the reverse) there was a cross, and the inscription gave the name of the moneyer (since

---

[31] *GS*, 160–1.

[32] *GS*, 148–51.

[33] The definitive treatment of the coinage of this reign is provided by Mark Blackburn, "Coinage and Currency," in King, *Anarchy*, 145–205.

he was responsible for the quality of his coins) and the place of issue. The names on Stephen's coins show that many of the moneyers at this period were of Saxon or Scandinavian descent – the moneyers in Hereford in his reign were Driu, Edric, Sibern, and Witric, and amongst those at York were Aschetil, Autgrim, Laisig, and Ulf.

There had been a strong discipline, as well as force of habit, behind the control of the coinage. Counterfeiting was seen as treason and the penalties were severe. Everyone knew the story of how the moneyers of England had fared at the Christmas court at Winchester in 1124–5, where Roger, bishop of Salisbury, presided. "All the moneyers of England" had been summoned to court and their treatment was exemplary. "When they came there, they were taken one by one, and each was deprived of his right hand and his testicles." The *Anglo-Saxon Chronicle*, which tells the story, is normally very sympathetic to the sufferings of the English but here showed no pity, "for they had ruined the country by the magnitude of their fraud."[34] Their guilt is very far from clear. The king was in Normandy, and it was later said that his troops had complained at the quality of the coins in which they were being paid;[35] but those writing in England, closer to the event, spoke instead of torrential summer rainfall, a poor harvest, high prices, and consequent high mortality.[36] It may be that the moneyers paid a heavy price for the vagaries of the English climate. A few of them were allowed to redeem their offence by payment of a fine.[37] And this was not the only benefit to the exchequer, for the fullers of Winchester proffered a mark of gold that they be not required to perform this distasteful operation upon their fellow professionals.[38]

One consequence of the tight control of the coinage is that English coin hoards are frequently dominated by coins of a particular issue. As a form of identifier, that issue is given the name of the place where a large find of coins is first documented. The first type of Stephen, issued from the beginning of his reign up to the mid-1140s, is called the "Watford" type, from Watford in Hertfordshire where a major find – of 477 coins of Henry I and 646 coins of the first type of Stephen – was discovered in 1818.[39] These numbers were overshadowed, and what might serve as an

---

[34] *ASC*, s.a. 1125.

[35] *GND*, ii. 236–8.

[36] This was the sequence in WM, *GP*, i. 662–3: and see also, HH, 474–5 (high prices); JW, iii. 156–7 (high prices *subsequently*); *ASC*, s.a. 1125 (poor weather; high prices; debased coinage). For modern comment on these events, see Green, *Government of England*, 88–91; Blackburn, "Coinage and Currency under Henry I," 64–5; Stewart, "Moneyers in the 1130 Pipe Roll."

[37] Brand of Chichester: *PR 31 Henry I*, 42 (and the mutilation of the moneyers is noted in the Chichester Annals, s.a. 1125, *UGQ*, 94); three moneyers at Winchester: Winchester Annals, s.a. 1125, *Ann. Mon.* ii. 47.

[38] *PR 31 Henry I*, 37.

[39] Blackburn, "Coinage and Currency," in King, *Anarchy*, 201–2.

alternative place-name for the type provided, by a find at Prestwich in Lancashire in 1972. This contained, as its two chief components, 66 coins from the last type of Henry I and 875 coins from the first type of Stephen.[40] Not the least of the interests of the Prestwich hoard is the comprehensive coverage of the type. There were forty-two mints of this type previously known, and Prestwich provided coins from all but two of them. This provides a remarkable indication – granted the remoteness of the find-spot from London and the south-east – of the integration of the English economy at this date. Stephen type 1 provides the base for the map. It shows the range and the depth of the authority that Stephen had inherited.

Other more recent finds demonstrate how Stephen's authority had been eroded and how the empress and her supporters had indeed brought much of the west country "under their own laws and ordinances." It has long been known that the empress issued coins of her own. The PERERIC type, fixed in aspic in the early summer of 1141, has already been considered, while the Prestwich hoard has a smattering of her later coins. The places of issue of these were Bristol, Cardiff, Wareham, and Oxford (this last clearly no later than 1142). Then on 8 June 1980, on the Coed-y-Wenallt hill outside Cardiff, two brothers working with metal detectors found a hoard of 102 coins.[41] These were predominantly coins of the empress, and this one find trebled the number of her coins recorded. It also added a second type for her coinage (see plate 12). This type was issued at Bristol and (chiefly) at Cardiff: in all, counting also the coins of Stephen, eighty-two coins from Wenallt were struck at the local mint. This suggests that these coins had a limited range of circulation. The element of localization is found also in a further remarkable find of coins at Box in Wiltshire, made in 1993–4. There were 104 coins or fragments in this hoard, forty-four of them struck in the name of Robert, earl of Gloucester. These coins show a lion rather than the more normal effigy and were based on the earl's seal, the image drawing attention to his status as the son of Henry I, who had used a lion as his emblem. Coins were struck, by three moneyers, at the earl's main base at Bristol, and there were coins also from Castle Combe, Marlborough, Salisbury, and Trowbridge, bases of his supporters in Wiltshire. One of the Bristol moneyers, Iordan, had earlier struck coins for Stephen and for the empress. This was a professional coinage, made with stamped not engraved dies. Robert of Gloucester knew how things ought to be done.[42]

So did David, king of Scots. By treaty he had control over the city of Carlisle, the regional capital of Cumbria, while his son, Henry, was earl of Northumberland and had taken the homage of many of the northern

---

[40] King, "The Anarchy of King Stephen's Reign," 149.
[41] This hoard was fully published in Boon, *Welsh Hoards 1979–1981*, 37–82.
[42] Archibald, "The Lion Coinage of Robert of Gloucester"; *Earldom of Gloucester Charters*, 24.

Mints of Stephen types 1, 2 and 6

barons. Stephen's grant to Henry had sought to exempt the capitals of
Northumbria, Newcastle, and Bamburgh from Scottish control, but he
had no power to stop their capture. Carlisle and Newcastle became important centres for David and Henry, and coins were issued in the names of
both men at these centres; they were of excellent quality, for with Carlisle
came control of the rich silver mines below Nenthead, near Alston.[43]
Henry also issued coins at Bamburgh and at Corbridge, upstream from
Newcastle upon Tyne. These are royal coins, showing Henry crowned and
holding a sceptre (see plate 13e); those from Corbridge are copied from
Stephen type 1, and are to be found in circulation in southern England.[44]
And to the monastic houses of Northumbria Henry granted privileges in
royal style. Tynemouth Priory had a comprehensive set of charters from
him, which its parent abbey of St Albans carefully preserved. It was to
have its court and its privileges, including rights to vessels wrecked on
the sea coast, as it had held them in the time of King Henry; it was to
enjoy its salmon fisheries; its men were to be exempt from works "on the
castle of Newcastle and on all other castles within Northumberland"; and
so also with army and escort service, "unless an army shall come upon me
and my land within Northumberland between the Tyne and the
Tweed."[45] The exemptions show the extent of the authority which Henry
claimed as earl of Northumberland. There was no criticism of its exercise
from the northern chroniclers, for he and his father had brought peace.
"The northern region, which as far as the river Tees had fallen under the
control of king David of Scotland, was peaceful through that king's
diligence."[46]

The situation south of the Tees was in marked contrast. The control of
York was the limit of Stephen's ambition, at very least to keep his lines of
communication open. He had come north in 1142, immediately after his
release from captivity, but had not stayed long and had then fallen ill. He
would not be in York again until 1149. In his absence, it was commonly
said, the true king in Yorkshire was the earl, William, count of Aumale,
and there were many such: "in England there were in a sense as many
kings, or rather tyrants, as there were lords of castles; each minted his own
coinage and each, like a king, had the power to lay down the law for his

[43] Stewart, "Scottish Mints," 191–202; Blanchard, "Lothian and Beyond"; Blackburn,
"Coinage and Currency," in King, *Anarchy*, 191–3.

[44] Bamburgh mint: Henry of Northumbria Scottish border Cross crosslet (North no.
914). Corbridge mint: Henry of Northumbria Scottish border as BMC 1 (North no. 912).
The Corbridge mint is well represented in single finds: pennies at Deal (Kent), Louth
(Lincs.), Wilbraham (Cambs.), Sedgefield (Co. Durham) (EMC 1993.0276; 2000.0331;
2003.0052; 2004.0129]; cut halfpennies at Keelby (Lincs.), Walmer (Kent), Hasketon (Suff.)
[EMC 1987.0199; 1991.0145; 1994.0291].

[45] *Charters of David I*, nos. 79, 84, 163, 169; and for charters of his father, David of Scots,
ibid., nos. 143–4.

[46] Newburgh, i. 70.

subjects."[47] William did indeed issue his own coins,[48] and so did several of the Yorkshire baronage. William of Newburgh, whose monastery was just 17 miles from York and who will have held the coins in his hand, would recall these York coins as symptomatic of the absence of legitimate authority.[49] The problems were compounded by the lack of authoritative church leadership. In both York and Durham the king should have been able to rely on the support of the diocesan bishops. The two sees, however, fell vacant in successive years, York with the death of Thurstan in February 1140, and Durham with the death of Geoffrey Rufus in May 1141. The two elections were disputed and went to lengthy processes of appeal, the York election calling to mind Jarndyce and Jarndyce in *Bleak House*, which for a decade and more "still drags its weary length before the Court, perennially hopeless." Henry of Winchester, the papal legate for the English Church, strove to bring order and resolution to the two cases, but his legation lapsed in 1143 with Innocent II's death, his reputation was blackened by the white monks, particularly by Bernard, abbot of Clairvaux,[50] and he became part of the problem rather than the solution. The Church in these years had the freedom from lay control by which it set so much store. It would prove a distinctly mixed blessing.[51]

The two disputed elections can only be considered briefly and it is helpful to consider them together.[52] The death of Archbishop Thurstan of York occurred on 6 February 1140, at the Cluniac priory of Pontefract, where he had taken the cowl. A number of successors were proposed: first Waldef, the prior of Kirkham, but he was a stepson of David of Scots, and Stephen refused to accept him; second up was Henry de Sully, who was Stephen's nephew, but he had just been appointed abbot of Fécamp and refused to resign his abbacy, at which point the pope refused to accept him; finally, William, the treasurer of York, was chosen, but the election was not unanimous and it was alleged that the earl of York had appeared in the chapter house saying that the king had ordered that William be elected. All this had taken a full year. William came to Lincoln in January 1141, and Stephen confirmed him in his temporalities, but within days the

---

[47] *Chron. Meaux*, i. 74; Newburgh, i. 70.

[48] A fine recently discovered coin is Cambridge, Fitzwilliam Museum, CM.692.2005.

[49] Blackburn, "Coinage and Currency," in King, *Anarchy*, 167–8.

[50] *Letters of St Bernard*, nos. 187–208, esp. nos. 187 (to Innocent II), 195 (to Henry of Winchester), 197 (to King Stephen), 198 (to Queen Matilda), 202 (to Celestine II), 204 (to Lucius II), 205–7 (to Eugenius III). The letters to Eugenius "must rank among the most vehement he ever wrote": Knowles, "St William of York," 87.

[51] Warren, *Henry II*, 420–6, provides an admirable brief meditation on this theme.

[52] There is full discussion of the York dispute in Knowles, "St William of York," and of the Durham dispute in Young, *William Cumin*. The main contemporary sources are JH, 306–22; SD, *Libellus*, 280–323. Knowles's study is a classic, and sets out the evidence meticulously, but it never underestimates the case against William the treasurer. Knowles believed, as did others when he wrote, that William the treasurer was one of the king's nephews, but Hollister showed that this was not the case: *Anglo-Norman World*, 215 n. 3.

king was captured. On 6 May the same year, with the empress recently appointed as lady of the English, Geoffrey Rufus, the bishop of Durham, died. In advance of any election, William Cumin, the chancellor of the king of Scots, seized control of the diocese, but he was opposed by the local clergy; at London in June he was about to receive the temporalities from the empress when she was driven out of the city. It was alleged that she had ordered the election of Cumin, just as it was alleged that Stephen had ordered the election of William the treasurer at York.[53] These allegations would in the long term prove fatal to each man. The two dioceses were to remain in a limbo of legitimacy for the best part of two years, with the various interested parties, which in the case of York included the abbots of the Cistercian houses of the diocese, taking their case to the papal court. In Rome on 7 March 1143 the pope gave his decision in the matter of York: the election of William the treasurer was to stand if the dean of York, William of St Barbe, would swear on oath that the election had been free. Just a week later, the chapter of Durham elected the same William of St Barbe as their bishop. There might have seemed to be little room for further dispute.

It was certainly the clear intention of the papal legate, Henry of Winchester, under no less clear instructions from the pope, to move matters on.[54] He consecrated William of St Barbe as bishop of Durham at Winchester on 20 June 1143. Three months later, on 24 September, again at Winchester, the legate consecrated William of York: an oath in support of William was sworn by the bishop of Orkney, a suffragan of York, and by the black-monk abbots of York and Whitby, William of St Barbe having sent apologies because of the problems he faced in his own diocese. The two newly consecrated bishops still faced problems, but they were of different kinds. The problem for the bishop of Durham was that he could not secure control over his own diocese. William Cumin had control of the cathedral city, the bishop's supporters were abused, in an ingenious variety of ways, and his lands devastated: "a place accustomed to be held in honour became for all a place of horrors and was called indeed a hell of tortures."[55] The bishop was not just excluded

---

[53] That the empress nominated Cumin to Durham is alleged in SD, *Libellus*, 286–9; for discussion, Chibnall, *Matilda*, 138–9. That the earl of York was present at, and anxious for, the election of William the treasurer to York is stated by John of Hexham; that he had ordered the election of William, *ex ore regis*, was the allegation made before the pope: JH, 307, 313.

[54] The key document here is Innocent's letter to Henry of Winchester, his legate, dated March 1143: *PUE*, 2/ii, no. 32. The charges against William were set out and how they were to be addressed was explained. "If all this is properly carried out on William's behalf, then invoking the Holy Spirit you should promote him and arrange to have him consecrated as bishop of the said church." Innocent did not expect the matter to come back to the papal court and, had he lived, it would not have done.

[55] SD, *Libellus*, 298–301. Other descriptions of tortures are to be found in WM, *HN*, 70–3, 76–7; *ASC*, s.a. 1137.

from Durham but found that "it was not sensible for him to remain south of the Tyne," and took refuge in Lindisfarne. He "placed his hope" in Henry, earl of Northumberland, and was not disappointed.[56] The archbishop of York and the bishop of Carlisle were also involved in mediation and a benign alliance of lay and Church authority proved decisive. At Durham on 18 October 1144 William Cumin withdrew his opposition and accepted penance for his crimes, and the Durham dispute was over.

The archbishop of York had helped bring peace to Durham but his own troubles were very far from over. As an archbishop he needed to be invested with the pallium by the pope. Two days after his consecration, however, on 26 September 1143, Innocent II died. Henry of Winchester's legation now lapsed and it would not be renewed, despite his best efforts.[57] The next eighteen months proved to be a period of transition in the papacy, with first Celestine II on 8 March 1144 and then Lucius II on 15 February 1145, dying after short reigns, the latter under a hail of stones trying to re-establish his authority in Rome, which had formed a commune headed by the brother of the previous antipope, Anacletus II. It was Lucius, in response to appeals from the clergy, who sent Imar of Tusculum to England as papal legate. Amongst his baggage there was a pallium for the archbishop of York. Had William moved quickly he might have had his pallium, but he did nothing, and the legate found himself surrounded by the insistent voices of senior clergy urging his involvement in their minor concerns.[58] He returned home after a few weeks, taking the pallium with him, after a visit that had been a total waste of time. At the end of 1145 William went in person to Rome to ask for his pallium but, under vitriolic attack from Bernard of Clairvaux (the pope's former superior) and with few friends, he found himself instead suspended from office. He took refuge in the court of his cousin, Roger, king of Sicily; in 1147 he was deposed and the severe Henry Murdac, abbot of Fountains, one of his chief opponents, was elected archbishop on 24 July 1147. This marked the end of a chapter, not the end of the story. It had brought little credit to anyone and lessons would be learned, not least that "appeals to Rome" needed to be used more sparingly. The narrative of the York dispute is provided by John of Hexham, and as he writes the northern province seems to withdraw within itself. The oppression of the monks of Ramsey by Geoffrey de Mandeville, the death of Miles of Gloucester, and

---

[56] SD, *Libellus*, 306–7: "in comite de Northumbria spem habebat, qui et scripto ei atque pacto firmauerat auxilio ei fore contra Willelmum." A charter confirming his *pactum* with the monks of Durham survives in the cathedral archives: *Charters of David I*, no. 123.

[57] JH, 315–16; HH, 742–5; Newburgh, i. 43–4; Winchester Annals, in *Ann. Mon.*, ii. 53; Waverley Annals, ibid., ii. 229; *Letters of St Bernard*, nos. 204, 205.

[58] Imar was in England in May–June 1145. Sources here: *Councils and Synods*, 810–13 (no. 146); Saltman, *Theobald*, no. 223, 450–1; *GF Letters*, nos. 41, 45, to Imar, and related letters, termed "The Cerne Letters" by Christopher Brooke and discussed by him, ibid., 507–9.

(subsequently) the empress's flight from Oxford[59] are noted, but thereafter the south of England is another country, and it would remain so until Stephen came to York in 1149.

REGIONAL KINGSHIP

Stephen's kingship had its foundation in a regional lordship. He and his wife had been among the greatest landowners in south-east England before he became king. This area contained the administrative centres of England. It was wealthy and becoming more so. It had been Stephen's strength in the south-east which had carried him through the dark days of 1141, even though he himself had been in captivity. The empress had managed just a few days in London and a few weeks in Winchester before she was driven out of the two cities. The Londoners and the queen and Henry of Winchester had shared the headlines, but ultimately it was the weight of money behind them that had carried the day. The king's party would learn the lessons of 1141 just as the empress's party had done. It should consolidate its power base. This had been the agreement in the autumn of 1141: "each should guard his own region to the best of his ability, as before."[60] By the spring of 1144, Normandy had been lost but in England the position had barely changed. In the south-east of England, Stephen and his officials could look to assert his lordship and enforce his rights. In this they had some success. When the king sought to extend his lordship beyond the south-east, however, he found himself constrained. The magnates kept a close eye on affairs but for the most part they held their distance. If they are found with the king, it is very often in areas where they shared lordship with him. As Henry of Huntingdon noted at this time, "the ceremonies of the court and the custom of royal crown-wearings, handed down from the ancient line, had completely died out."[61] In saying that it was not important to know where the king was, he reflected the views of the landowners of the midlands whom he met from day to day. The nature of national politics had changed. Forces were small; objectives were limited; the crown had to accommodate its interests to those of the great magnates.

In East Anglia the disgrace and death of Geoffrey de Mandeville had altered the landscape of power. His son, bearing his father's name and inheriting his father's expectations, sought out the empress at Devizes. She

---

[59] JH, 314–15, 317. The empress's escape, placed at the end of events of the year 1144, is certainly misdated but whether by the chronicler or by a later copyist is not clear. Todd and Offler, "A Medieval Chronicle from Scotland," 154, remark that a new edition of the work would "deprive of most of its point the charge of chronological confusion so often laid against John of Hexham."

[60] WM, *HN*, 106–7: "quisque partes suas pro posse, sicut et prius, tutaretur."

[61] HH, 724–5. The text was first "published" in the fourth version of the chronicle, which concluded with the crown-wearing at Lincoln at Christmas 1146: HH, lxviii–lxix, lxxv, 748–9 and n. 140.

granted him his "whole inheritance" and "all tenures which she had conceded to his father," but there was no attempt to revive the earldom of Essex for him.[62] The document might provide Geoffrey with some insurance should the political situation change but for the moment it was the king who had secure possession of the Mandeville lands. Stephen was cautious about what he granted and on what terms. The authority that Geoffrey de Mandeville had enjoyed as a royal official would now be exercised by Richard de Lucy, a man of evident executive ability who kept out of the limelight but who was all but continuously at the king's side. He was local justice in London, Middlesex, and Essex, and custodian of the Tower of London. He was building a barony from what was formerly a manor of the Boulogne fee, at Ongar in Essex, with a castle to symbolize his power.[63] Of the Mandeville demesne manors, Waltham seems to have come to Richard de Lucy while Saffron Walden was granted to the royal constable, Turgis of Avranches.

The fall of Turgis of Avranches, shortly thereafter, came as a surprise. It was intended to. It was surprising, indeed it seemed "quite incredible to everyone who heard of it," because he was an important royal confidant, and had become rich from his association with the royal court. "The cause and source was the castle of Walden and all the neighbouring district, which the king had given him to guard rather than possess." When Turgis attempted to turn the custody of Walden castle into a more permanent lordship he was in for a shock. He is presented as very much the local squire, hunting from his castle – "the hounds were straining with keen-scented nostrils and others were pursuing the quarry with headlong speed, while Turgis himself was following joyfully, sounding his horn." The king arrived unexpectedly, Turgis was captured and threatened with hanging unless the castle was surrendered. And so it was. Turgis had mistaken his role and possibly also failed to notice a change of mood. There is a clear tightening of royal control over the financial administration of East Anglia at this time. Forest rights in Essex were being closely monitored, and there may have been a requirement – for these events must have taken place quite close to Michaelmas 1144 – that some at least of the profits of the Mandeville manors be accounted for. Turgis had his hopes of growing to baronial rank dashed; he lost his position at the court; and he ended his days as a household knight in the entourage of Earl Simon of Senlis.[64]

Any tightening of royal control in East Anglia would need to involve Hugh Bigod, "the most restless opponent of the king's sovereignty," and

---

[62] *Regesta*, iii, no. 277, and for comment, Holt, "1153," in King, *Anarchy*, 298–9.

[63] Round, "The Honour of Ongar"; Amt, "Richard de Lucy."

[64] On this episode: for the story, exactly observed, see *GS*, 174–7; for forest rights see Vincent, "New Charters of King Stephen," 913–17; for Turgis in the entourage of Simon of Senlis, see BL, Cotton MS Vesp. E. xvii, fo. 224r; Farrer, *Honors and Knights' Fees*, ii. 297–8 (after 19 Dec. 1148); *Records of Harrold Priory*, 16, 18–19.

this was early business in 1145.[65] Hugh had earlier been a supporter of the king and was one of the earls who had fought for him at the battle of Lincoln.[66] But he had withdrawn from the court and reportedly had been in league with Geoffrey de Mandeville at the time of his revolt.[67] Stephen seems to have contemplated a showdown, but all we are told is that his men captured some of Hugh's knights, devastated his lands and built siege-castles. Had there been a major siege we would have been told of it, but there was not. Hugh did not offer a military threat. In Norfolk he had some demesne lands but no power base, Norwich was the provincial capital, its life lit up in the aftermath of the death of the boy William, who was allegedly killed by the Jews at Eastertide 1144.[68] The authority of the sheriff, John de Chesney, is taken for granted in what became a saint's life,[69] while there is no mention of the earl. Hugh Bigod's castles were at Bungay and Framlingham in Suffolk and Walton on the Naze in northern Essex. The castle of Eye was inland from Framlingham and it was probably in this area that any skirmishing took place. It has been plausibly argued that in the period 1140–5, "the central administration lost control of finance and local government in Suffolk,"[70] and the recapturing of control may have been the most enduring outcome of the "considerable time" that Stephen spent there in the early months of 1145. During this visit the king is recorded at Bury St Edmunds, in the company of Imar of Tusculum, the papal legate, Rotrou, bishop of Evreux, who had clearly accompanied the legate from Normandy, and Robert, bishop of Hereford.[71] Another outcome of the visit may have been the deposition of the local bishop, Everard of Norwich. Everard set out for Rome, perhaps initially to appeal against his sentence, stopped at the Cistercian monastery of Fontenay in the Côte d'Or, and stayed there. It was reportedly the wealth of his diocese that paid for the construction of the abbey

[65] GS, 174–5

[66] HH, 728–31, 736–7.

[67] GS, 166–7.

[68] Thomas of Monmouth, Life of St William; Anderson, A Saint at Stake; Langmuir, "Thomas of Monmouth."

[69] The sheriff was a consistent supporter of the Jews and gave them shelter in the castle when popular feelings against them ran high: Thomas of Monmouth, Life of St William, 28–9, 46–8, 94–5; the editors comment, xxxiv, that "the chief magistracy was in good hands." This seems to have been the king's view also, for he granted John the manor of Blythburgh and his brother William (who succeeded him in 1146–7) the manor of Acle: ibid., 111–12; Regesta, iii, nos. 174–6. On the brothers and their networks there is an excellent discussion in Sibton Abbey Cartularies, i. 7–21.

[70] Wareham, "Bigod Family," 237.

[71] Regesta, iii, no. 460 (facs. ibid., iv, plate XXXI), issued "at the request" of Richard de Belmeis, archdeacon of Middlesex. The king was attended by three earls, William of Warenne, Gilbert of Clare, and Aubrey de Vere, and by William of Ypres and Henry of Essex (lord of Haughley in Suffolk). While the legate's party was at Bury St Edmunds, Rotrou of Evreux consecrated the chapel at St Peter's hospital outside the walls: Customary of Bury St Edmunds, 119.

church and his fine tomb can still be seen within it. Everard's loyalty may have been suspect and a papal legation would have provided a convenient opportunity to secure his removal.[72]

The legation would have been an appropriate time also for the king to be publicly reconciled with Nigel, bishop of Ely. This was done with some ceremony at "the royal town" of Ipswich, through the mediation of his neighbours and members of the nobility.[73] Nigel would later be heard to say that unlike those around him, who adulterated the coinage and put their own image on coins, he struck coins in the proper form at the proper weight.[74] As a former royal treasurer, he knew the standard, and it may not be coincidence that his return to the king's camp was followed by a new issue of Stephen's coinage, the first since the beginning of the reign, with which he had also been involved. It was indeed in the proper form, the dies being produced at the official workshop in London and distributed from there. The mints recorded are London itself, and Oxford, three mints in Norfolk (Norwich, Thetford, and Castle Rising), three in Suffolk (Ipswich, Bury St Edmunds, and Dunwich), Colchester in Essex, three mints in Kent (Canterbury, Dover, and Sandwich), and four in Sussex (Hastings, Lewes, Pevensey, and Rye).[75] The regional pattern is clear, and appropriately it was a hoard found at Wicklewood near Wymondham in Norfolk, in 1989, that in a way put the type 2 coinage on the map. Ipswich and in particular Norwich were the most important of the provincial mints of this type; these were prosperous communities, growing rich on the profits of trade. In one of the miracles of St William, he cures Ralph the moneyer of Norwich of a severe disease; and on another occasion we are given a picture of the moneyers and their workmen busy at their tasks; when one of the workmen had a seizure the whole workplace downed tools and prayed successfully for his recovery.[76] The coins of type 2 which they were making are stylish coins; the king wears an arched crown with pendants, and looks alert (see plate 13a–b).

---

[72] Henry of Huntingdon says that both Everard of Norwich and Seffrid of Chichester were deposed, and Seffrid's deposition is confirmed by the local annals: HH, 610–11, 612–13; Chichester Annals, s.a. 1145, *UGQ*, 95. See further, *First Register of Norwich*, 70–1; *EEA* 6: *Norwich 1070–1214*, ed. Christopher Harper-Bill, xxxiii (arguing for resignation rather than deposition); Auberger, *Mystère de Fontenay*, 49, 82.

[73] *Liber Eliensis*, 332–3: "die statuto adductus fuisset a propinquis et nobilibus regni ante eum in Gepeswich villa regia"; dramatizing *Regesta*, iii, no. 267: "pacem de me habet et concordiam mecum fecit." The terms of the agreement were that he should pay 300 marks and give his son, Richard Fitz Nigel, as a hostage.

[74] *Liber Eliensis*, 322: "numisma quoque et es et commercii formam quisque apud se transmutavit, imminuit et adulteravit in suis finibus et, quam voluit, inpressit imaginem, preter dragmam de Ely, quod integrum servabatur ex argento electo ac pondere publico per episcopum extitisse memoratur."

[75] Blackburn, "Coinage and Currency," in King, *Anarchy*, 154–7 (list of mints), 162–6 (discussion of the type), 194–9 (review of the dating).

[76] Thomas of Monmouth, *Life of St William*, 168–9. We are not told the nature of Ralph's illness but his colleagues and their wives were much troubled by gout: ibid., 154, 223. Coins struck by Ralph in type 2 survive.

He needed to be. Stephen was looking for opportunities to break out from this strong enclave in south-eastern England and take the battle to his enemies. He will have felt that he had no option but to continue to fight to recapture territory that he had lost. The garrison at Lincoln was a particular reproach to him and he sought to evict it. At some point in 1144 he appeared in the city and ordered the building of an earthwork against the castle walls; but this collapsed and nearly eighty workmen were buried alive: "so the king withdrew in confusion, leaving the business unfinished."[77] The main base for any offensive operations was Oxford, from which the empress had escaped so dramatically at the end of the year 1142. It is likely to have been from here that Stephen launched a raid on Winchcombe in Gloucestershire, one of the castles of the earl of Hereford, and captured it. His men also garrisoned Malmesbury in Wiltshire, which was very much an outlier in hostile territory. His opponents remained active. William Peverel of Dover built a castle at Cricklade, and the earl of Gloucester built a number of siege-castles. These developments provoked a response from the king. He gathered together "a vast army," arrived "suddenly and unexpectedly," and attempted to take Tetbury, which may have been one of the siege-castles; but here too he was forced to withdraw.[78] The impact of all this on the monks of Malmesbury is not hard to imagine. Gilbert Foliot was moved to write to the pope:

> Just as once the wolf has got into the sheepfold there can be no escape from its jaws, so the monastery is afflicted by the castle which is situated on its land and within its enclosure; it is hemmed in by the fortifications and those living therein, and it laments the disappearance of almost all that contributes to its bodily welfare and spiritual well-being. It could hardly be any worse, for it has been brought to the extremes of desolation and its sons have been dispersed. At a place where the praise of God has resounded since the time of St Aldhelm, there now an armed rabble of retainers and a troop of knights ready for the most reprehensible deeds debauch themselves.[79]

For the abbot of Gloucester, the state of this one monastery exemplified the state of the country as a whole: "the churches of the whole of England wear a look of total devastation."

There were continuing operations in the upper Thames valley in the summer of 1145. William of Dover left Cricklade, and it was entrusted to Philip, one of several younger sons of the earl of Gloucester, "a man of strife, supreme in savagery, in truth a past master at every kind of wickedness."[80] Opposed to him was William de Chesney, "governor of the city of

[77] HH, 744–5.
[78] GS, 166–75.
[79] GF Letters, no. 35.
[80] In the uncomplimentary if somewhat routine characterization of GS, 180–1.

Oxford and leader and commander of the king's troops" there.[81] The recapture of Oxford would have been a major prize for the empress both in strategic terms and in terms of the morale of her men. Robert of Gloucester built a castle at Faringdon, 20 miles south-west of Oxford, and considerable resources were committed there. The king arrived, "at the head of a formidable and numerous army of Londoners." This was not the first time that the London militia had provided crucial resources for the king: they had earlier done so in the siege of Winchester in 1141. There was heavy fighting; Robert of Gloucester refused to commit forces that would match the king's, which would have been necessary to raise the siege; and the leaders of the garrison surrendered the castle under terms. The capture of Faringdon was widely reported as a great triumph for the king's party.[82] Henry of Huntingdon, indeed, writing a year or so later, could interpret it as the turning point of the war. "Now at last the king's fortunes began to change for the better and took an upward turn."[83] This may seem surprising, for Faringdon was not a major fortress and its capture by the king served only to restore the status quo ante. But both sides saw this as a trial of strength and Wallingford was now left totally exposed. And the report of victory was important in itself. It confirms the impression that the king's party was starting – belatedly – to manage the news and with it establish some control over the political agenda. The king's opponents would, each in their different ways, have to review their position in the light of these changing perceptions. It is this process of review that provides the context for the politics of the year 1146.

RANULF OF CHESTER

One man above all was seen as the dominant figure in 1146. This was Ranulf, earl of Chester. Around the turn of the year, he "came to the king in humility and submission," repenting of his past deeds, and "was restored to favour after the pact of their old friendship had been renewed between them."[84] The terms of this "pact" have survived.[85] In it the political realities of 1146 overlie and in part adjust the ambition of late 1140. The first sentence introduces one element that is new. The king "gave and conceded to Ranulf earl of Chester the castle of Lincoln and the city, [to hold] until such time as the king should let him have his Norman lands and all his castles." The loss of the Norman lands was one factor leading to a rapprochement with the king. That Ranulf had lost these lands may

---

[81] GS, 180–1. On this family see Eynsham, i. 411–23; on William, see Amt, Accession, 50–4.

[82] GS, 180–3.

[83] HH, 746–7.

[84] GS, 184–5: "ueteris amicitie renouato inter eos foedere"; HH, 748–9: "iam regi concordia coniunctus."

[85] Regesta, iii, no. 178: "concordia inter regem Stephanum et Ranulphum comitem Cestrie" (early fourteenth-century heading of an abstract of an agreement between the two). This was clearly based on an earlier agreement, just as the chroniclers stated.

seem surprising, but the evidence for it is clear. The *caput* of the Norman honour of the earls of Chester, at Briquessart, had been one of the places taken by the Angevins in 1142.[86] And in September 1146, at Devizes, Robert of Gloucester made an agreement with the bishop of Bayeux, by which he was permitted to hold of the bishop the land which Ranulf of Chester held, "until there should come an heir whom the duke of Normandy would recognise as the rightful heir of Ranulf earl of Chester."[87] In these circumstances, Ranulf's recovery of his Norman estates could only be seen as some way off. Even were they to be recovered, Stephen made substantial grants to the earl, in large part "renewing" those he had made earlier. These included Stephen's own lands in the midlands and the north of England, "all the land of Roger of Poitou from Northampton up to Scotland, except the land of Roger of Montbegon in Lincolnshire," also "the honour of Lancaster with its appurtenances and all the land between Ribble and Mersey," granted to him in inheritance. According to the *Gesta Stephani* Ranulf "had encroached on almost a third part of England."[88] Much of it he seems here to have retained, as a royal grant.

Why then was Stephen, who was reasserting his rights elsewhere, prepared to come to terms with Ranulf of Chester and to promise him so much? In part because he had little choice. He was in need of support and in need of resources, and these the earl supplied. Ranulf's allegiance was of immediate value in the publicity war. In the longer term he offered the king the opportunity to extend the area under his direct control. As part of the agreement with the king, made at Stamford,[89] Ranulf was required to remain at court. A pattern was by now established and Ranulf was being treated in just the same way as Robert, earl of Gloucester, had been when he accepted Stephen in April 1136, and Eustace Fitz John similarly after the battle of the Standard in August 1138. It was an integral part of the deal that Ranulf "accompanied the king." First they went to Bedford, "which had always been in opposition to the royal power." This is a slightly surprising statement. Bedford was, for example, one of the mint towns that struck coins for the king throughout the reign. It is most likely that Stephen required the surrender of the castle, from Miles de Beauchamp or another member of that family, and put in his own custodian.[90] The next stage in the progress of king and earl was St Albans. Here on 12 May 1146 – a precise date at last – he was at the abbey for the installation of a new abbot.[91] The elect was Ralph Gubiun, a member of

---

[86] WM, *HN*, 126–7.

[87] *Regesta*, iii, no. 58: "donec talis heres adveniat quem dux Normannorum iustum heredem ipsius Ranulfi comitis Cestrie recognoscat."

[88] *GS*, 184–5.

[89] *ASC*, s.a. 1140, gives the place.

[90] Miles had regained the castle in 1141: *GS*, 116–17.

[91] Roger of Wendover, *Chronica*, ii. 237; Matthew Paris, *Historia Minor*, i. 276–7; *Heads*, 67.

a family that held of the honour of Huntingdon, a further indication of the influence of Simon of Senlis. Next came the siege of Wallingford, the fortress of Brian Fitz Count in the Thames valley, potentially the biggest prize of all. The earl was there "with a retinue of three hundred stout-hearted cavalry"; a siege-castle was built, "a work of wondrous toil and skill"; and the court remained there for some time.[92] Charters were issued "at the siege," confirming the presence of Ranulf of Chester, along with Earl Aubrey de Vere, Richard de Lucy, William Martel, and Baldwin Fitz Gilbert de Clare.[93] The monks of Abingdon, a few miles upriver, once again brought their charters for the king to inspect.[94] But the garrison of Wallingford remained resolute; the siege was not hard-pressed; and all that was achieved was "to check for a time their accustomed raids throughout the district."[95]

In practical terms not much may have been achieved but the publicity value was considerable. It confirmed the impression that the king's cause was on the up. It provoked division amongst his opponents and a desire to make peace. The division was seen even in the family most closely associ-ated with the empress's cause, that of Robert, earl of Gloucester. Philip, one of the younger sons, either at the time of or shortly after the surrender of Faringdon, "entered upon a pact of peace and concord" with the king, "gave hostages and paid him homage," and then actively fought on the king's side. At some point in the summer of 1146, his uncle Reginald, earl of Cornwall, fell into Philip's hands. It turned out, whether or not Philip knew this, that the earl of Cornwall was riding under a safe conduct from the king, as an emissary to explore the possibilities for peace. The king, as always in matters involving a breach of chivalric etiquette, was greatly offended and he ordered the earl's release. There were then peace discus-sions, noted by just one chronicler and in general terms:

When the king with his supporters, and the countess with hers, had met together to establish peace, since an overweening spirit prevailed on each side and both parties courted strife they accomplished nothing. The countess's adherents, claiming the sovereignty for her by right, were trying to deprive the king of the royal title and the king's honour; he on his side not only claimed that what he held was held by right but firmly stated that he would not make them any concession at all with regard to anything that he had got in any way whatsoever. As there was this difference of opinion between the two parties they went back again to their former condition of hostility.[96]

[92] *GS*, 184–5.
[93] *Regesta* iii, nos. 11 (for Abingdon abbey), 992 (for St Peter's hospital, York).
[94] *Regesta*, iii, nos. 11–12.
[95] *GS*, 184–5.
[96] *GS*, 186–7.

There is not much to go on here. It is likely, however, that the initiative
came from the empress's side. In or near Oxford would be a possible
venue for the meeting.[97] At that meeting the two sides got no further than
making a preliminary statement of the rightness of their cause. Invited
then to come to specifics, and to distinguish between his various comital
lands and the crown of England, as had certainly been discussed at earlier
meetings, the king flatly refused to do so. That concluded the business.
The breakdown of the talks was not surprising for the options were
narrowing. Geoffrey of Anjou was now duke of Normandy, so Normandy
was no longer a bargaining counter for the empress's party, while Stephen
could not abandon his claims to the duchy without compromising his
whole position and breaking any agreements he might have made with his
own supporters, such as that with Ranulf of Chester, which involved the
restitution of their Norman lands. Stephen's own strategy was to consolidate his power base in the south-east of England and work out from there.
Most significantly perhaps, Eustace of Boulogne and Henry Fitz Empress,
the heirs to the two competing claims, were now of an age when they
would wish to speak for themselves.

The reconciliation with Ranulf of Chester had taken place when the
bishop of Lincoln was in Rome.[98] This may not have been a coincidence, for
the bishop was no disinterested observer of the power struggle between king
and earl, and his animus against the earl is transparent. As he sought to
protect his diocese, envisaging that he would die in the middle of a civil war,
Bishop Alexander of Lincoln saw his castles – at Newark, at Sleaford, and at
Banbury – as a bulwark of its independence and a defence of its integrity.

> No one, whether it be the king or some magnate or servants of the
> same, should presume to occupy the castles of the church of Lincoln on
> the death of a bishop, whether as custodians or for some other cause.
> Rather they should remain in the protective custody of those who are
> liege men of the church, and in the power of that church, until they can
> be returned freely into the power of the bishop who has been canonic-
> ally substituted in his place.[99]

The papal chancellor who authenticated this instrument was Robert
Pullen. He was an Englishman, born near Sherborne, a famous teacher in
the schools of Oxford and of Paris, and a largely non-resident archdeacon

---

[97] The upper Thames valley had been the sphere of operation of Philip of Gloucester.
Regesta, iii, no. 485, the work of *scriptor* xxi (facs. in *Reg. Ant.* i, plate viii), was issued at
Oxford around this time. The witnesses were Robert de Vere, William of Ypres, Richard
de Lucy, Henry of Essex, and Adam de Beaunay.

[98] He was honourably received by the pope, and charters were issued for him at
Trastavere on 5, 6 and 9 Feb. 1146: HH, 748–9 and n. 134. These sources indicates that
Alexander left England late in 1145; he is likely to have returned to his diocese soon after
Easter 1146.

[99] *Reg. Ant.* i, 195–7 (no. 251).

of Rochester.[100] As the litany of names was read out to him – Banbury "with its castle and market," Cropredy, Thame, and Dorchester, "with all their liberties and appurtenances," the abbey of Eynsham "with its fair" – they may have brought back some memories. The bishop of Lincoln returned to England in the spring and was warmly welcomed back to his diocese. It may be no accident that in the months immediately following his return, the king in a number of ways would help promote the integrity of his diocese, for his residence at Bedford had been singled out for protection in the papal bull and the vacancy at St Albans would be filled by one of his former clerks. The bishop was certainly involved in the royal court, if not resident, in the summer of 1146.

In late August 1146 the court met at Northampton.[101] This would be the scene of the arrest of another of the great magnates, in circumstances that in several ways replicated the events of June 1139 at Oxford (when the bishop of Lincoln had been one of the bishops arrested) and of August 1143 at St Albans (when Geoffrey de Mandeville had been arrested). The person now singled out was Ranulf, earl of Chester. After the siege of Wallingford, he had returned to his earldom, taking his forces with him.[102] Here in the north-west there was work for them to do. Owain, prince of Gwynedd, had raided over the River Clyd and into Tegeingl, capturing Mold, one of the chief castles of the honour of Chester and the seat of its steward, Robert de Montealto.[103] Ranulf came to this court, with just a small escort, asking for the king's support against this clear threat to the integrity of his earldom. He promised – so it was said – that the king would thereby gain great glory at limited expense, for "he stated that the enemy would be alarmed merely by hearing the king's name," and he would pay the costs of the expedition. In normal times, this would be an invitation that a king would wish to accept,[104] aside from any reciprocal obligation he might have recognized in respect of the troops that the earl had supplied to him earlier in the year. The king initially said that he would go, but he was dissuaded from doing so by his chief counsellors. There were other priorities, it was urged; the expedition was dangerous; and any gains that were made might prove difficult to hold. All these were reasonable enough points, as recent experience would testify, and certainly sufficient to support a polite refusal. But the atmosphere here was highly charged and there was a suspicion of treachery. On 29 August 1146 Ranulf of Chester was arrested and detained.

---

[100] Luscombe, "Pullen, Robert." Robert was the first English cardinal.

[101] GS, 192–9, the chief source for the following paragraph; HH, 748–9; *Annales Cestrienses*, 20–1; ASC, s.a. 1140.

[102] HH, 748–9, says that Ranulf went direct from Wallingford to Northampton, but his treatment is highly condensed, and GS, 184–5, insists there was a gap. This must be likely. The demand for hostages would have made little sense if the earl had been continuously at court.

[103] *Brut*, s.a. 1146; for discussion, Crouch, "The March and the Welsh Kings," in King, *Anarchy*, 278–9.

[104] Lloyd, *A History of Wales*, ii. 479–80.

The story of the arrest seems a familiar one and such detail as is given seems formulaic. On the one side there are allegations of treachery, on the other an outraged innocence, a court that had been unified now suddenly rent apart. There is, however, some indication of the issues that lay behind the rhetoric. The king's side wanted a proper accounting. Whatever had been granted to the earl in the renewal of the agreement at Stamford, it was a small part of what he had taken: "let him first restore the king's property that he had unjustly taken for his own use."[105] They also asked for better security: he should publicly swear fealty and offer hostages. While at the king's court he had been a hostage in his own person; when he left it clearly no security had been asked for. Now, after only a few weeks, he had returned, and when challenged by the king's party his response came without hesitation. The chronicle gives no more than what would now be called "bullet points" but they hit their targets. The earl said, first, that he had not come to court for this reason: the court was a formal body; he may have been individually summoned to attend; certainly his arrival will have been announced and his concerns intimated. He had not, he said further, been given advance notice of the charges that were now levelled against him. Nor had he been offered any opportunity to receive counsel from his men.[106] The basic concerns of proper procedure – we may be sure we are not leading the witness in saying this – which the earl would have offered to any defendant in his own court, were here simply being ignored in the highest court in the land. Here was a man – and this man was the king of England – who did not know how to behave. The chorus, the voices of all who commented on the arrests, whatever their views on the succession dispute or their assessment of the earl's character, were as one in saying that what had been done was improper.[107]

The immediate consequence of the arrest of Ranulf of Chester, and perhaps its chief objective, was the recapture by the king of the castle of Lincoln.[108] Stephen summoned the Christmas court of 1146 to meet in the city and there he wore his crown, defying a superstition that to do so would be unlucky. "This shows that King Stephen possessed great boldness and a spirit that was not fearful of danger."[109] It was a moment he had waited for for some time, a feeling clearly evoked in a charter for the bishop, restoring rights over two military tenants as they had been held "on the

---

[105] GS, 196–7: "redderet prius que de suis iniuste usurpauerat."

[106] Ibid.: "non ad hoc curiam uenisse, sed nec de his premonitum, uel cum suis consilium accepisse."

[107] Annales Cestrienses, 20–1: "dolo captus est"; GS, 236–7: "curiam suam [the king's] subintrasset de pace sibi indulta securus"; HH, 748–9: "pacifice venisset . . . nichil tale metuentem"; ASC, s.a. 1140: the king and the earl "had sworn oaths and confirmed pledges that neither of them should betray the other," but still "the king captured him at Northampton through bad counsel, and put him in prison, and soon he let him out through worse counsel."

[108] GS, 196–9; HH, 748–9. It was marked also by a Welsh invasion of Cheshire, which was repulsed: Crouch, "The March and the Welsh Kings," in King, Anarchy, 278–9.

[109] HH, 748–9.

day on which I first came to the siege of Lincoln."[110] This charter is attested by the queen and so can be dated to the Christmas court, when she too would have worn her crown. Another, also for the diocese, confirmed a charter of William the Conqueror, which had been brought and read "before my barons at Lincoln," a charter that was then carefully returned to the archives, for it still survives.[111] Among the barons present were Earl Simon of Senlis, Earl William d'Aubigny, and Gilbert de Gant. Their names come from charters issued in favour of two new Cistercian monasteries, Sawtry Abbey in Huntingdonshire (the foundation of Simon of Senlis) and Rufford Abbey in Nottinghamshire (the foundation of Gilbert de Gant).[112] Perhaps at Lincoln also was the abbot of the best-established Cistercian house in the county, 20 miles from the city, at Revesby. This was Aelred, who had come from Rievaulx and in 1147 would return there as abbot. Aelred's biographer, Walter Daniel, finds a context for Aelred's ministry in the support of the local bishop, Alexander, and the ready patronage of laymen, which they offered the more readily because of the confusion of the times:

> The bishop orders him to preach to the clergy in their local synods and he does so; to bring priests to a better way of life, as he does not fail to do; to accept grants of lands from knights in generous free-alms, and he obeys, since he had realised that in this unsettled time such gifts profited knights and monks alike, for in those days it was hard for anyone to lead a good life unless they were monks or members of some religious order, so disturbed and chaotic was the land, reduced almost to a desert by the malice, slaughters and harryings of evil men. And so he desired that land, for which almost all men were fighting to the death, should pass into the hands of the monks for their good.[113]

The memories of monastic houses, preserved in their foundation narratives, would keep alive this image of "the unsettled time" of Stephen's reign.[114]

---

[110] *Regesta*, iii, no. 471: "sicut illos tenuit die qua primum veni ad obsidionem Lincolnie"; facs. in *Reg. Ant.* 1, no. 77, in hand of *scriptor* xxii.

[111] *Regesta*, iii, no. 487: "quam testificor me vidisse coram baronibus meis in Lincolnia." For the original charter of William I see *Reg. Ant.*1, 2–4, with facs. and discussion by F. M. Stenton, and *Regesta Regum Anglo-Normannorum. The Acta of William I*, 587–9 (no. 177).

[112] The royal charter for Sawtry, not in *Regesta*, is printed and discussed in Stringer, "Charters of Sawtry Abbey," 333; that for Rufford is *Regesta*, iii, no. 736, discussed in *Rufford Charters* 1, xx–xxvi.

[113] Walter Daniel, 28.

[114] *Sibton Abbey Cartularies*, iii, no. 470; *Walden*, 12–15; *Battle*, 140–3; Hugh Candidus, 104–5; *Waltham*, 76–7; *Historia Ecclesie Abbendonensis*, ii. 314–15; *Liber Eliensis*, 320. It is found also in the genealogical rolls of the kings of England, intended mainly for a lay audience: *Feudal Manuals of English History*, p. 29 ("this Stephen . . . retained the crown all the time of his life in war and labour"); Clanchy, *From Memory to Written Record*, p. 142 and plate xiii.

THE SECOND CRUSADE

A new incentive to religious benefaction, and a new factor in the politics of the later months of 1146, was the preaching of what would become the Second Crusade. The idea of the Crusade and the commitment to the defence of the Crusader Kingdom of Jerusalem were well established in the minds of the aristocracy of western Europe. When challenged by Henry, bishop of Winchester, not to emulate the wife of Lot, and look back, Brian Fitz Count told him about the First Crusade. He looked back with some pride at the deeds of the great men, including the bishop's father, "who by assault and force of arms conquered Jerusalem like good knights, and established there a good and lawful king by the name of Godfrey."[115] Eugenius III, in promulgating the crusade, also looked back: "we have learned from the accounts of writers of former times and we have found written in their *gesta* how much our predecessors (*quantum prede-cessores*) the Roman pontiffs laboured for the liberation of the eastern church."[116] Whilst the pope initiated the crusade, and went into some detail in outlining the practicalities, its preaching fell to one man especially, Bernard of Clairvaux. He could adapt his appeal to the circumstances of each region. This was his specific appeal to "the people of England":

> Your land is well known to be rich in young and vigorous men. The world is full of their praises and the renown of their courage is on the lips of all. Gird yourselves like men and take up arms with joy and with zeal for your Christian name, in order to "take vengeance on the heathen and curb the nations." For how long will your men continue to shed Christian blood; for how long will they continue to fight among themselves? You attack each other, you slay each other and by each other you are slain. What is this savage craving of yours? Put a stop to it now, for it is not fighting but foolery.[117]

The passage just quoted from the *Life* of Aelred of Rievaulx suggests that the English Cistercians made their appeals to the laity in very much the same terms.

There is no muster roll of those who went on the Second Crusade. Nonetheless from charters, chronicles, and other literary sources, a good list can be put together, enough to confirm that a sizeable contingent came from England.[118] There were two Anglo-Norman earls, William, Earl

---

[115] King, "Brian Fitz Count," 90. Brian certainly did not view Stephen as "a good and lawful king."

[116] JL, no. 8796; in trans. in Otto of Freising, *Deeds of Barbarossa*, 71–3.

[117] *Letters of St Bernard*, no. 391.

[118] HH, 750–1: "et multi de gente Anglorum"; *GS*, 196–9. Essential reading are, Tyerman, *England and the Crusades*; Constable, "The Second Crusade."

Warenne, and Waleran, count of Meulan. There were two Anglo-Norman bishops, Arnulf of Lisieux and Roger of Chester. There were magnates and gentry from the north of England, the west country, and East Anglia. There were sailors and their chaplains from London, Southampton, Hastings, Bristol, Dover, and other ports. The East Anglian presence was particularly strong. Hervey de Glanville commanded the local fleet and he was hardly a "young man," for just a few years later he would say that he had been coming to the Suffolk county court for fifty years.[119] At least one member of the Clare family, Walter Fitz Gilbert de Clare of Maldon, went on the crusade and proceedings which involved him were placed on hold until he should return.[120] Hugh Tirel, the son of the man who (allegedly) fired the arrow which killed William Rufus, mortgaged his one English property, the manor of Langham near Colchester, to Gervase of Cornhill. It enabled him to raise 100 marks "for his journey to Jerusalem."[121] Across the Channel, St Bernard's appeal found a ready response among the men of the county of Boulogne, who are recorded as a distinct component of the naval force that attacked Lisbon.[122] One man who did not make the journey, however, was the king himself. The campaign for the relief of the crusader kingdom, an enterprise in which the family of the counts of Boulogne had invested so much, now simply passed them by. There was no way that Stephen could have gone, granted the continuing challenge to his authority within England, but still he lost some prestige as a result. The English noted in a matter-of-fact way, perhaps even with pride, that their leader was the king of France.[123]

In the spring of 1147 Paris was the centre not just of France but of the whole of Christendom, for the pope was in the city and visitors could remark upon "a double marvel," the king of France, Louis VII, and the pope, Eugenius III, united in fostering the crusade.[124] Their presence

---

[119] *English Lawsuits*, i. 288–91, no. 331, giving a date of 1150.

[120] *Regesta*, iii, nos. 546 ("usque ad diem qua Walterus filius Gilberti perrexit Jerosolimam"), 547 ("donec Walterus redeat in Angliam").

[121] *Book of Seals*, nos. 84, 105 ("ad iter suum de Jerusalem"); *RHF*, xvi.10; Round, *Feudal England*, 468–79.

[122] *De expugnatione Lyxbonensi*, 54–5, 104–5. Bernard of Clairvaux spent three months preaching the crusade in the Low Countries: Phillips, "St Bernard of Clairvaux, the Low Countries, and the Second Crusade."

[123] *Register of St Benet of Holme*, i. 87: "post profeccionem regis Francie et aliorum baronum atque ipsius Philippi [Philip Basset] in Ierusalem"; *Book of Seals*, no. 8: "antequam ego [Roger de Mowbray] primo arriperem iter eundi Jerosolimam cum rege Francorum Ludouico." David, king of Scots, issued a charter on 3 May 1147, "videlicet illo anno in quo rex Francie et multi Cristiani perrexerunt Ierusalem," whilst there is a similar charter of his son Henry, given at Michaelmas "postquam Ludouicus rex Francie iter Ierosolimitanum aggressus est": *Charters of David I*, nos. 158, 163. A charter of Roger de Fraxineto, the king's constable, for Lewes Priory, refers to the valuation of his grant "die Pentecostes ante mocionem regis Gallie in Ierusolimam": BL, Cotton MS Vesp. F. xv, fo. 95v.

[124] Odo of Deuil, *De profectione Ludovici VII*, 14–17.

offered excellent opportunities for the conduct of business and for networking.[125] So it was that the best-attested English property transaction of the decade took place in Paris, shortly after Easter, in 1147. It concerned an estate at Hitchin in Hertfordshire, which was granted by Bernard de Balliol to the Templars, in the presence of the pope, the king of France, four archbishops (including Hugh of Rouen), and 130 Knights Templar, "robed in their white mantles."[126] It must have been quite a sight. A month later a further settlement involving property in England, between the monks of Bec and the canons of St Frideswide's, Oxford, was concluded in Paris, in the presence of the pope and the archbishops of Canterbury and Rouen. The number of important men in the city was still a matter of remark.[127] Then on 11 June, at the time of the Lendit fair, there was a further ceremony. The oriflamme, the banner of the count of the Vexin, was taken from above the high altar of St Denis by Abbot Suger, blessed by the pope, and entrusted to the king.[128] A new window in the abbey church showed scenes from the First Crusade.[129] Immediately thereafter the main French contingent set out. Not without a backward glance or two. The French king was particularly concerned about the security of Gisors.[130]

The largest gathering of which there is record in England in the spring of 1147 was not a meeting of the royal court, but it did involve a crusader. This was the dedication, organized by William de Warenne, of the new conventual church at Lewes Priory. He made sure it was a great occasion. The consecration was performed by four bishops: Theobald, archbishop of Canterbury, and the bishops of Winchester, Bath, and Rochester. A part of the ceremony was a confirmation of privileges, and the monks were put in seisin of the resources thus transferred by hair of the earl and Ralph de Warenne his brother, "which Henry bishop of Winchester cut from our heads with a knife before the altar."[131] The barber himself had a very fine beard. Watching, possibly remarking this fact, there were the abbots of Reading and Battle, the prior of Canterbury, William d'Aubigny, earl of Sussex, as well as other Warenne family and vassals. The ceremony came at the end of, and should be seen as part of, a lengthy period of preparation for the crusade, one filled with all the uncertainty

---

[125] The scene is well realized in Crouch, *Beaumont Twins*, 66–7.

[126] *Templars*, 213–15 (dated 27 Apr. 1147): "alba clamide indutis."

[127] *Cart. St Frideswide's*, ii. 324 (dated 25 May 1147): "cum multis aliis et nominatissimis viris."

[128] Odo of Deuil, *De Profectione*, 16–17.

[129] On the windows, see Brown and Cothren, "The Twelfth-Century Crusading Window of Saint-Denis"; for the argument for this date, Grant, *Suger*, 158 n. 14.

[130] *RHF* xv. 487.

[131] *EYC* 8: *Warenne*, 84–5 (no. 32): "quos abscidit cum cultello de capitibus nostris ante altare Henricus episcopus Wintoniensis." Hair and knife would have been placed on the altar and may thereafter have been "filed" with the charter that makes mention of them. They served as "props in the theatre of memory": Clanchy, *From Memory to Written Record*, 38–9.

and excitement of a long journey and a shared endeavour. The earl had taken the cross some time before.[132] He had taken an aid from his vassals, and he had made arrangements for the safekeeping of his lands while he was away, during which time he would enjoy the protection afforded to all crusaders' lands. In the circumstances of a civil war, the terms of that protection would need to be defined with some care. In response to a request for guidance from the bishop of Salisbury, the pope stated that church sanctions should not be invoked, "in respect of those men whom our beloved son Stephen the illustrious king of the English or his adversaries disinherited on the occasion of the war held for the realm before they took the cross."[133] This was good law but also sound politics. Any intervention would have involved taking sides.

Several distinct armies set out on crusade, of which those commanded by the king of France and the German emperor are the best recorded.[134] Many of the English joined an Anglo-Flemish naval force which helped the king of France to capture Lisbon before – some at least of them – travelling on to the Holy Land.[135] There were inevitable tensions in these composite armies, among the common soldiers, competing for food and lodgings, and among their leaders also. "The Germans were unbearable even to us," said the French monk, Odo of Deuil, but he had the sense to recognize that linguistic differences lay behind many of the confrontations, "for when one person accuses another in a very loud voice without understanding him there is a brawl."[136] Louis VII, in one of his letters to Suger, smoothed all this over. He reported that with God's help they had arrived safely in Constantinople and had been honourably received by the emperor. As his forces travelled on, however, he had met with disaster. In January 1148, as he crossed Mount Cadmus, he had become detached from the vanguard of his army and his escort had been cut down, with the loss amongst others of his cousin, William de Warenne. He was too upset to say more. Not much more is known. Odo of Deuil explained as best he could to a home audience that this was territory inhospitable for cavalry.[137] The various Western armies came together in the Holy Land between March and June 1148. But they remained divided. They could do nothing

---

[132] William de Warenne referred to "palmiferis fratribus meis" in his charter for the priory of the Holy Sepulcre, Thetford: *EYC* 8, 93–4 (no. 45).

[133] *Epistolae Pontificum Romanorum ineditae*, 103–4 (no. 199); and for comment, Robinson, *Papacy*, 340–1. Brian Kemp's reconstruction of the bishop's letter saw it as being specifically concerned with properties granted to monasteries by laymen who had already lost control of them: *EEA* 19: *Salisbury 1217–28*, 387.

[134] There are good, accessible accounts in: Odo of Deuil, *De Profectione*; Otto of Freising, *Deeds of Barbarossa*; JS, *HP*, 11–12, 52–9.

[135] *De expugnatione Lyxbonensi*.

[136] Odo of Deuil, *De Profectione*, 42–5: "Nostris etiam erant importabiles Alemanni."

[137] *RHF*, xv. 495–6; William of Tyre, *History*, ii. 175–7, at 176 describing William of Warenne as "a man pre-eminent even among great lords"; Odo of Deuil, *De Profectione*, 118–23.

to recapture Edessa. They decided to attack Damascus but after a week of heavy fighting, in danger of being cut off by fresh Muslim forces, they were forced to withdraw.[138] The crusade in the East had been a total failure. As news of this reached the West, and as the crusaders returned, there were lengthy discussions as to what had gone wrong. In England Alured of Lincoln raised the matter in one of his conversations with the hermit, Wulfric of Haselbury. The holy man informed him that this was the judgement of God, "who abandoned the false pilgrims, and shamed the great men of the world because they sought not the Lord in truth."[139] Otto of Freising concluded, more philosophically, that the pilgrimage, and the privations of the route, had a value in themselves and had contributed to "the salvation of many souls."[140]

The participants may well have seen their journeys to the Holy Land in these terms. Certainly what is found in the English records is a series of individual histories, each of them incomplete, each with an inbuilt capacity to grow in the telling. The pilgrims had set out with enthusiasm, asking for the prayers of friends and family, and anticipating their safe return.[141] Those left behind waited anxiously for news.[142] Not all were destined to return. Of the two Anglo-Norman bishops who set out, only one returned. Roger of Chester died and was buried at Antioch.[143] Arnulf of Lisieux, who had served as one of the main diplomats in a bitterly divisive campaign, returned with his reputation diminished.[144] Of the two Anglo-Norman counts as well, only one returned. Waleran of Meulan was more fortunate than William de Warenne, but he narrowly survived a shipwreck on his return journey, and he founded a monastery in gratitude for his escape.[145] Some died in action.[146] Some remained in the Holy Land.[147] The majority will have returned. They, and the affinities of those

---

[138] Loud, "The Failure of the Second Crusade."

[139] *Wulfric of Haselbury*, 116.

[140] Otto of Freising, *Deeds of Barbarossa*, 105–6; for commentary on the inquest, Constable, "Second Crusade," 266–76.

[141] Roger de Mowbray wrote to the monks of Garendon at this stage, requiring "vestris orationes et precibus dum in hac peregrinatione fuero," and promising every assistance "cum rediero": *Charters of the Honour of Mowbray*, 116 (no. 155).

[142] See the charters of Reginald de Warenne, *EYC* 8, nos. 49 ("si dominus Jesus Christus dominum comitem Warennie reduxerit"), 50 ("si Deus comitem reduxerit").

[143] *Monasticon*, vi. 1242; *EEA* 14, *Coventry and Lichfield 1072–1159*, 124–5.

[144] JS, *HP*, 54–6; for good discussion see Chibnall, ibid., xxxv–xxxvii, and Barlow in *Letters of Arnulf of Lisieux*, xxv–xxvii.

[145] *Chron. Valassense*, 8–9; Crouch, *Beaumont Twins*, 68 and n. 48.

[146] Roger de Mandeville made grants to Montacute Priory, "for the soul of Stephen his father, who died in an engagement on the road to Jerusalem": *Two Cartularies of Bruton and Montacute*, nos. 167–8. William Peverel of Dover "died a blessed death": *GS*, 178–9.

[147] Philip, son of Robert, earl of Gloucester: his resolution is recorded in *GS*, 190–1; that he went and stayed on is suggested by Roger, bishop of Worcester's complaint to Henry II that he had hounded one of his brothers to such an extent "that he gave himself for ever to the Hospital of Jerusalem": *MTB*, iii. 104–5. The aristocratic bishop evidently did not consider this a particularly honourable end.

who had died, kept alive the memories of their exploits. John of Hexham had the story of Roger de Mowbray killing a Saracen in single combat, very likely from Roger himself.[148] Roger survived to go on a second – that is the third – crusade, forty years later. His time as a crusader, who had more than once taken "the blessed road to Jerusalem," is a leitmotiv of his charters and must have been a recurring topic in his conversation.[149] The crusade was a part of his sense of identity, as Brian Fitz Count had claimed it to be a part of his.

[148] JH, 319: "promeruit celebrem gloriam Rogerus de Mulbrai, singulari certamine de quodam pagano tyranno triumphans."

[149] *Charters of the Honour of Mowbray*, xxxi–xxxii, nos. 111–12, 155, 174: "antequam prima vice irem ad Jerusalem in peregrinatione"; *Book of Seals*, no. 8.

Chapter 8

THE FAMILY

The king, in the presence of the magnates, ceremonially girded Eustace with the belt of knighthood, . . . and after most bountifully endowing him with lands and possessions, and giving him the special distinction of a most splendid retinue of knights, advanced him in rank to the dignity of earl.[1]

The Augustinian priory of Holy Trinity, Aldgate, was one of the most important religious houses within the walls of the city of London. It had been founded in the reign of Henry I and was particularly associated with his queen, Matilda, who was buried there.[2] The close relationship with the crown was continued by Stephen and his queen, and the house was no less a focus of their piety.[3] Within the abbey church two of their children, Baldwin and Matilda, lay buried. In front of their tombs, at some point during the winter of 1147–8, grants were made for the repose of their souls.[4] This was a solemn occasion, attended by the archbishop of Canterbury and five other bishops, including Robert of London, who until recently had refused to swear fealty to the king and may have been excluded from court as a result.[5] The laymen present were prominent members of the royal household – William of Ypres, Robert de Vere, William Martel, Henry of Essex, Richard de Lucy, and Warner de Lusors. What was granted was a rent charge on the manor of Braughing in Hertfordshire, a member of the honour of Boulogne, and the queen confirmed the transaction. The canons were also recompensed for a small-holding which they had given the queen next to the Tower of London, where she had founded the hospital of St Katharine. On another occasion, possibly just before the Christmas court of 1147 had dissolved, the king in proprietorial fashion granted the abbacy of Bury St Edmunds to

---

[1] *GS*, 208–9.
[2] *Cart. Aldgate*, xiii–xvi; Brooke, *London*, 314–25.
[3] There is an archive of twenty-two charters in *Regesta*, iii, nos. 499–520.
[4] *Regesta*, iii, nos. 511–12: "pro requie animarum scilicet Balduini filii mei et Matildis filie mee qui in eadem ecclesia sepulti requiescunt."
[5] The pope wrote separately to the king and queen on this matter on 26 June 1147: JL, nos. 9088–9, printed *PL* 180, cols. 1248–9. He advised them not to make an issue of it and to accept a simple oath, "quod laesionem tibi vel terrae tuae non inferat."

Ording, a monk of the house.[6] The appointment was evidently made in the royal court. A witness to both documents was "the earl Eustace, the king's son." He was the only earl present.

In the hopes and aspirations of those named at court, in their inter-action, can be found the themes of the years 1147–52. This is a distinct period, and it has a clear dynamic. It is a period that sees a change of generation. Robert, earl of Gloucester, the chief supporter of the empress, died on 31 October 1147,[7] and the empress herself left Devizes and settled in Normandy shortly thereafter.[8] The focus of ambition of the empress's party now lay in the person of Henry, whose first excursion to England had ended in failure in the spring of 1147. Concomitantly, the focus of the ambition of Stephen and his queen was the elder of their sons, Eustace, newly made an earl. They wished to see Eustace crowned in his father's lifetime, as was customary in France, and his promotion to comital rank had been a means to that end. The bench of bishops would have a say in whether or not these plans succeeded, in particular Theobald, the primate of the English Church, who had an adventurous year in prospect. The charters for Holy Trinity, Aldgate, are characteristic not least in showing the presence together of the archbishop and the queen. The queen would be the most persuasive advocate of her son's and her family's cause.

The honour of Boulogne, "the lands of count Eustace" as they were referred to long after that count's death,[9] had been kept distinct since Stephen, who had held the lands as count in succession to Eustace, had become king of England. Matilda's charters as queen, almost without exception, deal with the lands which she had brought to her marriage.[10] Her son, in turn, was seen as having particular rights to them; and the awareness of those rights was heightened in the summer of 1141, when his succession to the honour was demanded by his uncles as a part of any settlement. Most of the other comital lands had been granted out, most recently in the confirmation of the honour of Lancaster to Ranulf of Chester.[11] That the lands of the honour of Boulogne were kept in hand was a conscious decision, reflecting the past history of the honour, animated by the queen's personal involvement, administered by the members of her own household. When Eustace came of age, "the king, in the presence of the magnates, ceremonially girded [him] with the belt of

---

[6] *Regesta*, iii, no. 760.

[7] Margam Annals, in *Ann. Mon.*, i. 14.

[8] Gervase, i. 133 ("before Lent" (1148); *Regesta*, iii, no. 794; *Sarum Charters*, 14–15 (showing the empress at Falaise on 10 June 1148); Chibnall, *Matilda*, 148–9.

[9] *Regesta*, iii, nos. 550, 555, 569.

[10] Ibid., nos. 24, 26, 76, 157, 195–6, 198, 207, 221, 224, 239b, 239d, 243, 301, 509, 512–13, 539, 541, 550, 553, 557, 843, 845, 850.

[11] Ibid., no. 178. Stephen may already have lost control of this northern honour, to David of Scots, around the time of his captivity in 1141: Barrow, "David I and the Honour of Lancaster."

knighthood . . . and after most bountifully endowing him with lands and possessions, and giving him the special distinction of a most splendid retinue of knights, advanced him in rank to the dignity of earl."[12] It is usually presumed that this passage refers to his becoming count of Boulogne but this is far from certain. What is said is that he was advanced, consequent on his knighting and his being given his own household, *ad consulatus*, to comital rank.[13] In what seem to be the earliest of his charters he does not describe himself as count of Boulogne,[14] and none of those in which he takes that title are certainly issued in his mother's lifetime. The most likely date of the ceremony was early in 1147.[15] Eustace was still a young man, perhaps sixteen or seventeen years old, but he took to his new responsibilities as to the manner born. He

> gained the highest honours of fame and glory at the very outset of his career as knight. He showed himself extremely generous and courteous; everywhere he stretched forth a generous hand in cheerful liberality; as he had a great deal of his father's disposition he could meet men on a footing of equality or superiority as occasion required; in one place he was entirely devoted to establishing pacts of peace, in another he confronted his enemies sternly and invincibly.[16]

Eustace was his father's son, with his father's easy manners, though – to another observer – he showed early the faults of those who were now his peers: "he robbed the lands and levied heavy taxes."[17]

Eustace's younger brother, William, was also provided for in the weeks preceding the setting out of the Second Crusade. He was married to the daughter of Earl William III de Warenne, and he would in due course become Earl William IV de Warenne. It seems appropriate that the king's son should be married to a great heiress, and so it is a natural presumption

[12] *GS*, 208–9. It was reported that his uncle, Henry of Winchester, had paid for the celebrations: JH, 323.

[13] Ibid.: "ad consulatus apicem excellenter prouexit."

[14] He describes himself as "earl Eustace, the king's son" ("comes Eustachius filius regis") in his own charters: e.g. Chichester, West Sussex RO, E VI/1/6 (Chichester D & C Liber Y), fo. 126r; BL, Cotton MS Vesp. F. xv, fos. 64v, 89v ("filius regis Anglie"); *Cartae Antiquae Rolls, 11–20*, 70. And this is how he is described in his father's charters: e.g., *Regesta*, iii, nos. 448–9 ("comes Eustachius filius meus"). When he appears as a witness to his parents' charters, he is invariably the first lay witness and attests simply as "comes Eustachius," while in a charter of Richard de Lucy he witnesses as "comes Eustachius filius regis": Oxford, Bodleian Library, Dugdale 18, fo. 41v.

[15] The relevant passage in *GS* comes after the arrest and revolt of Ranulf of Chester in autumn 1146, "about the same time" as the spring 1147 expedition of Henry of Anjou, and before the death of Robert of Gloucester later that year. *Regesta*, iii, no. 694, holds the date to early in 1147, for it is witnessed by Eustace as earl and by the bishop of Chester, who did not return from the Second Crusade. HH, 754–5, notes it alongside the 1149 knighting of Henry of Anjou, as also does JH, 323.

[16] *GS*, 208–9.

[17] *ASC*, s.a. 1140.

that the betrothal took place when news had been received that the earl had died. It may have been so, but there is every indication that a settlement had been made before the earl's departure. A charter of Reginald de Warenne, a brother of the third earl, acting as custodian of the estates, survives from the time of uncertainty, when there was no firm news from the Holy Land. It granted to the burgesses of Lewes their guild merchant, and said that this was the agreement he had made with them, that if God brought the earl safe home, "I so far as I can will secure that he grants them their guild on these terms; if not, then so far as I can I will ensure that my lord earl William, the king's son, will grant that guild to them."[18] One of the witnesses to the charter is "Eustace the clerk of earl William the king's son." He could keep an eye on the drafting. His presence, described in these terms, suggests that William, like his brother, had been advanced to comital rank before he was seen as having inherited the title Earl Warenne. It may even be that the one ceremony served for both promotions. In any event, the death of Earl William III de Warenne was a shock neither to the English polity nor to the men of the honour. The vacancy had already been filled.

The king's ambition for his children, both now elevated to the highest rank of the aristocracy, had implications for other of the magnates, implications that they may have been a little slow to realize. It might explain, what is otherwise somewhat puzzling, the eclipse of the house of Clare. The two earls Gilbert, the elder the earl of Pembroke, the younger his nephew, the earl of Hertford, had been closely associated with Stephen from the beginning of the reign. They wrote to him in terms of some intimacy.[19] They had different spheres of interest, but occasionally are found together, once in a charter linked to the launch of the crusade.[20] And yet events would set them, one against another, and both – for a time at least – against the king. A cause of this, though far from a complete explanation, is to be found in the ties of kinship between the house of Clare and the earls of Chester. Richard Fitz Gilbert de Clare had married Alice, the sister of Ranulf II (de Gernons), earl of Chester. The earl of Chester was thus the brother-in-law of Gilbert, earl of Pembroke, of Baldwin Fitz Gilbert, of Walter Fitz Gilbert (a crusader), and of sisters who were married to William de Montfichet, William de Percy, Baderon of Monmouth, and Aubrey de Vere, earl of Oxford. The earl of Chester was the uncle of Gilbert de Clare, earl of Hertford, and their relationship was a close one.[21] When, in consequence, the king required hostages for the

---

[18] *EYC* 8, no. 50: "tali conuentione quod si Deus comitem reduxerit. pro posse meo faciam quod ipse eis predicto pacto prefatam ghildam concedet. sin autem. faciam pro posse meo quod dominus meus comes Willelmus filius regis eis eandem concedet ghildam."

[19] BL, Harley MS 4757, fo. 3v.

[20] *Book of Seals*, 58–9 (no. 84), a charter of Gilbert de Clare, earl of Hertford, witnessed by Earl Gilbert of Pembroke.

[21] As evidenced by a number of Earl Ranulf's charters. In the first of them, Gilbert Fitz Richard and "Adeliza my sister" were with him soon after the death of her husband in 1136: *Chester Charters*, no. 39. Later charters, by which time Gilbert is an earl, are ibid., nos. 45, 64, 89.

release of Ranulf of Chester after his arrest at court in 1146, the one hostage named in the sources was "Gilbert Fitz Richard, a man of illustrious descent." The agreement for Earl Ranulf's release had been that he would then act peaceably, and "enjoy the resources of his own earldom only." He did not, nor can it ever have been expected that he would have done so. He went back to Lincoln, to try to recapture it, but it had been strongly garrisoned by the king, and he was forced to withdraw. The earl's behaviour placed his nephew, himself an earl, in some peril. Gilbert of Clare may have been held in custody for a time. Certainly he was required, "as his only means of avoiding exile and banishment," to surrender his own castles.[22] He is found shortly thereafter at Chester, in the company of his uncle, as also of Cadwaladr, "king of the Welsh."[23] He may have remained there for several months.

At this point, with the earl of Clare absent from the court and his castles held confiscate (if not actually in the king's hand), his uncle, the earl of Pembroke, thought that he saw an opportunity. He demanded the castles of the honour from the king, "claiming that they were his by hereditary right." The request was refused. The earl had misread the script. So at least is suggested by the sequel, for it was the earl of Pembroke not the earl of Clare whose castles were invested, and the campaigning was not around Clare in Suffolk but in Kent and in Sussex. The earl of Pembroke, notwithstanding his seniority and military experience, represented the younger branch of the family, and he had little by inheritance. He had, however, been generously treated by his family and by the crown, as David Crouch well shows.[24] His power was considerable. He wrote expansively to the archbishop of Canterbury, referring him to "a place in Wales called Dungleddy," which lay "in those regions which by divine mercy have recently been added to our authority."[25] He wrote in similar terms to the monks of Lewes, granting them whatever he held in the rape of Pevensey, "as long as I or my heirs be lord and ruler" thereof.[26] It would not be very long at all.

In looking for the reason for the earl of Pembroke's fall, one can point to a greater emphasis on the accountability of those who held estates and offices by grant of the crown and not by hereditary right. But there was always a particular reason for accountability to be made an issue. Here, the focus of attention was the rape of Pevensey in Sussex. It had originally been a Mortain fee.[27] It was needed now for Eustace, for "the great lands and honours" he had reportedly been given were not in fact extensive. He

---

[22] The main authority for this episode is *GS*, 200–5, from which the quotations are taken. Other notices are in Diceto, i. 255–6, and JH, 324.

[23] *Chester Charters*, no. 64.

[24] Crouch, "The March," in King, *Anarchy*, 274–5 and n. 46.

[25] *Cart. Worcester*, no. 252.

[26] BL, Cotton MS Vesp. F. xv, fo. 73r: "quamdiu ego inde dominus et potens fuero aut heredes mei."

[27] *Cal. Charter Rolls*, i. 31; Thompson, "Rape of Pevensey," 209–11.

had the city of Cambridge, which may have been his wife's dower,[28] and the honour of Pevensey, which had to be taken by force. First the king took "the castle of the earl that lay nearest to hand." The author of the *Gesta Stephani* likes to name castles, but he seems to have little familiarity with this area. This may have been Leeds castle in Kent.[29] Two other castles were taken, and the royal army then came to Pevensey. This he clearly does know. "Pevensey is a castle rising on a very lofty mound, fortified on every side by a most beautiful wall, fenced impregnably by the washing waves of the sea, almost inaccessible owing to the difficulty of the ground."[30] The castle was invested and finally captured, some of Earl Gilbert's men being taken prisoner and forced to ransom themselves.[31] Eustace established himself in Pevensey very quickly, taking up residence and surrounding himself with his family. One of his grants to Lewes Priory was addressed to his men of the honour and issued at Ripe, one of its main demesne manors.[32] Another, of the fishery, makes provision for his anniversary, which the endowment would ensure would be a joyful celebration.[33] An emphasis on ceremonial is found also in the position at court offered to Hilary, the new bishop of Chichester and formerly dean of Christchurch, soon after his consecration. He and his successors should be chaplains to the queen: "when invited on the great feast days they should come and serve as her private chaplain."[34] There is some confidence shown in these documents. The family was drawing together.

In the spring of 1147, when final preparations were being made for the crusade, one of the monks of Bec recorded the welcome given to a distinguished visitor. "Henry, son of duke Geoffrey and the empress, coming

[28] *Regesta*, iii, no. 239a, a charter of Eustace given at Cambridge, is witnessed by "Countess Constance," and she made grants to the nuns of St Radegund's after Eustace's death: Gray, *Priory of St Radegund*, 75. She was well regarded in the neighbouring monastery of Peterborough: *ASC*, s.a. 1140.

[29] OV, vi. 520–1, notes that Gilbert of Clare captured Leeds castle after Robert of Gloucester's rebellion in 1138, and saw him as able to network with other landholders – "amici uel affines eorum" – in the region. Davis says "possibly Tonbridge (Kent) where Gilbert had an important castle": *GS*, 202 n. 2; it is possible, certainly, but this was a castle of the honour of Clare and it was not necessarily in the hands of the earl of Pembroke.

[30] *GS*, 202–5.

[31] BL Cotton Vesp. F. xv, fo. 68r: "pro hac donacione predicti monachi dederunt mihi .xx. marcas argenti in auxilium redempcionis mee quando fui captus apud Peuensele."

[32] Ibid., fo. 64v. Stephen's confirmation of this grant was issued at Lewes and witnessed by his other son, Earl William: *Regesta*, iii, no. 449, iv, plate XXXVa.

[33] BL Cotton Vesp. F. xv, fo. 89v, witnessed by "Willelmo comite de Warenne fratre meo." Stephen's confirmation of this grant was also issued at Lewes, possibly on the same occasion: *Regesta*, iii, no. 448, iv, plate XXXIVb.

[34] *Regesta*, iii, no. 184: "ad festa eius invitati tamquam proprii capellani eius venient et ei inde servient." A later copy than the one printed shows the place of issue as London; it must date from after the consecration of Bishop Hilary on 3 Aug. 1147 and before his departure for the council of Rheims, held during Lent 1148. Eustace's own charter in this regard was issued *c.*1149, during a meeting of the royal court at St Albans: West Sussex RO, E VI/1/6, fo. 126r, calendared *Cart. Chichester*, 80 (no. 292), where "the earl of Surrey" should read "Earl Simon (of Senlis)."

into Normandy from England, was received by a solemn procession on Ascension Day."[35] This fell on 29 May. Henry had no title at this time, other than as the son of his parents. He was just fourteen years old. Where he had been in England, for how long, and what he had achieved are all questions to which this bland extract offers no answers. Fortunately, however, some answers are found in another source, and the story it tells is a remarkable one.[36] It is likely that Henry had crossed to England early in April. He was accompanied, it was said, by "a fine company of knights." The size of his force grew as news of its arrival spread, till it comprised many thousands of men, men with a clear strategy and able to call upon unlimited funds. Those on Henry's side were naturally encouraged, "and it seemed to them that a new light had dawned," while the king's party was dismayed. But only for a short space of time.

It was all a charade. Henry had only a few troops with him, and they were not his, for he had no household of his own. They were mercenaries, and of a particularly volatile kind, for they had not been paid. They came, presumably via Wareham, and tried to capture Cricklade and a place called *Burtuna*, possibly Purton in Wiltshire, a few miles south of Cricklade. This area was not chosen at random. When we last heard of it – and probably when Henry last heard of it – it was in the hands of Philip, one of the sons of Robert of Gloucester, who had come to an agreement with Stephen and was now supporting him (though he had resolved to go – and may possibly have been about to go – on crusade).[37] This to Henry was a personal betrayal, by a cousin whom he had been close to for a time. His animus towards Philip of Gloucester was to be long remembered.[38] However poorly Henry was supported, there can be no doubt that he nourished the ambition that his supporters had cherished on his earlier visit, that the very sight of him "would inspire others to fight for the cause of the lawful heir."[39] But it had not had this effect back in 1143, and nor did it have now. The two minor towns that his men attacked were too strongly held; he had no idea what to do next, and some of his forces drifted away.

Henry at least had the sense to cut his losses. He had known all along – and it was soon clear to all – that this expedition represented his private initiative, and was not sanctioned by his family. When he did turn to his family, so the story was told, he found them unreceptive. He applied first for help to his mother, but she declined, for she had no money. There

---

[35] Torigni, 154: "Henricus filius ducis Gaufridi et imperatricis, de Anglia in Normanniam veniens, susceptus est a conventu Becci sollenni processione, die ascensionis Domini."

[36] *GS*, 204–9; Poole, "Henry Plantagenet's early visits to England," 451–2.

[37] *GS*, 186–7, 190–1.

[38] By another of the sons of Robert of Gloucester, Roger, bishop of Worcester, in animated correspondence with Henry (now king) in 1170: *MTB*, iii. 104–5; for comment, WM, *HN*, xcii–xciii.

[39] WM, *HN*, 126–7.

is no reason to doubt this. The empress, since her widowhood, had never had resources commensurate with her rank. So Henry turned to his uncle, Robert of Gloucester. He certainly did have the cash, but he declined to make it available in this cause, perhaps because Henry's expedition was predicated on divisions in his own family, perhaps because he was already ill (for he was to die later in the year). There is no reason to doubt this story either, nor that Henry would find himself third time lucky, in applying to one of his relatives, who did have money and who was prepared to help him. This was the king himself. The request, made by Henry's emissaries, obviously had to be drafted with care. The messengers "begged him in friendly and imploring terms to regard with pity the poverty that weighed upon him and hearken compassionately to one who was bound to him by close ties of relationship and well disposed to him as far as it depended on himself." The king sent a remittance by return. No one was surprised when they heard of this development. While the same authority had said that Henry of Winchester's behaviour in not confronting the empress in 1139 had seemed "almost incredible,"[40] the king's character was by now well set, and some even saw his avuncular behaviour as bringing him credit, "because the more kindly and humanely a man behaves to an enemy the feebler he makes him and the more he weakens him."[41]

Henry's time was not yet. But it is not to use any measure of hindsight to say that his time would come. The laconic entry in the Bec chronicle is in this respect transparent. The monks greeted him with all the ceremonial of a formal *adventus*, as their future duke. If Henry in his expedition had been running a little ahead of his next promotion, the monks' reception of him shows them doing the same. Over the next few years more and more people would do so, treating him not just as the putative duke of Normandy, but at his own evaluation, as "the lawful heir of England." The author of the *Gesta Stephani*, resolutely loyal to the king, would give Henry this title in 1147 and in 1149, in introducing his English expeditions.[42] There would, however, be no significant change in Henry's circumstances until he could be treated as an adult, knighted, himself given comital rank, just as his rival had been early in 1147. For it was Eustace who was his rival. The two years between Whitsun 1147, when Henry had just returned from England, and Whitsun 1149, when Henry was knighted, have as their centrepiece a church council, that at Rheims at mid-Lent 1148, and a dynamic in Theobald's assertion of his primacy. We often have to rely on Canterbury sources and there is a distinct Canterbury line, with king, queen, and jack being trumped continuously by the archbishop, and Henry of Winchester cast as the joker in the pack. The Canterbury narrative is at times economical with the truth. What it

[40] *GS*, 88–9.
[41] The main source for this paragraph is *GS*, 206–9.
[42] *GS*, 204–5, 214–15; for comment King, "*Gesta Stephani*," 202–3.

conceals is that the council of Rheims precipitated a major crisis in the English Church, which Theobald struggled to control, and that in the face of challenge to his regalian rights over the Church the king was able to hold his ground.

It is likely that it was in February 1148 that the royal court met to decide its response to the summoning of the archbishop of Canterbury, and the other bishops of England, to the council at Rheims.[43] To the previous council, in 1139, a small delegation had been sent, "since it seemed dangerous when war was imminent that all the prelates of England should leave the country,"[44] and it was intended again to follow this precedent. The bishops chosen to go were Robert of Hereford and the two most recently consecrated bishops, Hilary of Chichester and William of Norwich. After the delegation had set off, Stephen came to Canterbury for the consecration on 14 March of two further bishops, Walter of Rochester and Nicholas of Llandaff.[45] The king thought it had been agreed that the archbishop should not travel to France; but Theobald changed his mind. He said that he had been prevented from going, and that he was caught between a rock and a hard place: if he went he would suffer sanctions from the king, if he did not he would be suspended from office by the pope and perhaps even deposed. The ports were being watched to prevent him crossing to France.[46] And so he was forced to hire a small fishing boat, which could hold no more than a dozen men and was totally devoid of "the necessary facilities," and thus he crossed the Channel "rather as a survivor from a shipwreck than in a ship," "swimming rather than sailing."[47] He was warmly welcomed by the pope and the fathers of the council, and the story of his adventure went the rounds.

Among the clerks of Theobald, sent ahead to present his apologies, were John of Salisbury, Roger of Pont l'Evêque, and Thomas Becket. When Roger was archbishop of York, and Thomas was archbishop of Canterbury and in exile in his turn, John wrote his *Memoirs of the Papal Court*. He started with events at the council of Rheims and continued to 1152, though there are some flashbacks, such as when he described proceedings at the Lateran Council in 1139. The work is in some ways like a modern political memoir,

---

[43] JS, *HP*, 6–7, states that the decisions were taken "by the king and queen and their council along with certain of the bishops." Gervase, i. 134, names Henry of Winchester. One may date to this meeting a charter of Stephen in favour of the diocese of Chichester, witnessed by the archbishop of Canterbury and the bishops of Winchester and Worcester: *Regesta*, iii, no. 182.

[44] *Christina*, 162–3.

[45] *Canterbury Professions*, nos. 89, 90, recording the presence of his three suffragans, Nigel of Ely, Robert of Exeter, and Maurice of Bangor.

[46] Gervase, i. 134, stating that Theobald had sought permission to go to the council but had been refused. The Annals of St Augustine's, Canterbury, s.a. 1147, say that the king expelled the papal nuncios who brought the summons to the council: *UGQ*, 81.

[47] JS, *HP*, 7: "sic non tam navigio quam quasi quodam naufragio transfretavit"; *Correspondence of Thomas Becket*, i. 718–19 (no. 153). It is shown, ibid. i. 719 n. 4, that these two texts date from very much the same time.

in that it takes almost as read the proceedings of the council and concentrates on the personalities. A meeting in the lodgings of Bernard, abbot of Clairvaux, provides a focus for the discussion of the trial of Gilbert de la Porrée, bishop of Poitiers.[48] Bernard sought to have Gilbert's views condemned, just as he had secured the condemnation of Abelard at Sens in 1140. He took his seminar, which included the archbishops of Canterbury and York and Abbot Suger, one by one through propositions which he claimed the bishop denied. Gilbert, who seemed to have read everything,[49] proved more than a match for his accusers when the case came to trial. There was additionally the danger of schism, with the French and English churches supporting the abbot and the cardinals and other episcopal benches supporting the bishop. John of Salisbury though writing nearly twenty years later was still fascinated by the issues and he produced only a token apology for his digression when he returned to papal history.

As the bishops and their clerks talked long into the night, reliving their student days, Robert of Hereford, a member of the official English delegation, lay dying in the guest-house of the abbey of St Nicaise. He had been taken ill after the council had been in session for just three days, took to his bed, and after much suffering, and having been anointed by the pope and consoled by the council fathers, he died on 16 April. His body was brought to England;[50] it worked its first miracle before it had even crossed the Channel, and – so the *Life* records – as the news of this spead, it was received with honour at every stopping place along the road to Hereford.[51] Its reception in London was particularly noteworthy. The bishop of Winchester, "a most illustrious and magnificent man," as soon as he had news of the hearse's approach, set out from his palace in Southwark, rode far out along the road, and then escorted it on foot. A man famed for his eloquence, he spoke at length, as the cart trundled slowly along the Old Kent Road, of the loss that the English Church had suffered. "Alas," he said, "we have lost a flower of our order, a holy man, a wise man, a man of wide friendship, without guile or avarice, a doughty warrior and a pillar of Holy Church, a model to us all of honesty and constancy, purity and chastity." On foot they came to London, and on foot they crossed the city – it was "a jolly long way"[52] – until they reached the Temple church. The bells were sounded and the citizens came out. The queen followed them, to greet in death a man whom in life she had dearly loved. The king, who was occupied in business elsewhere, immediately broke off and hastened to the church. There they all sat for some time, united in grief. Not every word of this account need be accepted as gospel, but it contains an important point. Time spent in church was time well spent. Here are the king, the queen, and the king's brother,

[48] JS, *HP*, 15–41 at 17–19. There is a useful brief account in Poole, *Illustrations*, 163–70, and commentary in Southern, *Scholastic Humanism* 2, 123–32.

[49] JS, *HP*, 21 and n. 1.

[50] In an ox hide, according to the "Anglo-Norman Chronicle of Wigmore," 427.

[51] "Vita Roberti de Betune," in *Anglia Sacra*, ii. 295–321.

[52] Ibid., ii. 320: "Londonie latitudinem quam spetiosa est."

men and women who knew how to behave, behaving in the way that was expected of them.

On the pope's initiative, so we are told, but we may suspect also on Theobald's advice, it was decided to make the king's attempt to control the movement of his bishops a trial of strength. All the bishops who had not attended the council at Rheims were to be held under penalty of suspension, from which the archbishop of Canterbury could release them, with the exception of Henry of Winchester, who could only be released by the pope. The target of this initiative was the king but rather than fold his hand he raised the stakes. Theobald returned to Canterbury at the end of April. The king was then in London. He straight away set off for Canterbury, "in a foul temper," and sending ahead his two most trusted household officers, Richard de Lucy and William Martel, required the archbishop to answer for his behaviour, "since he had dared to attend the council in defiance of the king's prohibition."[53] Theobald's response was not to defend himself but to go into exile. He spent some time in France, but the queen and William of Ypres were sent after him, asking him at least to settle in St Omer.[54] There royal messengers would know where to find him. There a settlement might be reached.

The first half of 1148 saw four vacancies in the Canterbury province, out of a total of thirteen sees. That at Rochester had been filled instantaneously, the archbishop having the right to do this without reference to the crown.[55] That at Chester/Coventry occurred in the Middle East and the vacancy was not yet notified. That at Lincoln was discussed at the council of Rheims. To succeed Alexander "the magnificent" the king and his brother put forward three candidates, Gervase, abbot of Westminster, Henry de Sully, abbot of Fécamp, and Hugh, abbot of St Benet, Holme. All three were their close kin. None was of transparent ability. The names were greeted almost with incredulity at the papal court, and they were rejected, so Gilbert Foliot reported, with evident relish, "indignantly and with harsh language."[56] The appointment went to Robert de Chesney, the archdeacon of Leicester, a member of a prominent family which was active in Stephen's support. This was a popular decision. The appointment to Hereford was more problematic. The vacancy had arisen at the papal court, and the pope in these circumstances had some claim to provide to it. There was a good candidate immediately to hand, and one moreover close to the archbishop. This was Gilbert Foliot, who was promptly elected, with papal approval. A consecration to the see of Lincoln would await the archbishop's return, but that to Hereford was not allowed to wait. There was the complication that in terms

[53] Gervase, i. 135: "ira commotus"; JS, *HP*, 41–2.

[54] *GF Letters*, no. 78 (showing the archbishop and himself at Arras in July); Gervase, i. 135.

[55] Gervase, i. 132–3; Saltman, *Theobald*, 103–5.

[56] Gilbert Foliot wrote while in exile to his cousin Robert de Chesney, archdeacon of Leicester: *GF Letters*, no. 75. It may have been intended to signal that Robert's own claims to election to the see were seen as strong.

of secular politics the city of Hereford was out of Stephen's control, and the Angevins could seek to turn the appointment, as they could the archbishop's exile, to their own advantage.[57] Theobald pressed ahead. The bishops of London, Salisbury, and Chichester were summoned from England to assist in Gilbert Foliot's consecration. They declined to do so, saying that "it was contrary to ancient custom for anyone to be consecrated outside the kingdom, especially if he had not received the royal assent or sworn fealty to the king."[58] Theobald went ahead anyway, on 5 September, at St Omer, with the bishops of Amiens, Cambrai, and Térouanne assisting in the ceremony.[59]

In the late summer months of 1148 there were all the makings of a major crisis. While Theobald was away from his see it was placed in the hands of royal custodians and its substantial revenues came to the crown. Theobald appealed to the pope for their, and for his own, restitution. He was given authority, if the king did not relent, to place the whole country under an interdict, while at Michaelmas – the time when the archbishop's rents would be paid into the royal coffers – the king himself was to be excommunicated.[60] The threat was ignored, and so the interdict was published, to come into effect on 12 September. It was to prove "an almost complete fiasco."[61] There was no appetite for sanctions this severe, sent from out of the country to a hierarchy that was divided, several of whose members felt that the king had a good case. Gilbert Foliot had remained at Theobald's side throughout, his position complicating any settlement, his personality unhelpful. Gilbert's first action on taking control of the see as its administrator, before his consecration, was to place it under an interdict, to teach the earl of Hereford the error of his ways.[62] The canons of Llanthony were distressed and frightened as they first learned of the death of the bishop, their former superior, and then found themselves embroiled in an international incident. It was Hilary of Chichester, one of the bishops now on Theobald's blacklist, who wrote to them sympathetically, while their

---

[57] JS, *HP*, 47–9: "in cuius potestate [Duke Henry's] tunc erat episcopatus electio." A little earlier in the year Geoffrey of Anjou had sought to reopen the question of Stephen's title, sending the bishop of Térouanne to England on his behalf: ibid., 44.

[58] Ibid., 48.

[59] Ibid.; *Canterbury Professions*, no. 91; Gervase, i. 135.

[60] Three letters were sent by the pope from Brescia on 29 July 1148: JL, nos. 9287–9. John of Salisbury evidently had them in front of him as he wrote and summarizes them as follows: "He wrote to all the bishops of England, both individually and as a body, ordering them to admonish the king to restore the archbishop's confiscated goods . . . if the king did not reply to their admonitions they were at once, without allowing any appeal, to place his land under an interdict and warn him that the lord pope would excommunicate him personally at Michaelmas. He wrote too to ask the bishops and princes of France to assist the archbishop to the best of their ability. Finally he commanded all in the province of Canterbury to show steadfast obedience to the archbishop, and answer his summons as readily as if he were in his see." JS, *HP*, 45–6.

[61] Saltman, *Theobald*, 29.

[62] *GF Letters*, no. 77.

spiritual lord wrote to the pope about the election to the bishopric of Arras.[63] Theobald won golden opinions from the poor of St Omer, while the poor of Canterbury, his cathedral city, were denied access to the sacraments.[64] This was not Theobald's finest hour.

It seems to have been Theobald who made the first move. He returned to England, crossing over not to one of the Channel ports but to Gosford in Suffolk, on a stretch of coast under the control of Hugh Bigod, earl of Norfolk. The archbishop used Hugh's castle at Framlingham as his base for a time, "until peace had been made in his regard."[65] This involved discussions with some of his suffragans. It will certainly also have involved agents of the king, very likely Richard de Lucy and William Martel, with whom he had been negotiating earlier in the year, to work out a programme to secure peace by resolving the issues between them; only then could he return to his own estates. It will have been insisted upon that Gilbert Foliot swear fealty to the king as a newly appointed bishop. This he did. The Angevins were disappointed when they had news of this, and reproached the archbishop. The reply came that "a bishop had no right to cause schism in the church by refusing fealty to the prince approved by the papacy."[66] This formulation represented far more than diplomatic sleight of hand. The principle of unity, however much it had been compromised by events of the past few months, was fundamental to Theobald's thinking: "although individual dignitaries followed different lords, the church as a whole followed only one."[67]

Theobald's first public engagement of which we have notice after his return was the consecration at Canterbury, on 11 November 1148, of the first abbot of a new monastery, at Faversham in Kent.[68] This engagement will have been part of the settlement, for this was not a small cloister set to struggle and compete in a harsh environment, but a royal foundation, intended from the first as the burial place of Stephen, his immediate family, and – it was hoped – of a long dynasty. The first abbot was Clarembald, prior of Bermondsey, who came with twelve monks, there having first been obtained a release from both the abbot of Cluny and the prior of La Charité from any claim of subjection to those houses. These letters of release, which were read out at the consecration, and of which the originals survive, indicate that the building works were already well

---

[63] "We and other friends of your dead father will keep a watch for you as we have been commissioned from above and we will gladly run those affairs of yours which have been entrusted to us as if they were our own": Mayr-Harting, *Bishops of Chichester*, 11; *GF Letters*, no. 78.

[64] JS, *HP*, 42.

[65] Gervase, i. 136; JS, *HP*, 49: "donec sibi pax reformata est."

[66] JS, *HP*, 49: "persuadens ei quod episcopo non licuerat ecclesiam scindere, ei subtrahendo fidelitatem quem ecclesia Romana recipiebat ut principem."

[67] Ibid., 47–8: "licet enim proceres diuisi diuersos principes sequerentur, unum tamen habebat ecclesia."

[68] Details come from Abbot Clarembald's profession, printed by Woodruff, "Professions of Canonical Obedience," 64–6.

advanced.[69] What may be taken as the foundation charter granted the royal manor of Faversham as the sole benefaction.[70] William of Ypres had previously had control of it, and he was offered an exact exchange. The consecration of the new abbot was followed a few days later by his installation at Faversham. Among those present was the queen. The new monastery was seen very much as her initiative; she had been there at the start of the building works and had spent much time in Canterbury driving them on; and she continued to take a personal interest in its affairs.[71] She had an additional reason for her continuing interest in this area of Kent, since she was at the same time establishing a new nunnery at Lillechurch (in Higham parish), near Rochester. Its first prioress would be her daughter, Mary (see plate 22), and the nuns whom she would rule came from the prestigious abbey of St Sulpice-la-Forêt in Brittany. As with Faversham, a complex series of transactions was necessary to endow the new house.[72] In all of this, the queen was in her element.

The four bishops present at these celebrations – Bath, Chichester, Exeter, and Worcester – moved from Faversham immediately to London. Hilary of Chichester was the most junior of them, but he was already starting to make his mark. A former advocate at the papal court, and before that a clerk in the household of Henry of Winchester, Hilary was an impressive figure.[73] On his appointment he had forthwith "started to investigate the rights and privileges of his church most thoroughly."[74] He had come to an arrangement with the count of Eu to secure the restitution of the manor of Bexhill, a valuable asset since there were jurisdictional powers attached to the hundred. The conveyance was made publicly in St Paul's Cathedral on 14 November 1148, "the day of the translation of St Earconwald, confessor," when the saint's relics were transferred to a new shrine behind the high altar. This was a high feast in the cathedral and a large crowd was present. The four visiting bishops were accompanied by members of their entourage, the bishop of Bath by the dean and two of the canons of Wells, the bishop of Chichester by two of his canons. There were representatives of three other dioceses, two of the canons of Salisbury, the archdeacon of Suffolk, and Master John of Pagham, one of the archbishop of Canterbury's clerks, soon to have a diocese of his own. Also

[69] The letter of Peter the Venerable, abbot of Cluny, is printed in trans. in Saltman, *Theobald*, 82.

[70] *Regesta*, iii, no. 300.

[71] Woodruff, "Professions of Canonical Obedience," 66; Gervase, i. 139; Saltman, *Theobald*, 283, no. 57, noting the archbishop's consecration of a cemetery at the abbey, "precibus Matildis regine Anglorum domine nostre inclinatus."

[72] Set out very fully in an excellent article by Judith Everard, "Saint-Sulpice-la-Forêt and Royal Patronage in England," 111–20.

[73] *Battle*, 146–7: "uiro magnifico," On the Battle chronicle see Vincent, "The Battle Chronicle Unmasked," 264–86. On Hilary see Mayr-Harting, *Bishops of Chichester*, 7–12; idem, "Hilary of Chichester and Henry II"; Knowles, *Episcopal Colleagues*, 24–7.

[74] *Battle*, 148–9.

present were four heads of house, the abbots of Westminster, Reading, and Waverley, and the prior of Lewes. It was a most impressive gathering.[75]

The occasion was designed to gain maximum publicity. There was plenty to occupy the eyes. The saint had a new shrine, "with images, with 130 precious stones ('it is said') and angels at either end."[76] There was much also to occupy the mind. For these conveyances were not routine. They represent new thinking, on how "the rights and privileges" of the churches might best be restored, in the circumstances of the civil war. The count's grant of Bexhill was the start of a process. "I restore in full to the church and bishop Hilary that township with all its churches and all its members, retaining no custom or service for myself and my heirs. I grant all rights which the title-deeds of the church of Chichester show to belong to the township, saving the king's service." The real prize was the grant of the hundred; but it was made clear that the hundred was not the count's to give. His bailiff of the rape of Hastings was given instructions to transfer the township to the bishop, "without any retention of demesne or service of the hundred."[77] The king then, early in the New Year and on an equally solemn occasion, transferred the hundred to the bishop.[78] All this was intended to serve, to those listening carefully, as an object lesson in the legitimacy of local power. The key was the emphasis on the rights of the crown.[79] The king and the senior clergy had found common ground. The election of the new bishop of Lincoln, Robert de Chesney, took place on 13 December 1148, at Westminster, in the presence of the king and queen.[80] The royal court was in regular session.[81]

On the progress of the civil war in 1147 and 1148 there is little to be said. There was continued skirmishing between the two sides, the details of which show the emergence of a new frontier. This was on the border of Hampshire and Wiltshire, defined in terms of castles, particularly those of the bishopric of Winchester. One of these was at Merdon, which in 1147 was captured by the men of Brian Fitz Count.[82] The bishop built siege-castles against his own castle; all the forces of the empress's party – so at

[75] West Sussex RO, E VI/1/6, fos. 126v–127r, printed *Monasticon*, vi. 1171. It is rare to find so full an attendance list as that given here.

[76] Brooke, *London*, 272.

[77] West Sussex RO, E VI/1/6, fo. 127r.

[78] *Regesta*, iii, no. 183.

[79] The episode is discussed in this context in King, "Anarchy of King Stephen's Reign," 140–1.

[80] *Canterbury Professions*, no. 92; Saltman, *Theobald*, 106–7; HH, 752–5.

[81] *Battle*, 150–3, sees business as being referred from one court to another (here from St Albans to London), as being settled "before the king, the bishops, and the barons," and the formalities of leave-taking being enforced.

[82] GS, 208–11, referring to the castle of *Lidelea*. Granted we are told that this castle, "fuit . . . ex episcopi Wintoniensis iure" (ibid.), and that Henry of Winchester had built a castle at Merdon (in *Hursley* parish) (Winchester Annals, in *Ann. Mon.*, ii. 51), and that in a typical hand of the late twelfth century H and Li are all but indistinguishable, this identification can be made with confidence, though it has caused difficulty to editors (Howlett, in *Chronicles*, iii. 133 n. 1; Davis, GS, 208 n. 2).

least we are told – were brought to bear against the bishop; but the king appeared and put them to flight. Some of the knights of Brian Fitz Count were imprisoned deep in the dungeons of the castle which they had previously controlled.[83] In the following year there was activity at Castle Cary, involving William, the new earl of Gloucester, and Henry de Tracy; at Christchurch between the men of Baldwin de Redvers and Walter de Pinkney; and at Downton in Wiltshire between Patrick, earl of Salisbury, and the bishop of Winchester.[84] Patrick of Salisbury was one of those magnates who issued his own coins at this time, his heavily jowled face, helmeted and clutching a large sword, providing as vivid an image of magnate power as appears on any of the coins of this period (see plate 13d).[85] His men captured Downton, just as those of Brian Fitz Count had captured Merdon, and in similar manner they in their turn were evicted. The bishop's agent here was his nephew Hugh du Puiset, the treasurer of York, summoned from the north, given a blank cheque and told to get on with the job.[86] Henry of Winchester could not pursue the siege in person, since he had been summoned to Rome.

The reasons for that summons have already been examined. Henry had not gone to the council of Rheims, and he stood accused of trying to prevent the archbishop of Canterbury from attending. He would have been excommunicated on the spot, had not Archbishop Theobald and all the English bishops, along with Gilbert Foliot, as well as Henry's brother Theobald, count of Blois, interceded on his behalf.[87] All they could do, however, was to negotiate a period of grace. Henry was given six months to seek a personal absolution from the pope.[88] He may be seen as leaving in the summer of 1148 and reaching the papal curia in the autumn. The controversy between the king and the archbishop of Canterbury was then at its height. For that, at least, Henry could claim he was in no way responsible, but he was not believed,[89] and it may be that the penance imposed

---

[83] *GF Letters*, no. 29, asks Bishop Henry to show pity on Roger Foliot, "quem homines uestri apud Merendune incarceratum tenent," and suggests that William de Chesney had been involved in his capture; no. 30 is to the prior of Winchester on the same subject: "ignominiose enim tenetur in carcere"; no. 75, from the council of Rheims in 1148, shows that the matter had been brought to the attention of the pope.

[84] *GS*, 210–15.

[85] North, no. 947; Fitzwilliam Museum, Cambridge, CM.1229–2001, 1230–2001.

[86] *GS*, 214–15: "thesauros suos ei aperuit." Hugh knew the territory, for he was at the same time one of the archdeacons of Winchester: *Fasti* 2: *Monastic Cathedrals*, 91–2.

[87] JS, *HP*, 10; *GF Letters*, no. 75: "domnus Cantuariensis et alii quamplures episcopi *et nos omnes* pro domno Wintoniensi supplicantes in nullo prorsus auditi sumus."

[88] Over the next two years Henry travelled at least once and probably twice to "Rome," a word that might serve either for the city or for the bishop of Rome, wherever he might be. There is a magisterial discussion of the sources in JS, *HP*, 91–4. I follow the suggestion of two visits, ibid., 94, but would reverse the return journeys, bringing him back via Compostela early in 1149 and via Cluny early in 1150. Some of the reasoning behind what can only be an alternative hypothesis will be found in subsequent notes.

[89] The story that became attached to this episode, related in ibid., 79, refers most obviously to the circumstances of late 1148.

on him was a pilgrimage to Compostela. This will have been no hardship. Henry was an inveterate traveller, and he had the constitution of an ox, avoiding the almost inevitable tummy troubles by taking his own private chef. Henry arrived back in England early in 1149,[90] but again in the following autumn set out for Rome, hoping that now the climate between church and state had improved he might secure the renewal of the lega- tion which he had lost in 1143.[91] He failed, and was reduced to trawling the antiques shops of Rome for fine pieces, which he arranged to have shipped home under separate cover. John of Salisbury has a wonderful picture of him at this time, clearly drawn from life.[92] On this occasion he travelled back via Cluny, his alma mater. He found the abbey grievously in debt, and was able from the wealth he had in the panniers of his horses to advance the monks a massive loan.[93] The terms for repayment were carefully specified. Henry was always a man to insist on strict accounting.

For Henry of Winchester's brother, the king of England, 1149 was a year in which he also spent much time on the road, and in which he continued to react to events. The initiative was taken by Henry Fitz Empress, and it is his single-mindedness in pursuit of his inheritance that is the chief feature of the politics of the year. You could not fail to notice him at this time, and that was an achievement in itself. No territory was gained, but in terms of the fight for men's minds – the real struggle in the period with which this chapter is concerned – there were significant devel- opments. One later chronicler, Ralph de Diceto, would see the knighting

[90] Given that he is absent from all the guest-lists that survive from Nov. and Dec. 1148, it seems all but certain that he was not in England at this time. He must, however, have returned early in 1149, for he is a witness to royal confirmation to Chichester in respect of the manor of Bexhill, *Regesta*, iii, no. 183. This charter would be taken to Rome later in the year, and granted it was attested by the archbishop and five other bishops, we may see the royal court here constituted at the same time as one of Theobald's councils. A likely time for this would be mid-Lent or Low Sunday 1149.

[91] On the legation, which he was prepared to discuss in any company at any time, JS, *HP*, 78. I would take as a fixed point Eugenius III's confirmation of the grant of Bexhill, given at Frascati south of Rome on 26 Nov. 1149, seeing Henry as here conducting business for his close associate, Hilary of Chichester.

[92] Ibid., 79–80: he was "conspicuous at the papal court for his long beard and philosophical solemnity."

[93] *EEA* 8: *Winchester 1070–1204*, no. 38, recording an agreement made in the chapter house at Cluny in "1149." If, as Chibnall suggests is "more probable," this year is seen as stretching from 25 Mar. 1149 to 24 Mar. 1150, the argument for the early months of 1150, returning from a second visit to the papal curia, becomes compelling. This is based not just on Henry's known itinerary, but from the provision tagged on at the end of the document to ensure there was no misunderstanding. "Prima vero quadragesima sequenti incipient pecuniam reddere, sicut prescriptum est"; and earlier it had been stated that the payments were due in Easter week (when the abbey's own rents would have been paid). Such a state- ment would be quite unnecessary in midsummer, much more necessary in midwinter. A time in Jan. or early Feb. 1150, which might have been suggested on other evidence, would seem to fit very well.

of Henry at Carlisle in 1149 as marking a new beginning in the history of England.[94]

HENRY FITZ EMPRESS

Henry will have crossed to England around the time of Easter, which fell on 3 April, in 1149. He made first for Devizes, where he was joined by the earls of his party, Roger, earl of Hereford, William, earl of Gloucester, his uncle Reginald, earl of Cornwall, Patrick, earl of Salisbury, and other experienced figures in John the Marshal, Gotso de Dinan, William de Beauchamp, and Elias Giffard.[95] Henry's very tenure of the castle in which his future strategy was planned was threatened by the local bishop, Jocelin of Salisbury, active in his turn in seeking to recover the historic rights of his diocese. He had already received restitution from William of Gloucester in respect of Sherborne.[96] Now he continued his campaign to recapture Devizes, treating Henry as he would any other earl. Henry answered him as a future king. He gave back the manor of [Bishops] Cannings, with the hundred rights and jurisdiction:

> with the exception of the castle of Devizes, which is situated within this manor of the church of Salisbury, and the borough and the park, and the service of the knights of that manor, [all of which] I retain in my hand because of my great need, with the full understanding and ready acquiescence of the bishop, until God has shown me that I may give it back to him.[97]

Henry's programme for the future was founded on his rights as "the lawful heir." He claimed to stand in the historic line of the English kings, making a grant to Quarr Abbey, "for the safety and preservation of the lord Geoffrey, duke of Normandy and count of Anjou, for the safety of the lady empress my mother, as also my own, for the well-being of the kingdom of England, and for the souls of king Henry my grandfather, and queen Matilda, and all my predecessors now deceased."[98] As he prayed for the safety of his kingdom, he looked ahead to a successful military campaign. He expected that would all be over in less than two years.

Things started well enough. From Devizes, Henry went north to Carlisle, where he was knighted on Whit Sunday, 22 May 1149.[99] He took

---

[94] Diceto, i. 291.

[95] *Regesta*, iii, nos. 420, 666, 704, 795 (dated 13 Apr. 1149).

[96] *Earldom of Gloucester Charters*, 155–6 (no. 171), also stopping short of surrendering the castle itself.

[97] *Regesta*, iii, no. 795: "quod ego adhuc propter necessitatem meam . . . retineo in bona sufferentia episcopi donec me deus exemplificet quod ego ei reddere possim."

[98] Ibid., no. 666.

[99] *GS*, 214–17; JH, 322–3; *Melrose*, s.a. 1147; Aelred, *Genealogia*, col. 713; Torigni, 159–60; HH, 754–5; Diceto, i. 291; Howden, i. 211; Newburgh, i. 70; Gervase, i. 140–1; *Chron. Meaux*, i. 130.

with him Roger, earl of Hereford, "and the sons of some men of birth, that they might receive the honour of a knight's arms at the same time as himself."[100] These massed investitures were splendid occasions and the Scots put on a fine show, while Henry himself was received "with the respect due to a king."[101] Those assisting the king of Scots in the ceremonial were his own son, and the king-designate, Henry, earl of Northumberland, and Ranulf, earl of Chester.[102] The presence of the earl of Chester at Carlisle is of some significance. Of the many territorial claims he nurtured, that to Carlisle was one of the best founded. His father, Ranulf I (Meschin), had been the chief architect of Norman power in the region, his vassals the first barons of Cumbria, his memory a feature of the landscape.[103] As the price of allowing a collateral succession to the earldom of Chester in 1120, Henry I had reclaimed Carlisle from Earl Ranulf's father, but the son had not forgotten. "Ranulf certainly regarded Carlisle as a lost portion of his patrimony."[104] And yet here he abandoned his claim in favour of the king of Scots. He did so as part of an agreement. He was granted in return the honour of Lancaster, contiguous to his earldom, previously held by King Stephen as count; and the peace was to be confirmed by the marriage of Ranulf's son to one of the daughters of Henry, son of the king of Scots.[105] Ranulf did homage to the king of Scots,[106] and to Henry of Anjou; and it would be Henry whom thereafter he referred to as his lord.[107]

Stephen did not lack intelligence of the events at Carlisle and he was well aware of the threat they posed. He hastened north and may have arrived in York in time for the Whitsun feast. If not, he certainly arrived within the following week.[108] He found a city in turmoil, apprehensive, turned in upon itself. In the previous year, Henry Murdac had arrived to take up residence in his cathedral city and had been turned away, though he had been warmly welcomed by his suffragans, at Durham and at Carlisle, where he had been received by the king of Scots. He had then

---

[100] *GS*, 214–15.

[101] JH, 323; *GS*, 216–17.

[102] JH, 322–3.

[103] King, "Ranulf (I), Third Earl of Chester."

[104] Green, "Earl Ranulf II and Lancashire," 103.

[105] The children were tiny; circumstances changed; and nothing came of this proposal.

[106] JH, 323.

[107] *Chester Charters*, no. 87.

[108] JH, 323, after noting events at Whitsun at Carlisle, says "his diebus rex Stephanus venit Eboracum." *Cart. Whitby*, i. 8–9, shows Richard, their abbot-elect, setting off from Peterborough, his former house, on Whit Monday, and being received by the king in York. The narrative follows from the resignation of the previous abbot on Ash Wednesday "1148," i.e. 17 Feb. 1149: the coincidence of fixed and moveable feasts later in the year makes it quite certain that the year is 1149 not 1148; and so the itineraries of king, archbishop, and abbot need to be modified (*Regesta*, iii, xliii; *EEA* 5: *York 1070–1154*, 119; *Heads*, 78). These events are treated fully from the Peterborough side in Hugh Candidus, 119–22.

taken up residence first at Ripon and then at Beverley.[109] From there he had excommunicated his opponents, William of Aumale, the earl of York, and Hugh du Puiset, the treasurer, who had control of the diocese, paying its revenues into the royal coffers and ensuring that services were maintained in spite of any local or national interdict. Hugh in his turn excommunicated those who supported the archbishop, and he wielded the temporal sword also (as has been seen) in fighting in southern England for the bishop of Winchester. All in all, "the situation could not have been more confused";[110] and this confusion the king of Scots and his allies could hope to turn to their advantage. They did not succeed because they too were divided. David of Scots and the new knight, Henry of Anjou, for a start. It was later claimed that, as part of the discussions at Carlisle, there had been an acceptance by Henry that when he acquired his hereditary right he would allow the Scots to keep the gains they had made in the earlier treaties of Durham.[111] We need not doubt that there was some discussion of this matter, in what was for Henry a difficult environment, surrounded by eager young men and over-obliging new allies. He had from the first, however, a strong sense of his own mission, and there were careful draughtsmen in his company; he would not have wanted, or have been allowed, to swear a categorical oath. The issue lay between them as they marched south to Lancaster. There Ranulf of Chester had promised to meet them, bringing with him forces that he had raised within his earldom. Thereafter, it was expected, he would combine forces with Henry and attack York. Opinions differ as to what happened next. According to the *Gesta Stephani* Henry and Ranulf "together with a vast number of Scots" got almost to the gates of York, where Stephen had drawn up his forces in battle array, before they turned back. According to the more local witness, John of Hexham, who is to be preferred, Ranulf never even made the muster at Lancaster. At this point, he says simply, Henry "went home"; and he was next sighted travelling south, on minor roads, making for Hereford, the centre of the lordship of the most prominent of his companions. It must be doubtful whether Henry ever crossed the Pennines.[112]

King Stephen spent some time in Yorkshire. He came to Beverley and levied a fine on the townsmen, who earlier in the year had received Henry Murdac; he would have constructed a castle there had he not received a monitory apparition from St John. In York he was able to tax the citizens individually, which demonstrates the maintenance of up-to-date financial

---

[109] JH, 322. *Cart. Whitby*, i. 8, shows Henry Murdac at Beverley on 17 Feb. 1149.

[110] JH, 322: "factaque est confusio maxima infidelitatis in ea."

[111] Newburgh, i. 105, referring to Malcolm IV conceding this territory in 1157, "quamvis posset obtendere juramentum quod avo suo David praestitisse dicebatur"; Howden, i. 211, says that the oath referred specifically to Newcastle and the lands between the Tweed and the Tyne.

[112] JH, 323; *GS*, 216–17; HH, 754–5, stating that the two kings kept well apart.

records. After noting the levying of this taxation, John of Hexham went on to a more general complaint about the standard of the coinage: "each man, according to his own artifice, debased the value of money and coin."[113] That the city had long since ceased to use dies issued in southern England goes almost without saying. The coins that were issued were stylistically quite distinct, consisting of up to a dozen "elaborately decorated or unusual pictorial types," which may show Flemish and even Sicilian influence.[114] The main royal issue here showed the king holding a banner not a sceptre, possibly an allusion to the battle of the Standard; another would seem to show the king and his son Eustace standing side by side, just as they are found in the chronicles (see plate 13f).[115] There was also a wide variety of coins issued in the names of the leading magnates of the county, including William of Aumale, earl of York (see plate 13c), Eustace Fitz John, and Robert de Stuteville.[116] This was an enclosed community then, but fiercely if defensively loyal: few places in England at this time were more devoid of sympathy for the empress or her son. If Henry Murdac wished to be received in his cathedral city he would need to be careful; and he would need to wait, for Stephen felt under no immediate pressure to settle with him. When the bells were silenced and services curtailed within the city, under the archbishop's excommunication, Eustace came and told them to start up again.[117]

By midsummer, Stephen had returned to southern England, and Eustace soon followed him. Through the summer, and for the remainder of the year, Stephen and his son would Box and Cox, dealing with threats from old adversaries, such as Ranulf of Chester, "the men of Bedford," and Hugh Bigod.[118] They seemed to be stuck in a groove. After a hasty and undignified retreat to the west country, during which he feared for his safety, Henry was able to regroup. He gained forces from both the earl of Hereford and the earl of Gloucester, and entered "the part of England called Devon," his concern an indication that not all of the west country was under his control. Bridport he captured, but before he could make any inroads into the position of Henry de Tracy at Barnstaple, he was called back to Devizes, from where he had started out. Both the king and Eustace had been active in Wiltshire, the king actively pursuing a scorched-earth policy:

[113] JH, 324: "unusquisque enim ad adinventionis suae libitum corrupit monetae et numismatis pretium."

[114] Blackburn, in King, *Anarchy*, 182–7, provides a magisterial review of an extensive literature.

[115] Ibid., 183–4, 186–7; North, nos. 919 (Flag type), 922 (Two-Figures type, in earlier literature most commonly seen as showing the king and queen).

[116] Ibid., 184–5; North, nos. 929–33. The William of Aumale coin was unknown until it was offered for sale at St James's Auctions, London, on 3 Oct. 2005, when it was acquired by the Fitzwilliam Museum, Cambridge.

[117] JH, 324.

[118] The sole source for these events is *GS*, 216–25.

he set himself to lay waste that fair and delightful district, so full of all good things, round Salisbury; they took and plundered everything they came upon, set fire to houses and churches, and, what was a more cruel and brutal sight, fired the crops that had been reaped and stacked all over the fields, consumed and brought to nothing everything edible that they found. They raged with this bestial cruelty especially around Marlborough, they showed it also very terribly round Devizes, and they had it in mind to do the same to their adversaries all over England.[119]

The king's behaviour could be defended as standard military practice. The author gives the defence, but still he seems unsettled. Understandably so. Here was the king of England, in the heart of Wessex, the historic centre of the English monarchy, treating it as hostile territory, as though he were a raider in a foreign land. It was a radical departure for Stephen, and one born of desperation. It did, however, achieve its immediate purpose. Henry went home.

In the next eighteen months in England there was much discussion but little action. That action showed the limitation on Stephen's power caused by the arrangements the magnates had made to limit the impact of the civil war on their own position. A demonstration, which could not have been better designed to illustrate the point, occurred in the summer of 1150, and then again in the following summer, in and around the city of Worcester.[120] Stephen had granted the earldom to Waleran, count of Meulan. Waleran had been in Normandy for the best part of a decade, but still he exercised some real authority there, as is shown by a remarkable letter he sent to William de Beauchamp, "my dear son," in favour of the monks of Worcester, who also were very dear to him: "you should know that there are no monks in all of my land whom I love more dearly or in whose prayers I have greater confidence."[121] In this letter he envisages William, the local sheriff, and Robert, earl of Leicester, his brother, as joint agents of an authority that he was able to exercise at a distance. It was an authority that Stephen now sought to challenge. He attacked "this most beautiful city," firing the buildings surrounding the castle, but still the garrison under William de Beauchamp remained secure in the castle. As the king's forces retreated, having taken much booty, they plundered the countryside as they "returned home through their enemies' lands."[122] This campaign is all that is known of Stephen's actions in 1150. It underlines the point that he would

---

[119] *GS*, 220–1.

[120] The two authorities here are *GS*, 228–31, and HH, 754–7, discussed by King, "Waleran of Meulan," 173–4. The authorities differ as to chronology and in that discussion I stated that "there seem no strong grounds for preferring one to the other." Having lived with each of them a little longer, I would now follow Henry of Huntingdon, who writes within an annalistic framework, as to the chronology.

[121] Davis, "Some Documents of the Anarchy," 170–1.

[122] HH, 754–5.

deal with parts of his kingdom, now including one of his cathedral cities, as enemy territory.

In the summer of 1151 the king was back. More effort was invested in the siege, and two siege-castles built. But the king's plans were frustrated by a careful deception on the part of the earl of Leicester, who not only demolished the siege-castles but captured William de Beauchamp and "kept him in close confinement."[123] To Henry of Huntingdon the explanation of events that might have seemed confusing was simple: "this was because the said earl was brother of the count of Meulan."[124] The earl of Leicester was still the liege man of the king, though totally estranged from the royal court, but in a context in which family property was involved his relationship with the king was not a constraint on his actions. It was all just as the earl's father, himself the most able of Henry I's councillors, had foreseen in making arrangements for his twin sons: "if it should happen that they should lose their inheritance on one side of the Channel or the other, then I grant and I concede that as brothers together they should together share what remains."[125] The brothers' solidarity now seemed a threat to those who had thought of themselves as their allies. The earl of Hereford was the liege man of Duke Henry, but at some point in these events he offered his support to the king, if the king would only restore to him the castle of his ally, William de Beauchamp.[126] It is difficult to be sure of the context of an approach cast in these terms. It may indicate that the king was seen as making some ground. Roger of Hereford would certainly also have considered the threat to his own earldom posed by Robert of Leicester, who had a claim to the earldom and *comitatus* of Hereford that Stephen had acknowledged back in 1140, after Miles of Gloucester had abandoned his cause. In any event, nothing came of the approach. The king withdrew and after an interval the situation was restored, the parties doubtless more wary of each other, if that were possible.

The author of the *Gesta Stephani*, in dealing with these events, may have been a little confused in his chronology, but still he goes to the heart of the matter in seeing what happened as royal initiative putting strains on local agreements, which might break for a time, but the parties would then regroup. A fine chapter – the final chapter – in Ralph Davis's biography was entitled "The magnates' peace."[127] There was an interlocking network of individual agreements, which kept the peace in the localities, and which served as the foundation of the final peace settlement. By a careful examination of the agreements that survive, and then adding a number of marriage alliances, he produced the following diagram:

[123] *GS*, 228–9.
[124] HH, 756–7.
[125] *Regesta*, ii, no. 843.
[126] *GS*, 228–9.
[127] Davis, *Stephen*, 108–24 (diagram 110)

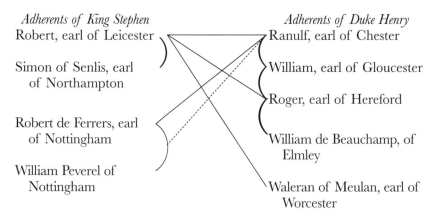

Adherents of King Stephen

Robert, earl of Leicester

Simon of Senlis, earl
of Northampton

Robert de Ferrers, earl
of Nottingham

William Peverel of
Nottingham

Adherents of Duke Henry

Ranulf, earl of Chester

William, earl of Gloucester

Roger, earl of Hereford

William de Beauchamp, of
Elmley

Waleran of Meulan, earl of
Worcester

As illustrating a network of interlocking alliances, not all of them identical in kind, but all of them reflecting reciprocal obligations, the diagram is most valuable. At its heart, however, is the concept of liege lordship, the idea that each individual supported either one side or the other in the succession dispute and that this allegiance shaped their actions and determined their alliances. In fact, as Davis pointed out, the magnates did not see the obligations of lordship as the single driving force in their lives. It was one factor only: ties of friendship, ties of family, ties of neighbourhood were no less important. No one of them was determinative.

Among the treaties of which a text survives, that concluded between the earls of Chester and Leicester has long been regarded as exemplary. "This is the agreement between earl Ranulf of Chester and Robert earl of Leicester, and the final peace and concord which was granted and arranged by them before Robert II, bishop of Lincoln and their own men."[128] At the heart of the agreement is the idea of territorial lordship that is found time and again in the charters of magnates of this period. "The earl of Leicester ought to guard the lands and goods of the earl of Chester, which are in the power of the earl of Leicester, without ill-will." Reciprocal promises were made, and so thereafter the earl of Chester promised to protect the possessions of the earl of Leicester within his territory. The charter was necessary because there were no neat divisions between such areas of power. In the north-east of Leicestershire the lands of the two earls lay side by side. Here there had been a series of disputes, which this agreement was intended to settle.[129] The area of concern is Leicestershire, defined in terms of the castles which ringed the county, which they sought to

---

[128] Original chirograph, BL Cotton MS Nero C. iii; New Palaeographical Soc., ii, no. 40 (facs.); printed, Stenton, *First Century*, 250–3 (trans.), 286–8 (text), *Chester Charters*, no. 110.

[129] On the local context, see Crouch, *Beaumont Twins*, 80–4; King, "Mountsorrel and its Region in Stephen's Reign."

make a demilitarized zone.[130] The focus of concern was the castle of Mountsorrel. As is shown by earlier agreements between the two men, the earl of Chester had renounced his proprietary rights to the castle in favour of the earl of Leicester, but he still retained rights of access:

> The earl of Leicester ought to receive earl Ranulf and his following in the borough and the baileys of Mountsorrel, as in his fee, to make war on whomsoever he wishes, and so that the earl of Leicester may not attack earl Ranulf therefrom for anything; and, if it shall be necessary for earl Ranulf, the earl of Leicester will receive him personally in the demesne castle of Mountsorrel, and so that the earl of Leicester will keep faith with earl Ranulf saving the faith due to his liege lord.[131]

The passage exemplifies the predatory lordship of which the monastic chroniclers complained, with the earl of Chester standing ready, with the connivance of a powerful neighbour, to "make war on anyone he wishes."

Yet the whole of the document shows that the power of each of the earls to behave as he liked was in practice limited. It was limited by other arrangements of this type which they had concluded earlier with other of their powerful relatives and neighbours. It was limited by the faith which they owed to their two different liege lords. And even its geographical range was limited, the mention of power as much an apology as a boast, the lands not in their power serving to define those that were, while within "their" areas individual castlemen, nominally their vassals, were able to behave much as they pleased. One castleman in Leicestershire, whose activities threatened the peace, was singled out in the agreement, clearly at the insistence of the earl of Chester. This was William de Launay, who had turned Ravenstone, "in the rugged Charnwood area of Leicestershire, into the lair of a robber-baron."[132] Ravenstone was to be destroyed, "unless earl Ranulf shall allow that it shall remain." At the time the treaty was made, this minor fortification exemplified what was becoming recognized as one of the major problems of the civil war. The Chester–Leicester agreement is unique in the emphasis it places on the control and building of castles, the need for monitoring and for severe sanctions against those who stepped out of line.

The arrangements with neighbouring magnates, if all were constructed with the care that went into the making of this document, will have been a powerful constraint on their independence also. "The earl of Leicester

---

[130] Stenton, *First Century*, 253: "Neither the earl of Chester nor the earl of Leicester ought to build any new castle between Hinckley and Coventry, nor between Hinckley and Hartshill, nor between Coventry and Donington, nor between Donington and Leicester, nor at Gotham nor at Kinoulton nor nearer, nor between Kinoulton and Belvoir, nor between Belvoir and Oakham, nor between Oakham and Rockingham nor nearer, except with the common consent of both. And if anyone shall build a castle in the aforesaid places or within the aforesaid limits, each shall aid the other without ill-will until the castle shall be destroyed."

[131] On the castle provisions, see Coulson, "The Chester–Leicester *conventio*."

[132] Crouch, *Beaumont Twins*, 81.

ought to help the earl of Chester against all men except against the earl of Leicester's liege lord and earl Simon." In any dispute between Ranulf of Chester and Simon of Senlis, Robert of Leicester would have the right to mediate, and he would become involved only if Simon (his brother-in-law) was the aggressor and refused to make restitution.[133] The two liege lords are nowhere named, but that the two men had two different liege lords was part of the dynamic of the agreement. The earl of Chester's lord was Duke Henry; the earl of Leicester's, King Stephen. The two men saw themselves as under an obligation consequent upon their fealty to offer personal service. They had to plan for a military showdown in the continuing struggle for the succession.[134] That remained the most likely way for the civil war to end. "If it be necessary for the earl of Leicester to go upon the earl of Chester with his liege lord he may not bring with him more than twenty knights, and if the earl of Leicester or those twenty knights shall take anything of the goods of the earl of Chester he will return the whole." In this document, wrote Sir Frank Stenton, the earls "speak like men to whom the rules and courtesies of feudal society are the highest law."[135] Just so. And because all references were to a shared code, some phrases in the document were shorthand. An example of this is the figure of twenty knights, which each earl promised would be the maximum force he would bring against the other. This figure was not plucked from the air. The same number, so the empress claimed, had been promised as the maximum number that Henry of Winchester would send against her if required to do so by his brother.[136] It did not represent either the military capacity of the honour, or the service due from it; rather it was a bare minimum, a figure calculated to meet the vassal's obligation to the lord, "so that he shall not lose land."[137]

The experience of such discussions was brought by the bishops to a council held in London in mid-Lent in 1151.[138] This meeting will have been in their diaries for some time, but there was a particular reason for

---

[133] It may be noted that Simon of Senlis is the first witness to *Reg. Ant.* 2, 16–17 (no. 324), in which Robert of Leicester made restitution to the previous bishop of Lincoln, Alexander, "in satisfaction of the damages inflicted by the earl or his men."

[134] A discussion of the date of the document must start from this point. It must be after 19 Dec. 1148, when Robert de Chesney was consecrated as bishop of Lincoln, and it must be before the death of Ranulf of Chester on 16 Dec. 1153. Barraclough, in his notes to *Chester Charters*, no. 110, argued that "the tenor of the agreement fits the situation in February–March 1153," but I would view it as otiose after the landing of Duke Henry in Jan. 1153. Crouch, *Stephen*, 253–4, argues for a date "closer to 1148 than 1153," and that would be my reading also.

[135] Stenton, *First Century*, 254.

[136] WM, *HN*, 110–11 and n. 261.

[137] In 1101 the count of Flanders in his agreement with Henry I promised if summoned by the French king into England to bring with him only "tam paruam fortitudinem hominum quam minorem poterit, ita tamen ne inde feodum suum . . . forisfaciat," and twenty knights were specified as such a token force: *English Diplomatic Documents* 1, 1–4 (no. 1); for discussion, Strickland, *War*, 236–8.

[138] *Councils and Synods*, 821–6 (no. 150).

this summons, for Archbishop Theobald was now papal legate.[139] It was an office that he had long sought and which he might have received earlier, had not the papal court been resident in northern France for more than two years (1146–8), allowing Eugenius III to deal directly with English affairs. This was the first legatine council that had been held since 1143. It took place in the presence of "King Stephen and his son Eustace and the magnates of England."[140] It was intended, so the preamble stated, to "seek out new remedies" for the diseases of the body politic. It continued:

> And so we ordain that the church and ecclesiastical possessions should remain free from works and exactions that are popularly called *tenserie* or tallages, concerning which no one shall presume to trouble them thereafter . . . only those works owing to the king are not prohibited, if they are specifically mentioned by a royal mandate.

The king at least will have had no quarrel with that, and nor with the canon which followed: "Since the churches throughout England have been grievously afflicted and destroyed on account of pleas that pertain to the crown, we do not wish that they should respond to barons in respect of such pleas." The crown and its customs are here the touchstone of legitimacy. The canons themselves are condensed, reading more as headings for discussion than decisions reached after debate. This could be because those involved were familiar with the issues. They were dealing with local cases in these terms. So too when they came to the third of the canons: those who had been bound by the chains of anathema for attacking and violating the possessions of the churches were not to be released until what had been taken away was restored in full, "or if the church that has suffered damage is satisfied that full restitution will be made in forty days." This represents a marked change from the equivalent provisions in 1143, the last legatine council of Henry of Winchester. In place of the reservation of quite minor offences to the bishops and even the pope, now the local church is given discretion to deal with the offender and come to terms. This is a legatine council, but of a new type, for at its heart lay the principle of subsidiarity.

As the council deliberated, the thoughts of Stephen and his son might well have drifted away from the bishops present and on to the archbishop of York, Henry Murdac, who was then, like so many of the English bishops before him, on his way to Rome. He had been sent as a royal ambassador, "on the business of the king and realm, of which the chief matter was that the king's son Eustace might be established by papal authority as heir to the throne."[141] Specifically, the point of this legation was to gain papal sanction for the coronation of Eustace in his father's lifetime. This was Capetian custom. It had been a key feature in preserving the stability of the dynasty,

---

[139] Ibid., 820–1 (no. 149), seeing the grant of the legation as having been made "probably in the early months of 1150."

[140] HH, 756–7.

[141] JH, 325–6.

and in the middle of a damaging civil war caused by a disputed succession it can only have seemed advantageous not just to the king and the potential heir but to their supporters and to some who wanted peace at whatever cost. Certainly we are told that it was the view of the royal court that Eustace should be crowned.[142] And so it was only after a private audience with Eustace himself that Henry Murdac was allowed access to his cathedral city and installed "with great pomp" on 25 January 1151. He set off south very soon thereafter, crossed the Channel, and was at Rome by Easter.[143]

John of Salisbury, whose *Memoirs of the Papal Court* are so vivid when he writes from direct experience, has no description of what happened when the king's request for the coronation of Eustace was discussed. A letter of his, however, suggests there was some support for the king's position, for Gregory, cardinal of St Angelo, reportedly spoke in his favour.[144] What came back, however, was a refusal. Henry of Huntingdon says that "it was understood that this was because Stephen had seized the kingdom contrary to the oath."[145] In fact, as might have been expected, a diplomatic mission came back with a diplomatic answer. John of Salisbury explains that there had been division earlier in the papal court, in 1139, when Cardinal Guy de Castello had opposed the confirmation of Stephen's title. In 1143 he became pope, as Celestine II, at which point:

he wrote to lord Theobald, archbishop of Canterbury, forbidding him to allow any change to be made in the English kingdom in the matter of the crown, for that matter was in dispute and so any claim for the transfer of the right was to be refused. His successors popes Lucius and Eugenius repeated the same prohibition. So it came about that the archbishop of York, as I was saying, could do nothing to further the coronation of Eustace.[146]

So this was not a new request.[147] The pope could cite precedent. And the refusal could be glossed in a way that saved face. It was not a decision by the papacy or the English Church to withdraw its support for the king. The churchmen had got their fingers very badly burnt in attempting to take the

---

[142] *Correspondence of Thomas Becket*, i, no. 153: "hoc fieri oportere decreuerat curia euis." An astrologer, possibly based in London, predicted that the king would soon force the issue: North, "Some Norman Horoscopes," 151 ("et iudicamus regem barones suos ad humagium filii sui compellere, et quid machinari quod perpetrare non poterit sine astrologo," dated to 16 Sept. 1151: see plate 23); Burnett, *Introduction of Arabic Learning*, 46–7 and n. 116.

[143] JH, 325–6.

[144] *Correspondence of Thomas Becket*, i, no. 170, dating from "after 2 July 1168." He is allowed the luxury of foreseeing "this tyranny," i.e. Henry II's assault on church liberties and persecution of Thomas Becket. Gregory was a friend of Henry of Winchester: JS, *HP*, 78.

[145] HH, 758–9.

[146] JS, *HP*, 85–6.

[147] *Correspondence of Thomas Becket*, i, no. 153, dating from "? December 1167," very soon after the date now suggested for the writing of the *Historia Pontificalis*: "prohibitionis apostolice *solutionem* a domino papa Eugenio impetrarent."

political initiative in 1141. On no account would they make the same mistake again. Rather they played for time. They said, which was unanswerable, that it was not the custom of the realm of England – customs to which the king referred repeatedly in his own dealings with the Church – to crown a son in the father's lifetime. The churchmen refused to set a precedent, while the question of the right to the succession, as distinct from Stephen's own rights of occupancy, remained in dispute. This was because the claims of Henry remained active. That point also was unanswerable.

Stephen and his court will not have been pleased to learn of the attitude of the papal curia. But it was the best part of a year later – during Easter week 1152 – before they decided to make an issue of it. Eustace was designated as Stephen's successor and oaths were sworn to him "by a good number of the nobles of England."[148] They then required the archbishop and the other bishops "to anoint Eustace as king and confirm him with their blessing." Again they were refused. "Consumed with deep chagrin and boiling with rage, father and son ordered them all to be shut up in a particular building, and putting them under strong coercion, urged them to do what they demanded."[149] Theobald escaped, according to another account, across the Thames, hotly pursued by a body of armed knights.[150] Peace was eventually made, though not before Archbishop Theobald had once again gone into exile in Flanders.[151] Some of the circumstantial detail in these accounts may be suspect, for the detention of "the bishops" in 1151 was seen as following the precedent set by the imprisonment of "the bishops" in 1139,[152] while the knights pursuing Theobald seem to prefigure the murderers of Thomas Becket. But the king's anger is not to be doubted,[153] and it might have lasted longer had he not been shocked out of it by a personal tragedy.

Queen Matilda died at Hedingham in Essex, the *caput* of Aubrey de Vere (see plate 15),[154] on 3 May 1152.[155] We know nothing of her illness,

---

[148] Annals of St Augustine's, Canterbury, s.a. 1152, *UGQ*, 82: "Hoc quoque anno adjurata est Anglia Eustachio filio regis Stephani a nonnullis nobilibus regni apud Westmonasterium 8 idus Aprilis" (6 Apr. 1152, the first Sunday after Easter); Waverley Annals, s.a. 1152, in *Ann. Mon.*, ii. 234: "apud Londoniam Eustachio filio Regis Stephani fide et jusjurando universi comites atque barones Anglie se subdiderunt."

[149] HH, 758–9.

[150] *Vita Theobaldi*, in *PL* 150, col. 734; Saltman, *Theobald*, 38.

[151] Gervase, i. 150–1, is the only source for the exile.

[152] HH, 758–9: "in domo quadam," going on to recall the imprisonment of two of the bishops in 1139.

[153] Ibid.: "intimo igitur dolore decoctus et ira nimia feruescens"; Gervase, i. 150 (glossing Henry of Huntingdon): "vehementer irati."

[154] Fernie, *Architecture*, 80–1: "building on this lavish and extravagent scale suggests an almost royal opulence."

[155] Place and date are given in an English text of the chronicle of Robert of Torigni: Torigni, xli, 166; date confirmed by the Lincoln obituary list, 157; *Holyrood*, s.a. 1152; Annals of St Augustine's, Canterbury, s.a. 1152, *UGQ*, 82; *Vita Theobaldi*, *PL* 150, col. 734 ("hebdomada enim ante Rogationes finem vivendi et regnandi regina subiit").

only that she was comforted for three days by Ralph, prior of Holy Trinity, Aldgate, who had been nominated to this office by Theobald in person.[156] She was buried at Faversham.[157] The loss to Stephen was severe, for the queen had not just been the partner in the raising of a family, but estate manager, peacemaker, and a point of reference in all his work. Confined increasingly to south-east England in the 1140s, the king would have enjoyed a domesticity unusual perhaps among rulers of the day. The loss to their son Eustace, whose birth they had awaited so eagerly, was no less severe. The queen's cultivation of Archbishop Theobald on her son's behalf is unmistakable, and although underpinned by a genuine piety it had a political purpose also. With the death of the queen, Eustace lost his best advocate. And earlier in the year there had been another significant loss to the family with the death of Theobald, count of Blois.[158]

If Eugenius III's refusal to allow the coronation of Eustace, a decision confirmed at Easter 1151, only provoked a confrontation a year later, after Easter 1152, the reason is to be found in events in northern France in the intervening period. Henry of Anjou, whose designs on the crown these manoeuvrings were intended to thwart, had returned to Normandy in January 1150, and when he did so he was invested as duke of Normandy. He had been regarded as duke since the time of his knighting at Carlisle at Whitsun 1149, if not before. The administration of Geoffrey of Anjou, as duke of Normandy, had been in the nature of a regency. The investiture "shows plainly that the count of Anjou had won and held Normandy for his son and not for himself."[159] Henry's own occupation of the duchy would cause problems, or rather compound problems,[160] in the relationship of the Angevins with the king of France. The investiture of the duchy had taken place without reference to, or permission from, the king of France, who had returned from crusade in November 1149. This was in contrast to events in 1144. These rights of overlordship were tenaciously defended by the Capetians as a matter of principle, and this particular

[156] *Cart. Aldgate*, 232. Charters in favour of the priory, issued at Hedingham, are *Regesta*, iii, nos. 503 (of the queen, also printed in *Book of Seals*, no. 424), 504 (of the king). It is suggested that the grant which they record was made on the queen's deathbed: "may safely be ascribed to," *Book of Seals*, no. 424; "possibly," *Regesta*, iii, no. 503. Against this attribution: (i) the king's confirmation nowhere mentions prayers for the queen's soul; (ii) the phrase he uses of her grant – "quod ipsa eis concessit coram me" – seems inappropriate for a deathbed grant; (iii) and there are no clergy present. The queen was not a lady to leave such matters to the last moment.
[157] JH, 327; Gervase, i. 151; *Cart. Aldgate*, 232; Dunstable Annals, in *Ann. Mon.* iii. 16 ("unde humiliatus est rex Stephanus"). The death is noted additionally in *Melrose*, s.a. 1152, but nowhere mentioned in either Henry of Huntingdon or *Gesta Stephani*, the contemporary "southern" chronicles.
[158] Torigni, 164; Annals of St Augustine's, Canterbury, *UGQ*, 82; *Chronique de Sens*, 200–1 ("famosus in nostro seculo").
[159] Haskins, 130–5 (quotation 131).
[160] On other tensions between Angevins and Capetians at this time see Grant, *Suger*, 283–6; Thompson, *Power and Border Lordship*, 89–90; Power, *Norman Frontier*, 394–6.

succession was significant because it impacted on the rights of Eustace, who was Louis VII's brother-in-law. "Thus," says Robert of Torigni, taking these points as read:

> a dispute having originated between the king and the duke, the former, accompanied by Eustace, the son of king Stephen, marched into Normandy with a large army, and sat down before the castle of Arques. On the other side was Henry, duke of Normandy, with a large army of the men of Normandy, Anjou, and Brittany; but the leaders of the army being men of more mature age and discretion, did not permit him to come into a collision with the king his lord, unless he should have received from him a greater injury than he had already experienced.[161]

These events were fixed in the chronicler's mind by events at his birthplace, Torigni-sur-Vire, which Duke Henry was besieging. No reason for this dispute is given, but granted that the lord of Torigni was one of the sons of Robert of Gloucester, we may suspect that the disloyalty of one son had called into question the loyalty of another.[162] When the king came into Normandy that siege was raised.

These events took place some time in 1150. They occur as a "flashback" in the chronicle, to help provide a context for events in August 1151, when the dispute moved quickly to a resolution. It started with another face-off. The French king mustered an army "on the banks of the Seine, between Meulan and Mantes." On learning of this Geoffrey of Anjou and Henry of Normandy "sat down on the borders of the duchy of Normandy to defend their own."[163] This was a serious challenge to Henry, but still there was an element of ritual in the behaviour of both sides. The king went to the frontiers of his territory but not beyond them. Negotiations for peace had being going on for several months. After Louis had suffered what was possibly a diplomatic illness, it was arranged that Henry's homage for Normandy would be accepted. The king exacted his price. The homage was performed in Paris, at the Capetian court, not on the borders of the duchy. The Norman Vexin, the lands between the rivers Epte and Andelle, would remain under the control of the French crown.[164] Even so, father and son were "rejoicing" when they set off from Paris,[165] a sentiment last recorded of this family when the empress had received news of Stephen's capture at the battle of Lincoln. They saw the event as marking a significant stage in the capture of power. Henry demonstrated this sense, a desire to seize the moment, by immediately summoning the baronage of Normandy to cross over with him to England. The place was Lisieux.

---

[161] Torigni, 161.
[162] *GND*, ii. 248–9.
[163] Torigni, 162: "in margine ducatus Normanniae sua defensuri consederunt."
[164] "Histoire du roi Louis VII," ed. Molinier, 161–2.
[165] Torigni, 162: "laeti discessissent."

Arnulf the bishop of Lisieux had been instrumental in arranging the peace with Louis, and he would now become the first administrative officer of Normandy, a position that his uncle had previously occupied.[166]

There was a lot to arrange before an invasion of England could be mounted and it was now late in the year but Henry might well have moved to the Channel and sailed to England had he not been unavoidably detained. What detained him was the death of his father. Geoffrey died on 14 September 1151 at the castle of St Germain-en-Laye. He was taken to Le Mans and buried in the cathedral church of St Julien. Henry succeeded to the county of Anjou as his father's nominated successor, while the second son, Geoffrey, received four castles.[167] This sudden accretion of power gave Henry fresh responsibilities, which detained him in Anjou. It also set up fresh tensions. His expectations seemed inequitable to his younger brothers, and it would later be claimed that a promise had been made to Geoffrey, the elder of them, that Anjou would be resigned to him should Henry become king of England.[168] The delay alarmed his supporters in England, who felt themselves to be under increasing pressure from the king's forces. In Lent 1152 Henry's uncle, Reginald, earl of Cornwall, crossed the Channel to deliver a personal appeal; and on Low Sunday the magnates of Normandy assembled again at Lisieux, to discuss the expedition into England.[169] On that very day, Stephen and his courtiers, well aware of these developments in Normandy,[170] summoned the bishops of England to London, hoping to persuade – and if not to coerce – them into crowning Eustace.

But Henry did not sail to England in 1152. Again he was delayed. This time by his own marriage. Everything happened very suddenly. On the pretext of consanguinity the marriage between the king and queen of France was dissolved. The divorce was pronounced during Lent by a church council meeting at Beaugency, first their relatives, and then the king and queen in person, swearing that they were related within the prohibited decrees.[171] No more formality was required for the union to be dissolved. The ex-queen returned to her home lands of Poitou, escaping, so it was said, more than one suitor who was lying in wait for her. Within

---

[166] *Letters of Arnulf of Lisieux*, xxvii–xxix.

[167] Torigni, 162–3. Chinon, Loudun, and Mirebeau are named in Newburgh, i. 113.

[168] Torigni, 165; Newburgh, i. 112–14. Hollister and Keefe, "The Making of the Angevin Empire," 265–6, take these sources as evidence that "Geoffrey le Bel by no means intended a permanent union of the two provinces [of Normandy and Anjou]," and this case is argued more fully in Keefe, "Geoffrey Plantagenet's Will and the Angevin Succession."

[169] Torigni, 164. *GS*, 228–31, for the situation in England.

[170] Gervase, i. 150, makes a connection between Henry's increasing strength and Stephen's increasing desperation: "rex autem S., novi ducis Normanniae et Aquitaniae et comitis Andegaviae H. probitatem simul et potentiam licet adolescentis valde suspectam habens, de successione regni Anglicani sollicitus erat."

[171] "Histoire du roi Louis VII," ed. Molinier, 163–4. Hugh, archbishop of Rouen, was among those present.

two months, "either suddenly or by design," as Robert of Torigni put it, she was married to Henry, count of Anjou and duke of Normandy.[172] This was about Whitsuntide, 18 May 1152. At the time, so far as can be judged, little was known in England about the ex-queen of France, Eleanor of Aquitaine. She had been married in July 1137, just a few days before her husband became king of France; to the Anglo-Norman chroniclers she was the heiress, unnamed, who had brought the great province of Aquitaine under the control of the Capetians, "which they were not known to have had since the days of Charlemagne."[173] She had accompanied Louis on the Second Crusade, and during that time "things were said about what happened there that had best been left unsaid."[174] John of Salisbury was not so fastidious; she was seen as having become much too closely involved with her uncle, Raymond, prince of Antioch: "his constant, indeed almost continuous, conversation with her aroused the king's suspicions."[175] These stories may already have circulated in England, and so also the story that the pope had blessed them in their marriage-bed on their return from crusade.[176] It was there, in their conjugal relations, that the story lay. In fifteen years of marriage the union had produced only two children, both of them girls, aged seven years and eighteen months respectively at the time of the divorce. In the absence of a male heir, divorce had become inevitable. The clergy seemed somewhat embarrassed but still were clear where their duty to the kingdom lay. You did not need to look far to see the dangers which might occur in even the strongest monarchies for the lack of a legitimate heir. The divorced parties would go on to marry new partners no less closely related to them.[177]

When Louis of France learned the name of Eleanor's new husband he was extremely angry.[178] He could not claim, as he could in his dealings with the dukes of Normandy, that he had to be consulted in the marriage, for the dukes of Aquitaine were not his vassals. But the prospects of his daughters were threatened by this second marriage, since any sons that Eleanor had with her new husband would take precedence over them. And Henry's marriage did not just represent an accretion of territory to a man already over-blessed: it changed the balance of power in France. It gave him the resources of a rich duchy and it meant that what later historians have termed "the Angevin empire" was clearly configured in the eyes

---

[172] Torigni, 165: "sive repentino sive premeditato consilio."

[173] WM, *HN*, 20–1: "in propriu dominatu Francorum reges non habuisse noscuntur"; there is a very simular formulation in OV vi. 490–1.

[174] Gervase, i. 149: "ex quibusdam forte que melius tacenda sunt que in illa peregrinatione contigerunt."

[175] JS, *HP*, 52–3. Jane Martindale points out that these rumours may have fed on incomprehension, for the queen's conversations with her uncle will most likely have been conducted in the *langue d'oc* and so "were perhaps not comprehensible to northerners": Martindale, "Eleanor of Aquitaine."

[176] Ibid., 61–2. This was in Oct. 1149.

[177] Bouchard, "The Uses of Consanguinity," 230–1.

of contemporaries. The list of those alarmed by the prospect was a long one and the French king brought them together: Eustace, the son of the king of England; Henry, count of Champagne, the nephew of the king of England; Robert, count of the Perche, the brother of the king of France; and Geoffrey of Anjou, the second of the empress's three sons. All save Geoffrey, who remained in Anjou, gathered at Neufmarché and laid siege to the castle. Henry, who had summoned an army to Barfleur on 24 June, ready to cross to England, was forced once more to postpone his expedition. It was a dangerous time for Henry, and no one at the time would bet on his success: "Nearly all of the Normans now thought that duke Henry would rapidly lose all of his possessions."[179] It is an arresting phrase, a political judgement quite devoid of any benefit of hindsight. Duke Henry was in trouble. King Stephen might yet pass on his kingdom to his son and heir.

[178] Torigni, 165: "commotus est contra eundem ducem."
[179] Ibid., 165–6: "omnes fere Normanni existimabant [dux] omnem terram suam in brevi amissurum."

Chapter 9

BLESSED ARE THE PEACEMAKERS

And so it came to pass, rather surprisingly, that the civil war was not concluded by force of arms. The two sides came to an agreement. The archbishop of Canterbury was closely involved in the discussions and was widely trusted; the bishop of Winchester took a close interest also. They were backed up by the other bishops, but what was still needed was the support of the great men, and counsel, and consensus.[1]

1153 was a decisive year. It was decisive in the history not just of England but of the British Isles, in the history not just of Normandy but of France. It was decisive in terms of a dynasty that might have been, that of Stephen and his sons; and of a dynasty in course of foundation, from the union of Henry of Anjou and Eleanor of Aquitaine. It was a decisive year for peace. That peace the two rival dynasties accepted rather than welcomed. It was forced on them by the political community of England. This made 1153 a year of bluster and hard talking, of rhetoric and accommodation. Some made peace because they had no alternative. Some made peace because they had made peace work in their own communities, and they found that the principles on which they made peace were good for the nation as a whole. What came to be agreed, as was inevitable after a long conflict, was not just a peace settlement but a peace process. It was the process which ensured that the settlement stuck. It is a remarkable story.

It started with Henry's arrival in England at Epiphany, 6 January 1153, or soon thereafter.[2] It was an auspicious day, for it was said that immediately on landing he sought out a church, to hear mass or listen to the word of the Lord, "or rather say his prayers in the manner of military men." There a clerk intoned the Introit. "See, he comes, our Lord and Ruler, armed with royal power and dominion." And he went on: "Grant to the king, O God, your own skill in judgement; to the inheritor of a throne, may he be just, as you are just."[3] These indeed, so it must have appeared, were texts for the times. Henry had come to claim his inheritance, the

---

[1] A loose translation from Diceto, i. 296.

[2] Gervase, i. 151 has Epiphany Day; Torigni, 171 has within the octave of the feast; while the Annals of St Augustine's, Canterbury, give a precise day within the octave, namely 11 Jan.: *UGQ*, 82.

[3] Gervase, i. 151–2; the readings in the Introit from Mal. 3 : 1, Ps. 71 : 1, in the translation of R. A. Knox from my *Roman Missal* (London, 1949), 64.

throne of England. Had he followed the route familiar to him from his earlier visits then he would have landed at Wareham in Dorset and travelled on to Devizes in Wiltshire. As his continued occupancy of Devizes would be the subject of renewed protest by the local bishop, it is safe to place Henry there for a time, during which he made contact with his chief supporters.

It was agreed that Henry should then go north from Devizes, to another of the castles formerly held by Roger of Salisbury, which he had erected within the precincts of Malmesbury Abbey. This was garrisoned by royal forces and there had been continued skirmishing here for some time.[4] Henry's intention now was to seek a confrontation. Stephen mustered at Cirencester just a few miles to the north.[5] Both king and duke had their core supporters with them. The king was accompanied by two earls, William d'Aubigny and Simon of Senlis, along with Richard de Lucy, William de Chesney, and William Martel.[6] It is not clear whether either of the king's sons was with him at this point.[7] The duke's support more than matched the king's in terms of men of rank, for he could call on four earls, Reginald of Cornwall, Roger of Hereford, William of Gloucester, and Patrick of Salisbury, along with experienced household officers from both England and Normandy.[8] These men did not want to miss the action, but the action they had in mind was not the action which their leaders looked for. They did not wish to miss the opportunity of privileged access to what was happening behind the scenes. Such action as there was at Malmesbury centred on the castle, which was defended by a royal garrison under the command of Jordan, who may have been a stipendiary soldier.[9] The castle was surrendered to the duke after Jordan had been allowed to go the king to seek help. According to the royalist side it was agreed that after the surrender the castle would be destroyed.[10] There was no fighting. The weather was dreadful, with "torrential rain and snow," and men and animals died in their hundreds.[11] These conditions favoured the duke: "whereas he and his men had the storm at their backs, it was in the faces of the king and his men, with the result that they could neither hold up

[4] GS, 170–3, 178–9; GF Letters, no. 35. In a bull of 30 Mar. 1151 the pope asked for action to be taken against various castellans who were injuring the monastery of Malmesbury: JL, no. 9467; Registrum Malmesburiense, i. 381.

[5] The place is given in Gervase, i. 152.

[6] These names are taken from Regesta, iii, no. 192, for Cirencester Abbey, which can be dated to between May 1152 and Aug. 1153, and was probably issued during this campaign.

[7] GS, 230–1 says that Eustace followed soon after Duke Henry crossed to England; Newburgh, i. 89, says that Eustace was present at Malmesbury.

[8] The officers were: Manasser Bisset, steward; Robert de Courcy, steward; Humphrey de Bohun, steward; Richard du Hommet, constable; John Fitz Gilbert, marshal. These names are taken from Regesta, iii, no. 180, for Ranulf, earl of Chester, issued by Duke Henry at Devizes.

[9] HH, 762–3, and GS, 232–3, both give the name but do not otherwise identify him.

[10] GS, 232–3.

[11] Gervase, i. 152; HH, 764–5.

their weapons nor handle their spears which were dripping with water."[12] In truth, no one wanted to fight. They wanted an agreed settlement to the succession dispute. This, behind the scenes, is what was now worked out.

In the weeks after the stand-off at Malmesbury, Henry went out of his way to be accommodating. In actions and words he was working towards a final settlement that would allow him *ius suum*, the rights which he claimed to the English crown. On 9 April 1153, ten days before Easter, he rode out to Stockbridge in Hampshire.[13] There his uncle, Robert of Gloucester, had been captured after "the rout of Winchester" in August 1141. It was a neutral place, offering Henry protection from ambush and the clergy some protection from imputations of treachery.[14] Riding out, possibly from Ludgershall, came Henry and his followers, the earls of Cornwall, Gloucester, and Salisbury, along with John the Marshal, Robert of Dunstanville, and William Fitz Hamo. Coming out from Winchester were the heavyweights of the English hierarchy, the archbishop of Canterbury, and the bishops of Winchester, Salisbury, Bath, and Chichester. These are men whom we have seen not just active in working for peace but with the ideas of the peace very clearly worked out. The declared business of the meeting was a further attempt to restore the castle of Devizes to the diocese of Salisbury. It was accepted that "the count," i.e. Duke Henry, should hold the castle for three years. If within that time he should have recovered his right, then he would immediately restore the castle, under terms to be negotiated with the bishops; and at the end of that time, in any event, the diocese would get it back. Henry offered recompense for damages, £10 of land immediately and a further £10 when he should have recovered his right. Each party to the agreement, Henry on the one side and the bishop of Salisbury on the other, swore to abide by its terms "in the hands of" Archbishop Theobald. In the short term it was Henry who gained most. Here, talking ostensibly about a single castle whose status was not to be changed, are to be found the leaders of Duke Henry's party and the leaders of the English episcopate. In riding out to meet him the bishops went a long way to accepting the right to the crown which Henry asserted. And yet there were limits to how far they would come at this time. They would not withdraw their fealty to the king. They would not welcome the duke coming to them and expecting to be received within their cathedral cities. They would not attend his court.[15] This they will have said.

---

[12] HH, 764–5.

[13] The date is given in the memorandum of their discussions contained in *Regesta*, iii, no. 796, a charter of Duke Henry given "ad vadum de Stocbrigge." It is not in the itinerary of the duke printed ibid., xlvii.

[14] The distances from Stockbridge are: Winchester, 8 miles; Ludgersall, 12 miles; Salisbury, 14 miles. Ludgershall and then Devizes had been the empress's route to safety after the rout of Winchester in 1141.

[15] This suggestion is made using the evidence of Henry's itinerary, of which there is a useful map in Davis, *Stephen*, 116, and *GF Letters*, nos. 104–6, which show the bishop sending apologies for meetings of the duke's court on the first Sunday in Lent (8 Mar. 1153), and on Palm Sunday (12 Apr.: on 9 Apr. the duke had been at Stockbridge).

What they would do was use their best efforts to work towards a consensus, one which the protagonists and the political community would accept.[16]

In establishing the consensus the lay magnates would supply the driving force. Even as the two sides confronted one another at Malmesbury, it was said, the king had seen his support slipping away: "he noticed that some of his leading barons were slack and very casual in their service and had already sent envoys by stealth and made a compact with the duke."[17] The one magnate mentioned was the earl of Leicester. His move, from being a nominal supporter of the king to having an active role as one of the chief counsellors of the duke, was among the chief news stories of the spring of 1153: "he started to take the duke's side and for some time supplied him with resources."[18] He may well have offered resources of men and money, but what was also needed was steady counsel, a good head for detail and the capacity to take a broad view: in a word, statesmanship. Robert of Leicester had it. On three distinct occasions during the period of civil war – the first regarding the grants of earldoms and counties in the period 1138–41; the second the formulating of the terms of what Ralph Davis termed "the magnates' peace" in the late 1140s; and now the making of a national peace in 1153 – where the historian has a range of texts to evaluate, it is the document perhaps drafted for but most certainly scrutinized by Robert of Leicester that proves to be exemplary.[19] In the second of these documents, the agreement between the earls of Chester and Leicester, the two men had looked to a time when they might have to fight for, or at least supply forces to, different liege lords. In arrangements that they made with Duke Henry, shortly after his arrival in 1153, they ensured that they would not. These arrangements are recorded in charters issued by the duke, two documents of great interest, the more valuable since they survive as originals.

The first of these was issued for the earl of Chester.[20] It seems old-fashioned, in that Henry was setting his seal to a long list of Ranulf's territorial claims. When it is compared with the equivalent grant by the king a decade before, however, two main differences are noteworthy. The first is that it starts with the Norman lands of the earldom of Chester. What Stephen earlier could only promise the duke now could deliver. His grants took immediate effect and were set out in detail: they included the castle of Vire, Barfleur with its *banlieue*, and extensive liberties within the

---

[16] Diceto, i. 296.

[17] *GS*, 232–3

[18] *GS*, 234–5; Gervase, i. 152–3: "cepit partem ducis fovere eique per aliquot tempus necessaria ministrare."

[19] The texts here are: (i) *Regesta*, iii, no. 437 (the grant of the *comitatus* of Hereford in 1140); (ii) Stenton, *First Century*, 286–8 (the Chester–Leicester *convencio*); (iii) *Regesta*, iii, nos. 438–9 (charters of Duke Henry in 1153). Note also his charter of war reparations in favour of the diocese of Lincoln, dating from no later than 1147, and so starting to set what would become a trend: *Reg. Ant.* 2, 16–17 (no. 324).

[20] *Regesta*, iii, no. 180.

Avranchin. To men such as Earl Ranulf, the opportunity to regain Norman estates that had been lost was not to be gainsaid. It was Henry's trump card. At the same time – and this is the second point of difference between Stephen's grant last confirmed in 1146 and Henry's of 1153 – the later charter is careful to note the need for judicial process before some of the grants could take effect. Belvoir had been granted by Stephen uncon-ditionally; Henry said that he would "do right" to Ranulf in respect of his claim to hold it by inheritance.[21] He granted the castle and the town of Nottingham, and the whole fee of William Peverel, "unless in the duke's court he could defend himself against charges of treachery."[22] Another estate was reserved for the earl, in respect of which two named claimants would have priority, if the men concerned were to come to terms with the duke. The second of those named was Earl Simon of Senlis: few men were so closely identified with Stephen's cause, yet he may have "sent envoys" and the duke would not refuse his homage were it to be offered. The grant of the *comitatus* of Stafford followed best practice in reserving the rights of the most important men of the shire, the tenants-in-chief of the crown, to hold in just these terms, directly of the king. In this respect Henry's clerk, *magister* Ralph, who drafted this charter, showed himself well aware of the usage of the English chancery.[23] The address, however, is distinctive. While the king's charters were characteristically addressed to "all his faithful men French and English in the whole of England," the duke's charters addressed "all his friends and faithful men both Norman and English": the reference to "friends" is new, as is the specific reference to "Normans." In the circumstances these cannot be casual changes. The duke was reaching out for support. He knew only too well, despite the assurances of Gilbert Foliot, that he was very far from being "the lord of the greater part of England."[24]

Henry spent some time in the late winter and early spring of 1153 in the west country, at Devizes, at Bristol, and at Gloucester, firmly within the area where his lordship was secure. At Bristol he appears at his most confident and expansive. He had spent a year here, in 1143, "instructed in the first elements of learning and good behaviour," alongside the younger sons of Robert, earl of Gloucester;[25] he could now thank the canons of St Augustine's, Bristol, for their sustaining support. He confirmed their

---

[21] Ibid.: "de Belvario tenebo ei rectum quam citius potero sicut de sua hereditate."

[22] Ibid.: "nisi poterit se dirationare in mea curia *de scelere et traditione*"; the same *phrase* is found in the empress's charter (M1) for Geoffrey de Mandeville, *Regesta*, iii, no. 274. On these charges, see below, p. 296 n. 119.

[23] This is *scriptor* xxiii, who in the next reign is found as "magister Radulfus clericus domini regis": Bishop, *Scriptores Regis*, 26, 30, plate xxiii; *Regesta*, iii, xxxv; iv, plates xl(a), xli; *Facsimiles of Charters in the British Mueseum*, no. 44. *Regesta*, iii, nos. 104, 180, 339, 379, 459 are in the hand of *scriptor* xxiii, while additionally nos. 44, 81, 90, 321, 362a, 458, 491, 492, 582, 837, 840, 962, which survive only in copies, also show his distinctive style. Here is one of the draughtsmen, if not the architects, of the peace.

[24] *GF Letters*, no. 104: "regni Anglorum pro magna portione domno."

[25] *MTB*, iii. 104–5.

lands and made grants of rents, £10 immediately and a further £10 "when by the grace of God I shall have acquired my inheritance."[26] At Bristol also, from one of the prominent burgesses, he gained much-needed financial help. This was Robert Fitz Harding. A man already closely linked with the local families who now stood around the duke of Normandy, Robert was given a great estate at Berkeley, with magnate privileges, a castle, a market, and a mint. When this transaction was fully complete he paid 500 marks by way of a relief.[27] The lands for which Robert Fitz Harding offered so handsome a consideration were not Henry's to give. They were acquired by means of a settlement upon the marriage of the son and heir of Robert and the eldest daughter of Roger of Berkeley. That marriage is recorded in an agreement between the two families. The record makes it very clear that a marriage was a business proposition, for the boys on the one side and the girls on the other might be substituted if the named children were to die. "The treaty which was drawn up in Robert Fitz Harding's house in Bristol was enacted in Henry's presence and with his consent, and both parties made Henry security for the agreement."[28] It would be easy to underestimate the significance of transactions of this kind. Henry was a young man, impatient to secure his right, yet in the house of one of his backers he was completely at home, sure in his role, the model of good lordship.[29]

Henry's accessibility was to be a feature of his success. One of those who sought him out at Bristol, doubtless after an exchange via messengers, was Robert, the eldest son of Robert, earl of Leicester. He was granted the English lands of the honour of Leicester as his father and his grandfather had held them. But, as had been the case also with the earl of Chester, it was the Norman lands that provided the bait: the honour of Breteuil, as William of Breteuil had held it, the honour of Pacy, as William of Pacy had held it, and the stewardship of England and Normandy were all granted to him.[30] It is clear that the son came to terms with the duke before his father the earl did so. Such an arrangement was unusual, but in

---

[26] *Regesta*, iii, no. 126: "cum hereditatem meam dei gratia adquisitus fuero"; he had made exactly the same offer to the bishop of Salisbury, ibid., no. 796, "quam cito ius suum recuperaverit sibi iure possidendas."

[27] The charters are *Regesta*, iii, nos. 309–10 (for Robert), 999 (for his son, Maurice). On the authenticity of this archive see Patterson, "*Acta* of Henry Fitz Empress in Berkeley Castle"; Holt, "1153," in King, *Anarchy*, 294 n. 15, 305 and n. 58; Vincent, "New Charters of Henry Plantagenet," no. 9 (Henry Hose). I offer these *acta* no other warranty other than that I believe them to be good as evidence for the exercise of Duke Henry's lordship in 1153.

[28] Patterson, "Robert Fitz Harding," 113; *Descriptive Catalogue of Charters at Berkeley Castle*, no. 4: "has pactiones affidaverunt Rodbertus filius Hardingi et Rogerus de Berckelai tenere et servare sine fallacia et dolo et posuerunt dominum Henricum ducem obsidem et justiciam inter se de servandis his pactionibus."

[29] There is an admirable treatment of Henry's *acta*, from this perspective, in White, *Restoration and Reform*, 46–50.

[30] *Regesta*, iii, no. 438.

the circumstances of 1153 it had advantages for both parties. It allowed the earl to keep his distance. It allowed the duke to set out what he would, and what he would not, accept as authority for the holding of lands in England. The grant to the earl's son took title back to the death of his grandfather, Robert of Meulan, in 1118. The earl, with his son's title secure, could then negotiate his own terms. He corrected with some care the charter which his son and his minders had brought back, and may have reprimanded the clerk responsible.[31] He obtained from the duke confirmation of all the lands which he held on Henry I's death. He made no claim, however, in respect of any grants that had been made to him by Stephen. Duke Henry claimed his succession as a matter of right. A variety of phrases reflected that belief in his charters, but the implication of all of them was the same. If King Stephen had no title to rule then by the same token he had no title to make grants to others. This was a major issue in 1153. All who came into contact with Henry would need to pay attention to the small print, as Robert of Leicester was well accustomed to doing.

The earl of Leicester may have come to Gloucester around Eastertide.[32] In the spring and for much of the early summer, Duke Henry was in the midlands. Here, during a relentless progress, centre after centre, nominally at least under Stephen's control, fell to Henry or accepted his lordship. At Whitsun he was at Leicester,[33] by invitation of the earl, and here he held court.[34] The monks of Haughmond Abbey, Shropshire, produced in evidence charters of the empress. So also did William Mauduit, when he vindicated his title to the chamberlainship of England and Normandy, "and specifically the castle of Porchester" in Hampshire. These charters show Gilbert de Lacy and William Fitz Alan at Henry's court; as were members of the Beauchamp family and their allies John de Bidun and Walchelin Maminot. Before arriving at Leicester, the duke had taken Tutbury from the garrison of Robert de Ferrers; he then moved to Warwick, where the earl, a kinsman of the earl of Leicester, had died shortly after the Whit feast.[35] It was reported that he had died of grief and shame on learning of the castle's surrender, the result of machinations in

---

[31] *Regesta*, iii, no. 439. Signs of correction: (i) Robert of Meulan is given his title of count; (ii) the manor of Sturminster (Dorset) was excluded from the grant of the lands of Robert of Meulan, for this had been given to Robert of Leicester's brother, Waleran of Meulan. Additionally the earl obtained confirmation of an exchange which he had made with Roger, earl of Warwick.

[32] Ibid., no. 840.

[33] Ibid., no. 459, refers to assarts made "usque Pentecosten que fui apud Legrecestriam."

[34] That there was a court held here is established not just by the this being one of the three main feasts of the year, but by the clutch of charters that survives, Ibid., nos. 104 (for Biddlesden Abbey), 379 (for Haughmond Abbey), 582 (for William Mauduit), and Vincent, "New Charters of Henry Plantagenet," no. 15 (for Stixwould Priory).

[35] *GS*, 234–5 (though saying that Tutbury was taken after Warwick); Torigni, 172. The *Rous Roll* gives 12 June as the date of the earl's death: *CP* 12/ii, 362 note d.

which the countess herself was involved.[36] The abbot of Radmore and the prior of Coventry were named as attending the duke at Warwick.[37] Most likely they were there for the obsequies of the earl. Otherwise, as had been agreed, the senior clergy kept their distance from the duke's court.

In July, seven months after his arrival in England, Duke Henry felt confident enough to come to Wallingford.[38] Stephen had placed a siege-castle there, on the opposite bank of the Thames, at Crowmarsh, controlling the bridge across the river. For a time, concomitantly, royalist forces continued the long-standing siege of Wallingford, while Henry's forces – who could now be called "the Normans" – started to besiege Crowmarsh.[39] Militarily not much happened. But with the leading men of both sides close together rapid advances could be made towards a peace agreement. Both king and duke found matters taken out of their hands.

> Certain religious persons moderated between them, and after discussions with the leading men of the duke's army a truce of five days was agreed, to allow king Stephen the opportunity of levelling the castle that he himself had erected, which was then under siege. He was allowed to remove eighty of his soldiers, while the duke had already captured twenty of his men and had beheaded sixty of his archers. When the duke learned of the terms agreed, which were honourable ones, he was very angry; he complained of loyalty of those of his friends who had accepted such terms; but rather than break the agreement he accepted them.[40]

It was a limited truce, which provided for the demilitarization of the area. The king and the duke spoke personally about the need for peace. "This was a foretaste of the peace treaty, but it was postponed to another time."[41] The civil war was not quite over, but here in the Thames valley the necessity for peace was finally accepted by the king himself.

The proof of this acceptance lay in the behaviour of Eustace. Whatever was agreed at the meeting between king and duke – and its very occurrence indicates that peace terms were well advanced, for the protagonists would not have become involved until at least the heads of an agreement had

---

[36] The earl was evidently away for some reason when the castle was surrendered, but he was not necessarily "in attendance on the king," which is the translation given in GS, 234–5, of "qui et eo tempore lateri regis adhærebat"; the translation should read rather that he "was on the king's side."

[37] Regesta, iii, no. 459; iv. plate xli.

[38] HH, 764–7; GS, 236–9; Gervase, i. 153–5; Torigni, 173–4. Regesta, iii, no. 44 (for Geoffrey Ridel), shows the duke accompanied at this point by the earls of Chester, Cornwall, Gloucester, and Hereford.

[39] Regesta, iii, no. 491, was given "apud Craumersam in obsidione"; it shows Archbishop Theobald involved in the peace discussions and also promoting the claims of his archdeacon, Roger of Pont l'Evêque, to the recently vacated archbishopric of York.

[40] Torigni, 173–4.

[41] HH, 766–7: "prelibatum est illud pacis negocium, sed tamen in aliud tempus dilatum est."

been reached – Eustace clearly felt betrayed. "Eustace for his part, greatly vexed and angry because the war, in his opinion, had reached no proper conclusion, left his father and went out of sight of the court, and met his death from grief within a few days."[42] "In a towering rage," he retreated to Cambridge, the nearest that he and his countess had to their own home.[43] He then plundered the lands of St Edmund of Bury, so the story was told, and that powerful figure took the most dreadful revenge. He died on 16 or 17 August 1153.[44] Almost on the same day, Eleanor of Aquitaine gave birth to her first child by Duke Henry, a son who was named William, the next heir to the inheritance that Henry claimed.[45] It is sometimes suggested that the death of Eustace was a key, perhaps even the key, factor in the making of the peace. In fact it did no more than remove a complication. The peace had been made, and Eustace's expectation to succeed his father as king formed no part of the terms on which that peace had been made. He had become one of yesterday's men and was given the briefest of obituary notices.[46]

With the peace terms not accepted by one of the protagonists, it was left to both sides to fight on. Henry's campaign was measured; anxious to maintain the momentum that he had built up, he was seeking to show his lordship in new territory. A new factor here was the death in mid-August, at the same time and reportedly of the same disease as Eustace, of Simon of Senlis.[47] Simon had been a stalwart supporter of the king to the very last. His death left a vacuum of lordship at the twin centres of his earldom, Huntingdon and Northampton, and, no less importantly, at Stamford. This could be described as "a strongly fortified castle, a wealthy community, and the chief town of a *comitatus*."[48] Even those closer to the east midlands than Robert of Torigni might find it difficult to describe the status of Rutland, but Stephen had been there often and its importance strategically is not in doubt. After spending some time at

[42] *GS*, 238–9: "bellum . . . ad effectum nequaquam processerat."

[43] Gervase, i. 155: "uehementer indignans."

[44] The Lincoln obituary list, 159, has 16 Aug.; the Annals of St Augustine's, Canterbury, *UGQ*, 82, have 17 Aug.; "around the octave of St Lawrence (17 August)" is the date given in Torigni, 176, after he had, "as some say" (including Gervase, i. 155) attacked the lands of Bury on the feast day (10 Aug.). He died "from grief," *GS*, 238–9; after a sudden seizure, Gervase, i. 155; "touched by an inward pain of the heart," JS, *Policraticus*, ed. Webb, ii. 52; ed. Nederman, 120.

[45] Torigni, 176.

[46] HH, 768–9, noting the burial at Faversham, and with a brief character sketch; *ASC*, s.a. 1140: "he died and his mother as well'; Plympton Annals, *UGQ*, 29: "and thus was peace made"; Annals of St Augustine's, Canterbury, ibid., 82; Winchester Annals, *Ann. Mon.*, ii. 55; Waverley Annals, ibid. ii. 235; Dunstable Annals, s.a. 1151, ibid. iii. 16; *Annales Cestrienses*, 23; *Melrose*, s.a. 1154; *Holyrood*, s.a.1153.

[47] HH, 768–9: "uterque iuuenis eodem morbo eadem deperierunt ebdomada"; and thence Gervase, i, 155; *GS*, 238–9; JH, 331; Torigni, 172; *Holyrood*, s.a. 1153; *CP*, vi. 643. The earl was remembered as having a fierce temper: Jocelin of Furness, "Vita sancti Waldeui," 257.

[48] Torigni, 174.

Wallingford, Henry went north, perhaps via Bedford,[49] and invested Stamford.[50] Here is another precise date, for the duke issued a charter in favour of the bishop and diocese of Lincoln, "at the siege of Stamford," on 31 August 1153.[51]

In September and October 1153 the precise details of the peace, whose main principles both the king and the duke had agreed to accept, were worked out. Once that agreement had been reached, the senior clergy could operate more openly as mediators between the two sides. Chief among them were the archbishop of Canterbury and the bishop of Winchester.[52] In 1141, the last occasion on which a peace might have been agreed, they had tried to lead events and had got their fingers burnt. Now they kept in step with the lay aristocracy. Theobald, as archbishop of Canterbury, and now as papal legate, played a leading role. He is described as speaking directly with the king on the matter of the peace on many occasions, whilst he was also frequently in communication with the duke, but only via intermediaries.[53] That would have been very correct, since he was the king's man; but he could stretch the point when the interests of his suffragans brought them into contact with the duke.[54] No less influential was the bishop of Winchester. The first peace discussions had been on his watch as papal legate for England. He no longer held that office, but still he had the memory of what had been said for a decade and more, he had in his chests sheaves of letters from the great men over two decades and more, and he had the confidence to sell the peace. It needed a clear vision and attention to detail. He was not unique in having these qualities, for laymen such as Robert of Leicester and Richard de Lucy were no less capable in this regard.[55] But he was family and the success of

---

[49] *GS*, 234–5: "ipsam ciuitatem graui depredatione spoliatam ignibus cremandam tradidit." In Bedford the smoke took a long time to clear. The burgesses claimed to have lost their charters in the conflagration: *Curia Regis Rolls*, xii. 513–14; one of the defenders had wounded the duke with a stone, ibid. iv. 270; while at Stamford the duke made reparations for the injuries he had done to the collegiate church of St Paul, Bedford (later Newnham Priory), *Regesta*, iii, no. 81. There is good discussion in Richardson and Sayles, *Governance of Medieval England*, 252 and n. 4.

[50] HH, 768–9; *GS*, 234–7; Torigni, 174.

[51] *Regesta*, iii, no. 492, reflecting his continuing involvement in the detailed arrangements that Ranulf of Chester was making with the bishop of Lincoln concerning his war reparations.

[52] *Melrose*, s.a. 1153; HH, 768–9 (giving Henry as the archbishop's *coadiutor*); thence Gervase, i. 156, and Diceto, i. 296; *GS*, 240–1 (mentioning only Henry); JH, 331 (similarly mentioning only Henry, and giving him a major role not just in the making of the peace but in its implementation).

[53] HH, 770–1.

[54] *Regesta*, iii, no. 796 (for Salisbury: 9 Apr. 1153); ibid., no. 491 (for Lincoln: late July–early Aug. 1153).

[55] Walter Daniel, 42, states that Aelred of Rievaulx kept up a considerable correspondence including, among others, "the most illustrious men of England and especially the earl of Leicester." It must be likely that some at least of these letters were sent during 1153: King, "Brian Fitz Count," 75–6.

the peace would turn, just as had earlier discussions, on the arrangements that would be made for Stephen's family.

The first meeting of the king and the duke, to ratify the terms that had been agreed, took place at Winchester during November.[56] The lay magnates and the higher clergy had been summoned to attend on the authority of both king and duke. In a ceremony that was carefully choreographed, Duke Henry was installed in the bishop's chair while the king was seated in his accustomed place on the opposite side of the choir.[57] Many but not all present would have known what was to be agreed but for most the precise form of words would have been new. It is possible to reconstruct much of what was said.

> Know that I, King Stephen, establish Henry, duke of Normandy, after me as my successor in the kingdom of England and as my heir by hereditary right; and in so doing I give and I confirm to him and his heirs the kingdom of England.

In the text that survives these words are in the present tense.[58] Stephen might on normal occasions have expected to have such a prepared text read out for him; but this was not a normal occasion, and it may well be that these are his words spoken viva voce. The king's grant was categorical. The matching statement from the duke was highly conditional, but it did involve him doing homage to the king.

> The duke in return for this honour and gift and confirmation which I have made to him has done homage to me and given me surety by oath. He has sworn that he will be my liege man and that he will guard my life and honour by every means in his power according to the agreements which have been made between us.

Many of these agreements related to the king's son, William, who next paid homage to the duke. The king then swore oaths in his turn. "I have also given an oath of security to the duke, that I will guard his life and honour by every means in my power, and that I will maintain him as my son and heir in all things, and that I will do all I can to guard him against all men." Stephen undertook to take advice from Henry but insisted that the royal power remained with him alone. "In the affairs of the kingdom I will act with the advice of the duke. I myself will exercise royal justice in the whole kingdom of England, both in the duke's territory and in my own." It may be that at this particular ceremony little more was said. The

---

[56] HH, 770–1, gives the place of the meeting but no date; Torigni, 177, and *Holyrood*, s.a. 1153, date the concord to 6 Nov. but do not give a place; the Tewkesbury Annals, in *Ann. Mon.*, i. 47–8, record the peace as being made "around the feast of St Martin (11 Nov.)"; Gervase, i. 156, says that the Winchester ceremony took place "in fine mensis."

[57] Gervase, i. 156.

[58] *Regesta*, iii, no. 272.

words served as it were as surtitles in the performance of an opera. What was most important and what was most clearly remembered was the inter-action of the king and the duke: the grant of the kingdom made by Stephen to Henry; the homage performed by Henry to Stephen; the oaths sworn and the undertakings given by Stephen to Henry; the homage performed to Henry by Earl William, King Stephen's son. At the end of the ceremony the two men exchanged the kiss of peace and there was not a dry eye in the house.[59] This was the *pax*.[60]

It was important that the main provisions of the peace were understood not just by those who saw them enacted in the cathedral but also by those who learned of them by report, particularly in England but in Normandy also. There was inevitably an element of what we would now call spin in the reports that went out. On Stephen's side it could be reported that Stephen "consented to the duke's inheriting England after his death provided he himself, as long as he lived, retained the majesty of the king's lofty position."[61] The Hexham chronicler saw the bishop of Winchester crowding into the picture, probably reflecting this ceremony extremely well. Through his mediation:

> his brother King Stephen and Duke Henry concluded an agreement for the establishment of peace, oaths being given and received on each side. It was agreed between them that Duke Henry would manage the affairs of the realm and be acknowledged heir to the throne after King Stephen; and that in all disputed points in the kingdom, Henry himself should yield to Henry bishop of Winchester as to a father.[62]

Of the Winchester agreement Henry of Huntingdon said simply that "the king adopted the duke as his son and made him heir to the kingdom."[63] In Normandy the arrangements were heard slightly differently. "The king in the sight of all adopted Henry as his son and granted him the government

---

[59] Newburgh, i. 91: "in mutuos, multis prae gaudio lacrimantibus, se dederunt amplexus."

[60] The peace was an agreement between the two men. It was an event. *Regesta*, iii, nos. 696 ("post compositionem inter me et H. ducem Normannie factam"), 866 ("post pacificationem et concordiam quam feci cum comite Normannorum"); *Eynsham*, i. 39: "in primo Pentecosten post factam inter regem et ducem Normannie concordiam," possibly picking up the phrase from a royal charter now lost; *English Lawsuits*, ii. 326 (no. 363): "Eo igitur anno quo rex S. et H. dux Normannie foederati sunt." Similarly in a variety of annals: Mont-Saint-Michel, in Robert of Torigni, ed. Delisle, ii. 227, 235: "S. rex Anglorum et H. dux Normannorum cognatus eius concordati sunt"; *Melrose*, s.a. 1153: "pax Anglie reddita est pacificatis ad invicem rege S. et H. duce Normannie"; Tewkesbury, in *Ann. Mon.*, i. 47–8: "rex S. cepit pacem"; Waverley, and others, ibid., ii. 236; *UGQ*, 48; "Winchcombe Annals 1049–1181," 130: "concordia facta est inter regem S. et H. ducem apud Wintoniam"; Dunstable, *Ann. Mon.*, iii. 16.

[61] *GS*, 240–1.

[62] JH, 331.

[63] HH, 770–1.

of the kingdom. In return, Henry accepted Stephen as a father, granting him the name of king and the resources of the kingship for so long as he lived."[64] Not all these statements may be exact, but they are valid statements nonetheless, for they reflect how news of the settlement reached the different constituencies of the Anglo-Norman realm. It is striking in fact how little they vary. The key points of the Winchester ceremony were not garbled. This was because they reflected a consensus, that Stephen had to be seen as the lawful king, if only to protect the integrity of the kingdom he ruled, while Henry was indeed now "the lawful heir."

The king and the duke then set out on something like a triumphal progress to London. As had happened in December 1135, and again in the spring and summer of 1141, the road to the crown in November 1153 started in Winchester and finished in London. This reflected the historic importance of the city of Winchester and the ability of its bishop to set the agenda. In the circumstances of 1153 an additional factor will have been the loyalty that the Londoners had shown to Stephen throughout his reign. London was Stephen's capital and the idea of Henry as "the lawful heir" had not taken root. The Londoners would be presented with a *fait accompli*. They received the duke "with splendid processions, as was fitting for so great a man."[65]

It was at Westminster that the charter was issued which spelt out the agreements that underpinned both Stephen's resignation of his son's claims to succeed and Henry's homage to the king. It was a charter issued in the king's name and addressed to the whole of England.[66] It set out first the arrangements between the king and the duke which had been discussed over the summer months and agreed at Winchester. The rights of William, the only surviving son of Stephen, were then spelt out. He was no less his father's heir than had been Eustace, his expectations no less. A substantial premium had to be offered for his support. We start with the main grants to him, of the lands which his father had held as count, and of the estates of the honour of Warenne:

> William my son has done liege homage and given surety to the duke of Normandy, and the duke has granted him to hold from him all the lands which I held before I acquired the kingdom of England, whether in England or in Normandy or in other places. He is also to hold whatever came with the daughter of the earl of Warenne, whether in England or in Normandy, and whatever pertains to those honours. And the duke will put William, my son, and the men of that honour into possession of all the lands, villages and boroughs and revenues which the duke has now in his demesne, and especially those which pertain to the honour of the earl of

---

[64] Torigni, 177.

[65] HH, 770–1; Gervase, i. 156.

[66] *Regesta*, iii, no. 272. The quotations which follow, pp. 282–8, are from my own translation of this document unless otherwise identified. Its status is considered by Holt, "1153", in King, *Anarchy*, 291–5.

Warenne, particularly the castle of Bellencombre and the castle of Mortemer: the agreement being that Reginald de Warenne shall, if he wish, keep the castle of Bellencombre and the castle of Mortemer, giving the duke hostages in respect of them; but if Reginald does not wish to do so, then other liege men of the earl of Warenne acceptable to the duke shall keep the said castles, likewise giving the duke good hostages. The duke shall return to him the other castles which belong to the count of Mortain, at my pleasure, when he can, for safe guard and with safe hostages, it being understood that all hostages shall be returned without dispute to my son when the duke comes into possession of the kingdom of England.

William did liege homage and gave security to his cousin, Duke Henry. It was that homage which gave William his own security; he had become Henry's man; and it was by grant of Henry that he held all the lands specified above. Also one sees introduced here what was evidently a major concern of the duke's side: the need for security in the holding of key fortifications. The phrases used will become recurrent, expressed in a shorthand that shows the confidence of all parties in what was involved: "safe custody," "safe hostages." Reginald de Warenne, the brother of the late earl, was clearly seen as a safe pair of hands.

These were substantial grants but they did not exhaust the duke's generosity to the earl of Warenne. He confirmed to him Norwich and the whole *comitatus* of Norfolk with land worth £700 a year:

The duke has agreed to the increment which I have given to my son, it being understood that the revenue of Norwich itself is included within those 700 librates; and the whole county of Norfolk, except what pertains to churches and prelates and abbots and earls, and excluding particularly the third penny which is received by Hugh Bigod as earl, and excepting in all things the rights of royal justice which are reserved. Also in order to increase my thanks and to strengthen my love towards him, the duke has given to my son, William, all those things which Richer of L'Aigle had from the honour of Pevensey.[67] And besides this the castle and town of Pevensey, and the service of Faramus (of Boulogne), apart from the castle and town of Dover, which pertains to the honour of Dover.[68]

What William was given in Norfolk amounted to the grant of an earldom in its own right. There seems to be a change of tone here and this may reflect a change in the terms previously agreed. These are additional grants and the king is particularly grateful for them. If a reason is sought, it may

[67] Thompson, "The Lords of Laigle"; eadem, "Rape of Pevensey," 213.
[68] Amt, *Accession*, 85–7; on Faramus's position as castellan of Dover see his letter to Theobald, Saltman, *Theobald*, 539–41.

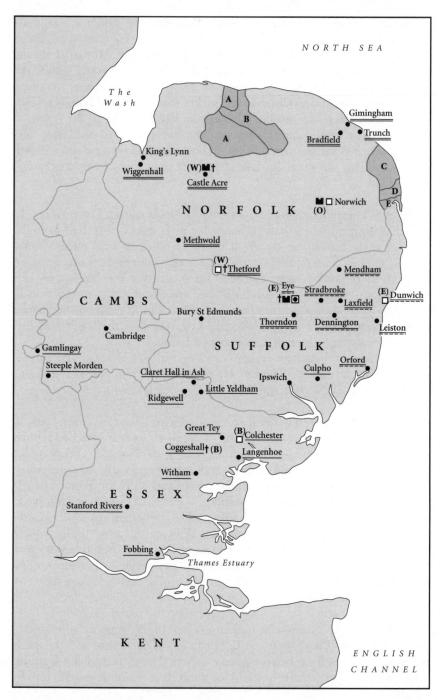

Lands held by William, Earl Warenne, in 1154

● <u>Methwold</u>   Demesne lands of the honour of Warenne, *c*.1154

(W)◼ <u>Castle Acre</u>   Castles of the honour of Warenne, *c*.1154

(W)◻ <u>Thetford</u>   Boroughs where the lord of the honour of Warenne had important interests

(W)† <u>Castle Acre</u>   Religious houses founded by the lords of the honour of Warenne

A   Private hundreds of the honour of Warenne
         A Brothercross Hundred
         B Gallow Hundred

● <u>Thorndon</u>   Demesne lands of the honour of Eye, *c*.1154

(E)◼ <u>Eye</u>   Castles of the honour of Eye, *c*.1154

(E)◻ <u>Dunwich</u>   Boroughs of the honour of Eye

(E)† <u>Eye</u>   Religious houses founded by the lords of the honour of Eye

● <u>Great Tey</u>   Demesne lands of the honour of Boulogne, *c*.1154

(B)◻ <u>Colchester</u>   Boroughs where the lord of the honour of Boulogne had important interests

(B)† <u>Coggeshall</u>   Religious houses founded by the lords of the honour of Boulogne

● <u>Culpho</u>   Demesne lands of the honour of Lancaster, *c*.1154

(O)◼ <u>Norwich</u>   Other castles held by Earl William, *c*.1154

(O)◻ <u>Norwich</u>   Other boroughs held by Earl William, *c*.1154

C   Other private hundreds held by Earl William
         C Happing Hundred
         D West Flegg Hundred
         E East Flegg Hundred

<u>Ipswich</u> ●   Other places not held by Earl William

be suggested that the grants that have just been listed were not intended originally as an "increment" for William but as additional provision for Eustace. Eustace at the beginning of 1153 was arguably less well provided for than his younger brother. He had a high-status bride but no land had come with her, while William had married the Warenne heiress. Eustace had been based in the fens and had been given control of the honour of Pevensey, but he had little time to establish his authority over the Boulogne lands after his mother's death. If this suggestion were to be accepted, it would have important implications for the chronology of the peace agreement. When the discussions for the peace were taken up in earnest in the summer of 1153 there were two sons of Stephen to be provided for. By the time of the second confrontation of king and duke, around the castle of Wallingford, not only was it accepted that Henry as Stephen's adopted son would inherit England, but a detailed and generous package was offered to each of Stephen's two sons. For Eustace whatever was offered was not enough, could never have been enough, for it did not contain the crown. But the offer had been made, in the presence of witnesses. On Eustace's death, Stephen and his advisers might have expected a refusal when they asked that the combined estates all go to William; but Henry held to what had been promised on his behalf, "so as not to break agreements that had been made." The result was to make William a figure of enormous wealth, far greater than he had ever envisaged. Henry for the moment made no great issue of it. All these lands were enjoyed by William as his man.

Finally, in the group of agreements that had been made with Stephen and his family, a terse statement relates to the abbey of Faversham in Kent. "The duke has confirmed the church of Faversham with all its appurtenances, and he will confirm all other things given or restored by me to other churches, on my advice and that of Holy Church." It was terse because of the difficulties of the issues involved. Henry had recognized Stephen as king for his lifetime but he did not wish it to be understood from this recognition that he would automatically accept as valid grants that Stephen had made, particularly where they concerned the rights and resources of the crown. Faversham had been a wealthy royal demesne manor, with market and hundredal rights attached to it.[69] Just as Stephen's son, William, now enjoyed his inherited lands and his father's gifts by grant of Henry, so Stephen's other son, Eustace, and his wife, Matilda, and he himself, when his time came, would rest in peace only because Henry "confirmed" their new foundation; he recognized that as cousins they had claims to his protection. Henry issued a charter to this effect when he got to Westminster.[70]

[69] It had been valued at £80 in 1086: *DB*, 7.
[70] Vincent, "New Charters of Henry Plantagenet," no. 3 (Faversham Abbey): "ego confirmo abbatiam quam Stephanus rex Anglorum fundauit in manerio de Fauresham ubi requiescunt *cognati mei*, videlicet Matillda regina uxor eiusdem Stephani regis et Eustachius filius eius." Henry, at the same place and probably on the same occasion, confirmed Stephen's grant of the manor of Letcombe Regis to the abbey of Cluny: *Regesta*, iii, no. 206.

With provision made as to their resting place the specific grants to Stephen and his family were concluded.[71] There then followed a notification of a more general exchange of homages:

> The earls and barons of the duke, who were never my men, in consideration for the honour which I have done to their lord, have sworn homage to me, saving only the agreements made between me and the duke; and the others who in previous times had done homage to me, have performed fealty to me as their lord. If the duke goes back from his promises, these shall altogether break their service to him until he corrects his errors; and my son also, following the counsel of Holy Church, shall act likewise in similar circumstances. My earls and my barons have done liege homage to the duke saving their fealty to me so long as I live and have the kingdom, with a similar understanding that if I go back on these agreements they will entirely withdraw from my service, until I have corrected my errors. The citizens of towns and the men of castles, which I have in my demesne, have likewise by my order done homage and given surety to the duke saving the fealty which they owe to me as long as I live and have the kingdom. Those who keep the castle of Wallingford have done homage and have given me hostages that they will keep their fealty to me.

It was all carefully worked out. In the detail of the provision that was made in this document these homages can easily be passed over. Yet for a majority of those who had gathered first at Winchester and then at Westminster this was the key provision. It provided that whosoever's lordship they had accepted up to this time, and whether or not they had changed their allegiance over time, they would now be received with an appearance of good grace, their homage would be accepted, by the other party. To many who had importuned him earlier in the year – and this significantly did not include men like Robert of Leicester, who had a clear view from the beginning of the terms on which peace would need to be made – Henry had promised lands from his earliest conquests.[72] Such men had hoped to profit from the discomfiture of the defeated. There would be no such. Henry had come to claim his inheritance. There would be no disinheritance built into the peace. It was a key to the integrity of the kingdom that the personal integrity of those who fought on either side was respected in this way.

---

[71] All at least that are on record. Stephen's daughter, Mary, prioress of Higham, was translated early in 1156 to the nunnery of Romsey (Hants.): Everard, "Saint-Sulpice-la-Forêt and Royal Patronage in England," 120–3. Her pre-election as abbess of this rich monastery may have been part of the peace settlement. Shortly thereafter, however, following the death in 1159 of her brother William without heirs, she was taken from her cloister and married to Matthew, son of the count of Flanders: Tanner, *Boulogne and Politics*, 202–3.

[72] *Regesta*, iii, nos. 180 (100 librates for each of six barons of the honour of Chester, "de his que mihi ex hostibus meis adquisita acciderint"), 582 (100 librates for William Mauduit, "in dominico meo et de terris mihi accidentibus de primis meis conquisitionibus").

This was all very well, but for the duke these principles did not in themselves protect his interests. A concern for his security is embedded in the charter. The duke asked for security in respect of the castles in Normandy pertaining to the honour of Warenne, while a slightly awkward form of words at least made clear that the frontier castles of the honour of Mortain might not be surrendered by the duke until he had succeeded as king. But for Henry's safe succession it was the castles in England that were the key:

> I have given surety to the duke concerning castles and fortifications, according to the counsel of Holy Church, so that the duke on my death may not in respect of these suffer loss or hindrance in his acquisition of the kingdom. The Tower of London and Windsor Castle have with the counsel of Holy Church been given into the keeping of Richard de Lucy. The said Richard has sworn in the hand of Holy Church, and has given his own son as pledge, that on my death he will hand over these castles to the duke. Likewise, with the counsel of Holy Church, Roger de Bussy is keeping the castle of Oxford, and Jordan de Bussy is keeping the castle of Lincoln; they are the liege men of the duke and they have sworn and given hostages in the hand of the archbishop that, when I die, they will hand over these castles to the duke without any dispute. The bishop of Winchester has pledged himself in the hand of the archbishop, in the presence of the bishops, that when I die he will hand over the castle of Winchester and the fortifications of Southampton to the duke. But if any one of those to whom castles have been entrusted shall make delay, or shall leave the castle to which he has been appointed, then, with the counsel of Holy Church, another custodian shall be appointed in his place until he returns. And if anyone who keeps my castles shall show himself contumacious or a rebel, namely concerning the castles which pertain to the crown, then the duke and I making common cause shall wage war upon him until he has been compelled to give satisfaction to both of us.

The list of castles in respect of which Henry required security was small. This was because many were already under the control of his liege men. It may be taken that Stamford, Bedford, and Nottingham, all important fortifications, were seen as secure. But the named castles included the two key fortifications in London and its environs, the Tower of London and Windsor Castle. Both had recently been under the control of Richard de Lucy and both he was allowed to retain. Granted that Richard had been Stephen's right-hand man for a decade and more, and would remain at his side, his acceptance now by Henry was a clear sign of the esteem in which he was held. He had, however, to deliver one of his sons as hostage. The same arrangements were followed in respect of Lincoln and Oxford castles, though the named custodians were the duke's liege men.[73] The

---

[73] They had served Stephen until comparatively recently: Amt, *Accession*, 56.

bishop of Winchester was allowed to offer the security of his own word that he would surrender Winchester and Southampton in the event of his brother's death.[74] These arrangements for the control of castles show Henry, in claiming his grandfather's kingdom, acknowledging the mistakes that could, and should, have led to the kingdom slipping from his grasp. Henry I twenty years earlier had simply refused to make any arrangements of this kind. When he refused, what the infant Henry's parents had envisaged might happen did happen, and when the old king died they found themselves divided and defenceless against Stephen's coup. A lesson had been learned and many of those who heard of the arrangements made as to the castles will have been reassured by them.

There were thirty-seven witnesses to the Westminster charter, attesting the unity of the political nation and standing behind the provisions of the peace agreement. They were headed by Theobald, archbishop of Canterbury, and all the bishops of the southern province (thirteen of them, with Henry of Winchester named first); following them were three other clergy, Geoffrey, bishop of St Asaph, Robert, prior of Bermondsey, and Osto, knight of the Temple. There were twelve earls, headed by William d'Aubigny, earl of Chichester, and Robert, earl of Leicester. And finally there were just eight other laymen: Richard de Lucy, William Martel, Richard du Hommet, Reginald de Warenne, Manasser Bisset, John de Port, Richard de Canville, and Henry of Essex. This was the largest court recorded since the Easter court of 1136, which had been followed by the issue of Stephen's "charter of liberties."[75] There are just four names common to the two documents: Henry, bishop of Winchester; Nigel, bishop of Ely; Hugh Bigod, listed simply as an earl; and William Martel. They had survived. The witnesses to any agreement are frequently those who helped to negotiate it. The two bishops first mentioned, Archbishop Theobald and Henry of Winchester, certainly fall into this category; so also the first two of the earls, William d'Aubigny and Robert of Leicester.[76] The attestations of those of slightly lower rank very likely indicate their active involvement also. Among the religious persons who had moderated at Wallingford earlier in the summer, the prior of Bermondsey can be identified with some confidence.[77] In mid-place between the churchmen and the laymen came Osto, knight of the Temple. His place at the top table must indicate not just the importance of the order but his continuing links with Stephen and his family, notably the queen, going back

---

[74] On his tenure of Southampton, WM, *HN*, 128–9.

[75] *Regesta*, iii, no. 271, which also has thirty-seven witnesses.

[76] Gervase, i. 154, on William d'Aubigny, "vir eloquentissimus"; HH, 770–1; *GS*, 234–5.

[77] *Regesta*, iii, no. 90. The itinerary in ibid., p. xlvii, includes this charter both in the spring (when it would be, along with no. 180, the duke's first charter after his arrival) and in the autumn (where it would precede "the peace" at Winchester). The involvement of the prior of Bermondsey, whose predecessor was the first abbot of Faversham, strongly argues for the latter date. Peter, abbot of Malmesbury, another Cluniac, was also with the duke at this time and later in London: ibid., nos. 837, 875. We are told that "certain religious men" mediated between the king and the duke: Torigni, 173. We may have two of them here, makers of the peace.

nearly thirty years.[78] Richard de Lucy, William Martel, Richard du Hommet, Manasser Bisset, Henry of Essex, and Richard de Canville are officers of the king's household and the duke's household, here combined. The importance of the Warenne honour, and his long experience, are enough to explain the presence of Reginald de Warenne. The most surprising name on this list is that of John de Port, one of the chief barons of Hampshire.[79] Rather than our inventing a specific role to account for his involvement, let him stand for all those in 1153 who were well respected in their communities but had managed to stay out of the headlines. These men had attended courts which in human drama and political importance had no rival since an earlier duke of Normandy had come, after the battle of Hastings, first to Berkhamstead and then to London to be crowned. They had shown themselves to be statesmen.

What the king and the duke and the political community had provided for was not just a peace agreement but a peace process. It was the process that allowed individuals to identify with the agreement; it would be by means of a process that *pax* made between king and duke "soon became a very good peace, such as there never was before."[80] "Immediately an edict went out to all regions," says John of Hexham.[81] The edict dealt with the suppression of violence, the prohibition of spoliation, the ejection from the kingdom of hired knights and archers from other nations, whilst "any fortifications built by individuals on their own possessions after the death of King Henry were to be destroyed." Of all the provisions of the edict, that dealing with castles is the best-attested and it may be that the Hexham chronicler here gives its precise wording.[82] All our witnesses emphasize that it is the castles built "in the time of sedition" that are to be destroyed: "all over the land since the death of Henry" is the formulation of Henry of Huntingdon, who is the most influential source for later writers.[83] There are other provisions of the edict, though it is more difficult to get at their precise wording and formulation.

---

[78] This on the assumption that the "Osto" who attests two of Stephen and Matilda's comital charters (Haigneré, "Chartes de l'abbaye de Samer," 117–23) is the "Osto of Boulogne" who is mentioned in 1126–9 and 1137 (BL, Harley 4757, fo. 8v–9r; *Regesta*, iii, no. 843) and the "Osto, master of the Temple," who occurs later in Stephen's reign (ibid., 848), and the "Osto, knight of the Temple" who is named here; for a full discussion, and other references, see *Templars*, xlvii–xlix, though his further identification there with an "Osto of St Omer" would seem to be more speculative.

[79] Sanders, *English Baronies*, 9; *CP*, xi. 319.

[80] *ASC*, s.a. 1140.

[81] JH, 331: "continuo exiit edictum ab eis per omnes provincias."

[82] Ibid.: "munitionesque quas quisque in sua possessione post mortem Henrici Regis construxerat dirui"; *GS*, 240–1: "castella nova diruentur."

[83] HH, 772–3: "castella post mortem Henrici regis in pessimos usus circumquaque constructa"; Torigni, 177: "de castellis etiam quæ post mortem prædicti regis facta fuerant ut everterentur"; *Walden*, 24–5: "castella etiam plurima seditionis tempore per patriam constructa solotenus confregit." Only one near-contemporary source uses the shorthand phrase, "adulterine castles": *Liber Eliensis*, 372: "castella adulterina diruit"; in support of the others' reticence, Coulson, *Castles in Medieval Society*, 117–27.

There was certainly an order for the restoration of peace: "arms should be laid down and peace restored," "there should be an end of violence and spoliation."[84] This must have stood at the head of any proclamation, before it got down to detail. John of Hexham is also clear that "hired knights and archers from other nations were to be ejected from the kingdom."[85] They were symbols of violence and they were not parties to the peace that had been made for that kingdom. Robert of Torigni says that lands are to be restored "to their ancient and legitimate possessors as they had held in the time of Henry, the very best of kings."[86] The edict gave notification of the process and was widely circulated. This much can be established. It is less certain that the edict dealt with those aspects of the Westminster charter which reflected "the agreements discussed between ourselves"(i.e. between the king and the duke). Some of this material was highly detailed; it concerned primarily the two families, and they had made their peace in the ceremony at Winchester. As the matter was remembered later: "The agreement was ratified by the swearing of oaths and the exchange of authentic documents."[87] The Westminster charter was one of these.[88]

At Winchester and again at Westminster the king had agreed to act in consultation with the duke, while reserving to himself the exercise of royal justice. "From this time on the king and the duke were as one in their governing of the kingdom and no discord arose between them."[89] This at least was the report. The process here involved a progression, the holding and promulgating of regular meetings of the royal court at which both king and duke were present. Holt calculates that there were six of these meetings between Winchester in November 1153 and Henry's departure for Normandy early in March 1154.[90] One of them was at Oxford in mid-January. Henry of Huntingdon, from his perspective in the east midlands, saw this as the main occasion at which oaths were sworn. "There, at the king's command, the English magnates paid to the duke the homage and fealty due to their lord."[91] The swearing of these homages did not happen

[84] GS, 240–1: "pax ubique in regno armis omnino depositis reformaretur"; JH, 331: "violentias comprimi, direptiones interdici."

[85] Ibid.: "milites conductitios et sagittarios exterarum nationum a regno ejici."

[86] Torigni, 177: "juramentum est etiam, quod possessiones, quae direptae erant ab invasoribus, ad antiquos et legitimos possessores revocarentur, quorum fuerant tempore Henrici optimi regis"; GS, 240–1: exheredati ad *propria* reuocarentur" (for comment on this *word*, Holt, "1153," in King, *Anarchy*, 297).

[87] *Walden*, 24–5: "conventione itaque sacramentis prestitis et scriptis autenticis utrinque roborata."

[88] *Regesta*, iii, no. 272. Another survivor from this "exchange" was Duke Henry's charter for the abbey of Faversham: Vincent, "New Charters of Henry Plantagenet," no. 3.

[89] Howden, i. 212: "Ab illo tempore rex et dux unanime exstiterunt in regimine regni, ita quod decetero inter illos nulla oriebatur discordia."

[90] Holt, "1153," in King, *Anarchy*, 307.

[91] HH, 770–3: "ibi principes Anglorum iussu regis hominium et domino debitam fidelitatem duci simul exhibuerunt"; cf. Winchester Annals, in *Ann. Mon.*, ii. 55: "fecerunt capitanei totius Anglie homagium predicti Henrico iussu predicti regis."

on just the one occasion.[92] It was part of the process. And the barons swore "at the king's command." The phrase is often found at this time.[93] It had evidently been agreed.

"After a short while they met again at Dunstable." Business was done here. Those wanting confirmation of their privileges could seek out the chanceries of the king and the duke, and some applied to both for extra security.[94] None of these joint courts, however, produced much in the way of written record. Most people had confidence in the promises that had been made to them and in the process in which they found themselves engaged. But not all. At Dunstable there was the first reported breach between the king and the duke. It concerned decommissioning: the destruction of castles. Some had been destroyed, it was asserted on Henry's side, but the king had favoured his own men and allowed them to retain their castles, showing at times his good nature and at other times his lack of faith. It was difficult, however; it was bound to be difficult when you turned from general principles to individual cases. The legitimacy of the castle was inextricably bound up with the legitimacy of the title to the ground on which the castle was built. Any disputed title would have to be settled by due process, in the king's court. The duke "regretfully let the matter pass in order not to appear to be snuffing out the lamp of recon-ciliation."[95] In fact, he had little choice but to do so. He had traded on his regard for due process since he had arrived in England. And he had accepted that Stephen should enjoy executive authority for the remainder of his reign. It was nonetheless reported that many castles had been destroyed and these reports had a value in themselves.[96]

The decommissioning issue was a part of the peace process, visible, verifiable. It is not surprising that the topic was raised, for what was at issue – perhaps – was less the castles themselves than the commitment to the process, and with the king reasserting his authority the duke and his followers needed reassurance on that commitment. It would have been

[92] There is further confirmation of this, if it were needed, in the form of words in the *ASC*, s.a., 1140: "Then the count [Duke Henry] was received in Winchester and in London with great honour, and all did him homage."

[93] It is stated in the Westminster charter that two groups, the citizens of towns and custo-dians of castles in the royal demesne, and the archbishops and bishops and abbots of the kingdom of England, had done homage to the duke "ex precepto meo" (*Regesta*, iii, no. 272); the duke's grant to the wife of Richard de Canville, who was one of the witnesses to the Westminster charter, was granted "petitione et precepto regis Stephani" (ibid., no. 140); Stephen's son, William, did homage to Henry "jubente patre" (Newburgh, i. 91).

[94] For charters of both king and duke to the same beneficiary see *Regesta*, iii, nos. 129–30, 583–4; for the king's confirmation of an earlier grant by the duke, ibid., no. 127; for other grants by the duke, ibid., no. 140; Crouch, "Earl William of Gloucester and the End of the Anarchy."

[95] HH, 772–3.

[96] *GS*, 240–1: "[the duke] plurima tandem castella quæ regno erant impedimento subruisset"; Howden, i. 213: "[the king] multa obsedit castella et obtinuit et multa ex eis prostravit."

surprising also had not some rumours circulated that the duke's person was in danger from "extremist groups," those unable to accept the terms agreed. After Dunstable, the court was next convened at Canterbury, where king and duke were escorted in procession into the cathedral church. Thence during Lent they travelled to Dover, where they held discussions with Thierry, count of Flanders, and his wife, who was Henry's aunt. What were these discussions about? No count of Flanders is known to have travelled to Dover since Robert II did so in 1110, to conclude the second of his treaties with Henry I. In 1154 Thierry would do so on no fewer than three occasions, the first here a family conference, the second in October to meet with Stephen, the third in December on his way to the coronation of Henry II. There will have been no single issue, but one issue that may not have been resolved was the succession of Stephen's son, William, to the county of Boulogne. The independence of the county has been stressed, but in the circumstances of 1153–4 this independence may have been a weakness rather than a strength. Whilst it has been argued that Stephen did not perform homage for Boulogne to the count of Flanders in 1128, his son may have been asked for homage in 1154, and Henry may not have seen any reason to discourage that request. This would have been more than enough to account for the heightened tension that certainly surrounded the first visit of the count of Flanders. After he had left, the king and the duke returned to Canterbury; and there a conspiracy was discovered, for "the Flemings wished to kill the duke, since they hated both him and the peace." It was rumoured that Stephen's son, William, was aware of these plans. Perhaps at a meeting with Duke Henry, at the meeting-place of the county court on Barham Down, William fell from his horse and broke his leg, "to the great distress of his followers." Very much here in the heartland of the king's territory the duke felt insecure, and he soon made for home, though only after correctly obtaining permission to leave the court and cross the Channel. He would not set eyes on Stephen again.[97]

The clearest evidence of the existence of a new regime, and of the restoration of the rights of the crown, came from the issuing of a new coinage. This was Stephen type 7, his fourth substantive issue.[98] The publicity gained from this move, a complex administrative matter, was obviously intended.[99] The number of mints from which coins have been found immediately indicates the change: there are at least forty-five, more than double the number of those that had issued coins in types 2 and 6,

---

[97] The main source for this paragraph is Gervase, i. 158. The meetings are discussed by Amt, *Accession*, 84. HH, 772–3, says simply that soon after the meeting at Dunstable, the duke received licence to depart from the court and returned to Normandy. Similarly, Newburgh, i. 91–2, notes William's broken leg but not in the context of any plot.

[98] Allen, "The English Coinage of 1153/4–1158"; Allen and Webb Ware, "Two Notes on Stephen *BMC* Type 7."

[99] One chronicler states that king and duke agreed on a reform of the coinage: Diceto, i. 297; cf. the comments of Howden, i. 211, discussed in Blackburn, "Coinage and Currency," in King, *Anarchy*, 168.

and not far short of those that had issued in type 1. There continued to be a strong showing in the south-east of England and in East Anglia. In the midlands, coins were issued at Lincoln, Stamford, Nottingham, Northampton, Huntingdon, and Bedford, in only the last of which had there been a continuity of official issues. In the north, coins survive from both York and Hedon, the latter one of those coins that are baronial in all but name for this small port on the Humber estuary was under the control of William of Aumale. Coins were issued also not just on the frontiers of, but from deep within, the areas where the empress and her supporters had been based and which were still in some manner under the duke's control.[100] Among them were Hereford, Worcester, Gloucester, Exeter, Taunton, Wilton, and Salisbury (near which a fascinating coin describing Duke Henry as "the future king" has recently come to light: see plate 24b).[101] There were coins struck at York and at Durham. All these were "official" coins, made from dies issued centrally, in London.[102] Any attempt at a portrait is difficult in this medium, but the issue is distinctive in showing the king bearded, and he seems noticeably older than in the previous issue (see plate 24a).[103] The quality of striking of the coins, however, is comparatively poor, perhaps inevitably, granted the number of new moneyers found in this issue and the lack of practice of even the more experienced of them. A good deal of effort and capital was put into this recoinage and no attempt was made to dismantle it when Stephen died in 1154. There was no recoinage until 1158 and the old king's image remained common currency for many years thereafter.[104]

The issuing of the new coinage necessitated the re-establishment of routine links between London and the provinces of England, many of which had been lost in the previous decade and more. This can only have given confidence to those associated with the king and the court. The Easter meeting of the court, immediately after the departure of Duke Henry, was probably held in London. It was well attended. Among the churchmen present were the archbishop of Canterbury, Henry of Winchester, Robert of Lincoln, and Richard of London, along with the prior of Bermondsey, and Thomas, a clerk of the archbishop waiting for preferment.[105] Some earls were at court: Aubrey de Vere, William

---

[100] *Regesta*, iii, no. 272: "in toto regno Anglie tam *in parte ducis* quam in mea."

[101] Cambridge, Fitzwilliam Museum, CM.1225–2001, bearing the inscription RE[X] [F]VTVRVS.

[102] A coin die for a Northampton issue of Stephen, possibly official, was found in 1991 in soil excavated from the Thames waterfront and seems to have been discarded from "the site of the die-making and/or die-cutting workshop": Archibald, "Four Early Medieval Coin Dies," 187–90, 197–9. It could have been surrendered at the time of this recoinage.

[103] The best-quality reproductions of coins are found in Boon, *Coins of the Anarchy*, here nos. 39, 38, 44.

[104] Noting the suggested dates of deposit given in the table of hoards in Blackburn, "Coinage and Currency," in King, *Anarchy*, 202–3.

[105] *Regesta*, iii, no. 866.

d'Aubigny, and Hugh Bigod.[106] Among the earls, Hugh was the most frequent attestor at this time.[107] If his very presence at Stephen's court, in the light of his earlier relationship, seems surprising, it should not. He was the layman most directly affected by the grants made in the peace agreement to William, the king's son. Hugh might be earl of Norfolk but the *comitatus*, the royal rights in the shire, had been granted to the king's son. Hugh had no choice but to come to terms. Indeed a spell of attendance at court may well have been required of him. Stephen had done this before. It made a point. Among the laymen who had been close to Stephen in the previous few years there is continuity. A grant of the abbey of Thorney, in proprietorial terms and perhaps in consequence not attested by any clergy, names Richard de Lucy, Henry of Essex, Warner de Lusors, Fulk d'Oilly, Baldwin Fitz Gilbert, and Hugh of Essarts.[108] Other names, secure at this place if not exactly at this time, are William Martel and Richard de Canville.[109] It was Warner de Lusors who attested a routine writ of freedom from toll in favour of the monks of Glastonbury, addressed by the king to William, earl of Gloucester, "and all his men of Bristol."[110] Not for the first time, Henry of Winchester was stepping in quickly to turn a national agreement to his local advantage. The monks preserved the writ. Whether the earl and his officials took any notice of it is another matter.

If the king continued to be firmly based in and around London, it was seen as a particular feature of 1154 that he had "traversed the provinces of England with regal pride, making public appearances as if he had just obtained the throne."[111] A definite progress can be identified in the summer months, one which took as its terminus the city of York. Now for much of his reign, when Stephen had thought of the north of England it will have been images of schism and secession which crowded into his mind. This was no longer the case. Death had totally transformed the landscape of power. Among churchmen, in the summer and autumn of 1153, there had died in quick succession: the pope, Eugenius III, on 8 July; the conscience of Europe, abbot Bernard of Clairvaux, on 19 August; and the archbishop of York, Henry Murdac, on 14 October.[112] All three were Cistercians. All three were hard men, single-minded, unaccommodating. The pope who succeeded, Anastasius IV, reigned for less than eighteen months, but this was time enough for him to set a different tone. He resolved the schism at York by restoring William Fitz Herbert to the see. He also accepted the choice of the chapter of Durham, who had elected

---

[106] *Regesta*, iii, nos. 137, 896.

[107] Ibid., nos. 28, 696, 896.

[108] Ibid., no. 896.

[109] Ibid., nos. 131, 239, 258.

[110] Ibid., no. 344, given at Windsor.

[111] Newburgh, i. 94.

[112] The three deaths are noted together in, e.g., the Tewkesbury, Waverley, Dunstaple, and Melrose annals, as also by John of Hexham and William of Newburgh: *Ann. Mon.*, i. 47, ii. 235, iii. 16; *Melrose*, s.a. 1153; JH, 331–2; Newburgh, i. 79.

the king's nephew Hugh du Puiset after the previous bishop had died on
3 November 1152, though Henry Murdac had opposed him. Both Hugh
du Puiset and William Fitz Herbert were accepted by the pope in Rome
in December 1153, at just the time of the general pacification in
England.[113] The pope was an old hand, he had been a cardinal for over
forty years, and he knew what he was doing. The acceptance of these two
candidates, the choices of the royal court, should be seen as a part of the
peace settlement.

In respect of lay authority in the north of England there had also been
significant changes. The heir to the king of Scots, Henry, earl of
Northumberland, had died on 12 June 1152, in his father's lifetime.[114] He
had been "effectively joint king of Scots with his father"; they sat together
at Carlisle, surrounded by their barons, and coins were struck in their
names. Then David himself had died, on 24 May 1153.[115] It was his
grandson, Malcolm IV, "the Maiden," who inherited the crown of
Scotland. He was no more than twelve years old. Aelred, abbot of
Rievaulx, wrote a eulogy of David of Scots, by way of a preface to his
work *De genealogia regum Anglorum*, which he addressed to Henry, duke of
Normandy, "now truly the heir to England."[116] As such, of course, he was
heir to the authority which Henry I, his grandfather, had exercised both at
Carlisle and at Newcastle. Aelred, well aware of this fact, begged Henry
to protect the "orphans" of the Scottish royal house. And there was
another significant death, for Ranulf, earl of Chester, died on 16
December 1153.[117] No man during the course of the reign had done more
to destabilize the north of England and none had proved so unconcili-
atory.[118] Now, in the middle of a month of reconciliation, and fully reconciled with the Church, he died. It seemed to some a little too convenient
and stories circulated that he had not died of natural causes.[119]

[113] On these two appointments see Newburgh, i. 78–80; JH, 328–32; Knowles, "St
William of York," 90–1; Scammell, *Hugh du Puiset*, 12–21.

[114] The date is given by *Holyrood*, s.a. 1152; and the death is noted additionally by *Melrose*,
s.a. 1152; Newburgh, i. 70–1; JH, 327; Torigni, 167. Interspersed with the eulogies can be
found some indications that Henry was a rough diamond: "hominem (ut accepimus)
mansuetum ac pium et bene morigeratum" (Jocelin of Furness, "Vita sancti Waldeui,"
251); "excepto quod paulo suauior fuerat, per omnia patri similis" (Aelred of Rievaulx,
Eulogium Davidis, ii. 277).

[115] The date is given by *Holyrood*, s.a. 1153; *Melrose*, s.a. 1153; JH, 330; the death is noted
additionally in Newburgh, i. 71; Torigni, 172; and for further references *Scottish Annals*, 230–1.

[116] Aelred, *Genealogia*, 737: "Angliae *vero gaudemus* haeredem." For further comment on the
context and the date of this work, see below, pp. 328–9 and n. 154.

[117] *GS*, 238–9; *Annales Cestrienses*, 23; *Brut*, s.a. 1153; Torigni, 177; *Holyrood*, s.a. 1153.

[118] He "afflicted the whole of the north with an unending persecution": *GS*, 166–7; after
1146, he "did worse than anything reported of him before": *ASC*, s.a. 1140.

[119] It was said that William Peverel of Nottingham had attempted to poison him: *GS*,
236–7; Gervase, i. 155 ("ut fama fuit"); if this is the "base conduct" referred to in Duke
Henry's charter for Ranulf of Chester, the occasion was several months before Ranulf's
death: *Regesta*, iii, no. 180: "nisi poterit se [William Peverel] dirationare in mea curia de
scelere et traditione."

The king's itinerary in the summer of 1154, travelling to and from York, took in Cambridge, Norwich, Lincoln, Worksop, and the castle of Drax. At Cambridge he met his widowed daughter-in-law, Constance of France, and confirmed her grants to the nuns of St Radegund's.[120] At Norwich he was a familiar figure.[121] At Lincoln, with the recoinage presumably now well under way, the bishop paid for the privilege of having a mint to strike coins "for ever" in the town of Newark, which his predecessor had developed with single-minded efficiency.[122] If it struck at all, it will have been in this year only, and no coins have survived. So also with the grant to the same bishop of the justiciarship of Lincolnshire. All the citizens and the men of the city were to come on the summons of the bishop's ministers to hold the royal pleas, just as they had done "in the time of king Henry my uncle."[123] This latter charter was issued at Drax, now the site of a power station and then of a castle, of no great strategic importance but a symbol of the lordship of the family of Paynel. The Paynels were a important baronial family with estates in eight counties in England and a significant estate in Normandy.[124] Stephen took up the siege of Drax "around harvest-time," so perhaps in early August 1154; the castle was captured and then destroyed.[125] It is the only named castle known to have suffered this fate, one intended for many of them by the terms of the peace process, during 1154. Its fate is the more surprising because it was almost certainly not a "new castle" of the reign. So why was it besieged? The answer may be found in a surviving charter of Duke Henry, which granted to Hugh Paynel his honour in Normandy "and the whole barony of his father both in Normandy and in England."[126] His ability to honour that grant with respect to England, after he had landed there and his claims had been accepted, was compromised by the grant of Drax, the English *caput* of the honour, to Hugh's half-sister, Alice Paynel. Alice was married to Robert de Gant, whom Stephen had created earl of Lincoln in the late 1140s, and who was also the nephew of Robert de Gant, the royal chancellor. Certainly Philip de Colville, named as defying the king and refusing to surrender the castle, was one of the knights of Robert de Gant. There was every incentive, granted the king's close relationship to the Gant family, for him to travel by another route and pass both castle and problem by. That he did not may indicate that he had given a precise undertaking to Duke Henry that on any journey north he would require

---

[120] *Regesta*, iii, no. 139.
[121] Ibid., no. 404; Thomas of Monmouth, *Life of St William*, 99: "euoluto denique aliquanti temporis spacio, cum Norwicum rex aduenisset."
[122] *Regesta*, iii, no. 489; King, "Economic Development," 11.
[123] *Regesta*, iii, no. 490.
[124] *EYC* 6: *Paynel*, 1–7.
[125] Newburgh, i. 94, gives the time of year; the siege is noted also in HH, 774–5, Howden, i. 213. *Regesta*, iii, no. 817, in favour of the monks of Selby, was issued "apud Dracas in obsidione."
[126] *Regesta*, iii, no. 653; see also *EYC* 6, 31–4, 96–8 (no. 19).

the surrender of Drax to a royal castellan, prior to a formal disposition as to the right.

The king was in York during a vacancy to the see, for William Fitz Herbert had died on 8 June, shortly after he had been warmly received into his cathedral.[127] No attempt was made to fill the vacancy at this time. Instead the northern clergy, either then or later, were given a day at Michaelmas to come to Westminster for this purpose. Hugh du Puiset had performed the archbishop's obsequies and for a time he was the senior churchman in the north of England.[128] Richard du Lucy, Richard de Canville, Hugh of Essarts, and Baldric de Sigillo, were among those who had travelled north with the king.[129] Eustace Fitz John, lord of Malton, who for a decade had been constable of the honour of Chester, came to court. It may be that his attendance was formally required. Henry de Lacy, the lord of Pontefract, was also at court at this time.[130] Among his chaplains may have been monks of Sawley Abbey in Craven, of which Henry was an important patron; but present also were monks of Selby Abbey, who had suffered from his attentions, and whose chronicle provides one of the most vivid accounts of the civil war in the north of England.[131] Stephen was also at Worksop, a place not often recorded on the itinerary of the kings of England, where laymen and monks from the north midlands sought him out.[132] William Peverel of Nottingham came before the king here, and may have made his peace,[133] but his long-term prospects were not good. When a king of England next travelled north on this road William would flee before him.[134]

Around Michaelmas, Stephen returned to London. There he held a council "with the bishops and nobles of England to attend to the business of the kingdom." The main item of business was the appointment of a new archbishop of York, in succession to William Fitz Herbert. "The senior figures of the church at York, and the abbots and priors of the province subject to it," were brought to London for the election.[135] In that place, away from their networks and their power base, they had little choice but to do what they were told. They elected Roger of Pont l'Evêque, the archdeacon of Canterbury. He was very clearly the southern candidate, although Theobald kept himself aloof from the proceedings.

---

[127] Newburgh, i. 80; Gervase, i. 158.

[128] Howden, i. 213.

[129] *Regesta*, iii, no. 490, 664, 739, 797, 817; BL Harley MS 3640, fo. 120.

[130] *Regesta*, iii, no. 664. On Henry de Lacy, see Wightman, *Lacy Family*, 76–80.

[131] *Regesta*, iii, no. 797, 817; "Historia Selebiensis Monasterii," i. [33]–[38]; Bartlett, *England under the Norman and Angevin Kings*, 284–5.

[132] *Regesta*, iii, no. 739 (an original in the hand of *scriptor* xxii, for Rufford Abbey); probably also ibid., iii, no. 923, for Welbeck Abbey (confirming a grant made by Ralph de Belfou "favente Stephano rege," witnessed by the bishop of Durham, Richard de Lucy, and Baldric de Sigillo).

[133] Ibid., no. 739.

[134] Gervase, i. 161; Torigni, 183; *CP*, iv, App. I, 761–70.

[135] Newburgh, i. 94–5.

Roger was consecrated in Westminster Abbey on 10 October 1154 in the king's presence.[136] There were also present a substantial number of bishops of the southern province: those of London, Lincoln, Hereford, Bath, Ely, Norwich, Worcester, and Rochester. Henry of Winchester sent his apologies.[137] No profession was made by York to Canterbury, and Theobald performed the consecration in his capacity as papal legate.[138] This may show statesmanship on Theobald's part but equally it may have been a part of the deal.[139] There had been quarrels enough regarding the see of York.

For good measure, however, Osbert of Bayeux, the archdeacon of York, who might in different circumstances have proved a match for the archdeacon of Canterbury, had his character blackened. It was the role of a deacon, assisting the celebrant at a solemn mass, to pass to him the chalice containing the wine that would be consecrated in the Eucharist. It was alleged that the chalice had been poisoned by or through the agency of Osbert. It was a charge inherently unlikely but impossible to disprove, and it was in the interests of the southern party to ensure that no quick resolution to the matter was obtained.[140] William of Newburgh, a local man, managed to get to the bottom of it: the archbishop had been given an antidote to poison, by his panicking staff as he lay dying, and the whole story had mushroomed from there.[141] From the point of view of the crown, however, the incident is of some interest for it shows the king dealing with a man who, allegedly, was a criminous clerk. This is how Archbishop Theobald described the proceedings in a letter to the pope:

One Symphorian, a clerk of the household of William of happy memory, archbishop of York, in the presence of King Stephen and the bishops and barons of England at a solemn council, cited Osbert, archdeacon of York, on a charge of poisoning: he alleged that the archbishop aforesaid was slain by poison which the archdeacon gave him to drink at the Lord's Table; and he promised steadfastly that he would prove this by the ordeal of white-hot iron or of boiling water or of single combat or any other form of trial. Osbert however most steadfastly denied the charge and replied that by privilege of his dignity and order he was not subject to lay jurisdiction, but only that of the church, and that he was ready, come what might, to abide by its judgement. So

---

[136] Gervase, i. 158–9, edits the king out; but Howden, i. 213, says that the appointment was made "dono regis Stephani," and the letter of Archbishop Theobald quoted in the next paragraph confirms the king's active involvement.

[137] He was evidently not present. His earlier letter of apology in the case of the London election of 1152 is condensed and – it may be – caricatured in Diceto, i. 295–6.

[138] Ibid., 298; Newburgh, i. 95.

[139] Saltman, *Theobald*, 122–5, argues for statesmanship.

[140] The poisoning is stated as fact in Gervase, i. 158; as an allegation in the Winchester and Melrose annals: *Ann. Mon.*, ii. 55 ("ut fertur"); *Melrose*, s.a. 1154 ("ut dicitur").

[141] Newburgh, i. 80–1.

both parties gave security that they would pursue their quarrel according to the custom of our nation in the king's hand, who, despite the resistance and opposition of ourselves and our brethren, said that it came under his jurisdiction, owing to the atrocity of the crime and to the fact that the case was initiated in his presence; thereupon the dispute was postponed till the octave of Epiphany.[142]

Stephen had all along been very tenacious of the rights of the crown, what Theobald here calls "the custom of our nation," over the English Church. In the circumstances of 1154 he was able to insist on them. He expected to hear the case again in his court early in January 1155.

If the king was ill at this time there is no indication of it now, though those who could read the king's face may have felt otherwise. Stephen now went again to Kent and at Dover he had further discussions with the count of Flanders. This may have been family business, if so reinforcing the impression that the king was winding up his affairs. The end came suddenly. "The count having taken his leave after these discussions, the king was violently assailed by a pain in his guts, accompanied by a discharge of blood (a long-standing ailment of his), and taking to his bed in the monastery there, he died on 25 October."[143] At Dover Priory the king would have got good-quality medical care and his attendants, when their best efforts had failed, would want to make a serious stab at giving a cause of death. Their first-hand testimony, reported at second hand by Gervase of Canterbury, is to be preferred to the third-hand and casual treatment of the author of the *Gesta Stephani*, who says that the king "caught a slight fever and departed this life."[144] The king was buried at Faversham, alongside his wife and son. There is no record of the funeral service. Attention skipped immediately to the new king. While the death of a king would normally cause instability, here it did not. It was seen rather as Stephen's final contribution to the peace.

---

[142] JS, *Letters*, i. 26–7 (no. 16).

[143] Gervase, i. 159. This is the received date: HH, 774–5; Torigni, 181; *Battle*, 152–3; *Holyrood*, s.a. 1154; William Thorne, *Chronicle of Saint Augustine's Canterbury*, 92; Lincoln obituary list, 162; and the annals of Margam, Waverley, Dunstable, and Bermondsey, in *Ann. Mon.*, i. 15; ii. 236; iii. 16, 439. Variant dates are found in Ralph of Coggeshall, 14 (24 Oct.); Annals of St Augustine's, Canterbury, *UGQ*, 82 (26 Oct.); Tewkesbury Annals, in *Ann. Mon.*, i. 48 (31 Oct.).

[144] *GS*, 240–1. *Liber Eliensis*, 371, says that he died of dysentry ("morbo dissenteriaco egrotavit"); HH, 774–5, followed by Newburgh, i. 95, simply says that he was taken ill and then died.

Chapter 10

APPRAISAL

It is not right that I should hide the truth, with all respect for a very kindly man; if he had acquired the kingdom in a lawful way, and in administering it had not lent trusting ears to those who wished him ill, then undoubtedly he would have lacked little that adorns the royal character.[1]

From this the disgrace of the kingdom is thrown away; from this comes its glory![2]

In December 1135 Stephen, count of Mortain, was chosen as king by the Anglo-Norman political community. Because he was chosen he came with a character reference. He was well known and well liked. Before his election, said William of Malmesbury, "because of his good nature and the way he would jest, sit and eat in the company even of the humblest, he had earned great affection, so great it can hardly be imagined."[3] He stood out amongst his peers, according to another authority, as being "rich and at the same time unassuming, generous and courteous."[4] He could be represented as a man of "great valour and boldness."[5] He was known equally to be "a pious and peaceable man."[6] His good character made him suitable for the kingship. He was known to have been close to his uncle, and so it was at least credible to claim that he was Henry's chosen successor, designated on his deathbed. "I present to you as king my comrade-in-arms, Stephen, an earl of mine, my most beloved kinsman, noble in his valour but exceedingly devout in his trust in God," Henry was represented as saying, before he breathed his last.[7] The author of the *Gesta Stephani* seems very close to the discussions in London which culminated in Stephen being crowned and he and the author of the *Liber Eliensis*, who reports Henry's designation, seem almost to be following the same text. It is tempting to suggest that their text was the proclamation of Stephen's

---

[1] WM, *HN*, 36–7.
[2] JS, *Entheticus*, i. 196–7, ll. 1395–6.
[3] WM, *HN*, 32–3.
[4] *GS*, 4–5.
[5] HH, 700–1.
[6] JW, iii. 242–3.
[7] *Liber Eliensis*, 285–6.

kingship, following his coronation, to the English political community.[8] Some evidently were not sure how well Stephen's character would stand up under pressure, but found it consoling that he would have the assistance of his very capable brothers, Theobald, count of Blois, and Henry, bishop of Winchester. Not mentioned at the time, but a no less familiar figure, was the new queen, Matilda of Boulogne, who would provide her husband with spirited and tenacious support.

It would be when he visited their churches that many of the chroniclers could observe Stephen at first hand. They found him relaxed and contented, as much at ease in church as in chapter house, enjoying the ceremonial. A monk of Gloucester described him as "delighted" by the welcome that he received there in 1138. It followed the ceremonial of the royal *adventus*. The citizens welcomed him outside the walls and escorted him in "with great joy," and the sheriff, Miles of Gloucester, "led him with honour to the royal palace." But first he had come to church, and he offered his royal ring on the high altar, which his chaplains then redeemed by offering the monks 500 shillings.[9] This must have been close to the going rate, for when he came to Peterborough in 1143, the monks showed him their most precious relic, the arm of St Oswald, and the king's ring was again offered and redeemed, though possibly via a credit note rather than for cash.[10] Such events were long remembered. When King John visited Bury St Edmunds in 1199 he borrowed his offering from the sacristy, failed to redeem it, and left only a miserly 13 shillings in the collection plate.[11] The monks of Bury and the other great monasteries had no such complaints about Stephen, who did everything in proper form. He would listen patiently and attentively as the privileges of the house were read out to him.[12] He would make new grants with proper ceremony. It was on the altar before the body of St Edmund that he offered some token that the knights of the abbey would henceforth be allowed to perform castle-guard at Bury rather than at Norwich.[13] The abbey of St Albans had relics of St Stephen, and on one of the king's visits the abbot plonked these down in front of the king, abased himself, and asked that the castle of Kingsbury, whose inhabitants were terrorizing the neighbourhood, should be destroyed.[14] It was late in the reign and the abbot here reflected the public mood. When the body of Robert de Béthune, bishop of Hereford, arrived at the Temple church in London, in 1148, on its return from France, the king dropped the business in which he was engaged and joined his wife in

[8] *GS*, 24–5, has the reference to the proclamation ("edicto per Angliam promulgato").
[9] JW, iii. 242–3.
[10] Hugh Candidus, 106, says that the king pardoned the monks 40 marks (i.e. 533s 4d), possibly in respect of a forest fine: cf. *Regesta*, iii, no. 655.
[11] Jocelin of Brakelond, 102–3.
[12] *Regesta*, iii, nos. 5 (Abingdon), 538 (St Martin le Grand, London); *Battle*, 152–3; *English Lawsuits*, i. 289–90 (Bury St Edmunds).
[13] *Regesta*, iii, no. 757.
[14] *GASA*, i. 121–2.

prayer, overcome with emotion. There seems nothing forced in his behaviour on these occasions. Stephen was "the pious king."[15] The epithet stuck to him.

The king attended mass on the morning of the battle of Lincoln, 2 February 1141. "As many men witnessed," there were suitable portents of the disaster which was to befall him later in the day.[16] It was said that the candle which he held during the ceremony broke in his hand, and that the pyx had fallen from above the high altar. This was one of the two things that everyone came to know about the battle of Lincoln. The other was that the king fought bravely, wielding both his sword and a double-headed axe to good effect before he was finally captured. The bravery, no less than the piety, was a part of the character which Stephen had brought with him. But is everything that we read in such accounts to be taken as gospel truth? To take the early morning mass first of all. Everyone knew that this was Candlemas, the Feast of the Purification. The story about the candle both fixed the date and provided a suitable portent. It was perfect for the occasion. Did it happen? It might have done. The king may well have experienced problems handling a ceremonial candle in a draughty church on a cold winter's morning. Did he even go to church that morning? Granted everything that is known of him, it is very likely that he did. As with the candle, so with the double-headed axe. In some accounts it was presented to him by one of the citizens of Lincoln. Everyone knew that Lincoln was in the Danelaw and that the double-headed axe was a Viking weapon. The story about the axe fixed the place. Did the king really fight with such a weapon and engage in lengthy hand-to-hand fighting with his enemies? There are grounds for scepticism. Did he fight bravely? That certainly was the reputation that he took from the battle, in marked contrast to many of his earls, and in such engagements reputation was all-important. Stephen was indeed "noble in his valour." The epithet stuck to him.[17]

The reports of Stephen's happiness, many of them presented in the context of ceremonial, come to us from eyewitnesses. If we ask what made him angry – which may be taken as another route to a man's character – the reports are more often at second hand. He is reported as being angry in 1137 while in Normandy, when his plans to attack the Angevins were thwarted by divisions in his camp, and "most of the leaders went off

[15] GASA, i. 122; Ralph of Coggeshall, 14; Liber Eliensis, 371; Walden, 12; Hist. Abingdon, ii. 346–7; Aelred, Genealogia, col. 757; JW, iii. 242–3.
[16] HH, 732–3; GS, 110–13; OV, vi. 544–5.
[17] In Normandy: OV, vi. 544–5 ("fortiter diminicauit"); Torigni, 140–1 (interpolating an encomium in verse into his text of Henry of Huntingdon). In northern England: SD, Libellus, 312–13 ("rebus bellicis eo tempore incomparabilis"); JH, 308 ("spiritu fortudinis"). In southern England: GS, 112–13 ("valide et constantissime repugnantem"); HH, 738–9 ("rex fortissimus"); Liber Eliensis, 321 ("viriliter et constanter agens"). Later: Walter Map, De Nugis Curialium, 474–5; Gervase of Tilbury, Otia Imperialia, 482–3.

without taking leave of the king." He chased after the offenders, who were described as "hot-headed youths," and remonstrated with them.[18] He was angry in 1138, when the bishop of Bath, having captured Geoffrey Talbot, then under duress allowed him to go free.[19] A year later, in 1139, he was angry when he heard that the empress had been allowed to land at Arundel; but he was not angry at her, rather "at those whose duty it was to guard the sea ports" – they had not done their job.[20] He was "beside himself with anger" in the autumn of 1143, on learning that Geoffrey de Mandeville had occupied the Isle of Ely, "and reckoned it was all due to the machinations of bishop Nigel."[21] He was angry in 1146, when one of the sons of Robert of Gloucester, who had come over to his side, captured Reginald, earl of Cornwall. Reginald was an acknowledged opponent of Stephen's regime but he should not have been captured, for he was under a safe conduct, perhaps engaged in the peace discussions of that year.[22] In 1148, in what is possibly a first-hand account from Canterbury, the king was angry when the archbishop of Canterbury, Theobald, left to attend the council of Rheims, having previously given undertakings that he would not.[23] And finally, in 1152, when Theobald and the whole bench of bishops refused to crown Eustace as king, both father and son were "boiling with anger at this crushing humiliation."[24] On each occasion the anger imputed to the king by the chroniclers is quite believable and would have been in every way in character. These episodes take us a little closer to the man and to his conception of his kingship.

The king's authority was manifested in his court. Stephen's court held at Easter 1136, at Westminster, was the most splendid that anyone could remember. It was to this court that Robert of Gloucester and others were summoned in order that they might pay homage to the king, "along with the other magnates and barons of the land." The magnates came to court as the result of a personal summons and they left court only with the king's permission. If their loyalty was suspect, they might be required to remain at court for an extended period. This is what happened to Robert of Gloucester when, "after being summoned many times," he joined the royal court at Oxford in April 1136; he travelled with the king down to the west country, and stayed for at least some of the three-month siege of Exeter. The same thing would happen to Ranulf, earl of Chester, when he approached the king, professing his loyalty, in 1146. That is why he was at the siege of Wallingford in that year. Others will have been placed under

---

[18] OV, vi. 486–7 ("nimis iratus est").

[19] JW, iii. 248–9 ("in episcopum . . . exardescit ira"); GS, 64–5, says that the king was slightly miffed.

[20] JW, iii. 268–9.

[21] Liber Eliensis, 328 ("rex Stephanus in iram graviter accensus omnia hec reputavit ab episcopo Nigello machinari").

[22] GS, 186–7 ("offensum regem liniuit"); Strickland, War, 49.

[23] Gervase, i. 135 ("ira commotus").

[24] HH, 758–9; Gervase, i. 150–1.

the same ceremonial constraint. Dating charters in terms of a witness's perceived loyalty misses this point and probably also misunderstands their perceptions. This in turn explains why the king was angry at those who departed without leave in Normandy: it was an offence against the constitution of the court and it placed his own security at risk. Similarly with his anger at those charged with defending the seaports, when the empress landed without permission. If this level of control seems surprising, it should be remembered that there were a limited number of natural ports in England, as in Normandy, and there were royal agents in each of them. It was not a figure of speech when Robert of Gloucester claimed that he needed to give undertakings as to his loyalty before being allowed to cross to England.[25] These same officials would stop papal legates at the coast until they were given permission to proceed, and at times they might refuse them entry.[26]

There is then no reason to doubt that the king was angry when Archbishop Theobald went without permission to the council of Rheims in 1148. This went against one of the acknowledged rights of the crown, which Henry II would later refer to as "the customs of my ancestors."[27] The archbishop could hardly claim ignorance of them. When Eadmer came to tell the story of Anselm's quarrels first with William Rufus and then with Henry I, he set out several of "the customs," saying that they were necessary for the reader to contextualize the quarrel that would follow.[28] When dignitaries of the church of York, in the middle of Henry I's reign, were challenged for crossing to France without licence, they did not plead ignorance but claimed that they were not important enough to need such permission.[29] And when the prayers of Christina of Markyate ensured that the abbot of St Albans would not have to travel to the papal court either in 1136 or 1139, though he was looking forward to the chance to meet up with his old friends there, these stories are predicated on the right of the royal court to decide who should go and who should stay.[30] William of Malmesbury heard the king's counsel directly challenging the bishops, when they threatened to appeal to Rome in 1139: if they left without permission, "contrary to the dignity of the crown," they might find it difficult to return.[31] When Theobald did just that, the king was as good as his word. The archbishop was only allowed to return, after several of the bishops had taken the king's part, after a deal which reasserted royal authority over the Church. It was part of the deal that Gilbert Foliot,

[25] WM, *HN*, 32–3.
[26] JS, *HP*, 6–7, 71; JW, iii. 244–5 (in 1138); Annals of St Augustine's Canterbury, s.a. 1147, *UGQ*, 81; Bernard of Clairvaux, *Life of St Malachy*, 120–1, 142 (in 1148); JH, 326–7 (in 1150).
[27] *Councils and Synods*, 852–93 (no. 159); Barlow, *Becket*, 99–102.
[28] Eadmer, 9–10.
[29] Hugh the Chanter, 78–9 ("huius momenti"). On the next occasion, they took care to travel separately: ibid., 112–13.
[30] *Christina*, 160–9.
[31] WM, *HN*, 58–9 ("regni *dignitatem*").

who had been consecrated abroad as bishop of Hereford, did homage to the king. The king had stood upon his dignity. In his charter of privileges for the Church he had specifically reserved the rights of the crown: "All these things I concede saving my royal and lawful dignity."[32] In his early charters he had spoken of the power given him by God.[33] He intended to exercise it.

In this context, "the arrest of the bishops" in 1139 is not to be seen as a one-off aberration on the king's part but rather as the best-publicized example of a sustained attempt to use the crown's rights to discipline clergy suspected of disloyalty during the civil war. The siege of Exeter in 1136 saw the garrison leave on honourable terms and the local bishop sent into honourable retirement. The siege of Shrewsbury in 1138 saw some of the garrison hanged and the local abbot deposed. On hearing of the release of Geoffrey Talbot in the same year, the king threatened the bishop of Bath with deposition also. He believed that he had the authority to do this, even if the threat was not carried out. After "the arrest of the bishops" in 1139 Alexander of Lincoln was certainly suspended for a time. Nigel of Ely was very fortunate to escape deposition and when he did come to terms with Stephen he was treated as a lay magnate, required to surrender his own son as hostage. The deposition of the bishops of Chichester and Norwich in 1145, very likely sanctioned by the visiting papal legate, went largely unnoticed. It is almost unsettling to find the tomb of Everard of Norwich in the austere Cistercian monastery of Fontenay in Burgundy. Those who wished to rest at peace in their own cathedrals would have to make their peace with the king. They were not allowed to plead divided loyalties. Several attempted to do so: Maurice of Bangor in 1139 was told by his peers to toe the party line; Gilbert Foliot in 1148 was required by Archbishop Theobald, "partly by threats partly by promises," to do the same. Gilbert's swearing of fealty followed a concordat with the Church. Robert de Sigillo, appointed bishop of London by the empress, refused to swear fealty to Stephen for several years, during which time he was not received at court and may not have enjoyed the revenues of his see. To secure his rehabilitation, he may have been required to negotiate the return of Theobald from exile as the king's emissary; more certainly, Henry Murdac, archbishop of York, was received at court in 1151 only when he promised to travel to Rome to make the case for Eustace's coronation. It is the king's own voice which we hear in these episodes. The higher clergy were the king's men and they were not allowed to forget it.

Stephen was a peace-loving man. It was a part of the reputation with which he came and which he sustained. The king, said the author of the

---

[32] *Regesta*, iii, no. 271: "Hec uero omnia concedo et confirmo salua regia et iusta *dignitate* mea." In his transcription of the charter, otherwise exact, William of Malmesbury left this clause out: WM, *HN*, 36–7 and n. 94.

[33] *Regesta*, iii, no. 99, iv. plate VI, drafted by the chief clerk, *scriptor* xiii: "Hec confirmo et regia auctoritate statuo et a deo mihi collata potestate . . . corroboro"; and similarly ibid., nos. 335, 716, 919.

Gesta Stephani, "preferred to settle all things in the love of peace and concord rather than encourage the schism of discord in any way"; and Orderic said much the same, that "he judged it prudent to make small concessions to preserve what mattered than to grasp at everything and deservedly forfeit the support of friends."[34] Stephen could not have acted in character otherwise than he did. At what point, however, did a love of peace in a king shade into appeasement, and encourage "the schism of discord"? The question was certainly asked. John of Worcester can be seen, without the benefit of hindsight, meditating on this issue, as news of events came in to him. In 1138, at the siege of Hereford, "the pious and peaceable king" had allowed the garrison to depart unharmed, and later in the same year "the peace-loving king" had not enforced any sanctions on the bishop of Bath. By 1139, on hearing that the empress had been allowed free passage to Bristol, he could not conceal his exasperation. "Stephen is the king of peace. If only he were the king of firm justice, crushing his enemies under foot, assessing all things with the balanced lance of judgement, protecting and strengthening with his mighty power the friends of peace."[35] His sentiments were widely shared.[36] Henry of Huntingdon, in many ways the best guide to public opinion, says the same thing. Had the king been more severe, then fewer castles would have been held against him. In response to such views, so it was said, "because many unruly men regarded his gentleness with contempt," the king would show much firmer justice to the garrison of Shrewsbury in 1138.[37] William of Malmesbury was in close contact with men who had already abandoned Stephen by this date. His judgement may well be theirs. "He was lenient to his enemies and easily appeased"; "he always managed to settle business with more loss to himself than to his opponents."[38] Such a perspective cannot have discouraged rebellion.

And yet, in the face of rebellion, Stephen kept going. This was a facet of his character which both friend and foe acknowledged. "In all the misfortunes of war and strife that befell him, the king never lost hope or was broken in spirit."[39] He kept smiling. "The king himself, though straightened on every side by calamities numberless and extreme, preserved always a firm courage and a cheerful countenance . . . as if already sure of ultimate victory."[40] Henry of Huntingdon, in the version of his text completed *c.*1147, concluded with the king wearing his crown at Lincoln: "This showed that King Stephen possessed great boldness and a spirit that was not fearful of danger."[41] This aspect of the king's character sustained the loyalty and

---

[34] *GS*, 36–7; OV, vi. 484–5.
[35] JW, iii. xxxix–xl, 216–17, 242–3, 248–9, 268–9.
[36] Ibid. 268–9; *GS*, 88–9; OV, vi. 534–5.
[37] HH, 708–9, 712–13; OV, vi. 520–1.
[38] WM, *HN*, 28–9, 40–1.
[39] *GS*, 86–9; cf. WM, *HN*, 41–2, 74–5.
[40] RH, 145.
[41] HH, 748–9.

affection of those who had helped bring him to power. When he was released after his captivity, early in November 1141, Stephen was "received by the English nobility with great rejoicing."[42] In what may be a London source, this reception is represented as again following the ceremonial of a formal *adventus*: "a superb and magnificent procession of barons went out to meet him and accompanied him as an escort . . . some of them shedding tears of joy out of friendship and out of piety."[43] In the decade which followed, the king's affinity increasingly focused upon London, its royal residences and religious houses, whose records show this same mix of friendship and piety. It drew in capable men – including Richard de Lucy, William of Ypres, Robert de Vere, and William d'Aubigny – who would remain loyal to him. They addressed him with proper ceremony.[44] They remembered him in their prayers. William d'Aubigny prayed "for the safety of Stephen, king of the English, of Queen Matilda his wife, of their sons, for his own welfare, and for the soul of Queen Adeliza, my wife."[45] William would have seen himself as a member of the royal family. It was this nexus of family and friends that allowed Stephen to keep going. At its centre was the queen.

FAMILY

In any appraisal of Stephen's kingship, the queen must be given a leading role. She sustained his kingship. And in 1141 she ensured its survival, very much against the odds. Contemporary writers were in no doubt as to her influence. Looking out from London, the author of the *Gesta Stephani* saw the queen, "a woman of subtlety and a man's resolution," as the key actor in Stephen's restoration to power.[46] Seen from Rouen, the capital of Normandy, the perspective was the same.[47] To the author of the *Liber Eliensis*, she appeared as "a second Sheba, outstanding for her wisdom and prudence."[48] The queen's efforts in 1141 were directed first to diplomacy, asking for her husband's release, which she cannot have expected, and the granting to her son, Eustace, of the lands his father had held under Henry I, which she might have hoped to achieve. When diplomacy failed, she turned to force and mustered an army on the south bank of the Thames. The Londoners knew that she meant business. When the empress was

---

[42] HH, 740–1.

[43] GS, 136–7. When the king arrived from the north, he would be met by the citizens at Knightsbridge: Round, *Geoffrey*, 84.

[44] BL, Harley MS 4757 (extracts from the lost Bermondsey cartulary), fos. 3v ("Carta domini Gilberti comitis de Clara . . . directa Stephano regi Anglie et Matilda regina"), 7v ("Stephano dei gracia regi Anglie domino suo . . . scripto presenti notifico uobis domino et regi dominum meum"); *Monasticon*, vi. 1171: grant of John, count of Eu, "assensu illustris Anglorum regis Stephani."

[45] *Monasticon*, vi. 419; Holdsworth, "The Church,", in King, *Anarchy*, 223–4.

[46] GS, 122–37; WM, *HN*, 94–109; OV, vi. 546–7; *ASC*, s.a. 1140; JH, 310; JW, iii. 296–7; HH, 738–9.

[47] Annals of Rouen, s.a. 1141, *RHF*, xii. 785.

[48] *Liber Eliensis*, 322–3.

driven out of London, the queen was immediately received there and she masterminded the fightback. She seems to have pursued Geoffrey de Mandeville into Hertfordshire, where he had attempted to seize Stortford castle.[49] She negotiated with the king's supporters and she persuaded Henry of Winchester, her brother-in-law, after a "family conference" at Guildford, to abandon his support for the empress. For William of Malmesbury this was the key defection, "the origin of all the evils that followed in England."[50] The queen was then seen as having a directive role at the siege of Winchester in the autumn, gaining the support of many of the earls supplemented by "a splendid body of troops and an invincible band of Londoners." After the empress and her supporters had been forced to retreat from Winchester, it was the queen who gave orders for Robert of Gloucester's imprisonment;[51] she then negotiated his exchange for her husband; and she travelled to Bristol to act as surety for his release. The queen's victory in 1141, for it was nothing less, was the result of clear thinking and unified direction, qualities lacking in her opponents. The queen had been resolute. The epithet stuck to her.

The queen, no less than her husband, was "pious and peace-loving." The promotion of peace was a part of the job description of a medieval queen, but it was a role which suited the temperament of Stephen's queen particularly well. It was first tested in the peace discussions with the Scots following the battle of the Standard in 1138. She took a leading role here, mediating with her husband, in conjunction with the papal legate, Alberic of Ostia. The legate, we are told, noted the queen's qualities very quickly and was content to leave negotiations in her hands. It is a nice testimonial from one of the outstanding diplomats of the day. The queen headed the deputation which travelled north and concluded the resultant treaty at Durham in April 1139. Then in February of the following year, she was in France for the betrothal of her son, Eustace, to Constance, the sister of the French king. It was an impressive alliance and the treasure amassed by Roger of Salisbury was reportedly used to "purchase" the bride. The queen's concern to promote the interests of Eustace is inescapable from this point on. It underpins all her actions. It was for Eustace that she was fighting in 1141. In the spring of 1142 he accompanied her in a visit to her county of Boulogne and her lordship of Lens. The visit served a number of useful purposes. It allowed the queen to reassert her own lordship after

---

[49] In a charter in favour of the diocese of London, of which only a damaged copy survives, Geoffrey de Mandeville regretted ". . . quoque que inter me et reginam fuerat de castello de Sto[rteford]", and promised restitution: Round, *Commune of London*, 119.

[50] WM, *HN*, 98–101.

[51] In one of the miracle stories of St Ithamar, the saint was appealed to by some men living in the suburbs of Rochester who had been imprisoned by a Queen Matilda, because their lord opposed the king: Bethell, "Miracles of St Ithamar," 435. The *queen* may be Matilda of Boulogne; the *lord* may be Robert of Gloucester; and the *date* may be late autumn 1141: the queen was in Rochester at this time and Robert of Gloucester was able to establish contact with his men in Kent (WM, *HN*, 114–17).

the disjuncture of 1141. She would also have been aware that the empress's party was now promoting the claims of her son, Henry, to succeed to the kingdom of England. The king had recently been very ill. The queen was introducing Eustace to her patrimony, which she hoped that he would subsequently rule, and at the same time protecting him from harm in the event that her husband should die. It may also have been necessary to make peace with the count of Flanders, for some Flemish observers believed that Stephen had conspired with the counts of Hainault and St Pol against the count of Flanders in 1140.[52]

During this visit the queen and her son were present at the consecration of Clairmarais Abbey, alongside Bernard, abbot of Clairvaux, the abbots of the region, and senior Knights Templar.[53] The queen would have a long association with Bernard, who in a playful letter claimed his part in the safe delivery of one of her younger sons.[54] In a more serious vein, in the following year, he would write to her in the matter of the election to the see of York, where he was orchestrating the opposition to the election of William Fitz Herbert. The same messenger carried a letter to the king and a letter to his brother, Henry, the papal legate, but it was to the queen that he wrote most fully and most directly: "do everything that you possibly can to prevent that man from occupying the see of York any longer."[55] The abbot respected the conventions. It was the queen's role to act as intercessor: "if you could arrange that the king should abjure before his bishops and princes the sacrilegious intrusion on the liberty of the chapter . . . know that it would be greatly to the honour of God, the well-being and security of the king and his friends, and to the profit of the whole realm." In the same vein, in 1146, Pope Eugenius III wrote to her on behalf of the bishop of London: she was instructed to work on her husband, "by means of threats, encouragement and advice," to ensure that the bishop was received at court.[56] The abbot of Ramsey, in similar difficulties in 1144, after the rebellion of Geoffrey de Mandeville, had followed the same path, first approaching the queen: "through her, though

---

[52] *Sigeberti Gemblacensis Chronica . . . Continuatio Burburgensis*, s.a. 1140, 457; thence, *Annales de Saint-Pierre de Gand et de Saint-Amand*, lx, 166; additional colour but no more solid information is provided by Buzelinus, *Annales Gallo-Flandriae*, 232; for the context, Tanner, "King Stephen's Continental Strategies," 106–7, and Crouch, "King Stephen and Northern France," 51–2.

[53] *Regesta*, iii, nos. 194–6.

[54] *Letters of St Bernard*, no. 376. He is following up on discussions he had had with the queen in Boulogne; cf. the story in the *Vita Prima* of Bernard about Matilda coming out from Boulogne to greet him though she was heavily pregnant: *PL* 185, cols. 324–5. The story may have become attached to Bernard's visit to Boulogne at the foundation of Longvilliers Abbey, 26 Mar. 1135: *Gallia Christiana*, x. 1615.

[55] *Letters of St Bernard*, nos. 195 (the legate), 197 (the king), 198 (the queen).

[56] *PL* 180, col. 1249: "apud virum tuum et dilectum filium nostrum Stephanum, insignem regem Anglorum, efficere studeas, ut *monitis, hortatu, et consilio tuo*, ipsum in benignitatem et dilectionem suam suscipiat."

not without difficulty, he gained the favour of the king."[57] The queen was a peacemaker. The epithet stuck to her.

The county of Boulogne, and the estates of the honour of Boulogne in England, were the queen's power base. They made her independently wealthy, in a way that earlier queens of England had not been. The English lands of the honour were substantial. Appearing before the Domesday commissioners, the jurors spoke in some awe of "the 100 manors" that Count Eustace II of Boulogne controlled.[58] They brought in an income of nearly £800 a year.[59] They were the more valuable because of their location, in the wealthy south-east of England, most notably in Essex, and because a high proportion of the estate was retained in demesne.[60] The honour had come early in the reign of Henry I to the queen's father, Count Eustace III of Boulogne, and she would insist that it took its identity from him. These were "the lands of count Eustace," and its tenants were "the knights of the honour of count Eustace."[61] The queen would emphasize that she held the lands and the rights which she transferred "in right of her father."[62] The branding of the estate was a deliberate exercise. It secured its preservation and her independence, which otherwise would have been at risk. The king's own comital estates passed quickly out of his direct control: he had granted out the honour of Eye, and by the 1140s the honour of Lancaster was in the hands of the Scots. The honour of Boulogne was kept in the queen's hands. It was hers, she said – "my manor,"[63] in which she exercised "my rights,"[64] managed by "my clerks" and household officers, in accordance with her instructions.[65] In such phrases we may detect echoes at least of the queen's own voice. It is more difficult to hear her voice in the county of Boulogne, but contemporaries took it as read that the resources of the county were available to the queen in England. At the siege of Dover, in 1138, "the queen sent word to her friends and kinsmen and dependants in Boulogne to blockade the foe by sea"; the castle was soon surrendered and placed in the hands of one of those kinsmen, Faramus of Boulogne.[66] It will not have been the last such request.[67] It was

---

[57] *Chron. Ramsey*, 335.

[58] *DB*, 975, 989 (Barstable Hundred, Essex).

[59] Hollister, *Anglo-Norman World*, 99, gives a figure of £770 a year for the English estate.

[60] Tanner, *Boulogne and Politics*, 125, gives a figure of £596 a year for estates kept in hand.

[61] *Regesta*, iii, nos. 541, 550, 555 ("de honore et terra comitis Eustacii"); *EEA* 8: *Winchester 1070–1204*, no. 52: "milites de honore comitis Eustachii."

[62] *Regesta*, iii, nos. 26 ("quam ex iure paterno hactenus tenui"), 207 ("sicut comes Eustachius pater meus et nos postea liberius . . . tenuimus"), 300 ("de hereditate regine").

[63] Ibid., nos. 301 ("manerium meum de Trenges"), 541, 845 ("manerium meum de Witham").

[64] Ibid., no. 541 ("quas constat fore de iure meo").

[65] Ibid., nos. 554 ("mando vobis et precipio ex parte regine et ex parte mea"), 556 ("ipse clericus meus est").

[66] *OV*, vi. 520–1. On Faramus, see Amt, *Accession*, 85–7.

[67] The queen was seen as particularly reliant on William of Ypres and Faramus of Boulogne while the king was in captivity in 1141: JH, 310.

the Boulogne lands that provided the queen with the resources for her political activity and for her religious patronage, which were not distinct but two sides of the same coin.

    Throughout her life, the queen was closely associated with the order of Knights Templar. Within England she was their major benefactor.[68] This commitment was in her blood. Her father, Eustace, had been a crusader and her two uncles, Godfrey and Baldwin, were the first rulers of the Latin kingdom of Jerusalem.[69] Crusading was a family enterprise and the queen saw the support of the Templars as a family obligation. While in Normandy in 1137 she granted them the manor and church of Cressing in Essex, and in the same county she later added the adjacent manor and the half-hundred of Witham, as well as land in Uphall in Great Tey; then early in 1139 she granted them "all my land" of Cowley in Oxfordshire.[70] The grants, whilst generous, were not munificent: there were no wholesale alienations of complete manors.[71] Also in Essex the queen founded a new Savignac house at Coggeshall. Here she did give a demesne manor of the honour. The date of foundation was later recorded as 3 August 1140.[72] This would be a good date for the queen's foundation charter, given in London, with five earls as witnesses, including Waleran of Meulan and Geoffrey de Mandeville.[73] The house did not grow significantly from this time onwards. A number of circumstances conspired against it. The king was captured and the group of potential supporters dispersed. The links of the English houses with the mother-house at Savigny weakened. The order submitted itself to Cîteaux at the general chapter in September 1147, which was held in the presence of the pope, and the new affiliation was promulgated by him at the council of Rheims in March 1148. Some of the English houses resisted the merger, most notably Furness, Stephen's own foundation, whose abbot resigned over the issue, but they were forced to accept it.[74] The queen had other claims on her generosity and other priorities. Another site was chosen for her major benefaction and the new house was given its independence.

    The place chosen was Faversham in Kent. This was a royal manor and the king when he was in giving mode had given "the whole county" of

    [68] *Templars*, xxxviii–xlvii.

    [69] On Eustace see the sources cited in Riley-Smith, *The First Crusaders*, 205; on Godfrey, Andressohn, *Life of Godfry of Bouillon*; on Baldwin, Mayer, "La Mort et la succession de Baudoin I."

    [70] *Regesta*, iii, nos. 843, 845, 850.

    [71] The exception here might appear to be Witham, "well-known" to have been part of her father's lands, but it had been a royal demesne manor in 1086: *DB*, 970. The Cowley land was valued at just 40s: *DB*, 432. Uphall was possibly the "berewick" in Great Tey listed in 1086 and not separately valued: *DB*, 991.

    [72] *DB*, 989 (render of £20); Ralph of Coggeshall, 11.

    [73] *Regesta*, iii, no. 207. Additional charters for Coggeshall, discovered by David Crouch, are printed in Davis, *Stephen*, 166–8.

    [74] Knowles, *Monastic Order*, 250–1; Burton, "English Monasteries and the Continent," 99–106.

Kent, the royal demesne lands and all royal rights in the county, to William of Ypres.[75] In order to found a monastery here the manor would have to be reclaimed and William given compensation. It was the queen who provided the resources to do this and who would supervise every aspect of the new foundation. She granted her manor of Lillechurch in Kent to William of Ypres, in compensation for his relinquishing his rights in Faversham; she also gave the abbey her manor of Tring in Hertfordshire.[76] She stayed at St Augustine's, Canterbury, when the building works were in progress, and when Theobald placed the city under an interdict she summoned monks from the cathedral to celebrate services for her. The building of the new monastery brought the queen close to Theobald, which must have been intended: she negotiated his return from exile, and procured privileges for the monastery from him.[77] It was all designed to further the coronation of Eustace. The consecration of the new church became a peace-making exercise. The monks of the house came from the Cluniac priory of Bermondsey, a daughter-house of La Charité, where Henry of Winchester had made his monastic profession. They were family. The new monastery was designed on a grand scale, built to the highest standards with the very best of materials, as a suitable mausoleum for a royal dynasty.[78] When that dynasty failed, the building plans were cut back but it was still impressive. In the maps of Matthew Paris it is shown as offering a convenient staging-post for travellers from London to the continent and thence to Rome (see plate 3).[79] In scale and in observance the model for Faversham was clearly Reading, which had gained a reputation for regal hospitality.

The queen did not spend much time on the road. Her base was in London and in the records of two of the London religious houses she appears in a domestic and a family setting. The first of these was Holy Trinity Priory, Aldgate. Here she buried two of her children. They are named in her grant to the priory, in the mid-1140s, of a quarter-share of her manor of Braughing in Hertfordshire, "for the repose of the souls of

---

[75] Gervase, ii. 73; *Battle*, 144–5; on such grants, Latimer, "Grants of 'Totus Comitatus.'" That William indeed possessed the county is shown by: (i) his having revenues from Kent of £454 in the 1156 pipe roll; (ii) his close association with the archbishop of Canterbury; and (iii) his own charters (Amt, *Accession*, 157–65; Saltman, *Theobald*, 271–2 (no. 44), 295–6 (no. 71); *Regesta*, iii, no. 519).

[76] *Regesta*, iii, nos. 300–1; Vincent, "New Charters of King Stephen," 901, 922 (no. 4). Lillechurch (in Higham) was shortly thereafter released by William of Ypres and supplied the site and main endowment of Higham Priory. It provided an establishment for the queen's daughter, Mary, who became the first prioress: Everard, "Saint-Sulpice-la-Forêt and Royal Patronage in England," 113–19.

[77] Gervase, i. 135, 139; Saltman, *Theobald*, 71, 283 (no. 57); JS, *HP*, 89.

[78] Fernie, *Architecture*, 42, 178–9, 251–2, 264, 296, citing in particular, Philp, *Excavations at Faversham, 1965*; Vincent, "New Charters of Henry Plantagenet," no. 3 (Faversham Abbey), with valuable discussion.

[79] Vaughan, *Matthew Paris*, plate xiii: "l'abbei de Feversham ke li rois estevene funda."

Baldwin my son and Matilda my daughter who are buried in that church."[80] The house narrative gives a little more detail. "Stephen and his queen held prior Ralph and our church in such high regard that they caused to be honourably buried in our church their son Baldwin and their daughter Matilda, formerly the wife of the count of Meulan, Baldwin to the north of the high altar and Matilda to the south." This suggests that there were monuments to be seen at the time he wrote. These are the only references to Baldwin, while his sister Matilda is only marginally better recorded.[81] Prior Ralph was the queen's confessor, appointed by Archbishop Theobald, and as the queen lay on her deathbed at Hedingham he heard her confession and gave her the last rites.[82] The canons also had custody of the hospital of St Katharine's by the Tower. They had surrendered some of their own land for the hospital and had been given an additional share of Braughing in compensation. They also received the lion's share of the revenues of Queenhithe, which had earlier been given to William of Ypres and which he now handed back, adding his prayers for the souls of Baldwin and Matilda.[83] They were to support in perpetuity thirteen paupers who would pray for the souls of Stephen, Matilda, and their sons Eustace and William. As with Faversham, this was seen as the queen's personal initiative: it was "the queen's hospital."[84]

If one can reduce any set of charters to a mood, then that of Holy Trinity Priory would be prayerful and contemplative. By contrast, that of the college of St Martin le Grand, with which the queen was also closely identified, could be seen as bureaucratic and managerial.[85] For much of Stephen's reign, the college was run as a family business: it was a royal chapel, which explains the king's interest; it was under the patronage of the lords of the honour of Boulogne, which explains the queen's involvement; and, after 1139 and in succession to Roger of Salisbury, its dean was Henry, bishop of Winchester, the king's brother. The life of the city crowds up against the walls of the college. The canons had rents from houses and stalls in Aldersgate and Cripplegate and they objected vigorously when the townsmen, probably the neighbouring butchers, dumped rubbish on their waste ground.[86] The townsmen were first with the news of the civil war,

[80] *Regesta*, iii, no. 512. The manor was valued at £20 in 1086: *DB*, 381.

[81] The bethrothal of an unnamed girl, aged two, to Waleran of Meulan, was noted by Orderic in 1136: OV, vi. 456–7. Waleran was married to Agnes, the daughter of the count of Evreux, by 1142: Crouch, *Beaumont Twins*, 52.

[82] *Cart. Aldgate*, 232.

[83] *Bibliotheca Topographica Britannica*, ii. 100–1 (A xviii, no. 5).

[84] Saltman, *Theobald*, 385–6 (no. 162): "hospitalis regine." The queen's final charter in favour of the hospital shows the only surviving copy of her seal: Northamptonshire Record Office, Finch-Hatton MS 170, fo. 89v (facsimile of c.1640 = *Regesta*, iii, no. 503; *Book of Seals*, no. 424).

[85] Davis, "St Martin-le-Grand," beautifully captures this tone; see also, Denton, *English Royal Free Chapels*, 28–40.

[86] *Regesta*, iii, nos. 523–34; Davis, "St Martin-le-Grand," 242–3.

and the first to react to it, particularly if it appeared that the dean of the college was out of favour with the king. On hearing of the arrest of Roger of Salisbury, some lads went out on the town and confiscated the canons' property in Aldersgate.[87] Henry of Winchester's absences were also viewed as an opportunity to pursue claims against the canons, on more than one occasion.[88] Henry would address the citizens of London as his "most dear friends," but he more than once threatened them with excommunication if his instructions were not obeyed.[89] Ralph Davis demonstrated the close links between the college and the royal court: "it was a college of civil servants."[90] Several of these men came from the Boulonnais and evidently owed their positions to the queen.[91] And there were more of them than could be accommodated in the college. "Two brothers from Boulogne," it would later be recalled, lived in digs with a prominent citizen of London, Gilbert Becket, and it was they who introduced Gilbert's son, Thomas, to Archbishop Theobald. For Thomas, the road to power, martyrdom, and sanctity started in the London suburbs.[92] There is a range of interaction here. The links between the queen and the dean of St Martin's and the Londoners were close. And these links sustained Stephen's kingship. He had come to power as one of a family team and it had been expected that the wisdom of his brothers might "bring to greater perfection whatever is thought to be lacking in him."[93] We now turn to the brothers and ask whether or not they did so.

The eldest of the brothers was Theobald, count of Blois. Theobald certainly took an interest in his brother's kingdom. He was sighted in Normandy after Henry I's death, when some thought that he should rule the Anglo-Norman realm.[94] He joined his brother when Stephen was in Normandy in 1137 and was awarded a pension of 2,000 marks a year. He cannot have received this pension in cash for very long but – almost certainly in lieu – he was given an English estate and was an absentee landlord in England. His main lands were in Essex and Hampshire. It

[87] The king's writ for Roger, *Regesta*, iii, no. 525, identifies them as the sons of Hubert *iuvenis*, and makes the context clear, for this happened "postquam discordiam incepit inter nos"; for the repercussions elsewhere in the country, King, "Economic Development," 17.

[88] *Regesta*, iii, nos. 534, 535 (the bishop is in Rome, "with my permission and at the apostolic command").

[89] *EEA* 8: *Winchester 1070–1204*, 49–50 (nos. 71–2).

[90] Davis, "St Martin-le-Grand," 253.

[91] The 1158 constitution agreed by Henry of Winchester as dean, and his nephew William, count of Boulogne, as advocate, lists Robert of Boulogne and Master Bernard of Boulogne, as canons: *EEA* 8: *Winchester 1070–1204*, 52–3 (no. 76). Robert was the son of Richard of Boulogne, who was the queen's senior clerk: *Regesta*, iii, p. xii.

[92] *MTB*, iii. 15; Barlow, *Becket*, 29–30. The two men were brothers, "Baldwin the archdeacon and Master Eustace." They appear as the queen's clerks in *Regesta*, iii, no. 541. Baldwin was archdeacon of Sudbury in the diocese of Norwich: *Fasti 2: Monastic Cathedrals*, 69.

[93] *GS*, 12–13: "fratrum sapientium."

[94] OV, vi. 42–3 (character and reputation), 454–5 (1135), 458–9, 464–5 (1136), 548–9 (1141).

cannot be coincidence that these were the centres of his family's estates, that of Stephen and his queen in Essex and that of Henry of Winchester in Hampshire. In Hampshire he was lord of Barton, a royal manor and hundredal centre, and he was granted the royal interest in Hurstbourne Tarrant and Burbage (Wilts.), after the fall of Roger of Salisbury.[95] In Essex he was given Maldon, the second town of the county, with its royal hall and 180 burgess households. In the hall he settled Walter of Provins, the steward of his estate, and other officials. They did not just collect rents but exercised an active lordship, which some found benign, others not.[96] But it lasted for just a short time – there is no trace of this lordship after Stephen's capture at the battle of Lincoln, though Geoffrey de Mandeville had envisaged that it might be restored.[97] Theobald would remain a corresponding member of the family team: he wrote letters to the pope in support of Stephen's coronation; he was involved in diplomacy with the French in 1137 and again in 1139–40, on each occasion in association with his brother, Henry of Winchester, and in support of his nephew, Eustace; after his brother's capture, he added his voice to those urging that Eustace succeed to the family lands; and finally, when Henry of Winchester was out of favour at the papal court in 1148, Theobald successfully argued for clemency.[98] On none of these occasions could it be said that Theobald's actions brought his brother's affairs "to perfection," but he helped to keep the show on the road.

Henry of Winchester, the youngest of the brothers, was far more significant. David Knowles stated that for the first eight years of his brother's reign, he was "unquestionably the most powerful agency in England both in secular and in ecclesiastical politics"; and his influence was not greatly diminished thereafter.[99] Henry was by training a Cluniac monk, professed at La Charité-sur-Loire and then moved to the mother-house at Cluny. He would retain his links with Cluny, and visited the house often. He was certainly there in 1134, 1149, and 1155–7. Archbishop Theobald sought to recall Henry from the last of these visits, after Stephen's death and Henry II's accession, by reminding him of his priorities: "you surely do not doubt that you are far more strongly bound to the churches of Winchester and Glastonbury than to that of Cluny?"[100] The question was well put but the answer may not have been the one that Theobald expected. As later with the Jesuits, so with the Cluniacs: give them the boy and they would have the man for life. Though they might leave the monastery and move to positions

---

[95] *EEA* 8, 40–1 (no. 59); *Regesta*, iii, no. 790; Vincent, "A Prebend in the Making," 92–3.

[96] *EEA* 8, 47 (no. 68); *Regesta*, iii, no. 543; BL MS Stowe 666, fo. 33r (no. 359) – another reference which I owe to the kindness of Nicholas Vincent; JS, *Letters*, i. 233–4 (no. 131).

[97] At Westminster in June 1141, the empress agreed that she would compensate Geoffrey de Mandeville in respect of 100 librates of land in Newport, Maldon, and elsewhere, should she return to Theobald "all the land which he held in England": *Regesta*, iii, no. 274.

[98] RH, 147–8; WM, *HN*, 52–3, 78–9; OV, vi. 548–9; JS, *HP*, 10; *GF Letters*, 109–10 (no. 75)

[99] Knowles, *Saints and Scholars*, 51–2.

[100] JS, *Letters*, i. 68 (no. 37).

of distinction, yet they remained bound to it, "children of the same womb."[101] The Cluniac training gave Henry an international perspective and a distinctive cast of mind. The house was particularly associated with the peace movement. The monks were known for the rigour of their liturgical observance and for the splendour of their buildings. Henry's early promotion, by his uncle, Henry I, first to Glastonbury and then to Winchester, gave him responsibilities that came naturally to him. They gave him his independence. Henry had the confidence born of high breeding, considerable charm,[102] and enormous wealth. He would always be ready to strike a deal and happy to offer cash if that would smooth the way. If the deal could be dramatized within a liturgical setting, then so much the better.

Deals did not come any bigger than the one which led to Henry's brother, Stephen, count of Mortain, being crowned king of England in Westminster Abbey on 22 December 1135. Henry took responsibility, while the pros and cons of Stephen's candidature were debated at length, to drive the matter through; he made himself guarantor of the agreement that was made with William of Corbeil, the archbishop of Canterbury, which secured Stephen's coronation. No show was more splendid than the Easter court of 1136. Henry remained a key figure in the early months of his brother's reign, clearing up after the sieges of Exeter (where he urged severity) and Bedford (where he urged accommodation), and claiming a leading role in church appointments. His desire to succeed to Canterbury came to nothing but the consolation prize he took away from his machinations, mediated by his Cluniac brother, Alberic of Ostia, was a role which he would play to perfection. This was the resident papal legation in England, which he held from early in 1139 to Innocent II's death in September 1143. In ordinary times the office did not amount to very much but these were not ordinary times and Henry was not inclined to understate the importance of his new position. "The control of the whole of the English church has been granted to me by reason of my office," he wrote to the Londoners.[103] "It was by authority of the pope that he took his place in England," he informed the legatine council which he convened in his cathedral city in April 1141.[104] In his prayers he asked that angels would guide him into Paradise, but not yet or the country would suffer, "since on him it depended for peace or war, agitation or rest." These were the words he gave to an engraver and that appear on enamel plaques now in the

---

[101] Iogna-Prat, *Cluny and Christendom*, 45–6. Henry thought of Cluny on his deathbed: *EEA* 8, no. 131.

[102] William of Malmesbury, *Early History of Glastonbury*, 164–7: "of illustrious birth, kind and friendly in his address and noble in the kindness of his heart"; *GS*, 8–9: "a man of inexpressible eloquence as well as wonderful wisdom"; for Henry's own self-assessment, see below n. 105.

[103] *EEA* 8, 49–50 (no. 72).

[104] WM, *HN*, 90–1.

British Museum (see plate 7).[105] They may be taken as the text for his legation.

Henry served as legate between 1139 and 1143. In a series of legatine councils, convened by him and with agendas set by him, the politics of those years became dramatized. The first council was held in April 1139, to call the king to account for "the arrest of the bishops." To those who might express surprise at this disloyalty to his brother, he had an answer ready to hand, one which stressed "the exalted office of the bishop" and his primary loyalty to the Church.[106] When later in the same year he negotiated with Robert of Gloucester he again caused surprise, but his concern as legate was to make peace, and he redoubled his efforts in 1140. The country depended on him. His activity here shows an early recognition that the civil war could be resolved only by compromise between his family and that of the empress. In 1141, the capture of Stephen at the battle of Lincoln offered Henry the opportunity, which he will have seen as a duty, to take a more directive role. He would now make a deal to rival – and which indeed would reverse – that of December 1135, with the ceremonial to match. He escorted the empress into the city of Winchester, and into his cathedral, on 3 March 1141, "in great state and pomp."[107] His brother's kingship, which he had done so much to fashion, was history: it was time to move on. In another legatine council, in April, the empress was offered authority to undertake the rule of England. Henry's mistake at this point, which he realized very quickly, was to hand power to the empress, in a council whose authority was unclear and which was poorly publicized, assuming that he could thereafter make a peace that would accommodate his family's interests. He totally failed to do so in the summer of 1141; he tried again after Robert of Gloucester's capture in September, and came within touching distance of success; but again he failed. The parties returned to their old positions.[108] It would be a decade and more before the chance came again.

In the 1140s, Henry of Winchester received a very bad press. He lost moral authority in 1141. He lost the authority of the legation in 1143. Henry of Huntingdon described him as "a new kind of monster, composed part pure and part corrupt, I mean part monk and part knight."[109] In truth, this

---

[105] BM, MLA. 52, 3–27, i; illustrated and discussed in *Romanesque*, 261–2 (no. 277a–b); Haney, "Mosan Sources for the Henry of Blois Enamels"; Stratford, *Catalogue of Medieval Enamels*, 53–8 (nos. 1–2). The inscriptions read: (*a*) "The aforementioned slave shapes gifts pleasing to God. May the angel take the giver to heaven after his gifts, but not just yet, lest England groan for it, for on him it depends for peace or war, agitation or rest." (*b*) "Art comes before gold and gems, the author before everything. Henry, alive in bronze, gives gifts to God. Henry, whose fame commends him to the heavens, a man equal in mind to the muses and in eloquence higher than Marcus (Cicero)."

[106] WM, *HN*, 52–5: "episcopalem celsitudinem."

[107] JW, iii. 294–5: "cum gloria et pompa magnifica"; *Regesta*, iii, no. 343; WM, *HN*, 88–91.

[108] *GS*, 136–7: "ad priorem dissensionis punctum ex integro redirent."

[109] HH, 608–11.

hybrid was a creation of the Norman settlement, for most of the bishops, many of the abbots, and even some of the abbesses owed quotas of military service to the crown. Henry was denigrated at every turn: ridiculed for promoting the claims of three of his nephews to the see of Lincoln in 1148; threatened by the pope with suspension for not attending the council of Rheims in the same year; teased by the same pope for his famous eloquence: "he could corrupt two nations by his tongue"; slandered by Bernard of Clairvaux: "would that their songs be silenced, that Winchester is greater than Rome"; satirized by John of Salisbury for his connoisseurship, touring the antiques shops of Rome looking for the finest pieces.[110] Much of the criticism related, at one remove or another, to his wealth. He could always think in terms of four figures and such a man, though he might be criticized, could never be ignored. In the 1140s, increasingly blatantly, he used his wealth in his brother's interest. It was the mobilization of this wealth that stopped the empress in her tracks in 1141. The "affair" of Wilton in 1143 was fought on his home ground. He paid for the knighting of his nephew in 1147. Criticism came to a head in 1148. The year saw a political crisis. But it was his position, not that of Theobald, that won the day. He defended the rights of the crown and maintained his family interests. Faversham was settled by Cluniac monks from Bermondsey, though – following the precedent set by Henry I's foundation of Reading – they were given their independence from the order. The reading of the letters of exemption, which he had procured from former brethren, doubtless for a consideration, introduced a cosmopolitan note at the new abbot's consecration.[111] They reminded everyone present of Henry's networks and influence.

There was yet one final deal that Henry would strike, and it was concluded with appropriate ceremonial in his cathedral church on 6 November 1153. On this occasion, unlike in 1141, the fine print had been agreed in advance and the deal held. It was far from being one man's effort – the archbishop of Canterbury, Theobald, by this time papal legate, was also heavily involved, as were several of the lay magnates. But Henry was family, and provision for his family was the key to Stephen's acceptance. The provision could not have been more generous. Even granted this, what the queen would have made of the settlement is an interesting question. She had been close to Eustace, her long-awaited and much-loved eldest son, and had rejected the provisions made for him in Henry of Winchester's peace proposals of 1140. But now both she and Eustace lay buried at Faversham, and Stephen was resigned to accepting his brother's proposals. Stephen would remain king for his lifetime and Henry of Winchester would be the young Henry's chief counsellor: "in all disputed points in the kingdom Henry himself should yield to Henry,

---

[110] *GF Letters*, 109–10 (no. 75); Gerald of Wales, "Vita S. Remigii," in *Opera*, vii. 46; *Letters of St Bernard*, 274–6 (no. 204); JS, *HP*, 10, 78–80.
[111] The letters, which survive in the Canterbury Cathedral Archives, were from Peter the Venerable, abbot of Cluny (printed in trans. in Saltman, *Theobald*, 82) and the prior of La Charité: Gervase, i. 138.

bishop of Winchester, as to a father."[112] This was how Henry wished to be remembered. He cannot be accused of inconsistency here, for he had made identical demands of his brother, Stephen, in December 1135 and of Henry's mother, the empress, in April 1141.[113] He had managed to reassert his influence on church appointments: William Fitz Herbert was reappointed as archbishop of York and placed on the road to sanctity; Henry's nephew, Hugh du Puiset, was appointed to Durham and would become a prince-bishop in his own right. From Winchester, Henry accompanied Henry Fitz Empress to London. One of the young Henry's first acts was to confirm the grant that Stephen had made, at the very beginning of his reign, to the monks of Cluny. At the same time he offered his protection to the abbey of Faversham. Henry of Winchester's two families, his blood relations and his spiritual relations, were thus provided for.

REVIEW – DIAGNOSIS – DECISION

The chapter up to this point has considered how Stephen was chosen as king, how his character informed his kingship, and how the loyalty of his family and close associates sustained it. It remains to be seen why ultimately he failed – for fail he certainly did. He was forced to accept that Henry Fitz Empress, not one of his own sons, would be his heir, and to agree to a peace process, which taken together would be presented as the Restoration. In the framing of the peace, "the national claims for good government were strongly insisted upon."[114] The interests of the nation and its people had been compromised by the civil war. This was the view of the international community. "England, hitherto prosperous, was subject to great disasters and many died in penury," was the perspective from Germany, while to the French, "both the Roman Empire and the kingdom of the English, for the lack of an heir, were subject to many disasters and seemed to come to the point of ruin."[115] It was the view of the local political commentators. It was the view of the people as a whole: the classic passage in the *Anglo-Saxon Chronicle* claims to represent their concerns and does so in their own language. "I have neither the ability nor the power to tell all the horrors nor all the torments" that were "inflicted upon the wretched people in this country; and that lasted the nineteen years while Stephen was king, and it was always going from bad to worse."[116] Henry of Huntingdon imagines

---

[112] JH, 331.

[113] WM, *HN*, 88–9: "all important business in England, especially gifts of bishoprics and abbacies, should be subject to his control."

[114] Stubbs, *Constitutional History of England*, i. 332. Stubbs cannot be accused of leading his witnesses here, though it is not to be doubted that he did so on other occasions: Bentley, *Modernizing England's Past*, 23–32.

[115] Otto of Freising, *The Two Cities*, 429–30; Suger, "Histoire de Louis VII," ed. Gasparri, 158–9.

[116] *ASC*, s.a. 1137; on the sufferings of the poor, more briefly, JW, iii. 216–17.

the country, "wretched England," welcoming Duke Henry as its saviour on his arrival in 1153. "Greatest descendant of great Henry, I am falling into ruin – I, noble England, am falling, though not yet in complete ruin."[117] The responsibily lay with the political classes. They had failed, and they knew it. Their review of what had gone wrong would involve a close reading of what William of Malmesbury called "those things that, by a wonderful dispensation of God, have happened in England in recent times,"[118] and an acknowledgement of the need to learn lessons from them. It will be followed initially as it evolved in the councils of the English Church and in the courts of the empress and her husband, the count of Anjou. In each of these centres the review was radical and unsentimental. We will start with the Church.

As the civil war came to the English countryside, the Church acted defensively, emphasizing the distinctiveness of its order, enforcing its own penalties, seeing the very exercise of lay power as a threat. The churchmen's chief penalty was excommunication. From a weapon of last resort it now became almost a routine punishment. It might be imposed on the highest of the land: Geoffrey de Mandeville, earl of Essex, Miles of Gloucester, earl of Hereford, and Reginald of Dunstanville, earl of Cornwall, were all excommunicated at some point in the 1140s.[119] It could simply be the penalty for political independence. In 1141, Henry of Winchester, in his legatine councils, first excommunicated "many of the king's supporters, most notably William Martel," and then later, after the king had been restored to power, "those disturbers of the peace who supported the countess of Anjou."[120] As the penalty became politicized, so inevitably it became less effective: "the bishops and the learned men were always excommunicating them, but they thought nothing of it."[121] The legate would later be blamed for this excess. Specifically, according to Henry of Huntingdon, he was responsible for cases being taken to Rome on appeal, something that had not been the custom in England before then.[122] This trend was inevitable. The 1139 Lateran Council had reserved to the pope the cases of those who laid violent hands on the clergy. It was a provision which resonated as the civil war took hold in England and it was widely reported and broadly interpreted. It was picked up and developed in Henry of Winchester's final legatine council in 1143.[123] All who invaded or diminished the possessions of the Church were to be excommunicated. They were to be deprived of all ministrations of the clergy.

---

[117] HH, 760–1. And the country is personified in earlier verses also, ibid., 724–5: "Stygian gloom has come, released from the underworld, and thickly veils the face of the realm."

[118] WM, *HN*, 2–3.

[119] *GS*, 166–7 (Geoffrey), 158–61 (Miles), 102–3 (Reginald).

[120] WM, *HN*, 96–7, 110–11.

[121] *ASC*, s.a. 1137.

[122] HH, 756–7.

[123] *Councils and Synods*, 794–800 (no. 144).

Those who had any dealings with them were themselves to be excommunicated. They were not to be buried in consecrated ground and any who had been so buried were to be disinterred. It would be nearly twenty years after his death before the body of Geoffrey de Mandeville was allowed to rest in peace.[124]

Where Henry had led, the other bishops and the higher clergy had for a time been more than ready to follow. The earliest letters of Gilbert Foliot, as abbot of Gloucester, show him urging the severest penalties on those who had invaded the possessions of his own church. He used suitably warlike language. The bishop of Hereford was urged to "go as a knight into his castle, ready to fight in the name of the lord'; the bishop of Worcester was asked to give his permission for the excommunication of William de Beauchamp, the castellan of Worcester, because of his "unjust exactions."[125] Gilbert responded to a begging letter from his uncle, William de Chesney, castellan of Oxford, with a gift of 15 marks and a long lecture. Should he not change his ways, William was told, then when he died "your castles would remain here," while the reproaches of the poor, the widows, and the orphans whom he had wronged would pursue him into the next world.[126] Like any good advocate, however, Gilbert could make the case for the defence no less effectively than the case for the prosecution. This is shown in his letter to Henry of Winchester, the legate, in defence of his kinsman, Miles of Gloucester, who had been excommunicated by Robert, bishop of Hereford; this had been done, he complained, even though he and two other heads of house were willing to stand as surety:

> Hence it happens that we the living are forbidden in our monasteries to bury the dead, the divine office has been interrupted, and severe penalties enacted though we are in no way at fault. We ask that through your diligent care a matter that has been blown up out of all proportion should be softened by prudent counsel, so that the vibrations of this affair should not be felt outside the boundaries of the province, but should be heard within the province and settled by men of the province, lest by chance a matter of little importance should be summoned before the apostolic see.[127]

This surely goes to the heart of the matter. The apostolic see itself could tire of appeals. Innocent II's last letter on the appointment to York, which he hoped would settle the issue, shows definite signs of exasperation. The dispute had been running for a very long time, he told the legate, and he and the cardinals had been listening to the parties for a very long time. It

[124] Round, *Geoffrey*, 223–6.
[125] *GF Letters*, nos. 2, 3.
[126] Ibid., no. 20.
[127] Ibid., no. 22.

was time to move on.[128] The 1151 legatine council, under Archbishop Theobald, shows a marked change of tone. Those who had been bound by the chains of anathema were now positively encouraged to make a deal to pay off the debt. They might even be allowed credit.[129] Charters of restitution for damage to churches proliferate in the late 1140s and the early 1150s. They seem almost routine, with common formulas being used.[130] These are local peaces, each with appropriate ceremonial, which underpinned the national peace. At times the local and the national seem to fuse into one. At the siege of Crowmarsh in the summer of 1153, Henry, duke of Normandy, acted as a guarantor of Ranulf of Chester's generous reparations to the diocese of Lincoln.[131] The archbishop of Canterbury was in attendance. The national peace was being negotiated between the king and the duke at the same time.[132]

In its review of the civil war, the Church came to focus on the crown as the sole source of legitimate authority. The first clauses of the 1151 legatine council home in on this point. "We ordain that the church and ecclesiastical possessions should remain free from works and exactions that are popularly called *tenserie* or tallages . . . only those works owing to the king are not prohibited." Also, they were concerned to stress, royal rights of jurisdiction had to be directly exercised. "Since the churches of all England have been grievously afflicted and destroyed on account of pleas that pertain to the crown, we do not wish that they should respond to barons in respect of such pleas."[133] The context in which they might have to respond to barons in respect of crown pleas was the hundred court, for many of these courts were in the hands of magnates and church corporations.[134] These provisions of the council reflected best practice as it had developed in individual dioceses. The key years here seem to be 1147 and 1148 and the key dioceses those of Chichester, Salisbury, and Winchester. A number of public gatherings were used to get across the issues involved. On 14 November 1148, at St Paul's Cathedral, when the body of St Earconwald was transferred to a new shrine, John, count of Eu, restored the manor of Bexhill to Hilary, bishop of Chichester. This was an important manor, which had valuable jurisdictional rights exercised through its hundred court. The rights over the hundred were granted by the king in a

---

[128] *PUE*, 2/ii, no. 32.

[129] *Councils and Synods*, 821–6 (no. 150).

[130] Ranulf of Chester, c.1150, and Robert of Leicester, no later than 1147, both made grants to the diocese of Lincoln in recompense for damages caused "per me seu per meos": *Reg. Ant.* 2, nos. 316, 324.

[131] *Regesta*, iii, no. 491, with the arrangements set out more fully at the siege of Stamford, ibid., no. 492. For other of Ranulf's charters of restitution, see *Chester Charters*, nos. 34 (St Werburgh's, Chester), 115 (Burton Abbey).

[132] HH, 766–7; Torigni, 174; King, "The Accession of Henry II," 29–30.

[133] *Councils and Synods*, 823–4. On the issues raised, and the examples given, in this paragraph see more fully, King, "Anarchy of King Stephen's Reign," 139–42.

[134] Cam, *The Hundred and the Hundred Rolls*, 137–45; eadem, "Manerium cum Hundredo."

separate transaction.[135] It was all carefully choreographed. Another such solemn occasion was the dedication of Lewes Priory church on 25 April 1147, with the bishops of Winchester and Chichester present. William de Warenne, about to go on crusade, added to the Church's endowment and specifically promised to pay directly the taxes "which belong to the king" on the land he transferred.[136] Similar provisions are found in charters of supporters of the empress as well as of the king.[137] The ideas trickled down. A grant to Missenden Abbey, datable to 1148, was made "excepting the service that particularly pertained to the king according to the common customs of the land."[138] The more such phrases were read out, the more they became embedded in the political consciousness.

If we turn finally here to the clergy's review of their proper place in determining the succession, the phrase "once bitten, twice shy" if a little colloquial would seem to be exact. They had been "bitten" in 1141, for after Stephen's imprisonment they had asserted that it was their "special prerogative to choose and consecrate a prince." In recanting their choice of the empress as lady of the English, they also recanted that claim. Thereafter they would keep in step with the rest of the political community. Their own review would reduce itself to two propositions: (i) they would not question Stephen's own title to rule; (ii) they would maintain a studied neutrality on the succession. John of Salisbury, who was on Archbishop Theobald's staff, records him speaking very precisely on these two – related – issues. There are two key passages.[139] In the first of them, Theobald deals with the complaint of Henry, son of the empress, that Gilbert Foliot, the newly consecrated bishop of Hereford, should have done homage to him and not to the king. Henry was told very firmly that "a bishop had no right to cause schism within the church by refusing fealty to the prince approved by the papacy." The Church would stand for unity: "while individual dignitaries followed different lords the church as a whole followed only one." It was here accepting, under pressure, the case put to it by the king and his court. With regard to the succession, however, which would become the key issue, it did not. In the second passage John of Salisbury explains why Theobald, following papal advice, would not crown

---

[135] *Monasticon*, vi. 1171, dated 14 Nov. 1148, is the count's grant; *Regesta*, iii, no. 183, is the royal grant. On this transaction, see above, pp. 249–50.

[136] *EYC* 8: *Warenne*, 84–5 (no. 32, with facsimile), dated 1147: "de danegeld et de omnibus aliis servitiis que ad regem pertinent." There is very similar phraseology in a grant of Henry of Winchester to his canons of St Martin le Grand in London: *EEA* 8, no. 75.

[137] Reginald, earl of Cornwall, on 21 June 1152; Mabel, countess of Gloucester, and her son William, earl of Gloucester, *c*.1148: *Sarum Charters*, 23–4; *Earldom of Gloucester Charters*, 155–6 (no. 171): "omnia placita ad idem manerium pertinentia salvis rectitudinibus corone."

[138] *Cart. Missenden*, iii. 74–5 (no. 653): "excepto servicio quod specialiter ad regem pertinet secundum communes consuetudines terre." Robert de Vere, the royal constable, is the first witness to this document.

[139] JS, *HP*, 47–9 (Gilbert Foliot), 83–6 (coronation of Eustace).

Eustace, son of the king, while his father was alive, and thus give him in his turn the status of an anointed king. The Church would follow custom. It was not the custom in England – though it was in France – for this to be done. It would be particularly improper to break with custom in the middle of a civil war, when the question of right to the crown, as distinct from possession, remained to be determined. It went unsaid, but any reading of recent history would have made clear, that the question of right might be determined on the battlefield. The Church was, perhaps rather ostentatiously, not taking sides. It would facilitate a peace when the time was right. John of Salisbury here provides the type of first-hand observation, combined with political sensitivity, that William of Malmesbury had provided earlier in the reign.

The review by the supporters of the empress was if anything more radical than that conducted by the senior churchmen. They would come to accept, tacitly, as the churchmen had done, that initially they had set off down paths which they would need to retrace before any progress could be made. The review proceeded most rapidly in the early 1140s, a time of retrospection and recrimination among the supporters of the empress, following their humiliation in the summer and autumn of 1141. It was first necessary – so it would be agreed – to focus on Henry's title rather than that of his mother. This would be the easy part. The more difficult task was to formulate that title in terms acceptable to the Anglo-Norman political community. The empress's marriage to Geoffrey of Anjou in 1128 had not been popular. Simeon of Durham, writing close to the event, represented it almost as a desperate measure on the king's part, a reaction to the threat posed by William Clito, who after the disaster of the White Ship was widely seen as being "the king's sole heir and judged worthy in the expectation of all."[140] William Clito died but the fact of the marriage remained. Henry was the eldest son of the count of Anjou. He would come to rule what appears in the literature as "the Angevin empire." It is an easy extension of this phrase to speak of Henry's vindication of his title as "the Angevin succession." In fact, a great deal of effort was expended in ensuring that it could not be represented in these terms. As long as Henry's inheritance of the English crown could be represented as the Angevin succession it was not going to happen.

Orderic Vitalis in 1141, as "he brought his work to its noble close,"[141] most certainly was thinking in terms of an Angevin succession. He records how Henry, bishop of Winchester, "went over to the Angevins"; how Rotrou of Mortagne "offered his support" to, and Robert, earl of Leicester, "made peace" with, the Angevins. He was resigned to the Normans having to accept "the lordship of count Geoffrey and Matilda" at this time, but when he had written of events in Normandy immediately after Henry I's death he had made his revulsion towards the Angevins clear. Then the

---

[140] SD, *Opera*, ii. 282; HH, 594–5.
[141] Haskins, 128.

Angevins had descended on the Normans and "committed every kind of atrocity"; "the men whom they shamelessly oppressed contemptuously called them all *Hilibecci* out of hatred and scorn"; those who resisted them, he said, "refused to bow their necks to the yoke of foreign domination."[142] The author of the *Gesta Stephani* always refers to Henry I's daughter not as "the empress" but as "the countess of Anjou."[143] In so doing he reflects the usage of Stephen and his supporters in London, their bastion and very likely his base also. He like Orderic stands squarely behind Stephen. Those more sympathetic to the claims of the empress and her son had to come at the problem more obliquely. They could not ignore it. William of Malmesbury makes a joke of it: "strangely enough", he says of Henry I, "that great man, though the mightiest of all kings in our recollection or that of our fathers, yet always regarded the power of the Angevins with suspicion."[144] In the refectory of Malmesbury Abbey that aside will have provoked a belly laugh; in the hall of Bristol castle, amongst the retainers of Robert of Gloucester, at best a rueful smile. When John of Salisbury, writing after Henry Fitz Empress had become king, wrote of the empress taking her appeal to the papal court in 1139, he imagined Ulger, the bishop of Angers, debating with Arnulf, archdeacon of Sées, who was making the case for Stephen. "Your whole race," he told Arnulf, "is garrulous and deserves to be held up as an example of sinful life and skill and effrontery in lying."[145] The antipathy was clearly reciprocated.[146] John here helps to show how difficult it was for the empress to make her case to succeed to England and Normandy with an Angevin bishop arguing for her against an English bishop and a Norman archdeacon. Ulger's shocked reaction to the suggestion that the empress was illegitimate suggests that he had not a clue about the recent history of the Anglo-Norman realm, to which his client laid claim.

When William of Malmesbury came to write his version of that recent history, he chose to start with the empress's return to England after the death of her husband and with the oaths sworn to her on New Year's Day 1127. The structure was intended to demonstrate that what was said there would determine what followed. He and his readers knew well enough, however, that nothing had been settled. It would be nearly eight years before Henry I died; much would change in the intervening period; and how the oaths were to be interpreted was very far from clear. Who exactly

---

[142] OV, vi. 466–75 (1135–6), 546–51 (1141).

[143] Or simply as "the countess": *GS*, 46–7 and *passim*; so also Orderic: OV, vi, p. xxvi; and so Henry of Winchester in Dec. 1141: WM, *HN*, 110–11 and n. 260. The Gloucester chronicler refers to her at times as the "ex-empress": JW, iii. 252–3, 268–9.

[144] WM, *HN*, 4–5.

[145] JS, *HP*, 83–5. Poole, in his edition of the *Historia Pontificalis*, III, speaks of Ulger's "irrelevant invective," but John of Salisbury had included it for a purpose.

[146] The author of the *Quadripartitus*, drawing on a series of racial stereotypes, sees Henry I as having triumphed over "the perjuries of the Angevins": Sharpe, "The Prefaces of 'Quadripartitus,'" 165

was the heir? There was no agreed answer to this basic question. Simeon of Durham thought that it would be the empress's husband, Geoffrey of Anjou, who would succeed, in the event that the king had no heir by his wife.[147] The author of the *Gesta Stephani* and Richard of Hexham represented Robert, earl of Gloucester, and David, king of Scots, the senior members of the family, as stressing the claims of the empress's son, Henry. This it would have promised Robert of Gloucester, in particular, during a minority, a continuity of the influence he had enjoyed during his father's reign. But the empress focused on her own claims to the succession and most commentators concentrated on her. She saw herself as the heir to the kingdom of England and the duchy of Normandy. We can be sure of this because one of her clerks, not trained in the austere traditions of the English chancery, at times uses her own words. Miles of Gloucester, she said, after her arrival in England, "received me as lady and as the rightful heir of the kingdom of England."[148] There is a more distant echo of these words in a charter of her son, Henry, in which he refers to "the day that Robert, earl of Gloucester, and other barons received my mother as the heir of England at Gloucester."[149] The Gloucester chronicler gives the date, Sunday, 15 October 1139. We seem to detect here some kind of ceremony, in which the original oaths to the empress were reformulated and reimposed. The magnates who supported her had been summoned as though to a crown-wearing.[150]

As this title was tested, however, after Stephen's capture at the battle of Lincoln, it would not prove robust enough to survive. It would be reformulated. The change can be seen in the words which William of Malmesbury gave to Henry I when he addressed the court when the oaths were first sworn. They were chosen with great care. The king's son, William, had he not died, would have claimed the kingdom as of right. "As it was, he said, his daughter remained, in whom alone lay the legitimate succession, since her grandfather, father and uncle had been kings, while on her mother's side the royal lineage went back for many centuries."[151] The empress was not the heir but the successor. She would hand on the title to her eldest son. It was Henry who was the heir. It is most unlikely that Henry had been quite so specific in 1127; rather this is what he should have said,

---

[147] SD, *Opera*, ii. 282: "ut regi, de legitima coniuge heredem non habenti, mortuo gener illius in regnum succederet."

[148] *Regesta*, iii, no. 391: "recepit me ut dominam et sicut illam quam justam heredem regni Anglie recognovit"; BL, MS Sloane 1301, fo. 422r–v, the fuller version of the charter, has the more succinct, "recepit ut dominam et regni heredem iustam." It seems likely that in Le Mans she spoke of herself in the same vein: *Actus pontificum Cenomannis*, 445 ("Matillis Romanorum regina regis Henrici filia et heres").

[149] Vincent, "New Charters of Henry Plantagenet," no. 9 (Henry Hose): "die qua comes Robertus et alii barones receperunt matrem meam ut heredem Anglie apud Glocestriam."

[150] JW, iii. 270–3: "expetens dominium et sumens hominium"; WM, *HN*, 62–3.

[151] WM, *HN*, 6–7: "cui iure regnum competeret (William) . . . cui soli legitima debeatur successio (Matilda)."

granted the wisdom of hindsight. After the empress had been driven out from London, in summer of 1141, she was told directly by Geoffrey de Mandeville that grants made in her name alone – whatever her title as lady of the English – did not carry sufficient authority. They would need to be ratified by her husband and by her son. And so she promised: "My lord count Geoffrey will give him security with his own hand to hold to this and so also will Henry my son." As would the king of France, if that were possible. She was as good as her word. Charters for Geoffrey de Mandeville and Aubrey de Vere were taken to Henry in Normandy. His advisers were careful to have him make his own grant independently in the same terms.[152] He was "Henry, the son of the daughter of King Henry, the rightful heir of England and Normandy." His title encapsulated the two key points, that the empress was the successor to her father, and that her son was the heir.

It would thereafter be claimed that Henry had all along been seen as the heir and that Stephen rather than Henry was the foreigner.

> Invading the kingdom, he disinherited and excluded the lord for whom, if there was any loyalty in the man, he was sworn to die both because of the merits of his predecessors in the office and by the necessity of his oath. He was devoted to corrupting neighbouring nations; he contracted marriages and alliances with their princes, lest by the intercession of God the child who was still crying in his cradle might claim his rightful inheritance.[153]

It is Henry here, "the child who was still crying in his cradle," whom Stephen has disinherited. His mother, the empress, is not mentioned. The emphasis is on the rights of her son. Henry was the true inheritor of the Anglo-Norman realm. This is the final stage of rebranding and again one can see it being done, this time in the pages of Aelred of Rievaulx's *De genealogia regum Anglorum*, which can be dated almost to the day in December 1153.[154] In this work, Aelred set out for Henry "your family line," which was traced "all the way back to Adam, the father of all mortals." Henry had been "bequeathed nobility of blood from the finest

---

[152] *Regesta*, iii, no. 635, for Aubrey de Vere. The editors' summary states that Henry here *confirms* his mother's grants, but this misses the point. They take their authority from him not her.

[153] JS, *Policraticus*, ed. Nederman, 119–20 (revised).

[154] Aelred, *Genealogia*, cols. 711–38, at 737, addresses Henry as "now truly the heir to England": "Angliae *vero gaudemus* haeredem." Powicke, in Walter Daniel xci–xcii, dated the work between 24 May 1153, when David of Scots died, and 25 Oct. 1154, when Stephen died, but Eustace's death in mid-Aug. 1153 supplies a narrower date, and if we emphasize the *vero* in the address we might suspect that he has news of the peace, in which that hereditary claim was recognized, in which case we might be looking at the last weeks of 1153 or the early weeks of 1154, while if we also emphasized *gaudemus* we could note that the third Sunday in Advent – *Gaudete* Sunday – fell within this period on 13 Dec. 1153.

on both sides" of his family, he was told, but a careful reader would have noted that Aelred skipped a generation in order to demonstrate this nobility. Henry's father, Geoffrey, count of Anjou, does not contribute to it. At the end of the work, Henry is envisaged as standing at the head of an extended cousinhood, now having responsibility equally for his two brothers, for Stephen's son, William, and for the three sons of Henry of Scots, to whom in particular Aelred urged Henry to "be merciful and to aid them in their necessity."[155]

The intellectual underpinning of Henry's claim had become very strong. It was nonetheless necessary to present the claim in a measured way, one which respected the sensitivities of the Anglo-Norman political class. The review of his party determined, whether fairly or not, that the failure in the summer of 1141 was to be ascribed to the empress herself. The lady of the English was not for turning. She said "no" to the Londoners, and evidently identified herself with the feelings of Geoffrey de Mandeville when he spoke of them as "his mortal enemies."[156] She said "no" to requests "from the chief men and highest nobles of England" that Stephen be restored to liberty should he surrender the crown. She said "no" to requests from the queen and from the king's brothers that Eustace be given his father's "counties," the lands which Stephen had held before he became king. It is clear that she intended to disinherit the family entirely. It could then be represented that all of the king's supporters would suffer the same fate. The queen and her brother-in-law, the legate, had the physical resources to impede the empress, and they briefed against her, in these terms, to considerable effect.[157] Any future review, by the empress's family, would need to assuage the magnates' fears about their title. Over the next few years, the takeover of Normandy by the forces of Geoffrey of Anjou would provide a "dummy run" for the takeover of England. It was achieved not by conquest but through consensus, with the connivance of the French king, the mediation of the great men, the sufferance of the Church, and, not least, the support of the citizens of Rouen. Geoffrey was duke of Normandy for just under six years, resigning the office when his son, Henry, reached the age of sixteen. This made the point, very publicly, as Haskins noted, "that the count of Anjou had won and held Normandy for his son and not for himself." He had exercised authority with this future handover in mind, following custom and avoiding innovation; the reader of his acts, to quote Haskins again, gets the impression "of a regency rather than of a permanent government."[158] Henry's later success would owe a lot to his father's reticence.

[155] Aelred, *Genealogia*, and in trans. in *The Historical Works*, ed. Dutton.

[156] *Regesta*, iii, no. 275: "quia inimici eius sunt mortales."

[157] WM, *HN*, 100–1: the legate's complaints against the empress "were borne throughout England."

[158] Haskins, 130–1, 135.

Henry made little impact on his first two independent visits to England. In 1147 he quickly ran out of money and it was left to Stephen to pay off his troops. In 1149, when he was knighted by David, king of Scots, he stayed longer but was unable to take the fight to Stephen within England, as he had hoped to do. Yet he spoke with complete conviction that his claim would be realized, telling the bishop of Salisbury that God would demonstrate when the castle of Devizes might be returned to him.[159] And there are signs that in the community at large, not just among his own supporters, that claim was gaining acceptance. The evidence for this is found in what is, at first sight, a surprising source. Henry's two visits were fully reported in the *Gesta Stephani*. The author writes particularly vividly about London, which was Stephen's base and may have been his base also. He was impeccably loyal to Stephen. Yet on each of these occasions he introduces Henry as "the lawful heir to the kingdom of England."[160] The phrase stands out and challenges the reader. Ralph Davis saw it as showing that by the time of writing "the author had changed his sympathies and ceased to support King Stephen."[161] This view presumes that a supporter of Stephen could not view Henry as the lawful heir.[162] Yet there is every indication that many of them did so: for them there was no inconsistency in seeing Stephen as the lawful king and Henry as the lawful heir. This represented the considered verdict of the whole political community, even though Stephen and his sons had not yet subscribed to it. Two questions then present themselves. Why was it agreed that Stephen would remain as king? And why did it become inescapable that Henry would be his successor? They will be taken in turn.

That Stephen would remain king for his lifetime was in the national interest. Stephen's captivity in 1141 had shamed the country. Otto of Freising wrote that "the king fell into the hands of that woman and became her prisoner"; Henry of Huntingdon stated that it was on the empress's orders that "the king, the Lord's anointed, was put in chains."[163] Henry's gloss must reflect widespread unease about the king's capture. It was in response to this that Robert of Gloucester wished it to be known that he had treated the king after his capture with great respect. In so doing, "he both showed kindness to a relative and had regard to the splendour of the crown."[164] Stephen's captivity shamed those who had fought against him, men who had been "ready to slay the Lord's anointed."[165] He would be reported as having reproached his opponents for "a monstrous

---

[159] *Regesta*, iii, no. 795.

[160] *GS*, 204–5 ("iustus regni Anglorum heres et appetitor": 1147), 214–15 ("iustus Anglorum heres": 1149).

[161] *GS*, xxi.

[162] King, "*Gesta Stephani*," 202–3.

[163] Otto of Freising, *The Two Cities*, 429; HH, 740–1. Also OV, vi. 550–1: "At this very moment Stephen, king of England, languishes wretchedly in a dungeon."

[164] WM, *HN*, 86–7.

[165] *Liber Eliensis*, 321: "occidere christum Domini parati."

crime in breaking their faith, condemning their oaths, caring nothing for
the homage they had pledged him, and rebelling so wickedly and so
abominably against the man that they had chosen of their own will as
their king and lord."[166] There can be no doubt that this represents an
accurate reporting of the views of Stephen and his family.[167] Nor that
Henry of Huntingdon accurately reflects the views of Stephen's followers,
when he has Baldwin Fitz Gilbert speaking for the king and calling them
to arms: "We stand by the king, risking our lives to keep what we vowed
before God against those of his men who are false to him."[168] A monk of
Peterborough could represent the king's opponents as traitors: "they had
done him homage and sworn oaths, but they kept no pledge; all of them
were perjured and their pledges nullified."[169]

The oaths that were sworn to Stephen are the forgotten oaths of the civil
war. They would prove durable. They were essential to the integrity of individuals and essential to the integrity of the kingdom. The peace would recognize this. When Henry landed in 1153, he assumed that he would reward his
supporters with the lands of his opponents, but he was quickly dispossessed
of this idea. A complex series of oaths was sworn, which the Westminster
charter recorded.[170] The supporters of Henry, here simply "the duke," did
homage to Stephen if they had not already done so, or swore fealty to him if
they had, "in consideration of the honour which I have done to their lord."
As a counterpart to this, the king's supporters swore liege homage to the
duke, "saving their fealty to me so long as I live and have the kingdom." A
similar oath was taken by "the citizens of towns and the men of castles, which
I have in my demesne." The garrison of the castle of Wallingford, alone of
the duke's men, gave the king hostages. The ceremonial of oath-taking was
the key element in the "road show" which followed the Winchester *pax*, king
and duke appearing together, which dramatized the unity of the kingdom.
No expense was spared. Henry of Huntingdon reported that the meeting at
Oxford in mid-January 1154 had been "a magnificent assembly."[171] The
oaths were not just important for the magnates, they were important to the
king. They restored his integrity. Those who had abandoned him had come
back. It was as though he had just gained the throne.[172]

And yet, as everybody knew, Stephen was now holding the kingdom in
trust, having renounced his family's interest. John of Salisbury did not pull
his punches: "he was constrained to disinherit his son and to concede the
royal succession to the Duke and to bind the nobility and troops to an
arrangement of loyalty." It was a humiliation. In looking for a reason for
it, and turning to the question why it had become imperative that Henry

---

[166] *GS*, 112–15.
[167] WM, *HN*, 40–1, 94–7.
[168] HH, 732–7.
[169] *ASC*, s.a. 1137; *Liber Eliensis*, 321, in similar vein.
[170] *Regesta*, iii, no. 272.
[171] HH, 770–3.
[172] Newburgh, i. 94.

should be the next ruler of England, we come back again to the common perception that during the civil war the country had been not just dishonoured but also impoverished. England, according to Herman of Tournai, had sunk "from earlier wealth to great poverty because of the devastation and expense of persistent dissension."[173] It was a view that found a ready echo in England, among those responsible for the crown estate, and in one family above all. The family is that of Nigel of Ely, and the view is articulated in a work written by his son, Richard Fitz Nigel, intended as a guide for administrators, the *Dialogue of the Exchequer*. He started by assuring them that theirs was an honourable craft, working in the service of kings:

> We ought to serve them by upholding not only those excellencies in which the glory of kingship displays itself but also the worldly wealth which accrues to kings by virtue of their position. Those confer distinction, this gives power. Their power indeed rises and falls as their portable wealth flows and ebbs. Those who lack it are a prey to their enemies, those who have it prey upon them.[174]

In writing in this way of those kings who lacked money and fell prey to their enemies, the author undoubtedly had King Stephen in mind. Stephen had ignored the basic principles of his craft. "He squandered his money like a fool."[175] William of Malmesbury reported the king saying of Roger of Salisbury: "By the birth of God, I would give him half of England if he asked for it, until his time shall come: he will grow tired of asking before I do of giving."[176] He was picking up on a phrase that was on everyone's lips in the late 1130s: "the king gave me." He gave manors, some of them centres of hundreds with jurisdictional rights attached; he gave towns; at times he gave whole counties, transferring to one of his followers royal rights and revenues within the shire. When William of Malmesbury came to comment more broadly on the king's generosity, he saw it as one manifestation of a society that was venal and corrupt: "everything in England was up for sale."[177] The king was held responsible.

The new regime went back to first principles. Nigel of Ely, "at the repeated insistence of Henry II, restored the knowledge of the Exchequer, which had almost perished in the long years of civil war."[178] In the first full financial year of the new reign, concluding at Michaelmas 1156, the work of reconstruction is seen to be under way. The king had restored one of the "customs" of his grandfather and levied a geld. It raised £2,391 in the year of its assessment, a sum not far short of the £2,480 that had been

---

[173] Herman of Tournai, 34.
[174] *Dialogus*, 1.
[175] *ASC*, s.a. 1137.
[176] WM, *HN*, 68–9.
[177] Ibid., 74–5.
[178] *Dialogus*, 50; and see the discussion in Yoshitake, "The Exchequer."

raised in 1130. But while in 1130 the sum of £1,837 had been pardoned, the equivalent figure in 1156 was £931, while £1,083 was recorded as waste. When the figures for each county are tabulated, the median is about 25 per cent recorded as waste. The range is considerable, from less than 5 per cent in Kent, Sussex, Norfolk, and Suffolk to over 50 per cent in Leicestershire, Warwickshire, Nottinghamshire, and Derbyshire.[179] How are these figures to be interpreted? The debate has been extensive.[180] For some they provide an exact measure of the devastation caused by civil war. For others they are a simple accounting device, which allowed the sheriff to write off sums which he could not levy and close his account. The discrepancies between the counties, the total sum levied, and the nature of medieval agriculture all urge caution in too literal interpretation of the figures. It is difficult to devastate half a county, but a single estate can be rendered unproductive by the simple expedient of selling the seedcorn and driving off the livestock which provided the plough teams. This happened very frequently. Gilbert Foliot complained that the servants of his uncle, William de Beauchamp, had stolen 44 measures of well-threshed corn, while after the depredations of Geoffrey de Mandeville, the incoming abbot of Ramsey found "on all the demesne lands of the abbey only one and a half plough teams and no provisions."[181] The 1156 pipe roll shows a total of £1,178 spent in twenty-one counties and eleven separately farmed estates on re-stocking manors.[182] As an example, at Taunton the sheriff paid in just over £1 as his proceeds from the estate, he was given credit for spending over £6 in buying in new stock, and it was noted that "from now on he should render to the treasury £13."[183] These are figures that can be read literally. The images they conjure up are not really those of poverty. They are those of an ineffectual and irresponsible lordship, of an estate in wardship, in which the interests of the heir were being compromised. The estate in question was the kingdom of England. The king was held responsible.

Stephen had come to power represented as a model count, a man who exemplified the chivalric virtues. This was the character that had been proclaimed after he had become king. As Henry Fitz Empress came to

[179] The figures are from the pipe roll of 1155–6, *PR 2–4 Henry II*, 3–68; the entries are tabulated in Amt, *Accession*, 139.

[180] Davis, "The Anarchy of Stephen's Reign"; Poole, *Domesday Book to Magna Carta*, 151–3; White, "Were the Midlands 'Wasted' during Stephen's Reign?"; Amt, "The Meaning of Waste"; Green, "Financing Stephen's War," 103–4. There has been a debate, over similar ground and on similar lines, as to the meaning of "waste" entries in Domesday Book: King, "The Anarchy of King Stephen's Reign," 143–4; Roffe, *Decoding Domesday*, 250–6.

[181] *GF Letters*, no. 3; *Chron. Ramsey*, 333–4, cited with related texts in Knowles, *Monastic Order*, 268–72.

[182] Amt, *Accession*, 142.

[183] Ibid., 146; *PR 2–4 Henry II*, 48. Taunton was one of the major estates of the bishopric of Winchester, taken in hand because Henry of Winchester was in exile.

power, Stephen was represented no less categorically, as having become not a model king but a tyrant.[184] The indictment, as John of Salisbury sets it out, may seem harsh but it drew on aspects of Stephen's character that his readers would readily have recognized. The king, so he claimed, had "neglected discipline to the extent that he did not so much rule as intimidate and bring clergy and people into conflict."[185] The picture of a king who was irresolute and easily led was drawn from the life. As lord of Alençon he had been misguided, trusting "like Rehoboam the fawning of sycophants not the counsel of the elders."[186] This comment from Orderic provides the first attempt at a character assessment of Stephen. It was a character that stayed with him. Abbot Geoffrey of St Albans told Christina of Markyate that he feared the "fickleness" of the king, a man, he said, "sometimes more inclined to believe flatterers than those who spoke the truth."[187] William of Malmesbury wrote in the same vein: the king was "easily manipulated" in his view, "too ready to lend a sympathetic ear to those who were ill-disposed."[188] The story of Stephen's reign was one of divided counsels. The theme provided a template for an analysis of the main events of the reign: at the siege of Exeter in 1136, when the king's supporters "changed him to another man"; at Normandy in 1137, when his army split into factions; in 1139, when his "excessive favour" to some of his magnates led to the arrest of the bishops; and in 1141 at Lincoln, when he "ignored the advice of prudent men" and offered battle.[189] The most protracted example of indecision came with his treatment of Ranulf of Chester in 1146. The earl approached the king and made an agreement with him: "it came to nothing, because after this the king captured him at Northampton through bad counsel, and put him in prison; and soon he let him out through worse counsel, on condition . . . that he would surrender his castles."[190] The way the story is told here in the *Anglo-Saxon Chronicle* suggests that the king's indecisiveness was something of a standing joke. The one time when Stephen's interests were pursued single-mindedly and with complete success was in the spring and summer of 1141, when he was in captivity and the direction lay with the queen and the legate.[191]

Stephen's opponents represented him not just as indecisive but also as underhand. He had come to power as a great courtier and his early courts had been splendid occasions. Yet as the reign wore on, with some regularity, a dispute would flare up and a prominent member of the court be arrested.

[184] JS, *Entheticus*, i. 190–1 (cap. 86), ii. 377–8.

[185] JS, *Policraticus*, bk vi, cap. 18, trans. Nederman, 119.

[186] OV, vi. 204–7; 2 Chron. 10:6–14. Orderic had used the same scriptural reference when writing of Robert, duke of Normandy: OV, iii. 98–101.

[187] *Christina*, 168–71.

[188] WM, *HN*, 32–3, 36–7.

[189] *GS*, 42–3 (1136); OV, vi. 484–7 (1137); WM, *HN*, 46–7 (1139); OV, vi. 540–3 (1141).

[190] *ASC*, s.a. 1140; with detail in *GS*, 184–5, 192–7.

[191] Henry of Winchester was never a man to a abandon a course of action once he had set his mind to it: WM, *HN*, 108–11.

The best-known episode is the first, the arrest of the bishops of Salisbury and Lincoln in 1139, "an extraordinary and scandalous event" in the view of one of their officials, one which would "prefigure the eventual fall of Stephen's house."[192] The attempted capture of Ranulf of Chester at Christmas 1140 showed many of the same features, as did the arrest of Geoffrey de Mandeville in 1143, and of Ranulf of Chester in 1146; "by the end no one felt secure in coming to his court."[193] On the king's side the arrests were represented as attempting to forestall potential treachery and as defending the rights of the crown. Geoffrey de Mandeville, it was claimed, "had cunningly appropriated all the royal prerogatives," while Ranulf of Chester "had appropriated the rights of the crown": the arrests were to ensure that the king recovered "what was recognised as belonging to the crown." The king's defence had been heard at the time with a large measure of sympathy but by the end of the reign the specific circumstances of each arrest had been lost to view. What was remembered was how the king had treated his own subjects within his court. On every occasion he had received the individuals peaceably and ceremoniously. They had been given no notice of the charges that would be levied against them. They were not given the chance to consult their advisers and mount a considered defence. All this meant that they never received a fair hearing. The reports make it clear that the arrests were seen as important, that the issues involved were actively debated, and the conclusions were not to the king's advantage. The king's court was a protected space and the king's men had been denied his protection. It was a shocking betrayal of trust.[194] The arrests were taken as symptomatic both of division and deceit. "And so the kingdom vacillated and the status of the kingdom with it, under a pitiable leader."[195]

The new regime would offer unity in place of division, clear direction in place of vacillation. The peace process was designed as a demonstration of what could be achieved. It was one aspect of the restoration of the integrity of the kingdom, singled out in the proclamation of the peace, that orders be given "for the dismissal from the kingdom of mercenary soldiers and archers of foreign nations."[196] Their arrival had been taken by William of Malmesbury as symptomatic of the breakdown of authority post-1135. "Knights of all kinds hastened to the king, as also those more lightly armed, especially from Flanders and Brittany. They were a class of men full of greed and violence."[197] Some of the worst atrocities of the civil war which followed had been, and continued to be, laid at their door. The removal of

[192] HH, 718–21; WM, *HN*, 45–6; *GS*, 74–7.

[193] WM, *HN*, 82–3; HH, 726–7 (1140); *Walden*, 14–15; HH, 338–9 n. 2, 742–3 (1143); HH, 748–9; *GS*, 196–7 (1146); JS, *Policraticus*, bk vi, cap. 18, trans. Nederman, 120

[194] Henry of Huntingdon, in referring to the *ius gentium*, "is describing dishonourable behaviour and seeking to draw attention to a betrayal of trust": HH, 338–9 n. 2, 742–3.

[195] *Waltham*, 76–7: "sic uacillaret regnum et regni status miserabili ductore."

[196] JH, 331.

[197] WM, *HN*, 32–3.

"this class of man" and the destruction of castles, some of which they had garrisoned, went together as a part of the process. Gervase of Canterbury makes much of the dangers threatened by "the Flemish wolves," and he lumps the Flemings, or rather all "foreigners," together: "it was made known that all foreigners were to be kicked out of the kingdom and that all those dreadful little castles the length and breadth of England were to be levelled to the ground."[198] It is not surprising that William of Ypres, the most loyal of Stephen's lieutenants, should now be identified as "that notorious tyrant and most grievous persecutor of our church" and "expelled from the realm of England."[199] It is slightly more surprising to find that Stephen himself – in specific contrast to Duke Henry – was now labelled as a "foreigner." This analysis drew on the insistence on Henry's English antecedents, as they had been seen set out by Aelred of Rievaulx. It drew also on the widespread support he had attracted after his arrival in England in 1153. At the siege of Crowmarsh, identified as a key episode by John of Salisbury,[200] the duke reportedly relied not on "men of foreign birth" but rather, for the most part, on "our chaps."[201]

John of Salisbury is here picking up on something important, a little surprising when viewed from a distance, but which those close to events would readily have recognized. Henry in all but name was offering a government of national unity. As duke of Normandy he had chosen his own men, notably his household officers, Manasser Bisset, the steward, Richard du Hommet, the constable, and Warin Fitz Gerald, the chamberlain. In terms of their backgrounds, these men already commanded a broad geographical range within the Anglo-Norman world, for Manasser Bisset was from the Pays de Caux, Richard Hommet was from western Normandy, while Warin Fitz Gerald came from Essex and was a member of a family in which household service was "an inherited tradition."[202] Henry would go on to work no less closely with men who joined him only after he came to England in 1153. Richard de Lucy had been at Stephen's side during the siege of Malmesbury, and he had led loyalist forces from Oxford at the siege of Wallingford, yet he is a key figure in the peace, holding the Tower of London and Windsor Castle on terms agreed by king and duke. He had been defending the rights of the crown, in Essex in particular,[203] for a decade and more, and he would become Henry's first justiciar. His co-justiciar was Robert, earl of Leicester, who had come to

[198] Gervase, i. 160–1.

[199] By Archbishop Theobald: JS, *Letters*, i. 37–8 (no. 23).

[200] Was he present? He was a clerk of Archbishop Theobald, who certainly was, and the reports may have come from him: *Regesta*, iii, no. 491.

[201] JS, *Policraticus*, ed. Webb, ii. 52–3. "Ne tamen hoc alienigenae ascribant uiribus suis, *nostro* praecipue *milite* nitebatur."

[202] Haskins, 161–3; Loyd, *Origins*, 15–16, 52; Vincent, "Warin and Henry Fitz Gerald, the King's Chamberlains," 233–52, at 251.

[203] See Vincent, "New Charters of King Stephen," 912–21, for evidence of "an alert forest administration" within the county.

terms with Henry earlier in the year and had offered him hospitality and
sound advice. There were others based in England, and thus to be
counted as "our chaps," who were evidently important as counsellors in
1153–4. William d'Aubigny, earl of Chichester, by now the widower of an
English queen, was certainly among them. Gervase of Canterbury attrib-
utes to him an eloquent speech on the need for national reconciliation at
the time of the siege of Wallingford.[204] William's chief agent was Jocelin
of Louvain, his brother-in-law, who has been seen as acting as intermediary betwen Duke Henry and the earl.[205] A similar role can be envisaged for Reginald de Warenne, the fixer in that formidable family,
solicitous for the interests of Earl William, the king's son.[206] These were
men of wide experience. They knew their lines. William d'Aubigny, at
Chichester, publicly repudiated a long list of his earlier exactions and
made "restitution for the damage which he had caused to the cathedral
church."[207] At Buckenham, the centre of his East Anglian estate, he seems
consciously to be making a fresh start, founding a new town and being
careful to specify that the castle on the original site was to be destroyed.[208]
These men now lined up behind the king and duke. They may be seen as
the "platform party" at what has been termed a "road show," as king and
duke received the homages which bound the nation together. The duke's
charter for Faversham gives perhaps the fullest list: after the king himself
and nine bishops it is witnessed by William, the king's son, William, earl of
Gloucester, Robert, earl of Leicester, Reginald, earl of Cornwall, William
Martel, Richard de Lucy, Manasser Bisset, and Richard du Hommet.
This was in Westminster.[209] Charters issued at Dunstable make the same
point.[210] To those attending, the sight of these men working together will
have been much more reassuring than any number of proclamations.

That this group of counsellors became a cohesive body who would
serve the new king, often for many years, must have been in one sense an
accident. The peace process was not what the protagonists wanted. Yet the
lengthy discussions that necessarily preceded the peace, "in order to take
the interests of both parties into account,"[211] gave those involved – the

---

[204] Gervase, i. 154: "vir eloquentissimus."

[205] Crouch, *Stephen*, 264–5, 269–70.

[206] *EYC* 8: *Warenne*, 47–51; Vincent, "Foundation of Wormegay Priory."

[207] Chichester, West Sussex Record Office, Ep. VI/1/6, fos. 126r–v ("hanc refutationem et libertatem concessionem"), 84r ("pro recompensatione dampnorum que eidem ecclesie feceram"), dated 2 Feb. 1148. He had reason to remember the date.

[208] *Facsimiles of Charters in the British Museum* i, no. 27, dated to Apr. 1151–Apr. 1152: "et castellum diruendum"; Beresford and St Joseph, *Medieval England: An Aerial Survey*, 226–8.

[209] Vincent, "New Charters of Henry Plantagenet," no. 3 (Faversham Abbey); a slightly shorter list is found in the equivalent charter issued for Cluny, *Regesta*, iii, no. 206.

[210] The king's charter for St Augustine's, Bristol, *Regesta*, iii. 127, is witnessed by William de Chesney, Richard de Canville, Richard du Hommet, constable, Manasser Bisset, steward, and Warin Fitz Gerald, chamberlain.

[211] *English Lawsuits*, i. 299: "secundum quod utriusque partis poscebat utilitas"; King, "Dispute Settlement," 124.

higher clergy and their secretaries, the magnates and their household officers – a common purpose. Those who had negotiated the peace remained responsible for it. While the Westminster charter spoke of two regions, and the charter witness lists seem to show two separate courts, it is still possible to speak of a common enterprise. Early in the new reign, in a matter-of-fact way, the chronicler of Battle Abbey speaks of Reginald, earl of Cornwall, and Richard du Hommet, the king's constable, along with Richard de Lucy and (his brother) Abbot Walter, as "joined together in a pact of friendship."[212] Such a pact might well have been made before Henry returned to Normandy in March 1154, taking Richard du Hommet with him, leaving Reginald of Cornwall responsible for his affairs in England, while Richard de Lucy remained at Stephen's court. Early in the new reign, John of Salisbury in his *Entheticus* provides a satirical view of the new Camelot.[213] We cannot be sure whose is the voice that states brusquely, "I speak of the king's profit"; or who is Mandroger," who boasts that "he alone preserves the Crown and is the father of the laws of the kingdom"; or who is "Antipater," who asserts that clergy and people should be governed by the same law.[214] One member of this confederacy would serve as well as another.[215] These men form "the new court under a youthful king," men confident of their mission: "from this the disgrace of the kingdom is thrown away; from this comes its glory!"[216] John of Salisbury here captures the authentic voice of the new regime.

In December 1135 Stephen, count of Mortain, was chosen as king by the Anglo-Norman political community. He would never forget it. He was quoted early in his reign as complaining that his support was drifting away. "When they have elected me king, why do they abandon me? By the birth of God, I will never be called a king without a throne!"[217] The way that he is made to pose the question, by a very shrewd observer, is interesting. He does not speak of entitlement to the throne, rather that it had been offered to him. It was something that had happened to him, not something to which he had been born. As we have attempted to follow the process of appraisal, which would give the nation's answer to the question Stephen posed, this is a point that has come across very strongly. Stephen never appears as his own man. He was the creation of others, used to further

[212] *Battle*, 160–1: "amicitie federeconiuncti erant"; for discussion, see Amt, "Richard de Lucy," 70–5.
[213] JS, *Entheticus*; for discussion of the date of composition, see Thomson, "What is the *Entheticus?*"
[214] JS, *Entheticus*, i. 190–1, l. 1324: "de regis utilitate loquar"; 194–5, ll. 1363–4: "qui se solum servare coronam / et legum regni iactitat esse patrem"; ll. 1389–90: "clerum populumque / decernit similem iure tenere locum."
[215] Another formulation found in *Battle*, 196–9 ("omnibus his sibi coherentibus"), for a group including Richard de Lucy, Robert of Leicester, and Reginald de Warenne.
[216] JS, *Entheticus*, i. 196–7, ll. 1395–6: "dedecus hinc regni vertitur, / inde decus"; 200–1, ll. 1463–4: nova curia rege / sub puero."
[217] WM, *HN*, 40–1.

their ambitions: of his uncle, Henry I, for whom he was a counter to William Clito, his promotion showing the extent of but also the limits to the king's generosity to his nephews; and then, after the king's death, of his younger brother, Henry, bishop of Winchester. Without Henry, so people said at the time, Stephen would have been nothing. This may originally have been a figure of speech but by the end of the reign it would have been viewed as a statement of fact. Stephen must be, as he was at the time, given credit for sustaining a strong marriage; but again, it appears on appraisal, the strength was derived from the queen. Stephen must also be given credit for keeping the loyalty of some capable men, but their attachment appears to be to the queen as much as to the king. She certainly had close ties to Richard de Lucy, whose honour was based on Boulogne property, to Aubrey de Vere,[218] in one of whose houses she died, and to William of Ypres. It was the queen not the king who was responsible for the religious benefactions of Stephen's reign. She was the builder. The queen had a clear sense of entitlement, as no less clearly did her brother-in-law, Henry of Winchester, and with it a sense of responsibility. With Henry you see a horror of alienation of any kind. He was outraged in the 1120s when a Glastonbury tenant declared as waste a fertile estate, which on inspection proved to contain "waving corn, golden in colour, making a soft murmur in the breeze."[219] He was distraught on his deathbed in 1171, confessing to the loss of two Winchester estates, which he saw as imperilling his immortal soul.[220] The concern in each case came from a sense of history, of lordship that was grounded in the English countryside. That of Stephen never was. He was acting a part. And never with real conviction. Henry of Huntingdon imagined the king, before the battle of Lincoln, as giving his lines to Baldwin Fitz Gilbert, "since he himself lacked a commanding voice."[221] This may stand as an image of Stephen's kingship (see plate 18). He never made his voice heard.

---

[218] *Regesta*, iii, no. 242; Crouch, "Aubrey III de Vere."

[219] *English Lawsuits*, i. 222 (no. 258).

[220] *EEA* 8, 93–4 (no. 131).

[221] HH, 732–3: "quia rex Stephanus festiua caret uoce." There is a nice drawing of the scene in BL, Arundel MS 48, fo. 168v, made *c.*1200. This is the "portrait" selected to illustrate King, "Stephen, King of England."

BIBLIOGRAPHY

PRIMARY SOURCES

Acta of the Bishops of Chichester 1075–1207, ed. H. Mayr-Harting (Canterbury and York Soc. 130, 1962)

Actes des comtes de Flandre 1071–1128, ed. F. Vercauteren, Recueil des Actes des Princes Belges (Brussels, 1938)

Actus pontificum Cenomannis in urbe degentium, ed. G. Busson and A. Ledru (Archives Historiques de Maine 2; Le Mans, 1901)

Adam of Domerham, *Historia de rebus gestis Glastoniensibus*, ed. T. Hearne, 2 vols (London, 1727)

Aelred of Rievaulx, *De genealogia regum Anglorum*, in *PL* 195, cols. 711–38

——, *Eulogium Davidis*, in *Pinkerton's Lives of the Scottish Saints*, ed. W. M. Metcalfe, 2 vols (Paisley, 1889), ii. 269–95

——, *Relatio venerabilis Aelredi, abbatis Rievallensis, de Standardo*, in *Chronicles*, iii. 181–99

——, *The Historical Works*, trans. Jane Patricia Freeland, ed. Marsha L. Dutton (Cistercian Fathers 56; Kalamazoo, Mich., 2005)

Albert of Aachen, *Historia Ierosolimitana: History of the Journey to Jerusalem*, ed. Susan B. Edgington (OMT, 2007)

"Anglo-Norman Chronicle of Wigmore Abbey," ed. J. C. Dickinson and P. T. Ricketts, *Trans. Woolhope Field Club* 39 (1969), 413–46

Anglo-Saxon Chronicle, ed. Dorothy Whitelock, rev. edn (London, 1965)

Annales Cestrienses: The Chronicle of the Abbey of St Werburgh, Chester, ed. R. C. Christie (Rec. Soc. of Lancashire and Cheshire 14, 1887)

Annales de Saint-Pierre de Gand et de Saint Amand, ed. Philip Grierson (Brussels, 1937)

Annales de l'abbaye Saint-Pierre de Jumièges, ed. Jean Laporte (Rouen, 1954)

Annales Monastici, ed. Henry Richards Luard, 5 vols (RS 36, 1864–9)

Baudri de Bourgueil, *Les Oeuvres poétiques de Baudri de Bourgueil (1046–1130)*, ed. Phyllis Abrahams (Paris, 1926)

Bernard of Clairvaux, *Life of St Malachy of Armagh*, ed. H. J. Lawlor (London, 1920)

Book of the Foundation of Walden Monastery, ed. Diana Greenway and Leslie Watkiss (OMT, 1999)

Book of St Gilbert, ed. Raymonde Foreville and Gillian Keir (OMT, 1987)

Brut Y Tywysogyon, or the Chronicle of the Princes: Red Book of Hergest Version, ed. Thomas Jones (Cardiff, 1955)

Calendar of the Charter Rolls, 6 vols (London, 1903–27)

Canterbury Professions, ed. Michael Richter (Canterbury and York Soc. 67, 1973)

Cartae Antiquae Rolls, 11–20, ed. J. Conway Davies (Pipe Roll Soc. NS 33, 1957)

Cartulaire d'Afflighem, ed. Edgar de Marneffe (Analectes pour server à l'histoire ecclésiastique de la Belgique 2: 1–5; Louvain, 1894)

Cartulaire de l'abbaye de Conques en Rouergue, ed. Gustave Desjardins (Paris, 1879)

Cartulaire de l'abbaye de Saint-Père de Chartres, ed. Benjamin E. C. Guérard, 2 vols (Paris, 1840)

Cartulaire de l'abbaye de la Sainte-Trinité de Tiron, ed. Lucien Merlet, 2 vols (Chartres, 1883)

Cartulaire de l'église Notre-Dame de Paris, ed. Benjamin E. C. Guérard, 4 vols (Paris, 1850)

Cartulaire de Marmoutier pour le Dunois, ed. Emile Mabille (Châteaudun, 1874)

Cartulaire de Notre-Dame de Chartres, ed. Eugène de Lépinois and Lucien Merlet, 2 vols (Chartres, 1862–5)

Cartulaire du prieuré de La Charité-sur-Loire (Nièvre), ordre de Cluni, ed. René de Lespinasse (Nevers and Paris, 1887)

Cartulaires de l'abbaye de Molesme, ed. Jacques Laurent, 2 vols (Paris, 1907–11)

Cartularium Abbathiae de Whiteby, ed. J. C. Atkinson, 2 vols (Surtees Soc. 69, 72; 1879–81)

Cartularium Monasterii de Rameseia, ed. William Henry Hart and Ponsonby A. Lyons, 3 vols (RS 79, 1884–94)

Cartularium Monasterii S. Johannis Baptiste de Colecestria, ed. S. A. Moore, 2 vols (Roxburghe Club, 1897)

Cartulary of Holy Trinity Aldgate, ed. Gerald A. J. Hodgett (London Rec. Soc. 7, 1971)

Cartulary of Missenden Abbey, ed. J. G. Jenkins, 3 vols (Buckinghamshire Rec. Soc. 2, 10, 12; 1938–62)

Cartulary of Shrewsbury Abbey, ed. Una Rees, 2 vols (Aberystwyth, 1975)

Cartulary of St Augustine's Abbey, Bristol, ed. David Walker (Bristol and Gloucestershire Archaeological Soc., Gloucestershire Rec. Series 10, 1998)

Cartulary of the Abbey of Mont-Saint-Michel, ed. K. S. B. Keats-Rohan (Donington, 2006)

Cartulary of the Monastery of St Frideswide in Oxford, ed. S. R. Wigram, 2 vols (Oxford Hist. Soc. 28, 31; 1895–6)

Cartulary of Worcester Cathedral Priory, ed. R. R. Darlington (Pipe Roll Soc. NS 38, 1968)

Charters of the Anglo-Norman Earls of Chester, c.1071–1237, ed. Geoffrey Barraclough (Rec. Soc. of Lancashire and Cheshire 126, 1988)

"Charters of the Earldom of Hereford, 1095–1201," ed. David Walker, in *Camden Miscellany XXII* (London, 1964), 1–75

Charters of the Honour of Mowbray 1107–1191, ed. D. E. Greenway (British Academy Records of Social and Economic History NS 1, 1972)

Charters of King David I: The Written Acts of King David I King of Scots, 1124–53, and of his son Henry Earl of Northumberland, 1139–52, ed. G. W. S. Barrow (Woodbridge, 1999)

Charters of the Redvers Family and the Earldom of Devon, 1090–1217, ed. Robert Bearman (Devon and Cornwall Rec. Soc. NS 37, 1994)

Chartulary of the High Church of Chichester, ed. W. D. Peckham (Sussex Rec. Soc. 46; 1946)

Chartulary of the Priory of St Pancras of Lewes, ed. L. F. Salzman, 2 vols (Sussex Rec. Soc. 38, 40; 1933–5)

Chronicle of Battle Abbey, ed. Eleanor Searle (OMT, 1980)

Chronicle of John of Worcester, ed. R. R. Darlington and P. McGurk, vols 2–3 (OMT, 1995–8)

Chronicle of Melrose, facsimile edn, ed. A. O. Anderson and M. O. Anderson (London, 1936)

Chronicles of the Reigns of Stephen, Henry II and Richard I, ed. Richard Howlett, 4 vols (RS 82, 1884–9)

Chronicon Angliae Petriburgense, ed. J. A. Giles (Caxton Soc. 2; 1845)

Chronicon Monasterii de Melsa, ed. Edward A. Bond, 3 vols (RS 43, 1866–8)

"Chronicon Sancti Sergii Andegavensis," in *Chroniques des églises d'Anjou*, ed. P. Marchegay and E. Mabille (Paris, 1869)

Chronicon Valassense, ed. F. Somménil (Rouen, 1868)

Chronique de Morigny (1095–1152), ed. Léon Mirot (Paris, 1909)

Chronique de Saint-Pierre-le-Vif de Sens, dite de Clarius, ed. Robert-Henri Bautier and Monique Gilles (Paris, 1979)

Chroniques des comtes d'Anjou et des seigneurs d'Amboise, ed. Louis Halphen and René Poupardin (Paris, 1913)

Correspondence of Thomas Becket, Archbishop of Canterbury, 1162–1170, ed. Anne Duggan, 2 vols (OMT, 2000)

Coucher Book of Furness Abbey, ed. J. C. Atkinson and J. Brownbill, 2 vols in 6 parts (Chetham Soc., NS, 9, 11, 14, 74, 76, 78; 1886–1919)

Councils and Synods with Other Documents Relating to the English Church 1, part 2: 1066–1204, ed. D. Whitelock, M. Brett, and C. N. L. Brooke (Oxford, 1981)

Coutumiers de Normandie, ed. Ernest-Joseph Tardif, Société de l'histoire de Normandie (Rouen, 1881)

Curia Regis Rolls. 20 vols (London, 1923–2006)

Customary of the Benedictine Abbey of Bury St Edmunds in Suffolk, ed. Antonia Gransden (Henry Bradshaw Soc. 99, 1973)

De expugnatione Lyxbonensi: The Conquest of Lisbon, ed. C. W. David (Columbia Records of Civilization 24; New York, 1936)

Dialogus de Scaccario, ed. Charles Johnson (NMT, 1950)

Diplomatic Documents Preserved in the Public Record Office 1: *1101–1272*, ed. Pierre Chaplais (London, 1964)

Documents historiques inédits, ed. J. J. Champollion Figeac, 5 vols (Paris, 1841–74)

Domesday Book: A Complete Translation, ed. Ann Williams and G. H. Martin (Harmondsworth, 2002)

Eadmer, *Historia Novorum*, ed. Martin Rule (RS 81, 1884)

——, *Eadmer's History of Recent Events in England*, trans. Geoffrey Bosanquet (London, 1964)

Earldom of Gloucester Charters: The Charters and Scribes of the Earls and Countesses of Gloucester to 1217, ed. Robert B. Patterson (Oxford, 1973)

Early Yorkshire Charters, 1–3, ed. W. Farrer (Edinburgh, 1914–16); 4–12, ed. C. T. Clay (Yorkshire Arch. Soc., 1935–65)

English Diplomatic Documents 1: *1101–1272*, ed. Pierre Chaplais (London, 1964)

English Episcopal Acta, 34 vols (London, 1980–2009)

English Lawsuits from William I to Richard I, ed. R. C. Van Caenegem, 2 vols (Selden Soc. 106–7, 1990–1)

English Register of Godstow Nunnery, ed. Andrew Clark, 3 vols (Early English Text Society 129–30, 142; 1905–11)

Epistolae Pontificum Romanorum ineditae, ed. S. Löwenfeld (Leipzig, 1885)

Eye Priory Cartulary and Charters, ed. Vivien Brown, 2 vols (Suffolk Charters 12–13, 1992–4)

Eynsham Cartulary, ed. H. E. Salter, 2 vols (Oxford Hist. Soc. 49, 51; 1907–8)

Facsimiles of Early Charters from Northamptonshire Collections, ed. F. M. Stenton (Northamptonshire Rec. Soc. 4, 1930)

Facsimiles of Royal & Other Charters in the British Museum 1: *William I–Richard I*, ed. George F. Warner and Henry J. Ellis (London, 1903)

Fasti Ecclesiae Anglicanae, 1066–1300, ed. Diana E. Greenway et al., 10 vols (London, 1968–2005)

Feudal Documents from the Abbey of Bury St Edmunds, ed. D. C. Douglas (British Academy Records of Social and Economic History 8; London, 1932)

First Register of Norwich Cathedral Priory, ed. H. W. Saunders (Norfolk Rec. Soc. 11, 1939)

Foundation History of the Abbeys of Byland and Jervaulx, ed. Janet Burton (Borthwick Texts and Studies 35; York, 2006)

Galbert of Bruges, *The Murder of Charles the Good, Count of Flanders*, ed. James Bruce Ross, rev. edn (New York, 1967)

Gallia Christiana, 16 vols (Paris, 1715–1865)

Geoffrey of Monmouth, *The History of the Kings of Britain*, ed. Michael D. Reeve and Neil Wright (Arthurian Studies 69; Woodbridge, 2007)

Gerald of Wales, *Opera*, ed. J. S. Brewer, James F. Dimock, and George F. Warner, 8 vols (RS 21, 1861–91)

Gervase of Canterbury, *Historical Works*, ed. William Stubbs, 2 vols (RS 73, 1879–80)

Gervase of Tilbury, *Otia Imperialia*, ed. S. E. Banks and J. W. Binns (OMT, 2002)

Gesta Abbatum Monasterii S. Albani, ed. H. T. Riley, 3 vols (RS 28:4, 1867–9)

Gesta Francorum: The Deeds of the Franks, ed. Rosalind Hill (NMT, 1962)

Gesta Normannorum Ducum of William of Jumièges, Orderic Vitalis and Robert of Torigni, ed. Elisabeth M. C. Van Houts, 2 vols (OMT, 1992–5)

Gesta Stephani, ed. K. R. Potter and R. H. C. Davis (OMT, 1976)

Gilbert of Mons, *Chronicle of Hainault*, trans. Laura Napran (Woodbridge, 2005)

Glanvill, ed. G. D. G. Hall (NMT, 1965)

Great Chartulary of Glastonbury, ed. Aelred Watkin, 3 vols (Somerset Rec. Soc. 59, 63–4; 1947–56)

Guibert of Nogent, *Dei Gesta per Francos*, ed. R. B. C. Huygens (Corpus Christianorum. Continuatio Medievalis 127A; Turnhout, 1996)

——, *The Deeds of God through the Franks*, trans. Robert Levine (Woodbridge, 1996)

Hariulf, *Chronique de l'Abbaye de Saint-Riquier*, ed. Ferdinand Lot (Paris, 1894)

"Haverholme Priory Charters," ed. C. W. Foster, *Lincolnshire Notes and Queries* 17 (1922–3), 7–48, 65–74, 89–98

Henry, Archdeacon of Huntingdon, *Historia Anglorum: The History of the English People*, ed. Diana Greenway (OMT, 1996)

Henry of Pytchley's Book of Fees, ed. W. T. Mellows (Northamptonshire Rec. Soc. 2, 1927)

Herman of Tournai, *The Restoration of the Monastery of Saint Martin of Tournai*, ed. Lynn H. Nelson (Washington, DC, 1996)

Histoire abrégée de l'abbaye de Saint-Florentin de Bonneval, ed. Victor Bigot (Châteaudun, 1875)

"Histoire du roi Louis VII," in *Vie de Louis le Gros par Suger*, ed. Auguste Molinier (Paris, 1887)

Historia Ecclesie Abbendonensis: The History of the Church of Abingdon, ed. John Hudson, 2 vols (OMT, 2002–7)

"Historia Selebiensis Monasterii," in *The Coucher Book of Selby*, ed. J. T. Fowler, 2 vols (Yorkshire Arch. Soc., Rec. Ser. 10, 13, 1891–3), i. [1]–[54]

History of William Marshal, ed. A. J. Holden, S. Gregory, and D. Crouch, 3 vols (Anglo-Norman Text Soc., Occasional Publications Series 4–6, 2002–6)

Hugh Candidus, *The Chronicle of Hugh Candidus, a Monk of Peterborough*, ed. W. T. Mellows (Oxford, 1949)

——, *The Peterborough Chronicle of Hugh Candidus*, trans. C. Mellows and W. T. Mellows, 2nd edn (Peterborough, 1966)

Hugh the Chanter, *The History of the Church of York 1066–1127*, ed. Charles Johnson, rev. M. Brett, C. N. L. Brooke, and M. Winterbottom (OMT, 1990)

Ivo of Chartres, *Correspondence* 1: *1090–1098*, ed. Jean Leclercq (Paris, 1949)

Jaffé, Philip *Regesta pontificum Romanorum*, ed. S. Löwenfeld, F. Kaltenbrunner, and P. Ewald (Leipzig, 1885–8)

Jocelin of Brakelond, *Chronicle of the Abbey of Bury St Edmunds*, ed. Diana Greenway and Jane Sayers (Oxford, 1989)

Jocelin of Furness, "Vita sancti Waldeui," in *Acta Sanctorum: Augustus* 1 (Antwerp, 1733), 241–77

John of Hexham, Continuation of Simeon of Durham's *Historia regum*, in SD, *Opera*, ii. 284–332

John of Marmoutier, "Historia Gaufredi ducis Normannorum et comitis Andegavorum," in *Chroniques des comtes d'Anjou*, 172–231

John of Salisbury, *Johannis Saresberiensis Episcopi Carnotensis Policratici*, ed. Clement C. J. Webb, 2 vols (Oxford, 1909)

——, *Iohannis Saresberiensis Historiae Pontificalis*, ed. Reginald L. Poole (Oxford, 1927)

——, *Historia Pontificalis: Memoirs of the Papal Court*, ed. Marjorie Chibnall (NMT, 1956)

——, *Entheticus Maior and Minor*, ed. Jan Van Laarhoven, 3 vols (Leiden, 1987)

——, *Policraticus*, ed. Cary J. Nederman (Cambridge, 1990)

Lancashire Pipe Rolls, also Early Lancashire Charters, ed. W. Farrer (Liverpool, 1902)

Letters and Charters of Gilbert Foliot, ed. Adrian Morey and C. N. L. Brooke (Cambridge, 1967)

Letters of Saint Anselm of Canterbury, trans. Walter Fröhlich, 3 vols (Cistercian Studies Series 96–7, 142; Kalamazoo, Mich., 1990–4)

Letters of Arnulf of Lisieux, ed. Frank Barlow (Camden 3 : 61, 1939)

Letters of St Bernard of Clairvaux, trans. Bruno Scott James, rev. edn (Stroud, 1998)

Letters of John of Salisbury, ed. W. J. Millor, H. E. Butler, and C. N. L. Brooke, 2 vols (OMT, 1955–79)

Letters of Osbert of Clare, ed. E. W. Williamson (Oxford, 1929)

Letters of Peter the Venerable, ed. Giles Constable, 2 vols (Harvard, Mass., 1967)

Liber Eliensis, ed. E. O. Blake (Camden 3 : 92, 1962)

Liber Eliensis: A History of the Isle of Ely from the Seventh Century to the Twelfth, trans. Janet Fairweather (Woodbridge, 2005)

Liber Monasterii de Hyda, ed. Edward Edwards (RS 45, 1866)
Liber Vitae of the New Minster and Hyde Abbey Winchester, ed. Simon Keynes (Early English Manuscripts in Facsimile 26; Copenhagen, 1996)
Life of Christina of Markyate, ed. C. H. Talbot (OMT, 2002)
Lincoln Cathedral obituary list, in Gerald of Wales, *Opera*, vii. 153–64
Lincolnshire Domesday and the Lindsey Survey, ed. C. W. Foster and T. Longley (Lincoln Rec. Soc. 19, 1924)
Un Manuscrit chartrain du XI siècle, ed. René Merlet and Jules A. Clerval (Chartres, 1893)
Materials for the History of Thomas Becket, ed. James Craigie Robertson, 7 vols (RS 67, 1875–85)
Matthew Paris, *Historia Minor*, ed. Frederic Madden, 3 vols (RS 44, 1866–9)
Memorials of the Abbey of St. Mary of Fountains, ed. J. R. Walbran and J. T. Fowler, 3 vols (Surtees Soc. 42, 67, 130; 1863–1918)
Monuments historiques, ed. Jules Tardif (Paris, 1866)
Norman Charters from English Sources: Antiquaries, Archives and the Rediscovery of the Anglo-Norman Past, ed. Nicholas Vincent (Pipe Roll Soc. 57, 2010)
Obituaires de la province de Sens 2: diocèse de Chartres, ed. Auguste Molinier (Paris, 1906)
Odo of Deuil, *De profectione Ludovici VII in orientem*, ed. Virginia Gingerich Berry, 2nd edn (New York, 1965)
De Oorkonden der Graven van Vlaanderen (Juli 1128–September 1191), 2/i. Regering van Diederik van de Elzas (Juli 1128–17 Januari 1168), ed. Thérèse de Hemptinne and Adriaan Verhulst (Brussels, 1988)
Orderic Vitalis, *The Ecclesiastical History*, ed. Marjorie Chibnall, 6 vols (OMT, 1969–80)
Otto of Freising, *The Deeds of Frederick Barbarossa*, ed. Charles Christopher Mierow (New York, 1953)
——, *The Two Cities: A Chronicle of Universal History to the Year 1146*, ed. Charles Christopher Mierow, rev. edn (New York, 2002)
Papsturkunden in England, ed. Walter Holtzmann, 3 vols (Berlin and Göttingen, 1930–52)
Patrilogia Cursus Completus, Series Latina, ed. J. P. Migne (Paris, 1841–64)
Pipe Roll 31 Henry I, ed. Joseph Hunter (London, 1833)
Pipe Rolls 2–3–4 Henry II, ed. Joseph Hunter (London, 1844)
Ralph of Coggeshall, *Chronicon Anglicanum*, ed. Joseph Stevenson (RS 66, 1875)
Ralph of Diceto, *Radulphi de Diceto Opera Historica*, ed. William Stubbs, 2 vols (RS 68, 1876)
Reading Abbey Cartularies, ed. B. R. Kemp (Camden 4 : 31, 33, 1986–7)
"Le Récit de la fondation de Mortemer", ed. J. Bouvet, *Collectanea Ordinis Cisterciensium Reformatorum* 20 (1960), 149–68
Records of Harrold Priory, ed. G. Herbert Fowler (Bedfordshire Hist. Rec. Soc. 17, 1935)
Records of the Templars in England in the Twelfth Century, ed. Beatrice A. Lees (British Academy Records of Social and Economic History 11, 1935)
Recueil des actes de Henri II, roi d'Angleterre et duc de Normandie, concernant les provinces françaises et les affaires de France, ed. L. Delisle and E. Berger, 3 vols (Paris, 1916–27)
Recueil des actes de Louis VI, roi de France (1108–1137), ed. Jean Dufour, 4 vols (Paris, 1992–4)
Recueil des actes des comtes de Ponthieu (1026–1279), ed. Clovis Brunel (Paris, 1930)
Recueil d'annales Angevines et Vendômoises, ed. Louis Halphen (Paris, 1903)
Recueil des chartes de l'abbaye de Cluny, ed. A. Bernard and A. Bruel, 6 vols (Paris, 1876–1903)
Recueil des historiens des Gaules et de la France, ed. M. Bouquet et al., 24 vols (Paris, 1738–1904)
Red Book of the Exchequer, ed. Hubert Hall, 3 vols (RS 99, 1896)
Regesta Regum Anglo-Normannorum, ed. H. W. C. Davis, C. Johnson, H. A. Cronne, and R. H. C. Davis, 4 vols (Oxford, 1913–69)
Regesta Regum Anglo-Normannorum. The Acta of William I (1066–1087), ed. David Bates (Oxford, 1988)
Reginald of Durham, *Libellus de vita et miraculis S. Godrici, heremitae de Finchale*, ed. Joseph Stevenson (Surtees Soc. 20, 1847)
Register of the Abbey of St. Benet of Holme, ed. J. R. West, 2 vols (Norfolk Rec. Soc. 2–3, 1932)
Registrum Antiquissimum of the Cathedral Church of Lincoln, ed. C. W. Foster and Kathleen Major, 10 vols (Lincoln Rec. Soc. 27–9, 32, 34, 41, 46, 51, 62, 67; 1931–73)

Registrum Malmesburiense, ed. J. S. Brewer and Charles Trice Martin, 2 vols (RS 72, 1879–80)

Rerum Anglicarum scriptorum veterum, ed. William Fulman (Oxford, 1684)

Richard of Hexham, *De gestis regis Stephani et de bello standardii*, in *Chronicles*, iii. 139–78

Robert of Torigni, *The Chronicle of Robert of Torigni*, in *Chronicles*, iv

——, *Chronique de Robert de Torigni*, ed. Léopold Delisle, 2 vols (Rouen and Paris, 1872–3)

Roger of Howden, *Chronica Rogeri de Houedene*, ed. William Stubbs, 4 vols (RS 51, 1868–71)

Roger of Wendover, *Chronica*, ed. Henry O. Coxe, 4 vols (English Hist. Soc., 1841–2)

Roman Missal: The Missal in Latin and English, being the text of the Missale Romanum with English Rubrics and a New Translation, ed. J. O'Connell and H. P. R. Finberg (London, 1949)

Rotuli Chartarum in Turri Londinensi Asservati 1199–1216, ed. T. D. Hardy (London, 1837)

Rufford Charters, ed. C. J. Holdsworth, 4 vols (Thoroton Soc. Rec. Series 29–30, 32, 34; 1972–80)

Sarum Charters and Documents, ed. W. Rich Jones and W. Dunn Macray (RS 97, 1891)

Scottish Annals from English Chroniclers, 500 to 1286, ed. Alan Orr Anderson, rev. edn (Stamford, 1991)

Scottish Chronicle known as the Chronicle of Holyrood, ed. M. O. Anderson (Scottish Hist. Soc. 3: 30; Edinburgh, 1938)

Sibton Abbey Cartularies and Charters, ed. Philippa Brown, 4 vols (Suffolk Rec. Soc., Suffolk Charters 7–10, 1985–8)

Sigeberti Gemblacensis Chronica . . . Continuatio Burgurgensis, in *MGH Scriptores* 6, 456–8

Simeon of Durham, *Historical Works*, ed. Thomas Arnold, 2 vols (RS 75, 1882–5)

——, *Libellus de Exordio atque Procursu istius hoc est Dunhelmensis Ecclesie*, ed. David Rollason (OMT, 2000)

Sir Christopher Hatton's Book of Seals, ed. Lewis C. Loyd and Doris Mary Stenton (Oxford, 1950)

Suger, *Vie de Louis VI le Gros*, ed. Henri Waquet (Paris, 1929)

——, *The Deeds of Louis the Fat*, trans. Richard C. Cusimano and John Moorhead (Washington, DC, 1992)

——, "De rebus in administratione sua gestis," in *Oeuvres* 1, ed. Françoise Gasparri (Paris, 1996), 54–155

——, "Histoire de Louis VII," ibid. 156–77

Thomas of Monmouth, *The Life and Miracles of St William of Norwich*, ed. Augustus Jessopp and Montagu Rhodes James (Cambridge, 1896)

Twelfth-Century English Archidiaconal and Vice-Archdiaconal Acta, ed. B. R. Kemp (Canterbury and York Soc. 92, 2001)

Two Cartularies of the Augustinian Priory of Bruton and the Cluniac Priory of Montacute (Somerset Rec. Soc. 8, 1894)

Ungedruckte Anglo-Normannische Geschichtsquellen, ed. F. Liebermann (Strasbourg, 1879)

"Vita domini Roberti de Betune, Herefordensis episcopi," in *Anglia Sacra*, ed. H. Wharton, 2 vols (London, 1691), ii. 295–321

Vita Prima of Bernard of Clairvaux, in PL 185, cols. 225–466

Wace, *The History of the Norman People: Wace's "Roman de Rou,"* ed. Glyn S. Burgess (Woodbridge, 2004)

Walter Daniel, *The Life of Ailred of Rievaulx*, ed. F. M. Powicke (NMT, 1950)

Walter Map, *De Nugis Curialium: Courtiers' Trifles*, ed. M. R. James, rev. C. N. L. Brooke and R. A. B. Mynors (OMT, 1983)

Walter of Thérouanne, "Vita Karoli Comitis Flandriae", *Monumenta Germaniae Historica Scriptores* 12, 537–61

Waltham Chronicle, ed. Leslie Watkiss and Marjorie Chibnall (OMT, 1994)

William of Malmesbury, *The Early History of Glastonbury: An Edition, Translation and Study of William of Malmesbury's "De Antiquitate Glastonie Ecclesie,"* ed. John Scott (Woodbridge, 1981)

——, *Historia Novella: The Contemporary History*, ed. Edmund King, trans. K. R. Potter (OMT, 1998)

——, *Gesta Regum Anglorum: The History of the English Kings*, ed. R. A. B. Mynors, R. M. Thomson, and M. Winterbottom, 2 vols (OMT, 1998–9)

——, *Gesta Pontificum Anglorum: The History of the English Bishops*, ed. R. M. Thomson and M. Winterbottom, 2 vols (OMT, 2007)

William of Newburgh, *Historia rerum Anglicarum*, in *Chronicles*, i

——, *The History of English Affairs, Book 1*, ed. P. G. Walsh and M. J. Kennedy (Warminster, 1988)

William of Poitiers, *Gesta Guillelmi*, ed. R. H. C. Davis and Marjorie Chibnall (OMT, 1998)

William of Tyre, *A History of Deeds done beyond the Sea*, ed. Emily Atwater Babcock and A. C. Krey, 2 vols (New York, 1943)

William Thorne, *Chronicle of Saint Augustine's Abbey Canterbury*, ed. A. H. Davis (Oxford, 1934)

"Winchcombe Annals 1049–1181," ed. R. R. Darlington, in *A Medieval Miscellany for Doris Mary Stenton*, ed. Patricia M. Barnes and C. F. Slade (Pipe Roll Soc. NS 36, 1962)

Wulfric of Haselbury by John, Abbot of Ford, ed. Maurice Bell (Somerset Rec. Soc. 47, 1933)

SECONDARY SOURCES

Allen, Martin, "The English Coinage of 1153/4–1158," *British Numismatic Journal* 76 (2006), 242–302

Allen, Martin and T. G. Webb Ware, "Two Notes on Stephen *BMC* Type 7," ibid. 77 (2007), 279–81

Amt, Emilie, "Richard de Lucy, Henry II's Justiciar," *Medieval Prosopography* 9 (1988), 61–87

——, "The Meaning of Waste in the Early Pipe Rolls of Henry II," *Economic History Review* 2 : 44 (1991), 240–8

——, *The Accession of Henry II in England: Royal Government Restored 1149–1159* (Woodbridge, 1993)

Anderson, M. D., *A Saint at Stake: The Strange Death of William of Norwich, 1144* (London, 1964)

Andressohn, J. C., *The Ancestry and Life of Godfry of Bouillon* (Bloomington, Ind., 1947)

Archibald, Marion M., "The Lion Coinage of Robert Earl of Gloucester and William Earl of Gloucester," *British Numismatic Journal* 71 (2002), 71–86

——, et al., "Four Early Medieval Coin Dies from the London Waterfront," *Numismatic Chronicle* 155 (1995), 163–200

Auberger, Jean-Baptiste, *Mystère de Fontenay: La spiritualité de saint Bernard en majesté* (Saint-Léger-Vauban, 2001)

Auvry, Claude, *Histoire de la congrégation de Savigny*, 3 vols (Rouen and Paris, 1896–8)

Barlow, Frank, *The English Church 1066–1154* (London, 1979)

——, *William Rufus* (London, 1983)

——, *Thomas Becket* (London, 1986)

——, "Corbeil, William de (d. 1136), Archbishop of Canterbury," *OxDNB*

Barrow, G. W. S., "King David I and the Honour of Lancaster," *EHR* 70 (1955), 85–9

——, *The Anglo-Norman Era in Scottish History* (Oxford, 1980)

——, "The Scots and the North of England," in King, *Anarchy*, 231–53

Bartlett, Robert, *England under the Norman and Angevin Kings 1075–1225* (Oxford, 2000)

Bates, David, *William the Conqueror* (Stroud, 2001)

Bayeux Tapestry, ed. F. M. Stenton, 2nd edn (London, 1965)

Bearman, Robert, "Baldwin de Redvers: Some Aspects of a Baronial Career in the Reign of King Stephen," *ANS* 18 (1996), 19–46

Beeler, John, *Warfare in England, 1066–1189* (Ithaca, NY, 1966)

Bentley, Michael, *Modernizing England's Past: English Historiography in the Age of Modernism, 1870–1970* (Cambridge, 2005)

Beresford, M. W. and J. K. S. St Joseph, *Medieval England: An Aerial Survey*, 2nd edn (Cambridge, 1979)

Bethell, Denis, "Richard of Belmeis and the Foundation of St Osyth's," *Trans. Essex Arch. Soc.*, 3 : 2/iii (1970), 299–328

——, "The miracles of St. Ithamar," *Analecta Bollandiana* 89 (1971), 421–37

Bibliotheca Topographica Britannica, ed. John Nichols, 10 vols (London, 1780–1800)

Biddle, Martin, "Seasonal Festivals and Residence: Winchester, Westminster and Gloucester in the Tenth to Twelfth Centuries," *ANS* 9 (1986), 51–72

Birch, W. de G., "On the Great Seals of King Stephen," *Trans. Royal Soc. of Literature*, 2:11 (1878), 1–29

Bishop, Edmund, "Gifts of Bishop Henry of Blois, Abbot of Glastonbury, to Winchester Cathedral," in *Liturgica Historica* (Oxford, 1918), 392–401

Bishop, T. A. M., *Scriptores Regis: Facsimiles to Identify and Illustrate the Hands of Royal Scribes in Original Charters of Henry I, Stephen, and Henry II* (Oxford, 1961)

Bisson, Thomas N., "The Lure of Stephen's England: *Tenserie*, Flemings and a Crisis of Circumstance," in *King Stephen's Reign (1135–1154)*, 171–81

——, *The Crisis of the Twelfth Century* (Princeton, NJ, 2009)

Blackburn, Mark, "Coinage and Currency under Henry I: A Review," *ANS* 13 (1990), 49–81

——, "Coinage and Currency," in King, *Anarchy*, 145–205

Blake, E. O., "The Formation of the 'Crusade Idea'," *Journal of Ecclesiastical History* 21 (1970), 11–31

Blanchard, Ian, "Lothian and Beyond: The Economy of the 'English Empire' of David I," in *Progress and Problems in Medieval England*, 23–45

Bloch, Marc, *Feudal Society*, 2nd edn (London, 1962)

Boon, George C., *Welsh Hoards 1979–1981* (Cardiff, 1986)

——, *Coins of the Anarchy 1135–54* (Cardiff, 1988)

Boüard, Michel de, "Sur les Origines de la Trève de Dieu en Normandie," *Annales de Normandie* 9 (1959), 169–89

Bouchard, Constance Brittain, "Eleanor's Divorce from Louis VII: The Uses of Consanguinity," in *Eleanor of Aquitaine: Lord and Lady*, 223–35

Boussard, J., "Le Comté de Mortain au XIe siècle," *Le Moyen Age* 4:7 (1952), 253–79

Boutemy, A., "Trois Oeuvres inédits de Godefroid de Reims," *Revue du moyen âge latin* 3 (1947), 335–66

Bradbury, Jim, "Battles in England and Normandy, 1066–1154," *ANS* 6 (1984), 1–12

Braun, H., "Notes on Newark Castle," *Trans. Thoroton Soc.* 39 (1935), 53–91

Brett, Martin, *The English Church under Henry I* (Oxford, 1975)

——, "The Annals of Bermondsey, Southwark and Merton," in *Church and City, 1000–1500: Essays in Honour of Christopher Brooke*, ed. David Abulafia, Michael Franklin, and Miri Rubin (Cambridge, 1992), 279–310

Brooke, Christopher N. L., *London 800–1216: The Shaping of a City* (London, 1975)

Brooks, N. P. and H. E. Walker, "The Authority and Interpretation of the Bayeux Tapestry," *ANS* 1 (1979), 1–34

Brown, A. E. and C. C. Taylor, "Cambridgeshire Earthwork Surveys 2," *Proceedings of the Cambridge Antiquarian Soc.* 67 (1977), 85–102

——, "Cambridgeshire Earthwork Surveys 3," ibid. 68 (1978), 59–75

Brown, Elizabeth A. R. and Michael W. Cothren, "The Twelfth-Century Crusading Window of the Abbey of Saint-Denis: *Praeteritorum enim recordatio futurorum est exhibitio*," *Journal of the Warburg and Courtauld Institutes* 49 (1986), 1–40

Brown, Shirley Ann and Michael W. Herren, "The *Adelae Comitissae* of Baudry of Bourgeuil and the Bayeux Tapestry," *ANS* 16 (1994), 55–73

Brownbill, J., "The Countess Lucy," *CP*, vii, App. J, 743–6

Brückmann, J., "The *Ordines* of the Third Recension of the Medieval English Coronation Order," in *Essays in Medieval History Presented to Bertie Wilkinson*, ed. T. A. Sandquist and M. R. Powicke (Toronto, 1969), 99–115

Brundage, James A., "An Errant Crusader: Stephen of Blois," *Traditio* 16 (1960), 380–95

Bur, Michel, *La Formation du comté de Champagne, v. 950–v.1150*. Mémoires des Annales de L'Est 54 (Nancy, 1977)

Burnett, Charles, *The Introduction of Arabic Learning into England* (London, 1997)

Burton, Janet, *The Monastic Order in Yorkshire, 1069–1215* (Cambridge, 1999)

——, "English Monasteries and the Continent in the Reign of King Stephen," in *King Stephen's Reign (1135–1154)*, 98–114

Buzelinus, Joannes, *Annales Gallo-Flandriae* (Douai, 1624)

Cam, Helen, *The Hundred and the Hundred Rolls* (London, 1930)

——, "Manerium cum Hundredo: The Hundred and the Hundredal Manor," *EHR* 47 (1932), 353–76

Carlin, Martha, "The Reconstruction of Winchester House, Southwark," *London Topographical Record* 25 (1985), 33–57

Catholic Encyclopedia, 17 vols (New York, 1907–18)

Chandler, Victoria, "The Last of the Montgomerys: Roger the Poitevin and Arnulf," *HR* 62 (1989), 1–14

Chédeville, André, *Chartres et ses campagnes (XIe–XIIIe s.)* (Paris, 1973)

Cheney, Mary G., *Roger, Bishop of Worcester 1164–1179* (Oxford, 1980)

Chibnall, Marjorie, *The World of Orderic Vitalis* (Oxford, 1964)

——, "The Empress Matilda and Bec-Hellouin," *ANS* 10 (1988), 35–48

——, "Anglo-French Relations in the Work of Orderic Vitalis," in *Documenting the Past: Essays in Medieval History Presented to G. P. Cuttino*, ed. J. S. Hamilton and P. J. Bradley (Woodbridge, 1989), 5–19

——, *The Empress Matilda: Queen Consort, Queen Mother and Lady of the English* (Oxford, 1991)

——, "The Charters of the Empress Matilda," in *Law and Government*, 276–96

——, "Normandy," in King, *Anarchy*, 93–115

Clanchy, M. T., *From Memory to Written Record: England 1066–1307*, 2nd edn (Oxford, 1993)

Clark, Cecily, *Words, Names and History: Selected Writings*, ed. Peter Jackson (Cambridge, 1995)

Clay, Charles, "Some Medieval Lincolnshire and Yorkshire Connections," *Lincolnshire Historian* 2 : 7 (1960), 1–15

Complete Peerage of England, Scotland, Ireland, Great Britain and the United Kingdom, by. G. E. C., rev. edn, 13 vols in 14 (London, 1910–59)

Constable, Giles, "The Second Crusade as Seen by Contemporaries," *Traditio* 9 (1953), 213–79

Coplestone-Crow, B., "Payn FitzJohn and Ludlow Castle," *Trans. of the Shropshire Arch. and Hist. Soc.* 70 (1995), 171–83

Corbett, W. J., "The Development of the Duchy of Normandy and the Norman Conquest of England," *Cambridge Medieval History* 5 (Cambridge, 1926), 481–520

Coulson, Charles, "The French Matrix of the Castle-Provisions of the Chester–Leicester *conventio*," *ANS* 17 (1995), 65–86

——, *Castles in Medieval Society: Fortresses in England, France and Ireland in the Central Middle Ages* (Oxford, 2003)

Cowdrey, H. E. J., "Pope Urban II's Preaching of the First Crusade," *History* 55 (1970), 177–88

——, *Lanfranc: Scholar, Monk, and Archbishop* (Oxford, 2003)

Cox, D. C., "Two Unpublished Charters of King Stephen for Wenlock Priory," *Trans. of the Shropshire Arch. and Hist. Soc.* 66 (1989), 56–9

Crick, J. C., "Oxford, Walter of (*d.* in or before 1151?)," *OxDNB*

Cronne, H. A., *The Reign of Stephen: Anarchy in England 1135–54* (London, 1970)

Crouch, David, "Robert, Earl of Gloucester, and the Daughter of Zelophehad," *Journal of Medieval History* 11 (1985), 227–43

——, *The Beaumont Twins: The Roots and Branches of Power in the Twelfth Century* (Cambridge, 1986)

——, "Vere, Aubrey (III) de, Count of Guînes and Earl of Oxford (*d.* 1194), *OxDNB*

——, "Earl William of Gloucester and the End of the Anarchy: New Evidence Relating to the Honor of Eudo Dapifer," *EHR* 88 (1988), 69–75

——, "The March and the Welsh Kings," in King, *Anarchy*, 255–89

——, "A Norman *convencio* and Bonds of Lordship in the Middle Ages," in *Law and Government*, 299–324

——, *The Reign of Stephen, 1135–1154* (London, 2000)

——, "Robert, First Earl of Gloucester (*b.* before 1000, *d.* 1147)," *OxDNB*

——, "Roger, Second Earl of Warwick (*d.* 1153)," *OxDNB*

——, "King Stephen and Northern France," in *King Stephen's Reign (1135–1154)*, 44–57

Dalton, Paul, "William Earl of York and Royal Authority in Yorkshire during the Reign of Stephen," *HSJ* 2 (1990), 155–65

——, "Aiming at the Impossible: Ranulf II, Earl of Chester, and Lincolnshire in the Reign of King Stephen," in *The Earldom of Chester and its Charters*, 109–34

——, "*In neutro latere*: The Armed Neutrality of Ranulf II, Earl of Chester, in King Stephen's Reign," *ANS* 14 (1991), 39–59

——, *Conquest, Anarchy and Lordship: Yorkshire, 1066–1154* (Cambridge, 1994)

——, "Eustace Fitz John and the Politics of Anglo-Norman England: The Rise and Survival of a Twelfth-Century Royal Servant," *Speculum* 71 (1996), 358–83

——, "Roumare, William de, First Earl of Lincoln (*c.*1096–1155×61)," *OxDNB*

Davies, R. R., *Conquest, Coexistence, and Change: Wales 1063–1415* (Oxford, 1987)

Davis, H. W. C., "The Anarchy of Stephen's Reign," *EHR* 18 (1903), 630–41

——, "Henry of Blois and Brian Fitz Count," *EHR* 25 (1910), 297–303

——, "Some Documents of the Anarchy," in *Essays in History presented to Reginald Lane Poole*, ed. H. W. C. Davis (Oxford, 1927), 168–89

Davis, R. H. C., "Geoffrey de Mandeville Reconsidered," *EHR* 79 (1964), 299–307

——, *King Stephen 1135–1154*, 3rd edn (London, 1990)

——, "The College of St Martin-le-Grand and the Anarchy, 1135–54," in *From Alfred the Great to Stephen* (London, 1991), 237–54

——, "The Ford, the River and the City," ibid., 281–91

Denton, J. H., *English Royal Free Chapels 1100–1300: A Constitutional Study* (Manchester, 1970)

Descriptive Catalogue of the Charters and Muniments at Berkeley Castle, ed. I. H. Jeayes (Bristol, 1892)

Desroches, Jean Jacques, *Histoire du Mont-Saint-Michel et de l'ancien diocèse d'Avranches*, 2 vols (Caen, 1838)

——, *Annales civiles, militaires et généalogiques du pays d'Avranches* (Caen, 1856)

Deville, É, *Analyse d'un ancien cartulaire de Saint- Etienne de Caen* (Evreux, 1905)

Duby, Georges, "Le Budget de l'abbaye de Cluny entre 1080 et 1155," in *Hommes et structures du moyen âge* (Paris, 1973), 61–82

Duchesne, A., *Histoire généalogique des maisons de Guines . . . de Coucy et quelques autres familles* (Paris, 1631)

Dugdale, William, *Monasticon Anglicanum*, ed. J. Caley, H. Ellis, and B. Bandinel, 8 vols (London, 1817–30)

Dunbabin, Jean, *France in the Making, 843–1180*, 2nd edn (Oxford, 2000)

Earldom of Chester and its Charters: A Tribute to Geoffrey Barraclough, ed. A. T. Thacker (*Journal of the Chester Arch. Soc.* 71, 1991)

Eleanor of Aquitaine: Lord and Lady, ed. Bonnie Wheeler and John Carmi Parsons (New York, 2002)

Elkins, Sharon K., *Holy Women of Twelfth-Century England* (Chapel Hill, NC, 1989)

England and Normandy in the Middle Ages, ed. David Bates and Anne Curry (London, 1994)

English Romanesque Art 1066–1200, ed. George Zarnecki, Janet Holt, and Tristram Holland (London, 1984)

Erdmann, Carl, *The Origin of the Idea of Crusade* (Princeton, NJ, 1977)

Everard, Judith, "The Abbey of Saint-Sulpice-la-Forêt and Royal Patronage in England, *c.*1150–1259," *Nottingham Medieval Studies* 47 (2003), 107–47

Farmer, David Hugh, "William of Malmesbury's Commentary on Lamentations," *Studia Monastica* 4 (1962), 283–311

Farrer, William, *Honors and Knights' Fees*, 3 vols (London and Manchester, 1923–5)

Faulkner, Kathryn, "Beauchamp, de, Family (*per. c.*1080–c.1265)," *OxDNB*

Fernie, Eric, *The Architecture of Norman England* (Oxford, 2000)

Finberg, H. P. R., "Uffculme," in *Lucerna: Studies of Some Problems in the Early History of England* (London, 1984), 204–21

Foot, Sarah, *Veiled Women 2: Female Religious Communities in England, 871–1066* (Aldershot, 1988)

Foreville, Raymonde, *Latran I, II, III et Latran IV* (Histoire des conciles oecuméniques 6; Paris, 1965)

Foulds, Trevor, "The Lindsey Survey and an Unknown Precept of King Henry I," *HR* 59 (1986), 212–15

Ganshof, F.-L., "Note sur le premier traité Anglo-Flamand de Douvres," *Revue du Nord* 40 (1958), 245–57

Garnett, George, "The Third Recension of the English Coronation *Ordo*: The Manuscripts," *HSJ* 11 (2003), 43–71

Gem, Richard, "Lincoln Minster: *ecclesia pulchra, ecclesia fortis*," in *Medieval Art and Architecture at Lincoln Cathedral* (British Arch. Association Conference Trans. 8, 1986), 9–28

Gillingham, John, "Doing Homage to the King of France," in *Henry II: New Interpretations*, 63–84

Giry, A., *Histoire de la ville de Saint-Omer et de ses institutions jusqu'au XIVe siècle* (Paris, 1877)

Golb, Norman, *The Jews in Medieval Normandy: A Social and Intellectual History* (Cambridge, 1998)

Gransden, Antonia, *Historical Writing in England, c.550–c.1307* (London, 1974)

Grant, Lindy, *Abbot Suger of St Denis* (London, 1998)

Gray, Arthur, *The Priory of St Radegund, Cambridge* (Cambridge, 1898)

Green, Judith A., " 'Praeclarum et magnificum antiquitatis monumentum': The Earliest Surviving Pipe Roll," *HR* 55 (1982), 1–17

——, *The Government of England under Henry I* (Cambridge, 1986)

——, "Earl Ranulf II and Lancashire," in *The Earldom of Chester and its Charters*, 97–108

——, "Financing Stephen's War," *ANS* 14 (1992), 92–114

——, "Family Matters: Family and the Formation of the Empress's Party in South-West England," in *Family Trees and the Roots of Politics: The Prosopography of Britain and France from the 10th to the 12th Century*, ed. K. S. B. Keats-Rohan (Woodbridge, 1997), 147–64

——, *Henry I: King of England and Duke of Normandy* (Cambridge, 2006)

Greenwell, William and C. Hunter Blair, "Durham Seals, Part VI: English Royal Seals," *Archaeologia Aeliana*, 3 : 13 (1916), 117–55

Grierson, Philip, "The Relations between England and Flanders before the Norman Conquest," *TRHS* 4 : 23 (1941), 71–112

Hagenmeyer, Heinrich, ed., *Die Kreuzzugsbriefe aus den Jahren 1088–1100* (Innsbruck, 1901)

Haigneré, Daniel, "Quelques Chartes de l'abbaye de Samer, 1107–1299," *Mémoires, de la société académique de Boulogne-sur-Mer* 12 (1881), 110–23

——, "Quelques Chartes inédites concernant les abbayes, les prieurés, ou les paroisses de l'ancien Boulonnais," ibid. 13 (1882–6), 413–78

Halsey, Richard, "The Earliest Architecture of the Cistercians in England," in *Cistercian Art and Architecture in the British Isles*, ed. Christopher Norton and David Park (Cambridge, 1986), 65–85

Handbook of British Chronology, ed. E. B. Fryde et al., 3rd edn (London, 1986)

Haney, K. E., "Some Mosan Sources for the Henry of Blois Enamels," *Burlington Magazine* 34 (1982), 220–30

Hare, Michael, "Kings, Crowns and Festivals: The Origins of Gloucester as a Royal Ceremonial Centre," *TBGAS* 115 (1997), 41–78

Harvey, B. F., "Abbot Gervase de Blois and the Fee-Farms of Westminster Abbey," *HR* 40 (1967), 127–42

Haskins, Charles Homer, *Norman Institutions* (Cambridge, Mass., 1918)

Heads of Religious Houses: England and Wales 1: *940–1216*, ed. David Knowles, C. N. L. Brooke, and Vera C. M. London, 2nd edn (Cambridge, 2001)

Henry II: New Interpretations, ed. Christopher Harper-Bill and Nicholas Vincent (Woodbridge, 2007)

Heslop, T. A., "Seals," in *English Romanesque Art*, 298–319

——, *Norwich Castle Keep: Romanesque Architecture and Social Context* (Norwich, 1994)

Hill, Bennett D., "The Counts of Mortain and the Origins of the Norman Congregation of Savigny," in *Order and Innovation in the Middle Ages: Essays in Honor of Joseph R. Strayer*, ed. William C. Jordan, Bruce McNab, and Teofilo F. Ruiz (Princeton, NJ, 1976), 237–53, 495–7

Hill, J. W. F., *Medieval Lincoln* (Cambridge, 1948)

Hill, Rosalind, "The Battle of Stockbridge, 1141," in *Studies in Medieval History presented to R. Allen Brown*, ed. Christopher Harper-Bill, Christopher Holdsworth, and Janet L. Nelson (Woodbridge, 1989), 173–7

Historical Manuscripts Commission Ninth Report 1 (1883)

History of the King's Works 1–2: *The Middle Ages*, ed. H. M. Colvin (London, 1963)

Holdsworth, Christopher, "The Church," in King, *Anarchy*, 207–29

Hollister, C. Warren, *Monarchy, Magnates and Institutions in the Anglo-Norman World* (London, 1986)

——, "London's First Charter of Liberties: Is it Genuine?" ibid., 191–208

——, "The Misfortunes of the Mandevilles," ibid., 117–27

——, "Royal Acts of Mutilation: The Case against Henry I," ibid., 291–301

——, "The Origins of the English Treasury," ibid., 209–22

——, *Henry I* (New Haven and London, 2001)

Hollister, C. Warren and Thomas K. Keefe, "The Making of the Angevin Empire," in Hollister, *Anglo-Norman World*, 247–71

Holt, J. C., *The End of the Anglo-Norman Realm* (British Academy Raleigh Lecture in History: London, 1975)

——, "1153: The Treaty of Winchester," in King, *Anarchy*, 291–316

Howell, Margaret, *Regalian Right in Medieval England* (London, 1962)

Hudson, John, "Administration Family and Perceptions of the Past in Late Twelfth-Century England: Richard FitzNigel and the Dialogue of the Exchequer," in *The Perception of the Past in Twelfth-Century Europe*, ed. Paul Magdalino (London, 1992), 75–98

Huneycutt, Lois L., *Matilda of Scotland: A Study in Medieval Queenship* (Woodbridge, 2003)

Hunter Blair, C., "Armorials in English Seals from the 12th to the 16th Centuries," *Archaeologia* 89 (1943), 1–26

Iogna-Prat, Dominique, *Order and Exclusion: Cluny and Christendom face Heresy, Judaism and Islam (1000–1150)* (Ithaca, NY, 2003)

Jones, Michael, "The Charters of Robert II de Ferrers, Earl of Nottingham, Derby and Ferrers," *Nottingham Medieval Studies* 24 (1980), 7–26

Juenin, Pierre, *Nouvelle Histoire de l'abbaye royale et collégiale de Saint Filibert, et de la ville de Tournus* (Dijon, 1733)

Kantorowicz, E. H. "The 'King's Advent,' " in *Selected Studies* (Locust Valley, NY, 1965), 37–51

Kealey, Edward J., *Roger of Salisbury: Viceroy of England* (Berkeley, 1972)

Keefe, Thomas K., "Geoffrey Plantagenet's Will and the Angevin Succession," *Albion* 6 (1974), 266–74

Keene, Derek, *Survey of Medieval Winchester*, 2 vols (Winchester Studies 2; Oxford, 1985)

——, "London from the post-Roman Period to 1300," in *The Cambridge Urban History of Britain* 1: *600–1540*, ed. D. M. Palliser (Cambridge, 2000), 187–216

Kemp, Brian, "The Miracles of the Hand of St James," *Berkshire Arch. Journal* 65 (1970), 1–19

Kempe, Alfred John, *Historical Notes of the Collegiate Church of St. Martin-le-Grand* (London, 1825)

Kenyon, John R., *Medieval Fortifications* (Leicester, 1990)

King, David James Cathcart, *Castellarium Anglicanum: An Index and Bibliography of the Castles in England, Wales and the Islands*, 2 vols (Millwood, NY, 1983)

King, Edmund, "Mountsorrel and its Region in King Stephen's Reign," *Huntington Library Quarterly* 44 (1980), 1–10

——, "The Anarchy of King Stephen's Reign," *TRHS* 5 : 34 (1984), 133–53

——, "Waleran, Count of Meulan, Earl of Worcester (1104–1166)," in *Tradition and Change: Essays in Honour of Marjorie Chibnall*, ed. Diana Greenway, Christopher Holdsworth, and Jane Sayers (Cambridge, 1985), 165–81

——, *Medieval England* (London, 1988)

——, "Dispute Settlement in Anglo-Norman England," *ANS* 14 (1992), 115–30

——, ed., *The Anarchy of King Stephen's Reign* (Oxford, 1994)

——, "Economic Development in the Early Twelfth Century," in *Progress and Problems in Medieval England*, 1–22

——,"Stephen of Blois, Count of Mortain and Boulogne," *EHR* 115 (2000), 271–96

——,"The Memory of Brian Fitz Count," *HSJ* 13 (2004), 75–99

——, "Ranulf (I), Third Earl of Chester (*d.* 1129)," *OxDNB*

——, "Stephen, King of England," *OxDNB*

——, "The *Gesta Stephani*," in *Writing Medieval Biography, 750–1250: Essays in Honour of Professor Frank Barlow*, ed. David Bates, Julia Crick, and Sarah Hamilton (Woodbridge, 2006), 195–206

——, "The Accession of Henry II," in *Henry II: New Interpretations*, 24–46

——, "A Week in Politics: Oxford, Late July 1141," in *King Stephen's Reign (1135–1154)*, 58–79

King Stephen's Reign (1135–1154), ed. Paul Dalton and Graeme J. White (Woodbridge, 2008)

Knowles, David, *The Episcopal Colleagues of Archbishop Thomas Becket* (Cambridge, 1951)

——, *Saints and Scholars: Twenty-Five Medieval Portraits* (Cambridge, 1962)

——, "The Case of St William of York," in *The Historian and Character and Other Essays* (Cambridge, 1963), 76–97

——, *The Monastic Order in England*, 2nd edn (Cambridge, 1963)

Koziol, Geoffrey, *Begging Pardon and Favor: Ritual and Political Order in Early Medieval France* (Ithaca, NY, 1992)

——, "England, France, and the Problem of Sacrality in Twelfth-Century Ritual," in *Cultures of Power: Lordship, Status and Process in Twelfth-Century Europe*, ed. Thomas N. Bisson (Philadelphia, 1995), 124–48

Krey, August C., *The First Crusade: The Accounts of Eye-witnesses and Participants* (Princeton, NJ, 1921)

Langmuir, Gavin I., "Thomas of Monmouth: Detector of Ritual Murder," *Speculum* 59 (1984), 820–46

Latimer, Paul, "The Earls in Henry II's Reign" (University of Sheffield Ph.D. thesis, 1982)

——, "Grants of 'Totus Comitatus' in Twelfth-Century England," *HR* 59 (1986), 137–45

Law and Government in Medieval England and Normandy: Essays in Honour of Sir James Holt, ed. George Garnett and John Hudson (Cambridge, 1994)

Le Patourel, John, *The Norman Empire* (Oxford, 1976)

Lethbridge, T. C., "Excavations at Burwell Castle, Cambridgeshire," *Proceedings of the Cambridge Antiquarian Soc.* 36 (1936), 121–33

Lewis, C. P., "The King and Eye: A Study in Anglo-Norman Politics," *EHR* 112 (1989), 569–89

Leyser, K. J., "Frederick Barbarossa, Henry II and the Hand of St James," *EHR* 90 (1975), 481–506

Liddiard, Robert, "Castle Rising, Norfolk: A 'Landscape of Lordship'?," *ANS* 22 (2000), 169–86

Lloyd, Sir John, *A History of Wales from the Earliest Times to the Edwardian Conquest*, 3rd edn, 2 vols (London, 1939)

LoPrete, Kimberley A., "The Anglo-Norman Card of Adela of Blois," *Albion* 22 (1990), 569–89

——, "Adela of Blois and Ivo of Chartres," *ANS* 14 (1992), 131–52

——, "A Female Ruler in Feudal Society: Adela of Blois (*ca.*1067–*ca.*1137)" (University of Chicago, Ph.D. dissertation, 1992)

——, "Adela of Blois as Mother and Countess," in *Medieval Mothering*, ed. John Carmi Parsons and Bonnie Wheeler (New York, 1996), 313–33

——, *Adela of Blois: Countess and Lord (c.1067–1137)* (Dublin, 2007)

Loud, Graham A., "Some Reflections on the Failure of the Second Crusade," *Crusades* 4 (2005), 1–14

Loyd, Lewis C., *The Origins of Some Anglo-Norman Families* (Harleian Soc. 103, 1951)

Luchaire, Achille, *Etude sur les actes de Louis VII* (Paris, 1885)

Luscombe, David, "Hugh (*d.* 1164), Abbot of Reading and Archbishop of Rouen," *OxDNB*

——, "Pullen, Robert (*d.* in or after 1146), Theologian and Cardinal," *OxDNB*

Lyon, Bryce D., *From Fief to Indenture: The Transition from Feudal to Non-Feudal Contract in Western Europe* (Cambridge, Mass., 1957)

McKisack, May, "London and the Succession to the Crown during the Middle Ages," in *Studies in History Presented to Frederick Maurice Powicke*, ed. R.W. Hunt, W. A. Pantin, and R. W. Southern (Oxford, 1948), 76–89

Maddicott, J. R., *Simon de Montfort* (Cambridge, 1994)

——, " 'An Infinite Multitude of Nobles': Quality, Quantity and Politics in the pre-Reform Parliaments of Henry III," *Thirteenth Century England* 7 (Woodbridge, 1999), 17–46

Martindale, Jane, "Eleanor [Eleanor of Aquitaine]," *OxDNB*

Mason, Emma, *Westminster Abbey and its People, c.1050–c.1216* (Woodbridge, 1996)

Mason, J. F. A., "Pain Fitz John (*d.* 1137)," *OxDNB*

Mayer, H. E., "La Mort et la succession de Baudoin I," in *Mélanges sur l'histoire du royaume latin de Jérusalem* (Mémoires de l'academie des inscriptions et belles-lettres, NS 5, Paris, 1984), 10–91

Mayr-Harting, H., *The Bishops of Chichester 1075–1207: Biographical Notes and Problems* (Chichester Papers 40, 1963)

——, "Hilary, Bishop of Chichester (1147–1169) and Henry II," *EHR* 78 (1963), 209–24

Miller, Edward, *The Abbey and Bishopric of Ely* (Cambridge, 1951)

Mills, D. R. and R. C. Wheeler, *Historic Town Plans of Lincoln 1610–1920* (Lincoln Rec. Soc. 92, 2004)

Morey, Adrian and C. N. L. Brooke, *Gilbert Foliot and his Letters* (Cambridge, 1965)

Nelson, Janet L., "The Rites of the Conqueror," *ANS* 4 (1982), 117–32, 210–21

New Palaeographical Society, *Facsimiles of Ancient Manuscripts*, ed. Edward Maunde Thompson et al., First Series, 2 vols (London, 1903–12)

Newton, R. R., *Medieval Chronicles and the Rotation of the Earth* (Baltimore, 1972)

Nicholl, Donald, *Thurstan Archbishop of York (1114–1140)* (York, 1964)

Norgate, Kate, *England under the Angevin Kings*, 2 vols (London, 1887)

North, J. D., "Some Norman Horoscopes," in *Adelard of Bath: An English Scientist and Arabist of the Early Twelfth Century*, ed. Charles Burnett (London, 1987), 147–61

North, J. J., *English Hammered Coinage* I: *Early Anglo-Saxon to Henry III, c.600–1272* (London, 1980)

Oliver, George, *Monasticon Diocesis Exoniensis* (Exeter, 1846–54)

Otter, Monika, "Baudri of Bourgueil, 'To Countess Adela'," *Journal of Medieval Latin* 11 (2001), 60–141

Owen, Dorothy M., *Church and Society in Medieval Lincolnshire* (Lincoln, 1971)

Oxford before the University: The Late Saxon and Norman Archaeology of the Thames Crossing, the Defences and the Town, ed. Anne Dodd (Oxford, 2003)

Oxford Companion to the Year, ed. Bonnie Blackburn and Leofranc Holford-Strevens (Oxford, 1999)

Oxford Dictionary of National Biography, ed. H. C. G. Matthew and Brian Harrison (Oxford, 2004)

Patterson, R. B., "Robert Fitz Harding of Bristol: Profile of an Early Angevin Burgess-Baron Patrician and his Family's Urban Involvement," *HSJ* 1 (1989), 109–22

——, "The Ducal and Royal *Acta* of Henry Fitz Empress in Berkeley Castle," *TBGAS* 109 (1991), 117–37

Paxton, Jennifer, "Charter and Chronicle in Twelfth-Century England: The House-Histories of the Fenland Abbeys" (Harvard University, Ph.D dissertation, 1999)

Phillips, Jonathan, "St Bernard of Clairvaux, the Low Countries, and the Lisbon Letter of the Second Crusade," *Journal of Ecclesiastical History* 48 (1997), 485–97

Philp, Brian, *Excavations at Faversham, 1965: The Royal Abbey, Roman Villa, and Belgic Farmstead* (Crawley, 1968)

Phythian-Adams, Charles, *Land of the Cumbrians: A Study of British Provincial Origins AD 400–1120* (Aldershot, 1996)

Plantagenêts et Capétiens: confrontations et héritages, ed. Martin Aurell and Noël-Yves Tonnerre (Turnhout, 2006)

Poole, Austin Lane, "Henry Plantagenet's Early Visits to England," *EHR* 47 (1932), 447–52

——, *From Domesday Book to Magna Carta 1087–1216*, 2nd edn (Oxford, 1955)

Poole, Reginald Lane, *Illustrations of the History of Medieval Thought and Learning*, 2nd edn (London, 1920)
——, *Studies in Chronology and History*, ed. Austin Lane Poole (Oxford, 1934)
——, "The Publication of Great Charters by the English Kings," ibid., 308–18
Pouëssel, Jean, "Les Structures militaires du comté de Mortain (XIe et XIIe siècles)," *Revue de l'Avranchin et du pays du Granville* 58 (1981), 11–74, 81–156
Poulle, Beatrice, "Savigny and England," in *England and Normandy*, 159–68
Power, Daniel, *The Norman Frontier in the Twelfth and Early Thirteenth Centuries* (Cambridge, 2004)
Powicke, F. M., "The Abbey of Furness," *VCH Lancashire* 2 (1908), 114–30
Prestwich, J. O., "The Treason of Geoffrey de Mandeville," *EHR* 103 (1988), 283–312
Progress and Problems in Medieval England: Essays in Honour of Edward Miller, ed. Richard Britnell and John Hatcher (Cambridge, 1996)
Richardson, H. G., "The Letters and Charters of Eleanor of Aquitaine," *EHR* 74 (1959), 193–213
——, "The Coronation in Medieval England," *Traditio* 16 (1960), 111–202
Richardson, H. G. and G. O. Sayles, *The Governance of Medieval England from the Conquest to Magna Carta* (Edinburgh, 1963)
Riley-Smith, Jonathan, *The First Crusade and the Idea of Crusading* (London, 1986)
——, *The First Crusaders, 1095–1131* (Cambridge, 1997)
Robinson, Ian S., "Gregory VII and the Soldiers of Christ," *History* 58 (1973), 169–92
——, *The Papacy 1073–1198: Continuity and Innovation* (Cambridge, 1990)
Roffe, David, *Domesday: The Inquest and the Book* (Oxford, 2000)
——, *Decoding Domesday* (Woodbridge, 2007)
Round, J. H., *Geoffrey de Mandeville* (London, 1892)
——, *Feudal England: Historical Studies on the XIth and XIIth Centuries* (London, 1895)
——, "Bernard, the King's Scribe," *EHR* 14 (1899), 417–30
——, *The Commune of London and Other Studies* (Westminster, 1899)
——, "The Honour of Ongar," *Trans. Essex Arch. Soc.* NS 7 (1900), 142–52
——, "The Counts of Boulogne as English Lords," in *Studies in Peerage and Family History* (London, 1901), 147–80
Salter, H. E., *Medieval Oxford* (Oxford Hist. Soc. 100, 1936)
Saltman, Avrom, *Theobald Archbishop of Canterbury* (London, 1956)
Sanders, I. J., *English Baronies: A Study of their Origin and Descent, 1086–1327* (Oxford, 1960)
Scammell, G. V., *Hugh du Puiset, Bishop of Durham* (Cambridge, 1956)
Sellar, W. C. and R. J. Yeatman, *1066 and All That* (Harmondsworth, 1960)
Sharpe, Richard, "The Prefaces of 'Quadripartitus'," in *Law and Government*, 148–72
——, "King Harold's Daughter," *HSJ* 19 (2008), 1–27
Southern, R. W., *Medieval Humanism and Other Studies* (Oxford, 1970)
——, "From Schools to University," in *The History of the University of Oxford* 1: *The Early Oxford Schools*, ed. J. I. Catto (Oxford, 1984), 1–36
——, *Saint Anselm: A Portrait in a Landscape* (Cambridge, 1990)
——, *Scholastic Humanism and the Unification of Europe* 2: *The Heroic Age* (Oxford, 2001)
Spear, David S., *The Personnel of the Norman Cathedrals during the Ducal Period, 911–1204* (London, 2006)
Spink, *The Coinex Sale: The Pimprez Hoard and Other Important Properties*, Catalogue 170 (London, 2004)
Stacey, Robert C., "Jewish Lending and the Medieval English Economy," in *A Commercialising Economy: England 1086 to c.1300*, ed. Richard H. Britnell and Bruce M.S. Campbell (Manchester, 1995), 78–101
Stacy, N. E., "Henry of Blois and the Lordship of Glastonbury," *EHR* 114 (1999), 1–33
Stalley, R. A., "A Twelfth-Century Patron of Architecture: A Study of the Buildings Erected by Roger, Bishop of Salisbury, 1102–1139," *Journal of the British Arch. Association* 3:34 (1971), 62–83
Stein, Henri, *Bibliographie générale des cartulaires français* (Paris, 1907)
Stenton, F. M., *The First Century of English Feudalism 1066–1166*, 2nd edn (Oxford, 1961)

Stewart, Ian, "Scottish Mints," in *Mints, Dies and Currency: Essays Dedicated to the Memory of Albert Baldwin*, ed. R. A. G. Carson (London, 1971), 165–289
——, "Moneyers in the 1130 Pipe Roll," *British Numismatic Journal* 61 (1992), 1–8
Stratford, Neil, *Catalogue of Medieval Enamels in the British Museum* 2: *Northern Romanesque Enamel* (London, 1993)
Strickland, Matthew, "Securing the North: Invasion and the Strategy of Defence in Twelfth-Century Anglo-Scottish Warfare," *ANS* 12 (1990), 177–9
——, "Against the Lord's Anointed: Aspects of Warfare and Baronial Rebellion in England and Normandy, 1075–1265," in *Law and Government*, 56–79
——, *War and Chivalry: The Conduct and Perception of War in England and Normandy, 1066–1217* (Cambridge, 1996)
Stringer, K. J., "A Cistercian Archive: The Earliest Charters of Sawtry Abbey," *Journal of the Society of Archivists* 6:6 (1980), 325–34
——, *Earl David of Huntingdon: A Study in Anglo-Scottish History* (Edinburgh, 1985)
——, "Henry, Earl of Northumberland (c.1115–1153)," *OxDNB*
Stubbs, William, *The Constitutional History of England* 1, 2nd edn (Oxford, 1875)
Styles, Dorothy, "The Early History of Alcester Abbey," *Birmingham Arch. Soc. Trans.* 64 (1946), 20–38
Tanner, Heather J., "The Expansion of the Power and Influence of the Counts of Boulogne under Eustace II, *ANS* 14 (1992), 251–86
——, "Reassessing King Stephen's Continental Strategies," *Medievalia et Humanistica* NS 26 (1999), 101–17
——, "Queenship: Office, Custom or Ad Hoc? The Case of Queen Matilda III of England (1135–1152)," in *Eleanor of Aquitaine: Lord and Lady*, 133–58
——, *Families, Friends and Allies: Boulogne and Politics in Northern France and England, c.879–1160* (Leiden, 2004)
Tatlock, J. S. P., *The Legendary History of Britain: Geoffrey of Monmouth's* Historia Regum Britanniae *and its Early Vernacular Versions* (Berkeley and Los Angeles, 1950)
Thompson, Kathleen, "William Talvas, Count of Ponthieu, and the Politics of the Anglo-Norman Realm," in *England and Normandy*, 169–84
——, "Arnoul de Montgommery: note de recherche," *Annales de Normandie* 45 (1995), 49–53
——, "The Lords of Laigle: Ambition and Insecurity on the Borders of Normandy," *ANS* 18 (1995), 176–99
——, "Lords, Castellans, Constables and Dowagers: The Rape of Pevensey from the 11th to the 13th Century," *Sussex Arch. Collections* 135 (1997), 209–20
——, "Queen Adeliza and the Lotharingian Connection," ibid. 140 (2002), 57–64
——, *Power and Border Lordship in Medieval France: The County of the Perche, 1000–1226* (London, 2002)
Thomson, Rodney M., "What is the *Entheticus?*" in *The World of John of Salisbury*, ed. M. Wilks (Studies in Church History: Subsidia 3, Oxford, 1984), 287–301
——, *William of Malmesbury*, rev. edn (Woodbridge, 2003)
Todd, J. M. and H. S. Offler, "A Medieval Chronicle from Scotland," *Scottish Historical Review* 47 (1968), 151–9
Tyerman, Christopher, *England and the Crusades, 1095–1588* (Chicago, 1988)
Van Houts, Elisabeth, "Les Femmes dans le royaume Plantagenêt: gendre, politique et nature," in *Plantagenêts et Capétiens*, 95–112
Van Moolenbroek, Jaap, *Vital l'Ermite, prédicateur itinérant, fondateur de l'abbaye normande de Savigny* (Assen-Maastricht, 1990)
Vaughan, Richard, *Matthew Paris* (Cambridge, 1958)
Victoria History of the Counties of England
Vincent, Nicholas, "The Origins of the Winchester Pipe Rolls," *Archives* 21 (1994), 25–42
——, *Peter des Roches: An Alien in English Politics, 1205–1238* (Cambridge, 1996)
——, "A Prebend in the Making: The Churches of Hurstbourne and Burbage 1100–1250," *Wiltshire Arch. and Natural Hist. Magazine* 90 (1997), 91–100

——, "The Foundation of Wormegay Priory," *Norfolk Archaeology* 43 (1999), 307–12

——, "New Charters of King Stephen with Some Reflections upon the Royal Forests during the Anarchy," *EHR* 114 (1999), 899–928

——, "Warin and Henry Fitz Gerald, the King's Chamberlains: The Origins of the FitzGeralds Revisited," *ANS* 21 (1999), 233–60

——, "King Henry II and the Monks of Battle: The Battle Chronicle Unmasked," in *Belief and Culture in the Middle Ages: Studies Presented to Henry Mayr-Harting*, ed. Richard Gameson and Henrietta Leyser (Oxford, 2001), 264–86

——, "The Murderers of Thomas Becket," in *Bischofsmord im Mittelalter: Murder of Bishops*, ed. Natalie Fryde and Dirk Reitz (Göttingen, 2003), 211–72

——, "Patronage, Politics and Piety in the Charters of Eleanor of Aquitaine," in *Plantagenêts et Capétiens*, 17–60

——, "New Charters of Henry Plantagenet before his Accession as King (1149–1154)," *HR* (forthcoming)

Waldman, T. G., "Hugh of Amiens, Archbishop of Rouen (1130–64), the Norman Abbots, and the Papacy: The Foundation of a 'Textual Community'," *HSJ* 2 (1990), 139–53

Walker, David, "Miles of Gloucester, Earl of Hereford," *TBGAS* 77 (1958), 66–84

——, "The 'Honours' of the Earls of Hereford in the Twelfth Century," *TBGAS* 79 (1960), 174–211

Walker, Simon, *Political Culture in Later Medieval England*, ed. Michael J. Braddick (Manchester, 2006)

Ward, J. C., "Royal Service and Reward: The Clare Family and the Crown, 1066–1154," *ANS* 11 (1989), 261–78

Wareham, Andrew, "The Motives and Politics of the Bigod Family, c.1066–1177," *ANS* 17 (1995), 223–42

Warren, W. L., *Henry II* (London, 1973)

——, *The Governance of Norman and Angevin England, 1086–1272* (London, 1987)

Wertheimer, Laura, "Adeliza of Louvain and Anglo-Norman Queenship," *HSJ* 7 (1997), 101–15

White, G. H. "King Stephen's Earldoms," *TRHS* 4 : 13 (1930), 51–82

White, Graeme J., "Were the Midlands 'Wasted' during Stephen's Reign?," *Midland History* 10 (1985), 26–46

——, *Restoration and Reform, 1153–1165: Recovery from Civil War in England* (Cambridge, 2000)

Wightman, W. E., "The Palatinate Earldom of William Fitz Osbern in Gloucestershire and Worcestershire (1066–71)," *EHR* 77 (1962), 6–17

——, *The Lacy Family in England and Normandy, 1066–1194* (Oxford, 1966)

Williams, D. and A. Vince, "The Early Norman Castle at Lincoln and a Re-evaluation of the Original West Tower of Lincoln Cathedral," *Medieval Archaeology* 41 (1997), 223–33

Winchester in the Early Middle Ages, ed. Martin Biddle (Winchester Studies 1; Oxford, 1976)

Winterbottom, Michael, "The *Gesta regum* of William of Malmesbury," *Journal of Medieval Latin* 5 (1995), 158–73

Wischermann, Else Maria, *Marcigny-sur-Loire: Gründungs- und Frühgeschichte der ersten Cluniacenserinnenpriorates (1055–1150)* (Munich, 1986)

Woodruff, C. Everleigh, "Some Early Professions of Canonical Obedience to the See of Canterbury by Heads of Religious Houses," *Archaeologia Cantiana* 37 (1925), 53–72

Yoshitake, Kenji, "The Exchequer in the Reign of Stephen," *EHR* 103 (1988), 950–9

Young, Alan, *William Cumin: Border Politics and the Bishopric of Durham 1141–1144* (Borthwick Papers 54; York, 1979)

Young, Charles R., *The Royal Forests of Medieval England* (Leicester, 1979)

Yver, Jean, "Les Châteaux forts en Normandie jusqu'au milieu du xiie siècle. Contribution à l'étude du pouvoir ducal," *Bulletin de la société des antiquaires de Normandie* 53 (1955–6), 28–115

INDEX OF ROYAL CHARTERS

An index to the charters printed in *Regesta Regum Anglo-Normannorum 1066–1154*, vol. iii, ed. H. A. Cronne and R. H. C. Davis (Oxford, 1968)

4	189 nn80, 81; 194 n109; 302 n12	183	324 n135
7	189 n81	184	241 n34
10	189 n81	189	122 n37; 124 n45
11	225 nn93, 94	192	271 n6
24	237 n10	194	180 n30; 310 n53
25	180 nn28, 30	195	180 n30; 257 n10; 310 n53
28	295 n106	195	180 n30; 257 n10; 310 n53
39	80 n227	198	257 n10
44	274 n23; 277 n38	204	68 n146; 126 n61
46	59 n105; 126 n61	206	286 n70; 337 n209
47	82 n6	207	257 n10; 311 n62; 312 n73
58	224 n87	210	194 n111
68	165 n109; 166 n118	218	339 n218
69	71 n160; 75 n190	221	257 n10
73	76 n191	224	257 n10
76	237 n10	239	295 n109
81	274 n23	239a	241 n28
90	274 n23; 289 n77	239b	237 n10
99	55 n73; 126 n61; 302 n33	239d	237 n10
104	274 n23; 276 n34	243	237 n10
114	150 n27	255	55 n73
119	126 n61	256	55 n73
121	126 n61	257	55 nn73, 78
126	185 n56; 275 n26	264	135 n117
127	292 n94; 337 n210	270	48 n37
129	292 n94	271	49 n40; 59 n105; 63 n116; 104 n127; 126 n61; 289 n75; 302 n32
130	292 n94		
131	295 n109	272	141 n147; 143 n155; 280 n58; 282 n66; 291 n88; 292 n93; 294 n100; 331 n170
132	71 n160; 90 n54		
137	295 n106		
139	297 n120	273	131 n89; 147 n12
140	292 nn93, 94	274	160 n81; 161 n83; 165 n110; 166 nn115, 117; 199 n138; 272 n22; 316 n97
157	237 n10		
163	190 n83		
174	220 n69	275	164 n105; 165 n107; 166 n116; 180 n32; 329 n156
175	220 n69		
176	220 n69	276	173 n157; 176 n7
178	147 n14; 223 n85; 237 n11	277	219 n62
180	273 n20; 274 nn21, 22, 23; 287 n72	278	126 n61
		281	76 n192

GENERAL INDEX

Aalst (East Flanders) 34
Abbotsbury (Dors.), abbot, *see* Geoffrey
Abelard 245
Abingdon (Berks.) 186; abbey 189, 225n,
302n; abbot, *see* Ingulph
Acle (Norf.) 220n
Ada de Warenne 106
Adam de Beaunay 69, 70, 84n, 178,
189, 226n
Adam, son of Robert de Bruce 92
Adela of Champagne, queen of
France xvii
Adela, countess of Blois, mother of
Stephen, birth (1067) xvi, 4; married to
Stephen, count of Blois (c.1083) 4;
widowed (1102) 7; activity as countess
8–10, 77; retires to Marcigny 17, 68,
learns there of Henry I's death 42n; her
death (1137) 72; father, *see* William I;
mother, *see* Matilda of Flanders; sons,
see Henry, bishop of Winchester, Odo,
Stephen, king of England, Theobald IV,
count of Blois, William, count of Sully
Adelelm, royal treasurer 52
Adeliza of Louvain (d. 1151), queen of
England, wife of Henry I xvi, 28, 31,
51–2, 124, 308; chancery 116n; marriage
to Henry I (1121) 19; marriage to
William d'Aubigny *pincerna* (c.1139) 116,
118n; receives empress at Arundel
(1139) 116
Adeliza, daughter of William the
Conqueror 3, 4n
Adeliza of Clare, countess of Oxford 239
Adeliza of Clare, wife of William de
Percy 239
Aelred, St, abbot of Rievaulx 91; abbot of
Revesby 229; works: *De spirituali amicitia*
91n; *De genealogia regum Anglorum* 296,
328–9; *Letters* 279n
Agnes de Sully, wife of William of Blois 8n
Agnes of Evreux, countess of Meulan 314n
Ailsi, son of Ulf, tenant of honour of
Lancaster 28

Alan Busel 55n
Alan III (d. 1146), count of Brittany, earl of
Richmond (*also* of Cornwall) 68, 107–8,
114n, 130n, 135, 137, 152n, 178, 179;
character 150
Alan, son of Flaad 89
Alberic, cardinal bishop of Ostia, papal
legate 94–5, 99–100, 104, 309
Alcester (Warw.), abbey 135
Aldreth (Cambs.), castle 125, 197
Alençon (Orne) 11, 14–15, 39, 334; battle
(1119) 15; burgesses 15
Alexander, king of Scots xvii
Alexander, bishop of Lincoln 37–8,
54n, 56, 68, 70n, 84n, 97, 100, 105,
114n, 124, 137, 145–6, 149, 156, 175,
191, 229, 246, 261n; arrested (1139)
107–8, 335, suspended 306; castles 109,
and see Newark, Sleaford; in Rome
226–7
Alexander, monk of Ely 101n
Alexius I Comnenus, Byzantine
emperor 6–7
Algar, bishop of Coutances 58, 69, 100n
Algrin of Etampes, chancellor of
France 140n
Alice Paynel, countess of Lincoln 297
Almenèches (Orne) 14
Alnwick (Northumb.), castle 53–4, 91
Alured of Lincoln 234
Amaury de Montfort 16
Amice, countess of Leicester 100
Amiens, bishop, *see* Thierry
Anacletus II, antipope 35, 217; death
(1138) 94
Anastasius IV, pope 295–6
Andelle, river 266
Andrew Buccuinte 69
Andrew of Baudemont, steward of
Theobald IV, count of Blois 21n, 28n,
72, 140n
Angers (Maine-et-Loire) 67n
Anglo-Saxon Chronicle 168, 211; description of
reign 206–7, 320